SECURITIES REGULATION
STATUTORY SUPPLEMENT

By

STEPHEN J. CHOI

Murray and Kathleen Bring Professor of Law
New York University Law School

and

A.C. PRITCHARD

Frances and George Skestos Professor of Law
University of Michigan Law School

2010 EDITION

FOUNDATION PRESS
2010

THOMSON REUTERS

© 2006–2009 THOMSON REUTERS/FOUNDATION PRESS
© 2010 By THOMSON REUTERS/FOUNDATION PRESS
   1 New York Plaza, 34th Floor
   New York, NY 10004
   Phone Toll Free 1–877–888–1330
   Fax 646–424–5201
   foundation-press.com
Printed in the United States of America

ISBN 978–1–59941–842–1

Mat #40999692

Federal Securities Laws
Selected Statutes, Rules and Forms

Securities Act – Statutes:

Section 1 – Short Title

This title may be cited as the "Securities Act of 1933."

Section 2 – Definitions; Promotion of Efficiency, Competition, and Capital Formation

a. Definitions

When used in this title, unless the context otherwise requires–

1.   The term "security" means any note, stock, treasury stock, security future, bond, debenture, evidence of indebtedness, certificate of interest or participation in any profit-sharing agreement, collateral-trust certificate, preorganization certificate or subscription, transferable share, investment contract, voting-trust certificate, certificate of deposit for a security, fractional undivided interest in oil, gas, or other mineral rights, any put, call, straddle, option, or privilege on any security, certificate of deposit, or group or index of

securities (including any interest therein or based on the value thereof), or any put, call, straddle, option, or privilege entered into on a national securities exchange relating to foreign currency, or, in general, any interest or instrument commonly known as a "security", or any certificate of interest or participation in, temporary or interim certificate for, receipt for, guarantee of, or warrant or right to subscribe to or purchase, any of the foregoing.

3. The term "sale" or "sell" shall include every contract of sale or disposition of a security or interest in a security, for value. The term "offer to sell", "offer for sale", or "offer" shall include every attempt or offer to dispose of, or solicitation of an offer to buy, a security or interest in a security, for value. The terms defined in this paragraph and the term "offer to buy" as used in subsection (c) of section 5 shall not include preliminary negotiations or agreements between an issuer (or any person directly or indirectly controlling or controlled by an issuer, or under direct or indirect common control with an issuer) and any underwriter or among underwriters who are or are to be in privity of contract with an issuer (or any person directly or indirectly controlling or controlled by an issuer, or under direct or indirect common control with an issuer). Any security given or delivered with, or as a bonus on account of, any purchase of securities or any other thing, shall be conclusively presumed to constitute a part of the subject of such purchase and to have been offered and sold for value. The issue or transfer of a right or privilege, when originally issued or transferred with a security, giving the holder of such security the right to convert such security into another security of the same issuer or of another person, or giving a right to subscribe to another security of the same issuer or of another person, which right cannot be exercised until some future date, shall not be deemed to be an offer or sale of such other security; but the issue or transfer of such other security upon the exercise of such right of conversion or subscription shall be deemed a sale of such other security. Any offer or sale of a security futures product by or on behalf of the issuer of the securities underlying the security futures product, an affiliate of the issuer, or an underwriter, shall constitute a contract for sale of, sale of, offer for sale, or offer to sell the underlying securities.

4. The term "issuer" means every person who issues or proposes to issue any security; except that with respect to certificates of deposit, voting-trust certificates, or collateral-trust certificates, or with respect to certificates of interest or shares in an unincorporated investment trust not having a board of directors (or persons performing similar functions) or of the fixed, restricted management, or unit type, the term "issuer" means the person or persons performing the acts and assuming the duties of depositor or manager pursuant to the provisions of the trust or other agreement or instrument under which such securities are issued; except that in the case of an unincorporated association which provides by its articles for limited liability of any or all of its members, or in the case of a trust, committee, or other legal entity, the trustees or members thereof shall not be individually liable as issuers of any security issued by the association, trust, committee, or other legal entity; except that with respect to equipment-trust certificates or like securities, the term "issuer" means the person by whom the equipment or property is or is to be used; and except that with respect to fractional undivided interests in oil, gas, or other

mineral rights, the term "issuer" means the owner of any such right or of any interest in such right (whether whole or fractional) who creates fractional interests therein for the purpose of public offering.

7. The term "interstate commerce" means trade or commerce in securities or any transportation or communication relating thereto among the several States or between the District of Columbia or any Territory of the United States and any State or other Territory, or between any foreign country and any State, Territory, or the District of Columbia, or within the District of Columbia.

10. The term "prospectus" means any prospectus, notice, circular, advertisement, letter, or communication, written or by radio or television, which offers any security for sale or confirms the sale of any security; except that (a) a communication sent or given after the effective date of the registration statement (other than a prospectus permitted under subsection (b) of section 10) shall not be deemed a prospectus if it is proved that prior to or at the same time with such communication a written prospectus meeting the requirements of subsection (a) of section 10 at the time of such communication was sent or given to the person to whom the communication was made, and (b) a notice, circular, advertisement, letter, or communication in respect of a security shall not be deemed to be a prospectus if it states from whom a written prospectus meeting the requirements of section 10 may be obtained and, in addition, does no more than identify the security, state the price thereof, state by whom orders will be executed, and contain such other information as the Commission, by rules or regulations deemed necessary or appropriate in the public interest and for the protection of investors, and subject to such terms and conditions as may be prescribed therein, may permit.

11. The term "underwriter" means any person who has purchased from an issuer with a view to, or offers or sells for an issuer in connection with, the distribution of any security, or participates or has a direct or indirect participation in any such undertaking, or participates or has a participation in the direct or indirect underwriting of any such undertaking; but such term shall not include a person whose interest is limited to a commission from an underwriter or dealer not in excess of the usual and customary distributors' or sellers' commission. As used in this paragraph the term "issuer" shall include, in addition to an issuer, any person directly or indirectly controlling or controlled by the issuer, or any person under direct or indirect common control with the issuer.

12. The term "dealer" means any person who engages either for all or part of his time, directly or indirectly, as agent, broker, or principal, in the business of offering, buying, selling, or otherwise dealing or trading in securities issued by another person.

Section 3 – Classes of Securities under this Title

a. **Exempted securities**
Except as hereinafter expressly provided, the provisions of this title shall not apply to any of the following classes of securities:

1. Reserved.

2. Any security issued or guaranteed by the United States or any territory thereof, or by the District of Columbia, or by any State of the United States, or by any political subdivision of a State or territory, or by any public instrumentality of one or more States or territories, or by any person controlled or supervised by and acting as an instrumentality of the Government of the United States pursuant to authority granted by the Congress of the United States; or any certificate of deposit for any of the foregoing; or any security issued or guaranteed by any bank; or any security issued by or representing an interest in or a direct obligation of a Federal Reserve bank; or any interest or participation in any common trust fund or similar fund that is excluded from the definition of the term "investment company" under section 3(c)(3) of the Investment Company Act of 1940; or any security which is an industrial development bond (as defined in section 103(c)(2) of the Internal Revenue Code of 1954) the interest on which is excludable from gross income under section 103(a)(1) of such Code if, by reason of the application of paragraph (4) or (6) of section 103(c) of such Code (determined as if paragraphs (4)(A), (5), and (7) were not included in such section 103(c)), paragraph (1) of such section 103(c) does not apply to such security; or any interest or participation in a single trust fund, or in a collective trust fund maintained by a bank, or any security arising out of a contract issued by an insurance company, which interest, participation, or security is issued in connection with (A) a stock bonus, pension, or profit-sharing plan which meets the requirements for qualification under section 401 of the Internal Revenue Code of 1954, (B) an annuity plan which meets the requirements for the deduction of the employer's contributions under section 404(a)(2) of such Code, (C) a governmental plan as defined in section 414(d) of such Code which has been established by an employer for the exclusive benefit of its employees or their beneficiaries for the purpose of distributing to such employees or their beneficiaries the corpus and income of the funds accumulated under such plan, if under such plan it is impossible, prior to the satisfaction of all liabilities with respect to such employees and their beneficiaries, for any part of the corpus or income to be used for, or diverted to, purposes other than the exclusive benefit of such employees or their beneficiaries, or (D) a church plan, company, or account that is excluded from the definition of an investment company under section 3(c)(14) of the Investment Company Act of 1940, other than any plan described in subparagraph (A), (B), (C), or (D) of this paragraph (i) the contributions under which are held in a single trust fund or in a separate account maintained by an insurance company for a single employer and under which an amount in excess of the employer's contribution is allocated to the purchase of securities (other than interests or participations in the trust or separate account itself) issued by the employer or any company directly or indirectly controlling, controlled by,

or under common control with the employer, (ii) which covers employees some or all of whom are employees within the meaning of section 401(c)(1) of such Code, or (iii) which is a plan funded by an annuity contract described in section 403(b) of such Code. The Commission, by rules and regulations or order, shall exempt from the provisions of section 5 of this title any interest or participation issued in connection with a stock bonus, pension, profit-sharing, or annuity plan which covers employees some or all of whom are employees within the meaning of section 401(c)(1) of the Internal Revenue Code of 1954, if and to the extent that the Commission determines this to be necessary or appropriate in the public interest and consistent with the protection of investors and the purposes fairly intended by the policy and provisions of this title. For purposes of this paragraph, a security issued or guaranteed by a bank shall not include any interest or participation in any collective trust fund maintained by a bank; and the term "bank" means any national bank, or any banking institution organized under the laws of any State, territory, or the District of Columbia, the business of which is substantially confined to banking and is supervised by the State or territorial banking commission or similar official; except that in the case of a common trust fund or similar fund, or a collective trust fund, the term "bank" has the same meaning as in the Investment Company Act of 1940;

3. Any note, draft, bill of exchange, or banker's acceptance which arises out of a current transaction or the proceeds of which have been or are to be used for current transactions, and which has a maturity at the time of issuance of not exceeding nine months, exclusive of days of grace, or any renewal thereof the maturity of which is likewise limited;

4. Any security issued by a person organized and operated exclusively for religious, educational, benevolent, fraternal, charitable, or reformatory purposes and not for pecuniary profit, and no part of the net earnings of which inures to the benefit of any person, private stockholder, or individual; or any security of a fund that is excluded from the definition of an investment company under section 3(c)(10)(B) of the Investment Company Act of 1940;

5. Any security issued (A) by a savings and loan association, building and loan association, cooperative bank, homestead association, or similar institution, which is supervised and examined by State or Federal authority having supervision over any such institution; or (B) by (i) a farmer's cooperative organization exempt from tax under section 521 of the Internal Revenue Code of 1954, (ii) a corporation described in section 501(c)(16) of such Code and exempt from tax under section 501(a) of such Code, or (iii) a corporation described in section 501(c)(2) of such Code which is exempt from tax under section 501(a) of such Code and is organized for the exclusive purpose of holding title to property, collecting income therefrom, and turning over the entire amount thereof, less expenses, to an organization or corporation described in clause (i) or (ii);

6. Any interest in a railroad equipment trust. For purposes of this paragraph "interest in a railroad equipment trust" means any interest in an equipment trust, lease, conditional sales contract, or other similar arrangement entered into, issued, assumed, guaranteed by, or for the benefit of, a common carrier to finance the acquisition of rolling stock, including motive power;

5

7. Certificates issued by a receiver or by a trustee or debtor in possession in a case under title 11 of the United States Code, with the approval of the court;

8. Any insurance or endowment policy or annuity contract or optional annuity contract, issued by a corporation subject to the supervision of the insurance commissioner, bank commissioner, or any agency or officer performing like functions, of any State or Territory of the United States or the District of Columbia;

9. Except with respect to a security exchanged in a case under title 11 of the United States Code, any security exchanged by the issuer with its existing security holders exclusively where no commission or other remuneration is paid or given directly or indirectly for soliciting such exchange;

10. Except with respect to a security exchanged in a case under title 11 of the United States Code, any security which is issued in exchange for one or more bona fide outstanding securities, claims or property interests, or partly in such exchange and partly for cash, where the terms and conditions of such issuance and exchange are approved, after a hearing upon the fairness of such terms and conditions at which all persons to whom it is proposed to issue securities in such exchange shall have the right to appear, by any court, or by any official or agency of the United States, or by any State or Territorial banking or insurance commission or other governmental authority expressly authorized by law to grant such approval;

11. Any security which is a part of an issue offered and sold only to persons resident within a single State or Territory, where the issuer of such security is a person resident and doing business within or, if a corporation, incorporated by and doing business within, such State or Territory.

12. Any equity security issued in connection with the acquisition by a holding company of a bank under section 3(a) of the Bank Holding Company Act of 1956 or a savings association under section 10(e) of the Home Owners' Loan Act, if–

    A. the acquisition occurs solely as part of a reorganization in which security holders exchange their shares of a bank or savings association for shares of a newly formed holding company with no significant assets other than securities of the bank or savings association and the existing subsidiaries of the bank or savings association;

    B. the security holders receive, after that reorganization, substantially the same proportional share interests in the holding company as they held in the bank or savings association, except for nominal changes in shareholders' interests resulting from lawful elimination of fractional interests and the exercise of dissenting shareholders' rights under State or Federal law;

    C. the rights and interests of security holders in the holding company are substantially the same as those in the bank or savings association prior to the transaction, other than as may be required by law; and

D.   the holding company has substantially the same assets and liabilities, on a consolidated basis, as the bank or savings association had prior to the transaction.

For purposes of this paragraph, the term "savings association" means a savings association (as defined in section 3(b) of the Federal Deposit Insurance Act) the deposits of which are insured by the Federal Deposit Insurance Corporation.

13.   Any security issued by or any interest or participation in any church plan, company or account that is excluded from the definition of an investment company under section 3(c)(14).

14.   Any security futures product that is—

A.   cleared by a clearing agency registered under section 17A of the Securities Exchange Act of 1934 or exempt from registration under subsection (b)(7) of such section 17A; and

B.   traded on a national securities exchange or a national securities association registered pursuant to section 15A(a) of the Securities Exchange Act of 1934.

b.   **Additional exemptions**

The Commission may from time to time by its rules and regulations, and subject to such terms and conditions as may be prescribed therein, add any class of securities to the securities exempted as provided in this section, if it finds that the enforcement of this title with respect to such securities is not necessary in the public interest and for the protection of investors by reason of the small amount involved or the limited character of the public offering; but no issue of securities shall be exempted under this subsection where the aggregate amount at which such issue is offered to the public exceeds $5,000,000.

Section 4 – Exempted Transactions

The provisions of section 5 shall not apply to—

1.   transactions by any person other than an issuer, underwriter, or dealer.

2.   transactions by an issuer not involving any public offering.

3.   transactions by a dealer (including an underwriter no longer acting as an underwriter in respect of the security involved in such transaction), except—

A.   transactions taking place prior to the expiration of forty days after the first date upon which the security was bona fide offered to the public by the issuer or by or through an underwriter,

B.   transactions in a security as to which a registration statement has been filed taking place prior to the expiration of forty days after the effective date of such registration statement or prior to the expiration of forty days after the first date upon which the security was bona fide offered to the public by the issuer or by or through an underwriter after such effective date, whichever is later (excluding in the computation of such forty days any time during which a stop order issued under section 8 is in effect as to the security), or such shorter period as the Commission may specify by rules and regulations or order, and

C.   transactions as to securities constituting the whole or a part of an unsold allotment to or subscription by such dealer as a participant in the distribution of such securities by the issuer or by or through an underwriter.

With respect to transactions referred to in clause (B), if securities of the issuer have not previously been sold pursuant to an earlier effective registration statement the applicable period, instead of forty days, shall be ninety days, or such shorter period as the Commission may specify by rules and regulations or order.

4.   brokers' transactions executed upon customers' orders on any exchange or in the over-the-counter market but not the solicitation of such orders.

Section 5 – Prohibitions Relating to Interstate Commerce and the Mails

a.   **Sale or delivery after sale of unregistered securities**
Unless a registration statement is in effect as to a security, it shall be unlawful for any person, directly or indirectly–

1.   to make use of any means or instruments of transportation or communication in interstate commerce or of the mails to sell such security through the use or medium of any prospectus or otherwise; or

2.   to carry or cause to be carried through the mails or in interstate commerce, by any means or instruments of transportation, any such security for the purpose of sale or for delivery after sale.

b.   **Necessity of prospectus meeting requirements of section 10**
It shall be unlawful for any person, directly or indirectly–

1.   to make use of any means or instruments of transportation or communication in interstate commerce or of the mails to carry or transmit any prospectus relating to any security with respect to which a registration statement has been filed under this title, unless such prospectus meets the requirements of section 10; or

2.   to carry or cause to be carried through the mails or in interstate commerce any such security for the purpose of sale or for delivery after sale, unless accompanied or preceded by a prospectus that meets the requirements of subsection (a) of section 10.

c.   **Necessity of filing registration statement**
It shall be unlawful for any person, directly or indirectly, to make use of any means or instruments of transportation or communication in interstate commerce or of the mails to offer to sell or offer to buy through the use or medium of any prospectus or otherwise any security, unless a registration statement has been filed as to such security, or while the registration statement is the subject of a refusal order or stop order or (prior to the effective date of the registration statement) any public proceeding or examination under section 8.

Section 6 – Registration of Securities

a.   **Method of registration**
Any security may be registered with the Commission under the terms and conditions hereinafter provided, by filing a registration statement in triplicate, at least one of

which shall be signed by each issuer, its principal executive officer or officers, its principal financial officer, its comptroller or principal accounting officer, and the majority of its board of directors or persons performing similar functions (or, if there is no board of directors or persons performing similar functions, by the majority of the persons or board having the power of management of the issuer), and in case the issuer is a foreign or Territorial person by its duly authorized representative in the United States; except that when such registration statement relates to a security issued by a foreign government, or political subdivision thereof, it need be signed only by the underwriter of such security. Signatures of all such persons when written on the said registration statements shall be presumed to have been so written by authority of the person whose signature is so affixed and the burden of proof, in the event such authority shall be denied, shall be upon the party denying the same. The affixing of any signature without the authority of the purported signer shall constitute a violation of this title. A registration statement shall be deemed effective only as to securities specified therein as proposed to be offered.

Section 7 – Information Required in Registration Statement

a. The registration statement, when relating to a security other than a security issued by a foreign government, or political subdivision thereof, shall contain the information, and be accompanied by the documents, specified in Schedule A, and when relating to a security issued by a foreign government, or political subdivision thereof, shall contain the information, and be accompanied by the documents, specified in Schedule B; except that the Commission may by rules or regulations provide that any such information or document need not be included in respect of any class of issuers or securities if it finds that the requirement of such information or document is inapplicable to such class and that disclosure fully adequate for the protection of investors is otherwise required to be included within the registration statement. If any accountant, engineer, or appraiser, or any person whose profession gives authority to a statement made by him, is named as having prepared or certified any part of the registration statement, or is named as having prepared or certified a report or valuation for use in connection with the registration statement, the written consent of such person shall be filed with the registration statement. If any such person is named as having prepared or certified a report or valuation (other than a public official document or statement) which is used in connection with the registration statement, but is not named as having prepared or certified such report or valuation for use in connection with the registration statement, the written consent of such person shall be filed with the registration statement unless the Commission dispenses with such filing as impracticable or as involving undue hardship on the person filing the registration statement. Any such registration statement shall contain such other information, and be accompanied by such other documents, as the Commission may by rules or regulations require as being necessary or appropriate in the public interest or for the protection of investors.

Section 8 – Taking Effect of Registration Statements and Amendments Thereto

a. **Effective date of registration statement.** Except as hereinafter provided, the effective date of a registration statement shall be the twentieth day after the filing thereof or such earlier date as the Commission may determine, having due regard to the adequacy of the information respecting the issuer theretofore available to the public, to the facility with which the nature of the securities to be registered, their relationship to the capital structure of the issuer and the rights of holders thereof can be understood, and to the public interest and the protection of investors. If any amendment to any such statement is filed prior to the effective date of such statement, the registration statement shall be deemed to have been filed when such amendment was filed; except that an amendment filed with the consent of the Commission, prior to the effective date of the registration statement, or filed pursuant to an order of the Commission, shall be treated as a part of the registration statement.

b. **Incomplete or inaccurate registration statement.** If it appears to the Commission that a registration statement is on its face incomplete or inaccurate in any material respect, the Commission may, after notice by personal service or the sending of confirmed telegraphic notice not later than ten days after the filing of the registration statement, and opportunity for hearing (at a time fixed by the Commission) within ten days after such notice by personal service or the sending of such telegraphic notice, issue an order prior to the effective date of registration refusing to permit such statement to become effective until it has been amended in accordance with such order. When such statement has been amended in accordance with such order the Commission shall so declare and the registration shall become effective at the time provided in subsection (a) of this section or upon the date of such declaration, whichever date is the later.

c. **Effective date of amendment to registration statement.** An amendment filed after the effective date of the registration statement, if such amendment, upon its face, appears to the Commission not to be incomplete or inaccurate in any material respect, shall become effective on such date as the Commission may determine, having due regard to the public interest and the protection of investors.

d. **Untrue statements or omissions in registration statement.** If it appears to the Commission at any time that the registration statement includes any untrue statement of a material fact or omits to state any material fact required to be stated therein or necessary to make the statements therein not misleading, the Commission may, after notice by personal service or the sending of confirmed telegraphic notice, and after opportunity for hearing (at a time fixed by the Commission) within fifteen days after such notice by personal service or the sending of such telegraphic notice, issue a stop order suspending the effectiveness of the registration statement. When such statement has been amended in accordance with such stop order, the Commission shall so declare and thereupon the stop order shall cease to be effective.

e. **Examination for issuance of stop order.** The Commission is empowered to make an examination in any case in order to determine whether a stop order should issue under subsection (d) of this section. In making such examination the Commission or any officer or officers designated by it shall have access to and may demand the production of any books and papers of, and may administer oaths and affirmations to and examine, the issuer, underwriter, or any other person, in respect of any matter relevant to the examination, and may, in its discretion, require the production of a balance sheet exhibiting the assets and liabilities of the issuer, or its income statement, or both, to be certified to by a public or certified accountant approved by the Commission. If the issuer or underwriter shall fail to cooperate, or shall obstruct or refuse to permit the making of an examination, such conduct shall be proper ground for the issuance of a stop order.

f.   **Notice requirements.**   Any notice required under this section shall be sent to or served on the issuer, or, in case of a foreign government or political subdivision thereof, to or on the underwriter, or, in the case of a foreign or Territorial person, to or on its duly authorized representative in the United States named in the registration statement, properly directed in each case of telegraphic notice to the address given in such statement.

Section 10 – Information Required in Prospectus

a.   **Information in registration statement; documents not required**

Except to the extent otherwise permitted or required pursuant to this subsection or subsections (c), (d), or (e)–

1.   a prospectus relating to a security other than a security issued by a foreign government or political subdivision thereof, shall contain the information contained in the registration statement, but it need not include the documents referred to in paragraphs (28) to (32), inclusive, of Schedule A;

2.   a prospectus relating to a security issued by a foreign government or political subdivision thereof shall contain the information contained in the registration statement, but it need not include the documents referred to in paragraphs (13) and (14) of Schedule B;

3.   notwithstanding the provisions of paragraphs (1) and (2) of this subsection (a) when a prospectus is used more than nine months after the effective date of the registration statement, the information contained therein shall be as of a date not more than sixteen months prior to such use, so far as such information is known to the user of such prospectus or can be furnished by such user without unreasonable effort or expense;

4.   there may be omitted from any prospectus any of the information required under this subsection (a) which the Commission may by rules or regulations designate as not being necessary or appropriate in the public interest or for the protection of investors.

b.   **Summarizations and omissions allowed by rules and regulations.**   In addition to the prospectus permitted or required in subsection (a), the Commission shall by rules or regulations deemed necessary or appropriate in the public interest or for the protection of investors permit the use of a prospectus for the purposes of subsection (b)(1) of section 5 which omits in part or summarizes information in the prospectus specified in subsection (a). A prospectus permitted under this subsection shall, except to the extent the Commission by rules or regulations deemed necessary or appropriate in the public interest or for the protection of investors otherwise provides, be filed as part of the registration statement but shall not be deemed a part of such registration statement for the purposes of section 11. The Commission may at any time issue an order preventing or suspending the use of a prospectus permitted under this subsection (b), if it has reason to believe that such prospectus has not been filed (if required to be filed as part of the registration statement) or includes any untrue statement of a material fact or omits to state any material fact required to be stated therein or necessary to make the statements therein, in the light of the circumstances under which such prospectus is or is to be used, not misleading. Upon issuance of an order under this subsection, the Commission shall give notice of the issuance of such order and opportunity for hearing by personal service or the sending of confirmed telegraphic notice. The Commission shall vacate or modify the order at any time for good cause or if such prospectus has been filed or amended in accordance with such order.

c. **Additional information required by rules and regulations.** Any prospectus shall contain such other information as the Commission may by rules or regulations require as being necessary or appropriate in the public interest or for the protection of investors.

d. **Classification of prospectuses.** In the exercise of its powers under subsections (a), (b), or (c), the Commission shall have authority to classify prospectuses according to the nature and circumstances of their use or the nature of the security, issue, issuer, or otherwise, and, by rules and regulations and subject to such terms and conditions as it shall specify therein, to prescribe as to each class the form and contents which it may find appropriate and consistent with the public interest and the protection of investors.

e. **Information in conspicuous part of prospectus.** The statements or information required to be included in a prospectus by or under authority of subsections (a), (b), (c), or (d), when written, shall be placed in a conspicuous part of the prospectus and, except as otherwise permitted by rules or regulations, in type as large as that used generally in the body of the prospectus.

f. **Prospectus consisting of radio or television broadcast.** In any case where a prospectus consists of a radio or television broadcast, copies thereof shall be filed with the Commission under such rules and regulations as it shall prescribe. The Commission may by rules and regulations require the filing with it of forms and prospectuses used in connection with the offer or sale of securities registered under this title.

Section 11 – Civil Liabilities on Account of False Registration Statement

a. **Persons possessing cause of action; persons liable.** In case any part of the registration statement, when such part became effective, contained an untrue statement of a material fact or omitted to state a material fact required to be stated therein or necessary to make the statements therein not misleading, any person acquiring such security (unless it is proved that at the time of such acquisition he knew of such untruth or omission) may, either at law or in equity, in any court of competent jurisdiction, sue–

1. every person who signed the registration statement;

2. every person who was a director of (or person performing similar functions) or partner in the issuer at the time of the filing of the part of the registration statement with respect to which his liability is asserted;

3. every person who, with his consent, is named in the registration statement as being or about to become a director, person performing similar functions, or partner;

4. every accountant, engineer, or appraiser, or any person whose profession gives authority to a statement made by him, who has with his consent been named as having prepared or certified any part of the registration statement, or as having prepared or certified any report or valuation which is used in connection with the registration statement, with respect to the statement in such registration statement, report, or valuation, which purports to have been prepared or certified by him;

5. every underwriter with respect to such security.

If such person acquired the security after the issuer has made generally available to its security holders an earning statement covering a period of at least twelve months beginning after the effective date of the registration statement, then the right of recovery under this subsection shall be conditioned on proof that such person acquired the security relying upon such untrue statement in the registration statement or relying upon the registration statement and not knowing of such omission, but such reliance may be established without proof of the reading of the registration statement by such person.

b. **Persons exempt from liability upon proof of issues.** Notwithstanding the provisions of subsection (a) of this section no person, other than the issuer, shall be liable as provided therein who shall sustain the burden of proof–

1. that before the effective date of the part of the registration statement with respect to which his liability is asserted (A) he had resigned from or had taken such steps as are permitted by law to resign from, or ceased or refused to act in, every office, capacity, or relationship in which he was described in the registration statement as acting or agreeing to act, and (B) he had advised the Commission and the issuer in writing that he had taken such action and that he would not be responsible for such part of the registration statement; or

2. that if such part of the registration statement became effective without his knowledge, upon becoming aware of such fact he forthwith acted and advised the Commission, in accordance with paragraph (1) of this subsection, and, in addition, gave reasonable public notice that such part of the registration statement had become effective without his knowledge; or

3. that (A) as regards any part of the registration statement not purporting to be made on the authority of an expert, and not purporting to be a copy of or extract from a report or valuation of an expert, and not purporting to be made on the authority of a public official document or statement, he had, after reasonable investigation, reasonable ground to believe and did believe, at the time such part of the registration statement became effective, that the

statements therein were true and that there was no omission to state a material fact required to be stated therein or necessary to make the statements therein not misleading; and (B) as regards any part of the registration statement purporting to be made upon his authority as an expert or purporting to be a copy of or extract from a report or valuation of himself as an expert,(i) he had, after reasonable investigation, reasonable ground to believe and did believe, at the time such part of the registration statement became effective, that the statements therein were true and that there was no omission to state a material fact required to be stated therein or necessary to make the statements therein not misleading, or(ii) such part of the registration statement did not fairly represent his statement as an expert or was not a fair copy of or extract from his report or valuation as an expert; and (C) as regards any part of the registration statement purporting to be made on the authority of an expert (other than himself) or purporting to be a copy of or extract from a report or valuation of an expert (other than himself), he had no reasonable ground to believe and did not believe, at the time such part of the registration statement became effective, that the statements therein were untrue or that there was an omission to state a material fact required to be stated therein or necessary to make the statements therein not misleading, or that such part of the registration statement did not fairly represent the statement of the expert or was not a fair copy of or extract from the report or valuation of the expert; and (D) as regards any part of the registration statement purporting to be a statement made by an official person or purporting to be a copy of or extract from a public official document, he had no reasonable ground to believe and did not believe, at the time such part of the registration statement became effective, that the statements therein were untrue, or that there was an omission to state a material fact required to be stated therein or necessary to make the statements therein not misleading, or that such part of the registration statement did not fairly represent the statement made by the official person or was not a fair copy of or extract from the public official document.

c. **Standard of reasonableness**. In determining, for the purpose of paragraph (3) of subsection (b) of this section, what constitutes reasonable investigation and reasonable ground for belief, the standard of reasonableness shall be that required of a prudent man in the management of his own property.

d. **Effective date of registration statement with regard to underwriters**. If any person becomes an underwriter with respect to the security after the part of the registration statement with respect to which his liability is asserted has become effective, then for the purposes of paragraph (3) of subsection (b) of this section such part of the registration statement shall be considered as having become effective with respect to such person as of the time when he became an underwriter.

e. **Measure of damages; undertaking for payment of costs**. The suit authorized under subsection (a) of this section may be to recover such damages as shall represent the difference between the amount paid for the security (not exceeding the price at which the security was offered to the public) and (1) the value thereof as of the time such suit was brought, or (2) the price at which such security shall have been disposed of in the market before suit, or (3) the price at which such security shall have been disposed of after suit but before judgment if such damages shall be less than the damages representing the difference between the amount paid for the security (not exceeding the price at which the security was offered to the public) and the value thereof as of the time such suit was brought: *Provided,* that if the defendant proves that any portion or all of such damages represents other than the depreciation in value of such security resulting from such part of the registration statement, with respect to which his liability is asserted, not being true or omitting to state a material fact required to be stated therein or necessary to make the statements therein not misleading, such portion of or all such damages shall not be recoverable. In no event shall any underwriter (unless such underwriter shall have knowingly received from the issuer for acting as an underwriter some benefit, directly or indirectly, in which all other underwriters similarly situated did not share in proportion to their respective interests in the underwriting) be liable in any suit or as a consequence of suits authorized under subsection (a) of this section for damages in excess of the total price at which the securities underwritten by him and distributed to the public were offered to the public. In any suit under this or any other section of this title the court may, in its discretion, require an undertaking for the payment of the costs of such suit, including reasonable attorney's fees, and if judgment shall be rendered against a party litigant, upon the motion of the other party litigant, such costs may be assessed in favor of such party litigant (whether or not such undertaking has been required) if the court believes the suit or the defense to have been without merit, in an amount sufficient to reimburse him for the reasonable expenses incurred by him, in connection with such suit, such costs to be taxed in the manner usually provided for taxing of costs in the court in which the suit was heard.

f.   **Joint and several liability; liability of outside director**
   1.   Except as provided in paragraph (2), all or any one or more of the persons specified in subsection (a) of this section shall be jointly and severally liable, and every person who becomes liable to make any payment under this section may recover contribution as in cases of contract from any person who, if sued separately, would have been liable to make the same payment, unless the person who has become liable was, and the other was not, guilty of fraudulent misrepresentation.
   2.   A.   The liability of an outside director under subsection (e) shall be determined in accordance with section 21D(f) of the Securities Exchange Act of 1934.
        B.   For purposes of this paragraph, the term "outside director" shall have the meaning given such term by rule or regulation of the Commission.

g.   **Offering price to public as maximum amount recoverable.** In no case shall the amount recoverable under this section exceed the price at which the security was offered to the public.

Section 12 – Civil Liabilities Arising in Connection with Prospectuses and Communications

  a. **In general**

Any person who–

1.   offers or sells a security in violation of section 5, or
2.   offers or sells a security (whether or not exempted by the provisions of section 3, other than paragraphs (2) and (14) of subsection (a) of said section), by the use of any means or instruments of transportation or communication in interstate commerce or of the mails, by means of a prospectus or oral communication, which includes an untrue statement of a material fact or omits to state a material fact necessary in order to make the statements, in the light of the circumstances under which they were made, not misleading (the purchaser not knowing of such untruth or omission), and who shall not sustain the burden of proof that he did not know, and in the exercise of reasonable care could not have known, of such untruth or omission,

shall be liable, subject to subsection (b), to the person purchasing such security from him, who may sue either at law or in equity in any court of competent jurisdiction, to recover the consideration paid for such security with interest thereon, less the amount of any income received thereon, upon the tender of such security, or for damages if he no longer owns the security.

  b. **Loss causation.** In an action described in subsection (a)(2), if the person who offered or sold such security proves that any portion or all of the amount recoverable under subsection (a)(2) represents other than the depreciation in value of the subject security resulting from such part of the prospectus or oral communication, with respect to which the liability of that person is asserted, not being true or omitting to state a material fact required to be stated therein or necessary to make the statement not misleading, then such portion or amount, as the case may be, shall not be recoverable.

Section 13 – Limitation of Actions

No action shall be maintained to enforce any liability created under section 11 or section 12(a)(2) unless brought within one year after the discovery of the untrue statement or the omission, or after such discovery should have been made by the exercise of reasonable diligence, or, if the action is to enforce a liability created under section 12(a)(1), unless brought within one year after the violation upon which it is based. In no event shall any such action be brought to enforce a liability created under section 11 or section 12(a)(1) more than three years after the security was bona fide offered to the public, or under section 12(a)(2) more than three years after the sale.

Section 14 – Contrary Stipulations Void

Any condition, stipulation, or provision binding any person acquiring any security to waive compliance with any provision of this title or of the rules and regulations of the Commission shall be void.

Section 15 – Liability of Controlling Persons

Every person who, by or through stock ownership, agency, or otherwise, or who, pursuant to or in connection with an agreement or understanding with one or more other persons by or through stock ownership, agency, or otherwise, controls any person liable under section 11 or 12, shall also be liable jointly and severally with and to the same extent as such controlled person to any person to whom such controlled person is liable, unless the controlling person had no knowledge of or reasonable ground to believe in the existence of the facts by reason of which the liability of the controlled person is alleged to exist.

Section 16 – Additional Remedies; Limitation on Remedies

a. **Remedies additional**
Except as provided in subsection (b), the rights and remedies provided by this title shall be in addition to any and all other rights and remedies that may exist at law or in equity.

b. **Class action limitations**
No covered class action based upon the statutory or common law of any State or subdivision thereof may be maintained in any State or Federal court by any private party alleging–
1. an untrue statement or omission of a material fact in connection with the purchase or sale of a covered security; or
2. that the defendant used or employed any manipulative or deceptive device or contrivance in connection with the purchase or sale of a covered security.

c. **Removal of covered class actions**
Any covered class action brought in any State court involving a covered security, as set forth in subsection (b), shall be removable to the Federal district court for the district in which the action is pending, and shall be subject to subsection (b).

d. **Preservation of certain actions**
1. Actions under State law of State of incorporation
   A. Actions preserved
   Notwithstanding subsection (b) or (c), a covered class action described in subparagraph (B) of this paragraph that is based upon the statutory or common law of the State in which the issuer is incorporated (in the case of a corporation) or organized (in the case of any other entity) may be maintained in a State or Federal court by a private party.
   B. Permissible actions
   A covered class action is described in this subparagraph if it involves–
      i. the purchase or sale of securities by the issuer or an affiliate of the issuer exclusively from or to holders of equity securities of the issuer; or
      ii. any recommendation, position, or other communication with respect to the sale of securities of the issuer that–
         I. is made by or on behalf of the issuer or an affiliate of the issuer to holders of equity securities of the issuer; and

17

          II.   concerns decisions of those equity holders with respect to voting their securities, acting in response to a tender or exchange offer, or exercising dissenters' or appraisal rights.

  2.   State actions

    A.   In general

    Notwithstanding any other provision of this section, nothing in this section may be construed to preclude a State or political subdivision thereof or a State pension plan from bringing an action involving a covered security on its own behalf, or as a member of a class comprised solely of other States, political subdivisions, or State pension plans that are named plaintiffs, and that have authorized participation, in such action.

    B.   State pension plan defined

    For purposes of this paragraph, the term "State pension plan" means a pension plan established and maintained for its employees by the government of the State or political subdivision thereof, or by any agency or instrumentality thereof.

  3.   Actions under contractual agreements between issuers and indenture trustees

  Notwithstanding subsection (b) or (c), a covered class action that seeks to enforce a contractual agreement between an issuer and an indenture trustee may be maintained in a State or Federal court by a party to the agreement or a successor to such party.

  4.   Remand of removed actions

  In an action that has been removed from a State court pursuant to subsection (c), if the Federal court determines that the action may be maintained in State court pursuant to this subsection, the Federal court shall remand such action to such State court.

e.   **Preservation of State jurisdiction**

The securities commission (or any agency or office performing like functions) of any State shall retain jurisdiction under the laws of such State to investigate and bring enforcement actions.

f.   **Definitions**

For purposes of this section, the following definitions shall apply:

  1.   Affiliate of the issuer

  The term "affiliate of the issuer" means a person that directly or indirectly, through one or more intermediaries, controls or is controlled by or is under common control with, the issuer.

  2.   Covered class action

    A.   In general

    The term "covered class action" means–

      i.   any single lawsuit in which–

        I.   damages are sought on behalf of more than 50 persons or prospective class members, and questions of law or fact common to those persons or members of the prospective class, without reference to issues of individualized reliance on an alleged misstatement or omission, predominate over

> any questions affecting only individual persons or members; or
>
> II. one or more named parties seek to recover damages on a representative basis on behalf of themselves and other unnamed parties similarly situated, and questions of law or fact common to those persons or members of the prospective class predominate over any questions affecting only individual persons or members; or
>
> ii. any group of lawsuits filed in or pending in the same court and involving common questions of law or fact, in which–
>
> I. damages are sought on behalf of more than 50 persons; and
>
> II. the lawsuits are joined, consolidated, or otherwise proceed as a single action for any purpose.

B. Exception for derivative actions

Notwithstanding subparagraph (A), the term "covered class action" does not include an exclusively derivative action brought by one or more shareholders on behalf of a corporation.

C. Counting of certain class members

For purposes of this paragraph, a corporation, investment company, pension plan, partnership, or other entity, shall be treated as one person or prospective class member, but only if the entity is not established for the purpose of participating in the action.

D. Rule of construction

Nothing in this paragraph shall be construed to affect the discretion of a State court in determining whether actions filed in such court should be joined, consolidated, or otherwise allowed to proceed as a single action.

3. Covered security

The term "covered security" means a security that satisfies the standards for a covered security specified in paragraph (1) or (2) of section 18(b) at the time during which it is alleged that the misrepresentation, omission, or manipulative or deceptive conduct occurred, except that such term shall not include any debt security that is exempt from registration under this title pursuant to rules issued by the Commission under section 4(2)

Section 17 – Fraudulent Interstate Transactions

a. **Use of interstate commerce for purpose of fraud or deceit.** It shall be unlawful for any person in the offer or sale of any securities or any security-based swap agreement (as defined in section 206B of the Gramm-Leach-Bliley Act) by the use of any means or instruments of transportation or communication in interstate commerce or by use of the mails, directly or indirectly–

1. to employ any device, scheme, or artifice to defraud, or

2. to obtain money or property by means of any untrue statement of a material fact or any omission to state a material fact necessary in order to make the statements made, in light of the circumstances under which they were made, not misleading; or

3. to engage in any transaction, practice, or course of business which operates or would operate as a fraud or deceit upon the purchaser.

Section 18 – Exemption from State Regulation of Securities Offerings

a. **Scope of exemption**

Except as otherwise provided in this section, no law, rule, regulation, or order, or other administrative action of any State or any political subdivision thereof–

1. requiring, or with respect to, registration or qualification of securities, or registration or qualification of securities transactions, shall directly or indirectly apply to a security that–

   i. is a covered security; or

   ii. will be a covered security upon completion of the transaction;

2. shall directly or indirectly prohibit, limit, or impose any conditions upon the use of–

   i. with respect to a covered security described in subsection (b), any offering document that is prepared by or on the behalf of the issuer; or

   ii. any proxy statement, report to shareholders, or other disclosure document relating to a covered security or the issuer thereof that is required to be and is filed with the Commission or any national thereof that is required to be and is filed with the Commission or any national securities organization registered under section 15A of the Securities Exchange Act of 1934, except that this subparagraph does not apply to the laws, rules, regulations, or orders, or other administrative actions of the State of incorporation of the issuer; or

3. shall directly or indirectly prohibit, limit, or impose conditions, based on the merits of such offering or issuer, upon the offer or sale of any security described in paragraph (1).

b. **Covered securities**

For the purposes of this section, the following are covered securities:

1. Exclusive federal registration of nationally traded securities

   A security is a covered security if such security is–

   i. listed, or authorized for listing, on the New York Stock Exchange or the American Stock Exchange, or listed, or authorized for listing, on the National Market System of the Nasdaq Stock Market (or any successor to such entities);

   ii. listed, or authorized for listing, on a national securities exchange (or tier or segment thereof) that has listing standards that the Commission determines by rule (on its own initiative or on the basis of a petition) are substantially similar to the listing standards applicable to securities describe in subparagraph (A); or

   iii. is a security of the same issuer that is equal in seniority or that is a senior security to a security described in subparagraph (A) or (B).

2. Exclusive federal registration of investment companies

   A security is a covered security if such security is a security issued by an investment company that is registered, or that has filed a registration statement, under the Investment Company Act of 1940.

3. Sales to qualified purchasers

   A security is a covered security with respect to the offer or sale of the security to qualified purchasers, as defined by the Commission by rule. In prescribing such rule, the Commission may define the term "qualified purchaser" differently with respect to different categories of securities, consistent with the public interest and the protection of investors.

4.   Exemption in connection with certain exempt offerings

A security is a covered security with respect to a transaction that is exempt from registration under this title pursuant to–

    i.   paragraph (1) or (3) of section 4, and the issuer of such security files reports with the Commission pursuant to section 13 or 15(d) of the Securities Exchange Act of 1934;

    ii.   section 4(4);

    iii.   section 3(a), other than the offer or sale of a security that is exempt from such registration pursuant to paragraph (4), (10) or (11) of such section, except that a municipal security that is exempt from such a registration pursuant to paragraph (2) of such section is not a covered security with respect to the offer or sale of such security in the State in which the issuer of such security is located; or

    iv.   Commission rules or regulations issued under section 4(2), except that this subparagraph does not prohibit a State from imposing notice filing requirements that are substantially similar to those required by rule or regulation under section 4(2) that are in effect on September 1, 1996.

c.   **Preservation of authority**

1.   Fraud authority

Consistent with this section, the securities commission (or agency or office performing like functions) of any State shall retain jurisdiction under the laws of such State to investigate and bring enforcement actions with respect to fraud or deceit, or unlawful conduct by a broker or dealer, in connection with securities or securities transactions.

2.   Preservation of filing requirements

    i.   Notice filings permitted

Nothing in this section prohibits the securities commission (or any agency or office performing like functions) of any State from requiring the filing of any document filed with the Commission pursuant to this title, together with annual or periodic reports of the value of securities sold or offered to be sold to persons located in the State (if such sales data is not included in documents filed with the Commission), solely for notice purposes and the assessment of any fee, together with a consent to service of process and any required fee.

    ii.   Preservation of fees

        a.   In general

Until otherwise provided by law, rule, regulation, or order, or other administrative action of any State, or any political subdivision thereof, adopted after the date of enactment of the National Securities Markets Improvement Act of 1996, filing or registration fees with respect to securities or securities transactions shall continue to be collected in amounts determined pursuant to State law as in effect on the day before such date.

    b. Schedule

        The fees required by this subparagraph shall be paid, and all necessary supporting data on sales or offers for sales required under subparagraph (A), shall be reported on the same schedule as would have been applicable had the issuer not relied on the exemption provided in subsection (a).

iii. Availability of preemption contingent on payment of fees

    a. In general

        During the period beginning on the date of enactment of the National Securities Markets Improvement Act of 1996 and ending 3 years after that date of enactment, the securities commission (or any agency or office performing like functions) of any State may require the registration of securities issued by any issuer who refuses to pay the fees required by subparagraph (B).

    b. Delays

        For purposes of this subparagraph, delays in payment of fees or underpayments of fees that are promptly remedied shall not constitute a refusal to pay fees.

iv. Fees not permitted on listed securities

    Notwithstanding subparagraphs (A), (B), and (C), no filing or fee may be required with respect to any security that is a covered security pursuant to subsection (b)(1), or will be such a covered security upon completion of the transaction, or is a security of the same issuer that is equal in seniority or that is a senior security to a security that is a covered security pursuant to subsection (b)(1).

3. Enforcement of requirements

    Nothing in this section shall prohibit the security commission (or any agency or office performing like functions) of any State from suspending the offer or sale of securities within such State as a result of the failure to submit any filing or fee required under law and permitted under this section.

d. **Definitions**

    For purposes of this section, the following definitions shall apply:

1. Offering document

    The term "offering document"–

    i. has the meaning given the term "prospectus" in section 2(a)(10), but without regard to the provisions of subparagraphs (a) and (b) of that section; and

    ii. includes a communication that is not deemed to offer a security pursuant to a rule of the Commission.

2. Prepared by or on behalf of the issuer

    Not later than 6 months after the date of enactment of the National Securities Markets Improvement Act of 1996 [enacted October 11, 1996], the Commission shall, by rule, define the term "prepared by or on behalf of the issuer" for purposes of this section.

3. State

    The term "State" has the same meaning as on section 3 of the Securities Exchange Act of 1934.

4. Senior security
The term "senior security" means any bond, debenture, note, or similar obligation or instrument constituting a security and evidencing indebtedness, and any stock of a class having priority over any other class as to distribution of assets or payments of dividends.

Section 24 – Penalties

Any person who willfully violates any of the provisions of this title, or the rules and regulations promulgated by the Commission under authority thereof, or any person who willfully, in a registration statement filed under this title, makes any untrue statement of a material fact or omits to state any material fact required to be stated therein or necessary to make the statements therein not misleading, shall upon conviction be fined not more than $10,000 or imprisoned not more than five years, or both.

Section 27 – Private Securities Litigation

a. **Private class actions**
1. In general
The provisions of this subsection shall apply to each private action arising under this title that is brought as a plaintiff class action pursuant to the Federal Rules of Civil Procedure.
2. Certification filed with complaint
A. In general
Each plaintiff seeking to serve as a representative party on behalf of a class shall provide a sworn certification, which shall be personally signed by such plaintiff and filed with the complaint, that–
   i. states that the plaintiff has reviewed the complaint and authorized its filing;
   ii. states that the plaintiff did not purchase the security that is the subject of the complaint at the direction of plaintiff's counsel or in order to participate in any private action arising under this title;
   iii. states that the plaintiff is willing to serve as a representative party on behalf of a class, including providing testimony at deposition and trial, if necessary;
   iv. sets forth all of the transactions of the plaintiff in the security that is the subject of the complaint during the class period specified in the complaint;
   v. identifies any other action under this title, filed during the 3-year period preceding the date on which the certification is signed by the plaintiff, in which the plaintiff has sought to serve, or served, as a representative party on behalf of a class; and
   vi. states that the plaintiff will not accept any payment for serving as a representative party on behalf of a class beyond the plaintiff's pro rata share of any recovery, except as ordered or approved by the court in accordance with paragraph (4).

B. Nonwaiver of attorney-client privilege
    The certification filed pursuant to subparagraph (A) shall not be construed to be a waiver of the attorney-client privilege.

3. Appointment of lead plaintiff
    A. Early notice to class members
        i. In general
            Not later than 20 days after the date on which the complaint is filed, the plaintiff or plaintiffs shall cause to be published, in a widely circulated national business-oriented publication or wire service, a notice advising members of the purported plaintiff class–
            I.   of the pendency of the action, the claims asserted therein, and the purported class period; and
            II. that, not later than 60 days after the date on which the notice is published, any member of the purported class may move the court to serve as lead plaintiff of the purported class.
        ii. Multiple actions
            If more than one action on behalf of a class asserting substantially the same claim or claims arising under this title is filed, only the plaintiff or plaintiffs in the first filed action shall be required to cause notice to be published in accordance with clause (i).
        iii. Additional notices may be required under Federal Rules
            Notice required under clause (i) shall be in addition to any notice required pursuant to the Federal Rules of Civil Procedure.
    B. Appointment of lead plaintiff
        i. In general
            Not later than 90 days after the date on which a notice is published under subparagraph (A)(i) , the court shall consider any motion made by a purported class member in response to the notice, including any motion by a class member who is not individually named as a plaintiff in the complaint or complaints, and shall appoint as lead plaintiff the member or members of the purported plaintiff class that the court determines to be most capable of adequately representing the interests of class members (hereafter in this paragraph referred to as the "most adequate plaintiff") in accordance with this subparagraph.
        ii. Consolidated actions
            If more than one action on behalf of a class asserting substantially the same claim or claims arising under this title has been filed, and any party has sought to consolidate those actions for pretrial purposes or for trial, the court shall not make the determination required by clause (i) until after the decision on the motion to consolidate is rendered. As soon as practicable after such decision is rendered, the court shall appoint the most adequate plaintiff as lead plaintiff for the consolidated actions in accordance with this subparagraph.

      iii.   Rebuttable presumption

          I.   In general

Subject to subclause (II), for purposes of clause (i), the court shall adopt a presumption that the most adequate plaintiff in any private action arising under this title is the person or group of persons that-

    (aa) has either filed the complaint or made a motion in response to a notice under Subparagraph (A)(i);

    (bb) in the determination of the court, has the largest financial interest in the relief sought by the class; and

    (cc) otherwise satisfies the requirements of Rule 23 of the Federal Rules of Civil Procedure.

         II.   Rebuttable evidence

The presumption described in subclause (I) may be rebutted only upon proof by a member of the purported plaintiff class that the presumptively most adequate plaintiff—

    (aa) will not fairly and adequately protect the interests of the class; or

    (bb) is subject to unique defenses that render such plaintiff incapable of adequately representing the class.

      iv.   Discovery

For purposes of this subparagraph, discovery relating to whether a member or members of the purported plaintiff class is the most adequate plaintiff may be conducted by a plaintiff only if the plaintiff first demonstrates a reasonable basis for a finding that the presumptively most adequate plaintiff is incapable of adequately representing the class.

      v.   Selection of lead counsel

The most adequate plaintiff shall, subject to the approval of the court, select and retain counsel to represent the class.

      vi.   Restrictions on professional plaintiffs

Except as the court may otherwise permit, consistent with the purposes of this section, a person may be a lead plaintiff, or an officer, director, or fiduciary of a lead plaintiff, in no more than 5 securities class actions brought as plaintiff class actions pursuant to the Federal Rules of Civil Procedure during any 3-year period.

4.   Recovery by plaintiffs

The share of any final judgment or of any settlement that is awarded to a representative party serving on behalf of a class shall be equal, on a per share basis, to the portion of the final judgment or settlement awarded to all other members of the class. Nothing in this paragraph shall be construed to limit the award of reasonable costs and expenses (including lost wages) directly relating to the representation of the class to any representative party serving on behalf of the class.

5.   Restrictions on settlements under seal
      The terms and provisions of any settlement agreement of a class action shall
      not be filed under seal, except that on motion of any party to the settlement, the
      court may order filing under seal for those portions of a settlement agreement
      as to which good cause is shown for such filing under seal. For purposes of this
      paragraph, good cause shall exist only if publication of a term or provision of a
      settlement agreement would cause direct and substantial harm to any party.

6.   Restrictions on payment of attorneys' fees and expenses
      Total attorneys' fees and expenses awarded by the court to counsel for the
      plaintiff class shall not exceed a reasonable percentage of the amount of any
      damages and prejudgment interest actually paid to the class.

7.   Disclosure of settlement terms to class members
      Any proposed or final settlement agreement that is published or otherwise
      disseminated to the class shall include each of the following statements, along
      with a cover page summarizing the information contained in such statements:

      A. Statement of plaintiff recovery
          The amount of the settlement proposed to be distributed to the parties to
          the action, determined in the aggregate and on an average per share basis.

      B. Statement of potential outcome of case

          i.   Agreement on the amount of damages
                If the settling parties agree on the average amount of damages per
                share that would be recoverable if the plaintiff prevailed on each
                claim alleged under this title, a statement concerning the average
                amount of such potential damages per share.

          ii.   Disagreement on the amount of damages
                If the parties do not agree on the average amount of damages per
                share that would be recoverable if the plaintiff prevailed on each
                claim alleged under this title, a statement from each settling party
                concerning the issue or issues on which the parties disagree.

          iii. Inadmissibility for certain purposes
                A statement made in accordance with clause (i) or (ii) concerning
                the amount of damages shall not be admissible in any Federal or
                State judicial action or administrative proceeding, other than an
                action or proceeding arising out of such statement.

      C. Statement of attorneys' fees or costs sought
          If any of the settling parties or their counsel intend to apply to the court for
          an award of attorneys' fees or costs from any fund established as part of
          the settlement, a statement indicating which parties or counsel intend to
          make such an application, the amount of fees and costs that will be sought
          (including the amount of such fees and costs determined on an average per
          share basis) , and a brief explanation supporting the fees and costs sought.

      D. Identification of lawyers' representatives
          The name, telephone number, and address of one or more representatives
          of counsel for the plaintiff class who will be reasonably available to
          answer questions from class members concerning any matter contained in
          any notice of settlement published or otherwise disseminated to the class.

E. Reasons for settlement

A brief statement explaining the reasons why the parties are proposing the settlement.

F. Other information: Such other information as may be required by the court.

8. Attorney conflict of interest

If a plaintiff class is represented by an attorney who directly owns or otherwise has a beneficial interest in the securities that are the subject of the litigation, the court shall make a determination of whether such ownership or other interest constitutes a conflict of interest sufficient to disqualify the attorney from representing the plaintiff class.

b. **Stay of discovery; preservation of evidence**

1. In general

In any private action arising under this title, all discovery and other proceedings shall be stayed during the pendency of any motion to dismiss, unless the court finds, upon the motion of any party, that particularized discovery is necessary to preserve evidence or to prevent undue prejudice to that party.

2. Preservation of evidence

During the pendency of any stay of discovery pursuant to this subsection, unless otherwise ordered by the court, any party to the action with actual notice of the allegations contained in the complaint shall treat all documents, data compilations (including electronically recorded or stored data) , and tangible objects that are in the custody or control of such person and that are relevant to the allegations, as if they were the subject of a continuing request for production of documents from an opposing party under the Federal Rules of Civil Procedure.

3. Sanction for willful violation

A party aggrieved by the willful failure of an opposing party to comply with paragraph (2) may apply to the court for an order awarding appropriate sanctions.

4. Circumvention of stay of discovery

Upon a proper showing, a court may stay discovery proceedings in any private action in a State court as necessary in aid of its jurisdiction, or to protect or effectuate its judgments, in an action subject to a stay of discovery pursuant to this subsection.

c. **Sanctions for abusive litigation**

1. Mandatory review by court

In any private action arising under this title, upon final adjudication of the action, the court shall include in the record specific findings regarding compliance by each party and each attorney representing any party with each requirement of Rule 11(b) of the Federal Rules of Civil Procedure as to any complaint, responsive pleading, or dispositive motion.

2.   Mandatory sanctions

If the court makes a finding under paragraph (1) that a party or attorney violated any requirement of Rule 11(b) of the Federal Rules of Civil Procedure as to any complaint, responsive pleading, or dispositive motion, the court shall impose sanctions on such party or attorney in accordance with Rule 11 of the Federal Rules of Civil Procedure. Prior to making a finding that any party or attorney has violated Rule 11 of the Federal Rules of Civil Procedure, the court shall give such party or attorney notice and an opportunity to respond.

3.   Presumptions in favor of attorneys' fees and costs

A.   In general

Subject to subparagraphs (B) and (C), for purposes of paragraph (2), the court shall adopt a presumption that the appropriate sanction—

i.   for failure of any responsive pleading or dispositive motion to comply with any requirement of Rule 11(b) of the Federal Rules of Civil Procedure is an award to the opposing party of the reasonable attorneys' fees and other expenses incurred as a direct result of the violation; and

ii.   for substantial failure of any complaint to comply with any requirement of Rule 11(b) of the Federal Rules of Civil Procedure is an award to the opposing party of the reasonable attorneys' fees and other expenses incurred in the action.

B.   Rebuttal evidence

The presumption described in subparagraph (A) may be rebutted only upon proof by the party or attorney against whom sanctions are to be imposed that—

i.   the award of attorneys' fees and other expenses will impose an unreasonable burden on that party or attorney and would be unjust, and the failure to make such an award would not impose a greater burden on the party in whose favor sanctions are to be imposed; or

ii.   the violation of Rule 11(b) of the Federal Rules of Civil Procedure was de minimis.

C.   Sanctions

If the party or attorney against whom sanctions are to be imposed meets its burden under subparagraph (B), the court shall award the sanctions that the court deems appropriate pursuant to Rule 11 of the Federal Rules of Civil Procedure.

d.   **Defendant's right to written interrogatories.** In any private action arising under this title in which the plaintiff may recover money damages only on proof that a defendant acted with a particular state of mind, the court shall, when requested by a defendant, submit to the jury a written interrogatory on the issue of each such defendant's state of mind at the time the alleged violation occurred.

Section 27A – Application of Safe Harbor for Forward-Looking Statements

a. **Applicability.** This section shall apply only to a forward-looking statement made by–

1. an issuer that, at the time that the statement is made, is subject to the reporting requirements of section 13(a) or section 15(d) of the Securities Exchange Act of 1934;

2. a person acting on behalf of such issuer;

3. an outside reviewer retained by such issuer making a statement on behalf of such issuer; or

4. an underwriter, with respect to information provided by such issuer or information derived from information provided by the issuer.

b. **Exclusions.** Except to the extent otherwise specifically provided by rule, regulation, or order of the Commission, this section shall not apply to a forward-looking statement–

1. that is made with respect to the business or operations of the issuer, if the issuer–

   A. during the 3-year period preceding the date on which the statement was first made–

     i. was convicted of any felony or misdemeanor described in clauses (i) through (iv) of section 15 (b)(4)(B) of the Securities Exchange Act of 1934; or

     ii. has been made the subject of a judicial or administrative decree or order arising out of a governmental action that–

       I. prohibits future violations of the antifraud provisions of the securities laws;

       II. requires that the issuer cease and desist from violating the antifraud provisions of the securities laws; or

       III. determines that the issuer violated the antifraud provisions of the securities laws;

   B. makes the forward-looking statement in connection with an offering of securities by a blank check company;

   C. issues penny stock;

   D. makes the forward-looking statement in connection with a rollup transaction;

   E. makes the forward-looking statement in connection with a going private transaction; or

2. that is–

   A. included in a financial statement prepared in accordance with generally accepted accounting principles;

   B. contained in a registration statement of, or otherwise issued by, an investment company;

   C. made in connection with a tender offer;

   D. made in connection with an initial public offering;

   E. made in connection with an offering by, or relating to the operations of, a partnership, limited liability company, or a direct participation investment program; or

F.   made in a disclosure of beneficial ownership in a report required to be filed with the Commission pursuant to section 13(d) of the Securities Exchange Act of 1934.

c. **Safe harbor**
1. In general

Except as provided in subsection (b), in any private action arising under this title that is based on an untrue statement of a material fact or omission of a material fact necessary to make the statement not misleading, a person referred to in subsection (a) shall not be liable with respect to any forward-looking statement, whether written or oral, if and to the extent that–

A.   the forward-looking statement is–

    i. identified as a forward-looking statement, and is accompanied by meaningful cautionary statements identifying important factors that could cause actual results to differ materially from those in the forward-looking statement; or

    ii. immaterial; or

B.   the plaintiff fails to prove that the forward-looking statement–

    i. if made by a natural person, was made with actual knowledge by that person that the statement was false or misleading; or

    ii. if made by a business entity, was–

        I. made by or with the approval of an executive officer of that entity, and

        II. made or approved by such officer with actual knowledge by that officer that the statement was false or misleading.

2. Oral forward-looking statements

In the case of an oral forward-looking statement made by an issuer that is subject to the reporting requirements of section 13(a) or section 15(d) of the Securities Exchange Act of 1934, or by a person acting on behalf of such issuer, the requirement set forth in paragraph (1) (A) shall be deemed to be satisfied–

A.   if the oral forward-looking statement is accompanied by a cautionary statement–

    i. that the particular oral statement is a forward-looking statement; and

    ii. that the actual results could differ materially from those projected in the forward-looking statement; and

B.   if–

    i. the oral forward-looking statement is accompanied by an oral statement that additional information concerning factors that could cause actual results to differ materially from those in the forward-looking statement is contained in a readily available written document, or portion thereof;

    ii. the accompanying oral statement referred to in clause (i) identifies the document, or portion thereof, that contains the additional information about those factors relating to the forward-looking statement; and

iii. the information contained in that written document is a cautionary statement that satisfies the standard established in paragraph (1) (A).

3. Availability

Any document filed with the Commission or generally disseminated shall be deemed to be readily available for purposes of paragraph (2) .

4. Effect on other safe harbors

The exemption provided for in paragraph (1) shall be in addition to any exemption that the Commission may establish by rule or regulation under subsection (g).

d. **Duty to update.** Nothing in this section shall impose upon any person a duty to update a forward-looking statement.

e. **Dispositive motion.** On any motion to dismiss based upon subsection (c) (1) , the court shall consider any statement cited in the complaint and cautionary statement accompanying the forward-looking statement, which are not subject to material dispute, cited by the defendant.

f. **Stay pending decision on motion.** In any private action arising under this title, the court shall stay discovery (other than discovery that is specifically directed to the applicability of the exemption provided for in this section) during the pendency of any motion by a defendant for summary judgment that is based on the grounds that—

1. the statement or omission upon which the complaint is based is a forward-looking statement within the meaning of this section; and

2. the exemption provided for in this section precludes a claim for relief.

g. **Exemption authority.** In addition to the exemptions provided for in this section, the Commission may, by rule or regulation, provide exemptions from or under any provision of this title, including with respect to liability that is based on a statement or that is based on projections or other forward-looking information, if and to the extent that any such exemption is consistent with the public interest and the protection of investors, as determined by the Commission.

h. **Effect on other authority of Commission.** Nothing in this section limits, either expressly or by implication, the authority of the Commission to exercise similar authority or to adopt similar rules and regulations with respect to forward-looking statements under any other statute under which the Commission exercises rulemaking authority.

i. **Definitions.** For purposes of this section, the following definitions shall apply:

1. Forward-looking statement

The term "forward-looking statement" means—

A. a statement containing a projection of revenues, income (including income loss), earnings (including earnings loss) per share, capital expenditures, dividends, capital structure, or other financial items;

B.　a statement of the plans and objectives of management for future operations, including plans or objectives relating to the products or services of the issuer;

C.　a statement of future economic performance, including any such statement contained in a discussion and analysis of financial condition by the management or in the results of operations included pursuant to the rules and regulations of the Commission;

D.　any statement of the assumptions underlying or relating to any statement described in subparagraph (A) , (B) , or (C) ;

E.　any report issued by an outside reviewer retained by an issuer, to the extent that the report assesses a forward-looking statement made by the issuer; or

F.　a statement containing a projection or estimate of such other items as may be specified by rule or regulation of the Commission.

2.　Investment company:　The term "investment company" has the same meaning as in section 3(a) of the Investment Company Act of 1940.

3.　Penny stock:　The term "penny stock" has the same meaning as in section 3(a)(51) of the Securities Exchange Act of 1934, and the rules and regulations, or orders issued pursuant to that section.

4.　Going private transaction:　The term "going private transaction" has the meaning given that term under the rules or regulations of the Commission issued pursuant to section 13(e) of the Securities Exchange Act of 1934.

5.　Security laws:　The term "securities laws" has the same meaning as in section 3 of the Securities Exchange Act of 1934.

6.　Person acting on behalf of an issuer:　The term "person acting on behalf of an issuer" means an officer, director, or employee of the issuer.

7.　Other terms:　The terms "blank check company", "rollup transaction", "partnership", "limited liability company", "executive officer of an entity" and "direct participation investment program", have the meanings given those terms by rule or regulation of the Commission.

Section 28 – General Exemptive Authority

The Commission, by rule or regulation, may conditionally or unconditionally exempt any person, security, or transaction, or any class of persons, securities, or transactions, from any provision or provisions of this title or of any rule or regulation issued under this title, to the extent that such exemption is necessary or appropriate in the public interest, and is consistent with the protection of investors.

Securities Act – Rules:

Rule 134 – Communications Not Deemed a Prospectus

Except as provided in paragraphs (e) and (g) of this section, the terms "prospectus" as defined in section 2(a)(10) of the Act or "free writing prospectus" as defined in Rule 405 shall not include a communication limited to the statements required or permitted by this section, provided that the communication is published or transmitted to any person only after a registration statement relating to the offering that includes a prospectus satisfying the requirements of section 10 of the Act (except as otherwise permitted in paragraph (a) of this section) has been filed.

a.   Such communication may include any one or more of the following items of information, which need not follow the numerical sequence of this paragraph, provided that, except as to paragraphs (a)(4), (a)(5), (a)(6), and (a)(17), the prospectus included in the filed registration statement does not have to include a price range otherwise required by rule:

1.   Factual information about the legal identity and business location of the issuer limited to the following: the name of the issuer of the security, the address, phone number, and e-mail address of the issuer's principal offices and contact for investors, the issuer's country of organization, and the geographic areas in which it conducts business;

2.   The title of the security or securities and the amount or amounts being offered, which title may include a designation as to whether the securities are convertible, exercisable, or exchangeable, and as to the ranking of the securities;

3.   A brief indication of the general type of business of the issuer, limited to the following:

    i.   In the case of a manufacturing company, the general type of manufacturing, the principal products or classes of products manufactured, and the segments in which the company conducts business;

    ii.   In the case of a public utility company, the general type of services rendered, a brief indication of the area served, and the segments in which the company conducts business;

    iii.   In the case of an asset-backed issuer, the identity of key parties, such as sponsor, depositor, issuing entity, servicer or servicers, and trustee, the asset class of the transaction, and the identity of any credit enhancement or other support; and

    iv.   In the case of any other type of company, a corresponding statement;

4.   The price of the security, or if the price is not known, the method of its determination or the bona fide estimate of the price range as specified by the issuer or the managing underwriter or underwriters;

5.   In the case of a fixed income security, the final maturity and interest rate provisions or, if the final maturity or interest rate provisions are not known, the probable final maturity or interest rate provisions, as specified by the issuer or the managing underwriter or underwriters;

6.   In the case of a fixed income security with a fixed (non-contingent) interest rate provision, the yield or, if the yield is not known, the probable yield range, as specified by the issuer or the managing underwriter or underwriters and the yield of fixed income securities with comparable maturity and security rating as referred to in paragraph (a)(17) of this section;

7.   A brief description of the intended use of proceeds of the offering, if then disclosed in the prospectus that is part of the filed registration statement;

8.   The name, address, phone number, and e-mail address of the sender of the communication and the fact that it is participating, or expects to participate, in the distribution of the security;

9.   The type of underwriting, if then included in the disclosure in the prospectus that is part of the filed registration statement;

10.   The names of underwriters participating in the offering of the securities, and their additional roles, if any, within the underwriting syndicate;

11.   The anticipated schedule for the offering (including the approximate date upon which the proposed sale to the public will begin) and a description of marketing events (including the dates, times, locations, and procedures for attending or otherwise accessing them);

12. A description of the procedures by which the underwriters will conduct the offering and the procedures for transactions in connection with the offering with the issuer or an underwriter or participating dealer (including procedures regarding account opening and submitting indications of interest and conditional offers to buy), and procedures regarding directed share plans and other participation in offerings by officers, directors, and employees of the issuer;

13. Whether, in the opinion of counsel, the security is a legal investment for savings banks, fiduciaries, insurance companies, or similar investors under the laws of any State or Territory or the District of Columbia, and the permissibility or status of the investment under the Employee Retirement Income Security Act of 1974;

14. Whether, in the opinion of counsel, the security is exempt from specified taxes, or the extent to which the issuer has agreed to pay any tax with respect to the security or measured by the income therefrom;

15. Whether the security is being offered through rights issued to security holders, and, if so, the class of securities the holders of which will be entitled to subscribe, the subscription ratio, the actual or proposed record date, the date upon which the rights were issued or are expected to be issued, the actual or anticipated date upon which they will expire, and the approximate subscription price, or any of the foregoing;

16. Any statement or legend required by any state law or administrative authority;

17. With respect to the securities being offered:
    i. Any security rating assigned, or reasonably expected to be assigned, by a nationally recognized statistical rating organization as defined in Rule 15c3-1(c)(2)(vi)(F) of the Securities Exchange Act of 1934 (Rule 15c3-1(c)(2)(vi)(F) of this chapter) and the name or names of the nationally recognized statistical rating organization(s) that assigned or is or are reasonably expected to assign the rating(s); and
    ii. If registered on Form F-9, any security rating assigned, or reasonably expected to be assigned, by any other rating organization specified in the Instruction to paragraph A.(2) of General Instruction I of Form F-9;

18. The names of selling security holders, if then disclosed in the prospectus that is part of the filed registration statement;

19. The names of securities exchanges or other securities markets where any class of the issuer's securities are, or will be, listed;

20. The ticker symbols, or proposed ticker symbols, of the issuer's securities;

21. The CUSIP number as defined in Rule 17Ad-19(a)(5) of the Securities Exchange Act of 1934 assigned to the securities being offered; and

22. Information disclosed in order to correct inaccuracies previously contained in a communication permissibly made pursuant to this section.

b. Except as provided in paragraph (c) of this section, every communication used pursuant to this section shall contain the following:
    1. If the registration statement has not yet become effective, the following statement:
    A registration statement relating to these securities has been filed with the Securities and Exchange Commission but has not yet become effective. These

securities may not be sold nor may offers to buy be accepted prior to the time the registration statement becomes effective; and

2.   The name and address of a person or persons from whom a written prospectus for the offering meeting the requirements of section 10 of the Act (other than a free writing prospectus as defined in Rule 405) including as to the identified paragraphs above a price range where required by rule, may be obtained.

c.   Any of the statements or information specified in paragraph (b) of this section may, but need not, be contained in a communication which:

    1.   Does no more than state from whom and include the uniform resource locator (URL) where a written prospectus meeting the requirements of section 10 of the Act (other than a free writing prospectus as defined in Rule 405) may be obtained, identify the security, state the price thereof and state by whom orders will be executed; or

    2.   Is accompanied or preceded by a prospectus or a summary prospectus, other than a free writing prospectus as defined in Rule 405, which meets the requirements of section 10 of the Act, including a price range where required by rule, at the date of such preliminary communication.

d.   A communication sent or delivered to any person pursuant to this section which is accompanied or preceded by a prospectus which meets the requirements of section 10 of the Act (other than a free writing prospectus as defined in Rule 405), including a price range where required by rule, at the date of such communication, may solicit from the recipient of the communication an offer to buy the security or request the recipient to indicate whether he or she might be interested in the security, if the communication contains substantially the following statement:

No offer to buy the securities can be accepted and no part of the purchase price can be received until the registration statement has become effective, and any such offer may be withdrawn or revoked, without obligation or commitment of any kind, at any time prior to notice of its acceptance given after the effective date.

Provided, that such statement need not be included in such a communication to a dealer.

e.   A section 10 prospectus included in any communication pursuant to this section shall remain a prospectus for all purposes under the Act.

f.   The provision in paragraphs (c)(2) and (d) of this section that a prospectus that meets the requirements of section 10 of the Act precede or accompany a communication will be satisfied if such communication is an electronic communication containing an active hyperlink to such prospectus.

g.   This section does not apply to a communication relating to an investment company registered under the Investment Company Act of 1940 or a business development company as defined in section 2(a)(48) of the Investment Company Act of 1940.

Rule 135 – Notice of Proposed Registered Offerings

a. **When notice is not an offer**. For purposes of section 5 of the Act only, an issuer or a selling security holder (and any person acting on behalf of either of them) that publishes through any medium a notice of a proposed offering to be registered under the Act will not be deemed to offer its securities for sale through that notice if:

1. Legend. The notice includes a statement to the effect that it does not constitute an offer of any securities for sale; and

2. Limited notice content. The notice otherwise includes no more than the following information:

    i.   The name of the issuer;

    ii. The title, amount and basic terms of the securities offered;

    iii. The amount of the offering, if any, to be made by selling security holders;

    iv. The anticipated timing of the offering;

    v.   A brief statement of the manner and the purpose of the offering, without naming the underwriters;

    vi. Whether the issuer is directing its offering to only a particular class of purchasers;

    vii. Any statements or legends required by the laws of any state or foreign country or administrative authority; and

    viii. In the following offerings, the notice may contain additional information, as follows:

    A. Rights offering. In a rights offering to existing security holders:

        1. The class of security holders eligible to subscribe;
        2. The subscription ratio and expected subscription price;
        3. The proposed record date;
        4. The anticipated issuance date of the rights; and
        5. The subscription period or expiration date of the rights offering.

    B. Offering to employees. In an offering to employees of the issuer or an affiliated company:

        1. The name of the employer;
        2. The class of employees being offered the securities;
        3. The offering price; and
        4. The duration of the offering period.

    C. Exchange offer. In an exchange offer:

        1. The basic terms of the exchange offer;
        2. The name of the subject company;
        3. The subject class of securities sought in the exchange offer.

    D. Rule 145(a) offering. In a Rule 145(a) offering:

        1. The name of the person whose assets are to be sold in exchange for the securities to be offered; The names of any other parties to the transaction;
        2. A brief description of the business of the parties to the transaction;
        3. The date, time and place of the meeting of security holders to vote on or consent to the transaction; and

4. A brief description of the transaction and the basic terms of the transaction.

b. **Corrections of misstatements about the offering.** A person that publishes a notice in reliance on this section may issue a notice that contains no more information than is necessary to correct inaccuracies published about the proposed offering.

Rule 135c – Notice of Certain Proposed Unregistered Offerings

a. For the purposes only of section 5 of the Act, a notice given by an issuer required to file reports pursuant to section 13 or 15(d) of the Securities Exchange Act of 1934 or a foreign issuer that is exempt from registration under the Securities Exchange Act of 1934 pursuant to Rule 12g3-2(b) of this chapter that it proposes to make, is making or has made an offering of securities not registered or required to be registered under the Act shall not be deemed to offer any securities for sale if:

1. Such notice is not used for the purpose of conditioning the market in the United States for any of the securities offered;

2. Such notice states that the securities offered will not be or have not been registered under the Act and may not be offered or sold in the United States absent registration or an applicable exemption from registration requirements; and

3. Such notice contains no more than the following additional information:
   i. The name of the issuer;
   ii. The title, amount and basic terms of the securities offered, the amount of the offering, if any, made by selling security holders, the time of the offering and a brief statement of the manner and purpose of the offering without naming the underwriters;
   iii. In the case of a rights offering to security holders of the issuer, the class of securities the holders of which will be or were entitled to subscribe to the securities offered, the subscription ratio, the record date, the date upon which the rights are proposed to be or were issued, the term or expiration date of the rights and the subscription price, or any of the foregoing;
   iv. In the case of an offering of securities in exchange for other securities of the issuer or of another issuer, the name of the issuer and the title of the securities to be surrendered in exchange for the securities offered, the basis upon which the exchange may be made, or any of the foregoing;
   v. In the case of an offering to employees of the issuer or to employees of any affiliate of the issuer, the name of the employer and class or classes of employees to whom the securities are offered, the offering price or basis of the offering and the period during which the offering is to be or was made or any of the foregoing; and
   vi. Any statement or legend required by State or foreign law or administrative authority.

b. Any notice contemplated by this section may take the form of a news release or a written communication directed to security holders or employees, as the case may be, or other published statements.

c. Notwithstanding the provisions of paragraphs (a) and (b) of this section, in the case of a rights offering of a security listed or subject to unlisted trading privileges on a national securities exchange or quoted on the NASDAQ inter-dealer quotation system information with respect to the interest rate, conversion ratio and subscription price may be disseminated through the facilities of the exchange, the consolidated transaction reporting system, the NASDAQ system or the Dow Jones broad tape, provided such information is already disclosed in a Form 8-K on file with the Commission, in a Form 6-K furnished to the Commission or, in the case of an issuer relying on Rule 12g3-2(b) of this chapter, in a submission made pursuant to that Section to the Commission.

d. The issuer shall file any notice contemplated by this section with the Commission under cover of Form 8-K or furnish such notice under Form 6-K, as applicable, and, if relying on Rule 12g3-2(b) of this chapter, shall furnish such notice to the Commission in accordance with the provisions of that exemptive Section.

Rule 137 – Publications or Distributions of Research Reports by Brokers or Dealers that are not Participating in an Issuer's Registered Distribution of Securities.

Under the following conditions, the terms "offers," "participates," or "participation" in section 2(a)(11) of the Act shall not be deemed to apply to the publication or distribution of research reports with respect to the securities of an issuer which is the subject of an offering pursuant to a registration statement that the issuer proposes to file, or has filed, or that is effective:

a. The broker or dealer (and any affiliate) that has distributed the report and, if different, the person (and any affiliate) that has published the report have not participated, are not participating, and do not propose to participate in the distribution of the securities that are or will be the subject of the registered offering.

b. In connection with the publication or distribution of the research report, the broker or dealer (and any affiliate) that has distributed the report and, if different, the person (and any affiliate) that has published the report are not receiving and have not received consideration directly or indirectly from, and are not acting under any direct or indirect arrangement or understanding with:
   1. The issuer of the securities;
   2. A selling security holder;
   3. Any participant in the distribution of the securities that are or will be the subject of the registration statement; or
   4. Any other person interested in the securities that are or will be the subject of the registration statement.

Instruction to Rule 137(b).
This paragraph (b) does not preclude payment of:
   1. The regular price being paid by the broker or dealer for independent research, so long as the conditions of this paragraph (b) are satisfied; or
   2. The regular subscription or purchase price for the research report.

c. The broker or dealer publishes or distributes the research report in the regular course of its business.

d. The issuer is not and during the past three years neither the issuer nor any of its predecessors was:

1. A blank check company as defined in Rule 419(a)(2);

2. A shell company, other than a business combination related shell company, each as defined in Rule 405; or

3. An issuer for an offering of penny stock as defined in Rule 3a51-1 of the Securities Exchange Act of 1934.

e. **Definition of research report.** For purposes of this section, research report means a written communication, as defined in Rule 405, that includes information, opinions, or recommendations with respect to securities of an issuer or an analysis of a security or an issuer, whether or not it provides information reasonably sufficient upon which to base an investment decision.

Rule 138 – Publications or Distributions of Research Reports by Brokers or Dealers about Securities other than those they are Distributing.

a. **Registered offerings**. Under the following conditions, a broker's or dealer's publication or distribution of research reports about securities of an issuer shall be deemed for purposes of sections 2(a)(10) and 5(c) of the Act not to constitute an offer for sale or offer to sell a security which is the subject of an offering pursuant to a registration statement that the issuer proposes to file, or has filed, or that is effective, even if the broker or dealer is participating or will participate in the registered offering of the issuer's securities:

1. i. The research report relates solely to the issuer's common stock, or debt securities, or preferred stock convertible into its common stock, and the offering involves solely the issuer's non-convertible debt securities or non-convertible, non-participating preferred stock; or

    ii. The research report relates solely to the issuer's non-convertible debt securities or non-participating preferred stock, and the offering involves solely the issuer's common stock, or debt securities, or preferred stock convertible into its common stock.

Instruction to paragraph (a)(1): If the issuer has filed a shelf registration statement under Rule 415(a)(1)(x) or pursuant to General Instruction I.D. of Form S-3 or General Instruction I.C. of Form F-3 with respect to multiple classes of securities, the conditions of paragraph (a)(1) of this section must be satisfied for the offering in which the broker or dealer is participating or will participate.

2. The issuer as of the date of reliance on this section:

    i. Is required to file reports, and has filed all periodic reports required during the preceding 12 months (or such shorter time that the issuer was required to file such reports) on Forms 10-K, 10-Q and 20-F) pursuant to section 13 or section 15(d) of the Securities Exchange Act of 1934; or

      ii. Is a foreign private issuer that:
          A. Meets all of the registrant requirements of Form F-3 other than the reporting history provisions of General Instructions I.A.1. & I.A.2(a) of Form F-3;
          B. Either:
             (1) Satisfies the public float threshold in General Instruction I.B.1. of Form F-3; or
             (2) Is issuing non-convertible investment grade securities meeting the provisions of General Instruction I.B.2. of Form F-3; and
          C. Either:
             (1) Has its equity securities trading on a designated offshore securities market as defined in Rule 902(b) and has had them so traded for at least 12 months; or
             (2) Has a worldwide market value of its outstanding common equity held by non-affiliates of $700 million or more.

3.   The broker or dealer publishes or distributes research reports on the types of securities in question in the regular course of its business; and

4.   The issuer is not, and during the past three years neither the issuer nor any of its predecessors was:
      i.   A blank check company as defined in Rule 419(a)(2);
      ii. A shell company, other than a business combination related shell company, each as defined in Rule 405; or
      iii. An issuer for an offering of penny stock as defined in Rule 3a51-1 of the Securities Exchange Act of 1934.

b.   **Rule 144A offerings**. If the conditions in paragraph (a) of this section are satisfied, a broker's or dealer's publication or distribution of a research report shall not be considered an offer for sale or an offer to sell a security or general solicitation or general advertising, in connection with an offering relying on Rule 144A.

c.   **Regulation S offerings**. If the conditions in paragraph (a) of this section are satisfied, a broker's or dealer's publication or distribution of a research report shall not:
1.   Constitute directed selling efforts as defined in Rule 902(c) for offerings under Regulation S; or
2.   Be inconsistent with the offshore transaction requirement in Rule 902(h) for offerings under Regulation S.

d.   **Definition of research report**. For purposes of this section, research report means a written communication, as defined in Rule 405, that includes information, opinions, or recommendations with respect to securities of an issuer or an analysis of a security or an issuer, whether or not it provides information reasonably sufficient upon which to base an investment decision.

Rule 139 – Publications or Distributions of Research Reports by Brokers or Dealers Distributing Securities.

    a.   **Registered offerings.** Under the conditions of paragraph (a)(1) or (a)(2) of this section, a broker's or dealer's publication or distribution of a research report about an issuer or any of its securities shall be deemed for purposes of sections 2(a)(10) and 5(c) of the Act not to constitute an offer for sale or offer to sell a security that is the subject of an offering pursuant to a registration statement that the issuer proposes to file, or has filed, or that is effective, even if the broker or dealer is participating or will participate in the registered offering of the issuer's securities:

    1.   Issuer-specific research reports.

        i.   The issuer either:

        (A)(1)   At the later of the time of filing its most recent Form S-3 or Form F-3 or the time of its most recent amendment to such registration statement for purposes of complying with section 10(a)(3) of the Act or, if no Form S-3 or Form F-3 has been filed, at the date of reliance on this section, meets the registrant requirements of such Form S-3 or Form F-3 and:

            (i)   either at such date meets the minimum float provisions of General Instruction I.B.1 of such Forms; or,

            (ii)   At the date of reliance on this section, is, or if a registration statement has not been filed, will be, offering securities meeting the requirements for the offering of investment grade securities pursuant to General Instruction I.B.2 of Form S-3 or Form F-3; or

            (iii)   At the date of reliance on this section is a well-known seasoned issuer as defined in Rule 405, other than a majority-owned subsidiary that is a well-known seasoned issuer by virtue of paragraph (1)(ii) of the definition of well known seasoned issuer in Rule 405; and

        (2)   As of the date of reliance on this section, has filed all periodic reports required during the preceding 12 months on Forms 10-K, 10-Q and 20-F pursuant to section 13 or section 15(d) of the Securities Exchange Act of 1934; or

        (B)   Is a foreign private issuer that as of the date of reliance on this section:

            (1)   Meets all of the registrant requirements of Form F-3 other than the reporting history provisions of General Instructions I.A.1. and I.A.2(a) of Form F-3 ;

            (2)   Either:

                (i)   Satisfies the public float threshold in General Instruction I.B.1. of Form F-3; or

                (ii)   Is issuing non-convertible investment grade securities meeting the provisions of General Instruction I.B.2. of Form F-3; and

(3) Either:
    (i) Has its equity securities trading on a designated offshore securities market as defined in Rule 902(b) and has had them so traded for at least 12 months; or
    (ii) Has a worldwide market value of its outstanding common equity held by non-affiliates of $700 million or more;

ii. The issuer is not and during the past three years neither the issuer nor any of its predecessors was:

(A) A blank check company as defined in Rule 419(a)(2);

(B) A shell company, other than a business combination related shell company, each as defined in Rule 405; or

(C) An issuer for an offering of penny stock as defined in Rule 3a51-1 of the Securities Exchange Act of 1934; and

iii. The broker or dealer publishes or distributes research reports in the regular course of its business and such publication or distribution does not represent the initiation of publication of research reports about such issuer or its securities or reinitiation of such publication following discontinuation of publication of such research reports.

2. Industry reports.

i. The issuer is required to file reports pursuant to section 13 or section 15(d) of the Securities Exchange Act of 1934 or satisfies the conditions in paragraph (a)(1)(i)(B) of this section;

ii. The condition in paragraph (a)(1)(ii) of this section is satisfied;

iii. The research report includes similar information with respect to a substantial number of issuers in the issuer's industry or sub-industry, or contains a comprehensive list of securities currently recommended by the broker or dealer;

iv. The analysis regarding the issuer or its securities is given no materially greater space or prominence in the publication than that given to other securities or issuers; and

v. The broker or dealer publishes or distributes research reports in the regular course of its business and, at the time of the publication or distribution of the research report, is including similar information about the issuer or its securities in similar reports.

b. **Rule 144A offerings**. If the conditions in paragraph (a)(1) or (a)(2) of this section are satisfied, a broker's or dealer's publication or distribution of a research report shall not be considered an offer for sale or an offer to sell a security or general solicitation or general advertising, in connection with an offering relying on Rule 144A.

c. **Regulation S offerings**. If the conditions in paragraph (a)(1) or (a)(2) of this section are satisfied, a broker's or dealer's publication or distribution of a research report shall not:

1. Constitute directed selling efforts as defined in Rule 902(c) for offerings under Regulation S; or

2.   Be inconsistent with the offshore transaction requirement in Rule 902(h) for offerings under Regulation S.

d.   **Definition of research report**. For purposes of this section, research report means a written communication, as defined in Rule 405, that includes information, opinions, or recommendations with respect to securities of an issuer or an analysis of a security or an issuer, whether or not it provides information reasonably sufficient upon which to base an investment decision.

Instruction to Rule 139

Projections. A projection constitutes an analysis or information falling within the definition of research report. When a broker or dealer publishes or distributes projections of an issuer's sales or earnings in reliance on paragraph (a)(2) of this section, it must:

1.   Have previously published or distributed projections on a regular basis in order to satisfy the "regular course of its business" condition;
2.   At the time of publishing or disseminating a research report, be publishing or distributing projections with respect to that issuer; and
3.   For purposes of paragraph (a)(2)(iii) of this section, include projections covering the same or similar periods with respect to either a substantial number of issuers in the issuer's industry or sub-industry or substantially all issuers represented in the comprehensive list of securities contained in the research report.

Rule 144 – Persons Deemed Not to be Engaged in a Distribution and Therefore Not Underwriters

Preliminary Note

Certain basic principles are essential to an understanding of the registration requirements in the Securities Act of 1933 (the Act or the Securities Act) and the purposes underlying Rule 144:

1.   If any person sells a non-exempt security to any other person, the sale must be registered unless an exemption can be found for the transaction.
2.   Section 4(1) of the Securities Act provides one such exemption for a transaction "by a person other than an issuer, underwriter, or dealer." Therefore, an understanding of the term "underwriter" is important in determining whether or not the Section 4(1) exemption from registration is available for the sale of the securities.

The term "underwriter" is broadly defined in Section 2(a)(11) of the Securities Act to mean any person who has purchased from an issuer with a view to, or offers or sells for an issuer in connection with, the distribution of any security, or participates, or has a direct or indirect participation in any such undertaking, or participates or has a participation in the direct or indirect underwriting of any such undertaking. The interpretation of this definition traditionally has focused on the words "with a view to" in the phrase "purchased from an issuer with a view to . . . distribution." An investment banking firm which arranges with an issuer for the public sale of its securities is clearly an "underwriter" under that section. However, individual investors who are not professionals in the securities business also may be "underwriters" if they act as links in a chain of transactions through which securities move from an issuer to the public.

Since it is difficult to ascertain the mental state of the purchaser at the time of an acquisition of securities, prior to and since the adoption of Rule 144, subsequent acts and circumstances have been considered to determine whether the purchaser took the securities "with a view to distribution" at the time of the acquisition. Emphasis has been placed on factors such as the length of time the person held the securities and whether there has been an unforeseeable change in circumstances of the holder. Experience has shown, however, that reliance upon such factors alone has led to uncertainty in the application of the registratition provisons of the Act.

The Commission adopted Rule 144 to establish specific criteria for determining whether a person is not engaged in a distribution. Rule 144 creates a safe harbor from the Section 2(a)(11) definition of "underwriter." A person satisfying the applicable conditions of the Rule 144 safe harbor is deemed not to be engaged in a distribution of the securities and therefore not an underwriter of the securities for purposes of Section 2(a)(11). Therefore, such a person is deemed not to be an underwriter when determining whether a sale is eligible for the Section 4(1) exemption for "transactions by any person other than an issuer, underwriter, or dealer." If a sale of securities complies with all of the applicable conditions of Rule 144:

1. Any affiliate or other person who sells restricted securities will be deemed not to be engaged in a distribution and therefore not an underwriter for that transaction
2. Any person who sells restricted or other securities on behalf of an affiliate of the issuer will be deemed not to be engaged in a distribution and therefore not an undewriter for that transaction; and
3. The purchaser in such transaction will receive securities that are not restricted securities.

Rule 144 is not an exclusive safe harbor. A person who does not meet all of the applicable conditions of Rule 144 still may claim any other available exemption under the Act for the sale of the securities. The Rule 144 safe harbor is not available to any person with respect to any transaction or series of transactions that, although in technical compliance with Rule 144, is part of a plan or scheme to evade the registration requirements of the Act.

    a.   **Definitions.** The following definitions shall apply for the purposes of this rule.

        1.   An **affiliate** of an issuer is a person that directly, or indirectly through one or more intermediaries, controls, or is controlled by, or is under common control with, such issuer.

        2.   The term **person** when used with reference to a person for whose account securities are to be sold in reliance upon this rule includes, in addition to such person, all of the following persons:

            i.   Any relative or spouse of such person, or any relative of such spouse, any one of whom has the same home as such person;

            ii.   Any trust or estate in which such person or any of the persons specified in paragraph (a)(2)(i) of this section collectively own ten percent or more of the total beneficial interest or of which any of such persons serve as trustee, executor or in any similar capacity; and

            iii.   Any corporation or other organization (other than the issuer) in which such person or any of the persons specified in paragraph (a)(2)(i) of this section are the beneficial owners collectively of ten percent or more of any class of equity securities or ten percent or more of the equity interest.

        3.   The term **restricted securities** means:

            i.   Securities acquired directly or indirectly from the issuer, or from an affiliate of the issuer, in a transaction or chain of transactions not involving any public offering;

    ii.   Securities acquired from the issuer that are subject to the resale limitations of Rule 502(d) under Regulation D or Rule 701(c);

    iii.   Securities acquired in a transaction or chain of transactions meeting the requirements of Rule 144A;

    iv.   Securities acquired from the issuer in a transaction subject to the conditions of Regulation CE;

    v.   Equity securities of domestic issuers acquired in a transaction or chain of transactions subject to the conditions of Rule 901 or Rule 903 under Regulation S (Rules 901 through 905 and Preliminary Notes);

    vi.   Securities acquired in a transaction made under Rule 801 to the same extent and proportion that the securities held by the security holder of the class with respect to which the rights offering was made were, as of the record date for the rights offering, "restricted securities" within the meaning of this paragraph (a)(3);

    vii.   Securities acquired in a transaction made under Rule 802 to the same extent and proportion that the securities that were tendered or exchanged in the exchange offer or business combination were "restricted securities" within the meaning of this paragraph (a)(3); and

    viii.   Securities acquired from the issuer in a transaction subject to an exemption under section 4(6) of the Act.

4.   The term **debt securities** means:

    i.   Any security other than an equity security as defined in Rule 405;

    ii.   Non-participatory preferred stock, which is defined as non-convertible capital stock, the holders of which are entitled to a preference in payment of dividends and in distribution of assets on liquidation, dissolution, or winding up of the issuer, but are not entitled to participate in residual earnings

    iii.   Asset-backed securities, as defined in Rule 1101 of this chapter.

b.   **Conditions to be Met.** Subject to paragraph (i) of this section, the following conditions must be met:

1.   **Non-Affiliates**.

    i.   If the issuer of the securities is, and has been for a period of at least 90 days immediately before the sale, subject to the reporting requirements of section 13 or 15(d) of the Securities Exchange Act of 1934 (the Exchange Act), any person who is not an affiliate of the issuer at the time of the sale, and has not been an affiliate during the preceding three months, who sells restricted securities of the issuer for his or her own account shall be deemed not to be an underwriter of those securities within the meaning of section 2(a)(11) of the Act if all of the conditions of paragraphs (c)(1) and (d) of are met. The requirements of paragraph (c)(1) of this section shall not apply to restricted securities sold for the account of a person who is not an affiliate of the issuer at the time of the sale and has not been an affiliate during the preceding three months, provided a period of one year has elapsed since the later of the date the securities were acquired from the issuer or from an affiliate of the issuer.

    ii.   If the issuer of the securities is not, or has not been for a period of at least 90 days immediately before the sale, subject to the reporting requirements of section 13 or 15(d) of the Exchange Act, any person who is not an affiliate of the issuer at the time of the sale, and has not been an affiliate during the preceding three months, who sells restricted securities of the issuer for his or her own account shall be deemed not to be underwriter of those securities within the meaning of section 2(a)(11) of the Act if the condition of paragraph (d) of this rule is met.

2. **Affiliates or persons selling on behalf of affiliates**. Any affiliate of the issuer, or any person who was an affiliate at any time during the 90 days immediately before the sale, who sells restricted securities, or any person who sells restricted or any other securities for the account of an affiliate of the issuer of such securities, or any person who sells restricted or any other securities for the account of a person who was an affiliate at any time during the 90 days immediately before the sale, shall be deemed not to be an underwriter of those securities within the meaning of section 2(a)(11) of the Act if all of the conditions of this section are met.

c. **Current Public Information**. Adequate current public information with respect to the issuer of the securities must be available. Such information will be deemed to be available only if the applicable condition set forth in this paragraph is met:

1. **Reporting Issuers**. The issuer is, and has been for a period of at least 90 days immediately before the sale, subject to the reporting requirements of section 13 or 15(d) of the Exchange Act and has:

    i. Filed all required reports under section 13 or 15(d) of the Exchange Act, as applicable, during the 12 months preceding such sale (or for such shorter period that the issuer was required to file such reports), other than Form 8-K reports; and

    ii. Submitted electronically and posted on its corporate Web site, if any, every Interactive Data File required to be submitted and posted pursuant to Rule 405 of Regulation S-T, during the 12 months preceding such sale (or for such shorter period that the issuer was required to submit and post such files); or or

2. **Non-reporting issuers**. If the issuer is not subject to Section 13 or 15(d) of the Securities Exchange Act of 1934, there is publicly available the information concerning the issuer specified in paragraphs (a)(5)(i) to (xiv), inclusive, and paragraph (a)(5)(xvi) of Rule 15c2-11 of this chapter or, if the issuer is an insurance company, the information specified in Section 12(g)(2)(G)(i) of the Exchange Act.

Note to Rule 144(c). With respect to paragraph (c)(1), the person can rely upon:

1. A statement in whichever is the most recent report, quarterly or annual, required to be filed and filed by the issuer that such issuer has:

    a. Filed all reports required under section 13 or 15(d) of the Exchange Act, as applicable, during the preceding 12 months (or for such shorter period that the issuer was required to file such reports), other than Form 8–K reports, and has been subject to such filing requirements for the past 90 days; and

    b. Submitted electronically and posted on its corporate Web site, if any, every Interactive Data File required to be submitted and posted pursuant to Rule 405 of Regulation S-T, during the preceding 12 months (or for such shorter period that the issuer was required to submit and post such files); or

2. A written statement from the issuer that it has complied with such reporting, submission or posting requirements.

3. Neither type of statement may be relied upon, however, if the person knows or has reason to believe that the issuer has not complied with such requirements..

d. **Holding Period for Restricted Securities.** If the securities sold are restricted securities, the following provisions apply:

1. **General Rule.**
   i. If the issuer of the securities is, and has been for a period of at least 90 days immediately before the sale, subject to the reporting requirements of section 13 or 15(d) of the Exchange Act, a minimum of six months must elapse between the later of the date of the acquisition of the securities from the issuer, or from an affiliate of the issuer, and any resale of such securities in reliance on this section for the account of either the acquiror or any subsequent holder of those securities.
   ii. If the issuer of the securities is not, or has not been for a period of at least 90 days immediately before the sale, subject to the reporting requirements of section 13 or 15(d) of the Exchange Act, a minimum of one year must elapse between the later of the date of the acquisition of the securities from the issuer, or from an affiliate of the issuer, and any resale of such securities in reliance on this section for the account of either the acquiror or any subsequent holder of those securities.
   iii. If the acquiror takes the securities by purchase, the holding period shall not begin until the full purchase price or other consideration is paid or given by the person acquiring the securities from the issuer or from an affiliate of the issuer.

2. **Promissory Notes, Other Obligations or Installment Contracts.** Giving the issuer or affiliate of the issuer from whom the securities were purchased a promissory note or other obligation to pay the purchase price, or entering into an installment purchase contract with such person, shall not be deemed full payment of the purchase price unless the promissory note, obligation or contract:
   i. provides for full recourse against the purchaser of the securities;
   ii. is secured by collateral, other than the securities purchased, having a fair market value at least equal to the purchase price of the securities purchased; and
   iii. shall have been discharged by payment in full prior to the sale of the securities.

3. **Determination of Holding Period.** The following provisions shall apply for the purpose of determining the period securities have been held:
   i. Stock Dividends, Splits and Recapitalizations. Securities acquired from the issuer as a dividend or pursuant to a stock split, reverse split or recapitalization shall be deemed to have been acquired at the same time as the securities on which the dividend or, if more than one, the initial dividend was paid, the securities involved in the split or reverse split, or the securities surrendered in connection with the recapitalization.

ii.   Conversions. If the securities sold were acquired from the issuer solely in exchange for other securities of the same issuer, the newly acquired securities shall be deemed to have been acquired at the same time as the securities surrendered for conversion or exchange, even if the securities surrendered were not convertible or exchangeable by their terms.;

Note to Rule 144(d)(3)(ii). If the surrendered securities originally did not provide for cashless conversion or exchange by their terms and the holder provided consideration, other than solely securities of the same issuer, in connection with the amendment of the surrendered securities to permit cashless conversion or exchange, then the newly acquired securities shall be deemed to have been acquired at the same time as such amendment to the surrendered securities, so long as, in the conversion or exchange, the securities sold were acquired from the issuer solely in exchange for other securities of the same issuer.

iii.   Contingent Issuance of Securities. Securities acquired as a contingent payment of the purchase price of an equity interest in a business, or the assets of a business, sold to the issuer or an affiliate of the issuer shall be deemed to have been acquired at the time of such sale if the issuer or affiliate was then committed to issue the securities subject only to conditions other than the payment of further consideration for such securities. An agreement entered into in connection with any such purchase to remain in the employment of, or not to compete with, the issuer or affiliate or the rendering of services pursuant to such agreement shall not be deemed to be the payment of further consideration for such securities.

iv.   Pledged Securities. Securities which are bona fide pledged by an affiliate of the issuer when sold by the pledgee, or by a purchaser, after a default in the obligation secured by the pledge, shall be deemed to have been acquired when they were acquired by the pledgor, except that if the securities were pledged without recourse they shall be deemed to have been acquired by the pledgee at the time of the pledge or by the purchaser at the time of purchase.

v.   Gifts of Securities. Securities acquired from an affiliate of the issuer by gift shall be deemed to have been acquired by the donee when they were acquired by the donor;

vi.   Trusts. Where a trust settlor is an affiliate of the issuer, securities acquired from the settlor by the trust, or acquired from the trust by the beneficiaries thereof, shall be deemed to have been acquired when such securities were acquired by the settlor;

vii.   Estates. Where a deceased person was an affiliate of the issuer, securities held by the estate of such person or acquired from such an estate by the estate beneficiaries shall be deemed to have been acquired when they were acquired by the deceased person, except that no holding period is required if the estate is not an affiliate of the issuer or if the securities are sold by a beneficiary of the estate who is not such an affiliate.

Note to Rule 144(d)(3(vii). While there is no holding period or amount limitation for estates and beneficiaries thereof which are not affiliates of the issuer, paragraphs (c), and (h) of this section apply to securities sold by such persons in reliance upon this section.

viii.   Rule 145(a) transactions. The holding period for securities acquired in a transaction specified in Rule 145(a) shall be deemed to commence on the date the securities were acquired by the purchaser in such transaction, except as otherwise provided in paragraphs (d)(3)(ii) and (ix) of this section.

ix.   Holding company formations. Securities acquired from the issuer in a transaction effected solely for the purpose of forming a holding company shall be deemed to have been acquired at the same time as the securities of the predecessor issuer exchanged in the holding company formation where:

A.   The newly formed holding company's securities were issued solely in exchange for the securities of the predecessor company as part of a reorganization of the predecessor company into a holding company structure;

B.   Holders received securities of the same class evidencing the same proportional interest in the holding company as they held in the predecessor, and the rights and interests of the holders of such securities are substantially the same as those they possessed as holders of the predecessor company's securitieis; and

C.   Immediately following the transaction, the holding company has no significant assets other than securities of the predecessor company and its existing subsidiaries and has substantially the same assets and liabilities on a consolidated basis as the predecessor company had before the transaction.

x.   Cashless exercise of options and warrants. If the securities sold were acquired from the issuer solely upon cashless exercise of options or warrants issued by the issuer, the newly acquired securities shall be deemed to have been acquired at the same time as the exercised options or warrants, even if the options or warrants exercised originally did not provide for cashless exercise by their terms.

Note 1 to Rule 144(d)(3)(x). If the options or warrants originally did not provide for cashless exercise by their terms and the holder provided consideration, other than solely securities of the same issuer, in connection with the amendment of the options or warrants to permit cashless exercise, then the newly acquired securities shall be deemed to have been acquired at the same time as such amendment to the options or warrants so long as the exercise itself was cashless.

Note 2 to Rule 144(d)(3)(x). If the options or warrants are not purchased for cash or property and do not create any investment risk to the holder, as in the case of employee stock options, the newly acquired securities shall be deemed to have been acquired at the time the options or warrants are exercised, so long as the full purchase price or other consideration for the newly acquired securities has been paid or given by the person acquiring the securities from the issuer or from an affiliate of the issuer at the time of exercise.

e. **Limitation on Amount of Securities Sold.** Except as hereinafter provided, the amount of securities sold for the account of an affiliate of the issuer in reliance upon this section shall be determined as follows:

1. If any securities are sold for the account of an affiliate of the issuer, regardless of whether those securities are restricted, the amount of securities sold, together with all sales of securities of the same class for the account of such person within the preceding three months, shall not exceed the greatest of

    i.   one percent of the shares or other units of the class outstanding as shown by the most recent report or statement published by the issuer, or

    ii. the average weekly reported volume of trading in such securities on all national securities exchanges and/or reported through the automated quotation system of a registered securities association during the four calendar weeks preceding the filing of notice required by paragraph (h), or if no such notice is required the date of receipt of the order to execute the transaction by the broker or the date of execution of the transaction directly with a market maker, or

    iii. the average weekly volume of trading in such securities reported through the consolidated transaction reporting system contemplated by Rule 11Aa3-1 under the Securities Exchange Act of 1934 during the four-week period specified in subdivision (ii) of this paragraph.

2. If the securities sold are debt securities, then the amount of debt securities sold for the account of an affiliate of the issuer, regardless of whether those securities are restricted, shall not exceed the greater of the limitation set forth in paragraph (e)(1) of this section or, together with all sales of securities of the same tranche (or class when the securities are on-participatory preferred stock) sold for the account of such person within the preceding three months, ten percent of the principal amount of the tranche (or class when the securities are non-participatory preferred stock) attributable to the securities sold..

3. Determination of Amount. For the purpose of determining the amount of securities specified in paragraph (e)(1) of this section and, applicable, paragraph (e)(2) of this section, the following provisions shall apply:

    i.   Where both convertible securities and securities of the class into which they are convertible are sold, the amount of convertible securities sold shall be deemed to be the amount of securities of the class into which they are convertible for the purpose of determining the aggregate amount of securities of both classes sold;

    ii. The amount of securities sold for the account of a pledgee of those securities, or for the account of a purchaser of the pledged securities, during any period of three months within six months (or within one year if the issuer of the securities is not, or has not been for a period of at least 90 days immediately before the sale, subject to the reporting requirements of section 13 or 15(d) of the Exchange Act) after a default in the obligation secured by the pledge, and the amount of securities sold during the same three-month period for the account of the pledgor shall not exceed, in the aggregate, the amount specified in paragraph (e)(1) or (2) of this section, whichever is applicable.

    Note to Rule 144(e)(3)(ii). Sales by a pledgee of securities pledged by a borrower will not be aggregated under paragraph (e)(3)(ii) with sales of the securities of the same issuer by other pledgees of such borrower in the absence of concerted action by such pledgees.

    iii. The amount of securities sold for the account of a donee of those securities during any three-month period within six months (or within one year if the issuer of the securities is not, or has not been for a period of at least 90 days immediately before the sale, subject to the reporting requirements of section 13 or 15(d) of the Exchange Act) after the donation, and the amount of securities sold during the same three-month period for the account of the donor, shall not exceed, in the aggregate, the amount specified in paragraph (e)(1) or (2), which is applicable.

    iv. Where securities were acquired by a trust from the settlor of the trust, the amount of such securities sold for the account of the trust during any period of three months within six months (or within one year if the issuer of the securities is not, or has not been for a period of at least 90 days immediately before the sale, subject to the reporting requirements of section 13 or 15(d) of the Exchange Act) after the acquisition of the securities by the trust, and the amount of securities sold during the same three-month period for the account of the settlor, shall not exceed, in the aggregate, the amount specified in paragraph (e)(1) or (2) of this section, whichever is applicable;

    v. The amount of securities sold for the account of the estate of a deceased person, or for the account of a beneficiary of such estate, during any three-month period and the amount of securities sold during the same three-month period for the account of the deceased person prior to his death shall not exceed, in the aggregate, the amount specified in subparagraph (1) or (2) of this section, whichever is applicable; *Provided,* That no limitation on amount shall apply if the estate or beneficiary thereof is not an affiliate of the issuer;

    vi. When two or more affiliates or other persons agree to act in concert for the purpose of selling securities of an issuer, all securities of the same class sold for the account of all such persons during any three-month period shall be aggregated for the purpose of determining the limitation on the amount of securities sold;

    vii. The following sales of securities need not be included in determining the amount of securities sold in reliance upon this section:

        A. securities sold pursuant to an effective registration statement under the Act;

        B. securities sold pursuant to an exemption provided by Regulation A under the Act;

        C. securities sold in a transaction exempt pursuant to Section 4 of the Act and not involving any public offering; and

        D. securities sold offshore pursuant to Regulation S under the Act.

f. **Manner of Sale**.

    1. The securities shall be sold in one of the following manners:

        i. *brokers' transactions* within the meaning of section 4(4) of the Act;

        ii. transactions directly with a *market maker,* as that term is defined in section 3(a)(38) of the Exchange Act; or

       iii.   *riskless principal transactions* where

          A.   the offsetting trades must be executed at the same price (exclusive of an explicitly disclosed markup or markdown, commission equivalent, or other fee);

          B.   the transaction is permitted to be reported as riskless under the rules of a self-regulatory organization; and the requirements of paragraphs (g)(2) (applicable to any markup or markdown, commission equivalent, or other fee, (g)(3), and (g)(4) of this section are met.

Note to Rule 144(f)(1)

For purposes of this paragraph, a riskless principal transaction means a principal transaction where, after having received from a customer an order to buy, a broker or dealer purchases the security as principal in the market to satisfy the order to buy or, after having received from a customer an order to sell, sells the security as principal to the market to satisfy the order to sell.

2.   The person selling the securities shall not:

       i.   solicit or arrange for the solicitation of orders to buy the securities in anticipation of or in connection with such transaction, or

       ii.   make any payment in connection with the offer or sale of the securities to any person other than the broker who executes the order to sell the securities.

3.   Paragraph (f) of this section shall not apply to:

       i.   Securities sold for the account of the estate of a deceased person or for the account of a beneficiary of such estate provided the estate or beneficiary thereof is not an affiliate of the issuer; or

       ii.   Debt securities.

g.   **Brokers' Transactions.** The term *brokers' transactions* in Section 4(4) of the Act shall for the purposes of this rule be deemed to include transactions by a broker in which such broker:

1.   does no more than execute the order or orders to sell the securities as agent for the person for whose account the securities are sold;

2.   receives no more than the usual and customary broker's commission;

3.   neither solicits nor arranges for the solicitation of customers' orders to buy the securities in anticipation of or in connection with the transaction; *provided*, that the foregoing shall not preclude

       i.   inquiries by the broker of other brokers or dealers who have indicated an interest in the securities within the preceding 60 days,

       ii.   inquiries by the broker of his customers who have indicated an unsolicited bona fide interest in the securities within the preceding 10 business days;

       iii.   the publication by the broker of bid and ask quotations for the security in an inter-dealer quotation system provided that such quotations are incident to the maintenance of a bona fide inter-dealer market for the security for the broker's own account and that the broker has published bona fide bid and ask quotations for the security in an inter-dealer quotation system on each of at least twelve days within the preceding thirty calendar days with no more than four business days in succession without such two-way quotations; or

iv. the publication by the broker of bid and ask quotations for the security in an alternative trading system, as defined in Rule 300 of this chapter, provided that the broker has published bona fide bid and ask quotations for the security in the alternative trading system on each of the last twelve business days; and

Note to Subparagraph (g)(3)(ii): The broker should obtain and retain in his files written evidence of indications of bona fide unsolicited interest by his customers in the securities at the time such indications are received.

4. after reasonable inquiry is not aware of circumstances indicating that the person for whose account the securities are sold is an underwriter with respect to the securities or that the transaction is a part of a distribution of securities of the issuer. Without limiting the foregoing, the broker shall be deemed to be aware of any facts or statements contained in the notice required by paragraph (h) below.

Notes

i. The broker, for his own protection, should obtain and retain in his files a copy of the notice required by paragraph (h).

ii. The reasonable inquiry required by paragraph (g)(3) of this section should include, but not necessarily be limited to, inquiry as to the following matters:

a. The length of time the securities have been held by the person for whose account they are to be sold. If practicable, the inquiry should include physical inspection of the securities;

b. The nature of the transaction in which the securities were acquired by such person;

c. The amount of securities of the same class sold during the past three months by all persons whose sales are required to be taken into consideration pursuant to paragraph (e) of this section;

d. Whether such person intends to sell additional securities of the same class through any other means;

e. Whether such person has solicited or made any arrangement for the solicitation of buy orders in connection with the proposed sale of securities;

f. Whether such person has made any payment to any other person in connection with the proposed sale of the securities; and

g. The number of shares or other units of the class outstanding, or the relevant trading volume.

h. **Notice of Proposed Sale**.

1. If the amount of securities to be sold in reliance upon the rule during any period of three months exceeds 5,000 shares or other units or has an aggregate sale price in excess of $50,000, three copies of a notice on Form 144 shall be filed with the Commission. If such securities are admitted to trading on any national securities exchange, one copy of such notice shall also be transmitted to the principal exchange on which such securities are so admitted.

2.   The Form 144 shall be signed by the person for whose account the securities are to be sold and shall be transmitted for filing concurrently with either the placing with a broker of an order to execute a sale of securities in reliance upon this rule or the execution directly with a market maker of such a sale. Neither the filing of such notice nor the failure of the Commission to comment thereon shall be deemed to preclude the Commission from taking any action it deems necessary or appropriate with respect to the sale of the securities referred to in such notice. The person filing the notice required by this paragraph shall have a bona fide intention to sell the securities referred to therein within a reasonable time after the filing of such notice.

i.   **Unavailability to securities of issuers with no or nominal operations and no or nominal non-cash assets.**
1.   This section is not available for the resale of securities initially issued by an issuer defined below:
   i.   An issuer, other than a business combination related shell company, as defined in   Rule 405, or an asset-backed issuer, as defined in Item 1101(b) of Regulation AB, that has:
      A. No or nominal operations; and
      B. Either:
         1. No or nominal assets;
         2. Assets consisting solely of cash and cash equivalents; or
         3. Assets consisting of any amount of cash and cash equivalents and nominal other assets; or
   ii.   An issuer that has been at any time previously an issuer described in paragraph (i)(1)(i).
2.   Notwithstanding paragraph (i)(1), if the issuer of the securities previously had been an issuer described in paragraph (i)(1)(i) but has ceased to be an issuer described in paragraph (i)(1)(i); is subject to the reporting requirements of section 13 or 15(d) of the Exchange Act; has filed all reports and other materials required to be filed by section 13 or 15(d) of the Exchange Act, as applicable, during the preceding 12 months (or for such shorter period that the issuer was required to file such reports and materials), other than Form 8-K reports; and has filed current "Form 10 information" with the Commission reflecting its status as an entity that is no longer an issuer described in paragraph (i)(1)(i), then those securities may be sold subject to the requirements of this section after one year has elapsed from the date that the issuer filed "Form 10 information" with the Commission.
3.   The term "Form 10 information" means the information that is required by Form 10 or Form 20-F, as applicable to the issuer of the securities, to register under the Exchange Act each class of securities being sold under this rule. The issuer may provide the Form 10 information in any filing of the issuer with the Commission. The Form 10 information is deemed filed when the initial filing is made with the Commission.

Rule 144A – Private Resales of Securities to Institutions

Preliminary Notes
1. This section relates solely to the application of section 5 of the Act and not to antifraud or other provisions of the federal securities laws.
2. Attempted compliance with this section does not act as an exclusive election; any seller hereunder may also claim the availability of any other applicable exemption from the registration requirements of the Act.
3. In view of the objective of this section and the policies underlying the Act, this section is not available with respect to any transaction or series of transactions that, although in technical compliance with this section, is part of a plan or scheme to evade the registration provisions of the Act. In such cases, registration under the Act is required.
4. Nothing in this section obviates the need for any issuer or any other person to comply with the securities registration or broker-dealer registration requirements of the Securities Exchange Act of 1934 (the *Exchange Act)*, whenever such requirements are applicable.
5. Nothing in this section obviates the need for any person to comply with any applicable state law relating to the offer or sale of securities.
6. Securities acquired in a transaction made pursuant to the provisions of this section are deemed to be *restricted securities* within the meaning of Rule 144(a)(3).
7. The fact that purchasers of securities from the issuer thereof may purchase such securities with a view to reselling such securities pursuant to this section will not affect the availability to such issuer of an exemption under section 4(2) of the Act, or Regulation D under the Act, from the registration requirements of the Act.

a. **Definitions**.
   1. For purposes of this section, **qualified institutional buyer** shall mean:
      i. Any of the following entities, acting for its own account or the accounts of other qualified institutional buyers, that in the aggregate owns and invests on a discretionary basis at least $100 million in securities of issuers that are not affiliated with the entity:
         A. Any *insurance company* as defined in section 2(a)(13) of the Act ;
         Note: A purchase by an insurance company for one or more of its separate accounts, as defined by section 2(a)(37) of the Investment Company Act of 1940 (the "Investment Company Act"), which are neither registered under section 8 of the Investment Company Act nor required to be so registered, shall be deemed to be a purchase for the account of such insurance company.
         B. Any *investment company* registered under the Investment Company Act or any *business development company* as defined in section 2(a)(48) of that Act;
         C. Any *Small Business Investment Company* licensed by the U.S. Small Business Administration under section 301(c) or (d) of the Small Business Investment Act of 1958;
         D. Any *plan* established and maintained by a state, its political subdivisions, or any agency or instrumentality of a state or its political subdivisions, for the benefit of its employees;

E. Any *employee benefit plan* within the meaning of title I of the Employee Retirement Income Security Act of 1974;

F. Any trust fund whose trustee is a bank or trust company and whose participants are exclusively plans of the types identified in paragraph (a)(1)(i)(D) or (E) of this section, except trust funds that include as participants individual retirement accounts or H.R. 10 plans.

G. Any *business development company* as defined in section 202(a)(22) of the Investment Advisers Act of 1940;

H. Any organization described in section 501(c) (3) of the Internal Revenue Code, corporation (other than a bank as defined in section 3(a)(2) of the Act or a savings and loan association or other institution referenced in section 3(a)(5)(A) of the Act or a foreign bank or savings and loan association or equivalent institution), partnership, or Massachusetts or similar business trust; and

I. Any *investment adviser* registered under the Investment Advisers Act.

ii. Any *dealer* registered pursuant to section 15 of the Exchange Act, acting for its own account or the accounts of other qualified institutional buyers, that in the aggregate owns and invests on a discretionary basis at least $10 million of securities of issuers that are not affiliated with the dealer, *Provided,* That securities constituting the whole or a part of an unsold allotment to or subscription by a dealer as a participant in a public offering shall not be deemed to be owned by such dealer;

iii. Any *dealer* registered pursuant to section 15 of the Exchange Act acting in a riskless principal transaction on behalf of a qualified institutional buyer;

Note: A registered dealer may act as agent, on a non-discretionary basis, in a transaction with a qualified institutional buyer without itself having to be a qualified institutional buyer.

iv. Any investment company registered under the Investment Company Act, acting for its own account or for the accounts of other qualified institutional buyers, that is part of a family of investment companies which own in the aggregate at least $100 million in securities of issuers, other than issuers that are affiliated with the investment company or are part of such family of investment companies. *Family of investment companies* means any two or more investment companies registered under the Investment Company Act, except for a unit investment trust whose assets consist solely of shares of one or more registered investment companies, that have the same investment adviser (or, in the case of unit investment trusts, the same depositor), *Provided* That, for purposes of this section:

A. Each series of a series company (as defined in Rule 18f-2 under the Investment Company Act) shall be deemed to be a separate investment company; and

B. Investment companies shall be deemed to have the same adviser (or depositor) if their advisers (or depositors) are majority-owned subsidiaries of the same parent, or if one investment company's adviser (or depositor) is a majority-owned subsidiary of the other investment company's adviser (or depositor);

v.   Any entity, all of the equity owners of which are qualified institutional buyers, acting for its own account or the accounts of other qualified institutional buyers; and

vi.   Any *bank* as defined in section 3(a)(2) of the Act, any savings and loan association or other institution as referenced in section 3(a)(5)(A) of the Act, or any foreign bank or savings and loan association or equivalent institution, acting for its own account or the accounts of other qualified institutional buyers, that in the aggregate owns and invests on a discretionary basis at least $100 million in securities of issuers that are not affiliated with it and that has an audited net worth of at least $25 million as demonstrated in its latest annual financial statements, as of a date not more than 16 months preceding the date of sale under the Rule in the case of a U.S. bank or savings and loan association, and not more than 18 months preceding such date of sale for a foreign bank or savings and loan association or equivalent institution.

2.   In determining the aggregate amount of securities owned and invested on a discretionary basis by an entity, the following instruments and interests shall be excluded: bank deposit notes and certificates of deposit; loan participations; repurchase agreements; securities owned but subject to a repurchase agreement; and currency, interest rate and commodity swaps.

3.   The aggregate value of securities owned and invested on a discretionary basis by an entity shall be the cost of such securities, except where the entity reports its securities holdings in its financial statements on the basis of their market value, and no current information with respect to the cost of those securities has been published. In the latter event, the securities may be valued at market for purposes of this section.

4.   In determining the aggregate amount of securities owned by an entity and invested on a discretionary basis, securities owned by subsidiaries of the entity that are consolidated with the entity in its financial statements prepared in accordance with generally accepted accounting principles may be included if the investments of such subsidiaries are managed under the direction of the entity, except that, unless the entity is a reporting company under section 13 or 15(d) of the Exchange Act, securities owned by such subsidiaries may not be included if the entity itself is a majority-owned subsidiary that would be included in the consolidated financial statements of another enterprise.

5.   For purposes of this section, *riskless principal transaction* means a transaction in which a dealer buys a security from any person and makes a simultaneous offsetting sale of such security to a qualified institutional buyer, including another dealer acting as riskless principal for a qualified institutional buyer.

6.   For purposes of this section, *effective conversion premium* means the amount, expressed as a percentage of the security's conversion value, by which the price at issuance of a convertible security exceeds its conversion value.

7.   For purposes of this section, *effective exercise premium* means the amount, expressed as a percentage of the warrant's exercise value, by which the sum of the price at issuance and the exercise price of a warrant exceeds its exercise value.

b. **Sales by Persons Other than Issuers or Dealers.** Any person, other than the issuer or a dealer, who offers or sells securities in compliance with the conditions set forth in paragraph (d) of this section shall be deemed not to be engaged in a distribution of such securities and therefore not to be an underwriter of such securities within the meaning of sections 2(a)(11) and 4(1) of the Act.

c. **Sales by Dealers.** Any dealer who offers or sells securities in compliance with the conditions set forth in paragraph (d) of this section shall be deemed not to be a participant in a distribution of such securities within the meaning of section 4(3)(C) of the Act and not to be an underwriter of such securities within the meaning of section 2(a)(11) of the Act, and such securities shall be deemed not to have been offered to the public within the meaning of section 4(3)(A) of the Act.

d. **Conditions to be Met.** To qualify for exemption under this section, an offer or sale must meet the following conditions:
    1. The securities are offered or sold only to a qualified institutional buyer or to an offeree or purchaser that the seller and any person acting on behalf of the seller reasonably believe is a qualified institutional buyer. In determining whether a prospective purchaser is a qualified institutional buyer, the seller and any person acting on its behalf shall be entitled to rely upon the following non-exclusive methods of establishing the prospective purchaser's ownership and discretionary investments of securities:
        i.   The prospective purchaser's most recent publicly available financial statements, *Provided,* That such statements present the information as of a date within 16 months preceding the date of sale of securities under this section in the case of a U.S. purchaser and within 18 months preceding such date of sale for a foreign purchaser;
        ii. The most recent publicly available information appearing in documents filed by the prospective purchaser with the Commission or another United States federal, state, or local governmental agency or self-regulatory organization, or with a foreign governmental agency or self-regulatory organization, *Provided,* That any such information is as of a date within 16 months preceding the date of sale of securities under this section in the case of a U.S. purchaser and within 18 months preceding such date of sale for a foreign purchaser;
        iii. The most recent publicly available information appearing in a recognized securities manual, *Provided,* That such information is as of a date within 16 months preceding the date of sale of securities under this section in the case of a U.S. purchaser and within 18 months preceding such date of sale for a foreign purchaser; or
        iv. A certification by the chief financial officer, a person fulfilling an equivalent function, or other executive officer of the purchaser, specifying the amount of securities owned and invested on a discretionary basis by the purchaser as of a specific date on or since the close of the purchaser's most recent fiscal year, or, in the case of a purchaser that is a member of a family of investment companies, a certification by an executive officer of the investment adviser specifying

the amount of securities owned by the family of investment companies as of a specific date on or since the close of the purchaser's most recent fiscal year;

2. The seller and any person acting on its behalf takes reasonable steps to ensure that the purchaser is aware that the seller may rely on the exemption from the provisions of section 5 of the Act provided by this section;

3. The securities offered or sold:

    i. Were not, when issued, of the same class as securities listed on a national securities exchange registered under section 6 of the Exchange Act or quoted in a U.S. automated inter-dealer quotation system; *Provided*, That securities that are convertible or exchangeable into securities so listed or quoted at the time of issuance and that had an effective conversion premium of less than 10 percent, shall be treated as securities of the class into which they are convertible or exchangeable; and that warrants that may be exercised for securities so listed or quoted at the time of issuance, for a period of less than 3 years from the date of issuance, or that had an effective exercise premium of less than 10 percent, shall be treated as securities of the class to be issued upon exercise; and *Provided further,* That the Commission may from time to time, taking into account then-existing market practices, designate additional securities and classes of securities that will not be deemed of the same class as securities listed on a national securities exchange or quoted in a U.S. automated inter-dealer quotation system; and

    ii. Are not securities of an open-end investment company, unit investment trust or face-amount certificate company that is or is required to be registered under section 8 of the Investment Company Act; and

4. i. In the case of securities of an issuer that is neither subject to section 13 or 15(d) of the Exchange Act, nor exempt from reporting pursuant to Rule 12g3-2(b) under the Exchange Act, nor a foreign government as defined in Rule 405 eligible to register securities under Schedule B of the Act, the holder and a prospective purchaser designated by the holder have the right to obtain from the issuer, upon request of the holder, and the prospective purchaser has received from the issuer, the seller, or a person acting on either of their behalf, at or prior to the time of sale, upon such prospective purchaser's request to the holder or the issuer, the following information (which shall be reasonably current in relation to the date of resale under this section): a very brief statement of the nature of the business of the issuer and the products and services it offers; and the issuer's most recent balance sheet and profit and loss and retained earnings statements, and similar financial statements for such part of the two preceding fiscal years as the issuer has been in operation (the financial statements should be audited to the extent reasonably available).

    ii. The requirement that the information be *reasonably current* will be presumed to be satisfied if:

        A. The balance sheet is as of a date less than 16 months before the date of resale, the statements of profit and loss and retained earnings are for the 12 months preceding the date of such balance sheet, and if such balance sheet is not as of a date less than 6 months before the date of resale, it shall be accompanied by additional statements of profit and loss and retained earnings for the period from the date of such balance sheet to a date less than 6 months before the date of resale; and

A. The statement of the nature of the issuer's business and its products and services offered is as of a date within 12 months prior to the date of resale; or

B. With regard to foreign private issuers, the required information meets the timing requirements of the issuer's home country or principal trading markets.

e. **Offers and Sales of Securities Pursuant to this Section** – shall be deemed not to affect the availability of any exemption or safe harbor relating to any previous or subsequent offer or sale of such securities by the issuer or any prior or subsequent holder thereof.

Rule 147 – "Part of an Issue," "Person Resident," and "Doing Business Within" for Purposes of Section 3(a)(11)

Preliminary Notes

1. This rule shall not raise any presumption that the exemption provided by Section 3(a)(11) of the Act is not available for transactions by an issuer which do not satisfy all of the provisions of the rule.

2. Nothing in this rule obviates the need for compliance with any state law relating to the offer and sale of the securities.

3. Section 5 of the Act requires that all securities offered by the use of the mails or by any means or instruments of transportation or communication in interstate commerce be registered with the Commission. Congress, however, provided certain exemptions in the Act from such registration provisions where there was no practical need for registration or where the benefits of registration were too remote. Among those exemptions is that provided by Section 3(a)(11) of the Act for transactions in "any security which is a part of an issue offered and sold only to persons resident within a single State or Territory, where the issuer of such security is a person resident and doing business within . . . such State or Territory." The legislative history of that Section suggests that the exemption was intended to apply only to issues genuinely local in character, which in reality represent local financing by local industries, carried out through local investment. Rule 147 is intended to provide more objective standards upon which responsible local businessmen intending to raise capital from local sources may rely in claiming the Section 3(a)(11) exemption.

All of the terms and conditions of the rule must be satisfied in order for the rule to be available. These are:

i.   that the issuer be a resident of and doing business within the state or territory in which all offers and sales are made; and

ii. that no part of the issue be offered or sold to nonresidents within the period of time specified in the rule. For purposes of the rule the definition of "issuer" in Section 2(a)(4) of the Act shall apply.

All offers, offers to sell, offers for sale, and sales which are part of the same issue must meet all of the conditions of Rule 147 for the rule to be available. The determination whether offers, offers to sell, offers for sale and sales of securities are part of the same issue (i.e., are deemed to be "integrated") will continue to be a question of fact and will depend on the particular circumstances. See Securities Act of 1933 Release No. 4434 (December 6, 1961). Release 33-4434 indicates that in determining whether offers and sales should be regarded as part of the same issue and thus should be integrated any one or more of the following factors may be determinative:

    i.   Are the offerings part of a single plan of financing;

    ii.   Do the offerings involve issuance of the same class of securities;

    iii.   Are the offerings made at or about the same time;

    iv.   Is the same type of consideration to be received; and

    v.   Are the offerings made for the same general purpose.

Subparagraph (b)(2) of the rule, however, is designed to provide certainty to the extent feasible by identifying certain types of offers and sales of securities which will be deemed not part of an issue, for purposes of the rule only.

Persons claiming the availability of the rule have the burden of proving that they have satisfied all of its provisions. However, the rule does not establish exclusive standards for complying with the Section 3(a)(11) exemption. The exemption would also be available if the issuer satisfied the standards set forth in relevant administrative and judicial interpretations at the time of the offering but the issuer would have the burden of proving the availability of the exemption. Rule 147 relates to transactions exempted from the registration requirements of Section 5 of the Act by Section 3(a)(11). Neither the rule nor Section 3(a)(11) provides an exemption from the registration requirements of Section 12(g) of the Securities Exchange Act of 1934, the anti-fraud provisions of the federal securities laws, the civil liability provisions of Section 12(a)(2) of the Act or other provisions of the federal securities laws.

Finally, in view of the objectives of the rule and the purposes and policies underlying the Act, the rule shall not be available to any person with respect to any offering which, although in technical compliance with the rule, is part of a plan or scheme by such person to make interstate offers or sales of securities. In such cases registration pursuant to the Act is required.

4.   The rule provides an exemption for offers and sales by the issuer only. It is not available for offers or sales of securities by other persons. Section 3(a)(11) of the Act has been interpreted to permit offers and sales by persons controlling the issuer, if the exemption provided by that Section would have been available to the issuer at the time of the offering. See Securities Act Release No. 4434 (December 6, 1961). Controlling persons who want to offer or sell securities pursuant to Section 3(a)(11) may continue to do so in accordance with applicable judicial and administrative interpretations.

a.   **Transactions Covered.** Offers, offers to sell, offers for sale and sales by an issuer of its securities made in accordance with all of the terms and conditions of this rule shall be deemed to be part of an issue offered and sold only to persons resident and doing business within such state or territory, within the meaning of Section 3(a)(11) of the Act.

b. **Part of an Issue.**
    1. For purposes of this rule, all securities of the issuer which are part of an issue shall be offered, offered for sale or sold in accordance with all of the terms and conditions of this rule.
    2. For purposes of this rule only, an issue shall be deemed not to include offers, offers to sell, offers for sale or sales of securities of the issuer pursuant to the exemptions provided by Section 3 or Section 4(2) of the Act or pursuant to a registration statement filed under the Act, that take place prior to the six month period immediately preceding or after the six month period immediately following any offers, offers for sale or sales pursuant to this rule, *Provided,* That, there are during either of said six month periods no offers, offers for sale or sales of securities by or for the issuer of the same or similar class as those offered, offered for sale or sold pursuant to the rule.

    Note: In the event that securities of the same or similar class as those offered pursuant to the rule are offered, offered for sale or sold less than six months prior to or subsequent to any offer, offer for sale or sale pursuant to this rule, see Preliminary Note 3 hereof, as to which offers, offers to sell, offers for sale, or sales are part of an issue.

c. **Nature of the Issuer.** The issuer of the securities shall at the time of any offers and the sales be a person resident and doing business within the state or territory in which all of the offers, offers to sell, offers for sale and sales are made.
    1. The issuer shall be deemed to be a resident of the state or territory in which:
        i.   it is incorporated or organized, if a corporation, limited partnership, trust or other form of business organization that is organized under state or territorial law;
        ii.   its principal office is located, if a general partnership or other form of business organization that is not organized under any state or territorial law;
        iii. his principal residence is located, if an individual.
    2. The issuer shall be deemed to be doing business within a state or territory if:
        i.   the issuer derived at least 80 percent of its gross revenues and those of its subsidiaries on a consolidated basis
            A. for its most recent fiscal year, if the first offer of any part of the issue is made during the first six months of the issuer's current fiscal year; or
            B. for the first six months of its current fiscal year or during the twelve month fiscal period ending with such six month period, if the first offer of any part of the issue is made during the last six months of the issuer's current fiscal year from the operation of a business or of real property located in or from the rendering of services within such state or territory; *provided, however,* that this provision does not apply to any issuer which has not had gross revenues in excess

of $5,000 from the sale of products or services or other conduct of its business for its most recent twelve month fiscal period;

ii.   the issuer had at the end of its most recent semi-annual fiscal period prior to the first offer of any part of the issue, at least 80 percent of its assets and those of its subsidiaries on a consolidated basis located within such state or territory;

iii.   the issuer intends to use and uses at least 80 percent of the net proceeds to the issuer from sales made pursuant to this rule in connection with the operation of a business or of real property, the purchase of real property located in, or the rendering of services within such state or territory; and

iv.   the principal office of the issuer is located within such state or territory.

d. **Offerees and Purchasers; Person Resident.** Offers, offers to sell, offers for sale and sales of securities that are part of an issue shall be made only to persons resident within the state or territory of which the issuer is a resident. For purposes of determining the residence of offerees and purchasers:

1. A corporation, partnership, trust or other form of business organization shall be deemed to be a resident of a state or territory if, at the time of the offer and sale to it, it has its principal office within such state or territory.

2. An individual shall be deemed to be a resident of a state or territory if such individual has, at the time of the offer and sale to him, his principal residence in the state or territory.

3. A corporation, partnership, trust or other form of business organization which is organized for the specific purpose of acquiring part of an issue offered pursuant to this rule shall be deemed not to be a resident of a state or territory unless all of the beneficial owners of such organization are residents of such state or territory.

e. **Limitation of Resales.** During the period in which securities that are part of an issue are being offered and sold by the issuer, and for a period of nine months from the date of the last sale by the issuer of such securities, all resales of any part of the issue, by any person, shall be made only to persons resident within such state or territory.

Notes:

1. In the case of convertible securities resales of either the convertible security, or if it is converted, the underlying security, could be made during the period described in paragraph (e) only to persons resident within such state or territory. For purposes of this rule a conversion in reliance on Section 3(a)(9) of the Act does not begin a new period.

2. Dealers must satisfy the requirements of Rule 15c2-11 under the Securities Exchange Act of 1934 prior to publishing any quotation for a security, or submitting any quotation for publication, in any quotation medium.

f. **Precautions against Interstate Offers and Sales.**

1. The issuer shall, in connection with any securities sold by it pursuant to this rule:

i.   Place a legend on the certificate or other document evidencing the security stating that the securities have not been registered under the Act and setting forth the limitations on resale contained in paragraph (e);

    ii.   Issue stop transfer instructions to the issuer's transfer agent, if any, with respect to the securities, or, if the issuer transfers its own securities, make a notation in the appropriate records of the issuer; and

    iii.   Obtain a written representation from each purchaser as to his residence.

2. The issuer shall, in connection with the issuance of new certificates for any of the securities that are part of the same issue that are presented for transfer during the time period specified in paragraph (e), take the steps required by subsections (f)(1)(i) and (ii).

3. The issuer shall, in connection with any offers, offers to sell, offers for sale or sales by it pursuant to this rule, disclose, in writing, the limitations on resale contained in paragraph (e) and the provisions of subsections (f)(1)(i) and (ii) and subparagraph (f)(2).

Rule 152 – Definition of "Transactions by an Issuer Not Involving Any Public Offering" in Section 4(2), for Certain Transactions

The phrase "transactions by an issuer not involving any public offering" in Section 4(2) shall be deemed to apply to transactions not involving any public offering at the time of said transactions although subsequently thereto the issuer decides to make a public offering and/or files a registration statement.

Rule 153 – Definition of "Preceded by a Prospectus," as Used in Section 5(b)(2), in Relation to Certain Transactions

a. **Definition of preceded by a prospectus**. The term preceded by a prospectus as used in section 5(b)(2) of the Act, regarding any requirement of a broker or dealer to deliver a prospectus to a broker or dealer as a result of a transaction effected between such parties on or through a national securities exchange or facility thereof, trading facility of a national securities association, or an alternative trading system, shall mean the satisfaction of the conditions in paragraph (b) of this section.

b. **Conditions**. Any requirement of a broker or dealer to deliver a prospectus for transactions covered by paragraph (a) of this section will be satisfied if:

1. Securities of the same class as the securities that are the subject of the transaction are trading on that national securities exchange or facility thereof, trading facility of a national securities association, or alternative trading system;

2. The registration statement relating to the offering is effective and is not the subject of any pending proceeding or examination under section 8(d) or 8(e) of the Act;

3. Neither the issuer, nor any underwriter or participating dealer is the subject of a pending proceeding under section 8A of the Act in connection with the offering; and

4. The issuer has filed or will file with the Commission a prospectus that satisfies the requirements of section 10(a) of the Act.

  c.   **Definitions**.

     1.   The term national securities exchange, as used in this section, shall mean a securities exchange registered as a national securities exchange under section 6 of the Securities Exchange Act of 1934.

     2.   The term trading facility, as used in this section, shall mean a trading facility sponsored and governed by the rules of a registered securities association or a national securities exchange.

     3.   The term alternative trading system, as used in this section, shall mean an alternative trading system as defined in Rule 300(a) of Regulation ATS under the Securities Exchange Act of 1934 registered with the Commission pursuant to Rule 301 of Regulation ATS under the Securities Exchange Act of 1934.

Rule 155 – Integration of Abandoned Offerings

Preliminary Note

Compliance with paragraph (b) or (c) of this section provides a non-exclusive safe harbor from integration of private and registered offerings. Because of the objectives of Rule 155 and the policies underlying the Act, Rule 155 is not available to any issuer for any transaction or series of transactions that, although in technical compliance with the rule, is part of a plan or scheme to evade the registration requirements of the Act.

  a.   **Definition of Terms.** For the purposes of this section only, a private offering means an unregistered offering of securities that is exempt from registration under Section 4(2) or 4(6) of the Act or Rule 506 of Regulation D.

  b.   **Abandoned Private Offering Followed by a Registered Offering**. A private offering of securities will not be considered part of an offering for which the issuer later files a registration statement if:

     1.   No securities were sold in the private offering;

     2.   The issuer and any person(s) acting on its behalf terminate all offering activity in the private offering before the issuer files the registration statement;

     3.   The Section 10(a) final prospectus and any Section 10 preliminary prospectus used in the registered offering disclose information about the abandoned private offering, including:

       i.   The size and nature of the private offering;

       ii.   The date on which the issuer abandoned the private offering;

       iii.   That any offers to buy or indications of interest given in the private offering were rejected or otherwise not accepted; and

       iv.   That the prospectus delivered in the registered offering supersedes any offering materials used in the private offering; and

     4.   The issuer does not file the registration statement until at least 30 calendar days after termination of all offering activity in the private offering, unless the issuer and any person acting on its behalf offered securities in the private offering only to persons who were (or who the issuer reasonably believes were):

       i.   Accredited investors (as that term is defined in Rule 501(a)); or

       ii.   Persons who satisfy the knowledge and experience standard of Rule 506(b)(2)(ii).

c. **Abandoned Registered Offering Followed by a Private Offering**. An offering for which the issuer filed a registration statement will not be considered part of a later commenced private offering if:

1. No securities were sold in the registered offering;
2. The issuer withdraws the registration statement under Rule 477;
3. Neither the issuer nor any person acting on the issuer's behalf commences the private offering earlier than 30 calendar days after the effective date of withdrawal of the registration statement under Rule 477;
4. The issuer notifies each offeree in the private offering that:
    i.   The offering is not registered under the Act;
    ii. The securities will be "restricted securities" (as that term is defined in Rule 144(a)(3)) and may not be resold unless they are registered under the Act or an exemption from registration is available;
    iii. Purchasers in the private offering do not have the protection of Section 11 of the Act; and
    iv. A registration statement for the abandoned offering was filed and withdrawn, specifying the effective date of the withdrawal; and
5. Any disclosure document used in the private offering discloses any changes in the issuer's business or financial condition that occurred after the issuer filed the registration statement that are material to the investment decision in the private offering.

Rule 158 – Definitions of Certain Terms in the Last Paragraph of Section 11(a)

a. An "earning statement" made generally available to securityholders of the registrant pursuant to the last paragraph of section 11(a) of the Act shall be sufficient for the purposes of such paragraph if:

1. There is included the information required for statements of income contained either:
    i.   In Item 8 of Form 10-K, part I, Item 1 of Form 10-Q, or rule 14a-3(b) under the Securities Exchange Act of 1934;
    ii. In Item 17 of Form 20-F, if appropriate; or
    iii. In Form 40-F; and
2. The information specified in the last paragraph of section 11(a) is contained in one report or any combination of reports either:
    i.   On Form 10-K, Form 10-Q, Form 8-K, or in the annual report to security holders pursuant to rule 14a-3 under the Securities Exchange Act of 1934; or
    ii. On Form 20-F, Form 40-F or Form 6-K.
         A subsidiary issuing debt securities guaranteed by its parent will be deemed to have met the requirements of this paragraph if the parent's income statements satisfy the criteria of this paragraph and information respecting the subsidiary is included to the same extent as was presented in the registration statement. An "earning statement" not meeting the requirements of this paragraph may otherwise be sufficient for purposes of the last paragraph of section 11(a).

b. For purposes of the last paragraph of section 11(a) only, the "earning statement" contemplated by paragraph (a) of this section shall be deemed to be "made generally available to its securityholders" if the registrant:

    1. Is required to file reports pursuant to section 13 or 15(d) of the Securities Exchange Act of 1934 and

    2. Has filed its report or reports on Form 10-K, Form 10-Q, Form 8-K, Form 20-F, Form 40-F, or Form 6-K, or has supplied to the Commission copies of the annual report sent to securityholders pursuant to rule 14a-3I, containing such information.

    A registrant may use other methods to make an earning statement "generally available to its securityholders" for purposes of the last paragraph of section 11(a).

c. For purposes of the last paragraph of section 11(a) of the Act only, the effective date of the registration statement is deemed to be the date of the latest to occur of:

    1. The effective date of the registration statement;

    2. The effective date of the last post-effective amendment to the registration statement next preceding a particular sale of the issuer's registered securities to the public filed for the purposes of:

        i. Including any prospectus required by section 10(a)(3) of the Act; or

        ii. Reflecting in the prospectus any facts or events arising after the effective date of the registration statement (or the most recent post-effective amendment thereof) which, individually or in the aggregate, represent a fundamental change in the information set forth in the registration statement;

    3. The date of filing of the last report of the issuer incorporated by reference into the prospectus that is part of the registration statement or the date that a form of prospectus filed pursuant to Rule 424(b) or Rule 497(b), (c), (d), or (e) is deemed part of and included in the registration statement, and relied upon in either case in lieu of filing a post-effective amendment for purposes of paragraphs (c)(2)(i) and (ii) of this section next preceding a particular sale of the issuer's registered securities to the public; or

    4. As to the issuer and any underwriter at that time only, the most recent effective date of the registration statement for purposes of liability under section 11 of the Act of the issuer and any such underwriter only at the time of or next preceding a particular sale of the issuer's registered securities to the public determined pursuant to Rule 430B.

Rule 159 – Information Available to Purchaser at Time of Contract of Sale.

a. For purposes of section 12(a)(2) of the Act only, and without affecting any other rights a purchaser may have, for purposes of determining whether a prospectus or oral statement included an untrue statement of a material fact or omitted to state a material fact necessary in order to make the statements, in the light of the circumstances under which they were made, not misleading at the time of sale (including, without limitation, a contract of sale), any information conveyed to the purchaser only after such time of sale (including such contract of sale) will not be taken into account.

b. For purposes of section 17(a)(2) of the Act only, and without affecting any other rights the Commission may have to enforce that section, for purposes of determining whether a statement includes or represents any untrue statement of a material fact or any omission to state a material fact necessary in order to make the statements made, in light of the circumstances under which they were made, not misleading at the time of sale (including, without limitation, a contract of sale), any information conveyed to the purchaser only after such time of sale (including such contract of sale) will not be taken into account.

c. For purposes of section 12(a)(2) of the Act only, knowing of such untruth or omission in respect of a sale (including, without limitation, a contract of sale), means knowing at the time of such sale (including such contract of sale).

Rule 159A – Certain Definitions for Purposes of Section 12(a)(2) of the Act.

a. **Definition of seller for purposes of section 12(a)(2) of the Act**. For purposes of section 12(a)(2) of the Act only, in a primary offering of securities of the issuer, regardless of the underwriting method used to sell the issuer's securities, seller shall include the issuer of the securities sold to a person as part of the initial distribution of such securities, and the issuer shall be considered to offer or sell the securities to such person, if the securities are offered or sold to such person by means of any of the following communications:

1. Any preliminary prospectus or prospectus of the issuer relating to the offering required to be filed pursuant to Rule 424 or Rule 497;

2. Any free writing prospectus as defined in Rule 405 relating to the offering prepared by or on behalf of the issuer or used or referred to by the issuer and, in the case of an issuer that is an open-end management company registered under the Investment Company Act of 1940, any profile relating to the offering provided pursuant to Rule 498;

3. The portion of any other free writing prospectus (or, in the case of an issuer that is an investment company registered under the Investment Company Act of 1940 or a business development company as defined in section 2(a)(48) of the Investment Company Act of 1940, any advertisement pursuant to Rule 482) relating to the offering containing material information about the issuer or its securities provided by or on behalf of the issuer; and

4. Any other communication that is an offer in the offering made by the issuer to such person.

Notes to paragraph (a) of Rule 159A:

1. For purposes of paragraph (a) of this section, information is provided or a communication is made by or on behalf of an issuer if an issuer or an agent or representative of the issuer authorizes or approves the information or communication before its provision or use. An offering participant other than the issuer shall not be an agent or representative of the issuer solely by virtue of its acting as an offering participant.

2. Paragraph (a) of this section shall not affect in any respect the determination of whether any person other than an issuer is a "seller" for purposes of section 12(a)(2) of the Act.

b. **Definition of by means of for purposes of section 12(a)(2) of the Act.**
  1.   For purposes of section 12(a)(2) of the Act only, an offering participant other than the issuer shall not be considered to offer or sell securities that are the subject of a registration statement by means of a free writing prospectus as to a purchaser unless one or more of the following circumstances shall exist:
     i.   The offering participant used or referred to the free writing prospectus in offering or selling the securities to the purchaser;
     ii.   The offering participant offered or sold securities to the purchaser and participated in planning for the use of the free writing prospectus by one or more other offering participants and such free writing prospectus was used or referred to in offering or selling securities to the purchaser by one or more of such other offering participants; or
     iii. The offering participant was required to file the free writing prospectus pursuant to the conditions to use in Rule 433.
  2.   For purposes of section 12(a)(2) of the Act only, a person will not be considered to offer or sell securities by means of a free writing prospectus solely because another person has used or referred to the free writing prospectus or filed the free writing prospectus with the Commission pursuant to Rule 433.

Rule 163 – Exemption from Section 5(c) of the Act for Certain Communications by or on Behalf of Well-Known Seasoned Issuers.

Preliminary Note
Attempted compliance with this section does not act as an exclusive election and the issuer also may claim the availability of any other applicable exemption or exclusion. Reliance on this section does not affect the availability of any other exemption or exclusion from the requirements of section 5 of the Act.

a. In an offering by or on behalf of a well-known seasoned issuer, as defined in Rule 405, that will be or is at the time intended to be registered under the Act, an offer by or on behalf of such issuer is exempt from the prohibitions in section 5(c) of the Act on offers to sell, offers for sale, or offers to buy its securities before a registration statement has been filed, provided that:
  1.   Any written communication that is an offer made in reliance on this exemption will be a free writing prospectus as defined in Rule 405 and a prospectus under section 2(a)(10) of the Act relating to a public offering of securities to be covered by the registration statement to be filed; and
  2.   The exemption from section 5(c) of the Act provided in this section for such written communication that is an offer shall be conditioned on satisfying the conditions in paragraph (b) of this section.

b. **Conditions**.
  1.   Legend
     i.   Every written communication that is an offer made in reliance on this exemption shall contain substantially the following legend:

The issuer may file a registration statement (including a prospectus) with the SEC for the offering to which this communication relates. Before you invest, you should read the prospectus in that registration statement and other documents the issuer has filed with the SEC for more complete information about the issuer and this offering. You may get these documents for free by visiting EDGAR on the SEC Web site at www.sec.gov. Alternatively, the company will arrange to send you the prospectus after filing if you request it by calling toll-free 1-8[xx-xxxxxxx].

ii.   The legend also may provide an e-mail address at which the documents can be requested and may indicate that the documents also are available by accessing the issuer's Web site, and provide the Internet address and the particular location of the documents on the Web site.

iii. An immaterial or unintentional failure to include the specified legend in a free writing prospectus required by this section will not result in a violation of section 5(c) of the Act or the loss of the ability to rely on this section so long as:

(A) A good faith and reasonable effort was made to comply with the specified legend condition;

(B) The free writing prospectus is amended to include the specified legend as soon as practicable after discovery of the omitted or incorrect legend; and

I. If the free writing prospectus has been transmitted without the specified legend, the free writing prospectus is retransmitted with the legend by substantially the same means as, and directed to substantially the same prospective purchasers to whom, the free writing prospectus was originally transmitted.

2. Filing condition.

i.   Subject to paragraph (b)(2)(ii) of this section, every written communication that is an offer made in reliance on this exemption shall be filed by the issuer with the Commission promptly upon the filing of the registration statement, if one is filed, or an amendment, if one is filed, covering the securities that have been offered in reliance on this exemption.

ii. The condition that an issuer shall file a free writing prospectus with the Commission under this section shall not apply in respect of any communication that has previously been filed with, or furnished to, the Commission or that the issuer would not be required to file with the Commission pursuant to the conditions of Rule 433 if the communication was a free writing prospectus used after the filing of the registration statement. The condition that the issuer shall file a free writing prospectus with the Commission under this section shall be satisfied if the issuer satisfies the filing conditions (other than timing of filing which is provided in this section) that would apply under Rule 433 if the communication was a free writing prospectus used after the filing of the registration statement.

iii. An immaterial or unintentional failure to file or delay in filing a free writing prospectus to the extent provided in this section will not result in a violation of section 5(c) of the Act or the loss of the ability to rely on this section so long as:

    (A) A good faith and reasonable effort was made to comply with the filing condition; and

    (B) The free writing prospectus is filed as soon as practicable after discovery of the failure to file.

3. Ineligible offerings. The exemption in paragraph (a) of this section shall not be available to:

    i. Communications relating to business combination transactions that are subject to Rule 165 or Rule 166;

    ii. Communications by an issuer that is an investment company registered under the Investment Company Act of 1940; or

    iii. Communications by an issuer that is a business development company as defined in section 2(a)(48) of the Investment Company Act of 1940.

c. For purposes of this section, a communication is made by or on behalf of an issuer if the issuer or an agent or representative of the issuer, other than an offering participant who is an underwriter or dealer, authorizes or approves the communication before it is made.

d. For purposes of this section, a communication for which disclosure would be required under section 17(b) of the Act as a result of consideration given or to be given, directly or indirectly, by or on behalf of an issuer is deemed to be an offer by the issuer and, if a written communication, is deemed to be a free writing prospectus of the issuer.

e. A communication exempt from section 5(c) of the Act pursuant to this section will not be considered to be in connection with a securities offering registered under the Securities Act for purposes of Rule 100(b)(2)(iv) of Regulation FD under the Securities Exchange Act of 1934.

Rule 163A – Exemption From Section 5(c) of the Act for Certain Communications Made By or On Behalf of Issuers More than 30 Days Before a Registration Statement is Filed.

Preliminary Note

Attempted compliance with this section does not act as an exclusive election and the issuer also may claim the availability of any other applicable exemption or exclusion. Reliance on this section does not affect the availability of any other exemption or exclusion from the requirements of section 5 of the Act.

a. Except as excluded pursuant to paragraph (b) of this section, in all registered offerings by issuers, any communication made by or on behalf of an issuer more than 30 days before the date of the filing of the registration statement that does not reference a securities offering that is or will be the subject of a registration statement shall not constitute an offer to sell, offer for sale, or offer to buy the securities being offered under the registration statement for purposes of section 5(c) of the Act, provided that the issuer takes reasonable steps within its control to prevent further distribution or

Must attempt to prevent

publication of such communication during the 30 days immediately preceding the date of filing the registration statement.

b.   The exemption in paragraph (a) of this section shall not be available with respect to the following communications:
  1.   Communications relating to business combination transactions that are subject to Rule 165 or Rule 166;
  2.   Communications made in connection with offerings registered on Form S-8, other than by well-known seasoned issuers;
  3.   Communications in offerings of securities of an issuer that is, or during the past three years was (or any of whose predecessors during the last three years was):
    i.   A blank check company as defined in Rule 419(a)(2);
    ii.   A shell company, other than a business combination related shell company, each as defined in Rule 405; or
    iii. An issuer for an offering of penny stock as defined in Rule 3a51-1 of the Securities Exchange Act of 1934; or
  4.   Communications made by an issuer that is:
    i.   An investment company registered under the Investment Company Act of 1940; or
    ii.   A business development company as defined in section 2(a)(48) of the Investment Company Act of 1940.

c.   For purposes of this section, a communication is made by or on behalf of an issuer if the issuer or an agent or representative of the issuer, other than an offering participant who is an underwriter or dealer, authorizes or approves the communication before it is made.

d.   A communication exempt from section 5(c) of the Act pursuant to this section will not be considered to be in connection with a securities offering registered under the Securities Act for purposes of Rule 100(b)(2)(iv) of Regulation FD under the Securities Exchange Act of 1934.

Rule 164 – Post-filing Free Writing Prospectuses in Connection with Certain Registered Offerings.

Preliminary Notes
  1.   This section is not available for any communication that, although in technical compliance with this section, is part of a plan or scheme to evade the requirements of section 5 of the Act.
  2.   Attempted compliance with this section does not act as an exclusive election and the person relying on this section also may claim the availability of any other applicable exemption or exclusion. Reliance on this section does not affect the availability of any other exemption or exclusion from the requirements of section 5 of the Act.

a.   In connection with a registered offering of an issuer meeting the requirements of this section, a free writing prospectus, as defined in Rule 405, of the issuer or any other offering participant, including any underwriter or dealer, after the filing of the registration statement will be a section 10(b) prospectus for purposes of section 5(b)(1) of the Act provided that the conditions set forth in Rule 433 are satisfied.

b. An immaterial or unintentional failure to file or delay in filing a free writing prospectus as necessary to satisfy the filing conditions contained in Rule 433 will not result in a violation of section 5(b)(1) of the Act or the loss of the ability to rely on this section so long as:

1. A good faith and reasonable effort was made to comply with the filing condition; and

2. The free writing prospectus is filed as soon as practicable after discovery of the failure to file.

c. An immaterial or unintentional failure to include the specified legend in a free writing prospectus as necessary to satisfy the legend condition contained in Rule 433 will not result in a violation of section 5(b)(1) of the Act or the loss of the ability to rely on this section so long as:

1. A good faith and reasonable effort was made to comply with the legend condition;

2. The free writing prospectus is amended to include the specified legend as soon as practicable after discovery of the omitted or incorrect legend; and

3. If the free writing prospectus has been transmitted without the specified legend, the free writing prospectus must be retransmitted with the legend by substantially the same means as, and directed to substantially the same prospective purchasers to whom, the free writing prospectus was originally transmitted.

d. Solely for purposes of this section, an immaterial or unintentional failure to retain a free writing prospectus as necessary to satisfy the record retention condition contained in Rule 433 will not result in a violation of section 5(b)(1) of the Act or the loss of the ability to rely on this section so long as a good faith and reasonable effort was made to comply with the record retention condition. Nothing in this paragraph will affect, however, any other record retention provisions applicable to the issuer or any offering participant.

e. **Ineligible issuers**.

1. This section and Rule 433 are available only if at the eligibility determination date for the offering in question, determined pursuant to paragraph (h) of this section, the issuer is not an ineligible issuer as defined in Rule 405 (or in the case of any offering participant, other than the issuer, the participant has a reasonable belief that the issuer is not an ineligible issuer);

2. Notwithstanding paragraph (e)(1) of this section, this section and Rule are available to an ineligible issuer with respect to a free writing prospectus that contains only descriptions of the terms of the securities in the offering or the offering (or in the case of an offering of asset-backed securities, contains only information specified in paragraphs (a)(1), (2), (3), (4), (6), (7), and (8) of the definition of ABS informational and computational materials in Item 1101 of Regulation AB, unless the issuer is or during the last three years the issuer or any of its predecessors was:

      i.   A blank check company as defined in Rule 419(a)(2);

      ii.   A shell company, other than a business combination related shell company, as defined in Rule 405; or

      iii. An issuer for an offering of penny stock as defined in Rule 3a51-1 of the Securities Exchange Act of 1934.

f.   **Excluded issuers.** This section and Rule 433 are not available if the issuer is an investment company registered under the Investment Company Act of 1940 or a business development company as defined in section 2(a)(48) of the Investment Company Act of 1940.

g.   **Excluded offerings.** This section and Rule 433 are not available if the issuer is registering a business combination transaction as defined in Rule 165(f)(1) or the issuer, other than a well-known seasoned issuer, is registering an offering on Form S-8.

h.   For purposes of this section and Rule 433, the determination date as to whether an issuer is an ineligible issuer in respect of an offering shall be:

      1.   Except as provided in paragraph (h)(2) of this section, the time of filing of the registration statement covering the offering; or

      2.   If the offering is being registered pursuant to Rule 415, the earliest time after the filing of the registration statement covering the offering at which the issuer, or in the case of an underwritten offering the issuer or another offering participant, makes a bona fide offer, including without limitation through the use of a free writing prospectus, in the offering.

Rule 165 – Offers Made in Connection with a Business Combination Transaction

Preliminary Note:
    This section is available only to communications relating to business combinations. The exemption does not apply to communications that may be in technical compliance with this section, but have the primary purpose or effect of conditioning the market for another transaction, such as a capital- raising or resale transaction.

a.   **Communications before a registration statement is filed**. Notwithstanding section 5(c) of the Act, the offeror of securities in a business combination transaction to be registered under the Act may make an offer to sell or solicit an offer to buy those securities from and including the first public announcement until the filing of a registration statement related to the transaction, so long as any written communication (other than non-public communications among participants) made in connection with or relating to the transaction (i.e., prospectus) is filed in accordance with Rule 425 and the conditions in paragraph I of this section are satisfied.

b.   **Communications after a registration statement is filed**. Notwithstanding section 5(b)(1) of the Act, any written communication (other than non-public communications among participants) made in connection with or relating to a business combination transaction (i.e., prospectus) after the filing of a registration statement related to the transaction need not satisfy the requirements of section 10 of the Act, so long as the prospectus is filed in accordance with Rule 424 or Rule 425 and the conditions in paragraph (c) of this section are satisfied.

c. **Conditions**. To rely on paragraphs (a) and (b) of this section:
    1. Each prospectus must contain a prominent legend that urges investors to read the relevant documents filed or to be filed with the Commission because they contain important information. The legend also must explain to investors that they can get the documents for free at the Commission's web site and describe which documents are available free from the offeror; and
    2. In an exchange offer, the offer must be made in accordance with the applicable tender offer rules (Rule 14d-1 through Rule 14e-8); and, in a transaction involving the vote of security holders, the offer must be made in accordance with the applicable proxy or information statement rules (Rule 14a-1 through Rule 14a-101 and Rule 14c-1 through Rule 14c-101).

d. **Applicability**. This section is applicable not only to the offeror of securities in a business combination transaction, but also to any other participant that may need to rely on and complies with this section in communicating about the transaction.

e. **Failure to file or delay in filing**. An immaterial or unintentional failure to file or delay in filing a prospectus described in this section will not result in a violation of section 5(b)(1) or (c) of the Act, so long as:
    1. A good faith and reasonable effort was made to comply with the filing requirement; and
    2. The prospectus is filed as soon as practicable after discovery of the failure to file.

f. **Definitions**.
    1. A business combination transaction means any transaction specified in Rule 145(a) or exchange offer;
    2. A participant is any person or entity that is a party to the business combination transaction and any persons authorized to act on their behalf; and
    3. Public announcement is any oral or written communication by a participant that is reasonably designed to, or has the effect of, informing the public or security holders in general about the business combination transaction.

Rule 168 – Exemption from Sections 2(a)(10) and 5(c) of the Act for Certain Communications of Regularly Released Factual Business Information and Forward-Looking Information

Preliminary Notes
1. This section is not available for any communication that, although in technical compliance with this section, is part of a plan or scheme to evade the requirements of section 5 of the Act.
2. This section provides a non-exclusive safe harbor for factual business information and forward-looking information released or disseminated as provided in this section. Attempted compliance with this section does not act as an exclusive election and the issuer also may claim the availability of any other applicable exemption or exclusion.

Reliance on this section does not affect the availability of any other exemption or exclusion from the definition of prospectus in section 2(a)(10) or the requirements of section 5 of the Act.

3. The availability of this section for a release or dissemination of a communication that contains or incorporates factual business information or forward-looking information will not be affected by another release or dissemination of a communication that contains all or a portion of the same factual business information or forward-looking information that does not satisfy the conditions of this section.

a. For purposes of sections 2(a)(10) and 5(c) of the Act, the regular release or dissemination by or on behalf of an issuer (and, in the case of an asset-backed issuer, the other persons specified in paragraph (a)(3) of this section) of communications containing factual business information or forward-looking information shall be deemed not to constitute an offer to sell or offer for sale of a security which is the subject of an offering pursuant to a registration statement that the issuer proposes to file, or has filed, or that is effective, if the conditions of this section are satisfied by any of the following:

1. An issuer that is required to file reports pursuant to section 13 or section 15(d) of the Securities Exchange Act of 1934;

2. A foreign private issuer that:
   i. Meets all of the registrant requirements of Form F-3 other than the reporting history provisions of General Instructions I.A.1. and I.A.2.(a) of Form F-3;
   ii. Either:
      (A) Satisfies the public float threshold in General Instruction I.B.1. of Form F-3; or
      (B) Is issuing non-convertible investment grade securities meeting the provisions of General Instruction I.B.2. of Form F-3; and
   iii. Either:
      (A) Has its equity securities trading on a designated offshore securities market as defined in Rule 902(b) and has had them so traded for at least 12 months; or
      (B) Has a worldwide market value of its outstanding common equity held by non-affiliates of $700 million or more; or

3. An asset-backed issuer or a depositor, sponsor, or servicer (as such terms are defined in Item 1101 of Regulation AB) or an affiliated depositor, whether or not such other person is the issuer.

b. **Definitions**.
1. Factual business information means some or all of the following information that is released or disseminated under the conditions in paragraph (d) of this section, including, without limitation, such factual business information contained in reports or other materials filed with, furnished to, or submitted to the Commission pursuant to the Securities Exchange Act of 1934:
   i. Factual information about the issuer, its business or financial developments, or other aspects of its business;
   ii. Advertisements of, or other information about, the issuer's products or services; and

        iii. Dividend notices.

   2.   Forward-looking information means some or all of the following information that is released or disseminated under the conditions in paragraph (d) of this section, including, without limitation, such forward-looking information contained in reports or other materials filed with, furnished to, or submitted to the Commission pursuant to the Securities Exchange Act of 1934:

        i.   Projections of the issuer's revenues, income (loss), earnings (loss) per share, capital expenditures, dividends, capital structure, or other financial items;

        ii. Statements about the issuer management's plans and objectives for future operations, including plans or objectives relating to the products or services of the issuer;

        iii. Statements about the issuer's future economic performance, including statements of the type contemplated by the management's discussion and analysis of financial condition and results of operation described in Item 303 of Regulations S-B and S-K or the operating and financial review and prospects described in Item 5 of Form 20-F; and

        iv. Assumptions underlying or relating to any of the information described in paragraphs (b)(2)(i), (b)(2)(ii) and (b)(2)(iii) of this section.

   3.   For purposes of this section, the release or dissemination of a communication is by or on behalf of the issuer if the issuer or an agent or representative of the issuer, other than an offering participant who is an underwriter or dealer, authorizes or approves such release or dissemination before it is made.

   4.   For purposes of this section, in the case of communications of a person specified in paragraph (a)(3) of this section other than the asset-backed issuer, the release or dissemination of a communication is by or on behalf of such other person if such other person or its agent or representative, other than an underwriter or dealer, authorizes or approves such release or dissemination before it is made.

c. **Exclusion**. A communication containing information about the registered offering or released or disseminated as part of the offering activities in the registered offering is excluded from the exemption of this section.

d. **Conditions to exemption**. The following conditions must be satisfied:

   1.   The issuer (or in the case of an asset-backed issuer, the issuer and the other persons specified in paragraph (a)(3) of this section, taken together) has previously released or disseminated information of the type described in this section in the ordinary course of its business;

   2.   The timing, manner, and form in which the information is released or disseminated is consistent in material respects with similar past releases or disseminations; and

   3.   The issuer is not an investment company registered under the Investment Company Act of 1940 or a business development company as defined in section 2(a)(48) of the Investment Company Act of 1940.

Rule 169 – Exemption from Sections 2(a)(10) and 5(c) of the Act for Certain Communications of Regularly Released Factual Business Information

Preliminary Notes

1. This section is not available for any communication that, although in technical compliance with this section, is part of a plan or scheme to evade the requirements of section 5 of the Act.

2. This section provides a non-exclusive safe harbor for factual business information released or disseminated as provided in this section. Attempted compliance with this section does not act as an exclusive election and the issuer also may claim the availability of any other applicable exemption or exclusion. Reliance on this section does not affect the availability of any other exemption or exclusion from the definition of prospectus in section 2(a)(10) or the requirements of section 5 of the Act.

3. The availability of this section for a release or dissemination of a communication that contains or incorporates factual business information will not be affected by another release or dissemination of a communication that contains all or a portion of the same factual business information that does not satisfy the conditions of this section.

a. For purposes of sections 2(a)(10) and 5(c) of the Act, the regular release or dissemination by or on behalf of an issuer of communications containing factual business information shall be deemed not to constitute an offer to sell or offer for sale of a security by an issuer which is the subject of an offering pursuant to a registration statement that the issuer proposes to file, or has filed, or that is effective, if the conditions of this section are satisfied.

b. **Definitions**.
    1. **Factual business information** means some or all of the following information that is released or disseminated under the conditions in paragraph (d) of this section:
        i.   Factual information about the issuer, its business or financial developments, or other aspects of its business; and
        ii. Advertisements of, or other information about, the issuer's products or services.
    2. For purposes of this section, the release or dissemination of a communication is by or on behalf of the issuer if the issuer or an agent or representative of the issuer, other than an offering participant who is an underwriter or dealer, authorizes or approves such release or dissemination before it is made.

c. **Exclusions**. A communication containing information about the registered offering or released or disseminated as part of the offering activities in the registered offering is excluded from the exemption of this section.

d. **Conditions to exemption.** The following conditions must be satisfied:
    1. The issuer has previously released or disseminated information of the type described in this section in the ordinary course of its business;

2.   The timing, manner, and form in which the information is released or disseminated is consistent in material respects with similar past releases or disseminations;

3.   The information is released or disseminated for intended use by persons, such as customers and suppliers, other than in their capacities as investors or potential investors in the issuer's securities, by the issuer's employees or agents who historically have provided such information; and

4.   The issuer is not an investment company registered under the Investment Company Act of 1940 or a business development company as defined in section 2(a)(48) of the Investment Company Act of 1940.

Rule 172 – Delivery of Prospectuses

a.   **Sending confirmations and notices of allocations**. After the effective date of a registration statement, the following are exempt from the provisions of section 5(b)(1) of the Act if the conditions set forth in paragraph (c) of this section are satisfied:

1.   Written confirmations of sales of securities in an offering pursuant to a registration statement that contain information limited to that called for in Rule 10b-10 under the Securities Exchange Act of 1934 and other information customarily included in written confirmations of sales of securities, which may include notices provided pursuant to Rule 173; and

2.   Notices of allocation of securities sold or to be sold in an offering pursuant to the registration statement that may include information identifying the securities (including the CUSIP number) and otherwise may include only information regarding pricing, allocation and settlement, and information incidental thereto.

b.   **Transfer of the security**. Any obligation under section 5(b)(2) of the Act to have a prospectus that satisfies the requirements of section 10(a) of the Act precede or accompany the carrying or delivery of a security in a registered offering is satisfied if the conditions in paragraph (c) of this section are met.

c.   **Conditions**.

1.   The registration statement relating to the offering is effective and is not the subject of any pending proceeding or examination under section 8(d) or 8(e) of the Act;

2.   Neither the issuer, nor an underwriter or participating dealer is the subject of a pending proceeding under section 8A of the Act in connection with the offering; and

3.   The issuer has filed with the Commission a prospectus with respect to the offering that satisfies the requirements of section 10(a) of the Act or the issuer will make a good faith and reasonable effort to file such a prospectus within the time required under Rule 424 and, in the event that the issuer fails to file timely such a prospectus, the issuer files the prospectus as soon as practicable thereafter.

4.   The condition in paragraph (c)(3) of this section shall not apply to transactions by dealers requiring delivery of a final prospectus pursuant to section 4(3) of the Act.

    d.   **Exclusions**. This section shall not apply to any:
        1.   Offering of any investment company registered under the Investment Company Act of 1940;
        2.   Offering of any business development company as defined in section 2(a)(48) of the Investment Company Act of 1940;
        3.   A business combination transaction as defined in Rule 165(f)(1); or
        4.   Offering registered on Form S-8.

Rule 173 – Notice of Registration

    a.   In a transaction that represents a sale by the issuer or an underwriter, or a sale where there is not an exclusion or exemption from the requirement to deliver a final prospectus meeting the requirements of section 10(a) of the Act pursuant to section 4(3) of the Act or Rule 174, each underwriter or dealer selling in such transaction shall provide to each purchaser from it, not later than two business days following the completion of such sale, a copy of the final prospectus or, in lieu of such prospectus, a notice to the effect that the sale was made pursuant to a registration statement or in a transaction in which a final prospectus would have been required to have been delivered in the absence of Rule 172.

    b.   If the sale was by the issuer and was not effected by or through an underwriter or dealer, the responsibility to send a prospectus, or in lieu of such prospectus, such notice as set forth in paragraph (a) of this section, shall be the issuer's.

    c.   Compliance with the requirements of this section is not a condition to reliance on Rule 172.

    d.   A purchaser may request from the person responsible for sending a notice a copy of the final prospectus if one has not been sent.

    e.   After the effective date of the registration statement with respect to an offering, notices as set forth in paragraph (a) of this section, are exempt from the provisions of section 5(b)(1) of the Act.

    f.   **Exclusions**. This section shall not apply to any:
        1.   Transaction solely between brokers or dealers in reliance on Rule 153;
        2.   Offering of any investment company registered under the Investment Company Act of 1940;
        3.   Offering of any business development company as defined in section 2(a)(48) of the Investment Company Act of 1940;
        4.   A business combination transaction as defined in Rule 165(f)(1); or
        5.   Offering registered on Form S-8.

Rule 174 – Delivery of Prospectus by Dealers; Exemptions Under Section 4(3) of the Act

The obligations of a dealer (including an underwriter no longer acting as an underwriter in respect of the security involved in such transactions) to deliver a prospectus in transactions in a security as to which a registration statement has been filed taking place prior to the expiration of the 40- or 90-day period specified in section 4(3) of the Act after the effective date of such registration statement or prior to the expiration of such period after the first date upon which the security was bona fide offered to the public by the issuer or by or through an underwriter after such effective date, whichever is later, shall be subject to the following provisions:

a.   No prospectus need be delivered if the registration statement is on Form F-6.

b.   No prospectus need be delivered if the issuer is subject, immediately prior to the time of filing the registration statement, to the reporting requirements of section 13 or 15(d) of the Securities Exchange Act of 1934.

c.   Where a registration statement relates to offerings to be made from time to time no prospectus need be delivered after the expiration of the initial prospectus delivery period specified in section 4(3) of the Act following the first bona fide offering of securities under such registration statement.

d.   If –
1.   the registration statement relates to the security of an issuer that is not subject, immediately prior to the time of filing the registration statement, to the reporting requirements of section 13 or 15(d) of the Securities Exchange Act of 1934, and
2.   as of the offering date, the security is listed on a registered national securities exchange or authorized for inclusion in an electronic inter-dealer quotation system sponsored and governed by the rules of a registered securities association, no prospectus need be delivered after the expiration of twenty-five calendar days after the offering date. For purposes of this provision, the term *offering date* refers to the later of the effective date of the registration statement or the first date on which the security was bona fide offered to the public.

e.   Notwithstanding the foregoing, the period during which a prospectus must be delivered by a dealer shall be:
1.   As specified in section 4(3) of the Act if the registration statement was the subject of a stop order issued under section 8 of the Act; or
2.   As the Commission may provide upon application or on its own motion in a particular case.

f.   Nothing in this section shall affect the obligation to deliver a prospectus pursuant to the provisions of section 5 of the Act by a dealer who is acting as an underwriter with respect to the securities involved or who is engaged in a transaction as to securities constituting the whole or a part of an unsold allotment to or subscription by such dealer as a participant in the distribution of such securities by the issuer or by or through an underwriter.

g.   If the registration statement relates to an offering of securities of a "blank check company," as defined in Rule 419 under the Act, the statutory period for prospectus delivery specified in section 4(3) of the Act shall not terminate until 90 days after the

4 (3) 90 day

date funds and securities are released from the escrow or trust account pursuant to Rule 419 under the Act.

h.   Any obligation pursuant to Section 4(3) of the Act and this section to deliver a prospectus, other than pursuant to paragraph (g) of this section, may be satisfied by compliance with the provisions of Rule 172.

Rule 176 – Circumstances Affecting the Determination of What Constitutes Reasonable Investigation and Reasonable Grounds for Belief Under Section 11 of the Securities Act

In determining whether or not the conduct of a person constitutes a reasonable investigation or a reasonable ground for belief meeting the standard set forth in section 11I, relevant circumstances include, with respect to a person other than the issuer.

a.   The type of issuer;

b.   The type of security;

c.   The type of person;

d.   The office held when the person is an officer;

e.   The presence or absence of another relationship to the issuer when the person is a director or proposed director;

f.   Reasonable reliance on officers, employees, and others whose duties should have given them knowledge of the particular facts ;

g.   When the person is an underwriter, the type of underwriting arrangement, the role of the particular person as an underwriter and the availability of information with respect to the registrant; and

h.   Whether, with respect to a fact or document incorporated by reference, the particular person had any responsibility for the fact or document at the time of the filing from which it was incorporated.

Rule 401 – Requirements as to Proper Form

a.   The form and contents of a registration statement and prospectus shall conform to the applicable rules and forms as in effect on the initial filing date of such registration statement and prospectus.

b.   If an amendment to a registration statement and prospectus is filed for the purpose of meeting the requirements of section 10(a)(3) of the Act or pursuant to the provisions of section 24(e) or 24(f) of the Investment Company Act of 1940, the form and contents of such an amendment shall conform to the applicable rules and forms as in effect on the filing date of such amendment.

c. An amendment to a registration statement and prospectus, other than an amendment described in paragraph (b) of this section, may be filed on any shorter Securities Act registration form for which it is eligible on the filing date of the amendment. At the issuer's option, the amendment also may be filed on the same Securities Act registration form used for the most recent amendment described in paragraph (b) of this section or, if no such amendment has been filed, the initial registration statement and prospectus.

d. The form and contents of a prospectus forming part of a registration statement which is the subject of a stop order entered under section 8(d) of the Act, if used after the date such stop order ceases to be effective, shall conform to the applicable rules and forms as in effect on the date such stop order ceases to be effective.

e. A prospectus filed as part of an amendment to an effective registration statement, or other amendment to such registration statement, on any form may be prepared in accordance with the requirements of any other form which would then be appropriate for the registration of securities to which the prospectus or other amendment relates, provided that all of the other requirements of such other form and applicable rules (including any required undertakings) are met.

f. Notwithstanding the provisions of this section, a registrant
    1. shall comply with the rules and forms as in effect at a date different from those specified in paragraphs (a), (b), (c) and (d) of this section if the rules or forms or amendments thereto specifically so provide; and
    2. may comply voluntarily with the rules and forms as in effect at dates subsequent to those specified in paragraphs (a), (b), (c) and (d) of this section, provided that all of the requirements of the particular rules and forms in effect at such dates (including any required undertakings) are met.

g. 1. Subject to paragraph (g)(2) of this section, except for registration statements and post-effective amendments that become effective immediately pursuant to Rule 462 and Rule 464, a registration statement or any amendment thereto is deemed filed on the proper registration form unless the Commission objects to the registration form before the effective date.
    2. An automatic shelf registration statement as defined in Rule 405 and any post-effective amendment thereto are deemed filed on the proper registration form unless and until the Commission notifies the issuer of its objection to the use of such form. Following any such notification, the issuer must amend its automatic shelf registration statement onto the registration form it is then eligible to use, *provided, however,* that any continuous offering of securities pursuant to Rule 415 that the issuer has commenced pursuant to the registration statement before the Commission has notified the issuer of its objection to the use of such form may continue until the effective date of a new registration statement or post-effective amendment to the registration statement that the issuer has filed on the proper registration form, if the issuer files promptly after notification the new registration statement or post-effective amendment and if

the offering is permitted to be made under the new registration statement or post-effective amendment.

Rule 405 – Definition of Terms

Unless the context otherwise requires, all terms used in Rule 400 to Rule 494, inclusive, or in the forms for registration have the same meanings as in the Act and in the general rules and regulations. In addition, the following definitions apply, unless the context otherwise requires:

Affiliate. An *affiliate* of, or person *affiliated* with, a specified person, is a person that directly, or indirectly through one or more intermediaries, controls or is controlled by, or is under common control with, the person specified.

Amount. The term *amount,* when used in regard to securities, means the principal amount if relating to evidences of indebtedness, the number of shares if relating to shares, and the number of units if relating to any other kind of security.

Associate. The term *associate,* when used to indicate a relationship with any person, means (1) a corporation or organization (other than the registrant or a majority-owned subsidiary of the registrant) of which such person is an officer or partner or is, directly or indirectly, the beneficial owner of 10 percent or more of any class of equity securities, (2) any trust or other estate in which such person has a substantial benefical interest or as to which such person serves as trustee or in a similar capacity, and (3) any relative or spouse of such person, or any relative of such spouse, who has the same home as such person or who is a director or officer of the registrant or any of its parents or subsidiaries.

Automatic shelf registration statement. The term *automatic shelf registration statement* means a registration statement filed on Form S-3 or Form F-3 by a well-known seasoned issuer pursuant to General Instruction I.D. or I.C. of such forms, respectively.

Business development company. The term *business development company* refers to a company which has elected to be regulated as a business development company under sections 55 through 65 of the Investment Company Act of 1940.

Certified. The term *certified,* when used in regard to financial statements, means examined and reported upon with an opinion expressed by an independent public or certified public accountant.

Charter. The term *charter* includes articles of incorporation, declarations of trust, articles of association or partnership, or any similar instrument, as amended, affecting (either with or without filing with any governmental agency) the organization or creation of an incorporated or unincorporated person.

Common equity. The term *common equity* means any class of common stock or an equivalent interest, including but not limited to a unit of beneficial interest in a trust or a limited partnership interest.

Commission. The term *Commission* means the Securities and Exchange Commission.

Control. The term *control* (including the terms *controlling, controlled by* and *under common control with*) means the possession, direct or indirect, of the power to direct or cause the direction of the management and policies of a person, whether through the ownership of voting securities, by contract, or otherwise.

Depositary share. The term *depositary share* means a security, evidenced by an American Depositary Receipt, that represents a foreign security or a multiple of or fraction thereof deposited with a depositary.

Director. The term *director* means any director of a corporation or any person performing similar functions with respect to any organization whether incorporated or unincorporated.

Dividend or interest reinvestment plan. The term *dividend or interest reinvestment plan* means a plan which is offered solely to the existing security holders of the registrant, which allows such persons to reinvest dividends or interest paid to them on securities issued by the registrant, and also may allow additional cash amounts to be contributed by the participants in the plan, provided the securities to be registered are newly issued, or are purchased for the account of plan participants, at prices not in excess of current market prices at the time of purchase, or at prices not in excess of an amount determined in accordance with a pricing formula specified in the plan and based upon average or current market prices at the time of purchase.

Electronic filer. The term *electronic filer* means a person or an entity that submits filings electronically pursuant to Rules 100 and 101 of Regulation S-T.

Electronic filing. The term *electronic filing* means a document under the federal securities laws that is transmitted or delivered to the Commission in electronic format.

Employee. The term *employee* does not include a director, trustee, or officer.

Employee benefit plan. The term *employee benefit plan* means any written purchase, savings, option, bonus, appreciation, profit sharing, thrift, incentive, pension or similar plan or written compensation contract solely for employees, directors, general partners, trustees (where the registrant is a business trust), officers, or consultants or advisors. However, consultants or advisors may participate in an employee benefit plan only if:
1. They are natural persons;
2. They provide bona fide services to the registrant; and
3. The services are not in connection with the offer or sale of securities in a capital-raising transaction, and do not directly or indirectly promote or maintain a market for the registrant's securities.

Equity security. The term *equity security* means any stock or similar security, certificate of interest or participation in any profit sharing agreement, preorganization certificate or subscription, transferable share, voting trust certificate or certificate of deposit for an equity security, limited partnership interest, interest in a joint venture, or certificate of interest in a business trust; any security future on any such security; or any security convertible, with or without consideration into such a security, or carrying any warrant or right to subscribe to or purchase such a security; or any such warrant or right; or any put, call, straddle, or other option or privilege of buying such a security from or selling such a security to another without being bound to do so.

Executive officer. The term *executive officer,* when used with reference to a registrant, means its president, any vice president of the registrant in charge of a principal business unit, division or function (such as sales, administration or finance), any other officer who performs a policy making function or any other person who performs similar policy making functions for the registrant. Executive officers of subsidiaries may be deemed executive officers of the registrant if they perform such policy making functions for the registrant.

Fiscal year. The term *fiscal year* means the annual accounting period or, if no closing date has been adopted, the calendar year ending on December 31.

Foreign government. The term *foreign government* means the government of any foreign country or of any political subdivision of a foreign country.

Foreign issuer. The term *foreign issuer* means any issuer which is a foreign government, a national of any foreign country or a corporation or other organization incorporated or organized under the laws of any foreign country.

Foreign private issuer. The term *foreign private issuer* means any foreign issuer other than a foreign government except an issuer meeting the following conditions:
1.   More than 50 percent of the outstanding voting securities of such issuer are directly or indirectly owned of record by residents of the United States; and

2.   Any of the following:
   i.   The majority of the executive officers or directors are United States citizens or residents;
   ii. More than 50 percent of the assets of the issuer are located in the United States; or
   iii. The business of the issuer is administered principally in the United States.

Instructions to paragraph (1): To determine the percentage of outstanding voting securities held by U.S. residents:
   A.   Use the method of calculating record ownership in Rule 12g3-2(a) under the Exchange Act, except that your inquiry as to the amount of shares represented by accounts of customers resident in the United States may be limited to brokers, dealers, banks and other nominees located in:
   1.   The United States,
   2.   Your jurisdiction of incorporation, and
   3.   The jurisdiction that is the primary trading market for your voting securities, if different than your jurisdiction of incorporation.
   B.   If, after reasonable inquiry, you are unable to obtain information about the amount of shares represented by accounts of customers resident in the United States, you may assume, for purposes of this definition, that the customers are residents of the jurisdiction in which the nominee has its principal place of business.

C.   Count shares of voting securities beneficially owned by residents of the United States as reported on reports of beneficial ownership that are provided to you or publicly filed and based on information otherwise provided to you.

Free writing prospectus. Except as otherwise specifically provided or the context otherwise requires, a *free writing prospectus* is any written communication as defined in this section that constitutes an offer to sell or a solicitation of an offer to buy the securities relating to a registered offering that is used after the registration statement in respect of the offering is filed (or, in the case of a well-known seasoned issuer, whether or not such registration statement is filed) and is made by means other than:

1. A prospectus satisfying the requirements of section 10(a) of the Act, Rule 430, Rule 430A, Rule 430B, Rule 430C, or Rule 431;
2. A written communication used in reliance on Rule 167 and Rule 426; or
3. A written communication that constitutes an offer to sell or solicitation of an offer to buy such securities that falls within the exception from the definition of prospectus in clause (a) of section 2(a)(10) of the Act.

Graphic communication. The term *graphic communication*, which appears in the definition of "write, written" in section 2(a)(9) of the Act and in the definition of written communication in this section, shall include all forms of electronic media, including, but not limited to, audiotapes, videotapes, facsimiles, CD-ROM, electronic mail, Internet Web sites, substantially similar messages widely distributed (rather than individually distributed) on telephone answering or voice mail systems, computers, computer networks and other forms of computer data compilation. Graphic communication shall not include a communication that, at the time of the communication, originates live, in real-time to a live audience and does not originate in recorded form or otherwise as a graphic communication, although it is transmitted through graphic means.

Ineligible issuer.
1. An *ineligible issuer* is an issuer with respect to which any of the following is true as of the relevant date of determination:
    i.   Any issuer that is required to file reports pursuant to section 13 or 15(d) of the Securities Exchange Act of 1934 that has not filed all reports and other materials required to be filed during the preceding 12 months (or for such shorter period that the issuer was required to file such reports pursuant to sections 13 or 15(d) of the Securities Exchange Act of 1934), other than reports on Form 8-K required solely pursuant to an item specified in General Instruction I.A.3(b) of Form S-3 (or in the case of an asset-backed issuer, to the extent the depositor or any issuing entity previously established, directly or indirectly, by the depositor (as such terms are defined in Item 1101 of Regulation AB are or were at any time during the preceding 12 calendar months required to file reports pursuant to section 13 or 15(d) of the Securities Exchange Act of 1934 with respect to a class of asset-backed securities involving the same asset class, such depositor and each such issuing entity must have filed all reports and other material required to be filed for such period (or such shorter period that each such entity was required to file such reports), other than reports on Form 8-K required solely pursuant to an item specified in General Instruction I.A.4 of Form S-3);

    ii.   The issuer is, or during the past three years the issuer or any of its predecessors was:

        A. A blank check company as defined in Rule 419(a)(2);

        B. A shell company, other than a business combination related shell company, each as defined in this section;

        C. An issuer in an offering of penny stock as defined in Rule 3a51-1 of the Securities Exchange Act of 1934;

    iii.   The issuer is a limited partnership that is offering and selling its securities other than through a firm commitment underwriting;

    iv.   Within the past three years, a petition under the federal bankruptcy laws or any state insolvency law was filed by or against the issuer, or a court appointed a receiver, fiscal agent or similar officer with respect to the business or property of the issuer subject to the following:

        A. In the case of an involuntary bankruptcy in which a petition was filed against the issuer, ineligibility will occur upon the earlier to occur of:

          (1) 90 days following the date of the filing of the involuntary petition (if the case has not been earlier dismissed); or

          (2) The conversion of the case to a voluntary proceeding under federal bankruptcy or state insolvency laws; and

        B. Ineligibility will terminate under this paragraph (1)(iv) if an issuer has filed an annual report with audited financial statements subsequent to its emergence from that bankruptcy, insolvency, or receivership process;

    v.   Within the past three years, the issuer or any entity that at the time was a subsidiary of the issuer was convicted of any felony or misdemeanor described in paragraphs (i) through (iv) of section 15(b)(4)(B) of the Securities Exchange Act of 1934;

    vi.   Within the past three years (but in the case of a decree or order agreed to in a settlement, not before [insert date 120 days after publication in the Federal Register]), the issuer or any entity that at the time was a subsidiary of the issuer was made the subject of any judicial or administrative decree or order arising out of a governmental action that:

        A. Prohibits certain conduct or activities regarding, including future violations of, the anti-fraud provisions of the federal securities laws;

        B. Requires that the person cease and desist from violating the anti-fraud provisions of the federal securities laws; or

        C. Determines that the person violated the anti-fraud provisions of the federal securities laws;

    vii.   The issuer has filed a registration statement that is the subject of any pending proceeding or examination under section 8 of the Act or has been the subject of any refusal order or stop order under section 8 of the Act within the past three years; or

    viii.   The issuer is the subject of any pending proceeding under section 8A of the Act in connection with an offering.

2.   An issuer shall not be an ineligible issuer if the Commission determines, upon a showing of good cause, that it is not necessary under the circumstances that the issuer be considered an ineligible issuer. Any such determination shall be without prejudice

to any other action by the Commission in any other proceeding or matter with respect to the issuer or any other person.

3. The date of determination of whether an issuer is an ineligible issuer is as follows:
    i. For purposes of determining whether an issuer is a well-known seasoned issuer, at the date specified for purposes of such determination in paragraph (2) of the definition of well-known seasoned issuer in this section; and
    ii. For purposes of determining whether an issuer or offering participant may use free writing prospectuses in respect of an offering in accordance with the provisions of Rules 164 and 433, at the date in respect of the offering specified in paragraph (h) of Rule 164.

Majority-owned subsidiary. The term *majority-owned subsidiary* means a subsidiary more than 50 percent of whose outstanding securities representing the right, other than as affected by events of default, to vote for the election of directors, is owned by the subsidiary's parent and/or one or more of the parent's other majority-owned subsidiaries.

Material. The term *material,* when used to qualify a requirement for the furnishing of information as to any subject, limits the information required to those matters to which there is a substantial likelihood that a reasonable investor would attach importance in determining whether to purchase the security registered.

Officer. The term *officer* means a president, vice president, secretary, treasurer or principal financial officer, comptroller or principal accounting officer, and any person routinely performing corresponding functions with respect to any organization whether incorporated or unincorporated.

Parent. A *parent* of a specified person is an affiliate controlling such person directly, or indirectly through one or more intermediaries.

Predecessor. The term *predecessor* means a person the major portion of the business and assets of which another person acquired in a single succession, or in a series of related successions in each of which the acquiring person acquired the major portion of the business and assets of the acquired person.

Principal underwriter. The term *principal underwriter* means an underwriter in privity of contract with the issuer of the securities as to which he is underwriter, the term *issuer* having the meaning given in sections 2(a)(4) and 2(a)(11) of the Act.

Promoter.
1. The term *promoter* includes:
    i. Any person who, acting alone or in conjunction with one or more other persons, directly or indirectly takes initiative in founding and organizing the business or enterprise of an issuer; or
    ii. Any person who, in connection with the founding and organizing of the business or enterprise of an issuer, directly or indirectly receives in consideration of services or property, or both services and property, 10 percent or more of any class of securities of the issuer or 10 percent or more of the proceeds from the

sale of any class of such securities. However, a person who receives such securities or proceeds either solely as underwriting commissions or solely in consideration of property shall not be deemed a promoter within the meaning of this paragraph if such person does not otherwise take part in founding and organizing the enterprise.

2. All persons coming within the definition of promoter in paragraph 1 of this definition may be referred to as *founders* or *organizers* or by another term provided that such term is reasonably descriptive of those persons' activities with respect to the issuer.

Prospectus. Unless otherwise specified or the context otherwise requires, the term *prospectus* means a prospectus meeting the requirements of section 10(a) of the Act.

Registrant. The term *registrant* means the issuer of the securities for which the registration statement is filed.

Share. The term *share* means a share of stock in a corporation or unit of interest in an unincorporated person.

Significant subsidiary. The term *significant subsidiary* means a subsidiary, including its subsidiaries, which meets any of the following conditions:

1. The registrant's and its other subsidiaries' investments in and advances to the subsidiary exceed 10 percent of the total assets of the registrant and its subsidiaries consolidated as of the end of the most recently completed fiscal year (for a proposed business combination to be accounted for as a pooling of interests, this condition is also met when the number of common shares exchanged or to be exchanged by the registrant exceeds 10 percent of its total common shares outstanding at the date the combination is initiated); or

2. The registrant's and its other subsidiaries' proportionate share of the total assets (after intercompany eliminations) of the subsidiary exceeds 10 percent of the total assets of the registrants and its subsidiaries consolidated as of the end of the most recently completed fiscal year; or

3. The registrant's and its other subsidiaries' equity in the income from continuing operations before income taxes, extraordinary items and cumulative effect of a change in accounting principle of the subsidiary exceeds 10 percent of such income of the registrant and its subsidiaries consolidated for the most recently completed fiscal year.

   Computational note. For purposes of making the prescribed income test the following guidance should be applied:

   1. When a loss has been incurred by either the parent and its subsidiaries consolidated or the tested subsidiary, but not both, the equity in the income or loss of the tested subsidiary should be excluded from the income of the registrant and its subsidiaries consolidated for purposes of the computation.

   2. If income of the registrant and its subsidiaries consolidated for the most recent fiscal year is at least 10 percent lower than the average of the income for the last five fiscal years, such average income should be substituted for purposes of the computation. Any loss years should be omitted for purposes of computing average income.

Smaller reporting company: As used in this part, the term *smaller reporting company* means an issuer that is not an investment company, an asset-backed issuer, or a majority-owned subsidiary of a parent that is not a smaller reporting company and that:

1. Had a public float of less than $ 75 million as of the last business day of its most recently completed second fiscal quarter, computed by multiplying the aggregate worldwide number of shares of its voting and non-voting common equity held by non-affiliates by the price at which the common equity was last sold, or the average of the bid and asked prices of common equity, in the principal market for the common equity; or

2. In the case of an initial registration statement under the Securities Act or Exchange Act for shares of its common equity, had a public float of less than $75 million as of a date within 30 days of the date of the filing of the registration statement, computed by multiplying the aggregate worldwide number of such shares held by non-affiliates before the registration plus, in the case of a Securities Act registration statement, the number of such shares included in the registration statement by the estimated public offering price of the shares; or

3. In the case of an issuer whose public float as calculated under paragraph (1) or (2) of this definition was zero, had annual revenues of less than $50 million during the most recently completed fiscal year for which audited financial statements are available.

4. Determination: Whether or not an issuer is a smaller reporting company is determined on an annual basis.

    i. For issuers that are required to file reports under section 13(a) or 15(d) of the Exchange Act, the determination is based on whether the issuer came within the definition of smaller reporting company using the amounts specified in paragraph (f)(2)(iii) of Item 10 of Regulation S-K as of the last business day of the second fiscal quarter of the issuer's previous fiscal year. An issuer in this category must reflect this determination in the information it provides in its quarterly report on Form 10-Q for the first fiscal quarter of the next year, indicating on the cover page of that filing, and in subsequent filings for that fiscal year, whether or not it is a smaller reporting company, except that, if a determination based on public float indicates that the issuer is newly eligible to be a smaller reporting company, the issuer may choose to reflect this determination beginning with its first quarterly report on Form 10-Q following the determination, rather than waiting until the first fiscal quarter of the next year.

    ii. For determinations based on an initial Securities Act or Exchange Act registration statement under paragraph (f)(1)(ii) of Item 10 of Regulation S-K, the issuer must reflect the determination in the information it provides in the registration statement and must appropriately indicate on the cover page of the filing, and subsequent filings for the fiscal year in which the filing is made, whether or not it is a smaller reporting company. The issuer must redetermine its status at the end of its second fiscal quarter and then reflect any change in status as provided in paragraph (4)(i) of this definition. In the case of a determination based on an initial Securities Act registration statement, an issuer that was not determined to be a smaller reporting company has the option to redetermine its status at the conclusion of the offering covered by the registration statement based on the actual offering price and number of shares sold.

iii. Once an issuer fails to qualify for smaller reporting company status, it will remain unqualified unless it determines that its public float, as calculated in accordance with paragraph (f)(1) of this definition, was less than $ 50 million as of the last business day of its second fiscal quarter or, if that calculation results in zero because the issuer had no public equity outstanding or no market price for its equity existed, if the issuer had annual revenues of less than $ 40 million during its previous fiscal year.

Note: The public float of a reporting company shall be computed by use of the price at which the stock was last sold, or the average of the bid and asked prices of such stock, on a date within 60 days prior to the end of its most recent fiscal year. The public float of a company filing an initial registration statement under the Exchange Act shall be determined as of a date within 60 days of the date the registration statement is filed.

In the case of an initial public offering of securities, public float shall be computed on the basis of the number of shares outstanding prior to the offering and the estimated public offering price of the securities.

Subsidiary. A *subsidiary* of a specified person is an affiliate controlled by such person directly, or indirectly through one or more intermediaries. (See also *majority owned subsidiary, significant subsidiary, totally held subsidiary,* and *wholly owned subsidiary.*)

Succession. The term *succession* means the direct acquisition of the assets comprising a going business, whether by merger, consolidation, purchase, or other direct transfer. The term does not include the acquisition of control of a business unless followed by the direct acquisition of its assets. The terms *succeed* and *successor* have meanings correlative to the foregoing.

Totally held subsidiary. The term *totally held subsidiary* means a subsidiary (1) substantially all of whose outstanding securities are owned by its parent and/or the parent's other totally held subsidiaries, and (2) which is not indebted to any person other than its parent and/or the parent's other totally held subsidiaries in an amount which is material in relation to the particular subsidiary, excepting indebtedness incurred in the ordinary course of business which is not overdue and which matures within one year from the date of its creation, whether evidenced by securities or not.

Voting securities. The term *voting securities* means securities the holders of which are presently entitled to vote for the election of directors.

Well-known seasoned issuer. A *well-known seasoned issuer* is an issuer that, as of the most recent determination date determined pursuant to paragraph (2) of this definition:

1. i. Meets all the registrant requirements of General Instruction I.A. of Form S-3 or Form F-3 and either:
   A. As of a date within 60 days of the determination date, has a worldwide market value of its outstanding voting and non-voting common equity held by nonaffiliates of $700 million or more; or
   B. 1. As of a date within 60 days of the determination date, has issued in the last three years at least $1 billion aggregate principal amount of non-

convertible securities, other than common equity, in primary offerings for cash, not exchange, registered under the Act; and

2. Will register only non-convertible securities, other than common equity, and full and unconditional guarantees permitted pursuant to paragraph (1)(ii) of this definition unless, at the determination date, the issuer also is eligible to register a primary offering of its securities relying on General Instruction I.B.1. of Form S-3 or Form F-3.

3. Provided that as to a parent issuer only, for purposes of calculating the aggregate principal amount of outstanding non-convertible securities under paragraph (1)(i)(B)(1) of this definition, the parent issuer may include the aggregate principal amount of non-convertible securities, other than common equity, of its majority-owned subsidiaries issued in registered primary offerings for cash, not exchange, that it has fully and unconditionally guaranteed, within the meaning of Rule 3-10 of Regulation S-Xin the last three years; or

ii. Is a majority-owned subsidiary of a parent that is a well-known seasoned issuer pursuant to paragraph (1)(i) of this definition and, as to the subsidiaries' securities that are being or may be offered on that parent's registration statement:

A. The parent has provided a full and unconditional guarantee, as defined in Rule 3-10 of Regulation S-X, of the payment obligations on the subsidiary's securities and the securities are non-convertible securities, other than common equity;

B. The securities are guarantees of:
   (1) Non-convertible securities, other than common equity, of its parent being registered; or
   (2) Non-convertible securities, other than common equity, of another majority-owned subsidiary being registered where there is a full and unconditional guarantee, as defined in Rule 3-10 of Regulation S-X, of such non-convertible securities by the parent; or

C. The securities of the majority-owned subsidiary meet the conditions of General Instruction I.B.2 of Form S-3 or Form F-3.

iii. Is not an ineligible issuer as defined in this section.

iv. Is not an asset-backed issuer as defined in Item 1101 of Regulation AB.

v. Is not an investment company registered under the Investment Company Act of 1940 or a business development company as defined in section 2(a)(48) of the Investment Company Act of 1940.

2. For purposes of this definition, the determination date as to whether an issuer is a well-known seasoned issuer shall be the latest of:

i. The time of filing of its most recent shelf registration statement; or

ii. The time of its most recent amendment (by post-effective amendment, incorporated report filed pursuant to section 13 or 15(d) of the Securities Exchange Act of 1934, or form of prospectus) to a shelf registration statement for purposes of complying with section 10(a)(3) of the Act (or if such amendment has not been made within the time period required by section 10(a)(3) of the Act, the date on which such amendment is required); or

iii. In the event that the issuer has not filed a shelf registration statement or amended a shelf registration statement for purposes of complying with section

10(a)(3) of the Act for sixteen months, the time of filing of the issuer's most recent annual report on Form 10-K or Form 20-F (or if such report has not been filed by its due date, such due date).

Wholly owned subsidiary. The term *wholly owned subsidiary* means a subsidiary substantially all of whose outstanding voting securities are owned by its parent and/or the parent's other wholly owned subsidiaries.

Written communication. Except as otherwise specifically provided or the context otherwise requires, a *written communication* is any communication that is written, printed, a radio or television broadcast, or a graphic communication as defined in this section.

Note to definition of "written communication." A communication that is a radio or television broadcast is a written communication regardless of the means of transmission of the broadcast.

Rule 408 – Additional Information

a. In addition to the information expressly required to be included in a registration statement, there shall be added such further material information, if any, as may be necessary to make the required statements, in the light of the circumstances under which they are made, not misleading.

b. Notwithstanding paragraph (a) of this section, unless otherwise required to be included in the registration statement, the failure to include in a registration statement information included in a free writing prospectus will not, solely by virtue of inclusion of the information in a free writing prospectus (as defined in Rule 405), be considered an omission of material information required to be included in the registration statement.

Rule 409 – Information Unknown or Not Reasonably Available

Information required need be given only insofar as it is known or reasonably available to the registrant. If any required information is unknown and not reasonably available to the registrant, either because the obtaining thereof could involve unreasonable effort or expense, or because it rests peculiarly within the knowledge of another person not affiliated with the registrant, the information may be omitted, subject to the following conditions:

a. The registrant shall give such information on the subject as it possesses or can acquire without unreasonable effort or expense, together with the sources thereof.

b. The registrant shall include a statement either showing that unreasonable effort or expense would be involved or indicating the absence of any affiliation with the person within whose knowledge the information rests and stating the result of a request made to such person for the information.

Rule 412 – Modified or Superseded Documents

a.   Any statement contained in a document incorporated or deemed to be incorporated by reference or deemed to be part of a registration statement or the prospectus that is part of the registration statement shall be deemed to be modified or superseded for purposes of the registration statement or the prospectus that is part of the registration statement to the extent that a statement contained in the prospectus that is part of the registration statement or in any other subsequently filed document which also is or is deemed to be incorporated by reference or deemed to be part of the registration statement or prospectus that is part of the registration statement modifies or replaces such statement. Any statement contained in a document that is deemed to be incorporated by reference or deemed to be part of a registration statement or the prospectus that is part of the registration statement after the most recent effective date or after the date of the most recent prospectus that is part of the registration statement may modify or replace existing statements contained in the registration statement or the prospectus that is part of the registration statement.

b.   The modifying or superseding statement may, but need not, state that it has modified or superseded a prior statement or include any other information set forth in the document which is not so modified or superseded. The making of a modifying or superseding statement shall not be deemed an admission that the modified or superseded statement, when made, constituted an untrue statement of a material fact, an omission to state a material fact necessary to make a statement not misleading, or the employment of a manipulative, deceptive, or fraudulent device, contrivance, scheme, transaction, act, practice, course of business or artifice to defraud, as those terms are used in the Act, the Securities Exchange Act of 1934, the Investment Company Act of 1940, or the rules and regulations thereunder.

Rule 413 – Registration of Additional Securities and Additional Classes of Securities.

a.   Except as provided in section 24(f) of the Investment Company Act of 1940 and in paragraph (b) of this section, where a registration statement is already in effect, the registration of additional securities shall only be effected through a separate registration statement relating to the additional securities.

b.   Notwithstanding paragraph (a) of this section, the following additional securities or additional classes of securities may be added to an automatic shelf registration statement already in effect by filing a post-effective amendment to that automatic shelf registration statement:
1.   Securities of a class different than those registered on the effective automatic shelf registration statement identified as provided in Rule 430B(a); or
2.   Securities of a majority-owned subsidiary that are permitted to be included in an automatic shelf registration statement, provided that the subsidiary and the securities are identified as provided in Rule 430B and the subsidiary satisfies the signature requirements of an issuer in the post-effective amendment.

Rule 415 – Delayed or Continuous Offering and Sale of Securities

a. Securities may be registered for an offering to be made on a continuous or delayed basis in the future, provided, that:

   1. The registration statement pertains only to:

      i. Securities which are to be offered or sold solely by or on behalf of a person or persons other than the registrant, a subsidiary of the registrant or a person of which the registrant is a subsidiary;

      ii. Securities which are to be offered and sold pursuant to a dividend or interest reinvestment plan or an employee benefit plan of the registrant;

      iii. Securities which are to be issued upon the exercise of outstanding options, warrants or rights;

      iv. Securities which are to be issued upon conversion of other outstanding securities;

      v. Securities which are pledged as collateral;

      vi. Securities which are registered on Form F-6;

      vii. Mortgage related securities, including such securities as mortgage backed debt and mortgage participation or pass through certificates;

      viii. Securities which are to be issued in connection with business combination transactions;

      ix. Securities the offering of which will be commenced promptly, will be made on a continuous basis and may continue for a period in excess of 30 days from the date of initial effectiveness;

      x. Securities registered (or qualified to be registered) on Form S-3 or Form F-3 which are to be offered and sold on an immediate, continuous or delayed basis by or on behalf of the registrant, a majority owned subsidiary of the registrant or a person of which the registrant is a majority-owned subsidiary; or

      xi. Shares of common stock which are to be offered and sold on a delayed or continuous basis by or on behalf of a registered closed-end management investment company or business development company that makes periodic repurchase offers pursuant to Rule 23c-3.

   2. Securities in paragraph (a)(1)(viii) of this section and securities in paragraph (a)(1)(ix) of this section that are not registered on Form S-3 or Form F-3 may only be registered in an amount which, at the time the registration statement becomes effective, is reasonably expected to be offered and sold within two years from the initial effective date of the registration.

   3. The registrant furnishes the undertakings required by Item 512(a) of Regulation S-K except that a registrant that is an investment company filing on Form N-2 must furnish the undertakings required by Item 34.4 of Form N-2.

   4. In the case of a registration statement pertaining to an at the market offering of equity securities by or on behalf of the registrant, the offering must come within paragraph (a)(1)(x) of this section. As used in this paragraph, the term "at the market offering" means an offering of equity securities into an existing trading market for outstanding shares of the same class at other than a fixed price.

5.   Securities registered on an automatic shelf registration statement and securities described in paragraphs (a)(1)(vii), (ix), and (x) of this section may be offered and sold only if not more than three years have elapsed since the initial effective date of the registration statement under which they are being offered and sold, *provided, however,* that if a new registration statement has been filed pursuant to paragraph (a)(6) of this section:

    i.   If the new registration statement is an automatic shelf registration statement, it shall be immediately effective pursuant to Rule 462(e); or

    ii.   If the new registration statement is not an automatic shelf registration statement:

      (A) Securities covered by the prior registration statement may continue to be offered and sold until the earlier of the effective date of the new registration statement or 180 days after the third anniversary of the initial effective date of the prior registration statement; and

      (B) A continuous offering of securities covered by the prior registration statement that commenced within three years of the initial effective date may continue until the effective date of the new registration statement if such offering is permitted under the new registration statement.

6.   Prior to the end of the three-year period described in paragraph (a)(5) of this section, an issuer may file a new registration statement covering securities described in such paragraph (a)(5) of this section, which may, if permitted, be an automatic shelf registration statement. The new registration statement and prospectus included therein must include all the information that would be required at that time in a prospectus relating to all offering(s) that it covers. Prior to the effective date of the new registration statement (including at the time of filing in the case of an automatic shelf registration statement), the issuer may include on such new registration statement any unsold securities covered by the earlier registration statement by identifying on the bottom of the facing page of the new registration statement or latest amendment thereto the amount of such unsold securities being included and any filing fee paid in connection with such unsold securities, which will continue to be applied to such unsold securities. The offering of securities on the earlier registration statement will be deemed terminated as of the date of effectiveness of the new registration statement.

b.   This section shall not apply to any registration statement pertaining to securities issued by a face-amount certificate company or redeemable securities issued by an open-end management company or unit investment trust under the Investment Company Act of 1940 or any registration statement filed by any foreign government or political subdivision thereof.

Rule 420 – Legibility of Prospectus

a.   The body of all printed prospectuses and all notes to financial statements and other tabular data included therein shall be in roman type at least as large and as legible as 10-point modern type.

However,

1. to the extent necessary for convenient presentation, financial statements and other tabular data, including tabular data in notes, and

2. prospectuses deemed to be omitting prospectuses under rule 482 may be in roman type at least as large and as legible as 8-point modern type. All such type shall be leaded at least 2 points.

b. Where a prospectus is distributed through an electronic medium, issuers may satisfy legibility requirements applicable to printed documents, such as paper size, type size and font, bold-face type, italics and red ink, by presenting all required information in a format readily communicated to investors, and where indicated, in a manner reasonably calculated to draw investor attention to specific information.

Rule 421 – Presentation of Information in Prospectuses

a. The information required in a prospectus need not follow the order of the items or other requirements in the form. Such information shall not, however, be set forth in such fashion as to obscure any of the required information or any information necessary to keep the required information from being incomplete or misleading. Where an item requires information to be given in a prospectus in tabular form it shall be given in substantially the tabular form specified in the item.

b. You must present the information in a prospectus in a clear, concise and understandable manner. You must prepare the prospectus using the following standards:

1. Present information in clear, concise sections, paragraphs, and sentences. Whenever possible, use short, explanatory sentences and bullet lists;

2. Use descriptive headings and subheadings;

3. Avoid frequent reliance on glossaries or defined terms as the primary means of explaining information in the prospectus. Define terms in a glossary or other section of the document only if the meaning is unclear from the context. Use a glossary only if it facilitates understanding of the disclosure; and

4. Avoid legal and highly technical business terminology.

Note to Rule 421(b): In drafting the disclosure to comply with this section, you should avoid the following:

1. Legalistic or overly complex presentations that make the substance of the disclosure difficult to understand;

2. Vague "boilerplate" explanations that are imprecise and readily subject to different interpretations;

3. Complex information copied directly from legal documents without any clear and concise explanation of the provision(s); and

4. Disclosure repeated in different sections of the document that increases the size of the document but does not enhance the quality of the information.

c. All information required to be included in a prospectus shall be clearly understandable without the necessity of referring to the particular form or to the general rules and regulations. Except as to financial statements and information required in a tabular form, the information set forth in a prospectus may be expressed in condensed or summarized form. In lieu of repeating information in the form of notes to financial statements, references may be made to other parts of the prospectus where such information is set forth.

    d.   1.   To enhance the readability of the prospectus, you must use plain English principles in the organization, language, and design of the front and back cover pages, the summary, and the risk factors section.

        2.   You must draft the language in these sections so that at a minimum it substantially complies with each of the following plain English writing principles:

> Short sentences;
> Definite, concrete, everyday words;
> Active voice;
> Tabular presentation or bullet lists for complex material, whenever possible;
> No legal jargon or highly technical business terms; and
> No multiple negatives.

        3.   In designing these sections or other sections of the prospectus, you may include pictures, logos, charts, graphs, or other design elements so long as the design is not misleading and the required information is clear. You are encouraged to use tables, schedules, charts and graphic illustrations of the results of operations, balance sheet, or other financial data that present the data in an understandable manner. Any presentation must be consistent with the financial statements and non-financial information in the prospectus. You must draw the graphs and charts to scale. Any information you provide must not be misleading.

Instruction to Rule 421: You should read Securities Act Release No. 33-7497 (January 28, 1998) for information on plain English principles.

Rule 424 – Filing of Prospectuses; Number of Copies

    a.   Except as provided in paragraph (f) of this section, five copies of every form of prospectus sent or given to any person prior to the effective date of the registration statement which varies from the form or forms of prospectus included in the registration statement as filed pursuant to Rule 402(a) shall be filed as a part of the registration statement not later than the date such form of prospectus is first sent or given to any person: *Provided, however,* That only a form of prospectus that contains substantive changes from or additions to a prospectus previously filed with the Commission as part of a registration statement need be filed pursuant to this paragraph (a).

    b.   Ten copies of each form of prospectus purporting to comply with section 10 of the Act, except for documents constituting a prospectus pursuant to Rule 428(a) or free writing prospectuses pursuant to Rule 164 and Rule 433, shall be filed with the Commission in the form in which it is used after the effectiveness of the registration statement and identified as required by paragraph (e) of this section; *provided, however,* that only a form of prospectus that contains substantive changes from or additions to a previously filed prospectus is required to be filed;

Provided, further, that this paragraph (b) shall not apply in respect of a form of prospectus contained in a registration statement and relating solely to securities offered at competitive bidding, which prospectus is intended for use prior to the opening of bids. Ten copies of the form of prospectus shall be filed or transmitted for filing as follows:

1. A form of prospectus that discloses information previously omitted from the prospectus filed as part of an effective registration statement in reliance upon Rule 430A under the Securities Act shall be filed with the commission no later than the second business day following the earlier of the date of determination of the offering price or the date it is first used after effectiveness in connection with a public offering or sales, or transmitted by a means reasonably calculated to result in filing with the Commission by that date.

2. A form of prospectus that is used in connection with a primary offering of securities pursuant to Rule 415(a)(1)(x) or a primary offering of securities registered for issuance on a delayed basis pursuant to Rule 415(a)(1)(vii) or (viii) and that, in the case of Rule 415(a)(1)(viii) discloses the public offering price, description of securities or similar matters, and in the case of Rule 415(a)(1)(vii) and (x) discloses information previously omitted from the prospectus filed as part of an effective registration statement in reliance on Rule 430B, shall be filed with the Commission no later than the second business day following the earlier of the date of the determination of the offering price or the date it is first used after effectiveness in connection with a public offering or sales, or transmitted by a means reasonably calculated to result in filing with the Commission by that date.

3. A form of prospectus that reflects facts or events other than those covered in paragraphs (b) (1), (2) and (6) of this section that constitute a substantive change from or addition to the information set forth in the last form of prospectus filed with the Commission under this section or as part of a registration statement under the Securities Act shall be filed with the Commission no later than the fifth business day after the date it is first used after effectiveness in connection with a public offering or sales, or transmitted by a means reasonably calculated to result in filing with the Commission by that date.

4. A form of prospectus that discloses information, facts or events covered in both paragraphs (b) (1) and (3) shall be filed with the Commission no later than the second business day following the earlier of the date of the determination of the offering price or the date it is first used after effectiveness in connection with a public offering or sales, or transmitted by a means reasonably calculated to result in filing with the Commission by that date.

5. A form of prospectus that discloses information, facts or events covered in both paragraphs (b) (2) and (3) shall be filed with the Commission no later than the second business day following the earlier of the date of the determination of the offering price or the date it is first used after effectiveness in connection with a public offering or sales, or transmitted by a means reasonably calculated to result in filing with the Commission by that date.

6. A form of prospectus used in connection with an offering of securities under Canada's National Policy Statement No. 45 pursuant to rule 415 under the Securities Act that is not made in the United States shall be filed with the

Commission no later than the date it is first used in Canada, or transmitted by a means reasonably calculated to result in filing with the Commission by that date.

7.   A form of prospectus that identifies selling security holders and the amounts to be sold by them that was previously omitted from the registration statement and the prospectus in reliance upon Rule 430B shall be filed with the Commission no later than the second business day following the earlier of the date of sale or the date of first use or transmitted by a means reasonably calculated to result in filing with the Commission by that date.

8.   A form of prospectus otherwise required to be filed pursuant to paragraph (b) of this section that is not filed within the time frames specified in paragraph (b) of this section must be filed pursuant to this paragraph as soon as practicable after the discovery of such failure to file.

Note to paragraph (b)(8) of Rule 424: A form of prospectus required to be filed pursuant to another paragraph of Rule 424(b) that is filed under Rule 424(b)(8) shall nonetheless be "required to be filed" under such other paragraph.

Instruction: Notwithstanding Rule 424 (b)(2) and (b)(5) above, a form of prospectus or prospectus supplement relating to an offering of mortgage-related securities on a delayed basis under Rule 415(a)(1)(vii) or asset-backed securities on a delayed basis under Rule 415(a)(1)(x) that is required to be filed pursuant to paragraph (b) of this section shall be filed with the Commission no later than the second business day following the date it is first used after effectiveness in connection with a public offering or sales, or transmitted by a means reasonably calculated to result in filing with the Commission by that date.

c.   If a form of prospectus, other than one filed pursuant to paragraph (b)(1) or (b)(4) of this Rule, consists of a prospectus supplement attached to a form of prospectus that

1.   previously has been filed or

2.   was not required to be filed pursuant to paragraph (b) because it did no contain substantive changes from a prospectus that previously was filed, only the prospectus supplement need be filed under paragraph (b) of this rule, provided that the first page of each prospectus supplement includes a cross reference to the date(s) of the related prospectus and any prospectus supplements thereto that together constitute the prospectus required to be delivered by Section 5(b) of the Securities Act with respect to the securities currently being offered or sold. The cross reference may be set forth in longhand, provided it is legible.

Note: Any prospectus supplement being filed separately that is smaller than a prospectus page should be attached to an 8-1/2" x 11" sheet of paper.

d.   Every prospectus consisting of a radio or television broadcast shall be reduced to writing. Five copies of every such prospectus shall be filed with the Commission in accordance with the requirements of this section.

e.   Each copy of a form of prospectus filed under this rule shall contain in the upper right corner of the cover page the paragraph of this rule, including the subparagraph if applicable, under which the filing is made, and the file number of the registration statement to which the prospectus relates. The information required by this paragraph may be set forth in longhand, provided it is legible.

f.   This rule shall not apply with respect to prospectuses of an investment company registered under the Investment Company Act of 1940 or a business development company.

g.   This rule shall not apply with respect to prospectuses of an investment company registered under the Investment Company Act of 1940 or a business development company.

h.   A form of prospectus filed pursuant to this section that operates to reflect the payment of filing fees for an offering or offerings pursuant to Rule 456(b) must include on its cover page the calculation of registration fee table reflecting the payment of such filing fees for the securities that are the subject of the payment.

Rule 425 – Filing of Certain Prospectuses and Communications under Rule 135 in Connection with Business Combination Transactions

a.   All written communications made in reliance on Rule 165 are prospectuses that must be filed with the Commission under this section on the date of first use.

b.   All written communications that contain no more information than that specified in Rule 135 must be filed with the Commission on or before the date of first use except as provided in paragraph (d)(1) of this section. A communication limited to the information specified in Rule 135 will not be deemed an offer in accordance with Rule 135 even though it is filed under this section.

c.   Each prospectus or Rule 135 communication filed under this section must identify the filer, the company that is the subject of the offering and the Commission file number for the related registration statement or, if that file number is unknown, the subject company's Exchange Act or Investment Company Act file number, in the upper right corner of the cover page.

d.   Notwithstanding paragraph (a) of this section, the following need not be filed under this section:
      1.   Any written communication that is limited to the information specified in Rule 135 and does not contain new or different information from that which was previously publicly disclosed and filed under this section.
      2.   Any research report used in reliance on Rule 137, Rule 138 and Rule 139;
      3.   Any confirmation described in Rule 10b-10; and
      4.   Any prospectus filed under Rule 424.

Notes to Rule 425:
      1.   File five copies of the prospectus or Rule 135 communication if paper filing is permitted.
      2.   No filing is required under Rule 13e-4(c), Rule 14a-12(b), Rule 14d-2(b), or Rule 14d-9(a), if the communication is filed under this section. Communications filed under this section also are deemed filed under the other applicable sections.

Rule 430 – Prospectus for Use Prior to Effective Date

a. A form of prospectus filed as a part of the registration statement shall be deemed to meet the requirements of section 10 of the Act for the purpose of section 5(b)(1) thereof prior to the effective date of the registration statement, provided such form of prospectus contains substantially the information required by the Act and the rules and regulations thereunder to be included in a prospectus meeting the requirements of section 10(a) of the Act for the securities being registered, or contains substantially that information except for the omission of information with respect to the offering price, underwriting discounts or commissions, discounts or commissions to dealers, amount of proceeds, conversion rates, call prices, or other matters dependent upon the offering price. Every such form of prospectus shall be deemed to have been filed as a part of the registration statement for the purpose of section 7 of the Act.

b. A form of prospectus filed as part of a registration statement on Form N-1A, Form N-2, Form N-3, Form N-4, or Form N-6 shall be deemed to meet the requirements of Section 10 of the Act for the purpose of Section 5(b)(1) thereof prior to the effective date of the registration statement, *Provided* that:
  1. Such form of prospectus meets the requirements of paragraph (a) of this section; and
  2. Such registration statement contains a form of Statement of Additional Information that is made available to persons receiving such prospectus upon written or oral request, and without charge, unless the form of prospectus contains the information otherwise required to be disclosed in the form of Statement of Additional Information. Every such form of prospectus shall be deemed to have been filed as part of the registration statement for the purpose of section 7 of the Act.

Rule 430A – Prospectus in a Registration Statement at the Time of Effectiveness

a. The form of prospectus filed as part of a registration statement that is declared effective may omit information with respect to the public offering price, underwriting syndicate (including any material relationships between the registrant and underwriters not named therein), underwriting discounts or commissions, discounts or commissions to dealers, amount of proceeds, conversion rates, call prices and other items dependent upon the offering price, delivery dates, and terms of the securities dependent upon the offering date; and such form of prospectus need not contain such information in order for the registration statement to meet the requirements of Section 7 of the Securities Act for the purposes of Section 5 thereof, *Provided* that:
  1. The securities to be registered are offered for cash;
  2. The registrant furnishes the undertakings required by Item 512(i) of Regulation S-K; and effective September 17, 1991.
  3. The information omitted in reliance upon paragraph (a) from the form of prospectus filed as part of a registration statement that is declared effective is contained in a form of prospectus filed with the Commission pursuant to Rule 424(b) or Rule 497(h) under the Securities Act; except that if such form of prospectus is not so filed by the later of fifteen business days after the effective date of the registration statement or fifteen business days after the effectiveness

of a post-effective amendment thereto that contains a form of prospectus, or transmitted by a means reasonably calculated to result in filing with the Commission by that date, the information omitted in reliance upon paragraph (a) must be contained in an effective post-effective amendment to the registration statement.

Instruction to paragraph (a): A decrease in the volume of securities offered or change in the bona fide estimate of the maximum offering price range from that indicated in the form of prospectus filed as part of a registration statement that is declared effective may be disclosed in the form of prospectus filed with the Commission pursuant to Rule 424(b) or Rule 497(h) under the Securities Act so long as the decrease in the volume or change in the price range would not materially change the disclosure contained in the registration statement at effectiveness. Notwithstanding the foregoing, any increase or decrease in volume (if the total dollar value of securities offered would not exceed that which was registered) and any deviation from the low or high end of the range may be reflected in the form of prospectus filed with the Commission pursuant to Rule 424(b)(1) or Rule 497(h) if, in the aggregate, the changes in volume and price represent no more than a 20% change in the maximum aggregate offering price set forth in the "Calculation of Registration Fee" table in the effective registration statement.

b.   The information omitted in reliance upon paragraph (a) from the form of prospectus filed as part of an effective registration statement, and contained in the form of prospectus filed with the Commission pursuant to Rule 424(b) or Rule 497(h) under the Securities Act, shall be deemed to be a part of the registration statement as of the time it was declared effective.

c.   When used prior to determination of the offering price of the securities, a form of prospectus relating to the securities offered pursuant to a registration statement that is declared effective with information omitted from the form of prospectus filed as part of such effective registration statement in reliance upon this Rule 430A need not contain information omitted pursuant to paragraph (a), in order to meet the requirements of Section 10 of the Securities Act for the purpose of section 5(b)(1) thereof. This provision shall not limit the information required to be contained in a form of prospectus meeting the requirements of section 10(a) of the Act for the purposes of section 5(b)(2) thereof or exception (a) of Section 2(a)(10) thereof.

d.   This rule shall not apply to registration statements for securities to be offered by competitive bidding.

e.   In the case of a registration statement filed on Form N-1A, Form N-2, Form N-3, Form N-4, or Form N-6, the references to "form of prospectus" in paragraphs (a) and (b) of this section and the accompanying Note shall be deemed also to refer to the form of Statement of Additional Information filed as part of such a registration statement.

f.   This section may apply to registration statements that are immediately effective pursuant to Rule 462(e) and (f).

Note: If information is omitted in reliance upon paragraph (a) from the form of prospectus filed as part of an effective registration statement, or effective post-effective amendment thereto, the registrant must ascertain promptly whether a form of prospectus transmitted for filing under Rule 424(b) of Rule 497(h) under the Securities Act actually was received for filing by the Commission and, in the event that it was not, promptly file such prospectus.

Rule 430B – Prospectus in a Registration Statement after Effective Date.

a.   A form of prospectus filed as part of a registration statement for offerings pursuant to Rule 415(a)(1)(vii) or (a)(1)(x) may omit from the information required by the form to be in the prospectus information that is unknown or not reasonably available to the issuer pursuant to Rule 409. In addition, a form of prospectus filed as part of an automatic shelf registration statement for offerings pursuant to Rule 415(a), other than Rule 415(a)(1)(vii) or (viii), also may omit information as to whether the offering is a primary offering or an offering on behalf of persons other than the issuer, or a combination thereof, the plan of distribution for the securities, a description of the securities registered other than an identification of the name or class of such securities, and the identification of other issuers. Each such form of prospectus shall be deemed to have been filed as part of the registration statement for the purpose of section 7 of the Act.

b.   A form of prospectus filed as part of a registration statement for offerings pursuant to Rule 415(a)(1)(i) by an issuer eligible to use Form S-3 or Form F-3 for primary offerings pursuant to General Instruction I.B.1 of such forms, may omit the information specified in paragraph (a) of this section, and may also omit the identities of selling security holders and amounts of securities to be registered on their behalf if:

   1.   The registration statement is an automatic shelf registration statement as defined in Rule 405; or

   2.   All of the following conditions are satisfied:

      i.   The initial offering transaction of the securities (or securities convertible into such securities) the resale of which are being registered on behalf of each of the selling security holders, was completed;

      ii.   The securities (or securities convertible into such securities) were issued and outstanding prior to the original date of filing the registration statement covering the resale of the securities;

      iii.   The registration statement refers to any unnamed selling security holders in a generic manner by identifying the initial offering transaction in which the securities were sold; and

      iv.   The issuer is not and during the past three years neither the issuer nor any of its predecessors was:

        (A) A blank check company as defined in Rule 419(a)(2);

        (B) A shell company, other than a business combination related shell company, each as defined in Rule 405; or

        (C) An issuer in an offering of penny stock as defined in Rule 3a51-1 of the Securities Exchange Act of 1934.

c.   A form of prospectus that is part of a registration statement that omits information in reliance upon paragraph (a) or (b) of this section meets the requirements of section 10 of the Act for the purpose of section 5(b)(1) thereof. This provision shall not limit the information required to be contained in a form of prospectus in order to meet the requirements of section 10(a) of the Act for the purposes of section 5(b)(2) thereof or exception (a) of section 2(a)(10) thereof.

d.   Information omitted from a form of prospectus that is part of an effective registration statement in reliance on paragraph (a) or (b) of this section may be included subsequently in the prospectus that is part of a registration statement by:

1.   A post-effective amendment to the registration statement;

2.   A prospectus filed pursuant to Rule 424(b); or

3.   If the applicable form permits, including the information in the issuer's periodic or current reports filed pursuant to section 13 or 15(d) of the Securities Exchange Act of 1934 that are incorporated or deemed incorporated by reference into the prospectus that is part of the registration statement in accordance with applicable requirements, subject to the provisions of paragraph (h) of this section.

e.   Information omitted from a form of prospectus that is part of an effective registration statement in reliance on paragraph (a) or (b) of this section and contained in a form of prospectus required to be filed with the Commission pursuant to Rule 424(b), other than as provided in paragraph (f) of this section, shall be deemed part of and included in the registration statement as of the date such form of filed prospectus is first used after effectiveness.

f.   1.   Information omitted from a form of prospectus that is part of an effective registration statement in reliance on paragraph (a) or (b) of this section and is contained in a form of prospectus required to be filed with the Commission pursuant to Rule 424(b)(2), (b)(5), or (b)(7), shall be deemed to be part of and included in the registration statement on the earlier of the date such subsequent form of prospectus is first used or the date and time of the first contract of sale of securities in the offering to which such subsequent form of prospectus relates.

2.   The date on which a form of prospectus is deemed to be part of and included in the registration statement pursuant to paragraph (f)(1) of this section shall be deemed, for purposes of liability under section 11 of the Act of the issuer and any underwriter at the time only, to be a new effective date of the part of such registration statement relating to the securities to which such form of prospectus relates, such part of the registration statement consisting of all information included in the registration statement and any prospectus relating to the offering of such securities (including information relating to the offering in a prospectus already included in the registration statement) as of such date and all information relating to the offering included in reports and materials incorporated by reference into such registration statement and prospectus as of such date, and in each case not modified or superseded pursuant to Rule 412. The offering of such securities at that time shall be deemed to be the initial bona fide offering thereof.

3.   If a registration statement is amended to include or is deemed to include, through incorporation by reference or otherwise, except as otherwise provided

in Rule 436, a report or opinion of any person made on such person's authority as an expert whose consent would be required under section 7 of the Act because of being named as having prepared or certified part of the registration statement, then for purposes of this section and for liability purposes under section 11 of the Act, the part of the registration statement for which liability against such person is asserted shall be considered as having become effective with respect to such person as of the time the report or opinion is deemed to be part of the registration statement and a consent required pursuant to section 7 of the Act has been provided as contemplated by section 11 of the Act.

4.   Except for an effective date resulting from the filing of a form of prospectus filed for purposes of including information required by section 10(a)(3) of the Act or pursuant to Item 512(a)(1)(ii) of Regulation S-K, the date a form of prospectus is deemed part of and included in the registration statement pursuant to this paragraph shall not be an effective date established pursuant to paragraph (f)(2) of this section as to:

i.   Any director (or person acting in such capacity) of the issuer;

ii. Any person signing any report or document incorporated by reference into the registration statement, except for such a report or document incorporated by reference for purposes of including information required by section 10(a)(3) of the Act or pursuant to Item 512(a)(1)(ii) of Regulation S-K (such person except for such reports being deemed not to be a person who signed the registration statement within the meaning of section 11(a) of the Act).

5.   The date a form of prospectus is deemed part of and included in the registration statement pursuant to paragraph (f)(2) of this section shall not be an effective date established pursuant to paragraph (f)(2) of this section as to:

i.   Any accountant with respect to financial statements or other financial information contained in the registration statement as of a prior effective date and for which the accountant previously provided a consent to be named as required by section 7 of the Act, unless the form of prospectus contains new audited financial statements or other financial information as to which the accountant is an expert and for which a new consent is required pursuant to section 7 of the Act or Rule 436; and

ii. Any other person whose report or opinion as an expert or counsel has, with their consent, previously been included in the registration statement as of a prior effective date, unless the form of prospectus contains a new report or opinion for which a new consent is required pursuant to section 7 of the Act or Rule 436.

g.   Notwithstanding paragraph (e) or (f) of this section or paragraph (a) of Rule 412, no statement made in a registration statement or prospectus that is part of the registration statement or made in a document incorporated or deemed incorporated by reference into the registration statement or prospectus that is part of the registration statement after the effective date of such registration statement or portion thereof in respect of an offering determined pursuant to this section will, as to a purchaser with a time of contract of sale prior to such effective date, supersede or modify any statement that was made in the registration statement or prospectus that was part of the registration statement or made in any such document immediately prior to such effective date.

h.   Where a form of prospectus filed pursuant to Rule 424(b) relating to an offering does not include disclosure of omitted information regarding the terms of the offering, the securities, or the plan of distribution, or selling security holders for the securities that are the subject of the form of prospectus, because such omitted information has been included in periodic or current reports filed pursuant to section 13 or 15(d) of the Securities Exchange Act of 1934 incorporated or deemed incorporated by reference into the prospectus, the issuer shall file a form of prospectus identifying the periodic or current reports that are incorporated or deemed incorporated by reference into the prospectus that is part of the registration statement that contain such omitted information. Such form of prospectus shall be required to be filed, depending on the nature of the incorporated information, pursuant to Rule 424(b)(2), (b)(5), or (b)(7).

i.   Issuers relying on this section shall furnish the undertakings required by Item 512(a) of Regulation S-K or Item 512(a) or (g) of Regulation S-B.

Note to Rule 430B: The provisions of paragraph (b) of Rule 401 shall apply to any prospectus filed for purposes of including information required by section 10(a)(3) of the Act.

Rule 430C – Prospectus in a Registration Statement Pertaining to an Offering other than Pursuant to Rule 430A or Rule 430B after the Effective Date.

a.   In offerings made other than in reliance on Rule 430B and other than for prospectuses filed in reliance on Rule 430A, information contained in a form of prospectus required to be filed with the Commission pursuant to Rule 424(b) or Rule 497(b), (c), (d), or (e), shall be deemed to be part of and included in the registration statement on the date it is first used after effectiveness.

b.   Notwithstanding paragraph (a) of this section or paragraph (a) of Rule 412, no statement made in a registration statement or prospectus that is part of the registration statement or made in a document incorporated or deemed incorporated by reference into the registration statement or prospectus that is part of the registration statement will, as to a purchaser with a time of contract of sale prior to such first use, supersede or modify any statement that was made in the registration statement or prospectus that was part of the registration statement or made in any such document immediately prior to such date of first use.

c.   Nothing in this section shall affect the information required to be included in an issuer's registration statement and prospectus.

e.   Issuers subject to paragraph (a) of this section shall furnish the undertakings required by Item 512(a) of Regulation S-K, or Item 34.4 of Form N-2, as applicable.

Rule 431 – Summary Prospectuses
a.   A summary prospectus prepared and filed (except a summary prospectus filed by an open-end management investment company registered under the Investment Company Act of 1940) as part of a registration statement in accordance with this

section shall be deemed to be a prospectus permitted under section 10(b) of the Act for the purposes of section 5(b)(1) of the Act if the form used for registration of the securities to be offered provides for the use of a summary prospectus and the following conditions are met:

1. i. The registrant is organized under the laws of the United States or any State or Territory or the District of Columbia and has its principal business operations in the United States or its territories; or

    ii. The registrant is a foreign private issuer eligible to use Form F-2;

2. The registrant has a class of securities registered pursuant to section 12(b) of the Securities Exchange Act of 1934 or has a class of equity securities registered pursuant to section 12(g) of that Act or is required to file reports pursuant to section 15(d) of that Act;

3. The registrant:

    i. Has been subject to the requirements of section 12 or 15(d) of the Securities Exchange Act of 1934 and has filed all the material required to be filed pursuant to sections 13, 14 or 15(d) of that Act for a period of at least thirty-six calendar months immediately preceding the filing of the registration statement; and

    ii. has filed in a timely manner all reports required to be filed during the twelve calendar months and any portion of a month immediately preceding the filing of the registration statement and, if the registrant has used (during the twelve calendar months and any portion of a month immediately preceding the filing of the registration statement) Rule 12b-25(b) under the Securities Exchange Act of 1934 with respect to a report or portion of a report, that report or portion thereof has actually been filed within the time period prescribed by that Rule; and

4. Neither the registrant nor any of its consolidated or unconsolidated subsidiaries has, since the end of its last fiscal year for which certified financial statements of the registrant and its consolidated subsidiaries were included in a report filed pursuant to section 13(a) or 15(d) of the Securities Exchange Act of 1934:

    i. failed to pay any dividend or sinking fund installment on preferred stock; or

    ii. defaulted on any installment or installments on indebtedness for borrowed money, or on any rental on one or more long term leases, which defaults in the aggregate are material to the financial position of the registrant and its consolidated and unconsolidated subsidiaries, taken as a whole.

b. A summary prospectus shall contain the information specified in the instructions as to summary prospectuses in the form used for registration of the securities to be offered. Such prospectus may include any other information the substance of which is contained in the registration statement except as otherwise specifically provided in the instructions as to summary prospectuses in the form used for registration. It shall not include any information the substance of which is not contained in the registration statement except that a summary prospectus may contain any information specified in Rule 134(a). No reference need be made to inapplicable terms and negative answers to any item of the form may be omitted.

c. All information included in a summary prospectus, other than the statement required by paragraph (e) of this section, may be expressed in such condensed or summarized form as may be appropriate in the light of the circumstances under which the prospectus is to be used. The information need not follow the numerical sequence of the items of the form used for registration. Every summary prospectus shall be dated approximately as of the date of its first use.

d. When used prior to the effective date of the registration statement, a summary prospectus shall be captioned a "Preliminary Summary Prospectus" and shall comply with the applicable requirements relating to a preliminary prospectus.

e. A statement to the following effect shall be prominently set forth in conspicuous print at the beginning or at the end of every summary prospectus:

    "Copies of a more complete prospectus may be obtained from" (Insert name(s), address(es) and telephone number(s)).

    Copies of a summary prospectus filed with the Commission pursuant to paragraph (g) of this section may omit the names of persons from whom the complete prospectus may be obtained.

f. Any summary prospectus published in a newspaper, magazine or other periodical need only be set in type at least as large as 7 point modern type. Nothing in this rule shall prevent the use of reprints of a summary prospectus published in a newspaper, magazine, or other periodical, if such reprints are clearly legible.

g. Eight copies of every proposed summary prospectus shall be filed as a part of the registration statement, or as an amendment thereto, at least 5 days (exclusive of Saturdays, Sundays and holidays) prior to the use thereof, or prior to the release for publication by any newspaper, magazine or other person, whichever is earlier. The Commission may, however, in its discretion, authorize such use or publication prior to the expiration of the 5-day period upon a written request for such authorization. Within 7 days after the first use or publication thereof, 5 additional copies shall be filed in the exact form in which it was used or published.

Rule 433 – Conditions to Permissible Post-filing Free Writing Prospectuses

a. **Scope of section**. This section applies to any free writing prospectus with respect to securities of any issuer (except as set forth in Rule 164 that are the subject of a registration statement that has been filed under the Act). Such a free writing prospectus that satisfies the conditions of this section may include information the substance of which is not included in the registration statement. Such a free writing prospectus that satisfies the conditions of this section will be a prospectus permitted under section 10(b) of the Act for purposes of sections 2(a)(10), 5(b)(1), and 5(b)(2) of the Act and will, for purposes of considering it a prospectus, be deemed to be public, without regard to its method of use or distribution, because it is related to the public offering of securities that are the subject of a filed registration statement.

b. **Permitted use of free writing prospectus.** Subject to the conditions of this paragraph (b) and satisfaction of the conditions set forth in paragraphs (c) through (g) of this section, a free writing prospectus may be used under this section and Rule 164 in connection with a registered offering of securities:

1. Eligibility and prospectus conditions for seasoned issuers and well-known seasoned issuers. Subject to the provisions of Rule 164(e), (f), and (g), the issuer or any other offering participant may use a free writing prospectus in the following offerings after a registration statement relating to the offering has been filed that includes a prospectus that, other than by reason of this section or Rule 431, satisfies the requirements of section 10 of the Act:

   i. Offerings of securities registered on Form S-3 pursuant to General Instruction I.B.1, I.B.2, I.B.5, I.C., or I.D. thereof;

   ii. Offerings of securities registered on Form F-3 pursuant to General Instruction I.A.5, I.B.1, I.B.2, or I.C. thereof;

   iii. Any other offering not excluded from reliance on this section and Rule 164 of securities of a well-known seasoned issuer; and

   iv. Any other offering not excluded from reliance on this section and Rule 164 of securities of an issuer eligible to use Form S-3 or Form F-3 for primary offerings pursuant to General Instruction I.B.1 of such Forms.

2. Eligibility and prospectus conditions for non-reporting and unseasoned issuers. If the issuer does not fall within the provisions of paragraph (b)(1) of this section, then, subject to the provisions of Rule 164(e), (f), and (g), any person participating in the offer or sale of the securities may use a free writing prospectus as follows:

   i. If the free writing prospectus is or was prepared by or on behalf of or used or referred to by an issuer or any other offering participant, if consideration has been or will be given by the issuer or other offering participant for the dissemination (in any format) of any free writing prospectus (including any published article, publication, or advertisement), or if section 17(b) of the Act requires disclosure that consideration has been or will be given by the issuer or other offering participant for any activity described therein in connection with the free writing prospectus, then a registration statement relating to the offering must have been filed that includes a prospectus that, other than by reason of this section or Rule 431, satisfies the requirements of section 10 of the Act, including a price range where required by rule, and the free writing prospectus shall be accompanied or preceded by the most recent such prospectus; *provided, however,* that use of the free writing prospectus is not conditioned on providing the most recent such prospectus if a prior such prospectus has been provided and there is no material change from the prior prospectus reflected in the most recent prospectus; *provided, further* that after effectiveness and availability of a final prospectus meeting the requirements of section 10(a) of the Act, no such earlier prospectus may be provided in satisfaction of this condition, and such final prospectus must precede or accompany any free writing prospectus provided after such availability, whether or not an earlier prospectus had been previously provided.

Notes to paragraph (b)(2)(i) of Rule 433.

1. The condition that a free writing prospectus shall be accompanied or preceded by the most recent prospectus satisfying the requirements of section 10 of the Act would be satisfied if a free writing prospectus that is an electronic communication contained an active hyperlink to such most recent prospectus; and

2. A communication for which disclosure would be required under section 17(b) of the Act as a result of consideration given or to be given, directly or indirectly, by or on behalf of an issuer or other offering participant is an offer by the issuer or such other offering participant as the case may be and is, if written, a free writing prospectus of the issuer or other offering participant.

    ii. Where paragraph (b)(2)(i) of this section does not apply, a registration statement relating to the offering has been filed that includes a prospectus that, other than by reason of this section or Rule 431 satisfies the requirements of section 10 of the Act, including a price range where required by rule. For purposes of paragraph (f) of this section, the prospectus included in the registration statement relating to the offering that has been filed does not have to include a price range otherwise required by rule.

3. Successors. A successor issuer will be considered to satisfy the applicable provisions of this paragraph (b) if:

    i. Its predecessor and it, taken together, satisfy the conditions, provided that the succession was primarily for the purpose of changing the state or other jurisdiction of incorporation of the predecessor or forming a holding company and the assets and liabilities of the successor at the time of succession were substantially the same as those of the predecessor; or

    ii. All predecessors met the conditions at the time of succession and the issuer has continued to do so since the succession.

c. **Information in a free writing prospectus.**

1. A free writing prospectus used in reliance on this section may include information the substance of which is not included in the registration statement but such information shall not conflict with:

    i. Information contained in the filed registration statement, including any prospectus or prospectus supplement that is part of the registration statement (including pursuant to Rule 430B or Rule 430C) and not superseded or modified; or

    ii. Information contained in the issuer's periodic and current reports filed or furnished to the Commission pursuant to section 13 or 15(d) of the Securities Exchange Act of 1934 that are incorporated by reference into the registration statement and not superseded or modified.

2.   i. A free writing prospectus used in reliance on this section shall contain substantially the following legend:

    The issuer has filed a registration statement (including a prospectus) with the SEC for the offering to which this communication relates. Before you invest, you should read the prospectus in that registration statement and other documents the issuer has filed with the SEC for more complete information about the issuer and this offering. You may get these documents for free by visiting EDGAR on the SEC Web site at www.sec.gov. Alternatively, the issuer, any underwriter or any dealer participating in the offering will arrange to send you the prospectus if you request it by calling toll-free 1-8[xx-xxx-xxxx].

ii.   The legend also may provide an e-mail address at which the documents can be requested and may indicate that the documents also are available by accessing the issuer's Web site and provide the Internet address and the particular location of the documents on the Web site.

d.   **Filing conditions**.

1.   Except as provided in paragraphs (d)(3), (d)(4), (d)(5), (d)(6), (d)(7), (d)(8), and (f) of this section, the following shall be filed with the Commission under this section by a means reasonably calculated to result in filing no later than the date of first use. The free writing prospectus filed for purposes of this section will not be filed as part of the registration statement:

   i.   The issuer shall file:

   (A) Any issuer free writing prospectus, as defined in paragraph (h) of this section;

   (B) Any issuer information that is contained in a free writing prospectus prepared by or on behalf of or used by any other offering participant (but not information prepared by or on behalf of a person other than the issuer on the basis of or derived from that issuer information); and

   (C) A description of the final terms of the issuer's securities in the offering or of the offering contained in a free writing prospectus or portion thereof prepared by or on behalf of the issuer or any offering participant, after such terms have been established for all classes in the offering; and

   ii.   Any offering participant, other than the issuer, shall file any free writing prospectus that is used or referred to by such offering participant and distributed by or on behalf of such person in a manner reasonably designed to lead to its broad unrestricted dissemination.

2.   Each free writing prospectus or issuer information contained in a free writing prospectus filed under this section shall identify in the filing the Commission file number for the related registration statement or, if that file number is unknown, a description sufficient to identify the related registration statement.

3.   The condition to file a free writing prospectus under paragraph (d)(1) of this section shall not apply if the free writing prospectus does not contain substantive changes from or additions to a free writing prospectus previously filed with the Commission.

4.   The condition to file issuer information contained in a free writing prospectus of an offering participant other than the issuer shall not apply if such information is included (including through incorporation by reference) in a prospectus or free writing prospectus previously filed that relates to the offering.

5.   Notwithstanding the provisions of paragraph (d)(1) of this section:

   i.   To the extent a free writing prospectus or portion thereof otherwise required to be filed contains a description of terms of the issuer's securities in the offering or of the offering that does not reflect the final terms, such free writing prospectus or portion thereof is not required to be filed; and

ii.   A free writing prospectus or portion thereof that contains only a description of the final terms of the issuer's securities in the offering or of the offerings shall be filed by the issuer within two days of the later of the date such final terms have been established for all classes of the offering and the date of first use.

6.   i.   Notwithstanding the provisions of paragraph (d) of this section, in an offering of asset-backed securities, a free writing prospectus or portion thereof required to be filed that contains only ABS informational and computational materials as defined in Item 1101(a) of Regulation AB, may be filed under this section within the timeframe permitted by Rule 426(b) and such filing will satisfy the filing conditions under this section.

ii.   In the event that a free writing prospectus is used in reliance on this section and Rule 164 and the conditions of this section and Rule 164 (which may include the conditions of paragraph (d)(6)(i) of this section) are satisfied with respect thereto, then the use of that free writing prospectus shall not be conditioned on satisfaction of the provisions, including without limitation the filing conditions, of Rule 167 and Rule 426. In the event that ABS informational and computational materials are used in reliance on Rule 167 and Rule 426 and the conditions of those rules are satisfied with respect thereto, then the use of those materials shall not be conditioned on the satisfaction of the conditions of Rule 164 and this section.

iii.   If a free writing prospectus used in an offering of asset-backed securities in reliance on this section and Rule 164 includes the specific address of or a hyperlink to an Internet Web site containing static pool information and is filed in accordance with this paragraph (d), the static pool information relating to the asset-backed securities offering at that specific address is included in the free writing prospectus, and the filing including such address or hyperlink satisfies the filing conditions under this section.

7.   The condition to file a free writing prospectus or issuer information pursuant to this paragraph (d) for a free writing prospectus used at the same time as a communication in a business combination transaction subject to Rule 425 shall be satisfied if:

i.   The free writing prospectus or issuer information is filed in accordance with the provisions of Rule 425, including the filing timeframe of Rule 425;

ii.   The filed material pursuant to Rule 425 indicates on the cover page that it also is being filed pursuant to Rule 433; and

iii.   The filed material pursuant to Rule 425 contains the information specified in paragraph (c)(2) of this section.

8.   Notwithstanding any other provision of this paragraph (d):

i.   A road show for an offering that is a written communication is a free writing prospectus, provided that, except as provided in paragraph (d)(8)(ii) of this section, a written communication that is a road show shall not be required to be filed; and

ii. In the case of a road show that is a written communication for an offering of common equity or convertible equity securities by an issuer that is, at the time of the filing of the registration statement for the offering, not required to file reports with the Commission pursuant to section 13 or section 15(d) of the Securities Exchange Act of 1934, such a road show is required to be filed pursuant to this section unless the issuer of the securities makes at least one version of a bona fide electronic road show available without restriction by means of graphic communication to any person, including any potential investor in the securities (and if there is more than one version of a road show for the offering that is a written communication, the version available without restriction is made available no later than the other versions).

Note to paragraph (d)(8): A communication that is provided or transmitted simultaneously with a road show and is provided or transmitted in a manner designed to make the communication available only as part of the road show and not separately is deemed to be part of the road show. Therefore, if the road show is not a written communication, such a simultaneous communication (even if it would otherwise be a graphic communication or other written communication) is also deemed not to be written. If the road show is written and not required to be filed, such a simultaneous communication is also not required to be filed. Otherwise, a written communication that is an offer contained in a separate file from a road show, whether or not the road show is a written communication, or otherwise transmitted separately from a road show, will be a free writing prospectus subject to any applicable filing conditions of paragraph (d) of this section.

e. **Treatment of information on, or hyperlinked from, an issuer's Web site**.
    1. An offer of an issuer's securities that is contained on an issuer's Web site or hyperlinked by the issuer from the issuer's Web site to a third party's Web site is a written offer of such securities by the issuer and, unless otherwise exempt or excluded from the requirements of section 5(b)(1) of the Act, the filing conditions of paragraph (d) of this section apply to such offer.
    2. Notwithstanding paragraph (e)(1) of this section, historical issuer information that is identified as such and located in a separate section of the issuer's Web site containing historical issuer information, that has not been incorporated by reference into or otherwise included in a prospectus of the issuer for the offering and that has not otherwise been used or referred to in connection with the offering, will not be considered a current offer of the issuer's securities and therefore will not be a free writing prospectus.

f. **Free writing prospectuses published or distributed by media**. Any written offer for which an issuer or any other offering participant or any person acting on its behalf provided, authorized, or approved information that is prepared and published or disseminated by a person unaffiliated with the issuer or any other offering participant that is in the business of publishing, radio or television broadcasting or otherwise disseminating written communications would be considered at the time of publication or dissemination to be a free writing prospectus prepared by or on behalf of the issuer or such other offering participant for purposes of this section subject to the following:

1. The conditions of paragraph (b)(2)(i) of this section will not apply and the conditions of paragraphs (c)(2) and (d) of this section will be deemed to be satisfied if:

   i. No payment is made or consideration given by or on behalf of the issuer or other offering participant for the written communication or its dissemination; and

   ii. The issuer or other offering participant in question files the written communication with the Commission, and includes in the filing the legend required by paragraph (c)(2) of this section, within four business days after the issuer or other offering participant becomes aware of the publication, radio or television broadcast, or other dissemination of the written communication.

2. The filing obligation under paragraph (f)(1)(ii) of this section shall be subject to the following:

   i. The issuer or other offering participant shall not be required to file a free writing prospectus if the substance of that free writing prospectus has previously been filed with the Commission;

   ii. Any filing made pursuant to paragraph (f)(1)(ii) of this section may include information that the issuer or offering participant in question reasonably believes is necessary or appropriate to correct information included in the communication; and

   iii. In lieu of filing the actual written communication as published or disseminated as required by paragraph (f)(1)(ii) of this section, the issuer or offering participant in question may file a copy of the materials provided to the media, including transcripts of interviews or similar materials, provided the copy or transcripts contain all the information provided to the media.

3. For purposes of this paragraph (f) of this section, an issuer that is in the business of publishing or radio or television broadcasting may rely on this paragraph (f) as to any publication or radio or television broadcast that is a free writing prospectus in respect of an offering of securities of the issuer if the issuer or an affiliate:

   i. Is the publisher of a bona fide newspaper, magazine, or business or financial publication of general and regular circulation or bona fide broadcaster of news including business and financial news;

   ii. Has established policies and procedures for the independence of the content of the publications or broadcasts from the offering activities of the issuer; and

   iii. Publishes or broadcasts the communication in the ordinary course.

g. **Record retention**. Issuers and offering participants shall retain all free writing prospectuses they have used, and that have not been filed pursuant to paragraph (d) or (f) of this section, for three years following the initial bona fide offering of the securities in question.

Note to paragraph (g).

To the extent that the record retention requirements of Rule 17a-4 of the Securities Exchange Act of 1934 apply to free writing prospectuses required to be retained by a broker-dealer under this section, such free writing prospectuses are required to be retained in accordance with such requirements.

h.   **Definitions.** For purposes of this section:
1.   An issuer free writing prospectus means a free writing prospectus prepared by or on behalf of the issuer or used or referred to by the issuer and, in the case of an asset-backed issuer, prepared by or on behalf of a depositor, sponsor, or servicer (as defined in Item 1101 of Regulation AB) or affiliated depositor or used or referred to by any such person.
2.   Issuer information means material information about the issuer or its securities that has been provided by or on behalf of the issuer.
3.   A written communication or information is prepared or provided by or on behalf of a person if the person or an agent or representative of the person authorizes the communication or information or approves the communication or information before it is used. An offering participant other than the issuer shall not be an agent or representative of the issuer solely by virtue of its acting as an offering participant.
4.   A road show means an offer (other than a statutory prospectus or a portion of a statutory prospectus filed as part of a registration statement) that contains a presentation regarding an offering by one or more members of the issuer's management (and in the case of an offering of asset-backed securities, management involved in the securitization or servicing function of one or more of the depositors, sponsors, or servicers (as such terms are defined in Item 1101 of Regulation AB) or an affiliated depositor) and includes discussion of one or more of the issuer, such management, and the securities being offered; and
5.   A bona fide electronic road show means a road show that is a written communication transmitted by graphic means that contains a presentation by one or more officers of an issuer or other persons in an issuer's management (and in the case of an offering of asset-backed securities, management involved in the securitization or servicing function of one or more of the depositors, sponsors, or servicers (as such terms are defined in Item 1101 of Regulation AB) or an affiliated depositor) and, if more than one road show that is a written communication is being used, includes discussion of the same general areas of information regarding the issuer, such management, and the securities being offered as such other issuer road show or shows for the same offering that are written communications.

Note to Rule 433.

This section does not affect the operation of the provisions of clause (a) of section 2(a)(10) of the Act providing an exception from the definition of "prospectus."

Rule 460 – Distribution of Preliminary Prospectus

a.   Pursuant to the statutory requirement that the Commission in ruling upon requests for acceleration of the effective date of a registration statement shall have due regard to the adequacy of the information respecting the issuer theretofore available to the public, the Commission may consider whether the persons making the offering have taken reasonable steps to make the information contained in the registration statement conveniently available to underwriters and dealers who it is reasonably anticipated will be invited to participate in the distribution of the security to be offered or sold.

b.

1. As a minimum, reasonable steps to make the information conveniently available would involve the distribution, to each underwriter and dealer who it is reasonably anticipated will be invited to participate in the distribution of the security, a reasonable time in advance of the anticipated effective date of the registration statement, of as many copies of the proposed form of preliminary prospectus permitted by Rule 430 as appears to be reasonable to secure adequate distribution of the preliminary prospectus.

2. In the case of a registration statement filed by a closed-end investment company on Form N-2, reasonable steps to make information conveniently available would involve distribution of a sufficient number of copies of the Statement of Additional Information required by Rule 430(b) as it appears to be reasonable to secure their adequate distribution either to each underwriter or dealer who it is reasonably anticipated will be invited to participate in the distribution of the security, or to the underwriter, dealer or other source named on the cover page of the preliminary prospectus as being the person investors should contact in order to obtain the Statement of Additional Information.

c. The granting of acceleration will not be conditioned upon

1. The distribution of a preliminary prospectus in any state where such distribution would be illegal; or

2. The distribution of a preliminary prospectus

    i. in the case of a registration statement relating solely to securities to be offered at competitive bidding, provided the undertaking in Item 512(d)(1) of Regulation S-K is included in the registration statement and distribution of prospectuses pursuant to such undertaking is made prior to the publication or distribution of the invitation for bids, or

    ii. In the case of a registration statement relating to a security issued by a face-amount certificate company or a redeemable security issued by an open-end management company or unit investment trust if any other security of the same class is currently being offered or sold, pursuant to an effective registration statement by the issuer or by or through an underwriter, or

    iii. In the case of an offering of subscription rights unless it is contemplated that the distribution will be made through dealers and the underwriters intend to make the offering during the stockholders' subscription period, in which case copies of the preliminary prospectus must be distributed to dealers prior to the effective date of the registration statement in the same fashion as is required in the case of other offerings through underwriters, or

    iv. In the case of a registration statement pertaining to a security to be offered pursuant to an exchange offer or transaction described in Rule 145.

Rule 461 – Acceleration of Effective Date

a.   Requests for acceleration of the effective date of a registration statement shall be made by the registrant and the managing underwriters of the proposed issue, or, if there are no managing underwriters, by the principal underwriters of the proposed issue, and shall state the date upon which it is desired that the registration statement shall become effective. Such requests may be made in writing or orally, provided that, if an oral request is to be made, a letter indicating that fact and stating that the registrant and the managing or principal underwriters are aware of their obligations under the Act must accompany the registration statement for a pre-effective amendment thereto) at the time of filing with the Commission. Written requests may be sent to the Commission by facsimile transmission. If, by reason of the expected arrangement in connection with the offering, it is to be requested that the registration statement shall become effective at a particular hour of the day, the Commission must be advised to that effect not later than the second business day before the day which it is desired that the registration statement shall become effective. A person's request for acceleration will be considered confirmation of such person's awareness of the person's obligations under the Act. Not later than the time of filing the last amendment prior to the effective date of the registration statement, the registrant shall inform the Commission as to whether or not the amount of compensation to be allowed or paid to the underwriters and any other arrangements among the registrant, the underwriters and other broker dealers participating in the distribution, as described in the registration statement, have been reviewed to the extent required by the National Association of Securities Dealers, Inc. and such Association has issued a statement expressing no objections to the compensation and other arrangements.

b.   Having due regard to the adequacy of information respecting the registrant theretofore available to the public, to the facility with which the nature of the securities to be registered, their relationship to the capital structure of the registrant issuer and the rights of holders thereof can be understood, and to the public interest and the protection of investors, as provided in section 8(a) of the Act, it is the general policy of the Commission, upon request, as provided in paragraph (a) of this section, to permit acceleration of the effective date of the registration statement as soon as possible after the filing of appropriate amendments, if any. In determining the date on which a registration statement shall become effective, the following are included in the situations in which the Commission considers that the statutory standards of section 8(a) may not be met and may refuse to accelerate the effective date:

   1.   Where there has not been a bona fide effort to make the prospectus reasonably concise, readable, and in compliance with the plain English requirements of Rule 421(d) of Regulation C in order to facilitate an understanding of the information in the prospectus.

   2.   Where the form of preliminary prospectus, which has been distributed by the issuer or underwriter, is found to be inaccurate or inadequate in any material respect, until the Commission has received satisfactory assurance that appropriate correcting material has been sent to all underwriters and dealers who received such preliminary prospectus or prospectuses in quantity sufficient for their information and the information of others to whom the inaccurate or inadequate material was sent.

3.   Where the Commission is currently making an investigation of the issuer, a person controlling the issuer, or one of the underwriters, if any, of the securities to be offered, pursuant to any of the Acts administered by the Commission.

4.   Where one or more of the underwriters, although firmly committed to purchase securities covered by the registration statement, is subject to and does not meet the financial responsibility requirements of Rule 15c3-1 under the Securities Exchange Act of 1934. For the purposes of this paragraph underwriters will be deemed to be firmly committed even though the obligation to purchase is subject to the usual conditions as to receipt of opinions of counsel, accountants, etc., the accuracy of warranties or representations, the happening of calamities or the occurrence of other events the determination of which is not expressed to be in the sole or absolute discretion of the underwriters.

5.   Where there have been transactions in securities of the registrant by persons connected with or proposed to be connected with the offering which may have artificially affected or may artificially affect the market price of the security being offered.

6.   Where the amount of compensation to be allowed or paid to the underwriters and any other arrangements among the registrant, the underwriters and other broker dealers participating in the distribution, as described in the registration statement, if required to be reviewed by the National Association of Securities Dealers, Inc. (NASD), have been reviewed by the NASD and the NASD has not issued a statement expressing no objections to the compensation and other arrangements.

7.   Where, in the case of a significant secondary offering at the market, the registrant, selling security holders and underwriters have not taken sufficient measures to insure compliance with Regulation M.

c.   Insurance against liabilities arising under the Act, whether the cost of insurance is borne by the registrant, the insured or some other person, will not be considered a bar to acceleration, unless the registrant is a registered investment company or a business development company and the cost of such insurance is borne by other than an insured officer or director of the registrant. In the case of such a registrant, the Commission may refuse to accelerate the effective date of the registration statement when the registrant is organized or administered pursuant to any instrument (including a contract for insurance against liabilities arising under the Act) that protects or purports to protect any director or officer of the company against any liability to the company or its security holders to which he or she would otherwise be subject by reason of willful misfeasance, bad faith, gross negligence or reckless disregard of the duties involved in the conduct of his or her office.

Rule 462 – Immediate Effectiveness of Certain Registration Statements and Post-Effective Amendments

a.   A registration statement on Form S-8 and a registration statement on Form S-3 or on Form F-3 for a dividend or interest reinvestment plan shall become effective upon filing with the Commission.

b. A registration statement and any post-effective amendment thereto shall become effective upon filing with the Commission if:

    1. The registration statement is for registering additional securities of the same class(es) as were included in an earlier registration statement for the same offering and declared effective by the Commission;

    2. The new registration statement is filed prior to the time confirmations are sent or given; and

    3. The new registration statement registers additional securities in an amount and at a price that together represent no more than 20% of the maximum aggregate offering price set forth for each class of securities in the "Calculation of Registration Fee" table contained in such earlier registration statement.

c. If the prospectus contained in a post-effective amendment filed prior to the time confirmations are sent or given contains no substantive changes from or additions to the prospectus previously filed as part of the effective registration statement, other than price-related information omitted from the registration statement in reliance on Rule 430A of the Act, such post-effective amendment shall become effective upon filing with the Commission.

d. A post-effective amendment filed solely to add exhibits to a registration statement shall become effective upon filing with the Commission.

e. An automatic shelf registration statement, including an automatic shelf registration statement filed in accordance with Rule 415(a)(6), and any post-effective amendment thereto, including a post-effective amendment filed to register additional classes of securities pursuant to Rule 413(b), shall become effective upon filing with the Commission.

f. A post-effective amendment filed pursuant to paragraph (e) of this section for purposes of adding a new issuer and its securities as permitted by Rule 413(b) that satisfies the requirements of Form S-3 or Form F-3, as applicable, including the signatures required by Rule 402(e), and contains a prospectus satisfying the requirements of Rule 430B, shall become effective upon filing with the Commission.

Rule 473 – Delaying Amendments

a. An amendment in the following form filed with a registration statement, or as an amendment to a registration statement which has not become effective, shall be deemed, for the purpose of section 8(a) of the Act, to be filed on such date or dates as may be necessary to delay the effective date of such registration statement

    1. until the registrant shall file a further amendment which specifically states as provided in paragraph (b) of this section that such registration statement shall thereafter become effective in accordance with section 8(a) of the Act, or

    2. until the registration statement shall become effective on such date as the Commission, acting pursuant to section 8(a), may determine:

        The registrant hereby amends this registration statement on such date or dates as may be necessary to delay its effective date until the registrant shall file a further amendment which specifically states that this registration statement shall thereafter become effective in accordance with section 8(a) of the Securities Act of 1933 or until the registration statement shall become effective on such date as the Commission acting pursuant to said section 8(a), may determine.

b. An amendment which for the purpose of paragraph (a)(1) of this section specifically states that a registration statement shall thereafter become effective in accordance with section 8(a) of the Act, shall be in the following form:

This registration statement shall hereafter become effective in accordance with the provisions of section 8(a) of the Securities Act of 1933.

c. An amendment pursuant to paragraph (a) of this section which is filed with a registration statement shall be set forth on the facing page thereof following the calculation of the registration fee. Any such amendment filed after the filing of the registration statement, any amendment altering the proposed date of public sale of the securities being registered, or any amendment filed pursuant to paragraph (b) of this section may be made by telegram, letter or facsimile transmission. Each such telegraphic amendment shall be confirmed in writing within a reasonable time by the filing of a signed copy of the amendment. Such confirmation shall not be deemed an amendment.

d. No amendments pursuant to paragraph (a) of this section may be filed with a registration statement on Form F-7, F-8 or F-80; on Form F-9 or F-10 relating to an offering being made contemporaneously in the United States and the registrant's home jurisdiction; on Form S-8; on Form S-3 or F-3 relating to a dividend or interest reinvestment plan; or on Form S-4 complying with General Instruction G of that Form.

Regulation A

Rule 251 – Scope of Exemption

A public offer or sale of securities that meets the following terms and conditions shall be exempt under section 3(b) from the registration requirements of the Securities Act of 1933 (the "Securities Act"):

a. **Issuer.** The issuer of the securities:
    1. is an entity organized under the laws of the United States or Canada, or any State, Province, Territory or possession thereof, or the District of Columbia, with its principal place of business in the United States or Canada;
    2. is not subject to section 13 or 15(d) of the Securities Exchange Act of 1934 (the "Exchange Act") immediately before the offering;
    3. is not a development stage company that either has no specific business plan or purpose, or has indicated that its business plan is to merge with an unidentified company or companies;
    4. is not an investment company registered or required to be registered under the Investment Company Act of 1940 ;
    5. is not issuing fractional undivided interests in oil or gas rights as defined in Rule 300 [Editor's note: Rule 300 under the Securities Act of 1933 is reserved], or a similar interest in other mineral rights; and
    6. is not disqualified because of Rule 262.

b. **Aggregate Offering Price.** The sum of all cash and other consideration to be received for the securities ("aggregate offering price") shall not exceed $5,000,000, including no more than $1,500,000 offered by all selling security holders, less the aggregate offering price for all securities sold within the twelve months before the start of and during the offering of securities in reliance upon Regulation A. No affiliate resales are permitted if the issuer has not had net income from continuing operations in at least one of its last two fiscal years.
    Note: Where a mixture of cash and non-cash consideration is to be received, the aggregate offering price shall be based on the price at which the securities are offered for cash. Any portion of the aggregate offering price attributable to cash received in a foreign currency shall be translated into United States currency at a currency exchange rate in effect on or at a reasonable time prior to the date of the sale of the securities. If securities are not offered for cash, the aggregate offering price shall be based on the value of the consideration as established by bona fide sales of that consideration made within a reasonable time, or, in the absence of sales, on the fair value as determined by an accepted standard. Valuations of non-cash consideration must be reasonable at the time made.

c. **Integration with Other Offerings.** Offers and sales made in reliance on this Regulation A will not be integrated with:
    1. prior offers or sales of securities; or
    2. subsequent offers or sales of securities that are:
        i.   registered under the Securities Act, except as provided in Rule 254(d);
        ii. made in reliance on Rule 701;

iii. made pursuant to an employee benefit plan;

iv. made in reliance on Regulation S; or

v. made more than six months after the completion of the Regulation A offering.

Note: If the issuer offers or sells securities for which the safe harbor rules are unavailable, such offers and sales still may not be integrated with the Regulation A offering, depending on the particular facts and circumstances. See Securities Act Release No. 4552.

d. **Offering Conditions.**

1. Offers.

    i. Except as allowed by Rule 254, no offer of securities shall be made unless a Form 1-A offering statement has been filed with the Commission.

    ii. After the Form 1-A offering statement has been filed:

    A. oral offers may be made;

    B. written offers under Rule 255 may be made;

    C. printed advertisements may be published or radio or television broadcasts made, if they state from whom a Preliminary Offering Circular or Final Offering Circular may be obtained, and contain no more than the following information:

    (1) the name of the issuer of the security;

    (2) the title of the security, the amount being offered and the per unit offering price to the public;

    (3) the general type of the issuer's business; and

    (4) a brief statement as to the general character and location of its property.

    iii. after the Form 1-A offering statement has been qualified, other written offers may be made, but only if accompanied with or preceded by a Final Offering Circular.

2. Sales.

    i. No sale of securities shall be made until:

    A. the Form 1-A offering statement has been qualified;

    B. A Preliminary Offering Circular or Final Offering Circular is furnished to the prospective purchaser at least 48 hours prior to the mailing of the confirmation of sale to that person; and

    C. A Final Offering Circular is delivered to the purchaser with the confirmation of sale, unless it has been delivered to that person at an earlier time.

    ii. Sales by a dealer (including an underwriter no longer acting in that capacity for the security involved in such transaction) that take place within 90 days after the qualification of the Regulation A offering statement may be made only if the dealer delivers a copy of the current offering circular to the purchaser before or with the confirmation of sale. The issuer or underwriter of the offering shall provide requesting dealers with reasonable quantities of the offering circular for this purpose.

3. Continuous or delayed offerings. Continuous or delayed offerings may be made under this Regulation A if permitted by Rule 415.

Rule 252 – Offering Statement

a. **Documents to be Included.** The offering statement consists of the facing sheet of Form 1-A , the contents required by the form and any other material information necessary to make the required statements, in the light of the circumstances under which they are made, not misleading.

b. **Paper, Printing, Language and Pagination.** The requirements for offering statements are the same as those specified in Rule 403 for registration statements under the Act.

c. **Confidential Treatment.** A request for confidential treatment may be made under Rule 406 for information required to be filed, and 17 CFR 200.83 for information not required to be filed.

d. **Signatures.** The issuer, its Chief Executive Officer, Chief Financial Officer, a majority of the members of its board of directors or other governing body, and each selling security holder shall sign the offering statement. If a signature is by a person on behalf of any other person, evidence of authority to sign shall be filed, except where an executive officer signs for the issuer. If the issuer is Canadian, its authorized representative in the United States shall sign. If the issuer is a limited partnership, a majority of the board of directors of any corporate general partner also shall sign.

e. **Number of Copies and Where to File.** Seven copies of the offering statement, at least one of which is manually signed, shall be filed with the Commission's main office in Washington, DC.

f. [**Removed** and reserved in Release No. 33-7331, effective Oct. 7, 1996, 61 F.R. 49957.]

g. **Qualification.**
   1. If there is no delaying notation as permitted by paragraph (g)(2) of this section or suspension proceeding under Rule 258, an offering statement is qualified without Commission action on the 20th calendar day after its filing.
   2. An offering statement containing the following notation can be qualified only by order of the Commission, unless such notation is removed prior to Commission action as described in paragraph (g)(3) of this section:
        This offering statement shall only be qualified upon order of the Commission, unless a subsequent amendment is filed indicating the intention to become qualified by operation of the terms of Regulation A.
   3. The delaying notation specified in paragraph (g)(2) of this section can be removed only by an amendment to the offering statement that contains the following language:
        This offering statement shall become qualified on the 20th calendar day following the filing of this amendment.

h. **Amendments.**
    1. If any information in the offering statement is amended, an amendment, signed in the same manner as the initial filing, shall be filed. Seven copies of every amendment shall be filed with the Commission's main Office in Washington, D.C.
    2. An amendment to include a delaying notation pursuant to paragraph (g)(2) or to remove one pursuant to paragraph (g)(3) of this section after the initial filing of an offering statement may be made by telegram, letter or facsimile transmission. Each such telegraphic amendment shall be confirmed in writing within a reasonable time by filing a signed copy. Such confirmation shall not be deemed an amendment.

Rule 253 – Offering Circular

a. **Contents.** An offering circular shall include the narrative and financial information required by Form 1-A.

b. **Presentation of Information.**
    1. Information in the offering circular shall be presented in a clear, concise and understandable manner and in a type size that is easily readable. Repetition of information should be avoided; cross-referencing of information within the document is permitted.
    2. Where an offering circular is distributed through an electronic medium, issuers may satisfy legibility requirements applicable to printed documents by presenting all required information in a format readily communicated to investors.

c. **Date.** An offering circular shall be dated approximately as of the date of the qualification of the offering statement of which it is a part.

d. **Cover Page Legend.** The cover page of every offering circular shall display the following statement in capital letters printed in boldfaced type at least as large as that used generally in the body of such offering circular:
    THE UNITED STATES SECURITIES AND EXCHANGE COMMISSION DOES NOT PASS UPON THE MERITS OF OR GIVE ITS APPROVAL TO ANY SECURITIES OFFERED OR THE TERMS OF THE OFFERING, NOR DOES IT PASS UPON THE ACCURACY OR COMPLETENESS OF ANY OFFERING CIRCULAR OR OTHER SELLING LITERATURE. THESE SECURITIES ARE OFFERED PURSUANT TO AN EXEMPTION FROM REGISTRATION WITH THE COMMISSION; HOWEVER, THE COMMISSION HAS NOT MADE AN INDEPENDENT DETERMINATION THAT THE SECURITIES OFFERED HEREUNDER ARE EXEMPT FROM REGISTRATION.

e. **Revisions.**
    1. An offering circular shall be revised during the course of an offering whenever the information it contains has become false or misleading in light of existing

2. circumstances, material developments have occurred, or there has been a fundamental change in the information initially presented.

3. An offering circular for a continuous offering shall be updated to include, among other things, updated financial statements, 12 months after the date the offering statement was qualified.

4. Every revised or updated offering circular shall be filed as an amendment to the offering statement and requalified in accordance with Rule 252.

Rule 254 – Solicitation of Interest Document for Use Prior to an Offering Statement

a. An issuer may publish or deliver to prospective purchasers a written document or make scripted radio or television broadcasts to determine whether there is any interest in a contemplated securities offering. Following submission of the written document or script of the broadcast to the Commission, as required by paragraph (b) of this section, oral communications with prospective investors and other broadcasts are permitted. The written documents, broadcasts and oral communications are each subject to the antifraud provisions of the federal securities laws. No solicitation or acceptance of money or other consideration, nor of any commitment, binding or otherwise, from any prospective investor is permitted. No sale may be made until qualification of the offering statement.

b. While not a condition to any exemption pursuant to this section:
   1. On or before the date of its first use, the issuer shall submit a copy of any written document or the script of any broadcast with the Commission's main office in Washington, D.C. (*Attention:* Office of Small Business Policy). The document or broadcast script shall either contain or be accompanied by the name and telephone number of a person able to answer questions about the document or the broadcast.
   Note: Only solicitation of interest material that contains substantive changes from or additions to previously submitted material needs to be submitted.
   2. The written document or script of the broadcast shall:
      i. state that no money or other consideration is being solicited, and if sent in response, will not be accepted;
      ii. state that no sales of the securities will be made or commitment to purchase accepted until delivery of an offering circular that includes complete information about the issuer and the offering;
      iii. state that an indication of interest made by a prospective investor involves no obligation or commitment of any kind; and
      iv. identify the chief executive officer of the issuer and briefly and in general its business and products.
   3. Solicitations of interest pursuant to this provision may not be made after the filing of an offering statement.
   4. Sales may not be made until 20 calendar days after the last publication or delivery of the document or radio or television broadcast.

c. Any written document under this section may include a coupon, returnable to the issuer indicating interest in a potential offering, revealing the name, address and telephone number of the prospective investor.

d. Where an issuer has a bona fide change of intention and decides to register an offering after using the process permitted by this section without having filed the offering statement prescribed by Rule 252, the Regulation A exemption for offers made in reliance upon this section will not be subject to integration with the registered offering, if at least 30 calendar days have elapsed between the last solicitation of interest and the filing of the registration statement with the Commission, and all solicitation of interest documents have been submitted to the Commission. With respect to integration with other offerings, see Rule 251(c).

e. Written solicitation of interest materials submitted to the Commission and otherwise in compliance with this section shall not be deemed to be a prospectus as defined in section 2(a)(10) of the Securities Act.

Rule 255 – Preliminary Offering Circulars

a. Prior to qualification of the required offering statement, but after its filing, a written offer of securities may be made if it meets the following requirements:

  1. The outside front cover page of the material bears the caption "Preliminary Offering Circular," the date of issuance, and the following statement, which shall run along the left hand margin of the page and be printed perpendicular to the text, in boldfaced type at least as large as that used generally in the body of such offering circular:

      An offering statement pursuant to Regulation A relating to these securities has been filed with the Securities and Exchange Commission.

      Information contained in this Preliminary Offering Circular is subject to completion or amendment. These securities may not be sold nor may offers to buy be accepted prior to the time an offering circular which is not designated as a Preliminary Offering Circular is delivered and the offering statement filed with the Commission becomes qualified. This Preliminary Offering Circular shall not constitute an offer to sell or the solicitation of an offer to buy nor shall there be any sales of these securities in any state in which such offer, solicitation or sale would be unlawful prior to registration or qualification under the laws of any such state.

  2. The Preliminary Offering Circular contains substantially the information required in an offering circular by Form 1-A, except that information with respect to offering price, underwriting discounts or commissions, discounts or commissions to dealers, amount of proceeds, conversion rates, call prices, or other matters dependent upon the offering price may be omitted. The outside front cover page of the Preliminary Offering Circular shall include a bona fide estimate of the range of the maximum offering price and maximum number of shares or other units of securities to be offered or a bona fide estimate of the principal amount of debt securities to be offered.

  3. The material is filed as a part of the offering statement.

b. If a Preliminary Offering Circular is inaccurate or inadequate in any material respect, a revised Preliminary Offering Circular or a complete Offering Circular shall be furnished to all persons to whom securities are to be sold at least 48 hours prior to the mailing of any confirmation of sale to such persons, or shall be sent to such persons under such circumstances that it would normally be received by them 48 hours prior to receipt of confirmation of the sale.

Rule 256 – Filing of Sales Material

While not a condition to an exemption pursuant to this provision, seven copies of any advertisement or written communication, or the script of any radio or television broadcast, shall be filed with the main Office of the Commission in Washington, D.C.
Note: Only sales material that contains substantive changes from or additions from previously filed material needs to be filed.

Rule 257 – Reports of Sales and Use of Proceeds

While not a condition to an exemption pursuant to this provision, the issuer and/or each selling security holder shall file seven copies of a report concerning sales and use of proceeds on Form 2-A, or other prescribed form with the main office of the Commission in Washington, D.C.

a. every six months after the qualification of the offering statement or any amendment until substantially all the proceeds have been applied; and

b. within 30 calendar days after the termination, completion or final sale of securities in the offering, or the application of the proceeds from the offering, whichever is the latest event. This report should be labeled the final report. For purposes of this section, the temporary investment of proceeds pending final application shall not constitute application of the proceeds.

Rule 258 – Suspension of the Exemption

a. The Commission may at any time enter an order temporarily suspending a Regulation A exemption if it has reason to believe that:
1. no exemption is available or any of the terms, conditions or requirements of the Regulation have not been complied with, including failures to provide the Commission a copy of the document or broadcast script under Rule 254, to file any sales material as required by Rule 256 or report as required by Rule 257;
2. the offering statement, any sales or solicitation of interest material contains any untrue statement of a material fact or omits to state a material fact necessary in order to make the statements made, in light of the circumstances under which they are made, not misleading;
3. the offering is being made or would be made in violation of section 17 of the Securities Act;
4. an event has occurred after the filing of the offering statement which would have rendered the exemption hereunder unavailable if it had occurred prior to such filing;

5.   any person specified in paragraph (a) of Rule 262 has been indicted for any crime or offense of the character specified in paragraph (a)3 of Rule 262, or any proceeding has been initiated for the purpose of enjoining any such person from engaging in or continuing any conduct or practice of the character specified in paragraph (a)4 of Rule 262;

6.   any person specified in paragraph (b) of Rule 262 has been indicted for any crime or offense of the character specified in paragraph (b)1 of Rule 262, or any proceeding has been initiated for the purpose of enjoining any such person from engaging in or continuing any conduct or practice of the character specified in paragraph (b)2 of Rule 262; or

7.   the issuer or any promoter, officer, director or underwriter has failed to cooperate, or has obstructed or refused to permit the making of an investigation by the Commission in connection with any offering made or proposed to be made in reliance on Regulation A.

b.   Upon the entry of an order under paragraph (a) of this section, the Commission will promptly give notice to the issuer, any underwriter and any selling security holder:

1.   that such order has been entered, together with a brief statement of the reasons for the entry of the order; and

2.   that the Commission, upon receipt of a written request within 30 calendar days after the entry of the order, will within 20 calendar days after receiving the request, order a hearing at a place to be designated by the Commission.

c.   If no hearing is requested and none is ordered by the Commission, an order entered under paragraph (a) of this section shall become permanent on the 30th calendar day after its entry and shall remain in effect unless or until it is modified or vacated by the Commission. Where a hearing is requested or is ordered by the Commission, the Commission will, after notice of and opportunity for such hearing, either vacate the order or enter an order permanently suspending the exemption.

d.   The Commission may, at any time after notice of and opportunity for hearing, enter an order permanently suspending the exemption for any reason upon which it could have entered a temporary suspension order under paragraph (a) of this section. Any such order shall remain in effect until vacated by the Commission.

e.   All notices required by this section shall be given by personal service, registered or certified mail to the addresses given by the issuer, any underwriter and any selling security holder in the offering statement.

Rule 259 – Withdrawal or Abandonment of Offering Statements

a.   If none of the securities which are the subject of an offering statement have been sold and such offering statement is not the subject of a proceeding under rule 258, the offering statement may be withdrawn with the Commission's consent. The application for withdrawal shall state the reason the offering statement is to be withdrawn, shall be signed by an authorized representative of the issuer and shall be provided to the main office of the Commission in Washington, D.C.

b. When an offering statement has been on file with the Commission for nine months without amendment and has not become qualified, the Commission may, in its discretion, proceed in the following manner to determine whether such offering statement has been abandoned by the issuer. If the offering statement has been amended, the 9-month period shall be computed from the date of the latest amendment.

    1.   Notice will be sent to the issuer, and to any counsel for the issuer named in the offering statement, by registered or certified mail, return receipt requested, addressed to the most recent addresses for the issuer and issuer's counsel as reflected in the offering statement. Such notice will inform the issuer and issuer's counsel that the offering statement or amendments thereto is out of date and must be either amended to comply with applicable requirements of Regulation A or be withdrawn within 30 calendar days after the notice.

    2.   If the issuer or issuer's counsel fail to respond to such notice by filing a substantive amendment or withdrawing the offering statement or does not furnish a satisfactory explanation as to why the issuer has not done so within 30 calendar days, the Commission may declare the offering statement abandoned.

Rule 260 – Insignificant Deviations from a Term, Condition or Requirement of Reg. A

a. A failure to comply with a term, condition or requirement of Regulation A will not result in the loss of the exemption from the requirements of section 5 of the Securities Act for any offer or sale to a particular individual or entity, if the person relying on the exemption establishes:

    1.   the failure to comply did not pertain to a term, condition or requirement directly intended to protect that particular individual or entity;

    2.   the failure to comply was insignificant with respect to the offering as a whole, provided that any failure to comply with paragraphs (a), (b), (d)(1) and (3) of rule 251 shall be deemed to be significant to the offering as a whole; and

    3.   a good faith and reasonable attempt was made to comply with all applicable terms, conditions and requirements of Regulation A.

b. A transaction made in reliance upon Regulation A shall comply with all applicable terms, conditions and requirements of the regulation. Where an exemption is established only through reliance upon paragraph (a) of this section, the failure to comply shall nonetheless be actionable by the Commission under section 20 of the Act.

c. This provision provides no relief or protection from a proceeding under rule 258.

Rule 261 – Definitions

As used in this Regulation A, all terms have the same meanings as in rule 405, except that all references to "registrant" in those definitions shall refer to the issuer of the securities to be offered and sold under Regulation A. In addition, these terms have the following meanings:

a. **Final Offering Circular** - The current offering circular contained in a qualified offering statement;

b. **Preliminary Offering Circular** - The offering circular described in rule 255(a).

Rule 262 – Disqualification Provisions

Unless, upon a showing of good cause and without prejudice to any other action by the Commission, the Commission determines that it is not necessary under the circumstances that the exemption provided by this Regulation A be denied, the exemption shall not be available for the offer or sale of securities, if:

a. the issuer, any of its predecessors or any affiliated issuer:

1. has filed a registration statement which is the subject of any pending proceeding or examination under section 8 of the Act, or has been the subject of any refusal order or stop order thereunder within 5 years prior to the filing of the offering statement required by rule 252;

2. is subject to any pending proceeding under rule 258 or any similar section adopted under section 3(b) of the Securities Act, or to an order entered thereunder within 5 years prior to the filing of such offering statement;

3. has been convicted within 5 years prior to the filing of such offering statement of any felony or misdemeanor in connection with the purchase or sale of any security or involving the making of any false filing with the Commission;

4. is subject to any order, judgment, or decree of any court of competent jurisdiction temporarily or preliminarily restraining or enjoining, or is subject to any order, judgment or decree of any court of competent jurisdiction, entered within 5 yrs prior to the filing of such offering statement, permanently restraining or enjoining, such person from engaging in or continuing any conduct or practice in connection with the purchase or sale of any security or involving the making of any false filing with the Commission; or

5. is subject to a United States Postal Service false representation order entered under 39 U.S.C. §3005 within 5 years prior to the filing of the offering statement, or is subject to a temporary restraining order or preliminary injunction entered under 39 U.S.C. §3007 with respect to conduct alleged to have violated 39 U.S.C. §3005. The entry of an order, judgment or decree against any affiliated entity before the affiliation with the issuer arose, if the affiliated entity is not in control of the issuer and if the affiliated entity and the issuer are not under the common control of a third party who was in control of the affiliated entity at the time of such entry does not come within the purview of this paragraph (a) of this section.

b. any director, officer or general partner of the issuer, beneficial owner of 10 percent or more of any class of its equity securities, any promoter of the issuer presently connected with it in any capacity, any underwriter of the securities to be offered, or any partner, director or officer of any such underwriter:

1. has been convicted within 10 years prior to the filing of the offering statement required by rule 252 of any felony or misdemeanor in connection with the purchase or sale of any security, involving the making of a false filing with the

Commission, or arising out of the conduct of the business of an underwriter, broker, dealer, municipal securities dealer, or investment adviser;

2. is subject to any order, judgment, or decree of any court of competent jurisdiction temporarily or preliminarily enjoining or restraining, or is subject to any order, judgment, or decree of any court of competent jurisdiction, entered within 5 years prior to the filing of such offering statement, permanently enjoining or restraining such person from engaging in or continuing any conduct or practice in connection with the purchase or sale of any security, involving the making of a false filing with the Commission, or arising out of the conduct of the business of an underwriter, broker, dealer, municipal securities dealer, or investment adviser;

3. is subject to an order of the Commission entered pursuant to section 15(b), 15B(a), or 15B(c) of the Exchange Act, or section 203(e) or (f) of the Investment Advisers Act of 1940;

4. is suspended or expelled from membership in, or suspended or barred from association with a member of, a national securities exchange registered under section 6 of the Exchange Act or a national securities association registered under section 15A of the Exchange Act for any act or omission to act constituting conduct inconsistent with just and equitable principles of trade; or

5. is subject to a United States Postal Service false representation order entered under 39 U.S.C. §3005 within 5 years prior to the filing of the offering statement required by rule 252, or is subject to a restraining order or preliminary injunction entered under 39 U.S.C. §3007 with respect to conduct alleged to have violated 39 U.S.C. §3005.

c. any underwriter of such securities was an underwriter or was named as an underwriter of any securities:

1. covered by any registration statement which is the subject of any pending proceeding or examination under section 8 of the Act, or is the subject of any refusal order or stop order entered thereunder within 5 years prior to the filing of the offering statement required by rule 252; or

2. covered by any filing which is subject to any pending proceeding under rule 258 or any similar rule adopted under section 3(b) of the Securities Act, or to an order entered thereunder within 5 years prior to the filing of such offering statement.

Rule 263 – Consent to Service of Process

a. If the issuer is not organized under the laws of any of the states of or the United States of America, it shall at the time of filing the offering statement required by rule 252, furnish to the Commission a written irrevocable consent and power of attorney on Form F-X.

b. Any change to the name or address of the agent for service of the issuer shall be communicated promptly to the Commission through amendment of the requisite form and referencing the file number of the relevant offering statement.

Regulation D – Preliminary Notes

1. The following rules relate to transactions exempted from the registration requirements of section 5 of the Securities Act of 1933 (the Act). Such transactions are not exempt from the anti fraud, civil liability, or other provisions of the federal securities laws. Issuers are reminded of their obligation to provide such further material information, if any, as may be necessary to make the information required under this regulation, in light of the circumstances under which it is furnished, not misleading.
2. Nothing in these rules obviates the need to comply with any applicable state law relating to the offer and sale of securities. Regulation D is intended to be a basic element in a uniform system of Federal-State limited offering exemptions consistent with the provisions of sections 18 and 19(c)of the Act. In those states that have adopted Regulation D, or any version of Regulation D, special attention should be directed to the applicable state laws and regulations, including those relating to registration of person who receive remuneration in connection with the offer and sale of securities, to disqualification of issuers and other persons associated with offerings based on state administrative orders or judgments, and to requirements for filings of notices of sales.
3. Attempted compliance with any rule in Regulation D does not act as an exclusive election; the issuer can also claim the availability of any other applicable exemption. For instance, an issuer's failure to satisfy all the terms and conditions of Rule 506 shall not raise any presumption that the exemption provided by section 4(2) of the Act is not available.
4. These rules are available only to the issuer of the securities and not to any affiliate of that issuer or to any other person for resales of the issuer's securities. The rules provide an exemption only for the transactions in which the securities are offered or sold by the issuer, not for the securities themselves.
5. These rules may be used for business combinations that involve sales by virtue of rule 145(a) or otherwise.
6. In view of the objectives of these rules and the policies underlying the Act, regulation D is not available to any issuer for any transaction or chain of transactions that, although in technical compliance with these rules, is part of a plan or scheme to evade the registration provisions of the Act. In such cases, registration under the Act is required.
7. Securities offered and sold outside the United States in accordance with Regulation S need not be registered under the Act. See Release No. 33-6863. Regulation S may be relied upon for such offers and sales even if coincident offers and sales are made in accordance with Regulation D inside the United States. Thus, for example, persons who are offered and sold securities in accordance with Regulation S would not be counted in the calculation of the number of purchasers under Regulation D. Similarly, proceeds from such sales would not be included in the aggregate offering price. The provisions of this note, however, do not apply if the issuer elects to rely solely on Regulation D for offers or sales to persons made outside the United States.

Rule 501 – Definitions and Terms Used in Regulation D

As used in Regulation D, the following terms shall have the meaning indicated:

a. **Accredited investor**. *Accredited investor* shall mean any person who comes within any of the following categories, or who the issuer reasonably believes comes within any of the following categories, at the time of the sale of the securities to that person:

1. Any bank as defined in section 3(a)(2) of the Act, or any savings and loan association or other institution as defined in section 3(a)(5)(A) of the Act whether acting in its individual or fiduciary capacity; any broker or dealer registered pursuant to section 15 of the Securities Exchange Act of 1934; any insurance company as defined in section 2(a)(13) of the Act; any investment company registered under the Investment Company Act of 1940 or a business development company as defined in section 2(a)(48) of that Act; any Small Business Investment Company licensed by the U.S. Small Business Administration under section 301(c) or (d) of the Small Business Investment Act of 1958; any plan established and maintained by a state, its political subdivisions, or any agency or instrumentality of a state or its political subdivisions, for the benefit of its employees, if such plan has total assets in excess of $5,000,000; any employee benefit plan within the meaning of the Employee Retirement Income Security Act of 1974 if the investment decision is made by a plan fiduciary, as defined in section 3(21) of such act, which is either a bank, savings and loan association, insurance company, or registered investment adviser, or if the employee benefit plan has total assets in excess of $5,000,000 or, if a self-directed plan, with investment decisions made solely by persons that are accredited investors;

2. Any private business development company as defined in section 202(a)(22) of the Investment Advisers Act of 1940;

3. Any organization described in section 501(c)(3) of the Internal Revenue Code, corporation, Massachusetts or similar business trust, or partnership, not formed for the specific purpose of acquiring the securities offered, with total assets in excess of $5,000,000;

4. Any director, executive officer, or general partner of the issuer of the securities being offered or sold, or any director, executive officer, or general partner of a general partner of that issuer;

5. Any natural person whose individual net worth, or joint net worth with that person's spouse, at the time of his purchase exceeds $1,000,000;

6. Any natural person who had an individual income in excess of $200,000 in each of the two most recent years or joint income with that person's spouse in excess of $300,000 in each of those years and has a reasonable expectation of reaching the same income level in the current year;

7. Any trust, with total assets in excess of $5,000,000, not formed for the specific purpose of acquiring the securities offered, whose purchase is directed by a sophisticated person as described in Rule 506(b)(2)(ii) and

8. Any entity in which all of the equity owners are accredited investors.

b. **Affiliate**. An *affiliate* of, or person *affiliated* with, a specified person shall mean a person that directly, or indirectly through one or more intermediaries, controls or is controlled by, or is under common control with, the person specified.

c. **Aggregate offering price**. *Aggregate offering price* shall mean the sum of all cash, services, property, notes, cancellation of debt, or other consideration to be received by an issuer for issuance of its securities. Where securities are being offered for both cash and non-cash consideration, the aggregate offering price shall be based on the price at which the securities are offered for cash. Any portion of the aggregate offering price attributable to cash received in a foreign currency shall be translated into United States currency at the currency exchange rate in effect at a reasonable time prior to or on the date of the sale of the securities. If securities are not offered for cash, the aggregate offering price shall be based on the value of the consideration as established by bona fide sales of that consideration made within a reasonable time, or, in the absence of sales, on the fair value as determined by an accepted standard. Such valuations of non-cash consideration must be reasonable at the time made.

d. **Business combination**. *Business combination* shall mean any transaction of the type specified in paragraph (a) of Rule 145 under the Act and any transaction involving the acquisition by one issuer, in exchange for all or a part of its own or its parent's stock, of stock of another issuer if, immediately after the acquisition, the acquiring issuer has control of the other issuer (whether or not it had control before the acquisition).

e. **Calculation of number of purchasers**. For purposes of calculating the number of purchasers under Rule 505(b) and Rule 506(b) only, the following shall apply:
1. The following purchasers shall be excluded:
    i.   Any relative, spouse or relative of the spouse of a purchaser who has the same principal residence as the purchaser;
    ii. Any trust or estate in which a purchaser and any of the persons related to him as specified in paragraph (e)(1)(i) or (e)(1)(iii) of this section collectively have more than 50 percent of the beneficial interest (excluding contingent interests);
    iii. Any corporation or other organization of which a purchaser and any of the persons related to him as specified in paragraph (e)(1)(i) or (e)(1)(ii) of this section collectively are beneficial owners of more than 50 percent of the equity securities (excluding directors' qualifying shares) or equity interests; and
    iv. Any accredited investor.
2. A corporation, partnership or other entity shall be counted as one purchaser. If, however, that entity is organized for the specific purpose of acquiring the securities offered and is not an accredited investor under paragraph (a)(8) of this section, then each beneficial owner of equity securities or equity interests in the entity shall count as a separate purchaser for all provisions of Regulation D, except to the extent provided in paragraph (e)(1) of this section.
3. A non-contributory employee benefit plan within the meaning of Title I of the Employee Retirement Income Security Act of 1974 shall be counted as one purchaser where the trustee makes all investment decisions for the plan.

f. **Executive officer**. *Executive officer* shall mean the president, any vice president in charge of a principal business unit, division or function (such as sales, administration or finance), any other officer who performs a policy making function, or any other person who performs similar policy making functions for the issuer. Executive officers of subsidiaries may be deemed executive officers of the issuer if they perform such policy making functions for the issuer.

g. **Issuer**. The definition of the term *issuer* in section 2(a)(4) of the Act shall apply, except that in the case of a proceeding under the Federal Bankruptcy Code, the trustee or debtor in possession shall be considered the issuer in an offering under a plan or reorganization, if the securities are to be issued under the plan.

h. **Purchaser representative**. *Purchaser representative* shall mean any person who satisfies all of the following conditions or who the issuer reasonably believes satisfies all of the following conditions:

1.   Is not an affiliate, director, officer or other employee of the issuer, or beneficial owner of 10 percent or more of any class of the equity securities or 10 percent or more of the equity interest in the issuer, except where the purchaser is:

i.   A relative of the purchaser representative by blood, marriage or adoption and not more remote than a first cousin;

ii.   A trust or estate in which the purchaser representative and any persons related to him as specified in paragraph (h)(1)(i) or (h)1(iii) of this section collectively have more than 50 percent of the beneficial interest (excluding contingent interest) or of which the purchaser representative serves as trustee, executor, or in any similar capacity; or

iii.   A corporation or other organization of which the purchaser representative and any persons related to him as specified in paragraph (h)(1)(i) or (h)(1)(ii) of this section collectively are the beneficial owners of more than 50 percent of the equity securities (excluding directors' qualifying shares) or equity interests;

2.   Has such knowledge and experience in financial and business matters that he is capable of evaluating, alone, or together with other purchaser representatives of the purchaser, or together with the purchaser, the merits and risks of the prospective investment;

3.   Is acknowledged by the purchaser in writing, during the course of the transaction, to be his purchaser representative in connection with evaluating the merits and risks of the prospective investment; and

4.   Discloses to the purchaser in writing a reasonable time prior to the sale of securities to that purchaser any material relationship between himself or his affiliates and the issuer or its affiliates that then exists, that is mutually understood to be contemplated, or that has existed at any time during the previous two years, and any compensation received or to be received as a result of such relationship.

Note 1: A person acting as a purchaser representative should consider the applicability of the registration and antifraud provisions relating to brokers and dealers under the Securities Exchange Act of 1934 (*Exchange Act*) and relating to investment advisers under the Investment Advisers Act of 1940.

Note 2: The acknowledgment required by paragraph (h)(3) and the disclosure required by paragraph (h)(4) of this section must be made with specific reference to each prospective investment. Advance blanket acknowledgment, such as for *all securities transactions* or *all private placements,* is not sufficient.

Note 3: Disclosure of any material relationships between the purchaser representative or his affiliates and the issuer or its affiliates does not relieve the purchaser representative of his obligation to act in the interest of the purchaser.

Rule 502 – General Conditions to Be Met

The following conditions shall be applicable to offers and sales made under Regulation D:

a. **Integration.** All sales that are part of the same Regulation D offering must meet all of the terms and conditions of Regulation D. Offers and sales that are made more than six months before the start of a Regulation D offering or are made more than six months after completion of a Regulation D offering will not be considered part of that Regulation D offering, so long as during those six month periods there are no offers or sales of securities by or for the issuer that are of the same or a similar class as those offered or sold under Regulation D, other than those offers or sales of securities under an employee benefit plan as defined in rule 405 under the Act.
   Note: The term *offering* is not defined in the Act or in Regulation D. If the issuer offers or sells securities for which the safe harbor rule in paragraph (a) of this Rule 502 is unavailable, the determination as to whether separate sales of securities are part of the same offering (i.e. are considered *integrated*) depends on the particular facts and circumstances. Generally, transactions otherwise meeting the requirements of an exemption will not be integrated with simultaneous offerings being made outside the United States in compliance with Regulation S. See Release No. 33-6863.

   The following factors should be considered in determining whether offers and sales should be integrated for purposes of the exemptions under Regulation D:
   a. Whether the sales are part of a single plan of financing;
   b. Whether the sales involve issuance of the same class of securities;
   c. Whether the sales have been made at or about the same time;
   d. Whether the same type of consideration is being received; and
   e. Whether the sales are made for the same general purpose.

b. **Information Requirements-**
   1. When information must be furnished. If the issuer sells securities under Rule 505 or Rule 506 to any purchaser that is not an accredited investor, the issuer shall furnish the information specified in paragraph (b)(2) of this section to such purchaser a reasonable time prior to sale. The issuer is not required to furnish the specified information to purchasers when it sells securities under Rule 504, or to any accredited investor.
      Note: When an issuer provides information to investors pursuant to paragraph (b)(1), it should consider providing such information to accredited investors as well, in view of the anti-fraud provisions of the federal securities laws.
   2. Type of information to be furnished.
      i. If the issuer is not subject to the reporting requirements of section 13 or 15(d) of the Exchange Act, at a reasonable time prior to the sale of securities the issuer shall furnish to the purchaser, to the extent material to an understanding of the issuer, its business and the securities being offered:
         A. Non-financial statement information. If the issuer is eligible to use Regulation A, the same kind of information as would be required in Part II of Form 1-A. If the issuer is not eligible to use Regulation A, the same kind of information as required in Part I of a registration

statement filed under the Securities Act on the form that the issuer would be entitled to use.

   B. Financial statement information.

      1. Offerings up to $2,000,000. The information required in Article 8 of Regulation X, except that only the issuer's balance sheet, which shall be dated within 120 days of the start of the offering, must be audited.

      2. Offerings up to $7,500,000. The financial statement information required in Form S-1 for smaller erporting companies. If an issuer, other than a limited partnership, cannot obtain audited financial statements without unreasonable effort or expense, then only the issuer's balance sheet, which shall be dated within 120 days of the start of the offering, must be audited. If the issuer is a limited partnership and cannot obtain the required financial statements without unreasonable effort or expense, it may furnish financial statements that have been prepared on the basis of Federal income tax requirements and examined and reported on in accordance with generally accepted auditing standards by an independent public or certified accountant.

      3. Offerings over $7,500,000. The financial statement as would be required in a registration statement filed under the Act on the form that the issuer would be entitled to use. If an issuer, other than a limited partnership, cannot obtain audited financial statements without unreasonable effort or expense, then only the issuer's balance sheet, which shall be dated within 120 days of the start of the offering, must be audited. If the issuer is a limited partnership and cannot obtain the required financial statements without unreasonable effort or expense, it may furnish financial statements that have been prepared on the basis of Federal income tax requirements and examined and reported on in accordance with generally accepted auditing standards by an independent public or certified accountant.

   C. If the issuer is a foreign private issuer eligible to use Form 20-F, the issuer shall disclose the same kind of information required to be included in a registration statement filed under the Act on the form that the issuer would be entitled to use. The financial statements need be certified only to the extent required by paragraph (b)2(i) (B) (*1*), (*2*) or (*3*) of this section, as appropriate.

  ii. If the issuer is subject to the reporting requirements of section 13 or 15(d) of the Exchange Act, at a reasonable time prior to the sale of securities the issuer shall furnish to the purchaser the information specified in paragraph (b)2(ii)(A) or (B) of this section, and in either event the information specified in paragraph (b)(2)(ii)(C) of this section:

   A. The issuer's annual report to shareholders for the most recent fiscal year, if such annual report meets the requirements of Rule 14a-3 or Rule14c-3 under the Exchange Act, the definitive proxy statement filed in connection with that annual report, and, if requested by the purchaser in writing, a copy of the issuer's most recent Form 10-K under the Exchange Act.

B. The information contained in an annual report on Form 10-K under the Exchange Act or in a registration statement on Form S-1 or S-11 under the Act or on Form 10 under the Exchange Act, whichever filing is the most recent required to be filed.

C. The information contained in any reports or documents required to be filed by the issuer under sections 13(a), 14(a), 14(c), and 15(d) of the Exchange Act since the distribution or filing of the report or registration statement specified in paragraphs (b)2(ii) (A) or (B), and a brief description of the securities being offered, the use of the proceeds from the offering, and any material changes in the issuer's affairs that are not disclosed in the documents furnished.

D. If the issuer is a foreign private issuer, the issuer may provide in lieu of the information specified in paragraph (b)2(ii) (A) or (B) of this section, the information contained in its most recent filing on Form 20-F or Form F-1.

iii. Exhibits required to be filed with the Commission as part of a registration statement or report, other than an annual report to shareholders or parts of that report incorporated by reference in a Form 10-K report, need not be furnished to each purchaser that is not an accredited investor if the contents of material exhibits are identified and such exhibits are made available to a purchaser, upon his written request, a reasonable time prior to his purchase.

iv. At a reasonable time prior to the sale of securities to any purchaser that is not an accredited investor in a transaction under Rule 505 or Rule 506, the issuer shall furnish to the purchaser a brief description in writing of any material written information concerning the offering that has been provided by the issuer to any accredited investor but not previously delivered to such unaccredited purchaser. The issuer shall furnish any portion or all of this information to the purchaser, upon his written request a reasonable time prior to his purchase.

v. The issuer shall also make available to each purchaser at a reasonable time prior to his purchase of securities in a transaction under Rule 505 or Rule 506 the opportunity to ask questions and receive answers concerning the terms and conditions of the offering and to obtain any additional information which the issuer possesses or can acquire without unreasonable effort or expense that is necessary to verify the accuracy of information furnished under paragraph (b)2(i) or (ii) of this section.

vi. For business combinations or exchange offers, in addition to information required by Form S-4, the issuer shall provide to each purchaser at the time the plan is submitted to security holders, or, with an exchange, during the course of the transaction and prior to sale, written information about any terms or arrangements of the proposed transactions that are materially different from those for all other security holders. For purposes of this subsection, an issuer which is not subject to the reporting requirements of section 13 or 15(d) of the Exchange Act may satisfy the requirements of Part I.B. or C. of Form S-4 by compliance with paragraph (b)2(i) of this Rule 502.

vii.   At a reasonable time prior to the sale of securities to any purchaser that is not an accredited investor in a transaction under Rule 505 or Rule 506, the issuer shall advise the purchaser of the limitations on resale in the manner contained in paragraph (d)2 of this section. Such disclosure may be contained in other materials required to be provided by this paragraph.

c.   **Limitation on Manner of Offering.** Except as provided in Rule 504(b)(1), neither the issuer nor any person acting on its behalf shall offer or sell the securities by any form of general solicitation or general advertising, including, but not limited to, the following:

1.   Any advertisement, article, notice or other communication published in any newspaper, magazine, or similar media or broadcast over television or radio; and

2.   Any seminar or meeting whose attendees have been invited by any general solicitation or general advertising;

Provided, however, that publication by an issuer of a notice in accordance with Rule 135c or filing with the Commission by an issuer of a notice of sales on Form D in which the issuer has made a good faith and reasonable attempt to comply with the requirements of such form, shall not be deemed to constitute general solicitation or general advertising for purposes of this section; *Provided further,* that, if the requirements of Rule 135e are satisfied, providing any journalist with access to press conferences held outside of the United States, to meetings with issuer or selling security holder representatives conducted outside of the United States, or to written press-related materials released outside the United States, at or in which a present or proposed offering of securities is discussed, will not be deemed to constitute general solicitation or general advertising for purposes of this section.

d.   **Limitations on Resale.** Except as provided in Rule 504(b)(1), securities acquired in a transaction under Regulation D shall have the status of securities acquired in a transaction under section 4(2) of the Act and cannot be resold without registration under the Act or an exemption therefrom. The issuer shall exercise reasonable care to assure that the purchasers of the securities are not underwriters within the meaning of section 2(a)(11) of the Act, which reasonable care may be demonstrated by the following:

1.   Reasonable inquiry to determine if the purchaser is acquiring the securities for himself or for other persons;

2.   Written disclosure to each purchaser prior to sale that the securities have not been registered under the Act and, therefore, cannot be resold unless they are registered under the Act or unless an exemption from registration is available; and

3.   Placement of a legend on the certificate or other document that evidences the securities stating that the securities have not been registered under the Act and setting forth or referring to the restrictions on transferability and sale of the securities.

While taking these actions will establish the requisite reasonable care, it is not the exclusive method to demonstrate such care. Other actions by the issuer may satisfy this provision. In addition, Rule 502(b)2(vii) requires the delivery of written disclosure of the limitations on resale to investors in certain instances.

Rule 503 – Filing of Notice of Sales

a. **When notice of sales on Form D is required and permitted to be filed.**
  1. An issuer offering or selling securities in reliance on Rule 504, Rule 505, or Rule 506 must file with the Commission a notice of sales containing the information required by Form D for each new offering of securities no later than 15 calendar days after the first sale of securities in the offering, unless the end of that period falls on a Saturday, Sunday or holiday, in which case the due date would be the first business day following.
  2. An issuer may file an amendment to a previously filed notice of sales on Form D at any time.
  3. An issuer must file an amendment to a previously filed notice of sales on Form D for an offering:
     i. To correct a material mistake of fact or error in the previously filed notice of sales on Form D, as soon as practicable after discovery of the mistake or error;
     ii. To reflect a change in the information provided in the previously filed notice of sales on Form D, as soon as practicable after the change, except that no amendment is required to reflect a change that occurs after the offering terminates or a change that occurs solely in the following information:
        A. The address or relationship to the issuer of a related person identified in response to Item 3 of the notice of sales on Form D;
        B. An issuer's revenues or aggregate net asset value;
        C. The minimum investment amount, if the change is an increase, or if the change, together with all other changes in that amount since the previously filed notice of sales on Form D, does not result in a decrease of more than 10%;
        D. Any address or state(s) of solicitation shown in response to Item 12 of the notice of sales on Form D;
        E. The total offering amount, if the change is a decrease, or if the change, together with all other changes in that amount since the previously filed notice of sales on Form D, does not result in an increase of more than 10%;
        F. The amount of securities sold in the offering or the amount remaining to be sold;
        G. The number of non-accredited investors who have invested in the offering, as long as the change does not increase the number to more than 35;
        H. The total number of investors who have invested in the offering; or
        I. The amount of sales commissions, finders' fees or use of proceeds for payments to executive officers, directors or promoters, if the change is a decrease, or if the change, together with all other

changes in that amount since the previously filed notice of sales on Form D, does not result in an increase of more than 10%; and

   iii. Annually, on or before the first anniversary of the filing of the notice of sales on Form D or the filing of the most recent amendment to the notice of sales on Form D, if the offering is continuing at that time.

4. An issuer that files an amendment to a previously filed notice of sales on Form D must provide current information in response to all requirements of the notice of sales on Form D regardless of why the amendment is filed.

b. **How notice of sales on Form D must be filed and signed.**

1. A notice of sales on Form D must be filed with the Commission in electronic format by means of the Commission's Electronic Data Gathering, Analysis, and Retrieval System (EDGAR) in accordance with EDGAR rules set forth in Regulation S-T.

2. Every notice of sales on Form D must be signed by a person duly authorized by the issuer.

Rule 504 – Exemption for Limited Offers and Sales of Securities Not Exceeding $1,000,000

a. **Exemption.** Offers and sales of securities that satisfy the conditions in paragraph (b) of this Rule 504 by an issuer that is not:

1. subject to the reporting requirements of section 13 or 15(d) of the Exchange Act,:

2. an investment company; or

3. a development stage company that either has no specific business plan or purpose or has indicated that its business plan is to engage in a merger or acquisition with an unidentified company or companies, or other entity or person, shall be exempt from the provision of section 5 of the Act under section 3(b) of the Act.

b. **Conditions to be Met.**

1. General conditions. To qualify for exemption under this Rule 504, offers and sales must satisfy the terms and conditions of Rule 501 and Rule 502 (a), (c) and (d), except that the provisions of Rule 502 (c) and (d) will not apply to offers and sales of securities under this Rule 504 that are made:

   i. Exclusively in one or more states that provide for the registration of the securities, and require the public filing and delivery to investors of a substantive disclosure document before sale, and are made in accordance with those state provisions;

   ii. In one or more states that have no provision for the registration of the securities or the public filing or delivery of a disclosure document before sale, if the securities have been registered in at least one state that provides for such registration, public filing and delivery before sale, offers and sales are made in that state in accordance with such provisions, and the disclosure document is delivered before sale to all purchasers (including those in the states that have no such procedure); or

      iii.   Exclusively according to state law exemptions from registration that permit general solicitation and general advertising so long as sales are made only to "accredited investors" as defined in Rule 501(a).

2.   The aggregate offering price for an offering of securities under this Rule 504, as defined in Rule 501(c), shall not exceed $1,000,000, less the aggregate offering price for all securities sold within the twelve months before the start of and during the offering of securities under this Rule 504, in reliance on any exemption under section 3(b), or in violation of section 5(a) of the Securities Act.

Note 1: The calculation of the aggregate offering price is illustrated as follows: If an issuer sold $900,000 on June 1, 1987 under this Rule 504 and an additional $4,100,000 on December 1, 1987 under Rule 505, the issuer could not sell any of its securities under this Rule 504 until December 1, 1988. Until then the issuer must count the December 1, 1987 sale towards the $1,000,000 limit within the preceding twelve months.

Note 2: If a transaction under Rule 504 fails to meet the limitation on the aggregate offering price, it does not affect the availability of this Rule 504 for the other transactions considered in applying such limitation. For example, if an issuer sold $1,000,000 worth of its securities on Jan. 1, 1988 under this Rule 504 and an additional $500,000 worth on July 1, 1988, this Rule 504 would not be available for the later sale, but would still be applicable to the Jan. 1, 1988 sale.

Rule 505 – Exemption for Limited Offers and Sales of Securities Not Exceeding $5,000,000

a.   **Exemption.** Offers and sales of securities that satisfy the conditions in paragraph (b) of this section by an issuer that is not an investment company shall be exempt from the provisions of section 5 of the Act under section 3(b) of the Act.

b.   **Conditions to be Met.**

    1.   General conditions. To qualify for exemption under this section, offers and sales must satisfy the terms and conditions of Rule 501 and Rule 502.

    2.   Specific conditions

        i.   Limitation on aggregate offering price. The aggregate offering price for an offering of securities under this Rule 505, as defined in Rule 501(c), shall not exceed $5,000,000, less the aggregate offering price for all securities sold within the twelve months before the start of and during the offering of securities under this Rule 505 in reliance on any exemption under section 3(b) of the Act or in violation of section 5(a) of the Act.

    Note: The calculation of the aggregate offering price is illustrated as follows: *Example 1.* If an issuer sold $2,000,000 of its securities on June 1, 1982 under this Rule 505 and an additional $1,000,000 on September 1, 1982, the issuer would be permitted to sell only $2,000,000 more under this Rule 505 until June 1, 1983. Until that date the issuer must count both prior sales towards the $5,000,000 limit. However, if the issuer made its third sale on

June 1, 1983, the issuer could then sell $4,000,000 of its securities because the June 1, 1982 sale would not be within the preceding twelve months

Example 2. If an issuer sold $500,000 of its securities on June 1, 1982 under Rule 504 and an additional $4,500,000 on December 1, 1982 under this Rule 505, then the issuer could not sell any of its securities under this Rule 505 until June 1, 1983. At that time it could sell an additional $500,000 of its securities.

    ii. Limitation on number of purchasers. There are no more than or the issuer reasonably believes that there are no more than 35 purchasers of securities from the issuer in any offering under this section.

    Note: See Rule 501(e) for the calculation of the number of purchasers and Rule 502 (a) for what may or may not constitute an offering under this section.

    iii. Disqualifications. No exemption under this section shall be available for the securities of any issuer described in Rule 262 of Regulation A, except that for purposes of this section only:

        A. The term "filing of the offering statement required by Rule 252 as used in Rule 262(a), (b) and (c) shall mean the first sale of securities under this section;

        B. The term "underwriter" as used in Rule 262 (b) and (c) shall mean a person that has been or will be paid directly or indirectly remuneration for solicitation of purchasers in connection with sales of securities under this section; and

        C. Paragraph (b) (2) (iii) of this Rule 505 shall not apply to any issuer if the Commission determines, upon a showing of good cause, that it is not necessary under the circumstances that the exemption be denied. Any such determination shall be without prejudice to any other action by the Commission in any other proceeding or matter with respect to the issuer or any other person.

Rule 506 – Exemption for Limited Offers and Sales Without Regard to Dollar Amount of Offering

a. **Exemption.** Offers and sales of securities by an issuer that satisfy the conditions in paragraph (b) of this Rule 506 shall be deemed to be transactions not involving any public offering within the meaning of section 4 (2) of the Act.

b. **Conditions to be Met-**

    1. General conditions. To qualify for an exemption under this section, offers and sales must satisfy all the terms and conditions of Rule 501 and Rule 502.

    2. Specific Conditions-

        i. Limitation on number of purchasers. There are no more than or the issuer reasonably believes that there are no more than 35 purchasers of securities from the issuer in any offering under this section.

        Note: See Rule 501(e) for the calculation of the number of purchasers and Rule 502(a) for what may or may not constitute an offering under this Rule 506.

ii.   Nature of purchasers. Each purchaser who is not an accredited investor either alone or with his purchaser representative(s) has such knowledge and experience in financial and business matters that he is capable of evaluating the merits and risks of the prospective investment, or the issuer reasonably believes immediately prior to making any sale that such purchaser comes within this description.

Rule 507 – Disqualifying Provision Relating to Exemptions Under Rules 504, 505 and 506

a.   No exemption under Rule 504, Rule 505 or Rule 506 shall be available for an issuer if such issuer, any of its predecessors or affiliates have been subject to any order, judgment, or decree of any court of competent jurisdiction temporarily, preliminary or permanently enjoining such person for failure to comply with Rule 503.

b.   Paragraph (a) of this section shall not apply if the Commission determines, upon a showing of good cause, that it is not necessary under the circumstances that the exemption be denied.

Rule 508 – Insignificant Deviations from a Term, Condition or Requirement of Reg. D

a.   A failure to comply with a term, condition or requirement of Rule 504, Rule 505 or Rule 506 will not result in the loss of the exemption from the requirements of section 5 of the Act for any offer or sale to a particular individual or entity, if the person relying on the exemption shows:
1.   The failure to comply did not pertain to a term, condition or requirement directly intended to protect that particular individual or entity; and
2.   The failure to comply was insignificant with respect to the offering as a whole, provided that any failure to comply with paragraph (c) of Rule 502, paragraph (b)(2) of Rule 504, paragraph (b)(2)(i) and paragraph(b)(2)(ii) of Rule 505 and paragraph (b)(2)(i) of Rule 506 shall be deemed to be significant to the offering as a whole; and
3.   A good faith and reasonable attempt was made to comply with all applicable terms, conditions and requirements of Rule 504, Rule 505 or Rule 506.

b.   A transaction made in reliance on Rule 504, Rule 505 or Rule 506 shall comply with all applicable terms, conditions and requirements of Regulation D. Where an exemption is established only through reliance upon paragraph (a) of this section, the failure to comply shall nonetheless be actionable by the Commission under section 20 of the Act.

Regulation S

Rule 901 – General Statement

For the purposes only of section 5 of the Act , the terms **offer, offer to sell, sell, sale,** and **offer to buy** shall be deemed to include offers and sales that occur within the United States and shall be deemed not to include offers and sales that occur outside the United States.

Rule 902 – Definitions

As used in Regulation S, the following terms shall have the meanings indicated.

    a.   **Debt securities.** *Debt securities* of an issuer is defined to mean any security other than an equity security as defined in Rule 405, as well as the following:

        1.   Non-participatory preferred stock, which is defined as non-convertible capital stock, the holders of which are entitled to a preference in payment of dividends and in distribution of assets on liquidation, dissolution, or winding up of the issuer, but are not entitled to participate in residual earnings or assets of the issuer; and

        2.   Asset-backed securities, which are securities of a type that either:

            i.   Represent an ownership interest in a pool of discrete assets, or certificates of interest or participation in such assets (including any rights designed to assure servicing, or the receipt or timeliness of receipt by holders of such assets, or certificates of interest or participation in such assets, of amounts payable thereunder), provided that the assets are not generated or originated between the issuer of the security and its affiliates; or

            ii.   Are secured by one or more assets or certificates of interest or participation in such assets, and the securities, by their terms, provide for payments of principal and interest (if any) in relation to payments or reasonable projections of payments on assets meeting the requirements of paragraph (a)(2)(i) of this section, or certificates of interest or participations in assets meeting such requirements.

           iii.   For purposes of paragraph (a)(2) of this section, the term "assets" means securities, installment sales, accounts receivable, notes, leases or other contracts, or other assets that by their terms convert into cash over a finite period of time.

    b.   **Designated offshore securities market.** *Designated offshore securities market* means:

        1.   The Eurobond market, as regulated by the International Securities Market Association; the Alberta Stock Exchange; the Amsterdam Stock Exchange; the Australian Stock Exchange Limited; the Bermuda Stock Exchange; the Bourse de Bruxelles; the Copenhagen Stock Exchange; the European Association of Securities Dealers Automated Quotation; the Frankfurt Stock Exchange; the Helsinki Stock Exchange; The Stock Exchange of Hong Kong Limited; the Irish Stock Exchange; the Istanbul Stock Exchange; the Johannesburg Stock Exchange; the London Stock Exchange; the Bourse de Luxembourg; the

Mexico Stock Exchange; the Borsa Valori di Milan; the Montreal Stock Exchange; the Oslo Stock Exchange; the Bourse de Paris; the Stock Exchange of Singapore Ltd.; the Stockholm Stock Exchange; the Tokyo Stock Exchange; the Toronto Stock Exchange; the Vancouver Stock Exchange; the Warsaw Stock Exchange and the Zurich Stock Exchange; and

2. Any foreign securities exchange or non-exchange market designated by the Commission. Attributes to be considered in determining whether to designate an offshore securities market, among others, include:
   i. Organization under foreign law;
   ii. Association with a generally recognized community of brokers, dealers, banks, or other professional intermediaries with an established operating history;
   iii. Oversight by a governmental or self-regulatory body;
   iv. Oversight standards set by an existing body of law;
   v. Reporting of securities transactions on a regular basis to a governmental or self-regulatory body;
   vi. A system for exchange of price quotations through common communications media; and
   vii. An organized clearance and settlement system.

c. **Directed selling efforts**.
   1. *Directed selling efforts* means any activity undertaken for the purpose of, or that could reasonably be expected to have the effect of, conditioning the market in the United States for any of the securities being offered in reliance on this Regulation S (Rule 901 through Rule 905, and Preliminary Notes). Such activity includes placing an advertisement in a publication "with a general circulation in the United States" that refers to the offering of securities being made in reliance upon this Reg. S.
   2. Publication "with a general circulation in the United States":
      i. Is defined as any publication that is printed primarily for distribution in the United States, or has had, during the preceding twelve months, an average circulation in the United States of 15,000 or more copies per issue; and
      ii. Will encompass only the U.S. edition of any publication printing a separate U.S. edition if the publication, without considering its U.S. edition, would not constitute a publication with a general circulation in the United States.
   3. The following are not "directed selling efforts":
      i. Placing an advertisement required to be published under U.S. or foreign law, or under rules or regulations of a U.S. or foreign regulatory or self-regulatory authority, provided the advertisement contains no more information than legally required and includes a statement to the effect that the securities have not been registered under the Act and may not be offered or sold in the United States (or to a U.S. person, if the advertisement relates to an offering under Category 2 or 3 (paragraph (b)(2) or (b)(3)) in Rule 903) absent registration or an applicable exemption from the registration requirements;

ii.   Contact with persons excluded from the definition of "U.S. person" pursuant to paragraph (k)(2)(vi) of this section or persons holding accounts excluded from the definition of "U.S. person" pursuant to paragraph (k)(2)(i) of this section, solely in their capacities as holders of such accounts;

iii. A tombstone advertisement in any publication with a general circulation in the United States, provided:

A.   The publication has less than 20% of its circulation, calculated by aggregating the circulation of its U.S. and comparable non-U.S. editions, in the United States;

B.   Such advertisement contains a legend to the effect that the securities have not been registered under the Act and may not be offered or sold in the United States (or to a U.S. person, if the advertisement relates to an offering under Category 2 or 3 (paragraph (b)(2) or (b)(3)) in Rule 903) absent registration or an applicable exemption from the registration requirements; and

C.   Such advertisement contains no more information than:

1.   The issuer's name;

2.   The amount and title of the securities being sold;

3.   A brief indication of the issuer's general type of business;

4.   The price of the securities;

5.   The yield of the securities, if debt securities with a fixed (non-contingent) interest provision;

6.   The name and address of the person placing the advertisement, and whether such person is participating in the distribution;

7.   The names of the managing underwriters;

8.   The dates, if any, upon which the sales commenced and concluded;

9.   Whether the securities are offered or were offered by rights issued to security holders and, if so, the class of securities that are entitled or were entitled to subscribe, the subscription ratio, the record date, the dates (if any) upon which the rights were issued and expired, and the subscription price; and

10. Any legend required by law or any foreign or U.S. regulatory or self- regulatory authority;

iv.   Bona fide visits to real estate, plants or other facilities located in the United States and tours thereof conducted for a prospective investor by an issuer, a distributor, any of their respective affiliates or a person acting on behalf of any of the foregoing;

v.   Distribution in the United States of a foreign broker-dealer's quotations by a third-party system that distributes such quotations primarily in foreign countries if:

A.   Securities transactions cannot be executed between foreign broker-dealers and persons in the United States through the system; and

B.   The issuer, distributors, their respective affiliates, persons acting on behalf of any of the foregoing, foreign broker-dealers and other participants in the system do not initiate contacts with U.S. persons or persons within the United States, beyond those contacts exempted under Rule 15a-6 under the Exchange Act.

vi. Publication by an issuer of a notice in accordance with Rule 135 or Rule 135c;

vii. Providing any journalist with access to press conferences held outside of the United States, to meetings with the issuer or selling security holder representatives conducted outside the United States, or to written press-related materials released outside the United States, at or in which a present or proposed offering of securities is discussed, if the requirements of Rule 135e are satisfied; and

viii. Publication or distribution of a research report by a broker or dealer in accordance with Rule 138(c) or Rule 139(b).

d. **Distributor**. *Distributor* means any underwriter, dealer, or other person who participates, pursuant to a contractual arrangement, in the distribution of the securities offered or sold in reliance on this Regulation S (Rule 901 through Rule 905, and Preliminary Notes).

e. **Domestic issuer/Foreign issuer.** *Domestic issuer* means any issuer other than a "foreign government" or "foreign private issuer" (both as defined in Rule 405). *Foreign issuer* means any issuer other than a *domestic issuer*.

f. **Distribution compliance period.** *Distribution compliance period* means a period that begins when the securities were first offered to persons other than distributors in reliance upon this Regulation S (Rule 901 through Rule 905, and Preliminary Notes) or the date of closing of the offering, whichever is later, and continues until the end of the period of time specified in the relevant provision of Rule 903, except that:

1. All offers and sales by a distributor of an unsold allotment or subscription shall be deemed to be made during the distribution compliance period;

2. In a continuous offering, the distribution compliance period shall commence upon completion of the distribution, as determined and certified by the managing underwriter or person performing similar functions;

3. In a continuous offering of non-convertible debt securities offered and sold in identifiable tranches, the distribution compliance period for securities in a tranche shall commence upon completion of the distribution of such tranche, as determined and certified by the managing underwriter or person performing similar functions; and

4. That in a continuous offering of securities to be acquired upon the exercise of warrants, the distribution compliance period shall commence upon completion of the distribution of the warrants, as determined and certified by the managing underwriter or person performing similar functions, if requirements of Rule 903(b)(5) are satisfied.

g. **Offering restrictions.** *Offering restrictions* means:

1. Each distributor agrees in writing:

    i. That all offers and sales of the securities prior to the expiration of the distribution compliance period specified in Category 2 or 3 (paragraph (b)(2) or (b)(3)) in Rule 903, as applicable, shall be made only in accordance with the provisions of Rule 903 or Rule 904; pursuant to registration of the securities under the Act; or pursuant to an available exemption from the registration requirements of the Act; and

ii.   For offers and sales of equity securities of domestic issuers, not to engage in hedging transactions with regard to such securities prior to the expiration of the distribution compliance period specified in Category 2 or 3 (para (b)(2) or (b)(3)) in Rule 903, as applicable, unless in compliance with the Act; and

2.   All offering materials and documents (other than press releases) used in connection with offers and sales of the securities prior to the expiration of the distribution compliance period specified in Category 2 or 3 (paragraph (b)(2) or (b)(3)) in Rule 903, as applicable, shall include statements to the effect that the securities have not been registered under the Act and may not be offered or sold in the United States or to U.S. persons (other than distributors) unless the securities are registered under the Act, or an exemption from the registration requirements of the Act is available. For offers and sales of equity securities of domestic issuers, such offering materials and documents also must state that hedging transactions involving those securities may not be conducted unless in compliance with the Act. Such statements shall appear:

i.   On the cover or inside cover page of any prospectus or offering circular used in connection with the offer or sale of the securities;

ii.   In the underwriting section of any prospectus or offering circular used in connection with the offer or sale of the securities; and

iii.   In any advertisement made or issued by the issuer, any distributor, any of their respective affiliates, or any person acting on behalf of any of the foregoing. Such statements may appear in summary form on prospectus cover pages and in advertisements.

h.   **Offshore transaction.**

1.   An offer or sale of securities is made in an *offshore transaction* if:

i.   The offer is not made to a person in the United States; and

ii.   Either:

A.   At the time the buy order is originated, the buyer is outside the United States, or the seller and any person acting on its behalf reasonably believe that the buyer is outside the United States; or

B.   For purposes of:

1.   Section Rule 903, the transaction is executed in, on or through a physical trading floor of an established foreign securities exchange that is located outside the United States; or

2.   Section Rule 904, the transaction is executed in, on or through the facilities of a designated offshore securities market described in paragraph (b) of this section, and neither the seller nor any person acting on its behalf knows that the transaction has been pre-arranged with a buyer in the United States.

2.   Notwithstanding paragraph (h)(1) of this section, offers and sales of securities specifically targeted at identifiable groups of U.S. citizens abroad, such as members of the U.S. armed forces serving overseas, shall not be deemed to be made in "offshore transactions."

3.   Notwithstanding paragraph (h)(1) of this section, offers and sales of securities to persons excluded from the definition of "U.S. person" pursuant to paragraph (k)(2)(vi) of this section or persons holding accounts excluded from the definition of "U.S. person" pursuant to paragraph (k)(2)(i) of this section, solely in their capacities as holders of such accounts, shall be deemed to be made in "offshore transactions."

4.   Notwithstanding paragraph (h)(1) of this section, publication or distribution of a research report in accordance with Rule 138(c) or Rule 139(b) by a broker or dealer at or around the time of an offering in reliance on Regulation S will not cause the transaction to fail to be an offshore transaction as defined in this section.

i.   **Reporting issuer.** *Reporting issuer* means an issuer other than an investment company registered or required to register under the 1940 Act that:

1.   Has a class of securities registered pursuant to Section 12(b) or 12(g) of the Exchange Act or is required to file reports pursuant to Section 15(d) of the Exchange Act; and

2.   Has filed all the material required to be filed pursuant to Section 13(a) or 15(d) of the Exchange Act for a period of at least twelve months immediately preceding the offer or sale of securities made in reliance upon this Regulation S (or for such shorter period that the issuer was required to file such material).

j.   **Substantial U.S. market interest**.

1.   *Substantial U.S. market interest* with respect to a class of an issuer's equity securities means:

   i.   The securities exchanges and inter-dealer quotation systems in the United States in the aggregate constituted the single largest market for such class of securities in the shorter of the issuer's prior fiscal year or the period since the issuer's incorporation; or

   ii.   20 percent or more of all trading in such class of securities took place in, on or through the facilities of securities exchanges and inter-dealer quotation systems in the United States and less than 55 percent of such trading took place in, on or through the facilities of securities markets of a single foreign country in the shorter of the issuer's prior fiscal year or the period since the issuer's incorporation.

2.   *Substantial U.S. market interest* with respect to an issuer's debt securities means:

   i.   Its debt securities, in the aggregate, are held of record (as that term is defined in Rule 12g5-1 under the Exchange Act and used for purposes of paragraph (j)(2) of this section) by 300 or more U.S. persons;

   ii. $1 billion or more of: The principal amount outstanding of its debt securities, the greater of liquidation preference or par value of its securities described in Rule 902(a)(1), and the principal amount or principal balance of its securities described in Rule 902(a)(2), in the aggregate, is held of record by U.S. persons; and

   iii.   20 percent or more of: The principal amount outstanding of its debt securities, the greater of liquidation preference or par value of its securities described in Rule 902(a)(1), and the principal amount or principal balance of its securities described in Rule 902(a)(1), in the aggregate, is held of record by U.S. persons.

3.   Notwithstanding paragraph (j)(2) of this section, substantial U.S. market interest with respect to an issuer's debt securities is calculated without reference to securities that qualify for the exemption provided by Section 3(a)(3) of the Act.

k.   **U.S. person.**

1.   *U.S. person* means:
   i.   Any natural person resident in the United States;
   ii.   Any partnership or corporation organized or incorporated under the laws of the United States;
   iii. Any estate of which any executor or administrator is a U.S. person;
   iv. Any trust of which any trustee is a U.S. person;
   v.   Any agency or branch of a foreign entity located in the United States;
   vi. Any non-discretionary account or similar account (other than an estate or trust) held by a dealer or other fiduciary for the benefit or account of a U.S. person;
   vii. Any discretionary account or similar account (other than an estate or trust) held by a dealer or other fiduciary organized, incorporated, or (if an individual) resident in the United States; and
   viii. Any partnership or corporation if:
       A. Organized or incorporated under the laws of any foreign jurisdiction; and
       B. Formed by a U.S. person principally for the purpose of investing in securities not registered under the Act, unless it is organized or incorporated, and owned, by accredited investors (as defined in Rule 501(a)) who are not natural persons, estates or trusts.

2.   The following are not *U.S. persons*:
   i.   Any discretionary account or similar account (other than an estate or trust) held for the benefit or account of a non-U.S. person by a dealer or other professional fiduciary organized, incorporated, or (if an individual) resident in the United States;
   ii.   Any estate of which any professional fiduciary acting as executor or administrator is a U.S. person if:
       A. An executor or administrator of the estate who is not a U.S. person has sole or shared investment discretion with respect to the assets of the estate; and
       B. The estate is governed by foreign law;
   iii. Any trust of which any professional fiduciary acting as trustee is a U.S. person, if a trustee who is not a U.S. person has sole or shared investment discretion with respect to the trust assets, and no beneficiary of the trust (and no settlor if the trust is revocable) is a U.S. person;

iv.   An employee benefit plan established and administered in accordance with the law of a country other than the United States and customary practices and documentation of such country;

v.   Any agency or branch of a U.S. person located outside the United States if:

   A.   The agency or branch operates for valid business reasons; and

   B.   The agency or branch is engaged in the business of insurance or banking and is subject to substantive insurance or banking regulation, respectively, in the jurisdiction where located; and

vi.   The International Monetary Fund, the International Bank for Reconstruction and Development, the Inter-American Development Bank, the Asian Development Bank, the African Development Bank, the United Nations, and their agencies, affiliates and pension plans, and any other similar international organizations, their agencies, affiliates and pension plans.

l.   **United States.** *United States* means the United States of America, its territories and possessions, any State of the United States, and the District of Columbia

Rule 903 – Offers or Sales of Securities by the Issuer, a Distributor, Any of their Respective Affiliates, or Any Person Acting on Behalf of Any of the Foregoing; Conditions Relating to Specific Securities

a.   An offer or sale of securities by the issuer, a distributor, any of their respective affiliates, or any person acting on behalf of any of the foregoing, shall be deemed to occur outside the United States within the meaning of Rule 901 if:

1.   The offer or sale is made in an offshore transaction;

2.   No directed selling efforts are made in the United States by the issuer, a distributor, any of their respective affiliates, or any person acting on behalf of any of the foregoing; and

3.   The conditions of paragraph (b) of this section, as applicable, are satisfied.

b.   **Additional Conditions.**

1.   **Category 1.** No conditions other than those set forth in paragraph (a) apply to securities in this category. Securities are eligible for this category if:

   i.   The securities are issued by a foreign issuer that reasonably believes at the commencement of the offering that:

      A.   There is no substantial U.S. market interest in the class of securities to be offered or sold (if equity securities are offered or sold);

      B.   There is no substantial U.S. market interest in its debt securities (if debt securities are offered or sold);

      C.   There is no substantial U.S. market interest in the securities to be purchased upon exercise (if warrants are offered or sold); and

      D.   There is no substantial U.S. market interest in either the convertible securities or the underlying securities (if convertible securities are offered or sold);

   ii. The securities are offered and sold in an overseas directed offering, which means:

        A. An offering of securities of a foreign issuer that is directed into a single country other than the United States to the residents thereof and that is made in accordance with the local laws and customary practices and documentation of such country; or

        B. An offering of non-convertible debt securities of a domestic issuer that is directed into a single country other than the United States to the residents thereof and that is made in accordance with the local laws and customary practices and documentation of such country, provided that the principal and interest of the securities (or par value, as applicable) are denominated in a currency other than U.S. dollars and such securities are neither convertible into U.S. dollar-denominated securities nor linked to U.S. dollars (other than through related currency or interest rate swap transactions that are commercial in nature) in a manner that in effect converts the securities to U.S. dollar- denominated securities.

   iii. The securities are backed by the full faith and credit of a foreign government; or

   iv. The securities are offered and sold to employees of the issuer or its affiliates pursuant to an employee benefit plan established and administered in accordance with the law of a country other than the United States, and customary practices and documentation of such country, provided that:

        A. The securities are issued in compensatory circumstances for bona fide services rendered to the issuer or its affiliates in connection with their businesses and such services are not rendered in connection with the offer or sale of securities in a capital-raising transaction;

        B. Any interests in the plan are not transferable other than by will or the laws of descent or distribution;

        C. The issuer takes reasonable steps to preclude the offer and sale of interests in the plan or securities under the plan to U.S. residents other than employees on temporary assignment in the United States; and

        D. Documentation used in connection with any offer pursuant to the plan contains a statement that the securities have not been registered under the Act and may not be offered or sold in the United States unless registered or an exemption from registration is available.

2. **Category 2.** The following conditions apply to securities that are not eligible for Category 1 (paragraph (b)(1)) of this section and that are equity securities of a reporting foreign issuer, or debt securities of a reporting issuer or of a non-reporting foreign issuer.

   i. Offering restrictions are implemented;

   ii. The offer or sale, if made prior to the expiration of a 40-day distribution compliance period, is not made to a U.S. person or for the account or benefit of a U.S. person (other than a distributor); and

   iii. Each distributor selling securities to a distributor, a dealer, as defined in section 2(a)(12) of the Act, or a person receiving a selling concession, fee or other remuneration in respect of the securities sold, prior to the expiration of a 40-day distribution compliance period, sends a confirmation or other notice to the purchaser stating that the purchaser is subject to the same restrictions on offers and sales that apply to a distributor.

3.   **Category 3**. The following conditions apply to securities that are not eligible for Category 1 or 2 (paragraph (b)(1) or (b)(2)) of this section:

i.   Offering restrictions are implemented;

ii.   In the case of debt securities:

A.   The offer or sale, if made prior to the expiration of a 40-day distribution compliance period, is not made to a U.S. person or for the account or benefit of a U.S. person (other than a distributor); and

B.   The securities are represented upon issuance by a temporary global security which is not exchangeable for definitive securities until the expiration of the 40-day distribution compliance period and, for persons other than distributors, until certification of beneficial ownership of the securities by a non-U.S. person or a U.S. person who purchased securities in a transaction that did not require registration under the Act;

iii. In the case of equity securities:

A.   The offer or sale, if made prior to the expiration of a one-year distribution compliance period (or a six-month distribution compliance period if the issuer is a reporting issuer), is not made to a U.S. person or for the account or benefit of a U.S. person (other than a distributor); and

B.   The offer or sale, if made prior to the expiration of a one-year distribution compliance period (or a six-month distribution compliance period if the issuer is a reporting issuer), is made pursuant to the following conditions:

1.   The purchaser of the securities (other than a distributor) certifies that it is not a U.S. person and is not acquiring the securities for the account or benefit of any U.S. person or is a U.S. person who purchased securities in a transaction that did not require registration under the Act;

2.   The purchaser of the securities agrees to resell such securities only in accordance with the provisions of this Regulation S (Rule 901 through Rule 905, and Preliminary Notes), pursuant to registration under the Act, or pursuant to an available exemption from registration; and agrees not to engage in hedging transactions with regard to such securities unless in compliance with the Act;

3.   The securities of a domestic issuer contain a legend to the effect that transfer is prohibited except in accordance with the provisions of this Regulation S (Rule 901 through Rule 905, and Preliminary Notes), pursuant to registration under the Act, or pursuant to an available exemption from registration; and that hedging transactions involving those securities may not be conducted unless in compliance with the Act;

4. The issuer is required, either by contract or a provision in its bylaws, articles, charter or comparable document, to refuse to register any transfer of the securities not made in accordance with the provisions of this Regulation S (Rule 901 through Rule 905, and Preliminary Notes), pursuant to registration under the Act, or pursuant to an available exemption from registration; *provided, however*, that if the securities are in bearer form or foreign law prevents the issuer of the securities from refusing to register securities transfers, other reasonable procedures (such as a legend described in paragraph (b)(3)(iii)(B)(3) of this section) are implemented to prevent any transfer of the securities not made in accordance with the provisions of this Regulation S; and

iv. Each distributor selling securities to a distributor, a dealer (as defined in section 2(a)(12) of the Act), or a person receiving a selling concession, fee or other remuneration, prior to the expiration of a 40-day distribution compliance period in the case of debt securities, or a one-year distribution compliance period (or a six-month distribution compliance period if the issuer is a reporting issuer) in the case of equity securities, sends a confirmation or other notice to the purchaser stating that the purchaser is subject to the same restrictions on offers and sales that apply to a distributor.

4. **Guaranteed securities**. Notwithstanding paragraphs (b)(1) through (b)(3) of this section, in offerings of debt securities fully and unconditionally guaranteed as to principal and interest by the parent of the issuer of the debt securities, only the requirements of paragraph (b) of this section that are applicable to the offer and sale of the guarantee must be satisfied with respect to the offer and sale of the guaranteed debt securities.

5. **Warrants**. An offer or sale of warrants under Category 2 or 3 (paragraph (b)(2) or (b)(3)) of this section also must comply with the following requirements:

i. Each warrant must bear a legend stating that the warrant and the securities to be issued upon its exercise have not been registered under the Act and that the warrant may not be exercised by or on behalf of any U.S. person unless registered under the Act or an exemption from such registration is available;

ii. Each person exercising a warrant is required to give:

A. Written certification that it is not a U.S. person and the warrant is not being exercised on behalf of a U.S. person; or

B. A written opinion of counsel to the effect that the warrant and the securities delivered upon exercise thereof have been registered under the Act or are exempt from registration thereunder; and

iii. Procedures are implemented to ensure that the warrant may not be exercised within the United States, and that the securities may not be delivered within the United States upon exercise, other than in offerings deemed to meet the definition of "offshore transaction" pursuant to Rule 902(h), unless registered under the Act or an exemption from such registration is available.

Rule 904 – Offshore Resales

a.   An offer or sale of securities by any person other than the issuer, a distributor, any of their respective affiliates (except any officer or director who is an affiliate solely by virtue of holding such position), or any person acting on behalf of any of the foregoing, shall be deemed to occur outside the United States within the meaning of Rule 901 if:

1.   The offer or sale are made in an offshore transaction;

2.   No directed selling efforts are made in the United States by the seller, an affiliate, or any person acting on their behalf; and

3.   The conditions of paragraph (b) of this section, if applicable, are satisfied.

b.   **Additional conditions**.

1.   Resales by dealers and persons receiving selling concessions. In the case of an offer or sale of securities prior to the expiration of the distribution compliance period specified in Category 2 or 3 (paragraph (b)(2) or (b)(3)) of Rule 903, as applicable, by a dealer, as defined in Section 2(a)(12) of the Act, or a person receiving a selling concession, fee or other remuneration in respect of the securities offered or sold:

    i.   Neither the seller nor any person acting on its behalf knows that the offeree or buyer of the securities is a U.S. person; and

    ii.   If the seller or any person acting on the seller's behalf knows that the purchaser is a dealer, as defined in Section 2(a)(12) of the Act, or is a person receiving a selling concession, fee or other remuneration in respect of the securities sold, the seller or a person acting on the seller's behalf sends to the purchaser a confirmation or other notice stating that the securities may be offered and sold during the distribution compliance period only in accordance with the provisions of this Regulation S (Rule 901 through Rule 905, and Preliminary Notes); pursuant to registration of the securities under the Act; or pursuant to an available exemption from the registration requirements of the Act.

2.   Resales by certain affiliates. In the case of an offer or sale of securities by an officer or director of the issuer or a distributor, who is an affiliate of the issuer or distributor solely by virtue of holding such position, no selling concession, fee or other remuneration is paid in connection with such offer or sale other than the usual and customary broker's commission that would be received by a person executing such transaction as agent.

Rule 905 – Resale Limitations

Equity securities of domestic issuers acquired from the issuer, a distributor, or any of their respective affiliates in a transaction subject to the conditions of Rule 901 or Rule 903 are deemed to be "restricted securities" as defined in Rule 144. Resales of any of such restricted securities by the offshore purchaser must be made in accordance with this Regulation S, the registration requirements of the Act or an exemption therefrom. Any "restricted securities," as defined in Rule 144, that are equity securities of a domestic issuer will continue to be deemed to be restricted securities, notwithstanding that they were acquired in a resale transaction made pursuant to Rule 901 or Rule 904.

Regulation S-K

Item 101 – Description of Business

   a.   **General development of business.** Describe the general development of the business of the registrant, its subsidiaries and any predecessor(s) during the past five years, or such shorter period as the registrant may have been engaged in business. Information shall be disclosed for earlier periods if material to an understanding of the general development of the business.

      1.   In describing developments, information shall be given as to matters such as the following: the year in which the registrant was organized and its form of organization; the nature and results of any bankruptcy, receivership or similar proceedings with respect to the registrant or any of its significant subsidiaries; the nature and results of any other material reclassification, merger or consolidation of the registrant or any of its significant subsidiaries; the acquisition or disposition of any material amount of assets otherwise than in the ordinary course of business; and any material changes in the mode of conducting the business.

      2.   Registrants, (i) filing a registration statement on Form S-1 under the Securities Act or on Form 10 under the Exchange Act, (ii) not subject to the reporting requirements of section 13(a) or 15(d) of the Exchange Act immediately prior to the filing of such registration statement, and (iii) that (including predecessors) have not received revenue from operations during each of the three fiscal years immediately prior to the filing of registration statement, shall provide the following information:

         A.   if the registration statement is filed prior to the end of the registrant's second fiscal quarter, a description of the registrant's plan of operation for the remainder of the fiscal year; or

         B.   if the registration statement is filed subsequent to the end of the registrant's second fiscal quarter, a description of the registrant's plan of operation for the remainder of the fiscal year and for the first six months of the next fiscal year. If such information is not available, the reasons for its not being available shall be stated. Disclosure relating to any plan shall include such matters as:

            1.   In the case of a registration statement on Form S-1, a statement in narrative form indicating the registrant's opinion as to the period of time that the proceeds from the offering will satisfy cash requirements and whether in the next six months it will be necessary to raise additional funds to meet the expenditures required for operating the business of the registrant; the specific reasons for such opinion shall be set forth and categories of expenditures and sources of cash resources shall be identified; however, amounts of expenditures and cash resources need not be provided; in addition, if the narrative statement is based on a cash budget, such budget shall be furnished to the Commission as supplemental information, but not as part of the registration statement;

2. An explanation of material product research and development to be performed during the period covered in the plan;

3. Any anticipated material acquisition of plant and equipment and the capacity thereof;

4. Any anticipated material changes in number of employees in the various departments such as research and development, production, sales or administration; and

5. Other material areas which may be peculiar to the registrant's business.

b. **Financial information about industry segments.** Report for each segment, as defined by generally accepted accounting principles, revenues from external customers, a measure of profit or loss and total assets. A registrant must report this information for each of the last three fiscal years or for as long as it has been in business, whichever period is shorter. If the information provided in response to this paragraph (b) conforms with generally accepted accounting principles, a registrant may include in its financial statements a cross reference to this data in lieu of presenting duplicative information in the financial statements; conversely, a registrant may cross reference to the financial statements.

1. If a registrant changes the structure of its internal organization in a manner that causes the composition of its reportable segments to change, the registrant must restate the corresponding information for earlier periods, including interim periods, unless it is impracticable to do so. Following a change in the composition of its reportable segments, a registrant shall disclose whether it has restated the corresponding items of segment information for earlier periods. If it has not restated the items from earlier periods, the registrant shall disclose in the year in which the change occurs segment information for the current period under both the old basis and the new basis of segmentation, unless it is impracticable to do so.

2. If the registrant includes, or is required by Article 3 of Regulation S-X to include, interim financial statements, discuss any facts relating to the performance of any of the segments during the period which, in the opinion of management, indicate that the three year segment financial data may not be indicative of current or future operations of the segment. Comparative financial information shall be included to the extent necessary to the discussion.

c. **Narrative description of business.**

1. Describe the business done and intended to be done by the registrant and its subsidiaries, focusing upon the registrant's dominant industry segment or each reportable industry segment about which financial information is presented in the financial statements. To the extent material to an understanding of the registrant's business taken as a whole, the description of each such segment shall include the information specified in paragraphs (c)(1) (i) through (x) of this section. The matters specified in paragraphs (c)(1) (xi) through (xiii) of this section shall be discussed with respect to the registrant's business in general; where material, the industry segments to which these matters are significant shall be identified.

    i.   The principal products produced and services rendered by the registrant in the industry segment and the principal markets for, and methods of distribution of, the segment's principal products and services. In addition, state for each of the last three fiscal years the amount or percentage of total revenue contributed by any class of similar products or services which accounted for 10 percent or more of consolidated revenue in any of the last three fiscal years or 15 percent or more of consolidated revenue, if total revenue did not exceed $50,000,000 during any of such fiscal years.

    ii.   A description of the status of a product or segment (*e.g.* whether in the planning stage, whether prototypes exist, the degree to which product design has progressed or whether further engineering is necessary), if there has been a public announcement of, or if the registrant otherwise has made public information about, a new product or industry segment that would require the investment of a material amount of the assets of the registrant or that otherwise is material. This paragraph is not intended to require disclosure of otherwise nonpublic corporate information the disclosure of which would affect adversely the registrant's competitive position.

    iii.   The sources and availability of raw materials.

    iv.   The importance to the industry segment and the duration and effect of all patents, trademarks, licenses, franchises and concessions held.

    v.   The extent to which the business of the industry segment is or may be seasonal.

    vi.   The practices of the registrant and the industry (respective industries) relating to working capital items (*e.g.,* where the registrant is required to carry significant amounts of inventory to meet rapid delivery requirements of customers or to assure itself of a continuous allotment of goods from suppliers; where the registrant provides rights to return merchandise; or where the registrant has provided extended payment terms to customers).

    vii.   The dependence of the segment upon a single customer, or a few customers, the loss of any one or more of which would have a material adverse effect on the segment. The name of any customer and its relationship, if any, with the registrant or its subsidiaries shall be disclosed if sales to the customer by one or more segments are made in an aggregate amount equal to 10 percent or more of the registrant's consolidated revenues and the loss of such customer would have a material adverse effect on the registrant and its subsidiaries taken as a whole. The names of other customers may be included, unless in the particular case the effect of including the names would be misleading. For purposes of this paragraph, a group of customers under common control or customers that are affiliates of each other shall be regarded as a single customer.

    viii.   The dollar amount of backlog orders believed to be firm, as of a recent date and as of a comparable date in the preceding fiscal year, together with an indication of the portion thereof not reasonably expected to be filled within the current fiscal year, and seasonal or other material aspects of the backlog. (There may be included as firm orders government orders that are firm but not yet funded and contracts awarded but not yet signed, provided an appropriate statement is added to explain the nature of such orders and the amount thereof. The portion of orders already included in sales or operating revenues on the basis of percentage of completion or program accounting shall be excluded.)

ix.   A description of any material portion of the business that may be subject to renegotiation of profits or termination of contracts or subcontracts at the election of the Government.

x.   Competitive conditions in the business involved including, where material, the identity of the particular markets in which the registrant competes, an estimate of the number of competitors and the registrant's competitive position, if known or reasonably available to the registrant. Separate consideration shall be given to the principal products or services or classes of products or services of the segment, if any. Generally, the names of competitors need not be disclosed. The registrant may include such names, unless in the particular case the effect of including the names would be misleading. Where, however, the registrant knows or has reason to know that one or a small number of competitors is dominant in the industry it shall be identified. The principal methods of competition (*e.g.,* price, service, warranty or product performance) shall be identified, and positive and negative factors pertaining to the competitive position of the registrant, to the extent that they exist, shall be explained if known or reasonably available to the registrant.

xi.   If material, the estimated amount spent during each of the last three fiscal years on company-sponsored research and development activities determined in accordance with generally accepted accounting principles. In addition, state, if material, the estimated dollar amount spent during each of such years on customer-sponsored research activities relating to the development of new products, services or techniques or the improvement of existing products, services or techniques.

xii.   Appropriate disclosure also shall be made as to the material effects that compliance with Federal, State and local provisions which have been enacted or adopted regulating the discharge of materials into the environment, or otherwise relating to the protection of the environment, may have upon the capital expenditures, earnings and competitive position of the registrant and its subsidiaries. The registrant shall disclose any material estimated capital expenditures for environmental control facilities for the remainder of its current fiscal year and its succeeding fiscal year and for such further periods as the registrant may deem materials.

xiii. The number of persons employed by the registrant.

d. **Financial information about geographic areas.**
   1.   State for each of the registrant's last three fiscal years, or for each fiscal year the registrant has been engaged in business, whichever period is shorter:
        i.   Revenues from external customers attributed to:

           A.   The registrant's country of domicile;

           B.   All foreign countries, in total, from which the registrant derives revenues; and

           C.   Any individual foreign country, if material. Disclose the basis for attributing revenues from external customers to individual countries.

      ii.   Long-lived assets, other than financial instruments, long-term customer relationships of a financial institution, mortgage and other servicing rights, deferred policy acquisition costs, and deferred tax assets, located in:

           A.   The registrant's country of domicile;

           B.   All foreign countries, in total, in which the registrant holds assets; and

           C.   Any individual foreign country, if material.

2.   A registrant shall report the amounts based on the financial information that it uses to produce the general-purpose financial statements. If providing the geographic information is impracticable, the registrant shall disclose that fact. A registrant may wish to provide, in addition to the information required by paragraph (d)(1) of this section, subtotals of geographic information about groups of countries. To the extent that the disclosed information conforms with generally accepted accounting principles, the registrant may include in its financial statements a cross reference to this data in lieu of presenting duplicative data in its financial statements; conversely, a registrant may cross-reference to the financial statements.

3.   A registrant shall describe any risks attendant to the foreign operations and any dependence on one or more of the registrant's segments upon such foreign operations, unless it would be more appropriate to discuss this information in connection with the description of one or more of the registrant's segments under paragraph (c) of this item.

4.   If the registrant includes, or is required by Article 3 of Regulation S-X, to include, interim financial statements, discuss any facts relating to the information furnished under this paragraph (d) that, in the opinion of management, indicate that the three year financial data for geographic areas may not be indicative of current or future operations. To the extent necessary to the discussion, include comparative information.

e.   **Available information.** Disclose the information in paragraphs (e)(1), (e)(2) and (e)(3) of this section in any registration statement you file under the Securities Act, and disclose the information in paragraphs (e)(3) and (e)(4) of this section if you are an accelerated filer (as defined in Rule 12b-2) filing an annual report on Form 10-K:

1.   Whether you file reports with the Securities and Exchange Commission. If you are a reporting company, identify the reports and other information you file with the SEC.

2.   That the public may read and copy any materials you file with the SEC at the SEC's Public Reference Room at 100 F Street, NE., Washington, DC 20549. State that the public may obtain information on the operation of the Public Reference Room by calling the SEC at 1-800-SEC-0330. If you are an electronic filer, state that the SEC maintains an Internet site that contains

reports, proxy and information statements, and other information regarding issuers that file electronically with the SEC and state the address of that site (*http://www.sec.gov*).

3. You are encouraged to give your Internet address, if available, except that if you are an accelerated filer filing your annual report on Form 10-K, you must disclose your Internet address, if you have one.

4.
    i. Whether you make available free of charge on or through your Internet website, if you have one, your annual report on Form 10-K, quarterly reports on Form 10-Q, current reports on Form 8-K, and amendments to those reports filed or furnished pursuant to Section 13(a) or 15(d) of the Exchange Act as soon as reasonably practicable after you electronically file such material with, or furnish it to, the SEC;

    ii. If you do not make your filings available in this manner, the reasons you do not do so (including, where applicable, that you do not have an Internet website); and

    iii. If you do not make your filings available in this manner, whether you voluntarily will provide electronic or paper copies of your filings free of charge upon request.

f. **Reports to security holders.** Disclose the following information in any registration statement you file under the Securities Act:

1. If the SEC's proxy rules or regulations, or stock exchange requirements, do not require you to send an annual report to security holders or to holders of American depository receipts, describe briefly the nature and frequency of reports that you will give to security holders. Specify whether the reports that you give will contain financial information that has been examined and reported on, with an opinion expressed "by" an independent public or certified public accountant.

2. For a foreign private issuer, if the report will not contain financial information prepared in accordance with U.S. generally accepted accounting principles, you must state whether the report will include a reconciliation of this information with U.S. generally accepted accounting principles.

g. **Enforceability of civil liabilities against foreign persons.** Disclose the following if you are a foreign private issuer filing a registration statement under the Securities Act:

1. Whether or not investors may bring actions under the civil liability provisions of the U.S. federal securities laws against the foreign private issuer, any of its officers and directors who are residents of a foreign country, any underwriters or experts named in the registration statement that are residents of a foreign country, and whether investors may enforce these civil liability provisions when the assets of the issuer or these other persons are located outside of the United States. The disclosure must address the following matters:

    i. The investor's ability to effect service of process within the United States on the foreign private issuer or any person;

    ii. The investor's ability to enforce judgments obtained in U.S. courts against foreign persons based upon the civil liability provisions of the U.S. federal securities laws;

  iii. The investor's ability to enforce, in an appropriate foreign court, judgments of U.S. courts based upon the civil liability provisions of the U.S. federal securities laws; and

  iv. The investor's ability to bring an original action in an appropriate foreign court to enforce liabilities against the foreign private issuer or any person based upon the U.S. federal securities laws.

 2. If you provide this disclosure based on an opinion of counsel, name counsel in the prospectus and file as an exhibit to the registration statement a signed consent of counsel to the use of its name and opinion.

h. **Smaller reporting companies.** A smaller reporting company, as defined by Rule 10(f)(1), may satisfy its obligations under this Item by describing the development of its business during the last three years. If the smaller reporting company has not been in business for three years, give the same information for predecessor(s) of the smaller reporting company if there are any. This business development description should include:

1. Form and year of organization;

2. Any bankruptcy, receivership or similar proceeding; and

3. Any material reclassification, merger, consolidation, or purchase or sale of a significant amount of assets not in the ordinary course of business.

4. Business of the smaller reporting company. Briefly describe the business and include, to the extent material to an understanding of the smaller reporting company:

  i. Principal products or services and their markets;

  ii. Distribution methods of the products or services;

  iii. Status of any publicly announced new product or service;

  iv. Competitive business conditions and the smaller reporting company's competitive position in the industry and methods of competition;

  v. Sources and availability of raw materials and the names of principal suppliers;

  vi. Dependence on one or a few major customers;

  vii. Patents, trademarks, licenses, franchises, concessions, royalty agreements or labor contracts, including duration;

  viii. Need for any government approval of principal products or services. If government approval is necessary and the smaller reporting company has not yet received that approval, discuss the status of the approval within the government approval process;

  ix. Effect of existing or probable governmental regulations on the business;

  x. Estimate of the amount spent during each of the last two fiscal years on research and development activities, and if applicable, the extent to which the cost of such activities is borne directly by customers;

  xi. Costs and effects of compliance with environmental laws (federal, state and local); and

  xii. Number of total employees and number of full-time employees.

5. Reports to security holders. Disclose the following in any registration statement you file under the Securities Act of 1933:

i.   If you are not required to deliver an annual report to security holders, whether you will voluntarily send an annual report and whether the report will include audited financial statements;

ii.   Whether you file reports with the Securities and Exchange Commission. If you are a reporting company, identify the reports and other information you file with the Commission; and

iii.   That the public may read and copy any materials you file with the Commission at the SEC's Public Reference Room at 100 F Street, NE., Washington, DC 20549, on official business days during the hours of 10 a.m. to 3 p.m. State that the public may obtain information on the operation of the Public Reference Room by calling the Commission at 1-800-SEC-0330. State that the Commission maintains an Internet site that contains reports, proxy and information statements, and other information regarding issuers that file electronically with the Commission and state the address of that site (http://www.sec.gov). You are encouraged to give your Internet address, if available.

6.   Foreign issuers. Provide the information required by Item 101(g) of Regulation S-K.

Instructions to Item 101:

1.   In determining what information about the industry segments is material to an understanding of the registrant's business taken as a whole and therefore required to be disclosed, pursuant to paragraph (c) of this Item, the registrant should take into account both quantitative and qualitative factors such as the significance of the matter to the registrant (e.g., whether a matter with a relatively minor impact on the registrant's business is represented by management to be important to its future profitability), the pervasiveness of the matter (e.g., whether it affects or may affect numerous items in the segment information), and the impact of the matter (e.g., whether it distorts the trends reflected in the segment information). Situations may arise when information should be disclosed about a segment, although the information in quantitative terms may not appear significant to the registrant's business taken as a whole.

2.   Base the determination of whether information about segments is required for a particular year upon an evaluation of interperiod comparability. For instance, interperiod comparability would require a registrant to report segment information in the current period even if not material under the criteria for reportability of SFAS No. 131 if a segment has been significant in the immediately preceding period and the registrant expects it to be significant in the future.

3.   The Commission, upon written request of the registrant and where consistent with the protection of investors, may permit the omission of any of the information required by this Item or the furnishing in substitution thereof of appropriate information of comparable character.

Item 102 – Description of Property

State briefly the location and general character of the principal plants, mines and other materially important physical properties of the registrant and its subsidiaries. In addition, identify the industry segment(s), as reported in the financial statements, that use the properties described. If any such property is not held in fee or is held subject to any major encumbrance, so state and describe briefly how held.

Instructions to Item 102:

1. What is required is such information as reasonably will inform investors as to the suitability, adequacy, productive capacity and extent of utilization of the facilities by the registrant. Detailed descriptions of the physical characteristics of individual properties or legal descriptions by metes and bounds are not required and shall not be given.

2. In determining whether properties should be described, the registrant should take into account both quantitative and qualitative factors. See Instruction 1 to Item 101 of Regulation S-K.

3. In the case of an extractive enterprise, material information shall be given as to production, reserves, locations, development and the nature of the registrant's interest. If individual properties are of major significance to an industry segment:

   A. More detailed information concerning these matters shall be furnished; and

   B. Appropriate maps shall be used to disclose location data of significant properties except in cases for which numerous maps would be required.

4.

   A. If reserve estimates are referred to in the document, the staff of the Office of Engineering, Division of Corporation Finance of the Commission, shall be consulted. That Office may request that a copy of the full report of the engineer or other expert who estimated the reserves be furnished as supplemental information and not as part of the filing. See Rule 418 of Regulation C and Rule 12b-4 of Regulation 12B with respect to the submission to, and return by, the Commission of supplemental information.

   B. If the estimates of reserves, or any estimated valuation thereof, are represented as being based on estimates prepared or reviewed by independent consultants, those independent consultants shall be named in the document.

5. Estimates of oil or gas reserves other than proved or, in the case of other extractive reserves, estimates other than proved or probable reserves, and any estimated values of such reserves shall not be disclosed in any document publicly filed with the Commission, unless such information is required to be disclosed in the document by foreign or state law; *provided, however*, that where such estimates previously have been provided to a person (or any of its affiliates) that is offering to acquire, merge or consolidate with the registrant or otherwise to acquire the registrant's securities, such estimates may be included in documents relating to such acquisition.

6. The definitions in Rule 4-10(a) of Regulation S-X shall apply to this Item with respect to oil and gas operations.

Item 103 – Legal Proceedings

Describe briefly any material pending legal proceedings, other than ordinary routine litigation incidental to the business, to which the registrant or any of its subsidiaries is a party or of which any of their property is the subject. Include the name of the court or agency in which the proceedings are pending, the date instituted, the principal parties thereto, a description of the factual basis alleged to underlie the proceeding and the relief sought. Include similar information as to any such proceedings known to be contemplated by governmental authorities.

Instructions to Item 103:

1. If the business ordinarily results in actions for negligence or other claims, no such action or claim need be described unless it departs from the normal kind of such actions.

2. No information need be given with respect to any proceeding that involves primarily a claim for damages if the amount involved, exclusive of interest and costs, does not exceed 10 percent of the current assets of the registrant and its subsidiaries on a consolidated basis. However, if any proceeding presents in large degree the same legal and factual issues as other proceedings pending or known to be contemplated, the amount involved in such other proceedings shall be included in computing such percentage.

3. Notwithstanding Instructions 1 and 2, any material bankruptcy, receivership, or similar proceeding with respect to the registrant or any of its significant subsidiaries shall be described.

4. Any material proceedings to which any director, officer or affiliate of the registrant, any owner of record or beneficially of more than five percent of any class of voting securities of the registrant, or any associate of any such director, officer, affiliate of the registrant, or security holder is a party adverse to the registrant or any of its subsidiaries or has a material interest adverse to the registrant or any of its subsidiaries also shall be described.

5. Notwithstanding the foregoing, an administrative or judicial proceeding (including, for purposes of A and B of this Instruction, proceedings which present in large degree the same issues) arising under any Federal, State or local provisions that have been enacted or adopted regulating the discharge of materials into the environment or primary for the purpose of protecting the environment shall not be deemed "ordinary routine litigation incidental to the business" and shall be described if:

    A. Such proceeding is material to the business or financial condition of the registrant;

    B. Such proceeding involves primarily a claim for damages, or involves potential monetary sanctions, capital expenditures, deferred charges or charges to income and the amount involved, exclusive of interest and costs, exceeds 10 percent of the current assets of the registrant and its subsidiaries on a consolidated basis; or

    C. A governmental authority is a party to such proceeding and such proceeding involves potential monetary sanctions, unless the registrant reasonably believes that such proceeding will result in no monetary sanctions, or in monetary sanctions, exclusive of interest and costs, of less than $100,000; *provided, however*, that such proceedings which are similar in nature may be grouped and described generically.

Item 201 – Market Price of and Dividends on the Registrant's Common Equity and Related Stockholder Matters

a. **Market information.**

    1.

        i.   Identify the principal United States market or markets in which each class of the registrant's common equity is being traded. Where there is no established public trading market for a class of common equity, furnish a statement to that effect. For purposes of this Item the existence of limited or sporadic quotations should not of itself be deemed to constitute an "established public trading market." In the case of foreign registrants, also identify the principal established foreign public trading market, if any, for each class of the registrant's common equity.

        ii. If the principal United States market for such common equity is an exchange, state the high and low sales prices for the equity for each full quarterly period within the two most recent fiscal years and any subsequent interim period for which financial statements are included, or are required to be included by Article 3 of Regulation S-X, as reported in the consolidated transaction reporting system or, if not so reported, as reported on the principal exchange market for such equity.

iii. If the principal United States market for such common equity is not an exchange, state the range of high and low bid information for the equity for each full quarterly period within the two most recent fiscal years and any subsequent interim period for which financial statements are included, or are required to be included by Article 3 of Regulation S-X, as regularly quoted in the automated quotation system of a registered securities association, or where the equity is not quoted in such a system, the range of reported high and low bid quotations, indicating the source of such quotations. Indicate, as applicable, that such over-the-counter market quotations reflect inter-dealer prices, without retail mark-up, mark-down or commission and may not necessarily represent actual transactions. Where there is an absence of an established public trading market, reference to quotations shall be qualified by appropriate explanation.

iv. Where a foreign registrant has identified a principal established foreign trading market for its common equity pursuant to paragraph (a)(1) of this Item, also provide market price information comparable, to the extent practicable, to that required for the principal United States market, including the source of such information. Such prices shall be stated in the currency in which they are quoted. The registrant may translate such prices into United States currency at the currency exchange rate in effect on the date the price disclosed was reported on the foreign exchange. If the primary United States market for the registrant's common equity trades using American Depositary Receipts, the United States prices disclosed shall be on that basis.

v. If the information called for by this Item is being presented in a registration statement filed pursuant to the Securities Act or a proxy or information statement filed pursuant to the Exchange Act, the document also shall include price information as of the latest practicable date, and, in the case of securities to be issued in connection with an acquisition, business combination or other reorganization, as of the date immediately prior to the public announcement of such transaction.

2. If the information called for by this paragraph (a) is being presented in a registration statement on Form S-1 under the Securities Act or on Form 10 under the Exchange Act relating to a class of common equity for which at the time of filing there is no established United States public trading market, indicate the amount(s) of common equity (i) that is subject to outstanding options or warrants to purchase, or securities convertible into, common equity of the registrant; (ii) that could be sold pursuant to Rule 144 under the Securities Act or that the registrant has agreed to register under the Securities Act for sale by security holders; or (iii) that is being, or has been publicly proposed to be, publicly offered by the registrant (unless such common equity is being offered pursuant to an employee benefit plan or dividend reinvestment plan), the offering of which could have a material effect on the market price of the registrant's common equity.

b. **Holders.**
  1.   Set forth the approximate number of holders of each class of common equity of the registrant as of the latest practicable date.
  2.   If the information called for by this paragraph (b) is being presented in a registration statement filed pursuant to the Securities Act or a proxy statement or information statement filed pursuant to the Exchange Act that relates to an acquisition, business combination or other reorganization, indicate the effect of such transaction on the amount and percentage of present holdings of the registrant's common equity owned beneficially by (i) any person (including any group as that term is used in section 13(d)(3) of the Exchange Act) who is known to the registrant to be the beneficial owner of more than five percent of any class of the registrant's common equity and (ii) each director and nominee and (iii) all directors and officers as a group, and the registrant's present commitments to such persons with respect to the issuance of shares of any class of its common equity.

c. **Dividends.**
  1.   State the frequency and amount of any cash dividends declared on each class of its common equity by the registrant for the two most recent fiscal years and any subsequent interim period for which financial statements are required to be presented by Article 3 of Regulation S-X. Where there are restrictions (including, where appropriate, restrictions on the ability of registrant's subsidiaries to transfer funds to the registrant in the form of cash dividends, loans or advances) that currently materially limit the registrant's ability to pay such dividends or that the registrant reasonably believes are likely to limit materially the future payment of dividends on the common equity so state and either (i) describe briefly (where appropriate quantify) such restrictions, or (ii) cross reference to the specific discussion of such restrictions in the Management's Discussion and Analysis of financial condition and operating results prescribed by Item 303 of Regulation S-K and the description of such restrictions required by Regulation S-X in the registrant's financial statements.
  2.   Where registrants have a record of paying no cash dividends although earnings indicate an ability to do so, they are encouraged to consider the question of their intention to pay cash dividends in the foreseeable future and, if no such intention exists, to make a statement of that fact in the filing. Registrants which have a history of paying cash dividends also are encouraged to indicate whether they currently expect that comparable cash dividends will continue to be paid in the future and, if not, the nature of the change in the amount or rate of cash dividend payments.

d. **Securities authorized for issuance under equity compensation plans.**
  1.   In the following tabular format, provide the information specified in paragraph (d)(2) of this Item as of the end of the most recently completed fiscal year with respect to compensation plans (including individual compensation arrangements) under which equity securities of the registrant are authorized for issuance, aggregated as follows:
    i.   All compensation plans previously approved by security holders; and
    ii.   All compensation plans not previously approved by security holders.

171

Equity Compensation Plan Information			
Plan category	Number of securities to be issued upon exercise of outstanding options, warrants and rights	Weighted-average exercise price of outstanding options, warrants and rights	Number of securities remaining available for future issuance under equity compensation plans (excluding securities reflected in column (a))
	(a)	(b)	(c)
Equity compensation plans approved by security holders			
Equity compensation plans not approved by security holders			
Total			

2. The table shall include the following information as of the end of the most recently completed fiscal year for each category of equity compensation plan described in paragraph (d)(1) of this Item:
   i. The number of securities to be issued upon the exercise of outstanding options, warrants and rights (column (a));
   ii. The weighted-average exercise price of the outstanding options, warrants and rights disclosed pursuant to paragraph (d)(2)(i) of this Item (column (b)); and
   iii. Other than securities to be issued upon the exercise of the outstanding options, warrants and rights disclosed in paragraph (d)(2)(i) of this Item, the number of securities remaining available for future issuance under the plan (column (c)).
3. For each compensation plan under which equity securities of the registrant are authorized for issuance that was adopted without the approval of security holders, describe briefly, in narrative form, the material features of the plan.

Instructions to Item 201(d):
1. Disclosure shall be provided with respect to any compensation plan and individual compensation arrangement of the registrant (or parent, subsidiary or affiliate of the registrant) under which equity securities of the registrant are authorized for issuance to employees or non-employees (such as directors, consultants, advisors, vendors, customers, suppliers or lenders) in exchange for consideration in the form of goods or services as described in Statement of Finan. Accounting Standards No. 123, *Accounting for Stock-Based Compensation*, or any successor standard. No disclosure is required with respect to:
   a. Any plan, contract or arrangement for the issuance of warrants or rights to all security holders of the registrant as such on a pro rata basis (such as a stock rights offering) or
   b. Any employee benefit plan that is intended to meet the qualification requirements of Section 401(a) of the Internal Revenue Code.

2. For purposes of this paragraph, an "individual compensation arrangement" includes, but is not limited to, the following: a written compensation contract within the meaning of "employee benefit plan" under Rule 405 under the Securities Act and a plan (whether or not set forth in any formal document) applicable to one person as provided under Item 402(a)(6)(ii) of Regulation S-K.

3. If more than one class of equity security is issued under its equity compensation plans, a registrant should aggregate plan information for each class of security.

4. A registrant may aggregate information regarding individual compensation arrangements with the plan information required under paragraph (d)(1)(i) and (ii) of this Item, as applicable.

5. A registrant may aggregate information regarding a compensation plan assumed in connection with a merger, consolidation or other acquisition transaction pursuant to which the registrant may make subsequent grants or awards of its equity securities with the plan information required under paragraph (d)(1)(i) and (ii) of this Item, as applicable. A registrant shall disclose on an aggregated basis in a footnote to the table the information required under paragraph (d)(2)(i) and (ii) of this Item with respect to any individual options, warrants or rights assumed in connection with a merger, consolidation or other acquisition transaction.

6. To the extent that the number of securities remaining available for future issuance disclosed in column (c) includes securities available for future issuance under any compensation plan or individual compensation arrangement other than upon the exercise of an option, warrant or right, disclose the number of securities and type of plan separately for each such plan in a footnote to the table.

7. If the description of an equity compensation plan set forth in a registrant's financial statements contains the disclosure required by paragraph (d)(3) of this Item, a cross-reference to such description will satisfy the requirements of paragraph (d)(3) of this Item.

8. If an equity compensation plan contains a formula for calculating the number of securities available for issuance under the plan, including, without limitation, a formula that automatically increases the number of securities available for issuance by a percentage of the number of outstanding securities of the registrant, a description of this formula shall be disclosed in a footnote to the table.

9. Except where it is part of a document that is incorporated by reference into a prospectus, the information required by this paragraph need not be provided in any registration statement filed under the Securities Act.

e. **Performance graph.**
    1. Provide a line graph comparing the yearly percentage change in the registrant's cumulative total shareholder return on a class of common stock registered under section 12 of the Exchange Act (as measured by dividing the sum of the cumulative amount of dividends for the measurement period, assuming dividend reinvestment, and the difference between the registrant's share price at the end and the beginning of the measurement period; by the share price at the beginning of the measurement period) with:
        i. The cumulative total return of a broad equity market index assuming reinvestment of dividends, that includes companies whose equity securities are traded on the same exchange or are of comparable market capitalization; *provided, however,* that if the registrant is a company

                    within the Standard & Poor's 500 Stock Index, the registrant must use that index; and

      ii.   The cumulative total return, assuming reinvestment of dividends, of:

          A.   A published industry or line-of-business index;

          B.   Peer issuer(s) selected in good faith. If the registrant does not select its peer issuer(s) on an industry or line-of-business basis, the registrant shall disclose the basis for its selection; or

          C.   Issuer(s) with similar market capitalization(s), but only if the registrant does not use a published industry or line-of-business index and does not believe it can reasonably identify a peer group. If the registrant uses this alternative, the graph shall be accompanied by a statement of the reasons for this selection.

2.   For purposes of paragraph (e)(1) of this Item, the term "measurement period" shall be the period beginning at the "measurement point" established by the market close on the last trading day before the beginning of the registrant's fifth preceding fiscal year, through and including the end of the registrant's last completed fiscal year. If the class of securities has been registered under section 12 of the Exchange Act for a shorter period of time, the period covered by the comparison may correspond to that time period.

3.   For purposes of paragraph (e)(1)(ii)(A) of this Item, the term "published industry or line-of-business index" means any index that is prepared by a party other than the registrant or an affiliate and is accessible to the registrant's security holders; *provided, however*, that registrants may use an index prepared by the registrant or affiliate if such index is widely recognized and used.

4.   If the registrant selects a different index from an index used for the immediately preceding fiscal year, explain the reason(s) for this change and also compare the registrant's total return with that of both the newly selected index and the index used in the immediately preceding fiscal year.

Instructions to Item 201(e):

1.   In preparing the required graphic comparisons, the registrant should:

   a.   Use, to the extent feasible, comparable methods of presentation and assumptions for the total return calculations required by paragraph (e)(1) of this Item; *provided, however*, that if the registrant constructs its own peer group index under paragraph (e)(1)(ii)(B), the same methodology must be used in calculating both the registrant's total return and that on the peer group index; and

   b.   Assume the reinvestment of dividends into additional shares of the same class of equity securities at the frequency with which dividends are paid on such securities during the applicable fiscal year.

2.   In constructing the graph:

   a.   The closing price at the measurement point must be converted into a fixed investment, stated in dollars, in the registrant's stock (or in the stocks represented by a given index) with cumulative returns for each subsequent fiscal year measured as a change from that investment; and

   b.   Each fiscal year should be plotted with points showing the cumulative total return as of that point. The value of the investment as of each point plotted on a given return line is the number of shares held at that point multiplied by the then-prevailing share price.

3. The registrant is required to present information for the registrant's last five fiscal years, and may choose to graph a longer period; but the measurement point, however, shall remain the same.

4. Registrants may include comparisons using performance measures in addition to total return, such as return on average common shareholders' equity.

5. If the registrant uses a peer issuer(s) comparison or comparison with issuer(s) with similar market capitalizations, the identity of those issuers must be disclosed and the returns of each component issuer of the group must be weighted according to the respective issuer's stock market capitalization at the beginning of each period for which a return is indicated.

6. A registrant that qualifies as a "smaller reporting company," as defined by Item 10(f)(1), is not required to provide the information required by paragraph (e) of this Item.

7. The information required by paragraph (e) of this Item need not be provided in any filings other than an annual report to security holders required by Exchange Act Rule 14a-3 or Exchange Act Rule 14c-3 that precedes or accompanies a registrant's proxy or information statement relating to an annual meeting of security holders at which directors are to be elected (or special meeting or written consents in lieu of such meeting). Such information will not be deemed to be incorporated by reference into any filing under the Securities Act or the Exchange Act, except to the extent that the registrant specifically incorporates it by reference.

8. The information required by paragraph (e) of this Item shall not be deemed to be "soliciting material" or to be "filed" with the Commission or subject to Regulation 14A or 14C, other than as provided in this item, or to the liabilities of section 18 of the Exchange Act, except to the extent that the registrant specifically requests that such information be treated as soliciting material or specifically incorporates it by reference into a filing under the Securities Act or the Exchange Act.

Instructions to Item 201:

1. Registrants, the common equity of which is listed for trading on more than one securities exchange registered under the Exchange Act, are required to indicate each such exchange pursuant to paragraph (a)(1)(i) of this Item; such registrants, however, need only report one set of price quotations pursuant to paragraph (a)(1)(ii) of this Item; where available, these shall be the prices as reported in the consolidated transaction reporting system and, where the prices are not so reported, the prices on the most significant (in terms of volume) securities exchange for such shares.

2. Market prices and dividends reported pursuant to this Item shall be adjusted to give retroactive effect to material changes resulting from stock dividends, stock splits and reverse stock splits.

3. The computation of the approximate number of holders of registrant's common equity may be based upon the number of record holders or also may include individual participants in security position listings. See Rule 17Ad-8 under the Exchange Act. The method of computation that is chosen shall be indicated.

4. If the registrant is a foreign issuer, describe briefly

   A. Any governmental laws, decrees or regulations in the country in which the registrant is organized that restrict the export or import of capital, including, but not limited to, foreign exchange controls, or that affect the remittance of dividends or other payments to nonresident holders of the registrant's common equity; and

B.   All taxes, including withholding provisions, to which United States common equity holders are subject under existing laws and regulations of the foreign country in which the registrant is organized. Include a brief description of pertinent provisions of any reciprocal tax treaty between such foreign country and the United States regarding withholding. If there is no such treaty, so state.

5.   If the registrant is a foreign private issuer whose common equity of the class being registered is wholly or partially in bearer form, the response to this Item shall so indicate together with as much information as the registrant is able to provide with respect to security holdings in the United States. If the securities being registered trade in the United States in the form of American Depositary Receipts or similar certificates, the response to this Item shall so indicate together with the name of the depositary issuing such receipts and the number of shares or other units of the underlying security representing the trading units in such receipts.

Item 202 – Description of Registrant's Securities

Note: If the securities being described have been accepted for listing on an exchange, the exchange may be identified. The document should not however, convey the impression that the registrant may apply successfully for listing of the securities on an exchange or that, in the case of an underwritten offering, the underwriters may request the registrant to apply for such listing, unless there is reasonable assurance that the securities to be offered will be acceptable to a securities exchange for listing.

a.   **Capital stock.** If capital stock is to be registered, state the title of the class and describe such of the matters listed in paragraphs (a)(1) through (5) as are relevant. A complete legal description of the securities need not be given.

1.   Outline briefly: (i) dividend rights; (ii) terms of conversion; (iii) sinking fund provisions; (iv) redemption provisions; (v) voting rights, including any provisions specifying the vote required by security holders to take action; (vi) any classification of the Board of Directors, and the impact of such classification where cumulative voting is permitted or required; (vii) liquidation rights; (viii) preemption rights; and (ix) liability to further calls or to assessment by the registrant and for liabilities of the registrant imposed on its stockholders under state statutes (e.g., to laborers, servants or employees of the registrant), unless such disclosure would be immaterial because the financial resources of the registrant or other factors make it improbable that liability under such state statues would be imposed; (x) any restriction on alienability of the securities to be registered; and (xi) any provision discriminating against any existing or prospective holder of such securities as a result of such security holder owning a substantial amount of securities.

2.   If the rights of holders of such stock may be modified otherwise than by a vote of a majority or more of the shares outstanding, voting as a class, so state and explain briefly.

3.   If preferred stock is to be registered, describe briefly any restriction on the repurchase or redemption of shares by the registrant while there is any

arrearage in the payment of dividends or sinking fund installments. If there is no such restriction, so state.

4.   If the rights evidenced by, or amounts payable with respect to, the shares to be registered are, or may be, materially limited or qualified by the rights of any other authorized class of securities, include the information regarding such other securities as will enable investors to understand such limitations or qualifications. No information need be given, however, as to any class of securities all of which will be retired, provided appropriate steps to ensure such retirement will be completed prior to or upon delivery by the registrant of the shares.

5.   Describe briefly or cross-reference to a description in another part of the document, any provision of the registrant's charter or by-laws that would have an effect of delaying, deferring or preventing a change in control of the registrant and that would operate only with respect to an extraordinary corporate transaction involving the registrant (or any of its subsidiaries), such as a merger, reorganization, tender offer, sale or transfer of substantially all of its assets, or liquidation. Provisions and arrangements required by law or imposed by governmental or judicial authority need not be described or discussed pursuant to this paragraph (a)(5). Provisions or arrangements adopted by the registrant to effect, or further, compliance with laws or governmental or judicial mandate are not subject to the immediately preceding sentence where such compliance did not require the specific provisions or arrangements adopted.

b.   **Debt securities.** If debt securities are to be registered, state the title of such securities, the principal amount being offered, and, if a series, the total amount authorized and the total amount outstanding as of the most recent practicable date; and describe such of the matter listed in paragraphs (b)(1) through (10) as are relevant. A complete legal description of the securities need not be given. For purposes solely of this Item, debt securities that differ from one another only as to the interest rate or maturity shall be regarded as securities of the same class. Outline briefly:

1.   Provisions with respect to maturity, interest, conversion, redemption, amortization, sinking fund, or retirement;

2.   Provisions with respect to the kind and priority of any lien securing the securities, together with a brief identification of the principal properties subject to such lien;

3.   Provisions with respect to the subordination of the rights of holders of the securities to other security holders or creditors of the registrant; where debt securities are designated as subordinated in accordance with Instruction 1 to this Item, set forth the aggregate amount of outstanding indebtedness as of the most recent practicable date that by the terms of such debt securities would be senior to such subordinated debt and describe briefly any limitation on the issuance of such additional senior indebtedness or state that there is no such limitation;

4.   Provisions restricting the declaration of dividends or requiring the maintenance of any asset ratio or the creation or maintenance of reserves;

5.   Provisions restricting the incurrence of additional debt or the issuance of additional securities; in the case of secured debt, whether the securities being

registered are to be issued on the basis of unbonded bondable property, the deposit of cash or otherwise; as of the most recent practicable date, the approximate amount of unbonded bondable property available as a basis for the issuance of bonds; provisions permitting the withdrawal of cash deposited as a basis for the issuance of bonds; and provisions permitting the release or substitution of assets securing the issue; *Provided, however,* That provisions permitting the release of assets upon the deposit of equivalent funds or the pledge of equivalent property, the release of property no longer required in the business, obsolete property, or property taken by eminent domain or the application of insurance moneys, and other similar provisions need not be described;

6.   The general type of event that constitutes a default and whether or not any periodic evidence is required to be furnished as to the absence of default or as to compliance with the terms of the indenture;

7.   Provisions relating to modification of the terms of the security or the rights of security holders;

8.   If the rights evidenced by the securities to be registered are, or may be, materially limited or qualified by the rights of any other authorized class of securities, the information regarding such other securities as will enable investors to understand the rights evidenced by the securities; to the extent not otherwise disclosed pursuant to this Item; no information need be given, however, as to any class of securities all of which will be retired, provided appropriate steps to ensure such retirement will be completed prior to or upon delivery by the registrant of the securities;

9.   If debt securities are to be offered at a price such that they will be deemed to be offered at an "original issue discount" as defined in paragraph (a) of section 1273 of the Internal Revenue Code, or if a debt security is sold in a package with another security and the allocation of the offering price between the two securities may have the effect of offering the debt security at such an original issue discount, the tax effects thereof pursuant to sections 1271-1278;

10.   The name of the trustee(s) and the nature of any material relationship with the registrant or with any of its affiliates; the percentage of securities of the class necessary to require the trustee to take action; and what indemnification the trustee may require before proceeding to enforce the lien.

c.   **Warrants and rights.** If the securities described are to be offered pursuant to warrants or rights state:

1.   The amount of securities called for by such warrants or rights;

2.   The period during which and the price at which the warrants or rights are exercisable;

3.   The amount of warrants or rights outstanding;

4.   Provisions for changes to or adjustments in the exercise price; and

5.   Any other material terms of such rights on warrants.

d.   **Other securities.** If securities other than capital stock, debt, warrants or rights are to be registered, include a brief description (comparable to that required in paragraphs (a), (b) and (c) of Item 202) of the rights evidenced thereby.

e. **Market information for securities other than common equity.** If securities other than common equity are to be registered and there is an established public trading market for such securities (as that term is used in Item 201 of Regulation S-K) provide market information with respect to such securities comparable to that required by paragraph (a) of Item 201 of Regulation S-K.

f. **American Depositary Receipts.** If Depositary Shares represented by American Depositary Receipts are being registered, furnish the following information:
     1. The name of the depositary and the address of its principal executive office.
     2. State the title of the American Depositary Receipts and identify the deposited security. Describe briefly the terms of deposit, including the provisions, if any, with respect to:
         i. The amount of deposited securities represented by one unit of American Depositary Receipts;
         ii. The procedure for voting, if any, the deposited securities;
         iii. The collection and distribution of dividends;
         iv. The transmission of notices, reports and proxy soliciting material;
         v. The sale or exercise of rights;
         vi. The deposit or sale of securities resulting from dividends, splits or plans of reorganization;
         vii. Amendment, extension or termination of the deposit;
         viii. Rights of holders of receipts to inspect the transfer books of the depositary and the list of holders of receipts;
         ix. Restrictions upon the right to deposit or withdraw the underlying securities;
         x. Limitation upon the liability of the depositary.
     3. Describe all fees and charges which may be imposed directly or indirectly against the holder of the American Depositary Receipts, indicating the type of service, the amount of fee or charges and to whom paid.

Instructions to Item 202:

1. Wherever the title of securities is required to be stated, there shall be given such information as will indicate the type and general character of the securities, including the following:
     A. In the case of shares, the par or stated value, if any; the rate of dividends, if fixed, and whether cumulative or non-cumulative; a brief indication of the preference, if any; and if convertible or redeemable, a statement to that effect;
     B. In the case of debt, the rate of interest; the date of maturity or, if the issue matures serially, a brief indication of the serial maturities, such as "maturing serially from 1955 to 1960"; if the payment of principal or interest is contingent, an appropriate indication of such contingency; a brief indication of the priority of the issue; and, if convertible or callable, a statement to that effect; or
     C. In the case of any other kind of security, appropriate information of comparable character.
2. If the registrant is a foreign registrant, include (to the extent not disclosed in the document pursuant to Item 201 of Regulation S-K or otherwise) in the description of the securities:
     A. A brief description of any limitations on the right of nonresident or foreign owners to hold or vote such securities imposed by foreign law or by the charter or other

constituent document of the registrant, or if no such limitations are applicable, so state;

B. A brief description of any governmental laws, decrees or regulations in the country in which the registrant is organized affecting the remittance of dividends, interest and other payments to nonresident holders of the securities being registered;

C. A brief outline of all taxes, including withholding provisions, to which United States security holders are subject under existing laws and regulations of the foreign country in which the registrant is organized; and

D. A brief description of pertinent provisions of any reciprocal tax treaty between such foreign country and the United States regarding withholding or, if there is no such treaty, so state.

3. Section 305(a)(2) of the Trust Indenture Act of 1939 ("Trust Indenture Act"), shall not be deemed to require the inclusion in a registration statement or in a prospectus of any information not required by this Item.

4. Where convertible securities or stock purchase warrants are being registered that are subject to redemption or call, the description of the conversion terms of the securities or material terms of the warrants shall disclose:

A. Whether the right to convert or purchase the securities will be forfeited unless it is exercised before the date specified in a notice of the redemption or call;

B. The expiration or termination date of the warrants;

C. The kinds, frequency and timing of notice of the redemption or call, including the cities or newspapers in which notice will be published (where the securities provide for a class of newspapers or group of cities in which the publication may be made at the discretion of the registrant, the registrant should describe such provision); and

D. In the case of bearer securities, that investors are responsible for making arrangements to prevent loss of the right to convert or purchase in the event of redemption of call, for example, by reading the newspapers in which the notice of redemption or call may be published.

5. The response to paragraph (f) shall include information with respect to fees and charges in connection with (A) the deposit or substitution of the underlying securities; (B) receipt and distribution of dividends; (C) the sale or exercise of rights; (D) the withdrawal of the underlying security; and (E) the transferring, splitting or grouping of receipts. Information with respect to the right to collect the fees and charges against dividends received and deposited securities shall be included in response to this item.

Item 301 – Selected Financial Data

Furnish in comparative columnar form the selected financial data for the registrant referred to below, for

a. Each of the last five fiscal years of the registrant (or for the life of the registrant and its predecessors, if less), and

b. Any additional fiscal years necessary to keep the information from being misleading.

Instructions to Item 301:

1. The purpose of the selected financial data shall be to supply in a convenient and readable format selected financial data which highlight certain significant trends in the registrant's financial condition and results of operations.

2. Subject to appropriate variation to conform to the nature of the registrant's business, the following items shall be included in the table of financial data: net sales or operating revenues; income (loss) from continuing operations; income (loss) from continuing operations per common share; total assets; long-term obligations and redeemable preferred stock (including long-term debt, capital leases, and redeemable preferred stock as defined in Rule 5-02.27(a) of Regulation S-X; and cash dividends declared per common share. Registrants may include additional items which they believe would enhance an understanding of and would highlight other trends in their financial condition and results of operations.

    Briefly describe, or cross-reference to a discussion thereof, factors such as accounting changes, business combinations or dispositions of business operations, that materially affect the comparability of the information reflected in selected financial data. Discussion of, or reference to, any material uncertainties should also be included where such matters might cause the data reflected herein not to be indicative of the registrant's future financial condition or results of operations.

3. All references to the registrant in the table of selected financial data and in this Item shall mean the registrant and its subsidiaries consolidated.

4. If interim period financial statements are included, or are required to be included, by Article 3 of Regulation S-X, registrants should consider whether any or all of the selected financial data need to be updated for such interim periods to reflect a material change in the trends indicated; where such updating information is necessary, registrants shall provide the information on a comparative basis unless not necessary to an understanding of such updating information.

5. A foreign private issuer shall disclose also the following information in all filings containing financial statements:

    A. In the forepart of the document and as of the latest practicable date, the exchange rate into U.S. currency of the foreign currency in which the financial statements are denominated;

    B. A history of exchange rates for the five most recent years and any subsequent interim period for which financial statements are presented setting forth the rates for period end, the average rates, and the range of high and low rates for each year; and

    C. If equity securities are being registered, a five year summary of dividends per share stated in both the currency in which the financial statements are denominated and United States currency based on the exchange rates at each respective payment date.

6. A foreign private issuer shall present the selected financial data in the same currency as its financial statements. The issuer may present the selected financial data on the basis of the accounting principles used in its primary financial statements but in such case shall present this data also on the basis of any reconciliations of such data to United States generally accepted accounting principles and Regulation S-X made pursuant to Rule 4-01 of Regulation S-X.

7. For purposes of this rule, the rate of exchange means the noon buying rate in New York City for cable transfers in foreign currencies as certified for customs purposes by the Federal Reserve Bank of New York. The average rate means the average of the exchange rates on the last day of each month during a year.

Item 302 – Supplementary Financial Information

a. **Selected quarterly financial data.** Registrants specified in paragraph (a)(5)of this Item shall provide the information specified below.

1. Disclosure shall be made of net sales, gross profit (net sales less costs and expenses associated directly with or allocated to products sold or services rendered), income (loss) before extraordinary items and cumulative effect of a change in accounting, per share data based upon such income (loss), net income (loss) and net income (loss) attributable to the registrant, for each full quarter within the two most recent fiscal years and any subsequent interim period for which financial statements are included or are required to be included by Article 3 of Regulation S-X.

2. When the data supplied pursuant to paragraph (a) of this section vary from the amounts previously reported on the Form 10-Q filed for any quarter, such as would be the case when a combination between entities under common control occurs or where an error is corrected, reconcile the amounts given with those previously reported and describe the reason for the difference.

3. Describe the effect of any disposals of segments of a business, and extraordinary, unusual or infrequently occurring items recognized in each full quarter within the two most recent fiscal years and any subsequent interim period for which financial statements are included or are required to be included by Article 3 of Regulation S-X, as well as the aggregate effect and the nature of year-end or other adjustments which are material to the results of that quarter.

4. If the financial statements to which this information relates have been reported on by an accountant, appropriate professional standards and procedures, as enumerated in the Statements of Auditing Standards issued by the Auditing Standards Board of the American Institute of Certified Public Accountants, shall be followed by the reporting accountant with regard to the data required by this paragraph (a).

5. This paragraph (a) applies to any registrant, except a foreign private issuer, that has securities registered pursuant to sections 12(b) (other than mutual life insurance companies) or 12(g) of the Exchange Act.

b. **Information about oil and gas producing activities.** Registrants engaged in oil and gas producing activities shall present the information about oil and gas producing activities (as those activities are defined in Regulation S-X, Rule 4-10(a)) specified in paragraphs 9-34 of Statement of Financial Accounting Standards ("SFAS") No. 69, "Disclosures about Oil and Gas Producing Activities." If such oil and gas producing activities are regarded as significant under one or more of the tests set forth in paragraph 8 of SFAS No. 69.

Instructions to Paragraph (b):

1. (a) SFAS No. 69 disclosures that relate to annual periods shall be presented for each annual period for which an income statement is required. (b) SFAS No. 69 disclosures required as of the end of an annual period shall be presented as of the date of each audited balance sheet required, and (c) SFAS No. 69 disclosures required as of the beginning of an annual period shall be presented as of the beginning of each annual period for which an income statement is required.

2.   This paragraph, together with Rule 4-10 of Regulation S-X, prescribes financial reporting standards for the preparation of accounts by persons engaged, in whole or in part, in the production of crude oil or natural gas in the United States, pursuant to Section 503 of the Energy Policy and Conservation Act of 1975 ("EPCA") and Section 11(c) of the Energy Supply and Environmental Coordination Act of 1974 ("ESECA") as amended by Section 506 of EPCA. The application of the paragraph to those oil and gas producing operations of companies regulated for ratemaking purposes on an individual-company-cost-of-service basis may, however, give appropriate recognition to differences arising because of the effect of the ratemaking process.

3.   Any person exempted by the Department of Energy from any record-keeping or reporting requirements pursuant to Section 11(c) of ESECA, as amended, is similarly exempted from the related provisions of this paragraph in the preparation of accounts pursuant to EPCA. This exemption does not affect the applicability of this paragraph to filings pursuant to the federal securities laws.

Item 303 – Management's Discussion and Analysis of Financial Condition and Results of Operations

a.   **Full fiscal years.** Discuss registrant's financial condition, changes in financial condition and results of operations. The discussion shall provide information as specified in paragraphs (a)(1) through (5) of this Item and also shall provide such other information that the registrant believes to be necessary to an understanding of its financial condition, changes in financial condition and results of operations. Discussions of liquidity and capital resources may be combined whenever the two topics are interrelated. Where in the registrant's judgment a discussion of segment information or of other subdivisions of the registrant's business would be appropriate to an understanding of such business, the discussion shall focus on each relevant, reportable segment or other subdivision of the business and on the registrant as a whole.

1.   *Liquidity.* Identify any known trends or any known demands, commitments, events or uncertainties that will result in or that are reasonably likely to result in the registrant's liquidity increasing or decreasing in any material way. If a material deficiency is identified, indicate the course of action that the registrant has taken or proposes to take to remedy the deficiency. Also identify and separately describe internal and external sources of liquidity, and briefly discuss any material unused sources of liquid assets.

2.   *Capital resources.*

   i.   Describe the registrant's material commitments for capital expenditures as of the end of the latest fiscal period, and indicate the general purpose of such commitments and the anticipated source of funds needed to fulfill such commitments.

   ii. Describe any known material trends, favorable or unfavorable, in the registrant's capital resources. Indicate any expected material changes in the mix and relative cost of such resources. The discussion shall consider changes between equity, debt and any off-balance sheet financing arrangements.

3. *Results of operations.*

    i. Describe any unusual or infrequent events or transactions or any significant economic changes that materially affected the amount of reported income from continuing operations and, in each case, indicate the extent to which income was so affected. In addition, describe any other significant components of revenues or expenses that, in the registrant's judgment, should be described in order to understand the registrant's results of operations.

    ii. Describe any known trends or uncertainties that have had or that the registrant reasonably expects will have a material favorable or unfavorable impact on net sales or revenues or income from continuing operations. If the registrant knows of events that will cause a material change in the relationship between costs and revenues (such as known future increases in costs of labor or materials or price increases or inventory adjustments), the change in the relationship shall be disclosed.

    iii. To the extent that the financial statements disclose material increases in net sales or revenues, provide a narrative discussion of the extent to which such increases are attributable to increases in prices or to increases in the volume or amount of goods or services being sold or to the introduction of new products or services.

    iv. For the three most recent fiscal years of the registrant, or for those fiscal years in which the registrant has been engaged in business, whichever period is shortest, discuss the impact of inflation and changing prices on the registrant's net sales and revenues and on income from continuing operations.

4. *Off-balance sheet arrangements.*

    i. In a separately-captioned section, discuss the registrant's off-balance sheet arrangements that have or are reasonably likely to have a current or future effect on the registrant's financial condition, changes in financial condition, revenues or expenses, results of operations, liquidity, capital expenditures or capital resources that is material to investors. The disclosure shall include the items specified in paragraphs (a)(4)(i)(A), (B), (C) and (D) of this Item to the extent necessary to an understanding of such arrangements and effect and shall also include such other information that the registrant believes is necessary for such an understanding.

        A. The nature and business purpose to the registrant of such off-balance sheet arrangements;

        B. The importance to the registrant of such off-balance sheet arrangements in respect of its liquidity, capital resources, market risk support, credit risk support or other benefits;

        C. The amounts of revenues, expenses and cash flows of the registrant arising from such arrangements; the nature and amounts of any interests retained, securities issued and other indebtedness incurred by the registrant in connection with such arrangements; and the nature and amounts of any other obligations or liabilities (including contingent obligations or liabilities) of the registrant arising from such arrangements that are or are reasonably likely to become material and the triggering events or circumstances that could cause them to arise; and

D. Any known event, demand, commitment, trend or uncertainty that will result in or is reasonably likely to result in the termination, or material reduction in availability to the registrant, of its off-balance sheet arrangements that provide material benefits to it, and the course of action that the registrant has taken or proposes to take in response to any such circumstances.

ii. As used in this paragraph (a)(4), the term *off-balance sheet arrangement* means any transaction, agreement or other contractual arrangement to which an entity unconsolidated with the registrant is a party, under which the registrant has:

A. Any obligation under a guarantee contract that has any of the characteristics identified in paragraph 3 of FASB Interpretation No. 45, *Guarantor's Accounting and Disclosure Requirements for Guarantees, Including Indirect Guarantees of Indebtedness of Others* (November 2002) ("FIN 45"), as may be modified or supplemented, and that is not excluded from the initial recognition and measurement provisions of FIN 45 pursuant to paragraphs 6 or 7 of that Interpretation;

B. A retained or contingent interest in assets transferred to an unconsolidated entity or similar arrangement that serves as credit, liquidity or market risk support to such entity for such assets;

C. Any obligation, including a contingent obligation, under a contract that would be accounted for as a derivative instrument, except that it is both indexed to the registrant's own stock and classified in stockholders' equity in the registrant's statement of financial position, and therefore excluded from the scope of FASB Statement of Financial Accounting Standards No. 133, *Accounting for Derivative Instruments and Hedging Activities* (June 1998), pursuant to paragraph 11(a) of that Statement, as may be modified or supplemented; or

D. Any obligation, including a contingent obligation, arising out of a variable interest (as referenced in FASB Interpretation No. 46, *Consolidation of Variable Interest Entities* (January 2003), as may be modified or supplemented) in an unconsolidated entity that is held by, and material to, the registrant, where such entity provides financing, liquidity, market risk or credit risk support to, or engages in leasing, hedging or research and development services with, the registrant.

5. *Tabular disclosure of contractual obligations.*

i. In a tabular format, provide the information specified in this paragraph (a)(5) as of the latest fiscal year end balance sheet date with respect to the registrant's known contractual obligations specified in the table that follows this paragraph (a)(5)(i). The registrant shall provide amounts, aggregated by type of contractual obligation. The registrant may disaggregate the specified categories of contractual obligations using other categories suitable to its business, but the presentation must include all of the obligations of the registrant that fall within the specified categories. A presentation covering at least the periods specified shall be included. The tabular presentation may be accompanied by footnotes to describe provisions that create, increase or accelerate obligations, or other pertinent data to the extent necessary for an understanding of the timing and amount of the registrant's specified contractual obligations.

Contractual obligations	Payments due by period				
	Total	Less than 1 year	1-3 years	3-5 years	More than 5 years
[Long-Term Debt Obligations]					
[Capital Lease Obligations]					
[Operating Lease Obligations]					
[Purchase Obligations]					
[Other Long-Term Liabilities Reflected on the Registrant's Balance Sheet under GAAP]					
Total					

    ii. *Definitions:* The following definitions apply to this paragraph (a)(5):
      A. *Long-Term Debt Obligation* means a payment obligation under long-term borrowings referenced in FASB Statement of Financial Accounting Standards No. 47 *Disclosure of Long-Term Obligations* (March 1981), as may be modified or supplemented.
      B. *Capital Lease Obligation* means a payment obligation under a lease classified as a capital lease pursuant to FASB Statement of Financial Accounting Standards No. 13 *Accounting for Leases* (November 1976), as may be modified or supplemented.
      C. *Operating Lease Obligation* means a payment obligation under a lease classified as an operating lease and disclosed pursuant to FASB Statement of Financial Accounting Standards No. 13 *Accounting for Leases* (November 1976), as may be modified or supplemented.
      D. *Purchase Obligation* means an agreement to purchase goods or services that is enforceable and legally binding on the registrant that specifies all significant terms, including: fixed or minimum quantities to be purchased; fixed, minimum or variable price provisions; and the approximate timing of the transaction.

Instructions to Item 303(a):
1. The registrant's discussion and analysis shall be of the financial statements and of other statistical data that the registrant believes will enhance a reader's understanding of its financial condition, changes in financial condition and

results of operations. Generally, the discussion shall cover the three year period covered by the financial statements and shall use year-to-year comparisons or any other formats that in the registrant's judgment enhance a reader's understanding. However, where trend information is relevant, reference to the five year selected financial data appearing pursuant to Item 301 of Regulation S-K may be necessary.

2. The purpose of the discussion and analysis shall be to provide to investors and other users information relevant to an assessment of the financial condition and results of operations of the registrant as determined by evaluating the amounts and certainty of cash flows from operations and from outside sources.

3. The discussion and analysis shall focus specifically on material events and uncertainties known to management that would cause reported financial information not to be necessarily indicative of future operating results or of future financial condition. This would include descriptions and amounts of (A) matters that would have an impact on future operations and have not had an impact in the past, and (B) matters that have had an impact on reported operations and are not expected to have an impact upon future operations.

4. Where the consolidated financial statements reveal material changes from year to year in one or more line items, the causes for the changes shall be described to the extent necessary to an understanding of the registrant's businesses as a whole; *Provided, however,* That if the causes for a change in one line item also relate to other line items, no repetition is required and a line-by-line analysis of the financial statements as a whole is not required or generally appropriate. Registrants need not recite the amounts of changes from year to year which are readily computable from the financial statements. The discussion shall not merely repeat numerical data contained in the consolidated financial statements.

5. The term "liquidity" as used in this Item refers to the ability of an enterprise to generate adequate amounts of cash to meet the enterprise's needs for cash. Except where it is otherwise clear from the discussion, the registrant shall indicate those balance sheet conditions or income or cash flow items which the registrant believes may be indicators of its liquidity condition. Liquidity generally shall be discussed on both a long-term and short-term basis. The issue of liquidity shall be discussed in the context of the registrant's own business or businesses. For example a discussion of working capital may be appropriate for certain manufacturing, industrial or related operations but might be inappropriate for a bank or public utility.

6. Where financial statements presented or incorporated by reference in the registration statement are required by Rule 4-08(e)(3) of Regulation S-X to include disclosure of restrictions on the ability of both consolidated and unconsolidated subsidiaries to transfer funds to the registrant in the form of cash dividends, loans or advances, the discussion of liquidity shall include a discussion of the nature and extent of such restrictions and the impact such restrictions have had and are expected to have on the ability of the parent company to meet its cash obligations.

7. Any forward-looking information supplied is expressly covered by the safe harbor rule for projections. See Rule 175 under the Securities Act , Rule 3b-6 under the Exchange Act and Securities Act Release No. 6084 (June 25, 1979) .

8. Registrants are only required to discuss the effects of inflation and other changes in prices when considered material. This discussion may be made in whatever manner appears appropriate under the circumstances. All that is required is a brief textual presentation of management's views. No specific numerical financial data need be presented except as Rule 3-20(c) of Regulation S-X otherwise requires. However, registrants may elect to voluntarily disclose supplemental information on the effects of changing prices as provided for in Statement of Financial Accounting Standards No. 89, "Financial Reporting and Changing Prices" or through other supplemental disclosures. The Commission encourages experimentation with these disclosures in order to provide the most meaningful presentation of the impact of price changes on the registrant's financial statements.

9. Registrants that elect to disclose supplementary information on the effects of changing prices as specified by SFAS No. 89, "Financial Reporting and Changing Prices," may combine such explanations with the discussion and analysis required pursuant to this Item or may supply such information separately with appropriate cross reference.

10. All references to the registrant in the discussion and in this Item shall mean the registrant and its subsidiaries consolidated.

11. Foreign private registrants also shall discuss briefly any pertinent governmental economic, fiscal, monetary, or political policies or factors that have materially affected or could materially affect, directly or indirectly, their operations or investments by United States nationals.

12. If the registrant is a foreign private issuer, the discussion shall focus on the primary financial statements presented in the registration statement or report. There shall be a reference to the reconciliation to United States generally accepted accounting principles, and a discussion of any aspects of the difference between foreign and United States generally accepted accounting principles, not discussed in the reconciliation, that the registrant believes is necessary for an understanding of the financial statements as a whole.

Instructions to Paragraph 303(a)(4):

1. No obligation to make disclosure under paragraph (a)(4) of this Item shall arise in respect of an off-balance sheet arrangement until a definitive agreement that is unconditionally binding or subject only to customary closing conditions exists or, if there is no such agreement, when settlement of the transaction occurs.

2. Registrants should aggregate off-balance sheet arrangements in groups or categories that provide material information in an efficient and understandable manner and should avoid repetition and disclosure of immaterial information. Effects that are common or similar with respect to a number of off-balance sheet arrangements must be analyzed in the aggregate to the extent the aggregation increases understanding. Distinctions in arrangements and their effects must be discussed to the extent the information is material, but the discussion should avoid repetition and disclosure of immaterial information.

3. For purposes of paragraph (a)(4) of this Item only, contingent liabilities arising out of litigation, arbitration or regulatory actions are not considered to be off-balance sheet arrangements.

4.   Generally, the disclosure required by paragraph (a)(4) shall cover the most recent fiscal year. However, the discussion should address changes from the previous year where such discussion is necessary to an understanding of the disclosure.

5.   In satisfying the requirements of paragraph (a)(4) of this Item, the discussion of off-balance sheet arrangements need not repeat information provided in the footnotes to the financial statements, provided that such discussion clearly cross-references to specific information in the relevant footnotes and integrates the substance of the footnotes into such discussion in a manner designed to inform readers of the significance of the information that is not included within the body of such discussion.

b.   **Interim periods.** If interim period financial statements are included or are required to be included by Article 3 of Regulation S-X, a management's discussion and analysis of the financial condition and results of operations shall be provided so as to enable the reader to assess material changes in financial condition and results of operations between the periods specified in paragraphs (b) (1) and (2) of this Item. The discussion and analysis shall include a discussion of material changes in those items specifically listed in paragraph (a) of this Item, except that the impact of inflation and changing prices on operations for interim periods need not be addressed.

1.   *Material changes in financial condition.* Discuss any material changes in financial condition from the end of the preceding fiscal year to the date of the most recent interim balance sheet provided. If the interim financial statements include an interim balance sheet as of the corresponding interim date of the preceding fiscal year, any material changes in financial condition from that date to the date of the most recent interim balance sheet provided also shall be discussed. If discussions of changes from both the end and the corresponding interim date of the preceding fiscal year are required, the discussions may be combined at the discretion of the registrant.

2.   *Material changes in results of operations.* Discuss any material changes in the registrant's results of operations with respect to the most recent fiscal year-to-date period for which an income statement is provided and the corresponding year-to-date period of the preceding fiscal year. If the registrant is required to or has elected to provide an income statement for the most recent fiscal quarter, such discussion also shall cover material changes with respect to that fiscal quarter and the corresponding fiscal quarter in the preceding fiscal year. In addition, if the registrant has elected to provide an income statement for the twelve-month period ended as of the date of the most recent interim balance sheet provided, the discussion also shall cover material changes with respect to that twelve-month period and the twelve-month period ended as of the corresponding interim balance sheet date of the preceding fiscal year. Notwithstanding the above, if for purposes of a registration statement a registrant subject to paragraph (b) of Rule 3-03 of Regulation S-X provides a statement of income for the twelve-month period ended as of the date of the most recent interim balance sheet provided in lieu of the interim income statements otherwise required, the discussion of material changes in that twelve-month period will be in respect to the preceding fiscal year rather than the corresponding preceding period.

Instructions to Paragraph 303(b):

1. If interim financial statements are presented together with financial statements for full fiscal years, the discussion of the interim financial information shall be prepared pursuant to this paragraph (b) and the discussion of the full fiscal year's information shall be prepared pursuant to paragraph (a) of this Item. Such discussions may be combined.

2. In preparing the discussion and analysis required by this paragraph (b), the registrant may presume that users of the interim financial information have read or have access to the discussion and analysis required by paragraph (a) for the preceding fiscal year.

3. The discussion and analysis required by this paragraph (b) is required to focus only on material changes. Where the interim financial statements reveal material changes from period to period in one or more significant line items, the causes for the changes shall be described if they have not already been disclosed: *Provided, however,* That if the causes for a change in one line item also relate to other line items, no repetition is required. Registrants need not recite the amounts of changes from period to period which are readily computable from the financial statements. The discussion shall not merely repeat numerical data contained in the financial statements. The information provided shall include that which is available to the registrant without undue effort or expense and which does not clearly appear in the registrant's condensed interim financial statements.

4. The registrant's discussion of material changes in results of operations shall identify any significant elements of the registrant's income or loss from continuing operations which do not arise from or are not necessarily representative of the registrant's ongoing business.

5. The registrant shall discuss any seasonal aspects of its business which have had a material effect upon its financial condition or results of operation.

6. Any forward-looking information supplied is expressly covered by the safe harbor rule for projections. See Rule 175 under the Securities Act, Rule 3b-6 under the Exchange Act and Securities Act Release No. 6084 (June 25, 1979).

7. The registrant is not required to include the table required by paragraph (a)(5) of this Item for interim periods. Instead, the registrant should disclose material changes outside the ordinary course of the registrant's business in the specified contractual obligations during the interim period.

c. **Safe harbor**.

1. The safe harbor provided in section 27A of the Securities Act of 1933 and section 21E of the Securities Exchange Act of 1934 ("statutory safe harbors") shall apply to forward-looking information provided pursuant to paragraphs (a)(4) and (5) of this Item, provided that the disclosure is made by: an issuer; a person acting on behalf of the issuer; an outside reviewer retained by the issuer making a statement on behalf of the issuer; or an underwriter, with respect to information provided by the issuer or information derived from information provided by the issuer.

2. For purposes of paragraph (c) of this Item only:

     i. All information required by paragraphs (a)(4) and (5) of this Item is deemed to be a *forward looking statement* as that term is defined in the statutory safe harbors, except for historical facts.

covering the fiscal period(s) subsequent to the date of the most recent financial statements covered by an audit report (including information that, unless resolved to the accountant's satisfaction, would prevent it from rendering an unqualified audit report on those financial statements), and

2.   Due to the accountant's resignation, dismissal or declination to stand for re-election, or for any other reason, the issue has not been resolved to the accountant's satisfaction prior to its resignation, dismissal or declination to stand for re-election.

2.   If during the registrant's two most recent fiscal years or any subsequent interim period, a new independent accountant has been engaged as either the principal accountant to audit the registrant's financial statements, or as an independent accountant to audit a significant subsidiary and on whom the principal accountant is expected to express reliance in its report, then the registrant shall identify the newly engaged accountant and indicate the date of such accountant's engagement. In addition, if during the registrant's two most recent fiscal years, and any subsequent interim period prior to engaging that accountant, the registrant (or someone on its behalf) consulted the newly engaged accountant regarding:

i.   Either: the application of accounting principles to a specified transaction, either completed or proposed; or the type of audit opinion that might be rendered on the registrant's financial statements, and either a written report was provided to the registrant or oral advice was provided that the new accountant concluded was an important factor considered by the registrant in reaching a decision as to the accounting, auditing or financial reporting issue; or

ii.   Any matter that was either the subject of a disagreement (as defined in paragraph (a)(1)(iv) and the related instructions to this item) or a reportable event (as described in paragraph (a)(1)(v)), then the registrant shall

A.   So state and identify the issues that were the subjects of those consultations;

B.   Briefly describe the views of the newly engaged accountant as expressed orally or in writing to the registrant on each such issue and, if written views were received by the registrant, file them as an exhibit to the report or registration statement requiring compliance with this Item 304(a);

C.   State whether the former accountant was consulted by the registrant regarding any such issues, and if so, provide a summary of the former accountant's views; and

D.   Request the newly engaged accountant to review the disclosure required by this Item 304(a) before it is filed with the Commission and provide the new accountant the opportunity to furnish the registrant with a letter addressed to the Commission containing any new information, clarification of the registrant's expression of its views, or the respects in which it does not agree with the statements made by the registrant in response to Item 304(a). The registrant shall file any such letter as an exhibit to the report or registration statement containing the disclosure required by this Item.

3.　The registrant shall provide the former accountant with a copy of the disclosures it is making in response to this Item 304(a) that the former accountant shall receive no later than the day that the disclosures are filed with the Commission. The registrant shall request the former accountant to furnish the registrant with a letter addressed to the Commission stating whether it agrees with the statements made by the registrant in response to this Item 304(a) and, if not, stating the respects in which it does not agree. The registrant shall file the former accountant's letter as an exhibit to the report on registration statement containing this disclosure. If the former accountant's letter is unavailable at the time of filing such report or registration statement, then the registrant shall request the former accountant to provide the letter as promptly as possible so that the registrant can file the letter with the Commission within ten business days after the filing of the report or registration statement. Notwithstanding the ten business day period, the registrant shall file the letter by amendment within two business days of receipt; if the letter is received on a Saturday, Sunday or holiday on which the Commission is not open for business, then the two business day period shall begin to run on and shall include the first business day thereafter. The former accountant may provide the registrant with an interim letter highlighting specific areas of concern and indicating that a more detailed letter will be forthcoming within the ten business day period noted above. If not filed with the report or registration statement containing the registrant's disclosure under this Item 304(a), then the interim letter, if any, shall be filed by the registrant by amendment within two business days of receipt.

b.　If:

1.　In connection with a change in accountants subject to paragraph (a) of this Item 304, there was any disagreement of the type described in paragraph (a)(1)(iv) or any reportable event as described in paragraph (a)(1)(v) of this Item;

2.　During the fiscal year in which the change in accountants took place or during the subsequent fiscal year, there have been any transactions or events similar to those which involved such disagreement or reportable event; and

3.　Such transactions or events were material and were accounted for or disclosed in a manner different from that which the former accountants apparently would have concluded was required, the registrant shall state the existence and nature of the disagreement or reportable event and also state the effect on the financial statements if the method had been followed which the former accountants apparently would have concluded was required.

These disclosures need not be made if the method asserted by the former accountants ceases to be generally accepted because of authoritative standards or interpretations subsequently issued.

Instructions to Item 304:

1.　The disclosure called for by paragraph (a) of this Item need not be provided if it has been previously reported as that term is defined in Rule 12b-2 under the Exchange Act; the disclosure called for by paragraph (a) must be *provided, however*, notwithstanding prior disclosure, if required pursuant to Item 9 of Schedule 14A. The disclosure called for by paragraph (b) of this section must be furnished, where required, notwithstanding any prior disclosure about accountant changes or disagreements.

2. When disclosure is required by paragraph (a) of this section in an annual report to security holders pursuant to Rule 14a-3 or Rule 14c-3, or in a proxy or information statement filed pursuant to the requirements of Schedule 14A or 14C , in lieu of a letter pursuant to paragraph (a)(2)(D) or (a)(3), prior to filing such materials with or furnishing such materials to the Commission, the registrant shall furnish the disclosure required by paragraph (a) of this section to any former accountant engaged by the registrant during the period set forth in paragraph (a) of this section and to the newly engaged accountant. If any such accountant believes that the statements made in response to paragraph (a) of this section are incorrect or incomplete, it may present its views in a brief statement, ordinarily expected not to exceed 200 words, to be included in the annual report or proxy or information statement. This statement shall be submitted to the registrant within ten business days of the date the accountant receives the registrant's disclosure. Further, unless the written views of the newly engaged accountant required to be filed as an exhibit by paragraph (a)(2)(B) of this Item 304 have been previously filed with the Commission the registrant shall file a Form 8-K concurrently with the annual report or proxy or information statement for the purpose of filing the written views as exhibits thereto.

3. The information required by Item 304(a) need not be provided for a company being acquired by the registrant that is not subject to the filing requirements of either section 13(a) or 15(d) of the Exchange Act, or, because of section 12(i) of the Exchange Act, has not furnished an annual report to security holders pursuant to Rule 14a-3 or Rule 14c-3 for its latest fiscal year.

4. The term "disagreements" as used in this Item shall be interpreted broadly, to include any difference of opinion concerning any matter of accounting principles or practices, financial statement disclosure, or auditing scope or procedure which (if not resolved to the satisfaction of the former accountant) would have caused it to make reference to the subject matter of the disagreement in connection with its report. It is not necessary for there to have been an argument to have had a disagreement, merely a difference of opinion. For purposes of this Item, however, the term disagreements does not include initial differences of opinion based on incomplete facts or preliminary information that were later resolved to the former accountant's satisfaction by, and providing the registrant and the accountant do not continue to have a difference of opinion upon, obtaining additional relevant facts or information.

5. In determining whether any disagreement or reportable event has occurred, an oral communication from the engagement partner or another person responsible for rendering the accounting firm's opinion (or their designee) will generally suffice as the accountant advising the registrant of a reportable event or as a statement of a disagreement at the "decision-making level" within the accounting firm and require disclosure under this Item.

Item 305 – Quantitative and Qualitative Disclosures about Market Risk

a. **Quantitative information about market risk.**
    1. Registrants shall provide, in their reporting currency, quantitative information about market risk as of the end of the latest fiscal year, in accordance with one of the following three disclosure alternatives. In preparing this quantitative information, registrants shall categorize market risk sensitive instruments into instruments entered into for trading purposes and instruments entered into for

purposes other than trading purposes. Within both the trading and other than trading portfolios, separate quantitative information shall be presented, to the extent material, for each market risk exposure category (i.e., interest rate risk, foreign currency exchange rate risk, commodity price risk, and other relevant market risks, such as equity price risk). A registrant may use one of the three alternatives set forth in this section for all of the required quantitative disclosures about market risk. A registrant also may choose, from among the three alternatives, one disclosure alternative for market risk sensitive instruments entered into for trading purposes and another disclosure alternative for market risk sensitive instruments entered into for other than trading purposes. Alternatively, a registrant may choose any disclosure alternative, from among the three alternatives, for each risk exposure category within the trading and other than trading portfolios. The three disclosure alternatives are:

i. A.

1. Tabular presentation of information related to market risk sensitive instruments; such information shall include fair values of the market risk sensitive instruments and contract terms sufficient to determine future cash flows from those instruments, categorized by expected maturity dates.

2. Tabular information relating to contract terms shall allow readers of the table to determine expected cash flows from the market risk sensitive instruments for each of the next five years. Comparable tabular information for any remaining years shall be displayed as an aggregate amount.

3. Within each risk exposure category, the market risk sensitive instruments shall be grouped based on common characteristics. Within the foreign currency exchange rate risk category, the market risk sensitive instruments shall be grouped by functional currency and within the commodity price risk category, the market risk sensitive instruments shall be grouped by type of commodity.

4. See the Appendix to this Item for a suggested format for presentation of this information; and

B. Registrants shall provide a description of the contents of the table and any related assumptions necessary to understand the disclosures required under paragraph (a)(1)(i)(A) of this Item 305; or

ii.

A. Sensitivity analysis disclosures that express the potential loss in future earnings, fair values, or cash flows of market risk sensitive instruments resulting from one or more selected hypothetical changes in interest rates, foreign currency exchange rates, commodity prices, and other relevant market rates or prices over a selected period of time. The magnitude of selected hypothetical changes in rates or prices may differ among and within market risk exposure categories; and

B. Registrants shall provide a description of the model, assumptions, and parameters, which are necessary to understand the disclosures required under paragraph (a)(1)(ii)(A) of this Item 305; or iii.

    A.   Value at risk disclosures that express the potential loss in future earnings, fair values, or cash flows of market risk sensitive instruments over a selected period of time, with a selected likelihood of occurrence, from changes in interest rates, foreign currency exchange rates, commodity prices, and other relevant market rates or prices;

    B.

        1.   For each category for which value at risk disclosures are required under paragraph (a)(1)(iii)(A) of this Item 305, provide either:

            i.   The average, high and low amounts, or the distribution of the value at risk amounts for the reporting period; or

            ii.   The average, high and low amounts, or the distribution of actual changes in fair values, earnings, or cash flows from the market risk sensitive instruments occurring during the reporting period; or

            iii.   The percentage or number of times the actual changes in fair values, earnings, or cash flows from the market risk sensitive instruments exceeded the value at risk amounts during the reporting period;

        2.   Information required under paragraph (a)(1)(iii)(B)(1) of this Item 305 is not required for the first fiscal year end in which a registrant must present Item 305 information; and

    C.   Registrants shall provide a description of the model, assumptions, and parameters, which are necessary to understand the disclosures required under paragraphs (a)(1)(iii)(A) and (B) of this Item 305.

2.   Registrants shall discuss material limitations that cause the information required under paragraph (a)(1) of this Item 305 not to reflect fully the net market risk exposures of the entity. This discussion shall include summarized descriptions of instruments, positions, and transactions omitted from the quantitative market risk disclosure information or the features of instruments, positions, and transactions that are included, but not reflected fully in the quantitative market risk disclosure information.

3.   Registrants shall present summarized market risk information for the preceding fiscal year. In addition, registrants shall discuss the reasons for material quantitative changes in market risk exposures between the current and preceding fiscal years. Information required by this paragraph (a)(3), however, is not required if disclosure is not required under paragraph (a)(1) of this Item 305 for the current fiscal year. Information required by this paragraph (a)(3) is not required for the first fiscal year end in which a registrant must present Item 305 information.

4.   If registrants change disclosure alternatives or key model characteristics, assumptions, and parameters used in providing quantitative information about market risk (e.g., changing from tabular presentation to value at risk, changing the scope of instruments included in the model, or changing the definition of

loss from fair values to earnings), and if the effects of any such change is material, the registrant shall:

    i.   Explain the reasons for the change; and

    ii.   Either provide summarized comparable information, under the new disclosure method, for the year preceding the current year or, in addition to providing disclosure for the current year under the new method, provide disclosures for the current year and preceding fiscal year under the method used in the preceding year.

Instructions to Paragraph 305(a):

1. Under paragraph 305(a)(1):

    A.   For each market risk exposure category within the trading and other than trading portfolios, registrants may report the average, high, and low sensitivity analysis or value at risk amounts for the reporting period, as an alternative to reporting year-end amounts.

    B.   In determining the average, high, and low amounts for the fiscal year under instruction 1.A. of the Instructions to Paragraph 305(a), registrants should use sensitivity analysis or value at risk amounts relating to at least four equal time periods throughout the reporting period (e.g., four quarter-end amounts, 12 month-end amounts, or 52 week-end amounts).

    C.   Functional currency means functional currency as defined by generally accepted accounting principles (see, e.g., FASB, Statement of Financial Accounting Standards No. 52, "Foreign Currency Translation", ("FAS 52") paragraph 20 (December 1981)).

    D.   Registrants using the sensitivity analysis and value at risk disclosure alternatives are encouraged, but not required, to provide quantitative amounts that reflect the aggregate market risk inherent in the trading and other than trading portfolios.

2. Under paragraph 305(a)(1)(i):

    A.   Examples of contract terms sufficient to determine future cash flows from market risk sensitive instruments include, but are not limited to:

        i.   Debt instruments–principal amounts and weighted average effective interest rates;

        ii.   Forwards and futures–contract amounts and weighted average settlement prices;

        iii.   Options–contract amounts and weighted average strike prices;

        iv.   Swaps–notional amounts, weighted average pay rates or prices, and weighted average receive rates or prices; and

        v.   Complex instruments–likely to be a combination of the contract terms presented in 2.A.i. through iv. of this Instruction;

    B.   When grouping based on common characteristics, instruments should be categorized, at a minimum, by the following characteristics, when material:

        i.   Fixed rate or variable rate assets or liabilities;

        ii.   Long or short forwards and futures;

        iii.   Written or purchased put or call options with similar strike prices;

        iv.   Receive fixed and pay variable swaps, receive variable and pay fixed swaps, and receive variable and pay variable swaps;

        v.   The currency in which the instruments' cash flows are denominated;

      vi.   Financial instruments for which foreign currency transaction gains and losses are reported in the same manner as translation adjustments under generally accepted accounting principles (see, e.g., FAS 52 paragraph 20 (December 1981)); and

      vii.   Derivatives used to manage risks inherent in anticipated transactions;

C. Registrants may aggregate information regarding functional currencies that are economically related, managed together for internal risk management purposes, and have statistical correlations of greater than 75% over each of the past three years;

D. Market risk sensitive instruments that are exposed to rate or price changes in more than one market risk exposure category should be presented within the tabular information for each of the risk exposure categories to which those instruments are exposed;

E. If a currency swap (see, e.g., FAS 52 Appendix E for a definition of currency swap) eliminates all foreign currency exposures in the cash flows of a foreign currency denominated debt instrument, neither the currency swap nor the foreign currency denominated debt instrument are required to be disclosed in the foreign currency risk exposure category. However, both the currency swap and the foreign currency denominated debt instrument should be disclosed in the interest rate risk exposure category; and

F. The contents of the table and related assumptions that should be described include, but are not limited to:

      i.   The different amounts reported in the table for various categories of the market risk sensitive instruments (e.g., principal amounts for debt, notional amounts for swaps, and contract amounts for options and futures);

      ii.   The different types of reported market rates or prices (e.g., contractual rates or prices, spot rates or prices, forward rates or prices); and

      iii. Key prepayment or reinvestment assumptions relating to the timing of reported amounts.

3. Under paragraph 305(a)(1)(ii):

A. Registrants should select hypothetical changes in market rates or prices that are expected to reflect reasonably possible near-term changes in those rates and prices. In this regard, absent economic justification for the selection of a different amount, registrants should use changes that are not less than 10 percent of end of period market rates or prices;

B. For purposes of instruction 3.A. of the Instructions to Paragraph 305(a), the term reasonably possible has the same meaning as defined by generally accepted accounting principles (see, e.g., FASB, Statement of Financial Accounting Standards No. 5, "Accounting for Contingencies," ("FAS 5") paragraph 3 (March 1975));

C. For purposes of instruction 3.A. of the Instructions to Paragraph 305(a), the term near term means a period of time going forward up to one year from the date of the financial statements (see generally AICPA, Statement of Position 94-6, "Disclosure of Certain Significant Risks and Uncertainties," ("SOP 94-6") at paragraph 7 (December 30, 1994));

D. Market risk sensitive instruments that are exposed to rate or price changes in more than one market risk exposure category should be included in the sensitivity analysis disclosures for each market risk category to which those instruments are exposed;

E. Registrants with multiple foreign currency exchange rate exposures should prepare foreign currency sensitivity analysis disclosures that measure the aggregate sensitivity to changes in all foreign currency exchange rate exposures, including the effects of changes in both transactional currency/functional currency exchange rate exposures and functional currency/reporting currency exchange rate exposures. For example, assume a French division of a registrant presenting its financial statements in U.S. dollars ($US) invests in a deutschmark(DM)-denominated debt security. In these circumstances, the $US is the reporting currency and the DM is the transactional currency. In addition, assume this division determines that the French franc (FF) is its functional currency according to FAS 52. In preparing the foreign currency sensitivity analysis disclosures, this registrant should report the aggregate potential loss from hypothetical changes in both the DM/FF exchange rate exposure and the FF/$US exchange rate exposure; and

F. Model, assumptions, and parameters that should be described include, but are not limited to, how loss is defined by the model (e.g., loss in earnings, fair values, or cash flows), a general description of the modeling technique (e.g., duration modeling, modeling that measures the change in net present values arising from selected hypothetical changes in market rates or prices, and a description as to how optionality is addressed by the model), the types of instruments covered by the model (e.g., derivative financial instruments, other financial instruments, derivative commodity instruments, and whether other instruments are included voluntarily, such as certain commodity instruments and positions, cash flows from anticipated transactions, and certain financial instruments excluded under instruction 3.C.ii. of the General Instructions to Paragraphs 305(a) and 305(b)), and other relevant information about the model's assumptions and parameters, (e.g., the magnitude and timing of selected hypothetical changes in market rates or prices used, the method by which discount rates are determined, and key prepayment or reinvestment assumptions).

4. Under paragraph 305(a)(1)(iii):

A. The confidence intervals selected should reflect reasonably possible near-term changes in market rates and prices. In this regard, absent economic justification for the selection of different confidence intervals, registrants should use intervals that are 95 percent or higher;

B. For purposes of instruction 4.A. of the Instructions to Paragraph 305(a), the term reasonably possible has the same meaning as defined by generally accepted accounting principles (see, e.g., FAS 5, paragraph 3 (March 1975));

C. For purposes of instruction 4.A. of the Instructions to Paragraphs 305(a), the term near term means a period of time going forward up to one year from the date of the financial statements (see generally SOP 94-6, at paragraph 7 (December 30, 1994));

D. Registrants with multiple foreign currency exchange rate exposures should prepare foreign currency value at risk analysis disclosures that measure the aggregate sensitivity to changes in all foreign currency exchange rate exposures, including the aggregate effects of changes in both transactional currency/functional currency exchange rate exposures and functional currency/reporting currency exchange rate exposures. For example, assume a French division of a registrant presenting its financial statements in U.S. dollars ($US) invests in a deutschmark (DM)-denominated debt security. In these circumstances, the $US is the reporting currency and the DM is the transactional currency. In addition, assume this division determines that the French franc (FF) is its functional currency according to FAS 52. In preparing the foreign currency value at risk disclosures, this registrant should report the aggregate potential loss from hypothetical changes in both the DM/FF exchange rate exposure and the FF/$US exchange rate exposure; and

E. Model, assumptions, and parameters that should be described include, but are not limited to, how loss is defined by the model (e.g., loss in earnings, fair values, or cash flows), the type of model used (e.g., variance/covariance, historical simulation, or Monte Carlo simulation and a description as to how optionality is addressed by the model), the types of instruments covered by the model (e.g., derivative financial instruments, other financial instruments, derivative commodity instruments, and whether other instruments are included voluntarily, such as certain commodity instruments and positions, cash flows from anticipated transactions, and certain financial instruments excluded under instruction 3.C.ii. of the General Instructions to Paragraphs 305(a) and 305(b)), and other relevant information about the model's assumptions and parameters, (e.g., holding periods, confidence intervals, and, when appropriate, the methods used for aggregating value at risk amounts across market risk exposure categories, such as by assuming perfect positive correlation, independence, or actual observed correlation).

5. Under paragraph 305(a)(2), limitations that should be considered include, but are not limited to:

A. The exclusion of certain market risk sensitive instruments, positions, and transactions from the disclosures required under paragraph 305(a)(1) (e.g., derivative commodity instruments not permitted by contract or business custom to be settled in cash or with another financial instrument, commodity positions, cash flows from anticipated transactions, and certain financial instruments excluded under instruction 3.C.ii. of the General Instructions to Paragraphs 305(a) and 305(b)). Failure to include such instruments, positions, and transactions in preparing the disclosures under paragraph 305(a)(1) may be a limitation because the resulting disclosures may not fully reflect the net market risk of a registrant; and

B. The ability of disclosures required under paragraph 305(a)(1) to reflect fully the market risk that may be inherent in instruments with leverage, option, or prepayment features (e.g., options, including written options, structured notes, collateralized mortgage obligations, leveraged swaps, and options embedded in swaps).

b. **Qualitative information about market risk.**
1. To the extent material, describe:
    i. The registrant's primary market risk exposures;
    ii. How those exposures are managed. Such descriptions shall include, but not be limited to, a discussion of the objectives, general strategies, and instruments, if any, used to manage those exposures; and
    iii. Changes in either the registrant's primary market risk exposures or how those exposures are managed, when compared to what was in effect during the most recently completed fiscal year and what is known or expected to be in effect in future reporting periods.
2. Qualitative information about market risk shall be presented separately for market risk sensitive instruments entered into for trading purposes and those entered into for purposes other than trading.

Instructions to Paragraph 305(b):
1. For purposes of disclosure under paragraph 305(b), primary market risk exposures means:
    A. The following categories of market risk: interest rate risk, foreign currency exchange rate risk, commodity price risk, and other relevant market rate or price risks (e.g., equity price risk); and
    B. Within each of these categories, the particular markets that present the primary risk of loss to the registrant. For example, if a registrant has a material exposure to foreign currency exchange rate risk and, within this category of market risk, is most vulnerable to changes in dollar/yen, dollar/pound, and dollar/peso exchange rates, the registrant should disclose those exposures. Similarly, if a registrant has a material exposure to interest rate risk and, within this category of market risk, is most vulnerable to changes in short-term U.S. prime interest rates, it should disclose the existence of that exposure.
2. For purposes of disclosure under paragraph 305(b), registrants should describe primary market risk exposures that exist as of the end of the latest fiscal year, and how those exposures are managed.

Instructions to Paragraphs 305(a) and 305(b):
1. The disclosures called for by paragraphs 305(a) and 305(b) are intended to clarify the registrant's exposures to market risk associated with activities in derivative financial instruments, other financial instruments, and derivative commodity instruments.
2. In preparing the disclosures under paragraphs 305(a) and 305(b), registrants are required to include derivative financial instruments, other financial instruments, and derivative commodity instruments.
3. For purposes of paragraphs 305(a) and 305(b), derivative financial instruments, other financial instruments, and derivative commodity instruments (collectively referred to as "market risk sensitive instruments") are defined as follows:
    A. Derivative financial instruments has the same meaning as defined by generally accepted accounting principles (see, e.g., FASB, Statement of Financial Accounting Standards No. 119, "Disclosure about Derivative Financial Instruments and Fair Value of Financial Instruments," ("FAS 119") paragraphs 5- 7 (October 1994)), and includes futures, forwards, swaps, options, and other financial instruments with similar characteristics;

B. Other financial instruments means all financial instruments as defined by generally accepted accounting principles for which fair value disclosures are required (see, e.g., FASB, Statement of Financial Accounting Standards No. 107, "Disclosures about Fair Value of Financial Instruments," ("FAS 107") paragraphs 3 and 8 (December 1991)), except for derivative financial instruments, as defined above;

C.

     i. Other financial instruments include, but are not limited to, trade accounts receivable, investments, loans, structured notes, mortgage-backed securities, trade accounts payable, indexed debt instruments, interest-only and principal-only obligations, deposits, and other debt obligations;

     ii. Other financial instruments exclude employers' and plans' obligations for pension and other post-retirement benefits, substantively extinguished debt, insurance contracts, lease contracts, warranty obligations and rights, unconditional purchase obligations, investments accounted for under the equity method, noncontrolling interests in consolidated enterprises, and equity instruments issued by the registrant and classified in stockholders' equity in the statement of financial position (see, e.g., FAS 107, paragraph 8 (December 1991)). For purposes of this item, trade accounts receivable and trade accounts payable need not be considered other financial instruments when their carrying amounts approximate fair value; and

D. Derivative commodity instruments include, to the extent such instruments are not derivative financial instruments, commodity futures, commodity forwards, commodity swaps, commodity options, and other commodity instruments with similar characteristics that are permitted by contract or business custom to be settled in cash or with another financial instrument. For purposes of this paragraph, settlement in cash includes settlement in cash of the net change in value of the derivative commodity instrument (e.g., net cash settlement based on changes in the price of the underlying commodity).

4.

A. In addition to providing required disclosures for the market risk sensitive instruments defined in instruction 2. of the General Instructions to Paragraphs 305(a) and 305(b), registrants are encouraged to include other market risk sensitive instruments, positions, and transactions within the disclosures required under paragraphs 305(a) and 305(b). Such instruments, positions, and transactions might include commodity positions, derivative commodity instruments that are not permitted by contract or business custom to be settled in cash or with another financial instrument, cash flows from anticipated transactions, and certain financial instruments excluded under instruction 3.C.ii. of the General Instructions to Paragraphs 305(a) and 305(b).

B. Registrants that voluntarily include other market risk sensitive instruments, positions and transactions within their quantitative disclosures about market risk under the sensitivity analysis or value at risk disclosure alternatives are not required to provide separate market risk disclosures for any voluntarily selected instruments, positions, or transactions. Instead, registrants selecting the sensitivity analysis and value at risk disclosure alternatives are permitted to present comprehensive market risk disclosures, which reflect the combined market risk exposures inherent in both the required and any voluntarily selected instruments, position, or transactions. Registrants that choose the tabular presentation disclosure alternative should present voluntarily selected instruments, positions, or transactions in a manner consistent with the requirements in Item 305(a) for market risk sensitive instruments.

C. If a registrant elects to include voluntarily a particular type of instrument, position, or transaction in their quantitative disclosures about market risk, that registrant should include all, rather than some, of those instruments, positions, or transactions within those disclosures. For example, if a registrant holds in inventory a particular type of commodity position and elects to include that commodity position within their market risk disclosures, the registrant should include the entire commodity position, rather than only a portion thereof, in their quantitative disclosures about market risk.

5.

A. Under paragraphs 305(a) and 305(b), a materiality assessment should be made for each market risk exposure category within the trading and other than trading portfolios.

B. For purposes of making the materiality assessment under instruction 5.A. of the General Instructions to Paragraphs 305(a) and 305(b), registrants should evaluate both:

    i. The materiality of the fair values of derivative financial instruments, other financial instruments, and derivative commodity instruments outstanding as of the end of the latest fiscal year; and

    ii. The materiality of potential, near-term losses in future earnings, fair values, and/or cash flows from reasonably possible near-term changes in market rates or prices.

    iii. If either paragraphs B.i. or B.ii. in this instruction of the General Instructions to Paragraphs 305(a) and 305(b) are material, the registrant should disclose quantitative and qualitative information about market risk, if such market risk for the particular market risk exposure category is material.

C. For purposes of instruction 5.B.i. of the General Instructions to Paragraphs 305(a) and 305(b), registrants generally should not net fair values, except to the extent allowed under generally accepted accounting principles (see, e.g., FASB Interpretation No. 39, "Offsetting of Amounts Related to Certain Contracts" (March 1992)). For example, under this instruction, the fair value of assets generally should not be netted with the fair value of liabilities.

D. For purposes of instruction 5.B.ii. of the General Instructions to Paragraphs 305(a) and 305(b), registrants should consider, among other things, the magnitude of:

    i. Past market movements;

    ii. Reasonably possible, near-term market movements; and

       iii.   Potential losses that may arise from leverage, option, and multiplier features.

    E.   For purposes of instructions 5.B.ii and 5.D.ii of the General Instructions to Paragraphs 305(a) and 305(b), the term near term means a period of time going forward up to one year from the date of the financial statements (see generally SOP 94-6, at paragraph 7 (December 30, 1994)).

    F.   For the purpose of instructions 5.B.ii. and 5.D.ii. of the General Instructions to Paragraphs 305(a) and 305(b), the term reasonably possible has the same meaning as defined by generally accepted accounting principles (see, e.g., FAS 5, paragraph 3 (March 1975)).

6.   For purposes of paragraphs 305(a) and 305(b), registrants should present the information outside of, and not incorporate the information into, the financial statements (including the footnotes to the financial statements). In addition, registrants are encouraged to provide the required information in one location. However, alternative presentation, such as inclusion of all or part of the information in Management's Discussion and Analysis, may be used at the discretion of the registrant. If information is disclosed in more than one location, registrants should provide cross-references to the locations of the related disclosures.

7.   For purposes of the instructions to paragraphs 305(a) and 305(b), trading purposes has the same meaning as defined by generally accepted accounting principles (see, e.g., FAS 119, paragraph 9a (October 1994)). In addition, anticipated transactions means transactions (other than transactions involving existing assets or liabilities or transactions necessitated by existing firm commitments) an enterprise expects, but is not obligated, to carry out in the normal course of business (see, e.g., FASB, Statement of Financial Accounting Standards No. 80, "Accounting for Futures Contracts," para 9, (Aug. 1984)).

c.   **Interim periods.** If interim period financial statements are included or are required to be included by Article 3 of Regulation S-X, discussion and analysis shall be provided so as to enable the reader to assess the sources and effects of material changes in information that would be provided under Item 305 of Regulation S-K from the end of the preceding fiscal year to the date of the most recent interim balance sheet.

Instructions to Paragraph 305(c):

1.   Information required under paragraph (c) of this Item 305 is not required until after the first fiscal year end in which this Item 305 is applicable.

d.   **Safe Harbor.**

1.   The safe harbor provided in Section 27A of the Securities Act of 1933 and Section 21E of the Securities Exchange Act of 1934 ("statutory safe harbors") shall apply, with respect to all types of issuers and transactions, to information provided pursuant to paragraphs (a), (b), and (c) of this Item 305, provided that the disclosure is made by: an issuer; a person acting on behalf of the issuer; an outside reviewer retained by the issuer making a statement on behalf of the issuer; or an underwriter, with respect to information provided by the issuer or information derived from information provided by the issuer.

2.   For purposes of paragraph (d) of this Item 305 only:

    i.   All information required by paragraphs (a), (b)(1)(i), (b)(1)(iii), and (c) of this Item 305 is considered forward looking statements for purposes of the statutory safe harbors, except for historical facts such as the terms of particular contracts and the number of market risk sensitive instruments held during or at the end of the reporting period; and

    ii.   With respect to paragraph (a) of this Item 305, the meaningful cautionary statements prong of the statutory safe harbors will be satisfied if a registrant satisfies all requirements of that same paragraph (a) of this Item 305.

e.   **Smaller Reporting Companies.** A smaller reporting company, as in 10(f)(1), is not required to provide the information required by this Item.

Instructions to Paragraphs 305(a) through 305(e):

1.   Bank registrants, thrift registrants, and non-bank and non-thrift registrants with market capitalizations on January 28, 1997 in excess of $2.5 billion should provide Item 305 disclosures in filings with the Commission that include annual financial statements for fiscal years ending after June 15, 1997. Non-bank and non-thrift registrants with market capitalizations on January 28, 1997 of $2.5 billion or less should provide Item 305 disclosures in filings with the Commission that include financial statements for fiscal years ending after June 15, 1998.

2.

    A.   For purposes of instruction 1. of the General Instructions to Paragraphs 305(a), 305(b), 305(c), 305(d), and 305(e), bank registrants and thrift registrants include any registrant which has control over a depository institution.

    B.   For purposes of instruction 2.A. of the General Instructions to Paragraphs 305(a), 305(b), 305(c), 305(d), and 305(e), a registrant has control over a depository institution if:

        i.   The registrant directly or indirectly or acting through one or more other persons owns, controls, or has power to vote 25% or more of any class of voting securities of the depository institution;

        ii.   The registrant controls in any manner the election of a majority of the directors or trustees of the depository institution; or

        iii.   The Federal Reserve Board or Office of Thrift Supervision determines, after notice and opportunity for hearing, that the registrant directly or indirectly exercises a controlling influence over the management or policies of the depository institution.

    C.   For purposes of instruction 2.B. of the General Instructions to Paragraphs 305(a), 305(b), 305(c), 305(d), and 305(e), a depository institution means any of the following:

        i.   An insured depository institution as defined in section 3(c)(2) of the Federal Deposit Insurance Act;

        ii.   An institution organized under the laws of the United States, any State of the United States, the District of Columbia, any territory of the United States, Puerto Rico, Guam, American Somoa, or the Virgin Islands, which both accepts demand deposits or deposits that the depositor may withdraw by check or similar means for payment to third parties or others and is engaged in the business of making commercial loans.

D. For purposes of instruction 1. of the General Instructions to Paragraphs 305(a), 305(b), 305(c), 305(d) and 305(e), market capitalization is the aggregate market value of common equity as set forth in General Instruction I.B.1. of Form S-3; *provided however*, that common equity held by affiliates is included in the calculation of market capitalization; and *provided further* that instead of using the 60 day period prior to filing referenced in General Instruction I.B.1. of Form S-3, the measurement date is January 28, 1997.

Appendix to Item 305–Tabular Disclosures

The tables set forth below are illustrative of the format that might be used when a registrant elects to present the information required by paragraph (a)(1)(i)(A) of Item 305 regarding terms and information about derivative financial instruments, other financial instruments, and derivative commodity instruments. These examples are for illustrative purposes only. Registrants are not required to display the information in the specific format illustrated below. Alternative methods of display are permissible as long as the disclosure requirements of the section are satisfied. Furthermore, these examples were designed primarily to illustrate possible formats for presentation of the information required by the disclosure item and do not purport to illustrate the broad range of derivative financial instruments, other financial instruments, and derivative commodity instruments utilized by registrants.

Interest Rate Sensitivity

The table below provides information about the Company's derivative financial instruments and other financial instruments that are sensitive to changes in interest rates, including interest rate swaps and debt obligations. For debt obligations, the table presents principal cash flows and related weighted average interest rates by expected maturity dates. For interest rate swaps, the table presents notional amounts and weighted average interest rates by expected (contractual) maturity dates. Notional amounts are used to calculate the contractual payments to be exchanged under the contract. Weighted average variable rates are based on implied forward rates in the yield curve at the reporting date. The information is presented in U.S. dollar equivalents, which is the Company's reporting currency. The instrument's actual cash flows are denominated in both U.S. dollars ($US) and German deutschmarks (DM), as indicated in parentheses.

December 31, 19X1								
	Expected maturity date							**Fair value**
	19X2	**19X3**	**19X4**	**19X5**	**19X6**	**There-after**	**Total**	
Liabilities	(US$ Equivalent in millions)							
Long-term Debt:								
Fixed Rate ($US)	$XXX	$XXX	$XXX	$XXX	$XXX	$XXX	$XXX	$XXX
Ave interest rate	X.X%	X.X%	X.X%	X.X%	X.X%	X.X%	X.X%	
Fixed Rate (DM)	XXX	XXX	XXX	XXX	XXX	XXX	XXX	XXX
Ave interest rate	X.X%	X.X%	X.X%	X.X%	X.X%	X.X%	X.X%	
Variable Rate ($US)	XXX	XXX	XXX	XXX	XXX	XXX	XXX	XXX
Ave interest rate	X.X%	X.X%	X.X%	X.X%	X.X%	X.X%	X.X%	
Interest Rate Derivatives	(In millions)							
Interest Rate Swaps								
Variable to Fixed ($US)	$XXX	$XXX	$XXX	$XXX	$XXX	$XXX	$XXX	$XXX
Average pay rate	X.X%	X.X%	X.X%	X.X%	X.X%	X.X%	X.X%	
Ave receive rate	X.X%	X.X%	X.X%	X.X%	X.X%	X.X%	X.X%	
Fixed to Variable ($US)	XXX	XXX	XXX	XXX	XXX	XXX	XXX	XXX
Average pay rate	X.X%	X.X%	X.X%	X.X%	X.X%	X.X%	X.X%	
Ave receive rate	X.X%	X.X%	X.X%	X.X%	X.X%	X.X%	X.X%	

Exchange Rate Sensitivity

The table below provides information about the Company's derivative financial instruments, other financial instruments, and firmly committed sales transactions by functional currency and presents such information in U.S. dollar equivalents. The table summarizes information on instruments and transactions that are sensitive to foreign currency exchange rates, including foreign currency forward exchange agreements, deutschmark (DM)-denominated debt obligations, and firmly committed DM sales transactions. For debt obligations, the table presents principal cash flows and related weighted average interest rates by expected maturity dates. For firmly committed DM-sales transactions, sales amounts are presented by the expected transaction date, which are not expected to exceed two years. For foreign currency forward exchange agreements, the table presents the notional amounts and weighted average exchange rates by expected (contractual) maturity dates. These notional amounts generally are used to calculate the contractual payments to be exchanged under the contract.

December 31, 19X1								
	Expected maturity date							**Fair value**
	19X2	**19X3**	**19X4**	**19X5**	**19X6**	**There-after**	**Total**	
On-Balance Sheet Financial Instruments	**(US$ Equivalent in millions)**							
$US Functional Currency:								
Liabilities								
Long-Term Debt:								
Fixed Rate (DM)	$XXX	$XXX	$XXX	$XXX	$XXX	$XXX	$XXX	$XXX
Avg interest rate	X.X	X.X	X.X	X.X	X.X	X.X	X.X	....
Anticipated Transactions and Related Derivatives	**Expected maturity or transaction date (US$ Equivalent in millions)**							
$US Functional Currency:								
Firmly committed Sales Contracts (DM)	$XXX	$XXX	....	....	....	....	$XXX	$XXX
Forward Exchange Agreements (Receive $US/Pay DM):								
Contract Amount	XXX	XXX	....	....	....	....	XXX	XXX
Average Contractual Exchange Rate	X.X	X.X	....	....	....	....	X.X	....

Commodity Price Sensitivity

The table below provides information about the Company's corn inventory and futures contracts that are sensitive to changes in commodity prices, specifically corn prices. For inventory, the table presents the carrying amount and fair value at December 31, 19x1. For the futures contracts the table presents the notional amounts in bushels, the weighted average contract prices, and the total dollar contract amount by expected maturity dates, the latest of which occurs one year from the reporting date. Contract amounts are used to calculate the contractual payments and quantity of corn to be exchanged under the futures contracts.

December 31, 19X1		
	Carrying amount	**Fair Value**
	(In millions)	
On Balance Sheet Commodity Position and Related Derivatives Corn Inventory	$XXX	$XXX
	Expected maturity 1992	**Fair value**
Related Derivatives Futures Contracts (Short):		
Contract Volumes (100,000 bushels)..............	XXX	....
Weighted Average Price (Per 100,000 bushels)..............	$X.XX	....
Contract Amount ($US in millions)..............	$XXX	$XXX

Item 401 – Directors, Executive Officers, Promoters and Control Persons

 a. **Identification of directors**. List the names and ages of all directors of the registrant and all persons nominated or chosen to become directors; indicate all positions and offices with the registrant held by each such person; state his term of office as director and any period(s) during which he has served as such; describe briefly any arrangement or understanding between him and any other person(s) (naming such person(s)) pursuant to which he was or is to be selected as a director or nominee.

Instructions to Paragraph 401(a):

1. Do not include arrangements or understandings with directors or officers of the registrant acting solely in their capacities as such.

2. No nominee or person chosen to become a director who has not consented to act as such shall be named in response to this Item. In this regard, with respect to proxy statements, see Rule 14a-4(d) under the Exchange Act.

3. If the information called for by this paragraph (a) is being presented in a proxy or information statement, no information need be given respecting any director whose term of office as a director will not continue after the meeting to which the statement relates.

4. With regard to proxy statements in connection with action to be taken concerning the election of directors, if fewer nominees are named than the number fixed by or pursuant to the governing instruments, state the reasons for this procedure and that the proxies cannot be voted for a greater number of persons than the number of nominees named.

5. With regard to proxy statements in connection with action to be taken concerning the election of directors, if the solicitation is made by persons other than management, information shall be given as to nominees of the persons making the solicitation. In all other instances, information shall be given as to directors

and persons nominated for election or chosen by management to become directors.

b. **Identification of executive officers**. List the names and ages of all executive officers of the registrant and all persons chosen to become executive officers; indicate all positions and offices with the registrant held by each such person; state his term of office as officer and the period during which he has served as such and describe briefly any arrangement or understanding between him and any other person(s) (naming such person) pursuant to which he was or is to be selected as an officer.

Instructions to Paragraph 401(b):

1. Do not include arrangements or understandings with directors or officers of the registrant acting solely in their capacities as such.

2. No person chosen to become an executive officer who has not consented to act as such shall be named in response to this Item.

3. The information regarding executive officers called for by this Item need not be furnished in proxy or information statements prepared in accordance with Schedule 14A under the Exchange Act by those registrants relying on General Instruction G of Form 10-K under the Exchange Act, *Provided,* That such information is furnished in a separate item captioned "Executive officers of the registrant" and included in Part I of the registrant's annual report on Form 10-K.

c. **Identification of certain significant employees.** Where the registrant employs persons such as production managers, sales managers, or research scientists who are not executive officers but who make or are expected to make significant contributions to the business of the registrant, such persons shall be identified and their background disclosed to the same extent as in the case of executive officers. Such disclosure need not be made if the registrant was subject to section 13(a) or 15(d) of the Exchange Act or was exempt from section 13(a) by section 12(g)(2)(G) of such Act immediately prior to the filing of the registration statement, report, or statement to which this Item is applicable.

d. **Family relationships.** State the nature of any family relationship between any director, executive officer, or person nominated or chosen by the registrant to become a director or executive officer.

Instruction to Paragraph 401(d):

The term "family relationship" means any relationship by blood, marriage, or adoption, not more remote than first cousin.

e. **Business experience–**

1. Background. Briefly describe the business experience during the past five years of each director, executive officer, person nominated or chosen to become a director or executive officer, and each person named in answer to paragraph (c) of Item 401, including: each person's principal occupations and employment during the past five years; the name and principal business of any corporation or other organization in which such occupations and employment were carried on; and whether such corporation or organization is a parent, subsidiary or other affiliate of the registrant. In addition, for each director or person nominated or chosen to become a director, briefly discuss the specific

experience, qualifications, attributes or skills that led to the conclusion that the person should serve as a director for the registrant at the time that the disclosure is made, in light of the registrant's business and structure. If material, this disclosure should cover more than the past five years, including information about the person's particular areas of expertise or other relevant qualifications. When an executive officer or person named in response to paragraph (c) of Item 401 has been employed by the registrant or a subsidiary of the registrant for less than five years, a brief explanation shall be included as to the nature of the responsibility undertaken by the individual in prior positions to provide adequate disclosure of his prior business experience. What is required is information relating to the level of his professional competence, which may include, depending upon the circumstances, such specific information as the size of the operation supervised.

2. Directorships. Indicate any other directorships held, including any other directorships held during the past five years, by each director or person nominated or chosen to become a director in any company with a class of securities registered pursuant to section 12 of the Exchange Act or subject to the requirements of section 15(d) of such Act or any company registered as an investment company under the Investment Company Act of 1940, naming such company.

Instruction to Paragraph 401(e):

For the purposes of paragraph (e)(2), where the other directorships of each director or person nominated or chosen to become a director include directorships of two or more registered investment companies that are part of a "fund complex" as that term is defined in Item 22(a) of Schedule 14A under the Exchange Act, the registrant may, rather than listing each such investment company, identify the fund complex and provide the number of investment company directorships held by the director or nominee in such fund complex.

f. **Involvement in certain legal proceedings.** Describe any of the following events that occurred during the past ten years and that are material to an evaluation of the ability or integrity of any director, person nominated to become a director or executive officer of the registrant:

1. A petition under the Federal bankruptcy laws or any state insolvency law was filed by or against, or a receiver, fiscal agent or similar officer was appointed by a court for the business or property of such person, or any partnership in which he was a general partner at or within two years before the time of such filing, or any corporation or business association of which he was an executive officer at or within two years before the time of such filing;

2. Such person was convicted in a criminal proceeding or is a named subject of a pending criminal proceeding (excluding traffic violations and other minor offenses);

3. Such person was the subject of any order, judgment, or decree, not subsequently reversed, suspended or vacated, of any court of competent jurisdiction, permanently or temporarily enjoining him from, or otherwise limiting, the following activities:

    i. Acting as a futures commission merchant, introducing broker, commodity trading advisor, commodity pool operator, floor broker, leverage transaction merchant, any other person regulated by the Commodity Futures Trading Commission, or an associated person of any of the foregoing, or as an investment adviser, underwriter, broker or dealer in securities, or as an affiliated person, director or employee of any investment company, bank, savings and loan association or insurance company, or engaging in or continuing any conduct or practice in connection with such activity;

    ii.   Engaging in any type of business practice; or

    iii.   Engaging in any activity in connection with the purchase or sale of any security or commodity or in connection with any violation of Federal or State securities laws or Federal commodities laws;

4.   Such person was the subject of any order, judgment or decree, not subsequently reversed, suspended or vacated, of any Federal or State authority barring, suspending or otherwise limiting for more than 60 days the right of such person to engage in any activity described in paragraph (f)(3)(i) of this section, or to be associated with persons engaged in any such activity;

5.   Such person was found by a court of competent jurisdiction in a civil action or by the Commission to have violated any Federal or State securities law, and the judgment in such civil action or finding by the Commission has not been subsequently reversed, suspended, or vacated;

6.   Such person was found by a court of competent jurisdiction in a civil action or by the Commodity Futures Trading Commission to have violated any Federal commodities law, and the judgment in such civil action or finding by the Commodity Futures Trading Commission has not been subsequently reversed, suspended or vacated;

7.   Such person was the subject of, or a party to, any Federal or State judicial or administrative order, judgment, decree, or finding, not subsequently reversed, suspended or vacated, relating to an alleged violation of:

    i.   Any Federal or State securities or commodities law or regulation; or

    ii.   Any law or regulation respecting financial institutions or insurance companies including, but not limited to, a temporary or permanent injunction, order of disgorgement or restitution, civil money penalty or temporary or permanent cease-and-desist order, or removal or prohibition order; or

    iii.   Any law or regulation prohibiting mail or wire fraud or fraud in connection with any business entity; or

8.   Such person was the subject of, or a party to, any sanction or order, not subsequently reversed, suspended or vacated, of any self-regulatory organization (as defined in Section 3(a)(26) of the Exchange Act), any registered entity (as defined in Section 1(a)(29) of the Commodity Exchange Act), or any equivalent exchange, association, entity or organization that has disciplinary authority over its members or persons associated with a member.

Instructions to Paragraph 401(f):

1.   For purposes of computing the ten-year period referred to in this paragraph, the date of a reportable event shall be deemed the date on which the final order, judgment or decree was entered, or the date on which any rights of appeal from preliminary orders, judgments, or decrees have lapsed. With respect to bankruptcy petitions, the computation date shall be the date of filing for

uncontested petitions or the date upon which approval of a contested petition became final.

2. If any event specified in this paragraph (f) has occurred and information in regard thereto is omitted on the grounds that it is not material, the registrant may furnish to the Commission, at time of filing (or at the time preliminary materials are filed, or ten days before definitive materials are filed in preliminary filing is not required, pursuant to Rule 14a-6 or 14c-5 under the Exchange Act), as supplemental information and not as part of the registration statement, report, or proxy or information statement, materials to which the omission relates, a description of the event and a statement of the reasons for the omission of information in regard thereto.

3. The registrant is permitted to explain any mitigating circumstances associated with events reported pursuant to this paragraph.

4. If the information called for by this paragraph (f) is being presented in a proxy or information statement, no information need be given respecting any director whose term of office as a director will not continue after the meeting to which the statement relates.

5. This paragraph (f)(7) shall not apply to any settlement of a civil proceeding among private litigants.

g. **Promoters and control persons.**

1. Registrants, which have not been subject to the reporting requirements of section 13(a) or 15(d) of the Exchange Act for the twelve months immediately prior to the filing of the registration statement, report, or statement to which this Item is applicable, and which had a promoter at any time during the past five fiscal years, shall describe with respect to anypromoter, any of the events enumerated in paragraphs (f)(1) through (f)(6) of this Item that occurred during the past five years and that are material to a voting or investment decision.

2. Registrants, which have not been subject to the reporting requirements of section 13(a) or 15(d) of the Exchange Act for the twelve months immediately prior to the filing of the registration statement, report, or statement to which this Item is applicable, shall describe with respect to any control person, any of the events enumerated in paragraphs (f)(1) through (f)(6) of this section that occurred during the past five years and that are material to a voting or investment decision.

Instructions to Paragraph 401(g):

1. Instructions 1 through 3 to paragraph (f) shall apply to this paragraph (g).

2. Paragraph (g) shall not apply to any subsidiary of a registrant which has been reporting pursuant to section 13(a) or 15(d) of the Exchange Act for the twelve months immediately prior to the filing of the registration statement, report or statement.

Item 402 – Executive compensation.

a **General**

1. Treatment of foreign private issuers. A foreign private issuer will be deemed to comply with this Item if it provides the information required by Items 6.B and

6.E.2 of Form 20-F, with more detailed information provided if otherwise made publicly available or required to be disclosed by the issuer's home jurisdiction or a market in which its securities are listed or traded.

2.   All compensation covered. This Item requires clear, concise and understandable disclosure of all plan and non-plan compensation awarded to, earned by, or paid to the named executive officers designated under paragraph (a)(3) of this Item, and directors covered by paragraph (k) of this Item, by any person for all services rendered in all capacities to the registrant and its subsidiaries, unless otherwise specifically excluded from disclosure in this Item. All such compensation shall be reported pursuant to this Item, even if also called for by another requirement, including transactions between the registrant and a third party where a purpose of the transaction is to furnish compensation to any such named executive officer or director. No amount reported as compensation for one fiscal year need be reported in the same manner as compensation for a subsequent fiscal year; amounts reported as compensation for one fiscal year may be required to be reported in a different manner pursuant to this Item.

3.   Persons covered. Disclosure shall be provided pursuant to this Item for each of the following (the "named executive officers"):

    i.   All individuals serving as the registrant's principal executive officer or acting in a similar capacity during the last completed fiscal year ("PEO"), regardless of compensation level;

    ii. All individuals serving as the registrant's principal financial officer or acting in a similar capacity during the last completed fiscal year ("PFO"), regardless of compensation level;

    iii. The registrant's three most highly compensated executive officers other than the PEO and PFO who were serving as executive officers at the end of the last completed fiscal year; and

    iv. Up to two additional individuals for whom disclosure would have been provided pursuant to paragraph (a)(3)(iii) of this Item but for the fact that the individual was not serving as an executive officer of the registrant at the end of the last completed fiscal year.

Instructions to Item 402(a)(3).

1.   Determination of most highly compensated executive officers. The determination as to which executive officers are most highly compensated shall be made by reference to total compensation for the last completed fiscal year (as required to be disclosed pursuant to paragraph (c)(2)(x) of this Item) reduced by the amount required to be disclosed pursuant to paragraph (c)(2)(viii) of this Item, *provided, however,* that nodisclosure need be provided for any executive officer, other than the PEO and PFO, whose total compensation, as so reduced, does not exceed $100,000.

2.   Inclusion of executive officer of subsidiary. It may be appropriate for a registrant to include as named executive officers one or more executive officers or other employees of subsidiaries in the disclosure required by this Item. See Rule 3b-7 under the Exchange Act.

3.   Exclusion of executive officer due to overseas compensation. It may be appropriate in limited circumstances for a registrant not to include in the disclosure required by this Item an individual, other than its PEO or PFO,

who is one of the registrant's most highly compensated executive officers due to the payment of amounts of cash compensation relating to overseas assignments attributed predominantly to such assignments.

4. *Information for full fiscal year.* If the PEO or PFO served in that capacity during any part of a fiscal year with respect to which information is required, information should be provided as to all of his or her compensation for the full fiscal year. If a named executive officer (other than the PEO or PFO) served as an executive officer of the registrant (whether or not in the same position) during any part of the fiscal year with respect to which information is required, information shall be provided as to all compensation of that individual for the full fiscal year.

5. *Omission of table or column.* A table or column may be omitted if there has been no compensation awarded to, earned by, or paid to any of the named executive officers or directors required to be reported in that table or column in any fiscal year covered by that table.

6. *Definitions.* For purposes of this Item:

   i. The term stock means instruments such as common stock, restricted stock, restricted stock units, phantom stock, phantom stock units, common stock equivalent units or any similar instruments that do not have option-like features, and the term option means instruments such as stock options, stock appreciation rights and similar instruments with option-like features. The term stock appreciation rights ("SARs") refers to SARs payable in cash or stock, including SARs payable in cash or stock at the election of the registrant or a named executive officer. The term equity is used to refer generally to stock and/or options.

   ii. The term plan includes, but is not limited to, the following: Any plan, contract, authorization or arrangement, whether or not set forth in any formal document, pursuant to which cash, securities, similar instruments, or any other property may be received. A plan may be applicable to one person. Registrants may omit information regarding group life, health, hospitalization, or medical reimbursement plans that do not discriminate in scope, terms or operation, in favor of executive officers or directors of the registrant and that are available generally to all salaried employees.

   iii. The term incentive plan means any plan providing compensation intended to serve as incentive for performance to occur over a specified period, whether such performance is measured by reference to financial performance of the registrant or an affiliate, the registrant's stock price, or any other performance measure. An equity incentive plan is an incentive plan or portion of an incentive plan under which awards are granted that fall within the scope of Financial Accounting Standards Board Statement of Financial Accounting Standards No. 123 (revised 2004), Share-Based Payment, as modified or supplemented ("FAS 123R"). A non-equity incentive plan is an incentive plan or portion of an incentive plan that is not an equity incentive plan. The term incentive plan award means an award provided under an incentive plan.

    iv. The terms <u>date of grant</u> or <u>grant date</u> refer to the grant date determined for financial statement reporting purposes pursuant to FAS 123R.

    v. <u>Closing market price</u> is defined as the price at which the registrant's security was last sold in the principal United States market for such security as of the date for which the closing market price is determined.

b. **Compensation discussion and analysis.**

    1. Discuss the compensation awarded to, earned by, or paid to the named executive officers. The discussion shall explain all material elements of the registrant's compensation of the named executive officers. The discussion shall describe the following:

        i. The objectives of the registrant's compensation programs;

        ii. What the compensation program is designed to reward;

        iii. Each element of compensation;

        iv. Why the registrant chooses to pay each element;

        v. How the registrant determines the amount (and, where applicable, the formula) for each element to pay; and

        vi. How each compensation element and the registrant's decisions regarding that element fit into the registrant's overall compensation objectives and affect decisions regarding other elements.

    2. While the material information to be disclosed under Compensation Discussion and Analysis will vary depending upon the facts and circumstances, examples of such information may include, in a given case, among other things, the following:

        i. The policies for allocating between long-term and currently paid out compensation;

        ii. The policies for allocating between cash and non-cash compensation, and among different forms of non-cash compensation;

        iii. For long-term compensation, the basis for allocating compensation to each different form of award (such as relationship of the award to the achievement of the registrant's long-term goals, management's exposure to downside equity performance risk, correlation between cost to registrant and expected benefits to the registrant);

        iv. How the determination is made as to when awards are granted, including awards of equity-based compensation such as options;

        v. What specific items of corporate performance are taken into account in setting compensation policies and making compensation decisions;

        vi. How specific forms of compensation are structured and implemented to reflect these items of the registrant's performance, including whether discretion can be or has been exercised (either to award compensation absent attainment of the relevant performance goal(s) or to reduce or increase the size of any award or payout), identifying any particular exercise of discretion, and stating whether it applied to one or more specified named executive officers or to all compensation subject to the relevant performance goal(s);

        vii. How specific forms of compensation are structured and implemented to reflect the named executive officer's individual performance and/or individual contribution to these items of the registrant's performance, describing the elements of individual performance and/or contribution that are taken into account;

viii.   Registrant policies and decisions regarding the adjustment or recovery of awards or payments if the relevant registrant performance measures upon which they are based are restated or otherwise adjusted in a manner that would reduce the size of an award or payment;

ix.   The factors considered in decisions to increase or decrease compensation materially;

x.   How compensation or amounts realizable from prior compensation are considered in setting other elements of compensation (e.g., how gains from prior option or stock awards are considered in setting retirement benefits);

xi.   With respect to any contract, agreement, plan or arrangement, whether written or unwritten, that provides for payment(s) at, following, or in connection with any termination or change-in-control, the basis for selecting particular events as triggering payment (e.g., the rationale for providing a single trigger for payment in the event of a change-in-control);

xii.   The impact of the accounting and tax treatments of the particular form of compensation;

xiii.   The registrant's equity or other security ownership requirements or guidelines (specifying applicable amounts and forms of ownership), and any registrant policies regarding hedging the economic risk of such ownership;

xiv.   Whether the registrant engaged in any benchmarking of total compensation, or any material element of compensation, identifying the benchmark and, if applicable, its components (including component companies); and

xv.   The role of executive officers in determining executive compensation.

Instructions to Item 402(b).

1.   The purpose of the Compensation Discussion and Analysis is to provide to investors material information that is necessary to an understanding of the registrant's compensation policies and decisions regarding the named executive officers.

2.   The Compensation Discussion and Analysis should be of the information contained in the tables and otherwise disclosed pursuant to this Item. The Compensation Discussion and Analysis should also cover actions regarding executive compensation that were taken after the registrant's last fiscal year's end. Actions that should be addressed might include, as examples only, the adoption or implementation of new or modified programs and policies or specific decisions that were made or steps that were taken that could affect a fair understanding of the named executive officer's compensation for the last fiscal year. Moreover, in some situations it may be necessary to discuss prior years in order to give context to the disclosure provided.

3.   The Compensation Discussion and Analysis should focus on the material principles underlying the registrant's executive compensation policies and decisions and the most important factors relevant to analysis of those policies and decisions. The Compensation Discussion and Analysis shall reflect the individual

circumstances of the registrant and shall avoid boilerplate language and repetition of the more detailed information set forth in the tables and narrative disclosures that follow.

4.   Registrants are not required to disclose target levels with respect to specific quantitative or qualitative performance-related factors considered by the compensation committee or the board of directors, or any other factors or criteria involving confidential trade secrets or confidential commercial or financial information, the disclosure of which would result in competitive harm for the registrant. The standard to use when determining whether disclosure would cause competitive harm for the registrant is the same standard that would apply when a registrant requests confidential treatment of confidential trade secrets or confidential commercial or financial information pursuant to Securities Act Rule 406 and Exchange Act Rule 24b-2, each of which incorporates the criteria for non-disclosure when relying upon Exemption 4 of the Freedom of Information Act and Rule 80(b)(4) thereunder. A registrant is not required to seek confidential treatment under the procedures in Securities Act Rule 406 and Exchange Act Rule 24b-2 if it determines that the disclosure would cause competitive harm in reliance on this instruction; however, in that case, the registrant must discuss how difficult it will be for the executive or how likely it will be for the registrant to achieve the undisclosed target levels or other factors.

5.   Disclosure of target levels that are non-GAAP financial measures will not be subject to Regulation G and Item 10(e); however, disclosure must be provided as to how the number is calculated from the registrant's audited financial statements.

c.   **Summary compensation table.**

1.   General. Provide the information specified in paragraph (c)(2) of this Item, concerning the compensation of the named executive officers for each of the registrant's last three completed fiscal years, in a Summary Compensation Table in the tabular format specified below.

SUMMARY COMPENSATION TABLE

Name and Principal Position	Year	Salary ($)	Bonus ($)	Stock Awards ($)	Option Awards ($)	Non-Equity Incentive Plan Compensation ($)	Change in Pension Value and Nonquali-fied Deferred Compensa-tion Earnings ($)	All Other Compen-sation ($)	Total ($)
(a)	(b)	(c)	(d)	(e)	(f)	(g)	(h)	(i)	(j)
PEO									
PFO									
A									
B									
C									

2. The Table shall include:

   i. The name and principal position of the named executive officer (column (a));

   ii. The fiscal year covered (column (b));

   iii. The dollar value of base salary (cash and non-cash) earned by the named executive officer during the fiscal year covered (column (c));

   iv. The dollar value of bonus (cash and non-cash) earned by the named executive officer during the fiscal year covered (column (d));

Instructions to Item 402(c)(2)(iii) and (iv).

   1. If the amount of salary or bonus earned in a given fiscal year is not calculable through the latest practicable date, a footnote shall be included disclosing that the amount of salary or bonus is not calculable through the latest practicable date and providing the date that the amount of salary or bonus is expected to be determined, and such amount must then be disclosed in a filing under Item 5.02(f) of Form 8-K.

   2. Registrants shall include in the salary column (column (c)) or bonus column (column (d)) any amount of salary or bonus forgone at the election of a named executive officer under which stock, equity-based or other forms of non-cash compensation instead have been received by the named executive officer. However, the receipt of any such form of non-cash compensation instead of salary or bonus must be disclosed in a footnote added to the salary or bonus column and, where applicable, referring to the Grants of Plan-Based Awards Table (required by paragraph (d) of this Item) where the stock, option or non-equity incentive plan award elected by the named executive officer is reported.

   v. For awards of stock, the aggregate grant date fair value computed in accordance with FASB ASC Topic 718 (column (e));

   vi. For awards of options, with or without tandem SARs (including awards that subsequently have been transferred), the aggregate grant date fair value computed in accordance with FASB ASC Topic 718 (column (f));

Instruction 1 to Item 402(c)(2)(v) and (vi).

For awards reported in columns (e) and (f), include a footnote disclosing all assumptions made in the valuation by reference to a discussion of those assumptions in the registrant's financial statements, footnotes to the financial statements, or discussion in the Management's Discussion and Analysis. The sections so referenced are deemed part of the disclosure provided pursuant to this Item.

Instruction 2 to Item 402(c)(2)(v) and (vi).

If at any time during the last completed fiscal year, the registrant has adjusted or amended the exercise price of options or SARs previously awarded to a named executive officer, whether through amendment, cancellation or replacement grants, or any other means ("repriced"), or otherwise has materially modified such awards, the registrant shall include, as awards required to be reported in column (f), the incremental fair value, computed as of the repricing or modification date in accordance with FASB ASC Topic 718, with respect to that repriced or modified award.

Instruction 3 to Item 402(c)(2)(v) and (vi). For any awards that are subject to performance conditions, report the value at the grant date based upon the probable outcome of such conditions. This amount should be consistent with the estimate of aggregate compensation cost to be recognized over the service period determined as of the grant date under FASB ASC Topic 718, excluding the effect of estimated forfeitures. In a footnote to the table, disclose the value of the award at the grant date assuming that the highest level of performance conditions will be achieved if an amount less than the maximum was included in the table. .

vii. The dollar value of all earnings for services performed during the fiscal year pursuant to awards under non-equity incentive plans as defined in paragraph (a)(6)(iii) of this Item, and all earnings on any outstanding awards (column (g));

Instructions to Item 402(c)(2)(vii).

1. If the relevant performance measure is satisfied during the fiscal year (including for a single year in a plan with a multi-year performance measure), the earnings are reportable for that fiscal year, even if not payable until a later date, and are not reportable again in the fiscal year when amounts are paid to the named executive officer.

2. All earnings on non-equity incentive plan compensation must be identified and quantified in a footnote to column (g), whether the earnings were paid during the fiscal year, payable during the period but deferred at the election of the named executive officer, or payable by their terms at a later date.

viii. The sum of the amounts specified in paragraphs (c)(2)(viii)(A) and (B) of this Item (column (h)) as follows:

A. The aggregate change in the actuarial present value of the named executive officer's accumulated benefit under all defined benefit and actuarial pension plans (including supplemental plans) from the pension plan measurement date used for financial statement reporting purposes with respect to the registrant's audited financial statements for the prior completed fiscal year to the pension plan measurement date used for financial statement reporting purposes with respect to the registrant's audited financial statements for the covered fiscal year; and

B. Above-market or preferential earnings on compensation that is deferred on a basis that is not tax-qualified, including such earnings on nonqualified defined contribution plans;

Instructions to Item 402(c)(2)(viii).

1. The disclosure required pursuant to paragraph (c)(2)(viii)(A) of this Item applies to each plan that provides for the payment of retirement benefits, or benefits that will be paid primarily following retirement, including but not limited to tax-qualified defined benefit plans and supplemental executive retirement plans, but excluding

tax-qualified defined contribution plans and nonqualified defined contribution plans. For purposes of this disclosure, the registrant should use the same amounts required to be disclosed pursuant to paragraph (h)(2)(iv) of this Item for the covered fiscal year and the amounts that were or would have been required to be reported for the executive officer pursuant to paragraph (h)(2)(iv) of this Item for the prior completed fiscal year.

2. Regarding paragraph (c)(2)(viii)(B) of this Item, interest on deferred compensation is above-market only if the rate of interest exceeds 120% of the applicable federal long-term rate, with compounding (as prescribed under section 1274(d) of the Internal Revenue Code) at the rate that corresponds most closely to the rate under the registrant's plan at the time the interest rate or formula is set. In the event of a discretionary reset of the interest rate, the requisite calculation must be made on the basis of the interest rate at the time of such reset, rather than when originally established. Only the above-market portion of the interest must be included. If the applicable interest rates vary depending upon conditions such as a minimum period of continued service, the reported amount should be calculated assuming satisfaction of all conditions to receiving interest at the highest rate. Dividends (and dividend equivalents) on deferred compensation denominated in the registrant's stock ("deferred stock") are preferential only if earned at a rate higher than dividends on the registrant's common stock. Only the preferential portion of the dividends or equivalents must be included. Footnote or narrative disclosure may be provided explaining the registrant's criteria for determining any portion considered to be above-market.

3. The registrant shall identify and quantify by footnote the separate amounts attributable to each of paragraphs (c)(2)(viii)(A) and (B) of this Item. Where such amount pursuant to paragraph (c)(2)(viii)(A) is negative, it should be disclosed by footnote but should not be reflected in the sum reported in column (h).

ix. All other compensation for the covered fiscal year that the registrant could not properly report in any other column of the Summary Compensation Table (column (i)). Each compensation item that is not properly reportable in columns (c) - (h), regardless of the amount of the compensation item, must be included in column (i). Such compensation must include, but is not limited to:

A. Perquisites and other personal benefits, or property, unless the aggregate amount of such compensation is less than $10,000;

B. All "gross-ups" or other amounts reimbursed during the fiscal year for the payment of taxes;

C. For any security of the registrant or its subsidiaries purchased from the registrant or its subsidiaries (through deferral of salary or bonus, or otherwise) at a discount from the market price of such security at the date of purchase, unless that discount is available generally, either to all security holders or to all salaried employees of the registrant, the compensation cost, if any, computed in accordance with FAS 123R;

D. The amount paid or accrued to any named executive officer pursuant to a plan or arrangement in connection with:

    1. Any termination, including without limitation through retirement, resignation, severance or constructive termination (including a change in responsibilities) of such executive officer's employment with the registrant and its subsidiaries; or

    2. A change in control of the registrant;

E. Registrant contributions or other allocations to vested and unvested defined contribution plans;

F. The dollar value of any insurance premiums paid by, or on behalf of, the registrant during the covered fiscal year with respect to life insurance for the benefit of a named executive officer; and

G. The dollar value of any dividends or other earnings paid on stock or option awards, when those amounts were not factored into the grant date fair value required to be reported for the stock or option award in column (e) or (f); and

Instructions to Item 402(c)(2)(ix).

1. Non-equity incentive plan awards and earnings and earnings on stock and options, except as specified in paragraph (c)(2)(ix)(G) of this Item, are required to be reported elsewhere as provided in this Item and are not reportable as All Other Compensation in column (i).

2. Benefits paid pursuant to defined benefit and actuarial plans are not reportable as All Other Compensation in column (i) unless accelerated pursuant to a change in control; information concerning these plans is reportable pursuant to paragraphs (c)(2)(viii)(A) and (h) of this Item.

3. Any item reported for a named executive officer pursuant to paragraph (c)(2)(ix) of this Item that is not a perquisite or personal benefit and whose value exceeds $10,000 must be identified and quantified in a footnote to column (i). This requirement applies only to compensation for the last fiscal year. All items of compensation are required to be included in the Summary Compensation Table without regard to whether such items are required to be identified other than as specifically noted in this Item.

4. Perquisites and personal benefits may be excluded as long as the total value of all perquisites and personal benefits for a named executive officer is less than $10,000. If the total value of all perquisites and personal benefits is $10,000 or more for any named executive officer, then each perquisite or personal benefit, regardless of its amount, must be identified by type. If perquisites and personal benefits are required to be reported for a named executive officer pursuant to this rule, then each perquisite or personal benefit that exceeds the greater of $25,000 or 10% of the total amount of perquisites and personal benefits for that officer must be quantified and disclosed in a footnote. The requirements for

identification and quantification apply only to compensation for the last fiscal year. Perquisites and other personal benefits shall be valued on the basis of the aggregate incremental cost to the registrant. With respect to the perquisite or other personal benefit for which footnote quantification is required, the registrant shall describe in the footnote its methodology for computing the aggregate incremental cost. Reimbursements of taxes owed with respect to perquisites or other personal benefits must be included in column (i) and are subject to separate quantification and identification as tax reimbursements (paragraph (c)(2)(ix)(B) of this Item) even if the associated perquisites or other personal benefits are not required to be included because the total amount of all perquisites or personal benefits for an individual named executive officer is less than $10,000 or are required to be identified but are not required to be separately quantified.

5. For purposes of paragraph (c)(2)(ix)(D) of this Item, an accrued amount is an amount for which payment has become due.

x. The dollar value of total compensation for the covered fiscal year (column (j)). With respect to each named executive officer, disclose the sum of all amounts reported in columns (c) through (i).

Instructions to Item 402(c).

1. Information with respect to fiscal years prior to the last completed fiscal year will not be required if the registrant was not a reporting company pursuant to section 13(a) or 15(d) of the Exchange Act at any time during that year, except that the registrant will be required to provide information for any such year if that information previously was required to be provided in response to a Commission filing requirement.

2. All compensation values reported in the Summary Compensation Table must be reported in dollars and rounded to the nearest dollar. Reported compensation values must be reported numerically, providing a single numerical value for each grid in the table. Where compensation was paid to or received by a named executive officer in a different currency, a footnote must be provided to identify that currency and describe the rate and methodology used to convert the payment amounts to dollars.

3. If a named executive officer is also a director who receives compensation for his or her services as a director, reflect that compensation in the Summary Compensation Table and provide a footnote identifying and itemizing such compensation and amounts. Use the categories in the Director Compensation Table required pursuant to paragraph (k) of this Item.

4. Any amounts deferred, whether pursuant to a plan established under section 401(k) of the Internal Revenue Code), or otherwise, shall be included in the appropriate column for the fiscal year in which earned.

d. **Grants of plan-based awards table**. (1) Provide the information specified in paragraph (d)(2) of this Item, concerning each grant of an award made to a named executive officer in the last completed fiscal year under any plan, including awards that subsequently have been transferred, in the following tabular format:

GRANTS OF PLAN-BASED AWARDS

Name	Grant Date	Estimated Future Payouts Under Non-Equity Incentive Plan Awards			Estimated Future Payouts Under Equity Incentive Plan Awards			All Other Stock Awards: Number of Shares of Stock or Units (#)	All Other Option Awards: Number of Securities Underlying Options (#)	Exercise or Base Price of Option Awards ($/Sh)	Grant Date Fair Value of Stock and Option Awards
		Thresh-old ($)	Target ($)	Maximum ($)	Thresh-old (#)	Target (#)	Maximum (#)				
(a)	(b)	(c)	(d)	(e)	(f)	(g)	(h)	(i)	(j)	(k)	(l)
PEO											
PFO											
A											
B											
C											

2. The Table shall include:

i. The name of the named executive officer (column (a));

ii. The grant date for equity-based awards reported in the table (column (b)). If such grant date is different than the date on which the compensation committee (or a committee of the board of directors performing a similar function or the full board of directors) takes action or is deemed to take action to grant such awards, a separate, adjoining column shall be added between columns (b) and (c) showing such date;

iii. The dollar value of the estimated future payout upon satisfaction of the conditions in question under non-equity incentive plan awards granted in the fiscal year, or the applicable range of estimated payouts denominated in dollars (threshold, target and maximum amount) (columns (c) through (e));

iv. The number of shares of stock, or the number of shares underlying options to be paid out or vested upon satisfaction of the conditions in question under equity incentive plan awards granted in the fiscal year, or the applicable range of estimated payouts denominated in the number of shares of stock, or the number of shares underlying options under the award (threshold, target and maximum amount) (columns (f) through (h));

v. The number of shares of stock granted in the fiscal year that are not required to be disclosed in columns (f) through (h) (column (i));

vi. The number of securities underlying options granted in the fiscal year that are not required to be disclosed in columns (f) through (h) (column (j)); and

vii. The per-share exercise or base price of the options granted in the fiscal year (column (k)). If such exercise or base price is less than the closing market price of the underlying security on the date of the grant, a separate, adjoining column showing the closing market price on the date of the grant shall be added after column (k).

viii. The grant date fair value of each equity award computed in accordance with FAS 123R (column (l)). If at any time during the last completed fiscal year, the registrant has adjusted or amended the exercise or base price of options, SARs or similar optionlike instruments previously awarded to a named executive officer, whether through amendment, cancellation or replacement grants, or any other means ("repriced"), or otherwise has materially modified such awards, the incremental fair value, computed as of the repricing or modification date in accordance with FAS 123R, with respect to that repriced or modified award, shall be reported.

Instructions to Item 402(d).

1. Disclosure on a separate line shall be provided in the Table for each grant of an award made to a named executive officer during the fiscal year. If grants of awards were made to a named executive officer during the fiscal year under more than one plan, identify the particular plan under which each such grant was made.

2. For grants of incentive plan awards, provide the information called for by columns (c), (d) and (e), or (f), (g) and (h), as applicable. For columns (c) and (f), threshold refers to the minimum amount payable for a certain level of performance under the plan. For columns (d) and (g), target refers to the amount payable if the specified performance target(s) are reached. For columns (e) and (h), maximum refers to the maximum payout possible under the plan. If the award provides only for a single estimated payout, that amount must be reported as the target in columns (d) and (g). In columns (d) and (g), registrants must provide a representative amount based on the previous fiscal year's performance if the target amount is not determinable.

3. In determining if the exercise or base price of an option is less than the closing market price of the underlying security on the date of the grant, the registrant may use either the closing market price as specified in paragraph (a)(6)(v) of this Item, or if no market exists, any other formula prescribed for the security. Whenever the exercise or base price reported in column (k) is not the closing market price, describe the methodology for determining the exercise or base price either by a footnote or accompanying textual narrative.

4. A tandem grant of two instruments, only one of which is granted under an incentive plan, such as an option granted in tandem with a performance share, need be reported only in column (i) or (j), as applicable. For example, an option granted in tandem with a performance share would be reported only as an option grant in column (j), with the tandem feature noted either by a footnote or accompanying textual narrative.

5. Disclose the dollar amount of consideration, if any, paid by the executive officer for the award in a footnote to the appropriate column.

6. If non-equity incentive plan awards are denominated in units or other rights, a separate, adjoining column between columns (b) and (c) shall be added quantifying the units or other rights awarded.

7. Options, SARs and similar option-like instruments granted in connection with a repricing transaction or other material modification shall be reported in this Table. However, the disclosure required by this Table does not apply to any repricing that occurs through a pre-existing formula or mechanism in the plan or award that results in the periodic adjustment of the option or SAR exercise or base price, an antidilution provision in a plan or award, or a recapitalization or similar transaction equally affecting all holders of the class of securities underlying the options or SARs.

8. For any equity awards that are subject to performance conditions, report in column (l) the value at the grant date based upon the probable outcome of such conditions. This amount should be consistent with the estimate of aggregate compensation cost to be recognized over the service period determined as of the grant date under FASB ASC Topic 718, excluding the effect of estimated forfeitures.

e. **Narrative disclosure to summary compensation table and grants of plan-based awards table**.

1. Provide a narrative description of any material factors necessary to an understanding of the information disclosed in the tables required by paragraphs (c) and (d) of this Item. Examples of such factors may include, in given cases, among other things:

    i.   The material terms of each named executive officer's employment agreement or arrangement, whether written or unwritten;

    ii. If at any time during the last fiscal year, any outstanding option or other equity-based award was repriced or otherwise materially modified (such as by extension of exercise periods, the change of vesting or forfeiture conditions, the change or elimination of applicable performance criteria, or the change of the bases upon which returns are determined), a description of each such repricing or other material modification;

    iii. The material terms of any award reported in response to paragraph (d) of this Item, including a general description of the formula or criteria to be applied in determining the amounts payable, and the vesting schedule. For example, state where applicable that dividends will be paid on stock, and if so, the applicable dividend rate and whether that rate is preferential. Describe any performance-based conditions, and any other material conditions, that are applicable to the award. For purposes of the Table required by paragraph (d) of this Item and the narrative disclosure required by paragraph (e) of this Item, performance-based conditions include both performance conditions and market conditions, as those terms are defined in FAS 123R; and

    iv. An explanation of the amount of salary and bonus in proportion to total compensation.

Instructions to Item 402(e)(1).

1. The disclosure required by paragraph (e)(1)(ii) of this Item would not apply to any repricing that occurs through a pre-existing formula or mechanism in the plan or award that results in the periodic adjustment of the option or SAR exercise or base price, an antidilution provision in a plan or award, or a

recapitalization or similar transaction equally affecting all holders of the class of securities underlying the options or SARs.

2. Instructions 4 and 5 to Item 402(b) apply regarding disclosure pursuant to paragraph (e)(1) of target levels with respect to specific quantitative or qualitative performance-related factors considered by the compensation committee or the board of directors, or any other factors or criteria involving confidential trade secrets or confidential commercial or financial information, the disclosure of which would result in competitive harm for the registrant.

3. Reserved.

f. **Outstanding equity awards at fiscal year-end table**.

1. Provide the information specified in paragraph (f)(2) of this Item, concerning unexercised options; stock that has not vested; and equity incentive plan awards for each named executive officer outstanding as of the end of the registrant's last completed fiscal year in the following tabular format:

OUTSTANDING EQUITY AWARDS AT FISCAL YEAR-END

Name	Option Awards					Stock Awards			
	Number of Securities Underlying Unexercised Options (#) Exercisable	Number of Securities Underlying Unexercised Options (#) Unexercisable	Equity Incentive Plan Awards: Number of Securities Underlying Unexercised Unearned Options (#)	Option Exercise Price ($)	Option Expiration Date	Number of Shares or Units of Stock That Have Not Vested (#)	Market Value of Shares or Units of Stock That Have Not Vested ($)	Equity Incentive Plan Awards: Number of Unearned Shares, Units or Other Rights That Have Not Vested (#)	Equity Incentive Plan Awards: Market or Payout Value of Unearned Shares, Units or Other Rights That Have Not Vested ($)
(a)	(b)	(c)	(d)	(e)	(f)	(g)	(h)	(i)	(j)
PEO									
PFO									
A									
B									
C									

2. The Table shall include:

i. The name of the named executive officer (column (a));

ii. On an award-by-award basis, the number of securities underlying unexercised options, including awards that have been transferred other than for value, that are exercisable and that are not reported in column (d) (column (b));

iii.   On an award-by-award basis, the number of securities underlying unexercised options, including awards that have been transferred other than for value, that are unexercisable and that are not reported in column (d) (column (c));

iv.   On an award-by-award basis, the total number of shares underlying unexercised options awarded under any equity incentive plan that have not been earned (column (d));

v.   For each instrument reported in columns (b), (c) and (d), as applicable, the exercise or base price (column (e));

vi.   For each instrument reported in columns (b), (c) and (d), as applicable, the expiration date (column (f));

vii.   The total number of shares of stock that have not vested and that are not reported in column (i) (column (g));

viii.   The aggregate market value of shares of stock that have not vested and that are not reported in column (j) (column (h));

ix.   The total number of shares of stock, units or other rights awarded under any equity incentive plan that have not vested and that have not been earned, and, if applicable the number of shares underlying any such unit or right (column (i)); and

x.   The aggregate market or payout value of shares of stock, units or other rights awarded under any equity incentive plan that have not vested and that have not been earned (column (j)).

Instructions to Item 402(f)(2).

1.   Identify by footnote any award that has been transferred other than for value, disclosing the nature of the transfer.

2.   The vesting dates of options, shares of stock and equity incentive plan awards held at fiscal-year end must be disclosed by footnote to the applicable column where the outstanding award is reported.

3.   Compute the market value of stock reported in column (h) and equity incentive plan awards of stock reported in column (j) by multiplying the closing market price of the registrant's stock at the end of the last completed fiscal year by the number of shares or units of stock or the amount of equity incentive plan awards, respectively. The number of shares or units reported in columns (d) or (i), and the payout value reported in column (j), shall be based on achieving threshold performance goals, except that if the previous fiscal year's performance has exceeded the threshold, the disclosure shall be based on the next higher performance measure (target or maximum) that exceeds the previous fiscal year's performance. If the award provides only for a single estimated payout, that amount should be reported. If the target amount is not determinable, registrants must provide a representative amount based on the previous fiscal year's performance.

4.   Multiple awards may be aggregated where the expiration date and the exercise and/or base price of the instruments is identical. A single award consisting of a combination of options, SARs and/or similar option-like instruments shall be reported as separate awards with respect to each tranche with a different exercise and/or base price or expiration date.

5.   Options or stock awarded under an equity incentive plan are reported in columns (d) or (i) and (j), respectively, until the relevant performance

condition has been satisfied. Once the relevant performance condition has been satisfied, even if the option or stock award is subject to forfeiture conditions, options are reported in column (b) or (c), as appropriate, until they are exercised or expire, or stock is reported in columns (g) and (h) until it vests.

g. **Option exercises and stock vested table.** (1) Provide the information specified in paragraph (g)(2) of this Item, concerning each exercise of stock options, SARs and similar instruments, and each vesting of stock, including restricted stock, restricted stock units and similar instruments, during the last completed fiscal year for each of the named executive officers on an aggregated basis in the following tabular format:

OPTION EXERCISES AND STOCK VESTED

Name	Option Awards		Stock Awards	
	Number of Shares Acquired on Exercise (#)	Value Realized on Exercise ($)	Number of Shares Acquired on Vesting (#)	Value Realized on Vesting ($)
(a)	(b)	(c)	(d)	(e)
PEO				
PFO				
A				
B				
C				

2. The Table shall include:
   i. The name of the executive officer (column (a));
   ii. The number of securities for which the options were exercised (column (b));
   iii. The aggregate dollar value realized upon exercise of options, or upon the transfer of an award for value (column (c));
   iv. The number of shares of stock that have vested (column (d)); and
   v. The aggregate dollar value realized upon vesting of stock, or upon the transfer of an award for value (column (e)).

Instruction to Item 402(g)(2).
Report in column (c) the aggregate dollar amount realized by the named executive officer upon exercise of the options or upon the transfer of such instruments for value. Compute the dollar amount realized upon exercise by determining the difference between the market price of the underlying securities at exercise and the exercise or base price of the options. Do not include the value of any related payment or other consideration provided (or to be provided) by the

registrant to or on behalf of a named executive officer, whether in payment of the exercise price or related taxes. (Any such payment or other consideration provided by the registrant is required to be disclosed in accordance with paragraph (c)(2)(ix) of this Item.) Report in column (e) the aggregate dollar amount realized by the named executive officer upon the vesting of stock or the transfer of such instruments for value. Compute the aggregate dollar amount realized upon vesting by multiplying the number of shares of stock or units by the market value of the underlying shares on the vesting date. For any amount realized upon exercise or vesting for which receipt has been deferred, provide a footnote quantifying the amount and disclosing the terms of the deferral.

h.   **Pension benefits**.
1.   Provide the information specified in paragraph (h)(2) of this Item with respect to each plan that provides for payments or other benefits at, following, or in connection with retirement, in the following tabular format:

PENSION BENEFITS

Name	Plan Name	Number of Years Credited Service (#)	Present Value of Accumulated Benefit ($)	Payments During Last Fiscal Year ($)
(a)	(b)	(c)	(d)	(e)
PEO				
PFO				
A				
B				
C				

2.   The Table shall include:
  i.   The name of the executive officer (column (a));
  ii. The name of the plan (column (b));
  iii. The number of years of service credited to the named executive officer under the plan, computed as of the same pension plan measurement date used for financial statement reporting purposes with respect to the registrant's audited financial statements for the last completed fiscal year (column (c));
  iv. The actuarial present value of the named executive officer's accumulated benefit under the plan, computed as of the same pension plan measurement date used for financial statement reporting purposes with respect to the registrant's audited financial statements for the last completed fiscal year (column (d)); and

      v.   The dollar amount of any payments and benefits paid to the named executive officer during the registrant's last completed fiscal year (column (e)).

Instructions to Item 402(h)(2).

1.   The disclosure required pursuant to this Table applies to each plan that provides for specified retirement payments and benefits, or payments and benefits that will be provided primarily following retirement, including but not limited to tax-qualified defined benefit plans and supplemental executive retirement plans, but excluding tax-qualified defined contribution plans and nonqualified defined contribution plans. Provide a separate row for each such plan in which the named executive officer participates.

2.   For purposes of the amount(s) reported in column (d), the registrant must use the same assumptions used for financial reporting purposes under generally accepted accounting principles, except that retirement age shall be assumed to be the normal retirement age as defined in the plan, or if not so defined, the earliest time at which a participant may retire under the plan without any benefit reduction due to age. The registrant must disclose in the accompanying textual narrative the valuation method and all material assumptions applied in quantifying the present value of the current accrued benefit. A benefit specified in the plan document or the executive's contract itself is not an assumption. Registrants may satisfy all or part of this disclosure by reference to a discussion of those assumptions in the registrant's financial statements, footnotes to the financial statements, or discussion in the Management's Discussion and Analysis. The sections so referenced are deemed part of the disclosure provided pursuant to this Item.

3.   For purposes of allocating the current accrued benefit between tax qualified defined benefit plans and related supplemental plans, apply the limitations applicable to tax qualified defined benefit plans established by the Internal Revenue Code and the regulations thereunder that applied as of the pension plan measurement date.

4.   If a named executive officer's number of years of credited service with respect to any plan is different from the named executive officer's number of actual years of service with the registrant, provide footnote disclosure quantifying the difference and any resulting benefit augmentation.

3.   Provide a succinct narrative description of any material factors necessary to an understanding of each plan covered by the tabular disclosure required by this paragraph. While material factors will vary depending upon the facts, examples of such factors may include, in given cases, among other things:

      i.   The material terms and conditions of payments and benefits available under the plan, including the plan's normal retirement payment and benefit formula and eligibility standards, and the effect of the form of benefit elected on the amount of annual benefits. For this purpose, normal retirement means retirement at the normal retirement age as defined in the plan, or if not so defined, the earliest time at which a participant may retire under the plan without any benefit reduction due to age;

ii. If any named executive officer is currently eligible for early retirement under any plan, identify that named executive officer and the plan, and describe the plan's early retirement payment and benefit formula and eligibility standards. For this purpose, early retirement means retirement at the early retirement age as defined in the plan, or otherwise available to the executive under the plan;

iii. The specific elements of compensation (e.g., salary, bonus, etc.) included in applying the payment and benefit formula, identifying each such element;

iv. With respect to named executive officers' participation in multiple plans, the different purposes for each plan; and

v.   Registrant policies with regard to such matters as granting extra years of credited service.

i. **Nonqualified defined contribution and other nonqualified deferred compensation plans.**

   1. Provide the information specified in paragraph (i)(2) of this Item with respect to each defined contribution or other plan that provides for the deferral of compensation on a basis that is not tax-qualified in the following tabular format:

NONQUALIFIED DEFERRED COMPENSATION

Name	Executive Contributions in Last FY ($)	Registrant Contributions in Last FY ($)	Aggregate Earnings in Last FY ($)	Aggregate Withdrawals/ Distributions ($)	Aggregate Balance at Last FYE ($)
(a)	(b)	(c)	(d)	(e)	(f)
PFO					
PEO					
A					
B					
C					

   2. The Table shall include:

      i.   The name of the executive officer (column (a));

      ii. The dollar amount of aggregate executive contributions during the registrant's last fiscal year (column (b));

      iii. The dollar amount of aggregate registrant contributions during the registrant's last fiscal year (column (c));

      iv. The dollar amount of aggregate interest or other earnings accrued during the registrant's last fiscal year (column (d));

      v.   The aggregate dollar amount of all withdrawals by and distributions to the executive during the registrant's last fiscal year (column (e)); and

      vi. The dollar amount of total balance of the executive's account as of the end of the registrant's last fiscal year (column (f)).

Instruction to Item 402(i)(2).

Provide a footnote quantifying the extent to which amounts reported in the contributions and earnings columns are reported as compensation in the last completed fiscal year in the registrant's Summary Compensation Table and amounts reported in the aggregate balance at last fiscal year end (column (f)) previously were reported as compensation to the named executive officer in the registrant's Summary Compensation Table for previous years.

3.   Provide a succinct narrative description of any material factors necessary to an understanding of each plan covered by tabular disclosure required by this paragraph. While material factors will vary depending upon the facts, examples of such factors may include, in given cases, among other things:

    i.   The type(s) of compensation permitted to be deferred, and any limitations (by percentage of compensation or otherwise) on the extent to which deferral is permitted;

    ii.   The measures for calculating interest or other plan earnings (including whether such measure(s) are selected by the executive or the registrant and the frequency and manner in which selections may be changed), quantifying interest rates and other earnings measures applicable during the registrant's last fiscal year; and

    iii.   Material terms with respect to payouts, withdrawals and other distributions.

j.   **Potential payments upon termination or change-in-control.** Regarding each contract, agreement, plan or arrangement, whether written or unwritten, that provides for payment(s) to a named executive officer at, following, or in connection with any termination, including without limitation resignation, severance, retirement or a constructive termination of a named executive officer, or a change in control of the registrant or a change in the named executive officer's responsibilities, with respect to each named executive officer:

1.   Describe and explain the specific circumstances that would trigger payment(s) or the provision of other benefits, including perquisites and health care benefits;

2.   Describe and quantify the estimated payments and benefits that would be provided in each covered circumstance, whether they would or could be lump sum, or annual, disclosing the duration, and by whom they would be provided;

3.   Describe and explain how the appropriate payment and benefit levels are determined under the various circumstances that trigger payments or provision of benefits;

4.   Describe and explain any material conditions or obligations applicable to the receipt of payments or benefits, including but not limited to non-compete, non-solicitation, non-disparagement or confidentiality agreements, including the duration of such agreements and provisions regarding waiver of breach of such agreements; and

5.   Describe any other material factors regarding each such contract, agreement, plan or arrangement.

Instructions to Item 402(j).

1. The registrant must provide quantitative disclosure under these requirements, applying the assumptions that the triggering event took place on the last business day of the registrant's last completed fiscal year, and the price per share of the registrant's securities is the closing market price as of that date. In the event that uncertainties exist as to the provision of payments and benefits or the amounts involved, the registrant is required to make a reasonable estimate (or a reasonable estimated range of amounts) applicable to the payment or benefit and disclose material assumptions underlying such estimates or estimated ranges in its disclosure. In such event, the disclosure would require forward-looking information as appropriate.

2. Perquisites and other personal benefits or property may be excluded only if the aggregate amount of such compensation will be less than $10,000. Individual perquisites and personal benefits shall be identified and quantified as required by Instruction 4 to paragraph (c)(2)(ix) of this Item. For purposes of quantifying health care benefits, the registrant must use the assumptions used for financial reporting purposes under generally accepted accounting principles.

3. To the extent that the form and amount of any payment or benefit that would be provided in connection with any triggering event is fully disclosed pursuant to paragraph (h) or (i) of this Item, reference may be made to that disclosure. However, to the extent that the form or amount of any such payment or benefit would be enhanced or its vesting or other provisions accelerated in connection with any triggering event, such enhancement or acceleration must be disclosed pursuant to this paragraph.

4. Where a triggering event has actually occurred for a named executive officer and that individual was not serving as a named executive officer of the registrant at the end of the last completed fiscal year, the disclosure required by this paragraph for that named executive officer shall apply only to that triggering event.

5. The registrant need not provide information with respect to contracts, agreements, plans or arrangements to the extent they do not discriminate in scope, terms or operation, in favor of executive officers of the registrant and that are available generally to all salaried employees.

k. **Compensation of directors.**

1. Provide the information specified in paragraph (k)(2) of this Item, concerning the compensation of the directors for the registrant's last completed fiscal year, in the following tabular format:

DIRECTOR COMPENSATION

Name	Fees Earned or Paid in Cash ($)	Stock Awards ($)	Option Awards ($)	Non-Equity Incentive Plan Compensation ($)	Change in Pension Value and Nonqualified Deferred Compensation Earnings	All Other Compensation ($)	Total ($)
(a)	(b)	(c)	(d)	(e)	(f)	(g)	(h)
A							
B							
C							
D							
E							

2. The Table shall include:

i. The name of each director unless such director is also a named executive officer under paragraph (a) of this Item and his or her compensation for service as a director is fully reflected in the Summary Compensation Table pursuant to paragraph (c) of this Item and otherwise as required pursuant to paragraphs (d) through (j) of this Item (column (a));

ii. The aggregate dollar amount of all fees earned or paid in cash for services as a director, including annual retainer fees, committee and/or chairmanship fees, and meeting fees (column (b));

iii. For awards of stock, the aggregate grant date fair value computed in accordance with FASB ASC Topic 718 (column (c));

iv. For awards of options, with or without tandem SARs (including awards that subsequently have been transferred), the aggregate grant date fair value computed in accordance with FASB ASC Topic 718 (column (d))

Instruction to Item 402(k)(2)(iii) and (iv).

For each director, disclose by footnote to the appropriate column: the grant date fair value of each equity award computed in accordance with FAS 123R; for each option, SAR or similar option like instrument for which the registrant has adjusted or amended the exercise or base price during the last completed fiscal year, whether through amendment, cancellation or replacement grants, or any other means ("repriced"), or otherwise has materially modified such awards, the incremental fair value, computed as of the repricing or modification date in accordance with FAS 123R; and the aggregate number of stock awards and the aggregate number of option awards outstanding at fiscal year end. However, the disclosure required by this Instruction does not apply to any repricing that occurs through a pre-existing formula or mechanism in the plan or award that results in the periodic adjustment of the option or SAR exercise or base price, an antidilution provision in a plan or award, or a recapitalization or similar transaction equally affecting all holders of the class of securities underlying the options or SARs.

v.   The dollar value of all earnings for services performed during the fiscal year pursuant to non-equity incentive plans as defined in paragraph (a)(6)(iii) of this Item, and all earnings on any outstanding awards (column (e));

vi.   The sum of the amounts specified in paragraphs (k)(2)(vi)(A) and (B) of this Item (column (f)) as follows:

A.   The aggregate change in the actuarial present value of the director's accumulated benefit under all defined benefit and actuarial pension plans (including supplemental plans) from the pension plan measurement date used for financial statement reporting purposes with respect to the registrant's audited financial statements for the prior completed fiscal year to the pension plan measurement date used for financial statement reporting purposes with respect to the registrant's audited financial statements for the covered fiscal year; and

B.   Above-market or preferential earnings on compensation that is deferred on a basis that is not tax-qualified, including such earnings on nonqualified defined contribution plans;

vii. All other compensation for the covered fiscal year that the registrant could not properly report in any other column of the Director Compensation Table (column (g)). Each compensation item that is not properly reportable in columns (b) - (f), regardless of the amount of the compensation item, must be included in column (g). Such compensation must include, but is not limited to:

A.   Perquisites and other personal benefits, or property, unless the aggregate amount of such compensation is less than $10,000;

B.   All "gross-ups" or other amounts reimbursed during the fiscal year for the payment of taxes;

C.   For any security of the registrant or its subsidiaries purchased from the registrant or its subsidiaries (through deferral of salary or bonus, or otherwise) at a discount from the market price of such security at the date of purchase, unless that discount is available generally, either to all security holders or to all salaried employees of the registrant, the compensation cost, if any, computed in accordance with FAS 123R;

D.   The amount paid or accrued to any director pursuant to a plan or arrangement in connection with:

1.   The resignation, retirement or any other termination of such director; or

2.   A change in control of the registrant;

E.   Registrant contributions or other allocations to vested and unvested defined contribution plans;

F.   Consulting fees earned from, or paid or payable by the registrant and/or its subsidiaries (including joint ventures)

G. The annual costs of payments and promises of payments pursuant to director legacy programs and similar charitable award programs;

H. The dollar value of any insurance premiums paid by, or on behalf of, the registrant during the covered fiscal year with respect to life insurance for the benefit of a director; and

I. The dollar value of any dividends or other earnings paid on stock or option awards, when those amounts were not factored into the grant date fair value required to be reported for the stock or option award in column (c) or (d); and

Instructions to Item 402(k)(2)(vii).

1. Programs in which registrants agree to make donations to one or more charitable institutions in a director's name, payable by the registrant currently or upon a designated event, such as the retirement or death of the director, are charitable awards programs or director legacy programs for purposes of the disclosure required by paragraph (k)(2)(vii)(G) of this Item. Provide footnote disclosure of the total dollar amount payable under the program and other material terms of each such program for which tabular disclosure is provided.

2. Any item reported for a director pursuant to paragraph (k)(2)(vii) of this Item that is not a perquisite or personal benefit and whose value exceeds $10,000 must be identified and quantified in a footnote to column (g). All items of compensation are required to be included in the Director Compensation Table without regard to whether such items are required to be identified other than as specifically noted in this Item.

3. Perquisites and personal benefits may be excluded as long as the total value of all perquisites and personal benefits for a director is less than $10,000. If the total value of all perquisites and personal benefits is $10,000 or more for any director, then each perquisite or personal benefit, regardless of its amount, must be identified by type. If perquisites and personal benefits are required to be reported for a director pursuant to this rule, then each perquisite or personal benefit that exceeds the greater of $25,000 or 10% of the total amount of perquisites and personal benefits for that director must be quantified and disclosed in a footnote. Perquisites and other personal benefits shall be valued on the basis of the aggregate incremental cost to the registrant. With respect to the perquisite or other personal benefit for which footnote quantification is required, the registrant shall describe in the footnote its methodology for computing the aggregate incremental cost. Reimbursements of taxes owed with respect to perquisites or other personal benefits must be included in column (g) and are subject to separate quantification and identification as tax reimbursements (paragraph (k)(2)(vii)(B) of this Item) even if the associated perquisites or other personal benefits are not required to be included because the total amount of all perquisites or personal benefits for an individual director is less

than $10,000 or are required to be identified but are not required to be separately quantified.

viii. The dollar value of total compensation for the covered fiscal year (column (h)). With respect to each director, disclose the sum of all amounts reported in columns (b) through (g).

Instruction to Item 402(k)(2).

Two or more directors may be grouped in a single row in the Table if all elements of their compensation are identical. The names of the directors for whom disclosure is presented on a group basis should be clear from the Table.

3.   Narrative to director compensation table.

Provide a narrative description of any material factors necessary to an understanding of the director compensation disclosed in this Table. While material factors will vary depending upon the facts, examples of such factors may include, in given cases, among other things:

i. A description of standard compensation arrangements (such as fees for retainer, committee service, service as chairman of the board or a committee, and meeting attendance); and

ii. Whether any director has a different compensation arrangement, identifying that director and describing the terms of that arrangement.

Instruction to Item 402(k).

In addition to the Instruction to paragraphs (k)(2)(iii) and (iv) and the Instructions to paragraph (k)(2)(vii) of this Item, the following apply equally to paragraph (k) of this Item: Instructions 2 and 4 to paragraph (c) of this Item; Instructions to paragraphs (c)(2)(iii) and (iv) of this Item; Instructions to paragraphs (c)(2)(v) and (vi) of this Item; Instructions to paragraph (c)(2)(vii) of this Item; Instructions to paragraph (c)(2)(viii) of this Item; and Instructions 1 and 5 to paragraph (c)(2)(ix) of this Item. These Instructions apply to the columns in the Director Compensation Table that are analogous to the columns in the Summary Compensation Table to which they refer and to disclosures under paragraph (k) of this Item that correspond to analogous disclosures provided for in paragraph (c) of this Item to which they refer.

***

s.   **Narrative disclosure of the registrant's compensation policies and practices as they relate to the registrant's risk management**. To the extent that risks arising from the registrant's compensation policies and practices for its employees are reasonably likely to have a material adverse effect on the registrant, discuss the registrant's policies and practices of compensating its employees, including non-executive officers, as they relate to risk management practices and risk-taking incentives. While the situations requiring disclosure will vary depending on the particular registrant and compensation policies and practices, situations that may trigger disclosure include, among others, compensation policies and practices: at a business unit of the company that carries a significant portion of the registrant's risk profile; at a business unit with compensation structured significantly differently than other units within the registrant; at a business unit that is significantly more profitable than others within the registrant; at a business unit where compensation expense is a significant percentage of the unit's revenues; and that vary significantly from the overall risk and reward structure of the registrant, such as when bonuses are awarded upon accomplishment of a task, while the income and risk to the registrant from the task extend over a significantly longer period of time. The purpose of this paragraph (s) is to provide investors material information concerning how the registrant compensates and incentivizes its employees that may create risks that are reasonably likely to have a material adverse effect on the registrant. While the information to be disclosed pursuant to this paragraph (s) will vary depending upon the nature of the registrant's business and the compensation approach, the following are examples of the issues that the registrant may need to address for the business units or employees discussed:

1.   The general design philosophy of the registrant's compensation policies and practices for employees whose behavior would be most affected by the incentives established by the policies and practices, as such policies and practices relate to or affect risk taking by employees on behalf of the registrant, and the manner of their implementation;

2.   The registrant's risk assessment or incentive considerations, if any, in structuring its compensation policies and practices or in awarding and paying compensation;

3.   How the registrant's compensation policies and practices relate to the realization of risks resulting from the actions of employees in both the short term and the long term, such as through policies requiring claw backs or imposing holding periods;

4.   The registrant's policies regarding adjustments to its compensation policies and practices to address changes in its risk profile;

5.   Material adjustments the registrant has made to its compensation policies and practices as a result of changes in its risk profile; and

6.   The extent to which the registrant monitors its compensation policies and practices to determine whether its risk management objectives are being met with respect to incentivizing its employees.

Instruction to Item 402. Specify the applicable fiscal year in the title to each table required under this Item which calls for disclosure as of or for a completed fiscal year.

Item 403 – Security Ownership of Certain Beneficial Owners and Management

a.   **Security ownership of certain beneficial owners.** Furnish the following information, as of the most recent practicable date, substantially in the tabular form indicated, with respect to any person (including any ``group'' as that term is used in section 13(d)(3) of the Exchange Act) who is known to the registrant to be the beneficial owner of more than five percent of any class of the registrant's voting securities. The address given in column (2) may be a business, mailing or residence address. Show in column (3) the total number of shares beneficially owned and in column (4) the percentage of class so owned. Of the number of shares shown in column (3), indicate by footnote or otherwise the amount known to be shares with respect to which such listed beneficial owner has the right to acquire beneficial ownership, as specified in Rule 13d-3(d)(1) under the Exchange Act.

(1) Title of Class	(2) Name and Address of Beneficial Owner	(3) Amount and Nature of Beneficial Ownership	(4) Percent of Class

b. **Security ownership of management**. Furnish the following information, as of the most recent practicable date, in substantially the tabular form indicated, as to each class of equity securities of the registrant or any of its parents or subsidiaries, including directors' qualifying shares, beneficially owned by all directors and nominees, naming them, each of the named executive officers as defined in Item 402(a)(3), and directors and executive officers of the registrant as a group, without naming them. Show in column (3) the total number of shares beneficially owned and in column (4) the percent of the class so owned. Of the number of shares shown in column (3), indicate, by footnote or otherwise, the amount of shares that are pledged as security and the amount of shares with respect to which such persons have the right to acquire beneficial ownership as specified in 13d-3(d)(1) of this chapter.

(1) Title of Class	(2) Name of Beneficial Owner	(3) Amount and Nature of Beneficial Ownership	(4) Percent of Class

c. **Changes in control.** Describe any arrangements, known to the registrant, including any pledge by any person of securities of the registrant or any of its parents, the operation of which may at a subsequent date result in a change in control of the registrant.

Instructions to Item 403:

1. The percentages are to be calculated on the basis of the amount of outstanding securities, excluding securities held by or for the account of the registrant or its subsidiaries, plus securities deemed outstanding pursuant to Rule 13d-3(d)(1) under the Exchange Act. For purposes of paragraph (b), if the percentage of shares beneficially owned by any director or nominee, or by all directors and officers of the registrant as a group, does not exceed one percent of the class so owned, the registrant may, in lieu of furnishing a precise percentage, indicate this fact by means of an asterisk and explanatory footnote or other similar means.

2. For the purposes of this Item, beneficial ownership shall be determined in accordance with Rule 13d-3 under the Exchange Act. Include such additional subcolumns or other appropriate explanation of column (3) necessary to reflect amounts as to which the beneficial owner has (A) sole voting power, (B) shared voting power, (C) sole investment power, or (D) shared investment power.

3. The registrant shall be deemed to know the contents of any statements filed with the Commission pursuant to section 13(d) or 13(g) of the Exchange Act. When applicable, a registrant may rely upon information set forth in such statements unless the registrant knows or has reason to believe that such information is not complete or accurate or that a statement or amendment should have been filed and was not.

4. For purposes of furnishing information pursuant to paragraph (a) of this Item, the registrant may indicate the source and date of such information.

5. Where more than one beneficial owner is known to be listed for the same securities, appropriate disclosure should be made to avoid confusion. For purposes of paragraph (b), in computing the aggregate number of shares owned by directors and officers of the registrant as a group, the same shares shall not be counted more than once.

6. Paragraph (c) of this Item does not require a description of ordinary default provisions contained in the charter, trust indentures or other governing instruments relating to securities of the registrant.

7. Where the holder(s) of voting securities reported pursuant to paragraph (a) hold more than five percent of any class of voting securities of the registrant pursuant to any voting trust or similar agreement, state the title of such securities, the amount held or to be held pursuant to the trust or agreement (if not clear from the table) and the duration of the agreement. Give the names and addresses of the voting trustees and outline briefly their voting rights and other powers under the trust or agreement.

Item 404 – Transactions with related persons, promoters and certain control persons.

a. **Transactions with related persons**. Describe any transaction, since the beginning of the registrant's last fiscal year, or any currently proposed transaction, in which the registrant was or is to be a participant and the amount involved exceeds $120,000, and in which any related person had or will have a direct or indirect material interest. Disclose the following information regarding the transaction:

  1. The name of the related person and the basis on which the person is a related person.

  2. The related person's interest in the transaction with the registrant, including the related person's position(s) or relationship(s) with, or ownership in, a firm, corporation, or other entity that is a party to, or has an interest in, the transaction.

  3. The approximate dollar value of the amount involved in the transaction.

  4. The approximate dollar value of the amount of the related person's interest in the transaction, which shall be computed without regard to the amount of profit or loss.

  5. In the case of indebtedness, disclosure of the amount involved in the transaction shall include the largest aggregate amount of principal outstanding during the period for which disclosure is provided, the amount thereof outstanding as of the latest practicable date, the amount of principal paid during the periods for which disclosure is provided, the amount of interest paid during the period for which disclosure is provided, and the rate or amount of interest payable on the indebtedness.

  6. Any other information regarding the transaction or the related person in the context of the transaction that is material to investors in light of the circumstances of the particular transaction.

Instructions to Item 404(a).

  1. For the purposes of paragraph (a) of this Item, the term related person means:

    a. Any person who was in any of the following categories at any time during the specified period for which disclosure under paragraph (a) of this Item is required:

      i.   Any director or executive officer of the registrant;

      ii.   Any nominee for director, when the information called for by paragraph (a) of this Item is being presented in a proxy or information statement relating to the election of that nominee for director; or

      iii.   Any immediate family member of a director or executive officer of the registrant, or of any nominee for director when the information called for by paragraph (a) of this Item is being presented in a proxy or information statement relating to the election of that nominee for director, which means any child, stepchild, parent, stepparent, spouse, sibling, mother-in-law, father-in-law, son-in-law, daughter-in-law, brother-in-law, or sister-in-law of such director, executive officer or nominee for director, and any person (other than a tenant or employee) sharing the household of such director, executive officer or nominee for director; and

  b.   Any person who was in any of the following categories when a transaction in which such person had a direct or indirect material interest occurred or existed:

      i.   A security holder covered by Item 403(a); or

      ii.   Any immediate family member of any such security holder, which means any child, stepchild, parent, stepparent, spouse, sibling, mother-in-law, father-in-law, son-in-law, daughter-in-law, brother-in-law, or sister-in-law of such security holder, and any person (other than a tenant or employee) sharing the household of such security holder.

2.   For purposes of paragraph (a) of this Item, a <u>transaction </u>includes, but is not limited to, any financial transaction, arrangement or relationship (including any indebtedness or guarantee of indebtedness) or any series of similar transactions, arrangements or relationships.

3.   The amount involved in the transaction shall be computed by determining the dollar value of the amount involved in the transaction in question, which shall include:

  a.   In the case of any lease or other transaction providing for periodic payments or installments, the aggregate amount of all periodic payments or installments due on or after the beginning of the registrant's last fiscal year, including any required or optional payments due during or at the conclusion of the lease or other transaction providing for periodic payments or installments; and

  b.   In the case of indebtedness, the largest aggregate amount of all indebtedness outstanding at any time since the beginning of the registrant's last fiscal year and all amounts of interest payable on it during the last fiscal year.

4.   In the case of a transaction involving indebtedness:

  a.   The following items of indebtedness may be excluded from the calculation of the amount of indebtedness and need not be disclosed: amounts due from the related person for purchases of goods and services subject to usual trade terms, for ordinary business travel and expense payments and for other transactions in the ordinary course of business;

  b.   Disclosure need not be provided of any indebtedness transaction for the related persons specified in Instruction 1.b. to paragraph (a) of this Item; and

  c.   If the lender is a bank, savings and loan association, or broker-dealer extending credit under Federal Reserve Regulation T and the loans are not disclosed as nonaccrual, past due, restructured or potential problems (see Item III.C.1. and 2. of Industry Guide 3, Statistical Disclosure by Bank Holding Companies), disclosure under paragraph (a) of this Item may consist of a statement, if such is the case, that the loans to such persons:

    i.   Were made in the ordinary course of business;

    ii.   Were made on substantially the same terms, including interest rates and collateral, as those prevailing at the time for comparable loans with persons not related to the lender; and

    iii.   Did not involve more than the normal risk of collectibility or present other unfavorable features.

5.   a.   Disclosure of an employment relationship or transaction involving an executive officer and any related compensation solely resulting from that employment relationship or transaction need not be provided pursuant to paragraph (a) of this Item if:

    i.   The compensation arising from the relationship or transaction is reported pursuant to Item 402; or

    ii.   The executive officer is not an immediate family member (as specified in Instruction 1 to paragraph (a) of this Item) and such compensation would have been reported under Item 402 as compensation earned for services to the registrant if the executive officer was a named executive officer as that term is defined in Item 402(a)(3), and such compensation had been approved, or recommended to the board of directors of the registrant for approval, by the compensation committee of the board of directors (or group of independent directors performing a similar function) of the registrant.

    b.   Disclosure of compensation to a director need not be provided pursuant to paragraph (a) of this Item if the compensation is reported pursuant to Item 402(k).

6.   A person who has a position or relationship with a firm, corporation, or other entity that engages in a transaction with the registrant shall not be deemed to have an indirect material interest within the meaning of paragraph (a) of this Item where:

    a.   The interest arises only:

       i.   From such person's position as a director of another corporation or organization that is a party to the transaction; or

       ii.   From the direct or indirect ownership by such person and all other persons specified in Instruction 1 to paragraph (a) of this Item, in the aggregate, of less than a ten percent equity interest in another person (other than a partnership) which is a party to the transaction; or iii. From both such position and ownership; or

    b.   The interest arises only from such person's position as a limited partner in a partnership in which the person and all other persons specified in Instruction 1 to paragraph (a) of this Item, have an interest of less than ten percent, and the person is not a general partner of and does not hold another position in the partnership.

7.   Disclosure need not be provided pursuant to paragraph (a) of this Item if:

    a.   The transaction is one where the rates or charges involved in the transaction are determined by competitive bids, or the transaction involves the rendering of services as a common or contract carrier, or public utility, at rates or charges fixed in conformity with law or governmental authority;

b. The transaction involves services as a bank depositary of funds, transfer agent, registrar, trustee under a trust indenture, or similar services; or

c. The interest of the related person arises solely from the ownership of a class of equity securities of the registrant and all holders of that class of equity securities of the registrant received the same benefit on a pro rata basis.

b. **Review, approval or ratification of transactions with related persons.**

1. Describe the registrant's policies and procedures for the review, approval, or ratification of any transaction required to be reported under paragraph (a) of this Item. While the material features of such policies and procedures will vary depending on the particular circumstances, examples of such features may include, in given cases, among other things:

    i. The types of transactions that are covered by such policies and procedures;

    ii. The standards to be applied pursuant to such policies and procedures;

    iii. The persons or groups of persons on the board of directors or otherwise who are responsible for applying such policies and procedures; and

    iv. A statement of whether such policies and procedures are in writing and, if not, how such policies and procedures are evidenced.

2. Identify any transaction required to be reported under paragraph (a) of this Item since the beginning of the registrant's last fiscal year where such policies and procedures did not require review, approval or ratification or where such policies and procedures were not followed.

Instruction to Item 404(b).

Disclosure need not be provided pursuant to this paragraph regarding any transaction that occurred at a time before the related person became one of the enumerated persons in Instruction 1.a.i., ii., or iii. to Item 404(a) if such transaction did not continue after the related person became one of the enumerated persons in Instruction 1.a.i., ii., or iii. to Item 404(a).

c. **Promoters and certain control persons**.

1. Registrants that are filing a registration statement on Form S-1 under the Securities Act or on Form 10 under the Exchange Act and that had a promoter at any time during the past five fiscal years shall:

    i. State the names of the promoter(s), the nature and amount of anything of value (including money, property, contracts, options or rights of any kind) received or to be received by each promoter, directly or indirectly, from the registrant and the nature and amount of any assets, services or other consideration therefore received or to be received by the registrant; and

    ii. As to any assets acquired or to be acquired by the registrant from a promoter, state the amount at which the assets were acquired or are to be acquired and the principle followed or to be followed in determining such amount, and identify the persons making the determination and their relationship, if any, with the registrant or any promoter. If the assets were acquired by the promoter within two years prior to their transfer to the registrant, also state the cost thereof to the promoter.

2. Registrants shall provide the disclosure required by paragraphs (c)(1)(i) and (c)(1)(ii) of this Item as to any person who acquired control of a registrant that is a shell company, or any person that is part of a group, consisting of two or more persons that agree to act together for the purpose of acquiring, holding, voting or disposing of equity securities of a registrant, that acquired control of a registrant that is a shell company. For purposes of this Item, shell company has the same meaning as in Rule 405 under the Securities Act and Rule 12b-2 under the Exchange Act.

d. **Smaller reporting companies**. A registrant that qualifies as a "smaller reporting company," as defined by Rule 229.10(f)(1), must provide the following information in order to comply with this Item:

1. The information required by paragraph (a) of this Item for the period specified there for a transaction in which the amount involved exceeds the lesser of $120,000 or one percent of the average of the smaller reporting company's total assets at year end for the last two completed fiscal years;

2. The information required by paragraph (c) of this Item; and

3. A list of all parents of the smaller reporting company showing the basis of control and as to each parent, the percentage of voting securities owned or other basis of control by its immediate parent, if any.

Instruction to Item 404(d)

1. Include information for any material underwriting discounts and commissions upon the sale of securities by the smaller reporting company where any of the persons specified in paragraph (a) of this Item was or is to be a principal underwriter or is a controlling person or member of a firm that was or is to be a principal underwriter.

2. For smaller reporting companies information shall be given for the period specified in paragraph (a) of this Item and, in addition, for the fiscal year preceding the small reporting company's last fiscal year.

Instructions to Item 404.

1. If the information called for by this Item is being presented in a registration statement filed pursuant to the Securities Act or the Exchange Act, information shall be given for the periods specified in the Item and, in addition, for the two fiscal years preceding the registrant's last fiscal year, unless the information is being incorporated by reference into a registration statement on Form S-4, in which case, information shall be given for the periods specified in the Item.

2. A foreign private issuer will be deemed to comply with this Item if it provides the information required by Item 7.B. of Form 20-F with more detailed information provided if otherwise made publicly available or required to be disclosed by the issuer's home jurisdiction or a market in which its securities are listed or traded.

Item 405 – Compliance with Section 16(a) of the Exchange Act

Every registrant having a class of equity securities registered pursuant to section 12 of the Exchange Act, every closed-end investment company registered under the Investment Company Act of 1940, shall:

a. Based solely upon a review of Forms 3 and 4 and amendments thereto furnished to the registrant under Rule16a-3(e) during its most recent fiscal year and Forms 5 and amendments thereto furnished to the registrant with respect to its most recent fiscal year, and any written representation referred to in paragraph (b)(1) of this section.

    1. Under the caption "Section 16(a) Beneficial Ownership Reporting Compliance," identify each person who, at any time during the fiscal year, was a director, officer, beneficial owner of more than ten percent of any class of equity securities of the registrant registered pursuant to section 12 of the Exchange Act, or any other person subject to section 16 of the Exchange Act with respect to the registrant because of the requirements of section 30 of the Investment Company Act Act ("reporting person") that failed to file on a timely basis, as disclosed in the above Forms, reports required by section 16(a) of the Exchange Act during the most recent fiscal year or prior fiscal years.

    2. For each such person, set forth the number of late reports, the number of transactions that were not reported on a timely basis, and any known failure to file a required Form. A known failure to file would include, but not be limited to, a failure to file a Form 3, which is required of all reporting persons, and a failure to file a Form 5 in the absence of the written representation referred to in paragraph (b)(1) of this section, unless the registrant otherwise knows that no Form 5 is required.

Note: The disclosure requirement is based on a review of the forms submitted to the registrant during and with respect to its most recent fiscal year, as specified above. Accordingly, a failure to file timely need only be disclosed once. For example, if in the most recently concluded fiscal year a reporting person filed a Form 4 disclosing a transaction that took place in the prior fiscal year, and should have been reported in that year, the registrant should disclose that late filing and transaction pursuant to this Item 405 with respect to the most recently concluded fiscal year, but not in material filed with respect to subsequent years.

b. With respect to the disclosure required by paragraph (a) of this section, if the registrant:

    1. Receives a written representation from the reporting person that no Form 5 is required; and

    2. Maintains the representation for two years, making a copy available to the Commission or its staff upon request, the registrant need not identify such reporting person pursuant to paragraph (a) of this section as having failed to file a Form 5 with respect to that fiscal year.

Item 406 – Code of Ethics

a. Disclose whether the registrant has adopted a code of ethics that applies to the registrant's principal executive officer, principal financial officer, principal accounting officer or controller, or persons performing similar functions. If the registrant has not adopted such a code of ethics, explain why it has not done so.

b. For purposes of this Item 406, the term *code of ethics* means written standards that are reasonably designed to deter wrongdoing and to promote:

1. Honest and ethical conduct, including the ethical handling of actual or apparent conflicts of interest between personal and professional relationships;

2. Full, fair, accurate, timely, and understandable disclosure in reports and documents that a registrant files with, or submits to, the Commission and in other public communications made by the registrant;

3. Compliance with applicable governmental laws, rules and regulations;

4. The prompt internal reporting of violations of the code to an appropriate person or persons identified in the code; and

5. Accountability for adherence to the code.

c. The registrant must:

1. File with the Commission a copy of its code of ethics that applies to the registrant's principal executive officer, principal financial officer, principal accounting officer or controller, or persons performing similar functions, as an exhibit to its annual report;

2. Post the text of such code of ethics on its Internet website and disclose, in its annual report, its Internet address and the fact that it has posted such code of ethics on its Internet Web site; or

3. Undertake in its annual report filed with the Commission to provide to any person without charge, upon request, a copy of such code of ethics and explain the manner in which such request may be made.

d. If the registrant intends to satisfy the disclosure requirement under Item 10 of Form 8-K regarding an amendment to, or a waiver from, a provision of its code of ethics that applies to the registrant's principal executive officer, principal financial officer, principal accounting officer or controller, or persons performing similar functions and that relates to any element of the code of ethics definition enumerated in paragraph (b) of this Item by posting such information on its Internet website, disclose the registrant's Internet address and such intention.

Instructions to Item 406:

1. A registrant may have separate codes of ethics for different types of officers. Furthermore, a code of ethics within the meaning of paragraph (b) of this Item may be a portion of a broader document that addresses additional topics or that applies to more persons than those specified in paragraph (a). In satisfying the requirements of paragraph (c), a registrant need only file, post or provide the portions of a broader document that constitutes a code of ethics as defined in paragraph (b) and that apply to the persons specified in paragraph (a).

2. If a registrant elects to satisfy paragraph (c) of this Item by posting its code of ethics on its website pursuant to paragraph (c)(2), the code of ethics must remain accessible on its Web site for as long as the registrant remains subject to the requirements of this Item and chooses to comply with this Item by posting its code on its Web site pursuant to paragraph (c)(2).

3. A registrant that is an Asset-Backed Issuer (as defined in Rule 13a-14(g) and 15d-14(g) under the Exchange Act) is not required to disclose the information required by this Item.

Item 407 – Corporate governance.

a. **Director independence**. Identify each director and, when the disclosure called for by this paragraph is being presented in a proxy or information statement relating to the election of directors, each nominee for director, that is independent under the independence standards applicable to the registrant under paragraph (a)(1) of this Item. In addition, if such independence standards contain independence requirements for committees of the board of directors, identify each director that is a member of the compensation, nominating or audit committee that is not independent under such committee independence standards. If the registrant does not have a separately designated audit, nominating or compensation committee or committee performing similar functions, the registrant must provide the disclosure of directors that are not independent with respect to all members of the board of directors applying such committee independence standards.

1. In determining whether or not the director or nominee for director is independent for the purposes of paragraph (a) of this Item, the registrant shall use the applicable definition of independence, as follows:

    i. If the registrant is a listed issuer whose securities are listed on a national securities exchange or in an inter-dealer quotation system which has requirements that a majority of the board of directors be independent, the registrant's definition of independence that it uses for determining if a majority of the board of directors is independent in compliance with the listing standards applicable to the registrant. When determining whether the members of a committee of the board of directors are independent, the registrant's definition of independence that it uses for determining if the members of that specific committee are independent in compliance with the independence standards applicable for the members of the specific committee in the listing standards of the national securities exchange or inter-dealer quotation system that the registrant uses for determining if a majority of the board of directors are independent. If the registrant does not have independence standards for a committee, the independence standards for that specific committee in the listing standards of the national securities exchange or inter-dealer quotation system that the registrant uses for determining if a majority of the board of directors are independent.

    ii. If the registrant is not a listed issuer, a definition of independence of a national securities exchange or of an inter-dealer quotation system which has requirements that a majority of the board of directors be independent, and state which definition is used. Whatever such definition the registrant chooses, it must use the same definition with respect to all directors and nominees for director. When determining whether the members of a specific committee of the board of directors are independent, if the national securities exchange or national securities association whose standards are used has independence standards for the members of a specific committee, use those committee specific standards.

    iii. If the information called for by paragraph (a) of this Item is being presented in a registration statement on Form S-1 under the Securities

Act or on a Form 10 under the Exchange Act where the registrant has applied for listing with a national securities exchange or in an inter-dealer quotation system which has requirements that a majority of the board of directors be independent, the definition of independence that the registrant uses for determining if a majority of the board of directors is independent, and the definition of independence that the registrant uses for determining if members of the specific committee of the board of directors are independent, that is in compliance with the independence listing standards of the national securities exchange or inter-dealer quotation system on which it has applied for listing, or if the registrant has not adopted such definitions, the independence standards for determining if the majority of the board of directors is independent and if members of the committee of the board of directors are independent of that national securities exchange or inter-dealer quotation system.

2.   If the registrant uses its own definitions for determining whether its directors and nominees for director, and members of specific committees of the board of directors, are independent, disclose whether these definitions are available to security holders on the registrant's Web site. If so, provide the registrant's Web site address. If not, include a copy of these policies in an appendix to the registrant's proxy statement or information statement that is provided to security holders at least once every three fiscal years or if the policies have been materially amended since the beginning of the registrant's last fiscal year. If a current copy of the policies is not available to security holders on the registrant's Web site, and is not included as an appendix to the registrant's proxy statement or information statement, identify the most recent fiscal year in which the policies were so included in satisfaction of this requirement.

3.   For each director and nominee for director that is identified as independent, describe, by specific category or type, any transactions, relationships or arrangements not disclosed pursuant to Item 404(a), or for investment companies, Item 22(b) of Schedule 14A, that were considered by the board of directors under the applicable independence definitions in determining that the director is independent.

Instructions to Item 407(a).

1.   If the registrant is a listed issuer whose securities are listed on a national securities exchange or in an inter-dealer quotation system which has requirements that a majority of the board of directors be independent, and also has exemptions to those requirements (for independence of a majority of the board of directors or committee member independence) upon which the registrant relied, disclose the exemption relied upon and explain the basis for the registrant's conclusion that such exemption is applicable. The same disclosure should be provided if the registrant is not a listed issuer and the national securities exchange or inter-dealer quotation system selected by the registrant has exemptions that are applicable to the registrant. Any national securities exchange or inter-dealer quotation system which has requirements that at least 50 percent of the members of a small business issuer's board of directors must be independent shall be considered a national securities exchange or inter-dealer quotation system which has requirements that a majority of the board of directors

be independent for the purposes of the disclosure required by paragraph (a) of this Item.

2. Registrants shall provide the disclosure required by paragraph (a) of this Item for any person who served as a director during any part of the last completed fiscal year, except that no information called for by paragraph (a) of this Item need be given in a registration statement filed at a time when the registrant is not subject to the reporting requirements of section 13(a) or 15(d) of the Exchange Act respecting any director who is no longer a director at the time of effectiveness of the registration statement.

3. The description of the specific categories or types of transactions, relationships or arrangements required by paragraph (a)(3) of this Item must be provided in such detail as is necessary to fully describe the nature of the transactions, relationships or arrangements.

b. **Board meetings and committees; annual meeting attendance**.

1. State the total number of meetings of the board of directors (including regularly scheduled and special meetings) which were held during the last full fiscal year. Name each incumbent director who during the last full fiscal year attended fewer than 75 percent of the aggregate of:

    i.   The total number of meetings of the board of directors (held during the period for which he has been a director); and

    ii. The total number of meetings held by all committees of the board on which he served (during the periods that he served).

2. Describe the registrant's policy, if any, with regard to board members' attendance at annual meetings of security holders and state the number of board members who attended the prior year's annual meeting.

    Instruction to Item 407(b)(2).

    In lieu of providing the information required by paragraph (b)(2) of this Item in the proxy statement, the registrant may instead provide the registrant's Web site address where such information appears.

3. State whether or not the registrant has standing audit, nominating and compensation committees of the board of directors, or committees performing similar functions. If the registrant has such committees, however designated, identify each committee member, state the number of committee meetings held by each such committee during the last fiscal year and describe briefly the functions performed by each such committee. Such disclosure need not be provided to the extent it is duplicative of disclosure provided in accordance with paragraph (c), (d) or (e) of this Item.

c. **Nominating committee**.

1. If the registrant does not have a standing nominating committee or committee performing similar functions, state the basis for the view of the board of directors that it is appropriate for the registrant not to have such a committee and identify each director who participates in the consideration of director nominees.

2. Provide the following information regarding the registrant's director nomination process:

i. State whether or not the nominating committee has a charter. If the nominating committee has a charter, provide the disclosure required by Instruction 2 to this Item regarding the nominating committee charter;

ii. If the nominating committee has a policy with regard to the consideration of any director candidates recommended by security holders, provide a description of the material elements of that policy, which shall include, but need not be limited to, a statement as to whether the committee will consider director candidates recommended by security holders;

iii. If the nominating committee does not have a policy with regard to the consideration of any director candidates recommended by security holders, state that fact and state the basis for the view of the board of directors that it is appropriate for the registrant not to have such a policy;

iv. If the nominating committee will consider candidates recommended by security holders, describe the procedures to be followed by security holders in submitting such recommendations;

v. Describe any specific minimum qualifications that the nominating committee believes must be met by a nominating committee-recommended nominee for a position on the registrant's board of directors, and describe any specific qualities or skills that the nominating committee believes are necessary for one or more of the registrant's directors to possess;

vi. Describe the nominating committee's process for identifying and evaluating nominees for director, including nominees recommended by security holders, and any differences in the manner in which the nominating committee evaluates nominees for director based on whether the nominee is recommended by a security holder, and whether, and if so how, the nominating committee (or the board) considers diversity in identifying nominees for director. If the nominating committee (or the board) has a policy with regard to the consideration of diversity in identifying director nominees, describe how this policy is implemented, as well as how the nominating committee (or the board) assesses the effectiveness of its policy;

vii. With regard to each nominee approved by the nominating committee for inclusion on the registrant's proxy card (other than nominees who are executive officers or who are directors standing for re-election), state which one or more of the following categories of persons or entities recommended that nominee: security holder, non-management director, chief executive officer, other executive officer, third-party search firm, or other specified source. With regard to each such nominee approved by a nominating committee of an investment company, state which one or more of the following additional categories of persons or entities recommended that nominee: security holder, director, chief executive officer, other executive officer, or employee of the investment company's investment adviser, principal underwriter, or any affiliated person of the investment adviser or principal underwriter;

viii. If the registrant pays a fee to any third party or parties to identify or evaluate or assist in identifying or evaluating potential nominees, disclose the function performed by each such third party; and

ix. If the registrant's nominating committee received, by a date not later than the 120th calendar day before the date of the registrant's proxy statement released to security holders in connection with the previous year's annual meeting, a recommended nominee from a security holder that beneficially owned more than 5% of the registrant's voting common stock for at least one year as of the date the recommendation was made, or from a group of security holders that beneficially owned, in the aggregate, more than 5% of the registrant's voting common stock, with each of the securities used to calculate that ownership held for at least one year as of the date the recommendation was made, identify the candidate and the security holder or security holder group that recommended the candidate and disclose whether the nominating committee chose to nominate the candidate, provided, however, that no such identification or disclosure is required without the written consent of both the security holder or security holder group and the candidate to be so identified.

Instructions to Item 407(c)(2)(ix).

1. For purposes of paragraph (c)(2)(ix) of this Item, the percentage of securities held by a nominating security holder may be determined using information set forth in the registrant's most recent quarterly or annual report, and any current report subsequent thereto, filed with the Commission pursuant to the Exchange Act (or, in the case of a registrant that is an investment company registered under the Investment Company Act of 1940, the registrant's most recent report on Form N-CSR, unless the party relying on such report knows or has reason to believe that the information contained therein is inaccurate.

2. For purposes of the registrant's obligation to provide the disclosure specified in paragraph (c)(2)(ix) of this Item, where the date of the annual meeting has been changed by more than 30 days from the date of the previous year's meeting, the obligation under that Item will arise where the registrant receives the security holder recommendation a reasonable time before the registrant begins to print and mail its proxy materials.

3. For purposes of paragraph (c)(2)(ix) of this Item, the percentage of securities held by a recommending security holder, as well as the holding period of those securities, may be determined by the registrant if the security holder is the registered holder of the securities. If the security holder is not the registered owner of the securities, he or she can submit one of the following to the registrant to evidence the required ownership percentage and holding period:

    a. A written statement from the "record" holder of the securities (usually a broker or bank) verifying that, at the time the security holder made the recommendation, he or she had held the required securities for at least one year; or

    b.   If the security holder has filed a Schedule 13D, Schedule 13G, Form 3, Form 4, and/or Form 5, or amendments to those documents or updated forms, reflecting ownership of the securities as of or before the date of the recommendation, a copy of the schedule and/or form, and any subsequent amendments reporting a change in ownership level, as well as a written statement that the security holder continuously held the securities for the one-year period as of the date of the recommendation.

    4.   For purposes of the registrant's obligation to provide the disclosure specified in paragraph (c)(2)(ix) of this Item, the security holder or group must have provided to the registrant, at the time of the recommendation, the written consent of all parties to be identified and, where the security holder or group members are not registered holders, proof that the security holder or group satisfied the required ownership percentage and holding period as of the date of the recommendation.

Instruction to Item 407(c)(2).

For purposes of paragraph (c)(2) of this Item, the term nominating committee refers not only to nominating committees and committees performing similar functions, but also to groups of directors fulfilling the role of a nominating committee, including the entire board of directors.

    3.   Describe any material changes to the procedures by which security holders may recommend nominees to the registrant's board of directors, where those changes were implemented after the registrant last provided disclosure in response to the requirements of paragraph (c)(2)(iv) of this Item, or paragraph (c)(3) of this Item.

Instructions to Item 407(c)(3).

    1.   The disclosure required in paragraph (c)(3) of this Item need only be provided in a registrant's quarterly or annual reports.

    2.   For purposes of paragraph (c)(3) of this Item, adoption of procedures by which security holders may recommend nominees to the registrant's board of directors, where the registrant's most recent disclosure in response to the requirements of paragraph (c)(2)(iv) of this Item, or paragraph (c)(3) of this Item, indicated that the registrant did not have in place such procedures, will constitute a material change.

d. **Audit committee**.

    1.   State whether or not the audit committee has a charter. If the audit committee has a charter, provide the disclosure required by Instruction 2 to this Item regarding the audit committee charter.

    2.   If a listed issuer's board of directors determines, in accordance with the listing standards applicable to the issuer, to appoint a director to the audit committee who is not independent (apart from the requirements in Rule 10A-3 of this chapter), including as a result of exceptional or limited or similar

circumstances, disclose the nature of the relationship that makes that individual not independent and the reasons for the board of directors' determination.

3.   i.   The audit committee must state whether:

        A.   The audit committee has reviewed and discussed the audited financial statements with management;

        B.   The audit committee has discussed with the independent auditors the matters required to be discussed by the statement on Auditing Standards No. 61, as amended as adopted by the Public Company Accounting Oversight Board in Rule 3200T;

        C.   The audit committee has received the written disclosures and the letter from the independent accountant required by applicable requirements of the Public Company Accounting Oversight Board regarding the independent accountant's communications with the audit committee concerning independence, and has discussed with the independent accountant the independent accountant's independence; and

        D.   Based on the review and discussions referred to in paragraphs (d)(3)(i)(A) through (d)(3)(i)(C) of this Item, the audit committee recommended to the board of directors that the audited financial statements be included in the company's annual report on Form 10-K (or, for closed-end investment companies registered under the Investment Company Act of 1940, the annual report to shareholders required by section 30(e) of the Investment Company Act of 1940 and Rule 30d-1 thereunder for the last fiscal year for filing with the Commission.

    ii.   The name of each member of the company's audit committee (or, in the absence of an audit committee, the board committee performing equivalent functions or the entire board of directors) must appear below the disclosure required by paragraph (d)(3)(i) of this Item.

4.   i.   If the registrant meets the following requirements, provide the disclosure in paragraph (d)(4)(ii) of this Item:

        A.   The registrant is a listed issuer, as defined in Rule 10A-3 of this chapter;

        B.   The registrant is filing either an annual report on Form 10-K or a proxy statement or information statement pursuant to the Exchange Act if action is to be taken with respect to the election of directors; and

        C.   The registrant is neither:

            1.   A subsidiary of another listed issuer that is relying on the exemption in Rule 10A-3(c)(2) of this chapter; nor

            2.   Relying on any of the exemptions in Rule 10A-3(c)(4) through (c)(7) of this chapter.

    ii.

        A.   State whether or not the registrant has a separately-designated standing audit committee established in accordance with section 3(a)(58)(A) of the Exchange Act, or a committee performing similar functions. If the registrant has such a committee, however designated, identify each committee member. If the entire board of directors is acting as the registrant's audit committee as specified in section 3(a)(58)(B) of the Exchange Act, so state.

B. If applicable, provide the disclosure required by Rule 10A-3(d) of this chapter regarding an exemption from the listing standards for audit committees.

5. Audit committee financial expert.

    i.   A. Disclose that the registrant's board of directors has determined that the registrant either:

    1. Has at least one audit committee financial expert serving on its audit committee; or

    2. Does not have an audit committee financial expert serving on its audit committee.

    B. If the registrant provides the disclosure required by paragraph (d)(5)(i)(A)(1) of this Item, it must disclose the name of the audit committee financial expert and whether that person is independent, as independence for audit committee members is defined in the listing standards applicable to the listed issuer.

    C. If the registrant provides the disclosure required by paragraph (d)(5)(i)(A)(2) of this Item, it must explain why it does not have an audit committee financial expert.

Instruction to Item 407(d)(5)(i).

If the registrant's board of directors has determined that the registrant has more than one audit committee financial expert serving on its audit committee, the registrant may, but is not required to, disclose the names of those additional persons. A registrant choosing to identify such persons must indicate whether they are independent pursuant to paragraph (d)(5)(i)(B) of this Item.

    ii. For purposes of this Item, an audit committee financial expert means a person who has the following attributes:

    A. An understanding of generally accepted accounting principles and financial statements;

    B. The ability to assess the general application of such principles in connection with the accounting for estimates, accruals and reserves;

    C. Experience preparing, auditing, analyzing or evaluating financial statements that present a breadth and level of complexity of accounting issues that are generally comparable to the breadth and complexity of issues that can reasonably be expected to be raised by the registrant's financial statements, or experience actively supervising one or more persons engaged in such activities;

    D. An understanding of internal control over financial reporting; and

    E. An understanding of audit committee functions.

    iii. A person shall have acquired such attributes through:

    A. Education and experience as a principal financial officer, principal accounting officer, controller, public accountant or auditor or experience in one or more positions that involve the performance of similar functions;

B. Experience actively supervising a principal financial officer, principal accounting officer, controller, public accountant, auditor or person performing similar functions;

C. Experience overseeing or assessing the performance of companies or public accountants with respect to the preparation, auditing or evaluation of financial statements; or

D. Other relevant experience.

iv. Safe harbor.

A. A person who is determined to be an audit committee financial expert will not be deemed an expert for any purpose, including without limitation for purposes of section 11 of the Securities Act, as a result of being designated or identified as an audit committee financial expert pursuant to this Item 407.

B. The designation or identification of a person as an audit committee financial expert pursuant to this Item 407 does not impose on such person any duties, obligations or liability that are greater than the duties, obligations and liability imposed on such person as a member of the audit committee and board of directors in the absence of such designation or identification.

C. The designation or identification of a person as an audit committee financial expert pursuant to this Item does not affect the duties, obligations or liability of any other member of the audit committee or board of directors.

Instructions to Item 407(d)(5).

1. The disclosure under paragraph (d)(5) of this Item is required only in a registrant's annual report. The registrant need not provide the disclosure required by paragraph (d)(5) of this Item in a proxy or information statement unless that registrant is electing to incorporate this information by reference from the proxy or information statement into its annual report pursuant to General Instruction G(3) to Form 10-K.

2. If a person qualifies as an audit committee financial expert by means of having held a position described in paragraph (d)(5)(iii)(D) of this Item, the registrant shall provide a brief listing of that person's relevant experience. Such disclosure may be made by reference to disclosures required under Item 401(e).

3. In the case of a foreign private issuer with a two-tier board of directors, for purposes of paragraph (d)(5) of this Item, the term board of directors means the supervisory or non-management board. In the case of a foreign private issuer meeting the requirements of Rule 10A-3(c)(3) of this chapter, for purposes of paragraph (d)(5) of this Item, the term board of directors means the issuer's board of auditors (or similar body) or statutory auditors, as applicable. Also, in the case of a foreign private issuer, the term generally accepted accounting principles in paragraph (d)(5)(ii)(A) of this Item means the body of generally accepted accounting principles used by that issuer in its primary financial statements filed with the Commission.

4. A registrant that is an Asset-Backed Issuer is not required to disclose the information required by paragraph (d)(5) of this Item.

Instructions to Item 407(d).

1. The information required by paragraphs (d)(1) - (3) of this Item shall not be deemed to be "soliciting material," or to be "filed" with the Commission or subject to Regulation 14A or 14C, other than as provided in this Item, or to the liabilities of section 18 of the Exchange Act, except to the extent that the registrant specifically requests that the information be treated as soliciting material or specifically incorporates it by reference into a document filed under the Securities Act or the Exchange Act. Such information will not be deemed to be incorporated by reference into any filing under the Securities Act or the Exchange Act, except to the extent that the registrant specifically incorporates it by reference.

2. The disclosure required by paragraphs (d)(1) - (3) of this Item need only be provided one time during any fiscal year.

3. The disclosure required by paragraph (d)(3) of this Item need not be provided in any filings other than a registrant's proxy or information statement relating to an annual meeting of security holders at which directors are to be elected (or special meeting or written consents in lieu of such meeting).

e. **Compensation committee.**

1. If the registrant does not have a standing compensation committee or committee performing similar functions, state the basis for the view of the board of directors that it is appropriate for the registrant not to have such a committee and identify each director who participates in the consideration of executive officer and director compensation.

2. State whether or not the compensation committee has a charter. If the compensation committee has a charter, provide the disclosure required by Instruction 2 to this Item regarding the compensation committee charter.

3. Provide a narrative description of the registrant's processes and procedures for the consideration and determination of executive and director compensation, including:

    i. A. The scope of authority of the compensation committee (or persons performing the equivalent functions); and

        B. The extent to which the compensation committee (or persons performing the equivalent functions) may delegate any authority described in paragraph (e)(3)(i)(A) of this Item to other persons, specifying what authority may be so delegated and to whom;

    ii. Any role of executive officers in determining or recommending the amount or form of executive and director compensation; and

    iii. Any role of compensation consultants in determining or recommending the amount or form of executive and director compensation (other than any role limited to consulting on any broad-based plan that does not discriminate in scope, terms, or operation, in favor of executive officers or directors of the registrant, and that is available generally to all salaried employees; or providing information that either is not customized for a particular registrant or that is customized based on parameters that are not developed by the compensation consultant, and about which the compensation consultant does not provide advice) during the registrant's last completed fiscal year, identifying such consultants, stating whether such consultants were engaged directly by the compensation committee (or persons performing the equivalent functions) or any other person, describing the nature and scope of their assignment, and the material elements of the instructions or directions given to the consultants with respect to the performance of their duties under the engagement:

A. If such compensation consultant was engaged by the compensation committee (or persons performing the equivalent functions) to provide advice or recommendations on the amount or form of executive and director compensation (other than any role limited to consulting on any broad-based plan that does not discriminate in scope, terms, or operation, in favor of executive officers or directors of the registrant, and that is available generally to all salaried employees; or providing information that either is not customized for a particular registrant or that is customized based on parameters that are not developed by the compensation consultant, and about which the compensation consultant does not provide advice) and the compensation consultant or its affiliates also provided additional services to the registrant or its affiliates in an amount in excess of $120,000 during the registrant's last completed fiscal year, then disclose the aggregate fees for determining or recommending the amount or form of executive and director compensation and the aggregate fees for such additional services. Disclose whether the decision to engage the compensation consultant or its affiliates for these other services was made, or recommended, by management, and whether the compensation committee or the board approved such other services of the compensation consultant or its affiliates.

B. If the compensation committee (or persons performing the equivalent functions) has not engaged a compensation consultant, but management has engaged a compensation consultant to provide advice or recommendations on the amount or form of executive and director compensation (other than any role limited to consulting on any broad-based plan that does not discriminate in scope, terms, or operation, in favor of executive officers or directors of the registrant, and that is available generally to all salaried employees; or providing information that either is not customized for a particular registrant or that is customized based on parameters that are not developed by the compensation consultant, and about which the compensation consultant does not provide advice) and such compensation consultant or its affiliates has provided additional services to the registrant in an amount in excess of $120,000 during the registrant's last completed fiscal year, then disclose the aggregate fees for determining or recommending the amount or form of executive and director compensation and the aggregate fees for any additional services provided by the compensation consultant or its affiliates.

4.   Under the caption "Compensation Committee Interlocks and Insider Participation":

     i.   Identify each person who served as a member of the compensation committee of the registrant's board of directors (or board committee performing equivalent functions) during the last completed fiscal year, indicating each committee member who:

          A.   Was, during the fiscal year, an officer or employee of the registrant;

          B.   Was formerly an officer of the registrant; or

          C.   Had any relationship requiring disclosure by the registrant under any paragraph of Item 404. In this event, the disclosure required by Item 404 shall accompany such identification.

     ii.   If the registrant has no compensation committee (or other board committee performing equivalent functions), the registrant shall identify each officer and employee of the registrant, and any former officer of the registrant, who, during the last completed fiscal year, participated in deliberations of the registrant's board of directors concerning executive officer compensation.

     iii.   Describe any of the following relationships that existed during the last completed fiscal year:

          A.   An executive officer of the registrant served as a member of the compensation committee (or other board committee performing equivalent functions or, in the absence of any such committee, the entire board of directors) of another entity, one of whose executive officers served on the compensation committee (or other board committee performing equivalent functions or, in the absence of any such committee, the entire board of directors) of the registrant;

          B.   An executive officer of the registrant served as a director of another entity, one of whose executive officers served on the compensation committee (or other board committee performing equivalent functions or, in the absence of any such committee, the entire board of directors) of the registrant; and

          C.   An executive officer of the registrant served as a member of the compensation committee (or other board committee performing equivalent functions or, in the absence of any such committee, the entire board of directors) of another entity, one of whose executive officers served as a director of the registrant.

     iv.   Disclosure required under paragraph (e)(4)(iii) of this Item regarding a compensation committee member or other director of the registrant who also served as an executive officer of another entity shall be accompanied by the disclosure called for by Item 404 with respect to that person.

Instruction to Item 407(e)(4).

For purposes of paragraph (e)(4) of this Item, the term entity shall not include an entity exempt from tax under section 501(c)(3) of the Internal Revenue Code).

5.   Under the caption "Compensation Committee Report:"
  i.   The compensation committee (or other board committee performing equivalent functions or, in the absence of any such committee, the entire board of directors) must state whether:
    A.   The compensation committee has reviewed and discussed the Compensation Discussion and Analysis required by Item 402(b) with management; and
    B.   Based on the review and discussions referred to in paragraph (e)(5)(i)(A) of this Item, the compensation committee recommended to the board of directors that the Compensation Discussion and Analysis be included in the registrant's annual report on Form 10-K, proxy statement on Schedule 14A or information statement on Schedule 14C.
  ii. The name of each member of the registrant's compensation committee (or other board committee performing equivalent functions or, in the absence of any such committee, the entire board of directors) must appear below the disclosure required by paragraph (e)(5)(i) of this Item.

Instructions to Item 407(e)(5).
1.   The information required by paragraph (e)(5) of this Item shall not be deemed to be "soliciting material," or to be "filed" with the Commission or subject to Regulation 14A or 14C, other than as provided in this Item, or to the liabilities of section 18 of the Exchange Act, except to the extent that the registrant specifically requests that the information be treated as soliciting material or specifically incorporates it by reference into a document filed under the Securities Act or the Exchange Act.
2.   The disclosure required by paragraph (e)(5) of this Item need not be provided in any filings other than an annual report on Form 10-K, a proxy statement on Schedule 14A or an information statement on Schedule 14C. Such information will not be deemed to be incorporated by reference into any filing under the Securities Act or the Exchange Act, except to the extent that the registrant specifically incorporates it by reference. If the registrant elects to incorporate this information by reference from the proxy or information statement into its annual report on Form 10-K pursuant to General Instruction G(3) to Form 10-K, the disclosure required by paragraph (e)(5) of this Item will be deemed furnished in the annual report on Form 10-K and will not be deemed incorporated by reference into any filing under the Securities Act or the Exchange Act as a result as a result of furnishing the disclosure in this manner.
3.   The disclosure required by paragraph (e)(5) of this Item need only be provided one time during any fiscal year.

f.   **Shareholder communications.**
1.   State whether or not the registrant's board of directors provides a process for security holders to send communications to the board of directors and, if the registrant does not have such a process for security holders to send communications to the board of directors, state the basis for the view of the board of directors that it is appropriate for the registrant not to have such a process.

2.   If the registrant has a process for security holders to send communications to the board of directors:

    i.   Describe the manner in which security holders can send communications to the board and, if applicable, to specified individual directors; and

    ii.   If all security holder communications are not sent directly to board members, describe the registrant's process for determining which communications will be relayed to board members.

Instructions to Item 407(f).

1.   In lieu of providing the information required by paragraph (f)(2) of this Item in the proxy statement, the registrant may instead provide the registrant's Web site address where such information appears.

2.   For purposes of the disclosure required by paragraph (f)(2)(ii) of this Item, a registrant's process for collecting and organizing security holder communications, as well as similar or related activities, need not be disclosed provided that the registrant's process is approved by a majority of the independent directors or, in the case of a registrant that is an investment company, a majority of the directors who are not "interested persons" of the investment company as defined in section 2(a)(19) of the Investment Company Act of 1940.

3.   For purposes of this paragraph, communications from an officer or director of the registrant will not be viewed as "security holder communications." Communications from an employee or agent of the registrant will be viewed as "security holder communications" for purposes of this paragraph only if those communications are made solely in such employee's or agent's capacity as a security holder.

4.   For purposes of this paragraph, security holder proposals submitted pursuant to Rule 14a-8 of this chapter, and communications made in connection with such proposals, will not be viewed as "security holder communications."

* * *

h.   **Board leadership structure and role in risk oversight.** Briefly describe the leadership structure of the registrant's board, such as whether the same person serves as both principal executive officer and chairman of the board, or whether two individuals serve in those positions, and, in the case of a registrant that is an investment company, whether the chairman of the board is an "interested person" of the registrant as defined in section 2(a)(19) of the Investment Company Act. If one person serves as both principal executive officer and chairman of the board, or if the chairman of the board of a registrant that is an investment company is an "interested person" of the registrant, disclose whether the registrant has a lead independent director and what specific role the lead independent director plays in the leadership of the board. This disclosure should indicate why the registrant has determined that its leadership structure is appropriate given the specific characteristics or circumstances of the registrant. In addition, disclose the extent of the board's role in the risk oversight of the registrant, such as how the board administers its oversight function, and the effect that this has on the board's leadership structure.

Instructions to Item 407.

1. For purposes of this Item:
    a. Listed issuer means a listed issuer as defined in Rule 10A-3 of this chapter;
    b. National securities exchange means a national securities exchange registered pursuant to section 6(a) of the Exchange Act;
    c. Inter-dealer quotation system means an automated inter-dealer quotation system of a national securities association registered pursuant to section 15A(a) of the Exchange Act; and
    d. National securities association means a national securities association registered pursuant to section 15A(a) of the Exchange Act that has been approved by the Commission (as that definition may be modified or supplemented).
2. With respect to paragraphs (c)(2)(i), (d)(1) and (e)(2) of this Item, disclose whether a current copy of the applicable committee charter is available to security holders on the registrant's Web site, and if so, provide the registrant's Web site address. If a current copy of the charter is not available to security holders on the registrant's Web site, include a copy of the charter in an appendix to the registrant's proxy or information statement that is provided to security holders at least once every three fiscal years, or if the charter has been materially amended since the beginning of the registrant's last fiscal year. If a current copy of the charter is not available to security holders on the registrant's Web site, and is not included as an appendix to the registrant's proxy or information statement, identify in which of the prior fiscal years the charter was so included in satisfaction of this requirement.

Item 501 – Forepart of Registration Statement and Outside Front Cover Page of Prospectus

The registrant must furnish the following information in plain English. See Rule 421(d) of Regulation C under the Securities Act.

   a. **Front cover page of the registration statement.** Where appropriate, include the delaying amendment legend from Rule 473 of Regulation C under the Securities Act.

   b. **Outside front cover page of the prospectus.** Limit the outside cover page to one page. If the following information applies to your offering, disclose it on the outside cover page of the prospectus.
       1. Name. The registrant's name. A foreign registrant must give the English translation of its name.
       Instruction to Paragraph 501(b)(1)
       If your name is the same as that of a company that is well known, include information to eliminate any possible confusion with the other company. If your name indicates a line of business in which you are not engaged or you are engaged only to a limited extent, include information to eliminate any misleading inference as to your business. In some circumstances, disclosure may not be sufficient and you may be required to change your name. You will not be required to change your name if you are an established company, the character of your business has changed, and the investing public is generally aware of the change and the character of your current business.

2. Title and amount of securities. The title and amount of securities offered. Separately state the amount of securities offered by selling security holders, if any. If the underwriter has any arrangement with the issuer, such as an over-allotment option, under which the underwriter may purchase additional shares in connection with the offering, indicate that this arrangement exists and state the amount of additional shares that the underwriter may purchase under the arrangement. Give a brief description of the securities except where the information is clear from the title of the security. For example, you are not required to describe common stock that has full voting, dividend and liquidation rights usually associated with common stock.

3. Offering price of the securities. Where you offer securities for cash, the price to the public of the securities, the underwriter's discounts and commissions, the net proceeds you receive, and any selling shareholder's net proceeds. Show this information on both a per share or unit basis and for the total amount of the offering. If you make the offering on a minimum/maximum basis, show this information based on the total minimum and total maximum amount of the offering. You may present the information in a table, term sheet format, or other clear presentation. You may present the information in any format that fits the design of the cover page so long as the information can be easily read and is not misleading:

Instruction to Paragraph 501(b)(3):

1. If a preliminary prospectus is circulated and you are not subject to the reporting requirements of Section 13(a) or 15(d) of the Exchange Act, provide, as applicable:

    A. A bona fide estimate of the range of the maximum offering price and the maximum number of securities offered; or

    B. A bona fide estimate of the principal amount of the debt securities offered.

2. If it is impracticable to state the price to the public, explain the method by which the price is to be determined. If the securities are to be offered at the market price, or if the offering price is to be determined by a formula related to the market price, indicate the market and market price of the securities as of the latest practicable date.

3. If you file a registration statement on Form S-8, you are not required to comply with this paragraph (b)(3).

4. Market for the securities. Whether any national securities exchange or the Nasdaq Stock Market lists the securities offered, naming the particular market(s), and identifying the trading symbol(s) for those securities;

5. Risk factors. A cross-reference to the risk factors section, including the page number where it appears in the prospectus. Highlight this cross- reference by prominent type or in another manner;

6. State legend. Any legend or statement required by the law of any state in which the securities are to be offered. You may combine this with any legend required by the SEC, if appropriate;

7. Commission legend. A legend that indicates that neither the Securities and Exchange Commission nor any state securities commission has approved or disapproved of the securities or passed upon the accuracy or adequacy of the

disclosures in the prospectus and that any contrary representation is a criminal offense. You may use one of the following or other clear, plain language:

Example A: Neither the Securities and Exchange Commission nor any state securities commission has approved or disapproved of these securities or passed upon the adequacy or accuracy of this prospectus. Any representation to the contrary is a criminal offense.

Example B: Neither the Securities and Exchange Commission nor any state securities commission has approved or disapproved of these securities or determined if this prospectus is truthful or complete. Any representation to the contrary is a criminal offense.

8. Underwriting.
   i. Name(s) of the lead or managing underwriter(s) and an identification of the nature of the underwriting arrangements;
   ii. If the offering is not made on a firm commitment basis, a brief description of the underwriting arrangements. You may use any clear, concise, and accurate description of the underwriting arrangements. You may use the following descriptions of underwriting arrangements where appropriate:

   Example A: Best efforts offering. The underwriters are not required to sell any specific number or dollar amount of securities but will use their best efforts to sell the securities offered.

   Example B: Best efforts, minimum-maximum offering. The underwriters must sell the minimum number of securities offered (insert number) if any are sold. The underwriters are required to use only their best efforts to sell the maximum number of securities offered (insert number).

   iii. If you offer the securities on a best efforts or best efforts minimum/maximum basis, the date the offering will end, any minimum purchase requirements, and any arrangements to place the funds in an escrow, trust, or similar account. If you have not made any of these arrangements, state this fact and describe the effect on investors;

9. Date of prospectus. The date of the prospectus;
10. Prospectus "Subject to Completion" legend. If you use the prospectus before the effective date of the registration statement, a prominent statement that:
    i. The information in the prospectus will be amended or completed;
    ii. A registration statement relating to these securities has been filed with the Securities and Exchange Commission;
    iii. The securities may not be sold until the registration statement becomes effective; and
    iv. The prospectus is not an offer to sell the securities and it is not soliciting an offer to buy the securities in any state where offers or sales are not permitted. The legend may be in the following or other clear, plain language:

       The information in this prospectus is not complete and may be changed. We may not sell these securities until the registration statement filed with the Securities and Exchange Commission is effective. This prospectus is not an offer to sell these securities and it is not soliciting an offer to buy these securities in any state where the offer or sale is not permitted.

11. If you use Rule 430A under the Securities Act to omit pricing information and the prospectus is used before you determine the public offering price, the information and legend in paragraph (b)(10) of this section.

Item 502 – Inside Front and Outside Back Cover Pages of Prospectus

The registrant must furnish this information in plain English. See Rule 421(d) of Regulation C.

a. **Table of contents.** On either the inside front or outside back cover page of the prospectus, provide a reasonably detailed table of contents. It must show the page number of the various sections or subdivisions of the prospectus. Include a specific listing of the risk factors section required by Item 503 of this Regulation S-K. You must include the table of contents immediately following the cover page in any prospectus you deliver electronically.

b. **Dealer prospectus delivery obligation.** On the outside back cover page of the prospectus, advise dealers of their prospectus delivery obligation, including the expiration date specified by Section 4(3) of the Securities Act and Rule 174 under such Act. If you do not know the expiration date on the effective date of the registration statement, include the expiration date in the copy of the prospectus you file under Rule 424(b) under the Securities Act. You do not have to include this information if dealers are not required to deliver a prospectus under Rule 174 under the Securities Act or Section 24(d) of the Investment Company Act. You may use the following or other clear, plain language:

Dealer Prospectus Delivery Obligation

Until (insert date), all dealers that effect transactions in these securities, whether or not participating in this offering, may be required to deliver a prospectus. This is in addition to the dealers' obligation to deliver a prospectus when acting as underwriters and with respect to their unsold allotments or subscriptions.

Item 503 – Prospectus Summary, Risk Factors, and Ratio of Earnings to Fixed Charges

The registrant must furnish this information in plain English. See Rule 421(d) of Regulation C of this chapter.

a. **Prospectus summary.** Provide a summary of the information in the prospectus where the length or complexity of the prospectus makes a summary useful. The summary should be brief. The summary should not contain, and is not required to contain, all of the detailed information in the prospectus. If you provide summary business or financial information, even if you do not caption it as a summary, you still must provide that information in plain English.

Instruction to Paragraph 503(a):

The summary should not merely repeat the text of the prospectus but should provide a brief overview of the key aspects of the offering. Carefully consider and identify those aspects of the offering that are the most significant and determine how best to highlight those points in clear, plain language.

b. **Address and telephone number.** Include, either on the cover page or in the summary section of the prospectus, the complete mailing address and telephone number of your principal executive offices.

c. **Risk factors.** Where appropriate, provide under the caption "Risk Factors" a discussion of the most significant factors that make the offering speculative or risky. This discussion must be concise and organized logically. Do not present risks that could apply to any issuer or any offering. Explain how the risk affects the issuer or the securities being offered. Set forth each risk factor under a subcaption that adequately describes the risk. The risk factor discussion must immediately follow the summary section. If you do not include a summary section, the risk factor section must immediately follow the cover page of the prospectus or the pricing information section that immediately follows the cover page. Pricing information means price and price-related information that you may omit from the prospectus in an effective registration statement based on Rule 430A(a) of this chapter. The risk factors may include, among other things, the following:
1. Your lack of an operating history;
2. Your lack of profitable operations in recent periods;
3. Your financial position;
4. Your business or proposed business; or
5. The lack of a market for your common equity securities or securities convertible into or exercisable for common equity securities.

d. **Ratio of earnings to fixed charges.** If you register debt securities, show a ratio of earnings to fixed charges. If you register preference equity securities, show the ratio of combined fixed charges and preference dividends to earnings. Present the ratio for each of the last five fiscal years and the latest interim period for which financial statements are presented in the document. If you will use the proceeds from the sale of debt or preference securities to repay any of your outstanding debt or to retire other securities and the change in the ratio would be ten percent or greater, you must include a ratio showing the application of the proceeds, commonly referred to as the pro forma ratio.

Instructions to Paragraph 503(d):
1. **Definitions.** In calculating the ratio of earnings to fixed charges, you must use the following definitions:
    A. **Fixed charges.** The term "fixed charges" means the sum of the following: (a) interest expensed and capitalized, (b) amortized premiums, discounts and capitalized expenses related to indebtedness, (c) an estimate of the interest within rental expense, and (d) preference security dividend requirements of consolidated subsidiaries.
    B. **Preference security dividend.** The term "preference security dividend" is the amount of pre-tax earnings that is required to pay the dividends on outstanding preference securities. The dividend requirement must be computed as the amount of the dividend divided by (1 minus the effective income tax rate applicable to continuing operations).

C. **Earnings.** The term "earnings" is the amount resulting from adding and subtracting the following items. Add the following: (a) pre-tax income from continuing operations before adjustment for income or loss from equity investees; (b) fixed charges; (c) amortization of capitalized interest; (d) distributed income of equity investees; and (e) your share of pre-tax losses of equity investees for which charges arising from guarantees are included in fixed charges. From the total of the added items, subtract the following: (a) interest capitalized; (b) preference security dividend requirements of consolidated subsidiaries; and (c) the noncontrolling interest in pre-tax income of subsidiaries that have not incurred fixed charges. Equity investees are investments that you account for using the equity method of accounting. Public utilities following SFAS 71 should not add amortization of capitalized interest in determining earnings, nor reduce fixed charges by any allowance for funds used during construction.

2. **Disclosure.** Disclose the following information when showing the ratio of earnings to fixed charges:
   A. **Deficiency.** If a ratio indicates less than one-to-one coverage, disclose the dollar amount of the deficiency.
   B. **Pro forma ratio.** You may show the pro forma ratio only for the most recent fiscal year and the latest interim period. Use the net change in interest or dividends from the refinancing to calculate the pro forma ratio.
   C. **Foreign private issuers.** A foreign private issuer must show the ratio based on the figures in the primary financial statement. A foreign private issuer must show the ratio based on the figures resulting from the reconciliation to U.S. generally accepted accounting principles if this ratio is materially different.
   D. **Summary Section.** If you provide a summary or similar section in the prospectus, show the ratios in that section.
3. **Exhibit.** File an exhibit to the registration statement to show the figures used to calculate the ratios. See paragraph (b)(12) of Item 601 of Regulation S-K.

Item 504 – Use of Proceeds

State the principal purposes for which the net proceeds to the registrant from the securities to be offered are intended to be used and the approximate amount intended to be used for each such purpose. Where registrant has no current specific plan for the proceeds, or a significant portion thereof, the registrant shall so state and discuss the principal reasons for the offering.

Instructions to Item 504:
1. Where less than all the securities to be offered may be sold and more than one use is listed for the proceeds, indicate the order of priority of such purposes and discuss the registrant's plans if substantially less than the maximum proceeds are obtained. Such discussion need not be included if underwriting arrangements with respect to such securities are such that, if any securities are sold to the public, it reasonably can be expected that the actual proceeds will not be substantially less than the aggregate proceeds to the registrant shown pursuant to Item 501 of Regulation S-K.
2. Details of proposed expenditures need not be given; for example, there need be furnished only a brief outline of any program of construction or addition of equipment. Consideration should be given as to the need to include a discussion of certain matters

addressed in the discussion and analysis of registrant's financial condition and results of operations, such as liquidity and capital expenditures.

3. If any material amounts of other funds are necessary to accomplish the specified purposes for which the proceeds are to be obtained, state the amounts and sources of such other funds needed for each such specified purpose and the sources thereof.

4. If any material part of the proceeds is to be used to discharge indebtedness, set forth the interest rate and maturity of such indebtedness. If the indebtedness to be discharged was incurred within one year, describe the use of the proceeds of such indebtedness other than short-term borrowings used for working capital.

5. If any material amount of the proceeds is to be used to acquire assets, otherwise than in the ordinary course of business, describe briefly and state the cost of the assets and, where such assets are to be acquired from affiliates of the registrant or their associates, give the names of the persons from whom they are to be acquired and set forth the principle followed in determining the cost to the registrant.

6. Where the registrant indicates that the proceeds may, or will, be used to finance acquisitions of other businesses, the identity of such businesses, if known, or, if not known, the nature of the businesses to be sought, the status of any negotiations with respect to the acquisition, and a brief description of such business shall be included. Where, however, pro forma financial statements reflecting such acquisition are not required by Regulation S-X to be included, in the registration statement, the possible terms of any transaction, the identification of the parties thereto or the nature of the business sought need not be disclosed, to the extent that the registrant reasonably determines that public disclosure of such information would jeopardize the acquisition. Where Regulation S-X would require financial statements of the business to be acquired to be included, the description of the business to be acquired shall be more detailed.

7. The registrant may reserve the right to change the use of proceeds, provided that such reservation is due to certain contingencies that are discussed specifically and the alternatives to such use in that event are indicated.

Item 505 – Determination of Offering Price

a. **Common equity.** Where common equity is being registered for which there is no established public trading market for purposes of paragraph (a) of Item 201 of Regulation S-K or where there is a material disparity between the offering price of the common equity being registered and the market price of outstanding shares of the same class, describe the various factors considered in determining such offering price.

b. **Warrants, rights and convertible securities.** Where warrants, rights or convertible securities exercisable for common equity for which there is no established public trading market for purposes of paragraph (a) of Item 201 of Regulation S-K are being registered, describe the various factors considered in determining their exercise or conversion price.

Item 506 – Dilution

Where common equity securities are being registered and there is substantial disparity between the public offering price and the effective cash cost to officers, directors, promoters and affiliated persons of common equity acquired by them in transactions during the past five years, or which they have the right to acquire, and the registrant is not subject to the reporting requirements of section 13(a) or 15(d) of the Exchange Act immediately prior to filing of the registration statement, there shall be included a comparison of the public contribution under the proposed public offering and the effective cash contribution of such persons. In such cases, and in other instances where common equity securities are being registered by a registrant that has had losses in each of its last three fiscal years and there is a material dilution of the purchasers' equity interest, the following shall be disclosed:

a.   The net tangible book value per share before and after the distribution;

b.   The amount of the increase in such net tangible book value per share attributable to the cash payments made by purchasers of the shares being offered; and

c.   The amount of the immediate dilution from the public offering price which will be absorbed by such purchasers.

Item 507 – Selling Security Holders

If any of the securities to be registered are to be offered for the account of security holders, name each such security holder, indicate the nature of any position, office, or other material relationship which the selling security holder has had within the past three years with the registrant or any of its predecessors or affiliates, and state the amount of securities of the class owned by such security holder prior to the offering, the amount to be offered for the security holder's account, the amount and (if one percent or more) the percentage of the class to be owned by such security holder after completion of the offering.

Item 508 – Plan of Distribution

a.   **Underwriters and underwriting obligation.** If the securities are to be offered through underwriters, name the principal underwriters, and state the respective amounts underwritten. Identify each such underwriter having a material relationship with the registrant and state the nature of the relationship. State briefly the nature of the obligation of the underwriter(s) to take the securities.
     Instruction to Paragraph 508(a):
     All that is required as to the nature of the underwriters' obligation is whether the underwriters are or will be committed to take and to pay for all of the securities if any are taken, or whether it is merely an agency or the type of *best efforts* arrangement under which the underwriters are required to take and to pay for only such securities as they may sell to the public. Conditions precedent to the underwriters' taking the securities, including *market-outs,* need not be described except in the case of an agency or *best efforts* arrangement.

b.   **New underwriters.** Where securities being registered are those of a registrant that has not previously been required to file reports pursuant to section 13(a) or 15(d) of the Exchange Act, or where a prospectus is required to include reference on its cover page to material risks pursuant to Item 501 of Regulation S-K, and any one or more of the managing underwriter(s) (or where there are no managing underwriters, a majority of the principal underwriters) has been organized, reactivated, or first registered as a broker-dealer within the past three years, these facts concerning such underwriter(s) shall be disclosed in the prospectus together with, where applicable, the disclosures that the principal business function of such underwriter(s) will be to sell the securities to be registered, or that the promoters of the registrant have a material relationship with such underwriter(s). Sufficient details shall be given to allow full appreciation of such underwriter(s) experience and its relationship with the registrant, promoters and their controlling persons.

c. **Other distributions.** Outline briefly the plan of distribution of any securities to be registered that are to be offered otherwise than through underwriters.

    1.   If any securities are to be offered pursuant to a dividend or interest reinvestment plan the terms of which provide for the purchase of some securities on the market, state whether the registrant or the participant pays fees, commissions, and expenses incurred in connection with the plan. If the participant will pay such fees, commissions and expenses, state the anticipated cost to participants by transaction or other convenient reference.

    2.   If the securities are to be offered through the selling efforts of brokers or dealers, describe the plan of distribution and the terms of any agreement, arrangement, or understanding entered into with broker(s) or dealer(s) prior to the effective date of the registration statement, including volume limitations on sales, parties to the agreement and the conditions under which the agreement may be terminated. If known, identify the broker(s) or dealer(s) which will participate in the offering and state the amount to be offered through each.

    3.   If any of the securities being registered are to be offered otherwise than for cash, state briefly the general purposes of the distribution, the basis upon which the securities are to be offered, the amount of compensation and other expenses of distribution, and by whom they are to be borne. If the distribution is to be made pursuant to a plan of acquisition, reorganization, readjustment or succession, describe briefly the general effect of the plan and state when it became or is to become operative. As to any material amount of assets to be acquired under the plan, furnish information corresponding to that required by Instruction 5 of Item 504 of Regulation S-K.

d. **Offerings on exchange.** If the securities are to be offered on an exchange, indicate the exchange. If the registered securities are to be offered in connection with the writing of exchange-traded call options, describe briefly such transactions.

e. **Underwriters' compensation.** Underwriter's compensation. Provide a table that sets out the nature of the compensation and the amount of discounts and commissions to be paid to the underwriter for each security and in total. The table must show the separate amounts to be paid by the company and the selling shareholders. In addition, include in the table all other items considered by the National Association of Securities Dealers to be underwriting compensation for purposes of that Association's Rules of Fair Practice.

Instructions to paragraph 508(e):

1.   The term "commissions" is defined in paragraph (17) of Schedule A of the Securities Act. Show separately in the table the cash commissions paid by the

registrant and selling security holders. Also show in the table commissions paid by other persons. Disclose any finder's fee or similar payments in the table.

2. Disclose the offering expenses specified in Item 511 of Regulation S-K.

3. If the underwriter has any arrangement with the issuer, such as an over- allotment option, under which the underwriter may purchase additional shares in connection with the offering, indicate that this arrangement exists and state the amount of additional shares that the underwriter may purchase under the arrangement. Where the underwriter has such an arrangement, present maximum-minimum information in a separate column to the table, based on the purchase of all or none of the shares subject to the arrangement. Describe the key terms of the arrangement in the narrative.

f. **Underwriter's representative on board of directors.** Describe any arrangement whereby the underwriter has the right to designate or nominate a member or members of the board of directors of the registrant. The registrant shall disclose the identity of any director so designated or nominated, and indicate whether or not a person so designated or nominated, or allowed to be designated or nominated by the underwriter is or may be a director, officer, partner, employee or affiliate of the underwriter.

g. **Indemnification of underwriters.** If the underwriting agreement provides for indemnification by the registrant of the underwriters or their controlling persons against any liability arising under the Securities Act, furnish a brief description of such indemnification provisions.

h. **Dealers' compensation.** State briefly the discounts and commissions to be allowed or paid to dealers, including all cash, securities, contracts or other considerations to be received by any dealer in connection with the sale of the securities. If any dealers are to act in the capacity of sub-underwriters and are to be allowed or paid any additional discounts or commissions for acting in such capacity, a general statement to that effect will suffice without giving the additional amounts to be sold.

i. **Finders.** Identify any finder and, if applicable, describe the nature of any material relationship between such finder and the registrant, its officers, directors, principal stockholders, finders or promoters or the principal underwriter(s), or if there is a managing underwriter(s), the managing underwriter(s), (including, in each case, affiliates or associates thereof).

j. **Discretionary accounts.** If the registrant was not, immediately prior to the filing of the registration statement, subject to the requirements of section 13(a) or 15(d) of the Exchange Act, identify any principal underwriter that intends to sell to any accounts over which it exercises discretionary authority and include an estimate of the amount of securities so intended to be sold. The response to this paragraph shall be contained in a pre-effective amendment which shall be circulated if the information is not available when the registration statement is filed.

k. **Passive market making.** If the underwriters or any selling group members intend to engage in passive market making transactions as permitted by Rule 103 of Regulation M, indicate such intention and briefly describe passive market making.

l. **Stabilization and other transactions.**
    1. Briefly describe any transaction that the underwriter intends to conduct during the offering that stabilizes, maintains, or otherwise affects the market price of the offered securities. Include information on stabilizing transactions, syndicate short covering transactions, penalty bids, or any other transaction that affects the offered security's price. Describe the nature of the transactions clearly and explain how the transactions affect the offered security's price. Identify the exchange or other market on which these transactions may occur. If true, disclose that the underwriter may discontinue these transactions at any time;
    2. If the stabilizing began before the effective date of the registration statement, disclose the amount of securities bought, the prices at which they were bought and the period within which they were bought. If you use Rule 430A of this chapter, the prospectus you file under Rule 424(b) of this chapter or include in a post-effective amendment must contain information on the stabilizing transactions that took place before the determination of the public offering price; and
    3. If you are making a warrants or rights offering of securities to existing security holders and any securities not purchased by existing security holders are to be reoffered to the public, disclose in a supplement to the prospectus or in the prospectus used in connection with the reoffering:
        i.   The amount of securities bought in stabilization activities during the offering period and the price or range of prices at which the securities were bought;
        ii. The amount of the offered securities subscribed for during the offering period;
        iii. The amount of the offered securities subscribed for by the underwriter during the offering period;
        iv. The amount of the offered securities sold during the offering period by the underwriter and the price or price ranges at which the securities were sold; and
        v.   The amount of the offered securities that will be reoffered to the public and the public offering price.

Item 509 – Interests of Named Experts and Counsel

If (a) any expert named in the registration statement as having prepared or certified any part thereof (or is named as having prepared or certified a report or valuation for use in connection with the registration statement), or (b) counsel for the registrant, underwriters or selling security holders named in the prospectus as having given an opinion upon the validity of the securities being registered or upon other legal matters in connection with the registration or offering of such securities, was employed for such purpose on a contingent basis, or at the time of such preparation, certification or opinion or at any time thereafter, through the date of effectiveness of the registration statement or that part of the registration statement to which such preparation, certification or opinion relates, had, or is to receive in connection with the offering, a substantial interest, direct or indirect, in the registrant or any of its parents or subsidiaries or was connected with the registrant or any of its parents or subsidiaries as a promoter, managing underwriter (or any principal underwriter, if there are no managing underwriters) voting trustee, director, officer, or employee, furnish a brief statement of the nature of such contingent basis, interest, or connection.

Instructions to Item 509:

1. The interest of an expert (other than an accountant) or counsel will not be deemed substantial and need not be disclosed if the interest, including the fair market value of all securities of the registrant owned, received and to be received, or subject to options, warrants or rights received or to be received by the expert or counsel does not exceed $50,000. For the purpose of this Instruction, the term *expert* or counsel includes the firm, corporation, partnership or other entity, if any, by which such expert or counsel is employed or of which he is a member or of counsel to and all attorneys in the case of counsel, and all nonclerical personnel in the case of named experts, participating in such matter on behalf of such firm, corporation, partnership or entity.

2. Accountants, providing a report on the financial statements, presented or incorporated by reference in the registration statement, should note Rule 2-01 of Regulation S-X for the Commission's requirements regarding "Qualification of Accountants" which discusses disqualifying interests.

Item 510 – Disclosure of Commission Position on Indemnification for Securities Act Liabilities

In addition to the disclosure prescribed by Item 702 of Regulation S-K, if the undertaking required by paragraph (h) of Item 512 of Regulation S-K is not required to be included in the registration statement because acceleration of the effective date of the registration statement is not being requested, and if waivers have not been obtained comparable to those specified in paragraph (h), a brief description of the indemnification provisions relating to directors, officers and controlling persons of the registrant against liability arising under the Securities Act (including any provision of the underwriting agreement which relates to indemnification of the underwriter or its controlling persons by the registrant against such liabilities where a director, officer or controlling person of the registrant is such an underwriter or controlling person thereof or a member of any firm which is such an underwriter) shall be included in the prospectus, together with a statement in substantially the following form:

> Insofar as indemnification for liabilities arising under the Securities Act of 1933 may be permitted to directors, officers or persons controlling the registrant pursuant to the foregoing provisions, the registrant has been informed that in the opinion of the Securities and Exchange Commission such indemnification is against public policy as expressed in the Act and is therefore unenforceable.

Item 511 – Other Expenses of Issuance and Distribution

Furnish a reasonably itemized statement of all expenses in connection with the issuance and distribution of the securities to be registered, other than underwriting discounts and commissions. If any of the securities to be registered are to be offered for the account of security holders, indicate the portion of such expenses to be borne by such security holder.

Instruction to Item 511:

Insofar as practicable, registration fees, Federal taxes, States taxes and fees, trustees' and transfer agents' fees, costs of printing and engraving, and legal, accounting, and engineering fees shall be itemized separately. Include as a separate item any premium paid by the registrant or any selling security holder on any policy obtained in connection with the offering and sale of the securities being registered which insures or indemnifies directors or officers against any liabilities they may incur in connection with the registration, offering, or sale of such securities. The information may be given as subject to future contingencies. If the amounts of any items are not known, estimates, identified as such, shall be given.

Item 512 – Undertakings

Include each of the following undertakings that is applicable to the offering being registered.

a. **Rule 415 Offering.** Include the following if the securities are registered pursuant to Rule 415 under the Securities Act:
   The undersigned registrant hereby undertakes:
   1. To file, during any period in which offers or sales are being made, a post-effective amendment to this registration statement:
       i. To include any prospectus required by section 10(a)(3) of the Securities Act of 1933;
       ii. To reflect in the prospectus any facts or events arising after the effective date of the registration statement (or the most recent post-effective amendment thereof) which, individually or in the aggregate, represent a fundamental change in the information set forth in the registration statement. Notwithstanding the foregoing, any increase or decrease in volume of securities offered (if the total dollar value of securities offered would not exceed that which was registered) and any deviation from the low or high end of the estimated maximum offering range may be reflected in the form of prospectus filed with the Commission pursuant to Rule 424(b) if, in the aggregate, the changes in volume and price represent no more than 20% change in the maximum aggregate offering price set forth in the "Calculation of Registration Fee" table in the effective registration statement.
       iii. To include any material information with respect to the plan of distribution not previously disclosed in the registration statement or any material change to such information in the registration statement;
       Provided, however, That:
       (A) Paragraphs (a)(1)(i) and (a)(1)(ii) of this section do not apply if the registration statement is on Form S-8, and the information required to be included in a post-effective amendment by those paragraphs is contained in reports filed with or furnished to the Commission by the registrant pursuant to section 13 or section 15(d) of the Securities Exchange Act of 1934 that are incorporated by reference in the registration statement; and 313
       (B) Paragraphs (a)(1)(i), (a)(1)(ii) and (a)(1)(iii) of this section do not apply if the registration statement is on Form S-3 or Form F-3 and the information required to be included in a post-effective amendment by those paragraphs is contained in reports filed with or furnished to the Commission by the registrant pursuant to section 13 or section 15(d) of the Securities Exchange Act of 1934 that are incorporated by reference in the registration statement, or is contained in a form of prospectus filed pursuant to Rule 424(b) that is part of the registration statement.

2. That, for the purpose of determining any liability under the Securities Act of 1933, each such post-effective amendment shall be deemed to be a new registration statement relating to the securities offered therein, and the offering of such securities at that time shall be deemed to be the initial bona fide offering thereof.

3. To remove from registration by means of a post-effective amendment any of the securities being registered which remain unsold at the termination of the offering.

4. If the registrant is a foreign private issuer, to file a post-effective amendment to the registration statement to include any financial statements required by Item 8.A. of Form 20-F at the start of any delayed offering or throughout a continuous offering. Financial statements and information otherwise required by Section 10(a)(3) of the Act need not be furnished, provided that the registrant includes in the prospectus, by means of a post-effective amendment, financial statements required pursuant to this paragraph (a)(4) and other information necessary to ensure that all other information in the prospectus is at least as current as the date of those financial statements. Notwithstanding the foregoing, with respect to registration statements on Form F-3, a post-effective amendment need not be filed to include financial statements and information required by Section 10(a)(3) of the Act or Rule 3-19 of this chapter if such financial statements and information are contained in periodic reports filed with or furnished to the Commission by the registrant pursuant to section 13 or section 15(d) of the Securities Exchange Act of 1934 that are incorporated by reference in the Form F-3.

5. That, for the purpose of determining liability under the Securities Act of 1933 to any purchaser:

    i.   If the registrant is relying on Rule 430B:

         (A) Each prospectus filed by the registrant pursuant to Rule 424(b)(3) shall be deemed to be part of the registration statement as of the date the filed prospectus was deemed part of and included in the registration statement; and

         (B) Each prospectus required to be filed pursuant to Rule 424(b)(2), (b)(5), or (b)(7) as part of a registration statement in reliance on Rule 430B relating to an offering made pursuant to Rule 415(a)(1)(i), (vii), or (x) for the purpose of providing the information required by section 10(a) of the Securities Act of 1933 shall be deemed to be part of and included in the registration statement as of the earlier of the date such form of prospectus is first used after effectiveness or the date of the first contract of sale of securities in the offering described in the prospectus. As provided in Rule 430B, for liability purposes of the issuer and any person that is at that date an underwriter, such date shall be deemed to be a new effective date of the registration statement relating to the securities in the registration statement to which that prospectus relates, and the offering of such securities at that time shall be deemed to be the initial bona fide offering thereof. *Provided, however,* that no statement made in a registration statement or prospectus that is part of the registration statement or made in a document incorporated or deemed incorporated by reference into the registration statement or prospectus that is part of the registration statement will, as to a purchaser with a time of contract of sale prior to such effective date, supersede or modify any statement that was made in the registration statement or prospectus that was part of the registration statement or made in any such document immediately prior to such effective date; or

ii.   If the registrant is subject to Rule 430C, each prospectus filed pursuant to Rule 424(b) as part of a registration statement relating to an offering, other than registration statements relying on Rule 430B or other than prospectuses filed in reliance on Rule 430A, shall be deemed to be part of and included in the registration statement as of the date it is first used after effectiveness. *Provided, however,* that no statement made in a registration statement or prospectus that is part of the registration statement or made in a document incorporated or deemed incorporated by reference into the registration statement or prospectus that is part of the registration statement will, as to a purchaser with a time of contract of sale prior to such first use, supersede or modify any statement that was made in the registration statement or prospectus that was part of the registration statement or made in any such document immediately prior to such date of first use.

6.   That, for the purpose of determining liability of the registrant under the Securities Act of 1933 to any purchaser in the initial distribution of the securities:

The undersigned registrant undertakes that in a primary offering of securities of the undersigned registrant pursuant to this registration statement, regardless of the underwriting method used to sell the securities to the purchaser, if the securities are offered or sold to such purchaser by means of any of the following communications, the undersigned registrant will be a seller to the purchaser and will be considered to offer or sell such securities to such purchaser:

i.   Any preliminary prospectus or prospectus of the undersigned registrant relating to the offering required to be filed pursuant to Rule 424;

ii.   Any free writing prospectus relating to the offering prepared by or on behalf of the undersigned registrant or used or referred to by the undersigned registrant;

iii.   The portion of any other free writing prospectus relating to the offering containing material information about the undersigned registrant or its securities provided by or on behalf of the undersigned registrant; and

iv.   Any other communication that is an offer in the offering made by the undersigned registrant to the purchaser.

i.   Include the following in a registration statement permitted by Rule 430A under the Securities Act of 1933:

The undersigned registrant hereby undertakes that:

1.   For purposes of determining any liability under the Securities Act of 1933, the information omitted from the form of prospectus filed as part of this registration statement in reliance upon Rule 430A and contained in a form of prospectus filed by the registrant pursuant to Rule 424(b) (1) or (4) or 497(h) under the Securities Act shall be deemed to be part of this registration statement as of the time it was declared effective.

2.   For the purpose of determining any liability under the Securities Act of 1933, each post-effective amendment that contains a form of prospectus shall be deemed to be a new registration statement relating to the securities offered therein, and the offering of such securities at that time shall be deemed to be the initial bona fide offering thereof.

Item 701 – Recent Sales of Unregistered Securities; Use of Proceeds from Registered Securities

Furnish the following information as to all securities of the registrant sold by the registrant within the past three years which were not registered under the Securities Act. Include sales of reacquired securities, as well as new issues, securities issued in exchange for property, services, or other securities, and new securities resulting from the modification of outstanding securities.

a.   **Securities sold.** Give the date of sale and the title and amount of securities sold.

b.   **Underwriters and other purchasers.** Give the names of the principal underwriters, if any. As to any such securities not publicly offered, name the persons or identify the class of persons to whom the securities were sold.

c.   **Consideration.** As to securities sold for cash, state the aggregate offering price and the aggregate underwriting discounts or commissions. As to any securities sold otherwise than for cash, state the nature of the transaction and the nature and aggregate amount of consideration received by the registrant.

d.   **Exemption from registration claimed.** Indicate the section of the Securities Act or the rule of the Commission under which exemption from registration was claimed and state briefly the facts relied upon to make the exemption available.

e.   **Terms of conversion or exercise.** If the information called for by this paragraph (e) is being presented on Form 8-K, Form 10-Q or Form 10-K under the Exchange Act, and where the securities sold by the registrant are convertible or exchangeable into equity securities, or are warrants or options representing equity securities, disclose the terms of conversion or exercise of the securities.

f.   **Use of Proceeds.** As required by Rule 463 of this chapter, following the effective date of the first registration statement filed under the Securities Act by an issuer, the issuer or successor issuer shall report the use of proceeds on its first periodic report filed pursuant to sections 13(a) and 15(d) of the Exchange Act after effectiveness of its Securities Act registration statement, and thereafter on each of its subsequent periodic reports filed pursuant to sections 13(a) and 15(d) of the Exchange Act through the later of disclosure of the application of all the offering proceeds, or disclosure of the termination of the offering. If a report of the use of proceeds is required with respect to the first effective registration statement of the predecessor issuer, the successor issuer shall provide such a report. The information provided pursuant to paragraphs (f)(2) through (f)(4) of this Item need only be provided with respect to the first periodic report filed pursuant to sections 13(a) and 15(d) of the Exchange Act after effectiveness of the registration statement filed under the Securities Act. Subsequent periodic reports filed pursuant to sections 13(a) and 15(d) of the Exchange Act need only provide the information required in paragraphs (f)(2) through (f)(4) of this Item if any of such required information has changed since the last periodic report filed. In disclosing the use of proceeds in the first periodic report filed pursuant to the Exchange Act, the issuer or successor issuer should include the following information:

1. The effective date of the Securities Act registration statement for which the use of proceeds information is being disclosed and the Commission file number assigned to the registration statement;

2. If the offering has commenced, the offering date, and if the offering has not commenced, an explanation why it has not;

3. If the offering terminated before any securities were sold, an explanation for such termination; and

4. If the offering did not terminate before any securities were sold, disclose:

    i. Whether the offering has terminated and, if so, whether it terminated before the sale of all securities registered;

    ii. The name(s) of the managing underwriter(s), if any;

    iii. The title of each class of securities registered and, where a class of convertible securities is being registered, the title of any class of securities into which such securities may be converted;

    iv. For each class of securities (other than a class of securities into which a class of convertible securities registered may be converted without additional payment to the issuer) the following information, provided for both the account of the issuer and the account(s) of any selling security holder(s): the amount registered, the aggregate price of the offering amount registered, the amount sold and the aggregate offering price of the amount sold to date;

    v. From the effective date of the Securities Act registration statement to the ending date of the reporting period, the amount of expenses incurred for the issuer's account in connection with the issuance and distribution of the securities registered for underwriting discounts and commissions, finders' fees, expenses paid to or for underwriters, other expenses and total expenses. Indicate if a reasonable estimate for the amount of expenses incurred is provided instead of the actual amount of expense. Indicate whether such payments were:

        A. Direct or indirect payments to directors, officers, general partners of the issuer or their associates; to persons owning ten (10) percent or more of any class of equity securities of the issuer; and to affiliates of the issuer; or

        B. Direct or indirect payments to others;

vi.   The net offering proceeds to the issuer after deducting the total expenses described in paragraph (f)(4)(v) of this Item;

vii.   From the effective date of the Securities Act registration statement to the ending date of the reporting period, the amount of net offering proceeds to the issuer used for construction of plant, building and facilities; purchase and installation of machinery and equipment; purchases of real estate; acquisition of other business(es); repayment of indebtedness; working capital; temporary investments (which should be specified); and any other purposes for which at least five (5) percent of the issuer's total offering proceeds or $100,000 (whichever is less) has been used (which should be specified). Indicate if a reasonable estimate for the amount of net offering proceeds applied is provided instead of the actual amount of net offering proceeds used. Indicate whether such payments were:

    A. Direct or indirect payments to directors, officers, general partners of the issuer or their associates; to persons owning ten (10) percent or more of any class of equity securities of the issuer; and to affiliates of the issuer; or

    B. Direct or indirect payments to others; and

viii. If the use of proceeds in paragraph (f)(4)(vii) of this Item represents a material change in the use of proceeds described in the prospectus, the issuer should describe briefly the material change.

Instructions to 701:

1. Information required by this Item 701 need not be set forth as to notes, drafts, bills of exchange, or bankers' acceptances which mature not later than one year from the date of issuance.

2. If the sales were made in a series of transactions, the information may be given by such totals and periods as will reasonably convey the information required.

Item 702 – Indemnification of Directors and Officers

State the general effect of any statute, charter provisions, by-laws, contract or other arrangements under which any controlling persons, director or officer of the registrant is insured or indemnified in any manner against liability which he may incur in his capacity as such.

Securities Act – Forms: S-1, S-3

UNITED STATES
SECURITIES AND EXCHANGE COMMISSION
Washington, D.C. 20549

FORM S-1

REGISTRATION STATEMENT UNDER THE SECURITIES ACT OF 1933

(Exact name of registrant as specified in its charter)

(State or other jurisdiction of incorporation or organization)

(Primary Standard Industrial Classification Code Number)

(I.R.S. Employer Identification Number)

(Address, including zip code, and telephone number, including area code,
of registrant's principal executive offices)

(Name, address, including zip code, and telephone number, including area code,
of agent for service)

(Approximate date of commencement of proposed sale to the public)

If any of the securities being registered on this Form are to be offered on a delayed or continuous basis pursuant to Rule 415 under the Securities Act of 1933 check the following box: ☐

If this Form is Filed to register additional securities for an offering pursuant to Rule 462(b) under the Securities Act, please check the following box and list the Securities Act registration statement number of the earlier effective registration statement for this same offering. ☐

If this Form is a post-effective amendment filed pursuant to Rule 462(c) under the Securities Act, check the following box and list the Securities Act registration statement number of the earlier effective registration statement for the same offering. D

If this Form is a post-effective amendment filed pursuant to Rule 462(d) under the Securities Act, check the following box and list the Securities Act registration statement number of the earlier effective registration statement for the same offering. ☐

CALCULATION OF REGISTRATION FEE

Title of Each Class of Securities to be Registered	Amount to be Registered	Proposed Maximum Offering Price Per Unit	Proposed Maximum Aggregate Offering Price	Amount of Registration Fee

Note: Specific details relating to the fee calculation shall be furnished in notes to the table, including references to provisions of Rule 457 relied upon, if the basis of the calculation is not otherwise evident from the information presented in the table. If the filing fee is calculated pursuant to Rule 457(o) under the Securities Act, only the title of the class of securities to be registered, the proposed maximum aggregate offering price for that class of securities and the amount of registration fee need to appear in the Calculation of Registration Fee table. Any difference between the dollar amount of securities registered for such offerings and the dollar amount of securities sold may be carried forward on a future registration statement pursuant to Rule 429 under the Securities Act.

GENERAL INSTRUCTIONS

I. Eligibility Requirements for Use of Form S-1

This Form shall be used for the registration under the Securities Act of 1933 ("Securities Act") of securities of all registrants for which no other form is authorized or prescribed, except that this Form shall not be used for securities of foreign governments or political subdivisions thereof.

II. Application of General Rules and Regulations

A. Attention is directed to the General Rules and Regulations under the Securities Act, particularly those comprising Regulation C thereunder. That Regulation contains general requirements regarding the preparation and filing of the registration statement.

B. Attention is directed to Regulation S-K for the requirements applicable to the content of the non-financial statement portions of registration statements under the Securities Act. Where this Form directs the registrant to furnish information required by Regulation S-K and the item of Regulation S-K so provides, information need only be furnished to the extent appropriate.

III. Exchange Offers

If any of the securities being registered are to be offered in exchange for securities of any other issuer, the prospectus shall also include the information which would be required by item 11 if the securities of such other issuer were registered on this Form. There shall also be included the information concerning such securities of such other issuer which would be called for by Item 9 if such securities were being registered. In connection with this instruction, reference is made to Rule 409.

IV.   Roll-up Transactions

If the securities to be registered on this Form will be issued in a roll-up transaction as defined in Item 901 (c) of Regulation S-K, attention is directed to the requirements of Form S-4 applicable to roll-up transactions, including, but not limited to, General Instruction I.

V.   Registration of Additional Securities

With respect to the registration of additional securities for an offering pursuant to Rule 462(b) under the Securities Act, the registrant may file a registration statement consisting only of the following: the facing page; a statement that the contents of the earlier registration statement, identified by file number, are incorporated by reference; required opinions and consents; the signature page; and any price-related information omitted from the earlier registration statement in reliance on Rule 430A that the registrant chooses to include in the new registration statement. The information contained in such a Rule 462(b) registration statement shall be deemed to be a part of the earlier registration statement as of the date of effectiveness of the Rule 462(b) registration statement. Any opinion or consent required in the Rule 462(b) registration statement may be incorporated by reference from the earlier registration statement with respect to the offering, if: (i) such opinion or consent expressly provides for such incorporation; and (ii) such opinion relates to the securities registered pursuant to Rule 462(b). *See* Rule 411(c) and Rule 439(b) under the Securities Act.

VI.   Offerings of Asset-Backed Securities.

The following applies if a registration statement on this Form S-1 is being used to register an offering of asset-backed securities. Terms used in this General Instruction VI. have the same meaning as in Item 1101 of Regulation AB.

>   A.   *Items that May be Omitted.*
>   Such registrants may omit the information called for by Item 11, Information with Respect to the Registrant.

>   B.   *Substitute Information to be Included.*
>   In addition to the Items that are otherwise required by this Form, the registrant must furnish in the prospectus the information required by Items 1102 through 1120 of Regulation AB.

>   C.   *Signatures.*
>   The registration statement must be signed by the depositor, the depositor's principal executive officer or officers, principal financial officer and controller or principal accounting officer, and by at least a majority of the depositor's board of directors or persons performing similar functions.

VII.   Eligibility to Use Incorporation by Reference

If a registrant meets the following requirements immediately prior to the time of filing a registration statement on this Form, it may elect to provide information required by Items 3 through 11 of this Form in accordance with Item 11A and Item 12 of this Form:

A. The registrant is subject to the requirement to file reports pursuant to Section 13 or Section 15(d) of the Securities Exchange Act of 1934 ("Exchange Act").

B. The registrant has filed all reports and other materials required to be filed by Sections 13(a), 14, or 15(d) of the Exchange Act during the preceding 12 months (or for such shorter period that the registrant was required to file such reports and materials).

C. The registrant has filed an annual report required under Section 13(a) or Section 15(d) of the Exchange Act for its most recently completed fiscal year.

D. The registrant is not:
   1. And during the past three years neither the registrant nor any of its predecessors was:
      (a) A blank check company as defined in Rule 419(a)(2);
      (b) A shell company, other than a business combination related shell company, each as defined in Rule 405; or
      (c) A registrant for an offering of penny stock as defined in Rule 3a51-1 of the Exchange Act.
   2. Registering an offering that effectuates a business combination transaction as defined in Rule 165(f)(1).

E. If a registrant is a successor registrant it shall be deemed to have satisfied conditions A., B., C., and D.2 above if:
   1. Its predecessor and it, taken together, do so, provided that the succession was primarily for the purpose of changing the state of incorporation of the predecessor or forming a holding company and that the assets and liabilities of the successor at the time of succession were substantially the same as those of the predecessor; or
   2. All predecessors met the conditions at the time of succession and the registrant has continued to do so since the succession.

F. The registrant makes its periodic and current reports filed pursuant to Section 13 or Section 15(d) of the Exchange Act that are incorporated by reference pursuant to Item 11A or Item 12 of this Form readily available and accessible on a Web site maintained by or for the registrant and containing information about the registrant.

PART I—INFORMATION REQUIRED IN PROSPECTUS

Item 1.   Forepart of the Registration Statement and Outside Front Cover Page of Prospectus.

Set forth in the forepart of the registration statement and on the outside front cover page of the prospectus the information required by Item 501 of Regulation S-K.

Item 2.   **Inside Front and Outside Back Cover Pages of Prospectus.**

Set forth on the inside front cover page of the prospectus or, where permitted, on the outside back cover page, the information required by Item 502 of Regulation S-K.

Item 3.   **Summary Information, Risk Factors and Ratio of Earnings to Fixed Charges.**

Furnish the information required by Item 503 of Regulation S-K.

Item 4.   **Use of Proceeds.**

Furnish the information required by Item 504 of Regulation S-K.

Item 5.   **Determination of Offering Price.**

Furnish the information required by Item 505 of Regulation S-K.

Item 6.   **Dilution.**

Furnish the information required by Item 506 of Regulation S-K.

Item 7.   **Selling Security Holders.**

Furnish the information required by Item 507 of Regulation S-K.

Item 8.   **Plan of Distribution.**

Furnish the information required by Item 508 of Regulation S-K.

Item 9.   **Description of Securities to be Registered.**

Furnish the information required by Item 202 of Regulation S-K.

Item 10.   **Interests of Named Experts and Counsel.**

Furnish the information required by Item 509 of Regulation S-K.

Item 11.   **Information with Respect to the Registrant.**

Furnish the following information with respect to the registrant:
(a)   Information required by Item 101 of Regulation S-K, description of business;
(b)   Information required by Item 102 of Regulation S-K, description of property;
(c)   Information required by Item 103 of Regulation S-K, legal proceedings;
(d)   Where common equity securities are being offered, information required by Item 201 of Regulation S-K, market price of and dividends on the registrant's common equity and related stockholder matters;

(e)   Financial statements meeting the requirements of Regulation S-X (Schedules required under Regulation S-X shall be filed as "Financial Statement Schedules" pursuant to Item 15, Exhibits and Financial Statement Schedules, of this Form), as well as any financial information required by Rule 3-05 and Article 11 of Regulation S-X;

(f)   Information required by Item 301 of Regulation S-K, selected financial data;

(g)   Information required by Item 302 of Regulation S-K, supplementary financial in formation;

(h)   Information required by Item 303 of Regulation S-K, management's discussion and analysis of financial condition and results of operations;

(i)   Information required by Item 304 of Regulation S-K, changes in and disagreements with accountants on accounting and financial disclosure;

(j)   Information required by Item 305 of Regulation S-K, quantitative and qualitative disclosures about market risk,

(k)   Information required by Item 401 of Regulation S-K, directors and executive officers;

(l)   Information required by Item 402 of Regulation S-K, executive compensation, and information required by paragraph (e)(4) of Item 407 of Regulation S-K, corporate governance;

(m)   Information required by Item 403 of Regulation S-K, security ownership of certain beneficial owners and management; and

(n)   Information required by Item 404 of Regulation S-K, transactions with related persons, promoters and certain control persons, and Item 407(a) of Regulation S-K, corporate governance.

Item 11A   Material Changes.

If the registrant elects to incorporate information by reference pursuant to General Instruction VII, describe any and all material changes in the registrant's affairs which have occurred since the end of the latest fiscal year for which audited financial statements were included in the latest Form 10-K and which have not been described in a Form 10-Q or Form 8-K filed under the Exchange Act.

Item 12.   Incorporation of Certain Information by Reference.

If the registrant elects to incorporate information by reference pursuant to General Instruction VII.:

(a)   It must specifically incorporate by reference into the prospectus contained in the registration statement the following documents by means of a statement to that effect in the prospectus listing all such documents:

     (1) The registrant's latest annual report on Form 10-K filed pursuant to Section 13(a) or Section 15(d) of the Exchange Act which contains financial statements for the registrant's latest fiscal year for which a Form 10-K was required to have been filed; and

     (2) All other reports filed pursuant to Section 13(a) or 15(d) of the Exchange Act or proxy or information statements filed pursuant to Section

14 of the Exchange Act since the end of the fiscal year covered by the annual report referred to in paragraph (a)(1) above.

Note to Item 12(a). Attention is directed to Rule 439 regarding consent to use of material incorporated by reference.

(b)   (1) The registrant must state:

         (i) That it will provide to each person, including any beneficial owner, to whom a prospectus is delivered, a copy of any or all of the reports or documents that have been incorporated by reference in the prospectus contained in the registration statement but not delivered with the prospectus;

         (ii) That it will provide these reports or documents upon written or oral request;

         (iii) That it will provide these reports or documents at no cost to the requester;

         (iv) The name, address, telephone number, and e-mail address, if any, to which the request for these reports or documents must be made; and

         (v) The registrant's Web site address, including the uniform resource locator (URL) where the incorporated reports and other documents may be accessed.

Note to Item 12(b)(1). If the registrant sends any of the information that is incorporated by reference in the prospectus contained in the registration statement to security holders, it also must send any exhibits that are specifically incorporated by reference in that information.

     (2) The registrant must:

         (i) Identify the reports and other information that it files with the SEC; and

         (ii) State that the public may read and copy any materials it files with the SEC at the SEC's Public Reference Room at 100 F Street, N.E., Washington, DC 20549. State that the public may obtain information on the operation of the Public Reference Room by calling the SEC at 1-800-SEC-0330. If the registrant is an electronic filer, state that the SEC maintains an Internet site that contains reports, proxy and information statements, and other information regarding issuers that file electronically with the SEC and state the address of that site (http://www.sec.gov).

Item 12A. Disclosure of Commission Position on Indemnification for Securities Act Liabilities.

Furnish the information required by Item 510 of Regulation S-K.

PART II—INFORMATION NOT REQUIRED IN PROSPECTUS

Item 13.   Other Expenses of Issuance and Distribution.

Furnish the information required by Item 511 of Regulation S-K.

Item 14.   Indemnification of Directors and Officers.

Furnish the information required by Item 702 of Regulation S-X.

Item 15.   Recent Sales of Unregistered Securities.

Furnish the information required by Item 701 of Regulation S-K.

Item 16.   Exhibits and Financial Statement Schedules.

(a) Subject to the rules regarding incorporation by reference, furnish the exhibits as required by Item 601 of Regulation S-K.

(b) Furnish the financial statement schedules required by Regulation S-X and Item ll(e) of this Form. These schedules shall be lettered or numbered in the manner described for exhibits in paragraph (a).

Item 17.   Undertakings.

Furnish the undertakings required by Item 512 of Regulation S-K.

SIGNATURES

Pursuant to the requirements of the Securities Act of 1933, the registrant has duly caused this registration statement to be signed on its behalf by the undersigned, thereunto duly authorized, in the City of _____, State of _____ _____, on _____, 20_____.

_____
(Registrant)

By _____
(Signature and Title)

Pursuant to the requirements of the Securities Act of 1933, this registration statement has been signed by the following persons in the capacities and on the dates indicated.

_____
(Signature)

_____
(Title)

_____
(Date)

Instructions.

1. The registration statement shall be signed by the registrant, its principal executive officer or officers, its principal financial officer, its controller or principal accounting officer and by at least a majority of the board of directors or persons performing similar functions. If the registrant is a foreign person, the registration statement shall also be signed by its authorized representative in the United States. Where the registrant is a limited partnership, the registration statement shall be signed by a majority of the board of directors of any corporate general partner signing the registration statement.

2. The name of each person who signs the registration statement shall be typed or printed beneath his signature. Any person who occupies more than one of the specified positions shall indicate each capacity in which he signs the registration statement. Attention is directed to Rule 402 concerning manual signatures and to Item 601 of Regulation S-K concerning signatures pursuant to powers of attorney.

INSTRUCTIONS AS TO SUMMARY PROSPECTUSES

1. A summary prospectus used pursuant to Rule 431, shall at the time of its use contain much of the information specified below as is then included in the registration statement. All other information and documents contained in the registration statement may be omitted.

    (a) As to Item 1, the aggregate offering price to the public, the aggregate underwriting discounts and commissions and the offering price per unit to the public;

    (b) As to Item 4, a brief statement of the principal purposes for which the proceeds are to be used;

    (c) As to Item 7, a statement as to the amount of the offering, if any, to be made for the account of security holders;

    (d) As to Item 8, the name of the managing underwriter or underwriters and a brief statement as to the nature of the underwriter's obligation to take the securities; if any securities to be registered are to be offered otherwise than through underwriters, a brief statement as to the manner of distribution; and, if securities are to be offered otherwise than for cash, a brief statement as to the general purposes of the distribution, the basis upon which the securities are to be offered, the amount of compensation and other expenses of distribution, and by whom they are to be borne;

    (e) As to Item 9, a brief statement as to dividend rights, voting rights, conversion rights, interest, maturity;

    (f) As to Item 11, a brief statement of the general character of the business done and intended to be done, the selected financial data (Item 301 of Regulation S-K) and a brief statement of the nature and present status of any material pending legal proceedings; and

(g) A tabular presentation of notes payable, long term debt, deferred credits, minority interests, if material, and the equity section of the latest balance sheet filed, as may be appropriate.

2. The summary prospectus shall not contain a summary or condensation of any other required financial information except as provided above.

3. Where securities being registered are to be offered in exchange for securities of any other issuer, the summary prospectus also shall contain that information as to Items 9 and 11 specified in paragraphs (e) and (f) above which would be required if the securities of such other issuer were registered on this Form.

4. The Commission may, upon the request of the registrant, and where consistent with the protection of investors, permit the omission of any of the information herein required or the furnishing in substitution therefor of appropriate information of comparable character. The Commission may also require the inclusion of other information in addition to, or in substitution for, the information herein required in any case where such information is necessary or appropriate for the protection of investors.

UNITED STATES
SECURITIES AND EXCHANGE COMMISSION
Washington, D.C. 20549

FORM S-3

REGISTRATION STATEMENT UNDER THE SECURITIES ACT OF 1933

(Exact name of registrant as specified in its charter)

(State or other jurisdiction of incorporation or organization)

(I.R.S. Employer Identification Number)

(Address, including zip code, and telephone number, including area code,
of registrant's principal executive offices)

(Name, address, including zip code, and telephone number, including area code,
of agent for service)

(Approximate date of commencement of proposed sale to the public)

If the only securities being registered on this Form are being offered pursuant to dividend or interest reinvestment plans, please check the following box: ❑

If any of the securities being registered on this Form are to be offered on a delayed or continuous basis pursuant to Rule 415 under the Securities Act of 1933, other than securities offered only in connection with dividend or interest reinvestment plans, check the following box: ❑

If this Form is filed to register additional securities for an offering pursuant to Rule 462(b) under the Securities Act, please check the following box and list the Securities Act registration statement number of the earlier effective registration statement for the same offering. ❑

If this Form is a post-effective amendment filed pursuant to Rule 462(c) under the Securities Act, check the following box and list the Securities Act registration statement number of the earlier effective registration statement for the same offering. ❑

If this Form is a registration statement pursuant to General Instruction I.D. or a post-effective amendment thereto that shall become effective upon filing with the Commission pursuant to Rule 462(e) under the Securities Act, check the following box. ❑

If this Form is a post-effective amendment to a registration statement filed pursuant to General Instruction I.D. filed to register additional securities or additional classes of securities pursuant to Rule 413(b) under the Securities Act, check the following box. ❑

Indicate by check mark whether the registrant is a large accelerated filer, an accelerated filer, a non-accelerated filer, or a smaller reporting company. See the definitions of "large accelerated filer," "accelerated filer" and "smaller reporting company" in Rule 12b-2 of the Exchange Act.

Large accelerated filer ❏   Accelerated filer ❏

Non-accelerated filer ❏   Smaller reporting company ❏

(Do not check if a smaller reporting company)

CALCULATION OF REGISTRATION FEE

Title of Each Class to be Registered	Amount to be Registered	Proposed Maximum Offering Price Per Unit	Proposed Maximum Aggregate Offering Price	Amount of Registration Fee

Note:

1.   Specific details relating to the fee calculation shall be furnished in notes to the Fee Table, including references to provisions of Rule 457 relied upon, if the basis of the calculation is not otherwise evident from the information presented in the Fee Table.

2.   If the filing fee is calculated pursuant to Rule 457(o) under the Securities Act, only the title of the class of securities to be registered, the proposed maximum aggregate offering price for that class of securities, and the amount of registration fee need to appear in the Fee Table. Where two or more classes of securities are being registered pursuant to General Instruction II.D., however, the Fee Table need only specify the maximum aggregate offering price for all classes; the Fee Table need not specify by each class the proposed maximum aggregate offering price (see General Instruction II.D.).

3.   If the filing fee is calculated pursuant to Rule 457(r) under the Securities Act, the Fee Table must state that it registers an unspecified amount of securities of each identified class of securities and must provide that the issuer is relying on Rule 456(b) and Rule 457(r). If the Fee Table is amended in a post-effective amendment to the registration statement or in a prospectus filed in accordance with Rule 456(b)(1)(ii), the Fee Table must specify the aggregate offering price for all classes of securities in the referenced offering or offerings and the applicable registration fee.

4.   Any difference between the dollar amount of securities registered for such offerings and the dollar amount of securities sold may be carried forward on a future registration statement pursuant to Rule 457 under the Securities Act.

GENERAL INSTRUCTIONS

I.   Eligibility Requirements for Use of Form S-3

This instruction sets forth registrant requirements and transaction requirements for the use of Form S-3. Any registrant which meets the requirements of I.A. below ("Registrant Requirements") may use this Form for the registration of securities under the Securities Act of 1933 ("Securities Act") which are offered in any transaction specified in I.B. below ("Transaction Requirement") provided that the requirement applicable to the specified transaction are met. With respect to majority-owned subsidiaries, see Instruction I.C. below. With respect to well-known seasoned issuers and majority-owned subsidiaries of well-known seasoned issuers, see Instruction I.D. below.

A. Registrant Requirements. Registrants must meet the following conditions in order to use this Form S-3 for registration under the Securities Act of securities offered in the transactions specified in I. B. below:

1. The registrant is organized under the laws of the United States or any State or Territory or the District of Columbia and has its principal business operations in the United States or its territories.

2. The registrant has a class of securities registered pursuant to Section 12(b) of the Securities Exchange Act of 1934 ("Exchange Act") or a class of equity securities registered pursuant to Section 12(g) of the Exchange Act or is required to file reports pursuant to Section 15(d) of the Exchange Act.

3. The registrant: (a) has been subject to the requirements of Section 12 or 15(d) of the Exchange Act and has filed all the material required to be filed pursuant to Sections 13, 14 or 15(d) for a period of at least twelve calendar months immediately preceding the filing of the registration statement on this Form; and (b) has filed in a timely manner all reports required to be filed during the twelve calendar months and any portion of a month immediately preceding the filing of the registration statement, other than a report that is required solely pursuant to Item 1.01, 1.02, 2.03, 2.04, 2.05, 2.06, 4.02(a) or 5.02(e) of Form 8-K. If the registrant has used (during the twelve calendar months and any portion of a month immediately preceding the filing of the registration statement) Rule 12b-25(b) under the Exchange Act with respect to a report or a portion of a report, that report or portion thereof has actually been filed within the time period prescribed by that rule.

4. The provisions of paragraphs A.2. and A.3.(a) of this section do not apply to any registered offerings of investment grade asset-backed securities as defined in I.B.5. below.

5. Neither the registrant nor any of its consolidated or unconsolidated subsidiaries have, since the end of the last fiscal year for which certified financial statements of the registrant and its consolidated subsidiaries were included in a report filed pursuant to Section 13(a) or 15(d) of the Exchange Act: (a) failed to pay any dividend or sinking fund installment on preferred stock; or (b) defaulted (i) on any installment or installments on indebtedness for borrowed money, or (ii) on any rental on one or more long term leases, which defaults in the aggregate are material to the financial position of the registrant and its consolidated and unconsolidated subsidiaries, taken as a whole.

6. A foreign issuer, other than a foreign government, which satisfies all of the above provisions of these registrant eligibility requirements except the

provisions in I.A.1. relating to organization and principal business shall be deemed to have met these registrant eligibility requirements provided that such a foreign issuer files the same reports with the Commission under Section 13(a) or 15(d) of the Exchange Act as a domestic registrant pursuant to I.A.3. above.

7. If the registrant is a successor registrant, it shall be deemed to have met conditions 1., 2., 3., and 5., above if: (a) its predecessor and it, taken together, do so, provided that the succession was primarily for the purpose of changing the state of incorporation of the predecessor or forming a holding company and that the assets and liabilities of the successor at the time of succession were substantially the same as those of the predecessor; or (b) if all predecessors met the conditions at the time of succession and the registrant has continued to do so since the succession.

8. *Electronic filings:* In addition to satisfying the foregoing conditions, a registrant subject to the electronic filing requirements of Rule 101 of Regulation S-T shall have:

    a. Filed with the Commission all required electronic filings, including electronic copies of documents submitted in paper pursuant to a hardship exemption as provided by Rule 201 or Rule 202(d) of Regulation S-T; and

    b. Submitted electronically to the Commission and posted on its corporate Web site, if any, all Interactive Data Files required to be submitted and posted pursuant to Rule 405 of Regulation S-T during the twelve calendar months and any portion of a month immediately preceding the filing of the registration statement on this Form (or for such shorter period of time that the registrant was required to submit and post such files).

B. **Transaction Requirements.** Security offerings meeting any of the following conditions and made by a registrant meeting the Registrant Requirements specified in I.A. above may be registered on this Form:

1. *Primary Offerings by Certain Registrants.* Securities to be offered for cash by or on behalf of a registrant, or outstanding securities to be offered for cash for the account of any person other than the registrant, including securities acquired by standby underwriters in connection with the call or redemption by the registrant of warrants or a class of convertible securities; *provided* that the aggregate market value of the voting and non-voting common equity held by non-affiliates of the registrant is $75 million or more.

    Instruction. For the purposes of this Form, "common equity" is as defined in Securities Act Rule 405. The aggregate market value of the registrant's outstanding voting and non-voting common equity shall be computed by use of the price at which the common equity was last sold, or the average of the bid and asked prices of such common equity, in the principal market for such common equity as of a date within 60 days prior to the date of filing. See the definition of "affiliate" in Securities Act Rule 405, as of a date within 60 days prior to the date of filing. See the definition of "affiliate" in Securities Act Rule 405.

2. *Primary Offerings of Non-convertible Investment Grade Securities.* Non-convertible securities to be offered for cash by or on behalf of a registrant, provided such securities at the time of sale are "investment grade securities," as defined below. A non-convertible security is an "investment grade security" if, at the time of sale, at least one nationally recognized statistical rating organization (as that term is used in Rule 15c3-1(c)(2)(vi)(F) under the Exchange Act has rated the security in one of its generic rating categories which signifies investment grade; typically, the four highest rating categories (within which there may be sub-categories or gradations indicating relative standing) signify investment grade.

3. *Transactions Involving Secondary Offerings.* Outstanding securities to be offered for the account of any person other than the issuer, including securities acquired by standby underwriters in connection with the call or redemption by the issuer of warrants or a class of convertible securities, if securities of the same class are listed and registered on a national securities exchange or are quoted on the automated quotation system of a national securities association. (In addition, attention is directed to General Instruction C to Form S-8 for the registration of employee benefit plan securities for resale.)

4. *Rights Offerings, Dividend or Interest Reinvestment Plans and Conversions or Warrants.* Securities to be offered (a) upon the exercise of outstanding rights granted by the issuer of the securities to be offered. If such rights are granted on a pro rata basis to all existing security holders of the class of securities to which the rights attach, or (b) pursuant to a dividend or interest reinvestment plan, or (c) upon the conversion of outstanding convertible securities or upon the exercise of outstanding transferable warrants issued by the issuer of the securities to be offered, or by an affiliate of such issuer: The issuer also must have provided, within the twelve calendar months immediately before the Form S-3 registration statement is filed, the information required by Items 401, 402, 403 and 407(c)(3), (d)(4), (d)(5) and (e)(4) of Regulation S-K to: all record holders of such rights, or to all participants in such plans, or to all record holders of such convertible securities or transferable warrants, respectively, material containing the information required by Rule 14a-3(b) under the Exchange Act and Items 401, 402 and 403 of Regulation S-K within the twelve calendar months immediately preceding the filing of the registration statement, except that the information required by Items 401, 402 and 403 of Regulation S-K need only be provided to holders of rights exercisable for common stock, holders of securities convertible into common stock, participants in plans which may invest in common stock, or in securities convertible into common stock or warrants exercisable for common stock, respectively.

5. *Offerings of Investment Grade Asset-backed Securities.* Asset-backed securities to be offered for cash, provided the securities are "investment grade securities," as defined in I.B.2. above (Primary Offerings of Non-convertible Investment Grade Securities). For purposes of this Form, the term "asset-packed security" means a security that is primarily serviced by the cashflows of a discrete pool of receivables or other financial assets, either fixed or revolving, that by their terms convert into cash within a finite time period plus any rights or other assets designed to assure the servicing or timely distribution of proceeds to the securityholders.

6. *Limited Primary Offerings by Certain Other Registrants.* Securities to be offered for cash by or on behalf of a registrant; provided that:
   a. the aggregate market value of securities sold by or on behalf of the registrant pursuant to this Instruction I.B.6. during the period of 12 calendar months immediately prior to, and including, the sale is no more than one-third of the aggregate market value of the voting and non-voting common equity held by non-affiliates of the registrant;
   b. the registrant is not a shell company (as defined in Rule 405 of this chapter) and has not been a shell company for at least 12 calendar months previously and if it has been a shell company at any time previously, has filed current Form 10 information with the Commission at least 12 calendar months previously reflecting its status as an entity that is not a shell company; and
   c. the registrant has at least one class of common equity securities listed and registered on a national securities exchange.

Instructions.
1. "Common equity" is as defined in Securities Act Rule 405. For purposes of computing the aggregate market value of the registrant's outstanding voting and non-voting common equity pursuant to General Instruction I.B.6., registrants shall use the price at which the common equity was last sold, or the average of the bid and asked prices of such common equity, in the principal market for such common equity as of a date within 60 days prior to the date of sale. See the definition of "affiliate" in Securities Act Rule 405.

2. For purposes of computing the aggregate market value of all securities sold by or on behalf of the registrant in offerings pursuant to General Instruction I.B.6. during any period of 12 calendar months, registrants shall aggregate the gross proceeds of such sales; provided, that, in the case of derivative securities convertible into or exercisable for shares of the registrant's common equity, registrants shall calculate the aggregate market value of any underlying equity shares in lieu of the market value of the derivative securities. The aggregate market value of the underlying equity shall be calculated by multiplying the maximum number of common equity shares into which the derivative securities are convertible or for which they are exercisable as of a date within 60 days prior to the date of sale, by the same per share market price of the registrant's equity used for purposes of calculating the aggregate market value of the registrant's outstanding voting and non-voting common equity pursuant to Instruction 1 to General Instruction I.B.6. If the derivative securities have been converted or

exercised, the aggregate market value of the underlying equity shall be calculated by multiplying the actual number of shares into which the securities were converted or received upon exercise, by the market price of such shares on the date of conversion or exercise.

3. If the aggregate market value of the registrant's outstanding voting and nonvoting common equity computed pursuant to General Instruction I.B.6. equals or exceeds $75 million subsequent to the effective date of this registration statement, then the one-third limitation on sales specified in General Instruction I.B.6(a) shall not apply to additional sales made pursuant to this registration statement on or subsequent to such date and instead the registration statement shall be considered filed pursuant to General Instruction I.B.1.

4. The term "Form 10 information" means the information that is required by Form 10 or Form 20-F, as applicable to the registrant, to register under the Securities Exchange Act of 1934 each class of securities being registered using this form. A registrant may provide the Form 10 information in another Commission filing with respect to the registrant.

5. The date used in Instruction 2 to General Instruction I.B.6. shall be the same date used in Instruction 1 to General Instruction I.B.6.

6. A registrant's eligibility to register a primary offering on Form S-3 pursuant to General Instruction I.B.6. does not mean that the registrant meets the requirements of Form S-3 for purposes of any other rule or regulation of the Commission apart from Rule 415(a)(1)(x).

7. Registrants must set forth on the outside front cover of the prospectus the calculation of the aggregate market value of the registrant's outstanding voting and nonvoting common equity pursuant to General Instruction I.B.6. and the amount of all securities offered pursuant to General Instruction I.B.6. during the prior 12 calendar month period that ends on, and includes, the date of the prospectus.

8. For purposes of General Instruction I.B.6(c), a "national securities exchange" shall mean an exchange registered as such under Section 6(a) of the Securities Exchange Act of 1934.

C. **Majority-owned Subsidiaries.** If a registrant is a majority-owned subsidiary, security offerings may be registered on this Form if:

1. the registrant-subsidiary itself meets the Registrant Requirements and the applicable Transaction Requirement;

2. the parent of the registrant-subsidiary meets the Registrant Requirements and the conditions of Transaction Requirement B.2. (Primary Offerings of Non-convertible Investment Grade Securities) are met;

3. the parent of the registrant-subsidiary meets the Registrant Requirements and the applicable Transaction Requirement, and provides a full and unconditional guarantee, as defined in Rule 3-10 of Regulation S-X, of the payment obligations on the securities being registered, and the securities being registered are non-convertible securities, other than common equity;

4. the parent of the registrant-subsidiary meets the Registrant Requirements and the applicable Transaction Requirement, and the securities of the registrant-subsidiary being registered are full and unconditional guarantees, as defined in Rule 3-10 of Regulation S-X, of the payment obligations on the parent's non-convertible securities, other than common equity, being registered; or

5. the parent of the registrant-subsidiary meets the Registrant Requirements and the applicable Transaction Requirement, and the securities of the registrant-subsidiary being registered are guarantees of the payment obligations on the non convertible securities, other than common equity, being registered by another majority-owned subsidiary of the parent where the parent provides a full and unconditional guarantee, as defined in Rule 3-10 of Regulation S-X, of such non-convertible securities.

Note to General Instruction I.C.: With regard to paragraphs I.C.3, I.C.4, and I.C.5 above, the guarantor is the issuer of a separate security consisting of the guarantee, which must be concurrently registered, but may be registered on the same registration statement as are the non-convertible guaranteed securities.

D. **Automatic Shelf Offerings by Well-known Seasoned Issuers**. Any registrant that is a well-known seasoned issuer as defined in Rule 405 at the most recent eligibility determination date specified in paragraph (2) of that definition may use this Form for registration under the Securities Act of securities offerings, other than pursuant to Rule 415(a)(1)(vii) or (viii), as follows:

1. The securities to be offered are:
    a. Any securities to be offered pursuant to Rule 415, Rule 430A, or Rule 430B by:
        i.   A registrant that is a well-known seasoned issuer by reason of paragraph (1)(i)(A) of the definition in Rule 405; or
        ii. A registrant that is a well-known seasoned issuer only by reason of paragraph (1)(i)(B) of the definition in Rule 405 if the registrant also is eligible to register a primary offering of its securities pursuant to Transaction Requirement I.B.1 of this Form;

    b. Non-convertible securities, other than common equity, to be offered pursuant to Rule 415, Rule 430A, or Rule 430B by a registrant that is a well-known seasoned issuer only by reason of paragraph (1)(i)(B) of the definition in Rule 405 and does not fall within Transaction Requirement I.B.1 of this Form;

    c. Securities of majority-owned subsidiaries of the parent registrant to be offered pursuant to Rule 415, Rule 430A, or Rule 430B if the parent registrant is a well-known seasoned issuer and the securities of the majority-owned subsidiary being registered meet the following requirements:
        i.   Securities of a majority-owned subsidiary that is a well-known seasoned issuer at the time it becomes a registrant, other than by

virtue of paragraph (1)(ii) of the definition of well-known seasoned issuer in Rule 405;

ii. Securities of a majority-owned subsidiary that are non-convertible securities, other than common equity, and the parent registrant provides a full and unconditional guarantee, as defined in Rule 3-10 of Regulation S-X, of the payment obligations on the non-convertible securities;

iii. Securities of a majority-owned subsidiary that are a guarantee of:

(A) Non-convertible securities, other than common equity, of the parent registrant being registered;

(B) Non-convertible securities, other than common equity, of another majority-owned subsidiary being registered and the parent registrant has provided a full and unconditional guarantee, as defined in Rule 3-10 of Regulation S-X, of the payment obligations on such non-convertible securities; or

iv. Securities of a majority-owned subsidiary that meet the conditions of Transaction Requirement I.B.2. of this Form (Primary Offerings of Non-Convertible Investment Grade Securities).

d. Securities to be offered for the account of any person other than the issuer ("selling security holders"), provided that the registration statement and the prospectus are not required to separately identify the selling security holders or the securities to be sold by such persons until the filing of a prospectus, prospectus supplement, posteffective amendment to the registration statement, or periodic or current report under the Exchange Act that is incorporated by reference into the registration statement and prospectus, identifying the selling security holders and the amount of securities to be sold by each of them and, if included in a periodic or current report, a prospectus or prospectus supplement is filed, as required by Rule 430B, pursuant to Rule 424(b)(7).

2. The registrant pays the registration fee pursuant to Rules 456(b) and 457(r) or in accordance with Rule 456(a).

3. If the registrant is a majority-owned subsidiary, it is required to file and has filed reports pursuant to Section 13 or Section 15(d) of the Exchange Act and satisfies the requirements of the Form with regard to incorporation by reference or information about the majority-owned subsidiary is included in the registration statement (or a post-effective amendment to the registration statement).

4. The registrant may register additional securities or classes of its or its majority-owned subsidiaries' securities on a post-effective amendment pursuant to Rule 413(b).

5. An automatic shelf registration statement and post-effective amendment will become effective immediately pursuant to Rule 462(e) and (f) upon filing.

All filings made on or in connection with automatic shelf registration statements on this Form become public upon filing with the Commission.

II.   Application of General Rules and Regulations

A.   Attention is directed to the General Rules and Regulations under the Securities Act, particularly Regulation C thereunder. That Regulation contains general requirements regarding the preparation and filing of registration statements.

B.   Attention is directed to Regulation S-K for the requirements applicable to the content of the non-financial statement portions of registration statements under the Securities Act. Where this Form directs the registrant to furnish information required by Regulation S-K and the item of Regulation S-K so provides, information need only be furnished to the extent appropriate. Notwithstanding Items 501 and 502 of Regulation S-K, no table of contents is required to be included in the prospectus or registration statement prepared on this Form. In addition to the information expressly required to be included in a registration statement on this Form S-3, registrants also may provide such other information as they deem appropriate.

C.   A "smaller reporting company," defined in Rule 405, that is eligible to use Form S-3 shall refer to the disclosure items in Regulation S-K with specific attention to the scaled disclosure provided for smaller reporting companies, if any. Smaller reporting companies may provide the financial information called for by Article 8 of Regulation S-X in lieu of the financial information called for by Item 11 in this form.

D.   *Non-Automatic Shelf Registration Statements.* Where two or more classes of securities being registered on this Form pursuant to General Instruction I.B.1. or I.B.2. are to be offered pursuant to Rule 415(a)(1)(x), and where this Form is not an automatic shelf registration statement, Rule 457(*o*) permits the registration fee to be calculated on the basis of the maximum offering price of all the securities listed in the Fee Table. In this event, while the Fee Table would list each of the classes of securities being registered and the aggregate proceeds to be raised, the Fee Table need not specify by each class information as to the amount to be registered, proposed maximum offering price per unit, and proposed maximum aggregate offering price.

E.   *Automatic Shelf Registration Statements.* Where securities are being registered on this Form pursuant to General Instruction I.D., Rule 456(b) permits, but does not require, the registrant to pay the registration fee on a pay-as-you-go basis and Rule 457(r) permits, but does not require, the registration fee to be calculated on the basis of the aggregate offering price of the securities to be offered in an offering or offerings off the registration statement. If a registrant elects to pay all or a portion of the registration fee on a deferred basis, the Fee Table in the initial filing must identify the classes of securities being registered and provide that the registrant elects to rely on Rule 456(b) and Rule 457(r), but the Fee Table does not need to specify any other information. When the registrant amends the Fee

Table in accordance with Rule 456(b)(1)(ii), the amended Fee Table must include either the dollar amount of securities being registered if paid in advance of or in connection with an offering or offerings or the aggregate offering price for all classes of securities referenced in the offerings and the applicable registration fee.

F. Information in Automatic and Non-Automatic Shelf Registration Statements. Where securities are being registered on this Form pursuant to General Instruction I.B.1, I.B.2, I.B.5, I.C., or I.D., information is only required to be furnished as of the date of initial effectiveness of the registration statement to the extent required by Rule 430A or Rule 430B. Required information about a specific transaction must be included in the prospectus in the registration statement by means of a prospectus that is deemed to be part of and included in the registration statement pursuant to Rule 430A or Rule 430B, a post-effective amendment to the registration statement, or a periodic or current report under the Exchange Act incorporated by reference into the registration statement and the prospectus and identified in a prospectus filed, as required by Rule 430B, pursuant to Rule 424(b).

G. Selling Security Holder Offerings. Where a registrant eligible to register primary offerings on this Form pursuant to General Instruction I.B.1 registers securities offerings on this Form pursuant to General Instruction I.B.1 or I.B.3 for the account of persons other than the registrant, if the offering of the securities, or securities convertible into such securities, that are being registered on behalf of the selling security holders was completed and the securities, or securities convertible into such securities, were issued and outstanding prior to the original date of filing the registration statement covering the resale of the securities, the registrant may, as permitted by Rule 430B(b), in lieu of identifying selling security holders prior to effectiveness of the resale registration statement, refer to unnamed selling security holders in a generic manner by identifying the initial transaction in which the securities were sold. Following effectiveness, the registrant must include in a prospectus filed pursuant to Rule 424(b)(7), a post-effective amendment to the registration statement, or an Exchange Act report incorporated by reference into the prospectus that is part of the registration statement (which Exchange Act report is identified in a prospectus filed, as required by Rule 430B, pursuant to Rule 424(b)(7)) the names of previously unidentified selling security holders and amounts of securities that they intend to sell. If this Form is being filed pursuant to General Instruction I.D. by a well-known seasoned issuer to register securities being offered for the account of persons other than the issuer, the registration statement and the prospectus included in the registration statement do not need to designate the securities that will be offered for the account of such persons, identify them, or identify the initial transaction in which the securities, or securities convertible into such securities, were sold until the registrant files a post-effective amendment to the registration statement, a prospectus pursuant to Rule 424(b), or an Exchange Act report (and prospectus filed, as required by Rule 430B, pursuant to Rule 424(b)(7)) containing information for the offering on behalf of such persons.

III.   Dividend or Interest Reinvestment Plans: Filing and Effectiveness of Registration Statement; Requests for Confidential Treatment

A registration statement on this Form S-3 relating solely to securities offered pursuant to dividend or interest reinvestment plans will become effective automatically (Rule 462) upon filing (Rule 456). Post-effective amendments to such a registration statement on this Form shall become effective upon filing (Rule 464). All filings made on or in connection with this Form become public upon filing with the Commission. As a result, requests for confidential treatment made under Rule 406 must be processed with the Commission staff prior to the filing of such a registration statement. The number of copies of the registration statement and of each amendment required by Rules 402 and 472 shall be filed with the Commission: *provided, however,* That the number of additional copies referred to in Rule 402(b) may be reduced from ten to three and the number of additional copies referred to in Rule 472(a) may be reduced from eight to three, one of which shall be marked clearly and precisely to indicate changes.

IV.   Registration of Additional Securities and Additional Classes of Securities

    A.   Registration of Additional Securities Pursuant to Rule 462(b). With respect to the registration of additional securities for an offering pursuant to Rule 462(b) under the Securities Act, the registrant may file a registration statement consisting only of the following: the facing page; a statement that the contents of the earlier registration statement, identified by file number, are incorporated by reference; required opinions and consents; the signature page; and any price-related information omitted from the earlier registration statement in reliance on Rule 430A that the registrant chooses to include in the new registration statement. The information contained in such a Rule 462(b) registration statement shall be deemed to be a part of the earlier registration statement as of the date of effectiveness of the Rule 462(b) registration statement. Any opinion or consent required in the Rule 462(b) registration statement may be incorporated by reference from the earlier registration statement with respect to the offering, if: (i) such opinion or consent expressly provides for such incorporation; and (ii) such opinion relates to the securities registered pursuant to Rule 462(b). *See* Rule 411(c) and Rule 439(b) under the Securities Act.

    B.   Registration of Additional Securities or Classes of Securities or Additional Registrants After Effectiveness. A well-known seasoned issuer relying on General Instruction I.D. of this Form may register additional securities or classes of securities, pursuant to Rule 413(b) by filing a post-effective amendment to the effective registration statement. The well-known seasoned issuer may add majority-owned subsidiaries as additional registrants whose securities are eligible to be sold as part of the automatic shelf registration statement by filing a post-effective amendment identifying the additional registrants, and the registrant and the additional registrants and other persons required to sign the registration statement must sign the post-effective amendment. The post-effective amendment must consist of the facing page; any disclosure required by this Form that is necessary to update the registration statement to reflect the additional securities, additional classes of securities, or additional registrants; any required opinions and consents; and the signature page. Required information, consents, or opinions may be included in the prospectus and the registration statement through a post-effective amendment or may be provided through a document incorporated or deemed incorporated by reference into the registration statement and the prospectus that is part of the registration statement, or, as to the required information only, contained in a prospectus filed pursuant to Rule 424(b) that is deemed part of and included in the registration statement and prospectus that is part of the registration statement.

PART I – INFORMATION REQUIRED IN PROSPECTUS

Item 1.   Forepart of the Registration Statement and Outside Front Cover Pages of Prospectus.

Set forth in the forepart of the registration statement and on the outside front cover page of the prospectus the information required by Item 501 of Regulation S-K.

Item 2.   Inside Front and Outside Back Cover Pages of Prospectus.

Set forth on the inside front cover page of the prospectus or, where permitted, on the outside back cover page, the information required by Item 502 of Regulation S-K.

Item 3.   Summary Information, Risk Factors and Ratio of Earnings to Fixed Charges.

Furnish the information required by Item 503 of Regulation S-K.

Item 4.   Use of Proceeds.

Furnish the information required by Item 504 of Regulation S-K.

Item 5.   Determination of Offering Price.

Furnish the information required by Item 505 of Regulation S-K.

Item 6.   Dilution.

Furnish the information required by Item 506 of Regulation S-K.

Item 7.   Selling Security Holders.

Furnish the information required by Item 507 of Regulation S-K.

Item 8.   Plan of Distribution.

Furnish the information required by Item 508 of Regulation S-K.

Item 9.   Description of Securities to be Registered.

Furnish the information required by Item 202 of Regulation S-K, unless capital stock is to be registered and securities of the same class are registered pursuant to Section 12 of the Exchange Act.

Item 10.   Interests of Named Experts and Counsel.

Furnish the information required by Item 509 of Regulation S-K.

Item 11.   Material Changes.

    a.   Describe any and all material changes in the registrant's affairs which have occurred since the end of the latest fiscal year for which certified financial statements were included in the latest annual report to security holders and which have not been described in a report on Form 10-Q or Form 8-K filed under the Exchange Act.

    b.   Include in the prospectus, if not incorporated by reference therein from the reports filed under the Exchange Act specified in Item 12(a), a proxy or information statement filed pursuant to Section 14 of the Exchange Act, a prospectus previously filed pursuant to Rule 424(b) or (c) under the Securities Act or, where no prospectus is required to be filed pursuant to Rule 424(b), the prospectus included in the registration statement at effectiveness, or a Form 8-K filed during either of the two preceding years: (i) information required by Rule 3-05 and Article 11 of Regulation S-X; (ii) restated financial statements prepared in accordance with Regulation S-X if there has been a change in accounting principles or a correction in an error where such change or correction requires a material retroactive restatement of financial statements; (iii) restated financial statements prepared in accordance with Regulation S-X where a combination of entities under common control has been consummated subsequent to the most recent fiscal year and the transferred businesses, considered in the aggregate, are significant pursuant to Rule 11-01(b), or (iv) any financial information required because of a material disposition of assets outside the normal course of business.

Item 12.   Incorporation of Certain Information by Reference.

    a.   The documents listed in (1) and (2) below shall be specifically incorporated by reference into the prospectus by means of a statement to that effect in the prospectus listing all such documents:

        1.   the registrant's latest annual report on Form 10-K filed pursuant to Section 13(a) or 15(d) of the Exchange Act which contains financial statements for the registrant's latest fiscal year for which a Form 10-K were required to have been filed; and

2. all other reports filed pursuant to Section 13(a) or 15(d) of the Exchange Act since the end of the fiscal year covered by the annual report referred to in (1) above; and

3. if capital stock is to be registered and securities of the same class are registered under Section 12 of the Exchange Act, the description of such class of securities which is contained in a registration statement filed under the Exchange Act, including any amendment or reports filed for the purpose of updating such description.

b. The prospectus shall also state that all documents subsequently filed by the registrant pursuant to Sections 13(a), 13(c), 14 or 15(d) of the Exchange Act, prior to the termination of the offering shall be deemed to be incorporated by reference into the prospectus.

Instruction. Attention is directed to Rule 439 regarding consent to use of material incorporated by reference.

c. 1. You must state
    (i) that you will provide to each person, including any beneficial owner, to whom a prospectus is delivered, a copy of any or all of the information that has been incorporated by reference in the prospectus but not delivered with the prospectus;
    (ii) that you will provide this information upon written or oral request;
    (iii) that you will provide this information at no cost to the requester; and
    (iv) the name, address, and telephone number to which the request for this information must be made.

    Note to Item 12(c)(1). If you send any of the information that is incorporated by reference in the prospectus to security holders, you also must send any exhibits that are specifically incorporated by reference in that information.

2. You must
    (i) identify the reports and other information that you file with the SEC; and
    (ii) state that the public may read and copy any materials you file with the SEC at the SEC's Public Reference Room at 100 F Street, N.E., Washington, D.C. 20549. State that the public may obtain information on the operation of the Public Reference Room by calling the SEC at 1-800-SEC-0330. If you are an electronic filer, state that the SEC maintains an Internet site that contains reports, proxy and information statements, and other information regarding issuers that file electronically with the SEC and state the address of that site (http://www.sec.gov). You are encouraged to give your Internet address, if available.

d. Any information required in the prospectus in response to Item 3 through Item 11 of this Form may be included in the prospectus through documents filed pursuant to Section 13(a), 14, or 15(d) of the Exchange Act that are incorporated or deemed incorporated by reference into the prospectus that is part of the registration statement.

Item 13. Disclosure of Commission Position on Indemnification for Securities Act Liabilities.

Furnish the information required by Item 510 of Regulation S-K.

PART II – INFORMATION NOT REQUIRED IN PROSPECTUS

Item 14. Other Expenses of Issuance and Distribution.

Furnish the information required by Item 511 of Regulation S-K.

Item 15. Indemnification of Directors and Officers.

Furnish the information required by Item 702 of Regulation S-K.

Item 16. Exhibits.

Subject to the rules regarding incorporation by reference, furnish the exhibits required by Item 601 of Regulation S-K.

Item 17. Undertakings.

Furnish the undertakings required by Item 512 of Regulation S-K.

SIGNATURES

Pursuant to the requirements of the Securities Act of 1933, the registrant certifies that it has reasonable grounds to believe that it meets all of the requirements for filing on Form S-3 and has duly caused this registration statement to be signed on its behalf by the undersigned, thereunto duly authorized, in the City of _____, State of _____ _____, on _____

_____
(Registrant)
By _____
(Signature and Title)

Pursuant to the requirements of the Securities Act of 1933, this registration statement has been signed by the following persons in the capacities and on the dates indicated.

_____
(Signature)

_____
(Title)

_____
(Date)

Instructions

1.   The registration statement shall be signed by the registrant, its principal executive officer or officers, its principal financial officer, its controller or principal accounting officer and by at least a majority of the board of directors or persons performing similar functions. If the registrant is a foreign person, the registration statement shall also be signed by its authorized representative in the United States. Where the registrant is a limited partnership, the registration statement shall be signed by a majority of the board of directors of any corporate general partner signing the registration statement.

2.   The name of each person who signs the registration statement shall be typed or printed beneath his signature. Any person who occupies more than one of the specified positions shall indicate each capacity in which he signs the registration statement. Attention is directed to Rule 402 concerning manual signatures and to Item 601 of Regulation S-K concerning signatures pursuant to powers of attorney.

3.   Where eligibility for use of the Form is based on the assignment of a security rating pursuant to Transaction Requirements B.2. or B.5., the registrant may sign the registration statement notwithstanding the fact that such security rating has not been assigned by the filing date, provided that the registrant reasonably believes, and so states, that the security rating requirement will be met by the time of sale.

Exchange Act – Statutes

Section 1 – Short Title

This Act may be cited as the "Securities Exchange Act of 1934."

Section 3(a) – Definitions

When used in this title, unless the context otherwise requires–

1. The term "exchange" means any organization, association, or group of persons, whether incorporated or unincorporated, which constitutes, maintains, or provides a market place or facilities for bringing together purchasers and sellers of securities or for otherwise performing with respect to securities the functions commonly performed by a stock exchange as that term is generally understood, and includes the market place and the market facilities maintained by such exchange.

10. The term "security" means any note, stock, treasury stock, security future, bond, debenture, certificate of interest or participation in any profit-sharing agreement or in any oil, gas, or other mineral royalty or lease, any collateral-trust certificate, preorganization certificate or subscription, transferable share, investment contract, voting-trust certificate, certificate of deposit for a security, any put, call, straddle,

option, or privilege on any security, certificate of deposit, or group or index of securities (including any interest therein or based on the value thereof), or any put, call, straddle, option, or privilege entered into on a national securities exchange relating to foreign currency, or in general, any instrument commonly known as a "security"; or any certificate of interest or participation in, temporary or interim certificate for, receipt for, or warrant or right to subscribe to or purchase, any of the foregoing; but shall not include currency or any note, draft, bill of exchange, or banker's acceptance which has a maturity at the time of issuance of not exceeding nine months, exclusive of days of grace, or any renewal thereof the maturity of which is likewise limited.

14. The terms "sale" and "sell" each include any contract to sell or otherwise dispose of. For security futures products, such term includes any contract, agreement, or transaction for future delivery.

Section 4C – Appearance and Practice Before the Commission

a. **Authority to Censure.** The Commission may censure any person, or deny, temporarily or permanently, to any person the privilege of appearing or practicing before the Commission in any way, if that person is found by the Commission, after notice and opportunity for hearing in the matter–

   highly unreasonable conduct

1. not to possess the requisite qualifications to represent others;
2. to be lacking in character or integrity, or to have engaged in unethical or improper professional conduct; or
3. to have willfully violated, or willfully aided and abetted the violation of, any provision of the securities laws or the rules and regulations issued thereunder.

b. **Definition.** With respect to any registered public accounting firm or associated person, for purposes of this section, the term 'improper professional conduct' means–

1. intentional or knowing conduct, including reckless conduct, that results in a violation of applicable professional standards; and
2. negligent conduct in the form of–
   A. a single instance of highly unreasonable conduct that results in a violation of applicable professional standards in circumstances in which the registered public accounting firm or associated person knows, or should know, that heightened scrutiny is warranted; or
   B. repeated instances of unreasonable conduct, each resulting in a violation of applicable professional standards, that indicate a lack of competence to practice before the Commission

Section 9 – Manipulation of Security Prices

a. **Transactions relating to purchase or sale of security.** It shall be unlawful for any person, directly or indirectly, by the use of the mails or any means or instrumentality of interstate commerce, or of any facility of any national securities exchange, or for any member of a national securities exchange–

1. For the purpose of creating a false or misleading appearance of active trading in any security registered on a national securities exchange, or a false or misleading appearance with respect to the market for any such security, (A) to

effect any transaction in such security which involves no change in the beneficial ownership thereof, or (B) to enter an order or orders for the purchase of such security with the knowledge that an order or orders of substantially the same size, at substantially the same time, and at substantially the same price, for the sale of any such security, has been or will be entered by or for the same or different parties, or (C) to enter any order or orders for the sale of any such security with the knowledge that an order or orders of substantially the same size, at substantially the same time, and at substantially the same price, for the purchase of such security, has been or will be entered by or for the same or different parties.

2.   To effect, alone or with one or more other persons, a series of transactions in any security registered on a national securities exchange or in connection with any security-based swap agreement (as defined in section 206B of the Gramm-Leach-Bliley Act) with respect to such security creating actual or apparent active trading in such security, or raising or depressing the price of such security, for the purpose of inducing the purchase or sale of such security by others.

3.   If a dealer or broker, or other person selling or offering for sale or purchasing or offering to purchase the security or a security-based swap agreement (as defined in section 206B of the Gramm-Leach-Bliley Act) with respect to such security, to induce the purchase or sale of any security registered on a national securities exchange or any security based swap agreement (as defined in section 206B of the Gramm-Leach Bliley Act) with respect to such security by the circulation or dissemination in the ordinary course of business of information to the effect that the price of any such security will or is likely to rise or fall because of market operations of any one or more persons conducted for the purpose of raising or depressing the price of such security.

4.   If a dealer or broker, or the person selling or offering for sale or purchasing or offering to purchase the security or a security-based swap agreement (as defined in section 206B of the Gramm-Leach-Bliley Act) with respect to such security, to make, regarding any security registered on a national securities exchange or any security-based swap agreement (as defined in section 206B of the Gramm-Leach-Bliley Act) with respect to such security, for the purpose of inducing the purchase or sale of such security or such security-based swap agreement, any statement which was at the time and in the light of the circumstances under which it was made, false or misleading with respect to any material fact, and which he knew or had reasonable ground to believe was so false or misleading.

5.   For a consideration, received directly or indirectly from a dealer or broker, or other person selling or offering for sale or purchasing or offering to purchase the security or a security-based swap agreement (as defined in section 206B of the Gramm-Leach-Bliley Act) with respect to such security, to induce the purchase of any security registered on a national securities exchange or any security-based swap agreement (as defined in section 206B of the Gramm-Leach-Bliley Act) with respect to such security by the circulation or dissemination of information to the effect that the price of any such security will or is likely to rise or fall because of the market operations of any one or

more persons conducted for the purpose of raising or depressing the price of such security.

6.   To effect either alone or with one or more other persons any series of transactions for the purchase and/or sale of any security registered on a national securities exchange for the purpose of pegging, fixing, or stabilizing the price of such security in contravention of such rules and regulations as the Commission may prescribe as necessary or appropriate in the public interest or for the protection of investors.

b.   **Transactions relating to puts, calls, straddles, or options**. It shall be unlawful for any person to effect, by use of any facility of a national securities exchange, in contravention of such rules and regulations as the Commission may prescribe as necessary or appropriate in the public interest or for the protection of investors–

1.   any transaction in connection with any security whereby any party to such transaction acquires (A) any put, call, straddle, or other option or privilege of buying the security from or selling the security to another without being bound to do so; or (B) any security futures product on the security; or

2.   any transaction in connection with any security with relation to which he has, directly or indirectly, any interest in any (A) such put, call, straddle, option, or privilege; or (B) such security futures product; or

3.   any transaction in any security for the account of any person who he has reason to believe has, and who actually has, directly or indirectly, any interest in any (A) such put, call, straddle, option, or privilege; or (B) such security futures product with relation to such security.

c.   **Endorsement or guarantee of puts, calls, straddles, or options.** It shall be unlawful for any member of a national securities exchange directly or indirectly to endorse or guarantee the performance of any put, call, straddle, option, or privilege in relation to any security registered on a national securities exchange, in contravention of such rules and regulations as the Commission may prescribe as necessary or appropriate in the public interest or for the protection of investors.

d.   **Registered warrant, right, or convertible security not included in "put", "call", "straddle", or "option."** The terms "put", "call", "straddle", or "option", or "privilege" as used in this section shall not include any registered warrant, right, or convertible security.

e.   **Persons liable; suits at law or in equity.** Any person who willfully participates in any act or transaction in violation of subsection (a), (b) or (c) of this section, shall be liable to any person who shall purchase or sell any security at a price which was affected by such act or transaction, and the person so injured may sue in law or in equity in any court of competent jurisdiction to recover the damages sustained as a result of any such act or transaction. In any such suit the court may, in its discretion, require an undertaking for the payment of the costs of such suit, and assess reasonable costs, including reasonable attorneys' fees, against either party litigant. Every person who becomes liable to make any payment under this subsection may recover contribution as in cases of contract from any person who, if joined in the original suit, would have been liable to make the same payment. No action shall be maintained to enforce any liability created under this section, unless brought within one year after the discovery of the facts constituting the violation and within three years after such violation.

f.   **Limitations on practices that affect market volatility.** It shall be unlawful for any person, by the use of the mails or any means or instrumentality of interstate commerce or of any facility of any national securities exchange, to use or employ any act or practice in connection with the purchase or sale of any equity security in contravention of such rules or regulations as the Commission may adopt, consistent with the public interest, the protection of investors, and the maintenance of fair and orderly markets–

a.   to prescribe means reasonably designed to prevent manipulation of price levels of the equity securities market or a substantial segment thereof; and

b.   to prohibit or constrain, during periods of extraordinary market volatility, any trading practice in connection with the purchase or sale of equity securities that the Commission determines (A) has previously contributed significantly to extraordinary levels of volatility that have threatened the maintenance of fair and orderly markets; and (B) is reasonably certain to engender such levels of volatility if not prohibited or constrained.

In adopting rules under paragraph (2), the Commission shall, consistent with the purposes of this subsection, minimize the impact on the normal operations of the market and a natural person's freedom to buy or sell any equity security.

Section 10 – Manipulative and Deceptive Devices

It shall be unlawful for any person, directly or indirectly, by the use of any means or instrumentality of interstate commerce or of the mails, or of any facility of any national securities exchange–

a.   1.   To effect a short sale, or to use or employ any stop-loss order in connection with the purchase or sale, of any security registered on a national securities exchange, in contravention of such rules and regulations as the Commission may prescribe as necessary or appropriate in the public interest or for the protection of investors.

2.   Paragraph (1) of this subsection shall not apply to security futures products.

b.   To use or employ, in connection with the purchase or sale of any security registered on a national securities exchange or any security not so registered * * * any manipulative or deceptive device or contrivance in contravention of such rules and regulations as the Commission may prescribe as necessary or appropriate in the public interest or for the protection of investors.

Section 10A – Audit Requirements

a.   **In General.** Each audit required pursuant to this title of the financial statements of an issuer by a registered public accounting firm shall include, in accordance with generally accepted auditing standards, as may be modified or supplemented from time to time by the Commission–

1.   procedures designed to provide reasonable assurance of detecting illegal acts that would have a direct and material effect on the determination of financial statement amounts;

2.   procedures designed to identify related party transactions that are material to the financial statements or otherwise require disclosure therein; and

3.   an evaluation of whether there is substantial doubt about the ability of the issuer to continue as a going concern during the ensuing fiscal year.

b.   **Required Response to Audit Discoveries**

1.   Investigation and report to management

If, in the course of conducting an audit pursuant to this title to which subsection (a) of this section applies, the registered public accounting firm detects or otherwise becomes aware of information indicating that an illegal act (whether or not perceived to have a material effect on the financial statements of the issuer) has or may have occurred, the firm shall, in accordance with generally accepted auditing standards, as may be modified or supplemented from time to time by the Commission–

A.

     i.   determine whether it is likely that an illegal act has occurred; and

     ii.   if so, determine and consider the possible effect of the illegal act on the financial statements of the issuer, including any contingent monetary effects, such as fines, penalties, and damages; and

B.   as soon as practicable, inform the appropriate level of the management of the issuer and assure that the audit committee of the issuer, or the board of directors of the issuer in the absence of such a committee, is adequately informed with respect to illegal acts that have been detected or have otherwise come to the attention of such firm in the course of the audit, unless the illegal act is clearly inconsequential.

2.   Response to failure to take remedial action

If, after determining that the audit committee of the board of directors of the issuer, or the board of directors of the issuer in the absence of an audit committee, is adequately informed with respect to illegal acts that have been detected or have otherwise come to the attention of the firm in the course of the audit of such firm, the registered public accounting firm concludes that–

A.   the illegal act has a material effect on the financial statements of the issuer;

B.   the senior management has not taken, and the board of directors has not caused senior management to take, timely and appropriate remedial actions with respect to the illegal act; and

C.   the failure to take remedial action is reasonably expected to warrant departure from a standard report of the auditor, when made, or warrant resignation from the audit engagement;

the registered public accounting firm shall, as soon as practicable, directly report its conclusions to the board of directors.

3.   Notice to Commission; response to failure to notify

An issuer whose board of directors receives a report under paragraph (2) shall inform the Commission by notice not later than 1 business day after the receipt of such report and shall furnish the registered public accounting firm making such report with a copy of the notice furnished to the Commission. If the registered public accounting firm fails to receive a copy of the notice before the expiration of the required 1-business-day period, the registered public accounting firm shall–

A.   resign from the engagement; or

B.   furnish to the Commission a copy of its report (or the documentation of any oral report given) not later than 1 business day following such failure to receive notice.

4.   Report after resignation

If a registered public accounting firm resigns from an engagement under paragraph (3)(A), the firm shall, not later than 1 business day following the failure by the issuer to notify the Commission under paragraph (3), furnish to the Commission a copy of the report of the firm (or the documentation of any oral report given).

c.   **Auditor Liability Limitation.** No registered public accounting firm shall be liable in a private action for any finding, conclusion, or statement expressed in a report made pursuant to paragraph (3) or (4) of subsection (b) of this section, including any rule promulgated pursuant thereto.

d.   **Civil Penalties in Cease-and-Desist Proceedings.** If the Commission finds, after notice and opportunity for hearing in a proceeding instituted pursuant to section 21C, that a registered public accounting firm has willfully violated paragraph (3) or (4) of subsection (b) of this section, the Commission may, in addition to entering an order under section 21C, impose a civil penalty against the registered public accounting firm and any other person that the Commission finds was a cause of such violation. The determination to impose a civil penalty and the amount of the penalty shall be governed by the standards set forth in section 21B.

e.   **Preservation of Existing Authority.** Except as provided in subsection (d) of this section, nothing in this section shall be held to limit or otherwise affect the authority of the Commission under this title.

f.   **Definitions.** As used in this section, the term "illegal act" means an act or omission that violates any law, or any rule or regulation having the force of law. As used in this section, the term 'issuer' means an issuer (as defined in section 3), the securities of which are registered under section 12, or that is required to file reports pursuant to section 15(d), or that files or has filed a registration statement that has not yet become effective under the Securities Act of 1933, and that it has not withdrawn.

g.   **Prohibited Activities.** Except as provided in subsection (h), it shall be unlawful for a registered public accounting firm (and any associated person of that firm, to the extent determined appropriate by the Commission) that performs for any issuer any audit required by this title or the rules of the Commission under this title or, beginning 180 days after the date of commencement of the operations of the Public Company Accounting Oversight Board established under section 101 of the Sarbanes-Oxley Act of 2002 (in this section referred to as the 'Board'), the rules of the Board, to provide to that issuer, contemporaneously with the audit, any non-audit service, including–

1. bookkeeping or other services related to the accounting records or financial statements of the audit client;
2. financial information systems design and implementation;
3. appraisal or valuation services, fairness opinions, or contribution-in-kind reports;
4. actuarial services;
5. internal audit outsourcing services;
6. management functions or human resources;
7. broker or dealer, investment adviser, or investment banking services;
8. legal services and expert services unrelated to the audit; and
9. any other service that the Board determines, by regulation, is impermissible.

h. **Preapproval Required for Non-Audit Services.** A registered public accounting firm may engage in any non-audit service, including tax services, that is not described in any of paragraphs (1) through (9) of subsection (g) for an audit client, only if the activity is approved in advance by the audit committee of the issuer, in accordance with subsection (i).

i. **Preapproval Requirements**
　1. In general
　　A. Audit committee action
　　　All auditing services (which may entail providing comfort letters in connection with securities underwritings or statutory audits required for insurance companies for purposes of State law) and non-audit services, other than as provided in subparagraph (B), provided to an issuer by the auditor of the issuer shall be preapproved by the audit committee of the issuer.
　　B. De minimis exception
　　　The preapproval requirement under subparagraph (A) is waived with respect to the provision of non-audit services for an issuer, if–
　　　　i. the aggregate amount of all such non-audit services provided to the issuer constitutes not more than 5 percent of the total amount of revenues paid by the issuer to its auditor during the fiscal year in which the nonaudit services are provided;
　　　　ii. such services were not recognized by the issuer at the time of the engagement to be non-audit services; and
　　　　iii. such services are promptly brought to the attention of the audit committee of the issuer and approved prior to the completion of the audit by the audit committee or by 1 or more members of the audit committee who are members of the board of directors to whom authority to grant such approvals has been delegated by the audit committee.
　2. Disclosure to investors
　　Approval by an audit committee of an issuer under this subsection of a non-audit service to be performed by the auditor of the issuer shall be disclosed to investors in periodic reports required by section 13(a).

3.   Delegation authority

The audit committee of an issuer may delegate to 1 or more designated members of the audit committee who are independent directors of the board of directors, the authority to grant preapprovals required by this subsection. The decisions of any member to whom authority is delegated under this paragraph to preapprove an activity under this subsection shall be presented to the full audit committee at each of its scheduled meetings.

4.   Approval of audit services for other purposes

In carrying out its duties under subsection (m)(2), if the audit committee of an issuer approves an audit service within the scope of the engagement of the auditor, such audit service shall be deemed to have been preapproved for purposes of this subsection.

j.   **Audit Partner Rotation.** It shall be unlawful for a registered public accounting firm to provide audit services to an issuer if the lead (or coordinating) audit partner (having primary responsibility for the audit), or the audit partner responsible for reviewing the audit, has performed audit services for that issuer in each of the 5 previous fiscal years of that issuer.

k.   **Reports to Audit Committees.** Each registered public accounting firm that performs for any issuer any audit required by this title shall timely report to the audit committee of the issuer–

1.   all critical accounting policies and practices to be used;

2.   all alternative treatments of financial information within generally accepted accounting principles that have been discussed with management officials of the issuer, ramifications of the use of such alternative disclosures and treatments, and the treatment preferred by the registered public accounting firm; and

3.   other material written communications between the registered public accounting firm and the management of the issuer, such as any management letter or schedule of unadjusted differences.

l.   **Conflicts of Interest**. It shall be unlawful for a registered public accounting firm to perform for an issuer any audit service required by this title, if a chief executive officer, controller, chief financial officer, chief accounting officer, or any person serving in an equivalent position for the issuer, was employed by that registered independent public accounting firm and participated in any capacity in the audit of that issuer during the 1-year period preceding the date of the initiation of the audit.

m.   **Standards Relating to Audit Committees**

1.   Commission rules

A.   In general

Effective not later than 270 days after the date of enactment of this subsection, the Commission shall, by rule, direct the national securities exchanges and national securities associations to prohibit the listing of any security of an issuer that is not in compliance with the requirements of any portion of paragraphs (2) through (6).

B.   Opportunity to cure defects

The rules of the Commission under subparagraph (A) shall provide for appropriate procedures for an issuer to have an opportunity to cure any defects that would be the basis for a prohibition under subparagraph (A), before the imposition of such prohibition.

2.   Responsibilities relating to registered public accounting firms

The audit committee of each issuer, in its capacity as a committee of the board of directors, shall be directly responsible for the appointment, compensation, and oversight of the work of any registered public accounting firm employed by that issuer (including resolution of disagreements between management and the auditor regarding financial reporting) for the purpose of preparing or issuing an audit report or related work, and each such registered public accounting firm shall report directly to the audit committee.

3.   Independence

A.   In general

Each member of the audit committee of the issuer shall be a member of the board of directors of the issuer, and shall otherwise be independent.

B.   Criteria

In order to be considered to be independent for purposes of this paragraph, a member of an audit committee of an issuer may not, other than in his or her capacity as a member of the audit committee, the board of directors, or any other board committee–

i.   accept any consulting, advisory, or other compensatory fee from the issuer; or

ii. be an affiliated person of the issuer or any subsidiary thereof.

C.   Exemption authority

The Commission may exempt from the requirements of subparagraph (B) a particular relationship with respect to audit committee members, as the Commission determines appropriate in light of the circumstances.

4.   Complaints

Each audit committee shall establish procedures for–

A.   the receipt, retention, and treatment of complaints received by the issuer regarding accounting, internal accounting controls, or auditing matters; and

B.   the confidential, anonymous submission by employees of the issuer of concerns regarding questionable accounting or auditing matters.

5.   Authority to engage advisers

Each audit committee shall have the authority to engage independent counsel and other advisers, as it determines necessary to carry out its duties.

6.   Funding

Each issuer shall provide for appropriate funding, as determined by the audit committee, in its capacity as a committee of the board of directors, for payment of compensation–

A.   to the registered public accounting firm employed by the issuer for the purpose of rendering or issuing an audit report; and

B.   to any advisers employed by the audit committee under paragraph (5).

Section 12 – Registration Requirements for Securities

a. **General requirement of registration.** It shall be unlawful for any member, broker, or dealer to effect any transaction in any security (other than an exempted security) on a national securities exchange unless a registration is effective as to such security for such exchange in accordance with the provisions of this title and the rules and regulations thereunder. The provisions of this subsection shall not apply in respect of a security futures product traded on a national securities exchange.

b. **Procedure for registration; information.** A security may be registered on a national securities exchange by the issuer filing an application with the exchange (and filing with the Commission such duplicate originals thereof as the Commission may require), which application shall contain–
   1.   Such information, in such detail, as to the issuer and any person directly or indirectly controlling or controlled by, or under direct or indirect common control with, the issuer, and any guarantor of the security as to principal or interest or both, as the Commission may by rules and regulations require, as necessary or appropriate in the public interest or for the protection of investors, in respect of the following:
      A.   the organization, financial structure, and nature of the business;
      B.   the terms, position, rights, and privileges of the different classes of securities outstanding;
      C.   the terms on which their securities are to be, and during the preceding three years have been, offered to the public or otherwise;
      D.   the directors, officers, and underwriters, and each security holder of record holding more than 10 per centum of any class of any equity security of the issuer (other than an exempted security), their remuneration and their interests in the securities of, and their material contracts with, the issuer and any person directly or indirectly controlling or controlled by, or under direct or indirect common control with, the issuer;
      E.   remuneration to others than directors and officers exceeding $20,000 per annum;
      F.   bonus and profit-sharing arrangements;
      G.   management and service contracts;
      H.   options existing or to be created in respect of their securities; (I) material contracts, not made in the ordinary course of business, which are to be executed in whole or in part at or after the filing of the application or which were made not more than two years before such filing, and every material patent or contract for a material patent right shall be deemed a material contract;
      I.   balance sheets for not more than the three preceding fiscal years, certified if required by the rules and regulations of the Commission by a registered public accounting firm;
      J.   balance sheets for not more than the three preceding fiscal years, certified if required by the rules and regulations of the Commission by a registered public accounting firm;

318

K. profit and loss statements for not more than the three preceding fiscal years, certified if required by the rules and regulations of the Commission by a registered public accounting firm; and

L. any further financial statements which the Commission may deem necessary or appropriate for the protection of investors.

2. Such copies of articles of incorporation, bylaws, trust indentures, or corresponding documents by whatever name known, underwriting arrangements, and other similar documents of, and voting trust agreements with respect to, the issuer and any person directly or indirectly controlling or controlled by, or under direct or indirect common control with, the issuer as the Commission may require as necessary or appropriate for the proper protection of investors and to insure fair dealing in the security.

3. Such copies of material contracts, referred to in paragraph (1)(I) above, as the Commission may require as necessary or appropriate for the proper protection of investors and to insure fair dealing in the security.

g. **Registration of securities by issuer; exemptions**

1. Every issuer which is engaged in interstate commerce, or in a business affecting interstate commerce, or whose securities are traded by use of the mails or any means or instrumentality of interstate commerce shall—

A. within one hundred and twenty days after the last day of its first fiscal year ended after July 1, 1964, on which the issuer has total assets exceeding $1,000,000 and a class of equity security (other than an exempted security) held of record by seven hundred and fifty or more persons; and

B. within one hundred and twenty days after the last day of its first fiscal year ended after two years from July 1, 1964, on which the issuer has total assets exceeding $1,000,000 and a class of equity security (other than an exempted security) held of record by five hundred or more but less than seven hundred and fifty persons,

register such security by filing with the Commission a registration statement (and such copies thereof as the Commission may require) with respect to such security containing such information and documents as the Commission may specify comparable to that which is required in an application to register a security pursuant to subsection (b) of this section. Each such registration statement shall become effective sixty days after filing with the Commission or within such shorter period as the Commission may direct. Until such registration statement becomes effective it shall not be deemed filed for the purposes of section 18. Any issuer may register any class of equity security not required to be registered by filing a registration statement pursuant to the provisions of this paragraph. The Commission is authorized to extend the date upon which any issuer or class of issuers is required to register a security pursuant to the provisions of this paragraph.

4. Registration of any class of security pursuant to this subsection shall be terminated ninety days, or such shorter period as the Commission may determine, after the issuer files a certification with the Commission that the number of holders of record of such class of security is reduced to less than three hundred persons. The Commission shall after notice and opportunity for

hearing deny termination of registration if it finds that the certification is untrue. Termination of registration shall be deferred pending final determination on the question of denial.

5.   For the purposes of this subsection the term "class" shall include all securities of an issuer which are of substantially similar character and the holders of which enjoy substantially similar rights and privileges. The Commission may for the purpose of this subsection define by rules and regulations the terms "total assets" and "held of record" as it deems necessary or appropriate in the public interest or for the protection of investors in order to prevent circumvention of the provisions of this subsection. For purposes of this subsection, a security futures product shall not be considered a class of equity security of the issuer of the securities underlying the security futures product.

j.   **Denial, suspension, or revocation of registration; notice and hearing.** The Commission is authorized, by order, as it deems necessary or appropriate for the protection of investors to deny, to suspend the effective date of, to suspend for a period not exceeding twelve months, or to revoke the registration of a security, if the Commission finds, on the record after notice and opportunity for hearing, that the issuer, of such security has failed to comply with any provision of this title or the rules and regulations thereunder. No member of a national securities exchange, broker, or dealer shall make use of the mails or any means or instrumentality of interstate commerce to effect any transaction in, or to induce the purchase or sale of, any security the registration of which has been and is suspended or revoked pursuant to the preceding sentence.

k.   **Trading suspensions; emergency authority**
1.   Trading suspensions
      If in its opinion the public interest and the protection of investors so require, the Commission is authorized by order–
      A.   summarily to suspend trading in any security (other than an exempted security) for a period not exceeding 10 business days, and
      B.   summarily to suspend all trading on any national securities exchange or otherwise, in securities other than exempted securities, for a period not exceeding 90 calendar days.
      The action described in subparagraph (B) shall not take effect unless the Commission notifies the President of its decision and the President notifies the Commission that the President does not disapprove of such decision. If the actions described in subparagraph (A) or (B) involve a security futures product, the Commission shall consult with and consider the views of the Commodity Futures Trading Commission.

Section 13 – Periodical and Other Reports

a.   **Reports by Issuer of Security; Contents.** Every issuer of a security registered pursuant to section 12 shall file with the Commission, in accordance with such rules and regulations as the Commission may prescribe as necessary or appropriate for the proper protection of investors and to insure fair dealing in the security–

1.   such information and documents (and such copies thereof) as the Commission shall require to keep reasonably current the information and documents required to be included in or filed with an application or registration statement filed pursuant to section 12, except that the Commission may not require the filing of any material contract wholly executed before July 1, 1962.

2.   such annual reports (and such copies thereof), certified if required by the rules and regulations of the Commission by independent public accountants, and such quarterly reports (and such copies thereof), as the Commission may prescribe.

Every issuer of a security registered on a national securities exchange shall also file a duplicate original of such information, documents, and reports with the exchange.

b.   **Form of Report; Books, Records, and Internal Accounting; Directives**

     1.   The Commission may prescribe, in regard to reports made pursuant to this title, the form or forms in which the required information shall be set forth, the items or details to be shown in the balance sheet and the earning statement, and the methods to be followed in the preparation of reports, in the appraisal or valuation of assets and liabilities, in the determination of depreciation and depletion, in the differentiation of recurring and nonrecurring income, in the differentiation of investment and operating income, and in the preparation, where the Commission deems it necessary or desirable, of separate and/or consolidated balance sheets or income accounts of any person directly or indirectly controlling or controlled by the issuer, or any person under direct or indirect common control with the issuer; but in the case of the reports of any person whose methods of accounting are prescribed under the provisions of any law of the United States, or any rule or regulation thereunder, the rules and regulations of the Commission with respect to reports shall not be inconsistent with the requirements imposed by such law or rule or regulation in respect of the same subject matter (except that such rules and regulations of the Commission may be inconsistent with such requirements to the extent that the Commission determines that the public interest or the protection of investors so requires).

     2.   Every issuer which has a class of securities registered pursuant to section 12 and every issuer which is required to file reports pursuant to section 15(d) shall–

         A.   make and keep books, records, and accounts, which, in reasonable detail, accurately and fairly reflect the transactions and dispositions of the assets of the issuer;

         B.   devise and maintain a system of internal accounting controls sufficient to provide reasonable assurances that–

             i.   transactions are executed in accordance with management's general or specific authorization;

             ii.   transactions are recorded as necessary (I) to permit preparation of financial statements in conformity with generally accepted accounting principles or any other criteria applicable to such statements, and (II) to maintain accountability for assets;

             iii.   access to assets is permitted only in accordance with management's general or specific authorization; and

            iv.   the recorded accountability for assets is compared with the existing assets at reasonable intervals and appropriate action is taken with respect to any differences; and

    C.   notwithstanding any other provision of law, pay the allocable share of such issuer of a reasonable annual accounting support fee or fees, determined in accordance with section 109 of the Sarbanes-Oxley Act of 2002.

3.   A.   With respect to matters concerning the national security of the United States, no duty or liability under paragraph (2) of this subsection shall be imposed upon any person acting in cooperation with the head of any Federal department or agency responsible for such matters if such act in cooperation with such head of a department or agency was done upon the specific, written directive of the head of such department or agency pursuant to Presidential authority to issue such directives. Each directive issued under this paragraph shall set forth the specific facts and circumstances with respect to which the provisions of this paragraph are to be invoked. Each such directive shall, unless renewed in writing, expire one year after the date of issuance.

    B.   Each head of a Federal department or agency of the United States who issues a directive pursuant to this paragraph shall maintain a complete file of all such directives and shall, on October 1 of each year, transmit a summary of matters covered by such directives in force at any time during the previous year to the Permanent Select Committee on Intelligence of the House of Representatives and the Select Committee on Intelligence of the Senate.

4.   No criminal liability shall be imposed for failing to comply with the requirements of paragraph (2) of this subsection except as provided in paragraph (5) of this subsection.

5.   No person shall knowingly circumvent or knowingly fail to implement a system of internal accounting controls or knowingly falsify any book, record, or account described in paragraph (2).

6.   Where an issuer which has a class of securities registered pursuant to section 12 of this title or an issuer which is required to file reports pursuant to section 15(d) holds 50 per centum or less of the voting power with respect to a domestic or foreign firm, the provisions of paragraph (2) require only that the issuer proceed in good faith to use its influence, to the extent reasonable under the issuer's circumstances, to cause such domestic or foreign firm to devise and maintain a system of internal accounting controls consistent with paragraph (2). Such circumstances include the relative degree of the issuer's ownership of the domestic or foreign firm and the laws and practices governing the business operations of the country in which such firm is located. An issuer which demonstrates good faith efforts to use such influence shall be conclusively presumed to have complied with the requirements of paragraph (2).

7.   For the purpose of paragraph (2) of this subsection, the terms "reasonable assurances" and "reasonable detail" mean such level of detail and degree of assurance as would satisfy prudent officials in the conduct of their own affairs.

c. **Alternative Reports**. If in the judgment of the Commission any report required under subsection (a) of this section is inapplicable to any specified class or classes of issuers, the Commission shall require in lieu thereof the submission of such reports of comparable character as it may deem applicable to such class or classes of issuers.

d. **Reports by Persons Acquiring More than Five Per Centum of Certain Classes of Securities**

1.   Any person who, after acquiring directly or indirectly the beneficial ownership of any equity security of a class which is registered pursuant to section 12, or any equity security of an insurance company which would have been required to be so registered except for the exemption contained in section 12(g)(2)(G), or any equity security issued by a closed-end investment company registered under the Investment Company Act of 1940 or any equity security issued by a Native Corporation pursuant to section 1629c(d)(6) of Title 43, is directly or indirectly the beneficial owner of more than 5 per centum of such class shall, within ten days after such acquisition, send to the issuer of the security at its principal executive office, by registered or certified mail, send to each exchange where the security is traded, and filed with the Commission, a statement containing such of the following information, and such additional information, as the Commission may by rules and regulations, prescribe as necessary or appropriate in the public interest or for the protection of investors—

   A.   the background, and identity, residence, and citizenship of, and the nature of such beneficial ownership by, such person and all other persons by whom or on whose behalf the purchases have been or are to be effected;

   B.   the source and amount of the funds or other consideration used or to be used in making the purchases, and if any part of the purchase price is represented or is to be represented by funds or other consideration borrowed or otherwise obtained for the purpose of acquiring, holding, or trading such security, a description of the transaction and the names of the parties thereto, except that where a source of funds is a loan made in the ordinary course of business by a bank, as defined in section 3(a)(6), if the person filing such statement so requests, the name of the bank shall not be made available to the public;

   C.   if the purpose of the purchases or prospective purchases is to acquire control of the business of the issuer of the securities, any plans or proposals which such persons may have to liquidate such issuer, to sell its assets to or merge it with any other persons, or to make any other major change in its business or corporate structure;

   D.   the number of shares of such security which are beneficially owned, and the number of shares concerning which there is a right to acquire, directly or indirectly, by (i) such person, and (ii) by each associate of such person, giving the background, identity, residence, and citizenship of each such associate; and

   E.   information as to any contracts, arrangements, or understandings with any person with respect to any securities of the issuer, including but not limited to transfer of any of the securities, joint ventures, loan or option arrangements, puts or calls, guaranties of loans, guaranties against loss or guaranties of profits, division of losses or profits, or the giving or withholding of proxies, naming the persons with whom such contracts, arrangements, or understandings have been entered into, and giving the details thereof.

2.   If any material change occurs in the facts set forth in the statements to the issuer and the exchange, and in the statement filed with the Commission, an amendment shall be transmitted to the issuer and the exchange and shall be filed with the Commission, in accordance with such rules and regulations as the Commission may prescribe as necessary or appropriate in the public interest or for the protection of investors.

3.   When two or more persons act as a partnership, limited partnership, syndicate, or other group for the purpose of acquiring, holding, or disposing of securities of an issuer, such syndicate or group shall be deemed a "person" for the purposes of this subsection.

4.   In determining, for purposes of this subsection, any percentage of a class of any security, such class shall be deemed to consist of the amount of the outstanding securities of such class, exclusive of any securities of such class held by or for the account of the issuer or a subsidiary of the issuer.

5.   The Commission, by rule or regulation or by order, may permit any person to file in lieu of the statement required by paragraph (1) of this subsection or the rules and regulations thereunder, a notice stating the name of such person, the number of shares of any equity securities subject to paragraph (1) which are owned by him, the date of their acquisition and such other information as the Commission may specify, if it appears to the Commission that such securities were acquired by such person in the ordinary course of his business and were not acquired for the purpose of and do not have the effect of changing or influencing the control of the issuer nor in connection with or as a participant in any transaction having such purpose or effect.

6.   The provisions of this subsection shall not apply to–

A.   any acquisition or offer to acquire securities made or proposed to be made by means of a registration statement under the Securities Act of 1933;

B.   any acquisition of the beneficial ownership of a security which, together with all other acquisitions by the same person of securities of the same class during the preceding twelve months, does not exceed 2 per centum of that class;

C.   any acquisition of an equity security by the issuer of such security;

D.   any acquisition or proposed acquisition of a security which the Commission, by rules or regulations or by order, shall exempt from the provisions of this subsection as not entered into for the purpose of, and not having the effect of, changing or influencing the control of the issuer or otherwise as not comprehended within the purposes of this subsection.

e.   **Purchase of Securities by Issuer**

1.   It shall be unlawful for an issuer which has a class of equity securities registered pursuant to section 12, or which is a closed-end investment company

registered under the Investment Company Act of 1940, to purchase any equity security issued by it if such purchase is in contravention of such rules and regulations as the Commission, in the public interest or for the protection of investors, may adopt (A) to define acts and practices which are fraudulent, deceptive, or manipulative, and (B) to prescribe means reasonably designed to prevent such acts and practices. Such rules and regulations may require such issuer to provide holders of equity securities of such class with such information relating to the reasons for such purchase, the source of funds, the number of shares to be purchased, the price to be paid for such securities, the method of purchase, and such additional information, as the Commission deems necessary or appropriate in the public interest or for the protection of investors, or which the Commission deems to be material to a determination whether such security should be sold.

g. **Statement of Equity Security Ownership**
1. Any person who is directly or indirectly the beneficial owner of more than 5 per centum of any security of a class described in subsection (d)(1) shall send to the issuer of the security and shall file with the Commission a statement setting forth, in such form and at such time as the Commission may, by rule, prescribe–
   A. such person's identity, residence, and citizenship; and
   B. the number and description of the shares in which such person has an interest and the nature of such interest.
2. If any material change occurs in the facts set forth in the statement sent to the issuer and filed with the Commission, an amendment shall be transmitted to the issuer and shall be filed with the Commission, in accordance with such rules and regulations as the Commission may prescribe as necessary or appropriate in the public interest or for the protection of investors.
3. When two or more persons act as a partnership, limited partnership, syndicate, or other group for the purpose of acquiring, holding, or disposing of securities of an issuer, such syndicate or group shall be deemed a "person" for the purposes of this subsection.
4. In determining, for purposes of this subsection, any percentage of a class of any security, such class shall be deemed to consist of the amount of the outstanding securities of such class, exclusive of any securities of such class held by or for the account of the issuer or a subsidiary of the issuer.
5. In exercising its authority under this subsection, the Commission shall take such steps as it deems necessary or appropriate in the public interest or for the protection of investors (A) to achieve centralized reporting of information regarding ownership, (B) to avoid unnecessarily duplicative reporting by and minimize the compliance burden on persons required to report, and (C) to tabulate and promptly make available the information contained in any report filed pursuant to this subsection in a manner which will, in the view of the Commission, maximize the usefulness of the information to other Federal and State agencies and the public.
6. The Commission may, by rule or order, exempt, in whole or in part, any person or class of persons from any or all of the reporting requirements of this

subsection as it deems necessary or appropriate in the public interest or for the protection of investors.

i. **Accuracy of Financial Reports.** Each financial report that contains financial statements, and that is required to be prepared in accordance with (or reconciled to) generally accepted accounting principles under this title and filed with the Commission shall reflect all material correcting adjustments that have been identified by a registered public accounting firm in accordance with generally accepted accounting principles and the rules and regulations of the Commission.

j. **Off-Balance Sheet Transactions.** Not later than 180 days after the date of enactment of the Sarbanes-Oxley Act of 2002 [enacted July 30, 2002], the Commission shall issue final rules providing that each annual and quarterly financial report required to be filed with the Commission shall disclose all material off-balance sheet transactions, arrangements, obligations (including contingent obligations), and other relationships of the issuer with unconsolidated entities or other persons, that may have a material current or future effect on financial condition, changes in financial condition, results of operations, liquidity, capital expenditures, capital resources, or significant components of revenues or expenses.

k. **Prohibition on Personal Loans to Executives**
   A. In general
      It shall be unlawful for any issuer (as defined in section 2 of the Sarbanes-Oxley Act of 2002), directly or indirectly, including through any subsidiary, to extend or maintain credit, to arrange for the extension of credit, or to renew an extension of credit, in the form of a personal loan to or for any director or executive officer (or equivalent thereof) of that issuer. An extension of credit maintained by the issuer on the date of enactment of this subsection shall not be subject to the provisions of this subsection, provided that there is no material modification to any term of any such extension of credit or any renewal of any such extension of credit on or after that date of enactment.
   B. Limitation
      Paragraph (1) does not preclude any home improvement and manufactured home loans (as that term is defined in section 5 of the Home Owners' Loan Act), consumer credit (as defined in section 103 of the Truth in Lending Act), or any extension of credit under an open end credit plan (as defined in section 103 of the Truth in Lending Act), or a charge card (as defined in section 127(c)(4)(e) of the Truth in Lending Act), or any extension of credit by a broker or dealer registered under section 15 of this title to an employee of that broker or dealer to buy, trade, or carry securities, that is permitted under rules or regulations of the Board of Governors of the Federal Reserve System pursuant to section 7 of this title (other than an extension of credit that would be used to purchase the stock of that issuer), that is–
         i. made or provided in the ordinary course of the consumer credit business of such issuer;
         ii. of a type that is generally made available by such issuer to the public; and

iii. made by such issuer on market terms, or terms that are no more favorable than those offered by the issuer to the general public for such extensions of credit.

C. Rule of construction for certain loans

Paragraph (1) does not apply to any loan made or maintained by an insured depository institution (as defined in section 3 of the Federal Deposit Insurance Act), if the loan is subject to the insider lending restrictions of section 22(h) of the Federal Reserve Act.

l. **Real Time Issuer Disclosures.** Each issuer reporting under section 13(a) or 15(d) shall disclose to the public on a rapid and current basis such additional information concerning material changes in the financial condition or operations of the issuer, in plain English, which may include trend and qualitative information and graphic presentations, as the Commission determines, by rule, is necessary or useful for the protection of investors and in the public interest

Section 14 – Proxies

a. **Solicitation of proxies in violation of rules and regulations.** It shall be unlawful for any person, by the use of the mails or by any means or instrumentality of interstate commerce or of any facility of a national securities exchange or otherwise, in contravention of such rules and regulations as the Commission may prescribe as necessary or appropriate in the public interest or for the protection of investors, to solicit or to permit the use of his name to solicit any proxy or consent or authorization in respect of any security (other than an exempted security) registered pursuant to section 12.

d. **Tender offer by owner of more than five per centum of class of securities; exceptions**

1. It shall be unlawful for any person, directly or indirectly, by use of the mails or by any means or instrumentality of interstate commerce or of any facility of a national securities exchange or otherwise, to make a tender offer for, or a request or invitation for tenders of, any class of any equity security which is registered pursuant to section 12, or any equity security of an insurance company which would have been required to be so registered except for the exemption contained in section 12(g)(2)(G), or any equity security issued by a closed-end investment company registered under the Investment Company Act of 1940, if, after consummation thereof, such person would, directly or indirectly, be the beneficial owner of more than 5 per centum of such class, unless at the time copies of the offer or request or invitation are first published or sent or given to security holders such person has filed with the Commission a statement containing such of the information specified in section 13(d), and such additional information as the Commission may by rules and regulations prescribe as necessary or appropriate in the public interest or for the protection of investors. All requests or invitations for tenders or advertisements making a tender offer or requesting or inviting tenders of such a security shall be filed as a part of such statement and shall contain such of the information contained in

such statement as the Commission may by rules and regulations prescribe. Copies of any additional material soliciting or requesting such tender offers subsequent to the initial solicitation or request shall contain such information as the Commission may by rules and regulations prescribe as necessary or appropriate in the public interest or for the protection of investors, and shall be filed with the Commission not later than the time copies of such material are first published or sent or given to security holders. Copies of all statements, in the form in which such material is furnished to security holders and the Commission, shall be sent to the issuer not later than the date such material is first published or sent or given to any security holders.

2.   When two or more persons act as a partnership, limited partnership, syndicate, or other group for the purpose of acquiring, holding, or disposing of securities of an issuer, such syndicate or group shall be deemed a "person" for purposes of this subsection.

3.   In determining, for purposes of this subsection, any percentage of a class of any security, such class shall be deemed to consist of the amount of the outstanding securities of such class, exclusive of any securities of such class held by or for the account of the issuer or a subsidiary of the issuer.

4.   Any solicitation or recommendation to the holders of such a security to accept or reject a tender offer or request or invitation for tenders shall be made in accordance with such rules and regulations as the Commission may prescribe as necessary or appropriate in the public interest or for the protection of investors.

5.   Securities deposited pursuant to a tender offer or request or invitation for tenders may be withdrawn by or on behalf of the depositor at any time until the expiration of seven days after the time definitive copies of the offer or request or invitation are first published or sent or given to security holders, and at any time after sixty days from the date of the original tender offer or request or invitation, except as the Commission may otherwise prescribe by rules, regulations, or order as necessary or appropriate in the public interest or for the protection of investors.

6.   Where any person makes a tender offer, or request or invitation for tenders, for less than all the outstanding equity securities of a class, and where a greater number of securities is deposited pursuant thereto within ten days after copies of the offer or request or invitation are first published or sent or given to security holders than such person is bound or willing to take up and pay for, the securities taken up shall be taken up as nearly as may be pro rata, disregarding fractions, according to the number of securities deposited by each depositor. The provisions of this subsection shall also apply to securities deposited within ten days after notice of an increase in the consideration offered to security holders, as described in paragraph (7), is first published or sent or given to security holders.

7.   Where any person varies the terms of a tender offer or request or invitation for tenders before the expiration thereof by increasing the consideration offered to holders of such securities, such person shall pay the increased consideration to each security holder whose securities are taken up and paid for pursuant to the tender offer or request or invitation for tenders whether or not such securities

have been taken up by such person before the variation of the tender offer or request or invitation.

8.   The provisions of this subsection shall not apply to any offer for, or request or invitation for tenders of, any security–

   A.   if the acquisition of such security, together with all other acquisitions by the same person of securities of the same class during the preceding twelve months, would not exceed 2 per centum of that class;

   B.   by the issuer of such security; or

   C.   which the Commission, by rules or regulations or by order, shall exempt from the provisions of this subsection as not entered into for the purpose of, and not having the effect of, changing or influencing the control of the issuer or otherwise as not comprehended within the purposes of this subsection.

e.   **Untrue statement of material fact or omission of fact with respect to tender offer.** It shall be unlawful for any person to make any untrue statement of a material fact or omit to state any material fact necessary in order to make the statements made, in the light of the circumstances under which they are made, not misleading, or to engage in any fraudulent, deceptive, or manipulative acts or practices, in connection with any tender offer or request or invitation for tenders, or any solicitation of security holders in opposition to or in favor of any such offer, request, or invitation. The Commission shall, for the purposes of this subsection, by rules and regulations define, and prescribe means reasonably designed to prevent, such acts and practices as are fraudulent, deceptive, or manipulative.

f.   **Election or designation of majority of directors of issuer by owner of more than five per centum of class of securities at other than meeting of security holders.** If, pursuant to any arrangement or understanding with the person or persons acquiring securities in a transaction subject to subsection (d) of this section or subsection (d) of section 13, any persons are to be elected or designated as directors of the issuer, otherwise than at a meeting of security holders, and the persons so elected or designated will constitute a majority of the directors of the issuer, then, prior to the time any such person takes office as a director, and in accordance with rules and regulations prescribed by the Commission, the issuer shall file with the Commission, and transmit to all holders of record of securities of the issuer who would be entitled to vote at a meeting for election of directors, information substantially equivalent to the information which would be required by subsection (a) or (c) to be transmitted if such person or persons were nominees for election as directors at a meeting of such security holders.

Section 15 – Registration and Regulation of Brokers and Dealers

c.   **Use of manipulative or deceptive devices; contravention of rules and regulations**

   4.   If the Commission finds, after notice and opportunity for a hearing, that any person subject to the provisions of section 12, 13, 14, or subsection (d) of this section or any rule or regulation thereunder has failed to comply with any such provision, rule, or regulation in any material respect, the Commission may publish its findings and issue an order requiring such person, and any person

who was a cause of the failure to comply due to an act or omission the person knew or should have known would contribute to the failure to comply, to comply, or to take steps to effect compliance, with such provision or such rule or regulation thereunder upon such terms and conditions and within such time as the Commission may specify in such order.

d. **Filing of supplementary and periodic information**. Each issuer which has filed a registration statement containing an undertaking which is or becomes operative under this subsection as in effect prior to August 20, 1964, and each issuer which shall after such date file a registration statement which has become effective pursuant to the Securities Act of 1933, as amended, shall file with the Commission, in accordance with such rules and regulations as the Commission may prescribe as necessary or appropriate in the public interest or for the protection of investors, such supplementary and periodic information, documents, and reports as may be required pursuant to section 13 in respect of a security registered pursuant to section 12. The duty to file under this subsection shall be automatically suspended if and so long as any issue of securities of such issuer is registered pursuant to section 12. The duty to file under this subsection shall also be automatically suspended as to any fiscal year, other than the fiscal year within which such registration statement became effective, if, at the beginning of such fiscal year, the securities of each class to which the registration statement relates are held of record by less than three hundred persons. For the purposes of this subsection, the term "class" shall be construed to include all securities of an issuer which are of substantially similar character and the holders of which enjoy substantially similar rights and privileges. The Commission may, for the purpose of this subsection, define by rules and regulations the term "held of record" as it deems necessary or appropriate in the public interest or for the protection of investors in order to prevent circumvention of the provisions of this subsection. Nothing in this subsection shall apply to securities issued by a foreign government or political subdivision thereof.

Section 16 – Directors, Officers, and Principal Stockholders

a. Every person who is directly or indirectly the beneficial owner of more than 10 per centum of any class of any equity security (other than an exempted security) which is registered pursuant to section 78l of this title, or who is a director or an officer of the issuer of such security, shall file, at the time of the registration of such security on a national securities exchange or by the effective date of a registration statement filed pursuant to section 78l (g) of this title, or within ten days after he becomes such beneficial owner, director, or officer, a statement with the Commission (and, if such security is registered on a national securities exchange, also with the exchange) of the amount of all equity securities of such issuer of which he is the beneficial owner, and within ten days after the close of each calendar month thereafter, if there has been a change in such ownership during such month, shall file with the Commission (and if such security is registered on a national securities exchange, shall also file with the exchange), a statement indicating his ownership at the close of the calendar month and such changes in his ownership as have occurred during such calendar month."

b. For the purpose of preventing the unfair use of information which may have been obtained by such beneficial owner, director, or officer by reason of his relationship to the issuer, any profit realized by him from any purchase and sale, or any sale and purchase, of any equity security of such issuer (other than an exempted security) within any period of less than six months, unless such security was acquired in good faith in connection with a debt previously contracted, shall inure to and be recoverable by the issuer, irrespective of any intention on the part of such beneficial owner, director, or officer in entering into such transaction of holding the security purchased or of not repurchasing the security sold for a period exceeding six months. Suit to recover such profit may be instituted at law or in equity in any court of competent jurisdiction by the issuer, or by the owner of any security of the issuer in the name and in behalf of the issuer if the issuer shall fail or refuse to bring such suit within sixty days after request or shall fail diligently to prosecute the same thereafter; but no such suit shall be brought more than two years after the date such profit was realized. This subsection shall not be construed to cover any transaction where such beneficial owner was not such both at the time of the purchase and sale, or the sale and purchase, of the security involved, or any transaction or transactions which the Commission by rules and regulations may exempt as not comprehended within the purpose of this subsection.

Section 18 – Liability for Misleading Statements

a. **Persons liable; persons entitled to recover; defense of good faith; suit at law or in equity; costs, etc.** Any person who shall make or cause to be made any statement in any application, report, or document filed pursuant to this title or any rule or regulation thereunder or any undertaking contained in a registration statement as provided in subsection (d) of section 15, which statement was at the time and in the light of the circumstances under which it was made false or misleading with respect to any material fact, shall be liable to any person (not knowing that such statement was false or misleading) who, in reliance upon such statement, shall have purchased or sold a security at a price which was affected by such statement, for damages caused by such reliance, unless the person sued shall prove that he acted in good faith and had no knowledge that such statement was false or misleading. A person seeking to enforce such liability may sue at law or in equity in any court of competent jurisdiction. In any such suit the court may, in its discretion, require an undertaking for the payment of the costs of such suit, and assess reasonable costs, including reasonable attorneys' fees, against either party litigant.

b. **Contribution.** Every person who becomes liable to make payment under this section may recover contribution as in cases of contract from any person who, if joined in the original suit, would have been liable to make the same payment.

c. **Period of limitations.** No action shall be maintained to enforce any liability created under this section unless brought within one year after the discovery of the facts constituting the cause of action and within three years after such cause of action accrued.

Section 20 – Liabilities of Controlling Persons and Persons Who Aid and Abet Violations

a. **Joint and several liability; good faith defense.** Every person who, directly or indirectly, controls any person liable under any provision of this title or of any rule orregulation thereunder shall also be liable jointly and severally with and to the same extent as such controlled person to any person to whom such controlled person is liable, unless the controlling person acted in good faith and did not directly or indirectly induce the act or acts constituting the violation or cause of action.

b. **Unlawful activity through or by means of any other person.** It shall be unlawful for any person, directly or indirectly, to do any act or thing which it would be unlawful for such person to do under the provisions of this title or any rule or regulation thereunder through or by means of any other person.

c. **Hindering, delaying, or obstructing the making or filing of any document, report, or information.** It shall be unlawful for any director or officer of, or any owner of any securities issued by, any issuer required to file any document, report, or information under this title or any rule or regulation thereunder without just cause to hinder, delay, or obstruct the making or filing of any such document, report, or information.

d. **Liability for trading in securities while in possession of material nonpublic information.** Wherever communicating, or purchasing or selling a security while in possession of, material nonpublic information would violate, or result in liability to any purchaser or seller of the security under any provisions of this title, or any rule or regulation thereunder, such conduct in connection with a purchase or sale of a put, call, straddle, option, privilege or security-based swap agreement (as defined in section 206B of the Gramm-Leach- Bliley Act) with respect to such security or with respect to a group or index of securities including such security, shall also violate and result in comparable liability to any purchaser or seller of that security under such provision, rule, or regulation.

e. **Prosecution of persons who aid and abet violations.** For purposes of any action brought by the Commission under paragraph (1) or (3) of section 21(d), any person that knowingly provides substantial assistance to another person in violation of a provision of this title, or of any rule or regulation issued under this title, shall be deemed to be in violation of such provision to the same extent as the person to whom such assistance is provided.

Section 20A – Liability to Contemporaneous Traders for Insider Trading

a. **Private rights of action based on contemporaneous trading.** Any person who violates any provision of this title or the rules or regulations thereunder by purchasing or selling a security while in possession of material, nonpublic information shall be liable in an action in any court of competent jurisdiction to any person who, contemporaneously with the purchase or sale of securities that is the subject of such violation, has purchased (where such violation is based on a sale of securities) or sold (where such violation is based on a purchase of securities) securities of the same class.

b. **Limitations on liability**

1. Contemporaneous trading actions limited to profit gained or loss avoided
   The total amount of damages imposed under subsection (a) of this section shall not exceed the profit gained or loss avoided in the transaction or transactions that are the subject of the violation.

2. Offsetting disgorgements against liability
   The total amount of damages imposed against any person under subsection (a) of this section shall be diminished by the amounts, if any, that such person may be required to disgorge, pursuant to a court order obtained at the instance of the Commission, in a proceeding brought under section 21(d) relating to the same transaction or transactions.

3. Controlling person liability
   No person shall be liable under this section solely by reason of employing another person who is liable under this section, but the liability of a controlling person under this section shall be subject to section 20(a).

4. Statute of limitations
   No action may be brought under this section more than 5 years after the date of the last transaction that is the subject of the violation.

c. **Joint and several liability for communicating.** Any person who violates any provision of this title or the rules or regulations thereunder by communicating material, nonpublic information shall be jointly and severally liable under subsection (a) of this section with, and to the same extent as, any person or persons liable under subsection (a) of this section to whom the communication was directed.

d. **Authority not to restrict other express or implied rights of action.** Nothing in this section shall be construed to limit or condition the right of any person to bring an action to enforce a requirement of this title or the availability of any cause of action implied from a provision of this title.

e. **Provisions not to affect public prosecutions.** This section shall not be construed to bar or limit in any manner any action by the Commission or the Attorney General under any other provision of this title, nor shall it bar or limit in any manner any action to recover penalties, or to seek any other order regarding penalties.

Section 21 – Investigations and Actions

a. **Authority and discretion of Commission to investigate violations**

1. The Commission may, in its discretion, make such investigations as it deems necessary to determine whether any person has violated, is violating, or is about to violate any provision of this title, the rules or regulations thereunder, the rules of a national securities exchange or registered securities association of which such person is a member or a person associated with a member, the rules of a registered clearing agency in which such person is a participant, the rules of the Public Company Accounting Oversight Board, of which such person is a

registered public accounting firm or a person associated with such a firm, or the rules of the Municipal Securities Rulemaking Board, and may require or permit any person to file with it a statement in writing, under oath or otherwise as the Commission shall determine, as to all the facts and circumstances concerning the matter to be investigated. The Commission is authorized in its discretion, to publish information concerning any such violations, and to investigate any facts, conditions, practices, or matters which it may deem necessary or proper to aid in the enforcement of such provisions, in the prescribing of rules and regulations under this title, or in securing information to serve as a basis for recommending further legislation concerning the matters to which this title relates.

2. On request from a foreign securities authority, the Commission may provide assistance in accordance with this paragraph if the requesting authority states that the requesting authority is conducting an investigation which it deems necessary to determine whether any person has violated, is violating, or is about to violate any laws or rules relating to securities matters that the requesting authority administers or enforces. The Commission may, in its discretion, conduct such investigation as the Commission deems necessary to collect information and evidence pertinent to the request for assistance. Such assistance may be provided without regard to whether the facts stated in the request would also constitute a violation of the laws of the United States. In deciding whether to provide such assistance, the Commission shall consider whether (A) the requesting authority has agreed to provide reciprocal assistance in securities matters to the Commission; and (B) compliance with the request would prejudice the public interest of the United States.

b. **Attendance of witnesses; production of records.** For the purpose of any such investigation, or any other proceeding under this title, any member of the Commission or any officer designated by it is empowered to administer oaths and affirmations, subpoena witnesses, compel their attendance, take evidence, and require the production of any books, papers, correspondence, memoranda, or other records which the Commission deems relevant or material to the inquiry. Such attendance of witnesses and the production of any such records may be required from any place in the United States or any State at any designated place of hearing.

c. **Judicial enforcement of investigative power of Commission; refusal to obey subpoena; criminal sanctions.** In case of contumacy by, or refusal to obey a subpoena issued to, any person, the Commission may invoke the aid of any court of the United States within the jurisdiction of which such investigation or proceeding is carried on, or where such person resides or carries on business, in requiring the attendance and testimony of witnesses and the production of books, papers, correspondence, memoranda, and other records. And such court may issue an order requiring such person to appear before the Commission or member or officer designated by the Commission, there to produce records, if so ordered, or to give testimony touching the matter under investigation or in question; and any failure to obey such order of the court may be punished by such court as a contempt thereof. All process in any such case may be served in the judicial district whereof such person is an inhabitant or wherever he may be found. Any person who shall, without just cause, fail or refuse to attend and testify or to answer any lawful inquiry or to produce books, papers, correspondence, memoranda, and other records, if in his power so to do, in obedience to the subpoena of the Commission, shall be guilty of a misdemeanor and, upon conviction, shall be subject to a fine of not more than $1,000 or to imprisonment for a term of not more than one year, or both.

d. **Injunction proceedings; authority of court to prohibit persons from serving as officers and directors; money penalties in civil actions**

1. Whenever it shall appear to the Commission that any person is engaged or is about to engage in acts or practices constituting a violation of any provision of this title, the rules or regulations thereunder, the rules of a national securities exchange or registered securities association of which such person is a member or a person associated with a member, the rules of a registered clearing agency in which such person is a participant, the rules of the Public Company Accounting Oversight Board, of which such person is a registered public accounting firm or a person associated with such a firm, or the rules of the Municipal Securities Rulemaking Board, it may in its discretion bring an action in the proper district court of the United States, the United States District Court for the District of Columbia, or the United States courts of any territory or other place subject to the jurisdiction of the United States, to enjoin such acts or practices, and upon a proper showing a permanent or temporary injunction or restraining order shall be granted without bond. The Commission may transmit such evidence as may be available concerning such acts or practices as may constitute a violation of any provision of this title or the rules or regulations thereunder to the Attorney General, who may, in his discretion, institute the necessary criminal proceedings under this title.

2. Authority of court to prohibit persons from serving as officers and directors
    In any proceeding under paragraph (1) of this subsection, the court may prohibit, conditionally or unconditionally, and permanently or for such period of time as it shall determine, any person who violated section 10(b) or the rules or regulations thereunder from acting as an officer or director of any issuer that has a class of securities registered pursuant to section 12 or that is required to file reports pursuant to section 15(d) if the person's conduct demonstrates unfitness to serve as an officer or director of any such issuer.

3. Money penalties in civil actions
    A. Authority of Commission
        Whenever it shall appear to the Commission that any person has violated any provision of this title, the rules or regulations thereunder, or a cease- and-desist order entered by the Commission pursuant to section 21C, other than by committing a violation subject to a penalty pursuant to section 21A, the Commission may bring an action in a United States district court to seek, and the court shall have jurisdiction to impose, upon a proper showing, a civil penalty to be paid by the person who committed such violation.
    B. Amount of penalty
        i. First tier
            The amount of the penalty shall be determined by the court in light of the facts and circumstances. For each violation, the

amount of the penalty shall not exceed the greater of (I) $5,000 for a natural person or $50,000 for any other person, or (II) the gross amount of pecuniary gain to such defendant as a result of the violation.

    ii. Second tier

Notwithstanding clause (i), the amount of penalty for each such violation shall not exceed the greater of (I) $50,000 for a natural person or $250,000 for any other person, or (II) the gross amount of pecuniary gain to such defendant as a result of the violation, if the violation described in subparagraph (A) involved fraud, deceit, manipulation, or deliberate or reckless disregard of a regulatory requirement.

    iii. Third tier

Notwithstanding clauses (i) and (ii), the amount of penalty for each such violation shall not exceed the greater of (I) $100,000 for a natural person or $500,000 for any other person, or (II) the gross amount of pecuniary gain to such defendant as a result of the violation, if–

(aa) the violation described in subparagraph (A) involved fraud, deceit, manipulation, or deliberate or reckless disregard of a regulatory requirement; and

(bb) such violation directly or indirectly resulted in substantial losses or created a significant risk of substantial losses to other persons.

C. Procedures for collection

    i. Payment of penalty to treasury

A penalty imposed under this section shall be payable into the Treasury of the United States, except as otherwise provided in section 308 of the Sarbanes-Oxley Act of 2002.

    ii. Collection of penalties

If a person upon whom such a penalty is imposed shall fail to pay such penalty within the time prescribed in the court's order, the Commission may refer the matter to the Attorney General who shall recover such penalty by action in the appropriate United States district court.

    iii. Remedy not exclusive

The actions authorized by this paragraph may be brought in addition to any other action that the Commission or the Attorney General is entitled to bring.

    iv. Jurisdiction and venue

For purposes of section 27, actions under this paragraph shall be actions to enforce a liability or a duty created by this title.

D. Special provisions relating to a violation of a cease-and-desist order

In an action to enforce a cease-and-desist order entered by the Commission pursuant to section 21C, each separate violation of such order shall be a separate offense, except that in the case of a violation through a continuing failure to comply with the order, each day of the failure to comply shall be deemed a separate offense.

4.   Prohibition of attorneys' fees paid from Commission disgorgement funds

Except as otherwise ordered by the court upon motion by the Commission, or, in the case of an administrative action, as otherwise ordered by the Commission, funds disgorged as the result of an action brought by the Commission in Federal court, or as a result of any Commission administrative action, shall not be distributed as payment for attorneys' fees or expenses incurred by private parties seeking distribution of the disgorged funds.

5.   Equitable Relief

In any action or proceeding brought or instituted by the Commission under any provision of the securities laws, the Commission may seek, and any Federal court may grant, any equitable relief that may be appropriate or necessary for the benefit of investors.

6.   Authority of a court to prohibit persons from participating in an offering of penny stock

A.   In general

In any proceeding under paragraph (1) against any person participating in, or, at the time of the alleged misconduct who was participating in, an offering of penny stock, the court may prohibit that person from participating in an offering of penny stock, conditionally or unconditionally, and permanently or for such period of time as the court shall determine.

B.   Definition

For purposes of this paragraph, the term 'person participating in an offering of penny stock' includes any person engaging in activities with a broker, dealer, or issuer for purposes of issuing, trading, or inducing or attempting to induce the purchase or sale of, any penny stock. The Commission may, by rule or regulation, define such term to include other activities, and may, by rule, regulation, or order, exempt any person or class of persons, in whole or in part, conditionally or unconditionally, from inclusion in such term.

e.   **Mandamus.** Upon application of the Commission the district courts of the United States and the United States courts of any territory or other place subject to the jurisdiction of the United States shall have jurisdiction to issue writs of mandamus, injunctions, and orders commanding (1) any person to comply with the provisions of this title, the rules, regulations, and orders thereunder, the rules of a national securities exchange or registered securities association of which such person is a member or person associated with a member, the rules of a registered clearing agency in which such person is a participant, the rules of the Public Company Accounting Oversight Board, of which such person is a registered public accounting firm or a person associated with such a firm, the rules of the Municipal Securities Rulemaking Board, or any undertaking contained in a registration statement as provided in subsection (d) of section 15, (2) any national securities exchange or registered securities association to enforce compliance by its members and persons associated with its members with the provisions of this title, the rules, regulations, and orders thereunder, and the rules of such exchange or association, or (3) any registered clearing agency to enforce compliance by its participants with the provisions of the rules of such clearing agency.

f. **Rules of self-regulatory organizations.** Notwithstanding any other provision of this title, the Commission shall not bring any action pursuant to subsection (d) or (e) of this section against any person for violation of, or to command compliance with, the rules of a self- regulatory organization or the Public Company Accounting Oversight Board unless it appears to the Commission that (1) such self- regulatory organization or the Public Company Accounting Oversight Board is unable or unwilling to take appropriate action against such person in the public interest and for the protection of investors, or (2) such action is otherwise necessary or appropriate in the public interest or for the protection of investors.

g. **Consolidation of actions; consent of Commission.** Notwithstanding the provisions of section 1407(a) of Title 28, or any other provision of law, no action for equitable relief instituted by the Commission pursuant to the securities laws shall be consolidated or coordinated with other actions not brought by the Commission, even though such other actions may involve common questions of fact, unless such consolidation is consented to by the Commission.

h. **Access to records**
    1. The Right to Financial Privacy Act of 1978 shall apply with respect to the Commission, except as otherwise provided in this subsection
    2. Notwithstanding section 1105 or 1107 of the Rights to Financial Privacy Act of 1978, the Commission may have access to and obtain copies of, or the information contained in financial records of a customer from a financial institution without prior notice to the customer upon an ex parte showing to an appropriate United States district court that the Commission seeks such financial records pursuant to a subpoena issued in conformity with the requirements of section 19(b) of the Securities Act of 1933, section 21(b) of the Securities Exchange Act of 1934, section 42(b) of the Investment Company Act of 1940, or section 209(b) of the Investment Advisers Act of 1940, and that the Commission has reason to believe that–
        A. delay in obtaining access to such financial records, or the required notice, will result in–
            i.   flight from prosecution;
            ii. destruction of or tampering with evidence;
            iii. transfer of assets or records outside the territorial limits of the United States;
            iv. improper conversion of investor assets; or
            v.   impeding the ability of the Commission to identify or trace the source or disposition of funds involved in any securities transaction;
        B. such financial records are necessary to identify or trace the record or beneficial ownership interest in any security;
        C. the acts, practices or course of conduct under investigation involve–
            i.   the dissemination of materially false or misleading information concerning any security, issuer, or market, or the failure to make disclosures required under the securities laws, which remain uncorrected; or

ii. a financial loss to investors or other persons protected under the securities laws which remains substantially uncompensated; or

D.   the acts, practices or course of conduct under investigation–

i.   involve significant financial speculation in securities; or

ii. endanger the stability of any financial or investment intermediary.

3. Any application under paragraph (2) for a delay in notice shall be made with reasonable specificity.

4.

A.   Upon a showing described in paragraph (2), the presiding judge or magistrate shall enter an ex parte order granting the requested delay for a period not to exceed ninety days and an order prohibiting the financial institution involved from disclosing that records have been obtained or that a request for records has been made.

B.   Extensions of the period of delay of notice provided in subparagraph (A) of up to ninety days each may be granted by the court upon application, but only in accordance with this subsection or section 1109(a), (b)(1), or (b)(2) of the Right to Financial Privacy Act of 1978.

C.   Upon expiration of the period of delay of notification ordered under subparagraph (A) or (B), the customer shall be served with or mailed a copy of the subpoena insofar as it applies to the customer together with the following notice which shall describe with reasonable specificity the nature of the investigation for which the Commission sought the financial records:

Records or information concerning your transactions which are held by the financial institution named in the attached subpoena were supplied to the Securities and Exchange Commission on (date). Notification was withheld pursuant to a determination by the (title of court so ordering) under section 21(h) of the Securities Exchange Act of 1934 that (state reason). The purpose of the investigation or official proceeding was (state purpose).

5. Upon application by the Commission, all proceedings pursuant to paragraphs (2) and (4) shall be held in camera and the records thereof sealed until expiration of the period of delay or such other date as the presiding judge or magistrate judge may permit.

6. The Commission shall compile an annual tabulation of the occasions on which the Commission used each separate subparagraph or clause of paragraph (2) of this subsection or the provisions of the Right to Financial Privacy Act of 1978 to obtain access to financial records of a customer and include it in its annual report to the Congress. Section 1121(b) of the Right to Financial Privacy Act of 1978 shall not apply with respect to the Commission.

7.

A.   Following the expiration of the period of delay of notification ordered by the court pursuant to paragraph (4) of this subsection, the customer may, upon motion, reopen the proceeding in the district court which issued the order. If the presiding judge or magistrate judge finds that the movant is the customer to whom the records obtained by the

Commission pertain, and that the Commission has obtained financial records or information contained therein in violation of this subsection, other than paragraph (1), it may order that the customer be granted civil penalties against the Commission in an amount equal to the sum of–

    i. $100 without regard to the volume of records involved;

    ii.   any out-of-pocket damages sustained by the customer as a direct result of the disclosure; and

    iii.   if the violation is found to have been willful, intentional, and without good faith, such punitive damages as the court may allow, together with the costs of the action and reasonable attorney's fees as determined by the court.

B.   Upon a finding that the Commission has obtained financial records or information contained therein in violation of this subsection, other than paragraph (1), the court, in its discretion, may also or in the alternative issue injunctive relief to require the Commission to comply with this subsection with respect to any subpoena which the Commission issues in the future for financial records of such customer for purposes of the same investigation.

C.   Whenever the court determines that the Commission has failed to comply with this subsection, other than paragraph (1), and the court finds that the circumstances raise questions of whether an officer or employee of the Commission acted in a willful and intentional manner and without good faith with respect to the violation, the Office of Personnel Management shall promptly initiate a proceeding to determine whether disciplinary action is warranted against the agent or employee who was primarily responsible for the violation. After investigating and considering the evidence submitted, the Office of Personnel Management shall submit its findings and recommendations to the Commission and shall send copies of the findings and recommendations to the officer or employee or his representative. The Commission shall take the corrective action that the Office of Personnel Management recommends.

8.   The relief described in paragraphs (7) and (10) shall be the only remedies or sanctions available to a customer for a violation of this subsection, other than paragraph (1), and nothing herein or in the Right to Financial Privacy Act of 1978 shall be deemed to prohibit the use in any investigation or proceeding of financial records, or the information contained therein, obtained by a subpoena issued by the Commission. In the case of an unsuccessful action under paragraph (7), the court shall award the costs of the action and attorney's fees to the Commission if the presiding judge or magistrate judge finds that the customer's claims were made in bad faith.

9.

A.   The Commission may transfer financial records or the information contained therein to any government authority if the Commission proceeds as a transferring agency in accordance with section 1112 of the Right to Financial Privacy Act of 1978, except that the customer notice required under section 1112(b) or (c) of such Act may be delayed upon a showing by the Commission, in accordance with the procedure set forth in paragraphs (4) and (5), that one or more of subparagraphs (A) through (D) of paragraph (2) apply.

    B.   The Commission may, without notice to the customer pursuant to section 1112 or the Right to Financial Privacy Act of 1978, transfer financial records or the information contained therein to a State securities agency or to the Department of Justice. Financial records or information transferred by the Commission to the Department of Justice or to a State securities agency pursuant to the provisions of this subparagraph may be disclosed or used only in an administrative, civil, or criminal action or investigation by the Department of Justice or the State securities agency which arises out of or relates to the acts, practices, or courses of conduct investigated by the Commission, except that if the Department of Justice or the State securities agency determines that the information should be disclosed or used for any other purpose, it may do so if it notifies the customer, except as otherwise provided in the Right to Financial Privacy Act of 1978, within 30 days of its determination, or complies with the requirements of section 1109 of such Act regarding delay of notice.

10.   Any government authority violating paragraph (9) shall be subject to the procedures and penalties applicable to the Commission under paragraph (7)(A) with respect to a violation by the Commission in obtaining financial records.

11.   Notwithstanding the provisions of this subsection, the Commission may obtain financial records from a financial institution or transfer such records in accordance with provisions of the Right to Financial Privacy Act of 1978.

12.   Nothing in this subsection shall enlarge or restrict any rights of a financial institution to challenge requests for records made by the Commission under existing law. Nothing in this subsection shall entitle a customer to assert any rights of a financial institution.

13.   Unless the context otherwise requires, all terms defined in the Right to Financial Privacy Act of 1978 which are common to this subsection shall have the same meaning as in such Act.

i.   **Information to CFTC.** The Commission shall provide the Commodity Futures Trading Commission with notice of the commencement of any proceeding and a copy of any order entered by the Commission against any broker or dealer registered pursuant to section 15(b)(11), any exchange registered pursuant to section 6(g), or any national securities association registered pursuant to section 15A(k).

Section 21A – Civil Penalties for Insider Trading

a. **Authority to impose civil penalties**
  1. Judicial actions by Commission authorized
     Whenever it shall appear to the Commission that any person has violated any provision of this title or the rules or regulations thereunder by purchasing or selling a security or security-based swap agreement (as defined in section 206B of the Gramm-Leach-Bliley Act) while in possession of material, nonpublic information in, or has violated any such provision by communicating such information in connection with, a transaction on or through the facilities of a national securities exchange or from or through a broker or dealer, and which is not part of a public offering by an issuer of securities other than standardized options or security futures products, the Commission–
     A. may bring an action in a United States district court to seek, and the court shall have jurisdiction to impose, a civil penalty to be paid by the person who committed such violation; and
     B. may, subject to subsection (b)(1) of this section, bring an action in a United States district court to seek, and the court shall have jurisdiction to impose, a civil penalty to be paid by a person who, at the time of the violation, directly or indirectly controlled the person who committed such violation.
  2. Amount of penalty for person who committed violation
     The amount of the penalty which may be imposed on the person who committed such violation shall be determined by the court in light of the facts and circumstances, but shall not exceed three times the profit gained or loss avoided as a result of such unlawful purchase, sale, or communication.
  3. Amount of penalty for controlling person
     The amount of the penalty which may be imposed on any person who, at the time of the violation, directly or indirectly controlled the person who committed such violation, shall be determined by the court in light of the facts and circumstances, but shall not exceed the greater of $1,000,000, or three times the amount of the profit gained or loss avoided as a result of such controlled person's violation. If such controlled person's violation was a violation by communication, the profit gained or loss avoided as a result of the violation shall, for purposes of this paragraph only, be deemed to be limited to the profit gained or loss avoided by the person or persons to whom the controlled person directed such communication.

b. **Limitations on liability**
  1. Liability of controlling persons
     No controlling person shall be subject to a penalty under subsection (a)(1)(B) of this section unless the Commission establishes that–
     A. such controlling person knew or recklessly disregarded the fact that such controlled person was likely to engage in the act or acts constituting the violation and failed to take appropriate steps to prevent such act or acts before they occurred; or

B.   such controlling person knowingly or recklessly failed to establish, maintain, or enforce any policy or procedure required under section 15(f) or section 204A of the Investment Advisers Act of 1940 and such failure substantially contributed to or permitted the occurrence of the act or acts constituting the violation.

2.   Additional restrictions on liability

No person shall be subject to a penalty under subsection (a) of this section solely by reason of employing another person who is subject to a penalty under such subsection, unless such employing person is liable as a controlling person under paragraph (1) of this subsection. Section 20(a) shall not apply to actions under subsection (a) of this section.

c.   **Authority of Commission.** The Commission, by such rules, regulations, and orders as it considers necessary or appropriate in the public interest or for the protection of investors, may exempt, in whole or in part, either unconditionally or upon specific terms and conditions, any person or transaction or class of persons or transactions from this section.

d.   **Procedures for collection**

1.   Payment of penalty to Treasury

A penalty imposed under this section shall (subject to subsection (e) of this section) be payable into the Treasury of the United States, except as otherwise provided in section 308 of the Sarbanes-Oxley Act of 2002.

2.   Collection of penalties

If a person upon whom such a penalty is imposed shall fail to pay such penalty within the time prescribed in the court's order, the Commission may refer the matter to the Attorney General who shall recover such penalty by action in the appropriate United States district court.

3.   Remedy not exclusive

The actions authorized by this section may be brought in addition to any other actions that the Commission or the Attorney General are entitled to bring.

4.   Jurisdiction and venue

For purposes of section 27, actions under this section shall be actions to enforce a liability or a duty created by this title.

5.   Statute of limitations

No action may be brought under this section more than 5 years after the date of the purchase or sale. This section shall not be construed to bar or limit in any manner any action by the Commission or the Attorney General under any other provision of this title, nor shall it bar or limit in any manner any action to recover penalties, or to seek any other order regarding penalties, imposed in an action commenced within 5 years of such transaction.

e.   **Authority to award bounties to informants.** Notwithstanding the provisions of subsection (d)(1) of this section, there shall be paid from amounts imposed as a penalty under this section and recovered by the Commission or the Attorney General, such sums, not to exceed 10 percent of such amounts, as the Commission deems appropriate, to the person or persons who provide information leading to the imposition of such penalty. Any determinations under this subsection, including whether, to whom, or in what amount to make payments, shall be in the sole discretion of the Commission, except that no such payment shall be made to any member, officer, or employee of any appropriate regulatory agency, the Department of Justice, or a self-regulatory organization. Any such determination shall be final and not subject to judicial review.

f.   **Definition.** For purposes of this section, "profit gained" or "loss avoided" is the difference between the purchase or sale price of the security and the value of that security as measured by the trading price of the security a reasonable period after public dissemination of the nonpublic information.

g.   **Limitation.** The authority of the Commission under this section with respect to security- based swap agreements (as defined in section 206B of the Gramm-Leach-Bliley Act) shall be subject to the restrictions and limitations of section 3A(b).

Section 21B – Civil Remedies In Administrative Proceedings

a.   **Commission authority to assess money penalties.** In any proceeding instituted pursuant to sections 15(b)(4), 15(b)(6), 15D, 15B, 15C, or 17A against any person, the Commission or the appropriate regulatory agency may impose a civil penalty if it finds, on the record after notice and opportunity for hearing, that such person–
1.   has willfully violated any provision of the Securities Act of 1933, the Investment Company Act of 1940, the Investment Advisers Act of 1940, or this title, or the rules or regulations thereunder, or the rules of the Municipal Securities Rulemaking Board;
2.   has willfully aided, abetted, counseled, commanded, induced, or procured such a violation by any other person;
3.   has willfully made or caused to be made in any application for registration or report required to be filed with the Commission or with any other appropriate regulatory agency under this title, or in any proceeding before the Commission with respect to registration, any statement which was, at the time and in the light of the circumstances under which it was made, false or misleading with respect to any material fact, or has omitted to state in any such application or report any material fact which is required to be stated therein; or
4.   has failed reasonably to supervise, within the meaning of section 15(b)(4)(E), with a view to preventing violations of the provisions of such statutes, rules and regulations, another person who commits such a violation, if such other person is subject to his supervision;

and that such penalty is in the public interest.

b.   **Maximum amount of penalty**
1.   First tier
   The maximum amount of penalty for each act or omission described in subsection (a) of this section shall be $5,000 for a natural person or $50,000 for any other person.
2.   Second tier
   Notwithstanding paragraph (1), the maximum amount of penalty for each such act or omission shall be $50,000 for a natural person or $250,000 for any other

person if the act or omission described in subsection (a) of this section involved fraud, deceit, manipulation, or deliberate or reckless disregard of a regulatory requirement.

3.   Third tier

Notwithstanding paragraphs (1) and (2), the maximum amount of penalty for each such act or omission shall be $100,000 for a natural person or $500,000 for any other person if–

A.   the act or omission described in subsection (a) of this section involved fraud, deceit, manipulation, or deliberate or reckless disregard of a regulatory requirement; and

B.   such act or omission directly or indirectly resulted in substantial losses or created a significant risk of substantial losses to other persons or resulted in substantial pecuniary gain to the person who committed the act or omission.

c.   **Determination of public interest.**   In considering under this section whether a penalty is in the public interest, the Commission or the appropriate regulatory agency may consider–

1.   whether the act or omission for which such penalty is assessed involved fraud, deceit, manipulation, or deliberate or reckless disregard of a regulatory requirement;

2.   the harm to other persons resulting either directly or indirectly from such act or omission;

3.   the extent to which any person was unjustly enriched, taking into account any restitution made to persons injured by such behavior;

4.   whether such person previously has been found by the Commission, another appropriate regulatory agency, or a self-regulatory organization to have violated the Federal securities laws, State securities laws, or the rules of a self-regulatory organization, has been enjoined by a court of competent jurisdiction from violations of such laws or rules, or has been convicted by a court of competent jurisdiction of violations of such laws or of any felony or misdemeanor described in section 15(b)(4)(B);

5.   the need to deter such person and other persons from committing such acts or omissions; and

6.   such other matters as justice may require.

d.   **Evidence concerning ability to pay.**   In any proceeding in which the Commission or the appropriate regulatory agency may impose a penalty under this section, a respondent may present evidence of the respondent's ability to pay such penalty. The Commission or the appropriate regulatory agency may, in its discretion, consider such evidence in determining whether such penalty is in the public interest. Such evidence may relate to the extent of such person's ability to continue in business and the collectability of a penalty, taking into account any other claims of the United States or third parties upon such person's assets and the amount of such person's assets.

e.   **Authority to enter order requiring accounting and disgorgement.**   In any proceeding in which the Commission or the appropriate regulatory agency may impose a penalty under this section, the Commission or the appropriate regulatory agency may enter an order requiring accounting and disgorgement, including reasonable interest. The Commission is authorized to adopt rules, regulations, and orders concerning payments to investors, rates of interest, periods of accrual, and such other matters as it deems appropriate to implement this subsection.

Section 21C – Cease-and-Desist Proceedings

a. **Authority of Commission.** If the Commission finds, after notice and opportunity for hearing, that any person is violating, has violated, or is about to violate any provision of this title, or any rule or regulation thereunder, the Commission may publish its findings and enter an order requiring such person, and any other person that is, was, or would be a cause of the violation, due to an act or omission the person knew or should have known would contribute to such violation, to cease and desist from committing or causing such violation and any future violation of the same provision, rule, or regulation. Such order may, in addition to requiring a person to cease and desist from committing or causing a violation, require such person to comply, or to take steps to effect compliance, with such provision, rule, or regulation, upon such terms and conditions and within such time as the Commission may specify in such order. Any such order may, as the Commission deems appropriate, require future compliance or steps to effect future compliance, either permanently or for such period of time as the Commission may specify, with such provision, rule, or regulation with respect to any security, any issuer, or any other person.

b. **Hearing.** The notice instituting proceedings pursuant to subsection (a) of this section shall fix a hearing date not earlier than 30 days nor later than 60 days after service of the notice unless an earlier or a later date is set by the Commission with the consent of any respondent so served.

c. **Temporary order**
   1. In general
      Whenever the Commission determines that the alleged violation or threatened violation specified in the notice instituting proceedings pursuant to subsection (a) of this section, or the continuation thereof, is likely to result in significant dissipation or conversion of assets, significant harm to investors, or substantial harm to the public interest, including, but not limited to, losses to the Securities Investor Protection Corporation, prior to the completion of the proceedings, the Commission may enter a temporary order requiring the respondent to cease and desist from the violation or threatened violation and to take such action to prevent the violation or threatened violation and to prevent dissipation or conversion of assets, significant harm to investors, or substantial harm to the public interest as the Commission deems appropriate pending completion of such proceedings. Such an order shall be entered only after notice and opportunity for a hearing, unless the Commission determines that notice and hearing prior to entry would be impracticable or contrary to the public interest. A temporary order shall become effective upon service upon the respondent and, unless set aside, limited, or suspended by the Commission or a court of competent jurisdiction, shall remain effective and enforceable pending the completion of the proceedings.

2.   Applicability

Paragraph (1) subsection shall apply only to a respondent that acts, or, at the time of the alleged misconduct acted, as a broker, dealer, investment adviser, investment company, municipal securities dealer, government securities broker, government securities dealer, registered public accounting firm (as defined in section 2 of the Sarbanes-Oxley Act of 2002), or transfer agent, or is, or was at the time of the alleged misconduct, an associated person of, or a person seeking to become associated with, any of the foregoing.

3.   Temporary freeze

A.   In general

     i.   Issuance of temporary order

Whenever, during the course of a lawful investigation involving possible violations of the Federal securities laws by an issuer of publicly traded securities or any of its directors, officers, partners, controlling persons, agents, or employees, it shall appear to the Commission that it is likely that the issuer will make extraordinary payments (whether compensation or otherwise) to any of the foregoing persons, the Commission may petition a Federal district court for a temporary order requiring the issuer to escrow, subject to court supervision, those payments in an interest-bearing account for 45 days.

     ii.   Standard

A temporary order shall be entered under clause (i), only after notice and opportunity for a hearing, unless the court determines that notice and hearing prior to entry of the order would be impracticable or contrary to the public interest.

     iii.   Effective period

A temporary order issued under clause (i) shall–

     I.   become effective immediately;

     II.   be served upon the parties subject to it; and

     III.   unless set aside, limited or suspended by a court of competent jurisdiction, shall remain effective and enforceable for 45 days.

     iv.   Extensions authorized

The effective period of an order under this subparagraph may be extended by the court upon good cause shown for not longer than 45 additional days, provided that the combined period of the order shall not exceed 90 days.

B.   Process on Determination of violations

     i.   Violations charged

If the issuer or other person described in subparagraph (A) is charged with any violation of the Federal securities laws before the expiration of the effective period of a temporary order under subparagraph (A) (including any applicable extension period), the order shall remain in effect, subject to court approval, until the conclusion of any legal proceedings related thereto, and the affected issuer or other person, shall have the right to petition the court for review of the order.

        ii.   Violations not charged

            If the issuer or other person described in subparagraph (A) is not charged with any violation of the Federal securities laws before the expiration of the effective period of a temporary order under subparagraph (A) (including any applicable extension period), the escrow shall terminate at the expiration of the 45-day effective period (or the expiration of any extension period, as applicable), and the disputed payments (with accrued interest) shall be returned to the issuer or other affected person.

d.   **Review of temporary orders**

    1.   Commission review

        At any time after the respondent has been served with a temporary cease and-desist order pursuant to subsection (c) of this section, the respondent may apply to the Commission to have the order set aside, limited, or suspended. If the respondent has been served with a temporary cease-and-desist order entered without a prior Commission hearing, the respondent may, within 10 days after the date on which the order was served, request a hearing on such application and the Commission shall hold a hearing and render a decision on such application at the earliest possible time.

    2.   Judicial review. Within–

        A.   10 days after the date the respondent was served with a temporary cease-and-desist order entered with a prior Commission hearing, or

        B.   10 days after the Commission renders a decision on an application and hearing under paragraph (1), with respect to any temporary cease-and desist order entered without a prior Commission hearing,

        the respondent may apply to the United States district court for the district in which the respondent resides or has its principal place of business, or for the District of Columbia, for an order setting aside, limiting, or suspending the effectiveness or enforcement of the order, and the court shall have jurisdiction to enter such an order. A respondent served with a temporary cease-and-desist order entered without a prior Commission hearing may not apply to the court except after hearing and decision by the Commission on the respondent's application under paragraph (1) of this subsection.

    3.   No automatic stay of temporary order

        The commencement of proceedings under paragraph (2) of this subsection shall not, unless specifically ordered by the court, operate as a stay of the Commission's order.

    4.   Exclusive review

        Section 25 shall not apply to a temporary order entered pursuant to this section.

e.   **Authority to enter order requiring accounting and disgorgement.** In any cease-and-desist proceeding under subsection (a), the Commission may enter an order requiring accounting and disgorgement, including reasonable interest. The Commission is authorized to adopt rules, regulations, and orders concerning payments to investors, rates of interest, periods of accrual, and such other matters as it deems appropriate to implement this subsection.

f. **Authority of the Commission to prohibit persons from serving as officers or directors.** In any cease-and-desist proceeding under subsection (a), the Commission may issue an order to prohibit, conditionally or unconditionally, and permanently or for such period of time as it shall determine, any person who has violated section 10(b) or the rules or regulations thereunder, from acting as an officer or director of any issuer that has a class of securities registered pursuant to section 12, or that is required to file reports pursuant to section 15(d), if the conduct of that person demonstrates unfitness to serve as an officer or director of any such issuer.

Section 21D – Private Securities Litigation

a. **Private class actions**
    1. In general
        The provisions of this subsection shall apply in each private action arising under this title that is brought as a plaintiff class action pursuant to the Federal Rules of Civil Procedure.
    2. Certification filed with complaint
        A. In general
            Each plaintiff seeking to serve as a representative party on behalf of a class shall provide a sworn certification, which shall be personally signed by such plaintiff and filed with the complaint, that–
            i.   states that the plaintiff has reviewed the complaint and authorized its filing;
            ii. states that the plaintiff did not purchase the security that is the subject of the complaint at the direction of plaintiff's counsel or in order to participate in any private action arising under this title;
            iii. states that the plaintiff is willing to serve as a representative party on behalf of a class, including providing testimony at deposition and trial, if necessary;
            iv. sets forth all of the transactions of the plaintiff in the security that is the subject of the complaint during the class period specified in the complaint;
            v.   identifies any other action under this title, filed during the 3-year period preceding the date on which the certification is signed by the plaintiff, in which the plaintiff has sought to serve as a representative party on behalf of a class; and
            vi. states that the plaintiff will not accept any payment for serving as a representative party on behalf of a class beyond the plaintiff's pro rata share of any recovery, except as ordered or approved by the court in accordance with paragraph (4).
        B. Nonwaiver of attorney-client privilege
            The certification filed pursuant to subparagraph (A) shall not be construed to be a waiver of the attorney-client privilege.
    3. Appointment of lead plaintiff
        A. Early notice to class members
            i.   In general
                 Not later than 20 days after the date on which the complaint is filed, the plaintiff or plaintiffs shall cause to be published, in a widely

circulated national business-oriented publication or wire service, a notice advising members of the purported plaintiff class–

    I. of the pendency of the action, the claims asserted therein, and the purported class period; and

    II. that, not later than 60 days after the date on which the notice is published, any member of the purported class may move the court to serve as lead plaintiff of the purported class.

  ii. Multiple actions

If more than one action on behalf of a class asserting substantially the same claim or claims arising under this title is filed, only the plaintiff or plaintiffs in the first filed action shall be required to cause notice to be published in accordance with clause (i).

  iii. Additional notices may be required under Federal rules

Notice required under clause (i) shall be in addition to any notice required pursuant to the Federal Rules of Civil Procedure.

B. Appointment of lead plaintiff

  i. In general

Not later than 90 days after the date on which a notice is published under subparagraph (A)(i), the court shall consider any motion made by a purported class member in response to the notice, including any motion by a class member who is not individually named as a plaintiff in the complaint or complaints, and shall appoint as lead plaintiff the member or members of the purported plaintiff class that the court determines to be most capable of adequately representing the interests of class members (hereafter in this paragraph referred to as the "most adequate plaintiff") in accordance with this subparagraph.

  ii. Consolidated actions

If more than one action on behalf of a class asserting substantially the same claim or claims arising under this title has been filed, and any party has sought to consolidate those actions for pretrial purposes or for trial, the court shall not make the determination required by clause (i) until after the decision on the motion to consolidate is rendered. As soon as practicable after such decision is rendered, the court shall appoint the most adequate plaintiff as lead plaintiff for the consolidated actions in accordance with this paragraph.

  iii. Rebuttable presumption

    I. In general

Subject to subclause (II), for purposes of clause (i), the court shall adopt a presumption that the most adequate plaintiff in any private action arising under this title is the person or group of persons that-

      (aa) has either filed the complaint or made a motion in response to a notice under subparagraph (A)(i);

      (bb) in the determination of the court, has the largest financial interest in the relief sought by the class; and (cc) otherwise satisfies the requirements of Rule 23 of the Federal Rules of Civil Procedure.

II. Rebuttal evidence

The presumption described in subclause (I) may be rebutted only upon proof by a member of the purported plaintiff class that the presumptively most adequate plaintiff–

(aa) will not fairly and adequately protect the interests of the class; or

(bb) is subject to unique defenses that render such plaintiff incapable of adequately representing the class.

iv. Discovery

For purposes of this subparagraph, discovery relating to whether a member or members of the purported plaintiff class is the most adequate plaintiff may be conducted by a plaintiff only if the plaintiff first demonstrates a reasonable basis for a finding that the presumptively most adequate plaintiff is incapable of adequately representing the class.

v. Selection of lead counsel

The most adequate plaintiff shall, subject to the approval of the court, select and retain counsel to represent the class.

vi. Restrictions on professional plaintiffs

Except as the court may otherwise permit, consistent with the purposes of this section, a person may be a lead plaintiff, or an officer, director, or fiduciary of a lead plaintiff, in no more than 5 securities class actions brought as plaintiff class actions pursuant to the Federal Rules of Civil Procedure during any 3-year period.

4. Recovery by plaintiffs

The share of any final judgment or of any settlement that is awarded to a representative party serving on behalf of a class shall be equal, on a per share basis, to the portion of the final judgment or settlement awarded to all other members of the class. Nothing in this paragraph shall be construed to limit the award of reasonable costs and expenses (including lost wages) directly relating to the representation of the class to any representative party serving on behalf of a class.

5. Restrictions on settlements under seal

The terms and provisions of any settlement agreement of a class action shall not be filed under seal, except that on motion of any party to the settlement, the court may order filing under seal for those portions of a settlement agreement as to which good cause is shown for such filing under seal. For purposes of this paragraph, good cause shall exist only if publication of a term or provision of a settlement agreement would cause direct and substantial harm to any party.

6. Restrictions on payment of attorneys' fees and expenses

Total attorneys' fees and expenses awarded by the court to counsel for the plaintiff class shall not exceed a reasonable percentage of the amount of any damages and prejudgment interest actually paid to the class.

7.   Disclosure of settlement terms to class members

Any proposed or final settlement agreement that is published or otherwise disseminated to the class shall include each of the following statements, along with a cover page summarizing the information contained in such statements:

A.   Statement of plaintiff recovery

The amount of the settlement proposed to be distributed to the parties to the action, determined in the aggregate and on an average per share basis.

B.   Statement of potential outcome of case

     i.   Agreement on amount of damages

If the settling parties agree on the average amount of damages per share that would be recoverable if the plaintiff prevailed on each claim alleged under this title, a statement concerning the average amount of such potential damages per share.

     ii.   Disagreement on amount of damages

If the parties do not agree on the average amount of damages per share that would be recoverable if the plaintiff prevailed on each claim alleged under this title, a statement from each settling party concerning the issue or issues on which the parties disagree.

     iii.   Inadmissibility for certain purposes

A statement made in accordance with clause (i) or (ii) concerning the amount of damages shall not be admissible in any Federal or State judicial action or administrative proceeding, other than an action or proceeding arising out of such statement.

C.   Statement of attorneys' fees or costs sought

If any of the settling parties or their counsel intend to apply to the court for an award of attorneys' fees or costs from any fund established as part of the settlement, a statement indicating which parties or counsel intend to make such an application, the amount of fees and costs that will be sought (including the amount of such fees and costs determined on an average per share basis), and a brief explanation supporting the fees and costs sought. Such information shall be clearly summarized on the cover page of any notice to a party of any proposed or final settlement agreement.

D.   Identification of lawyers' representatives

The name, telephone number, and address of one or more representatives of counsel for the plaintiff class who will be reasonably available to answer questions from class members concerning any matter contained in any notice of settlement published or otherwise disseminated to the class.

E.   Reasons for settlement

A brief statement explaining the reasons why the parties are proposing the settlement.

F.   Other information

Such other information as may be required by the court.

8.   Security for payment of costs in class actions

In any private action arising under this title that is certified as a class action pursuant to the Federal Rules of Civil Procedure, the court may require an undertaking from the attorneys for the plaintiff class, the plaintiff class, or both, or from the attorneys for the defendant, the defendant, or both, in such proportions and at such times as the court determines are just and equitable, for the payment of fees and expenses that may be awarded under this subsection.

9. Attorney conflict of interest

If a plaintiff class is represented by an attorney who directly owns or otherwise has a beneficial interest in the securities that are the subject of the litigation, the court shall make a determination of whether such ownership or other interest constitutes a conflict of interest sufficient to disqualify the attorney from representing the plaintiff class.

b. **Requirements for securities fraud actions**

1. Misleading statements and omissions

In any private action arising under this title in which the plaintiff alleges that the defendant–

A. made an untrue statement of a material fact; or

B. omitted to state a material fact necessary in order to make the statements made, in the light of the circumstances in which they were made, not misleading;

the complaint shall specify each statement alleged to have been misleading, the reason or reasons why the statement is misleading, and, if an allegation regarding the statement or omission is made on information and belief, the complaint shall state with particularity all facts on which that belief is formed.

2. Required state of mind

In any private action arising under this title in which the plaintiff may recover money damages only on proof that the defendant acted with a particular state of mind, the complaint shall, with respect to each act or omission alleged to violate this title, state with particularity facts giving rise to a strong inference that the defendant acted with the required state of mind.

3. Motion to dismiss; stay of discovery

A. Dismissal for failure to meet pleading requirements

In any private action arising under this title, the court shall, on the motion of any defendant, dismiss the complaint if the requirements of paragraphs (1) and (2) are not met.

B. Stay of discovery

In any private action arising under this title, all discovery and other proceedings shall be stayed during the pendency of any motion to dismiss, unless the court finds upon the motion of any party that particularized discovery is necessary to preserve evidence or to prevent undue prejudice to that party.

C. Preservation of evidence

i. In general

During the pendency of any stay of discovery pursuant to this paragraph, unless otherwise ordered by the court, any party to the action with actual notice of the allegations contained in the complaint shall treat all documents, data compilations (including electronically recorded or stored data), and tangible objects that are in the custody or control of such person and that are relevant to the allegations, as if they were the subject of a continuing request for production of documents from an opposing party under the Federal Rules of Civil Procedure.

    ii. Sanction for willful violation

A party aggrieved by the willful failure of an opposing party to comply with clause (i) may apply to the court for an order awarding appropriate sanctions.

D. Circumvention of stay of discovery

Upon a proper showing, a court may stay discovery proceedings in any private action in a State court, as necessary in aid of its jurisdiction, or to protect or effectuate its judgments, in an action subject to a stay of discovery pursuant to this paragraph.

4. Loss causation

In any private action arising under this title, the plaintiff shall have the burden of proving that the act or omission of the defendant alleged to violate this title caused the loss for which the plaintiff seeks to recover damages.

c. **Sanctions for abusive litigation**

1. Mandatory review by court

In any private action arising under this title, upon final adjudication of the action, the court shall include in the record specific findings regarding compliance by each party and each attorney representing any party with each requirement of Rule 11(b) of the Federal Rules of Civil Procedure as to any complaint, responsive pleading, or dispositive motion.

2. Mandatory sanctions

If the court makes a finding under paragraph (1) that a party or attorney violated any requirement of Rule 11(b) of the Federal Rules of Civil Procedure as to any complaint, responsive pleading, or dispositive motion, the court shall impose sanctions on such party or attorney in accordance with Rule 11 of the Federal Rules of Civil Procedure. Prior to making a finding that any party or attorney has violated Rule 11 of the Federal Rules of Civil Procedure, the court shall give such party or attorney notice and an opportunity to respond.

3. Presumption in favor of attorneys' fees and costs

A. In general

Subject to subparagraphs (B) and (C), for purposes of paragraph (2), the court shall adopt a presumption that the appropriate sanction–

    i. for failure of any responsive pleading or dispositive motion to comply with any requirement of Rule 11(b) of the Federal Rules of Civil Procedure is an award to the opposing party of the reasonable attorneys' fees and other expenses incurred as a direct result of the violation; and

    ii. for substantial failure of any complaint to comply with any requirement of Rule 11(b) of the Federal Rules of Civil Procedure is an award to the opposing party of the reasonable attorneys' fees and other expenses incurred in the action.

B. Rebuttal evidence

The presumption described in subparagraph (A) may be rebutted only upon proof by the party or attorney against whom sanctions are to be imposed that–

  i. the award of attorneys' fees and other expenses will impose an unreasonable burden on that party or attorney and would be unjust, and the failure to make such an award would not impose a greater burden on the party in whose favor sanctions are to be imposed; or

  ii. the violation of Rule 11(b) of the Federal Rules of Civil Procedure was de minimis.

C. Sanctions

If the party or attorney against whom sanctions are to be imposed meets its burden under subparagraph (B), the court shall award the sanctions that the court deems appropriate pursuant to Rule 11 of the Federal Rules of Civil Procedure.

d. **Defendant's right to written interrogatories**. In any private action arising under this title in which the plaintiff may recover money damages, the court shall, when requested by a defendant, submit to the jury a written interrogatory on the issue of each such defendant's state of mind at the time the alleged violation occurred.

e. **Limitation on damages**

1. In general

Except as provided in paragraph (2), in any private action arising under this title in which the plaintiff seeks to establish damages by reference to the market price of a security, the award of damages to the plaintiff shall not exceed the difference between the purchase or sale price paid or received, as appropriate, by the plaintiff for the subject security and the mean trading price of that security during the 90-day period beginning on the date on which the information correcting the misstatement or omission that is the basis for the action is disseminated to the market.

2. Exception

In any private action arising under this title in which the plaintiff seeks to establish damages by reference to the market price of a security, if the plaintiff sells or repurchases the subject security prior to the expiration of the 90-day period described in paragraph (1), the plaintiff's damages shall not exceed the difference between the purchase or sale price paid or received, as appropriate, by the plaintiff for the security and the mean trading price of the security during the period beginning immediately after dissemination of information correcting the misstatement or omission and ending on the date on which the plaintiff sells or repurchases the security.

3. Definition

For purposes of this subsection, the "mean trading price" of a security shall be an average of the daily trading price of that security, determined as of the close of the market each day during the 90-day period referred to in paragraph (1).

f. **Proportionate liability**
  1.   Applicability
      Nothing in this subsection shall be construed to create, affect, or in any manner modify, the standard for liability associated with any action arising under the securities laws.
  2.   Liability for damages
     A.   Joint and several liability
        Any covered person against whom a final judgment is entered in a private action shall be liable for damages jointly and severally only if the trier of fact specifically determines that such covered person knowingly committed a violation of the securities laws.
     B.   Proportionate liability
       i.   In general
          Except as provided in subparagraph (A), a covered person against whom a final judgment is entered in a private action shall be liable solely for the portion of the judgment that corresponds to the percentage of responsibility of that covered person, as determined under paragraph (3).
      ii.   Recovery by and costs of covered person
          In any case in which a contractual relationship permits, a covered person that prevails in any private action may recover the attorney's fees and costs of that covered person in connection with the action.
  3.   Determination of responsibility
     A.   In general
        In any private action, the court shall instruct the jury to answer special interrogatories, or if there is no jury, shall make findings, with respect to each covered person and each of the other persons claimed by any of the parties to have caused or contributed to the loss incurred by the plaintiff, including persons who have entered into settlements with the plaintiff or plaintiffs, concerning–
       i.   whether such person violated the securities laws;
      ii.   the percentage of responsibility of such person, measured as a percentage of the total fault of all persons who caused or contributed to the loss incurred by the plaintiff; and
     iii.   whether such person knowingly committed a violation of the securities laws.
     B.   Contents of special interrogatories or findings
        The responses to interrogatories, or findings, as appropriate, under subparagraph (A) shall specify the total amount of damages that the plaintiff is entitled to recover and the percentage of responsibility of each covered person found to have caused or contributed to the loss incurred by the plaintiff or plaintiffs.
     C.   Factors for consideration
        In determining the percentage of responsibility under this paragraph, the trier of fact shall consider–
       i.   the nature of the conduct of each covered person found to have caused or contributed to the loss incurred by the plaintiff or plaintiffs; and

        ii.   the nature and extent of the causal relationship between the conduct of each such person and the damages incurred by the plaintiff or plaintiffs.

4.   Uncollectible share

    A.   In general

Notwithstanding paragraph (2)(B), upon motion made not later than 6 months after a final judgment is entered in any private action, the court determines that all or part of the share of the judgment of the covered person is not collectible against that covered person, and is also not collectible against a covered person described in paragraph (2)(A), each covered person described in paragraph (2)(B) shall be liable for the uncollectible share as follows:

    i.   Percentage of net worth

Each covered person shall be jointly and severally liable for the uncollectible share if the plaintiff establishes that–

        I.   the plaintiff is an individual whose recoverable damages under the final judgment are equal to more than 10 percent of the net worth of the plaintiff; and

        II.   the net worth of the plaintiff is equal to less than $200,000.

    ii.   Other plaintiffs

With respect to any plaintiff not described in subclauses (I) and (II) of clause (i), each covered person shall be liable for the uncollectible share in proportion to the percentage of responsibility of that covered person, except that the total liability of a covered person under this clause may not exceed 50 percent of the proportionate share of that covered person, as determined under paragraph (3)(B).

    iii.   Net worth

For purposes of this subparagraph, net worth shall be determined as of the date immediately preceding the date of the purchase or sale (as applicable) by the plaintiff of the security that is the subject of the action, and shall be equal to the fair market value of assets, minus liabilities, including the net value of the investments of the plaintiff in real and personal property (including personal residences).

    B.   Overall limit

In no case shall the total payments required pursuant to subparagraph (A) exceed the amount of the uncollectible share.

    C.   Covered persons subject to contribution

A covered person against whom judgment is not collectible shall be subject to contribution and to any continuing liability to the plaintiff on the judgment.

5.   Right of contribution

To the extent that a covered person is required to make an additional payment pursuant to paragraph (4), that covered person may recover contribution–

    A.   from the covered person originally liable to make the payment;

    B.   from any covered person liable jointly and severally pursuant to paragraph (2)(A);

        C.   from any covered person held proportionately liable pursuant to this paragraph who is liable to make the same payment and has paid less than his or her proportionate share of that payment; or

        D.   from any other person responsible for the conduct giving rise to the payment that would have been liable to make the same payment.

6.   Nondisclosure to jury

The standard for allocation of damages under paragraphs (2) and (3) and the procedure for reallocation of uncollectible shares under paragraph (4) shall not be disclosed to members of the jury.

7.   Settlement discharge

        A.   In general

A covered person who settles any private action at any time before final verdict or judgment shall be discharged from all claims for contribution brought by other persons. Upon entry of the settlement by the court, the court shall enter a bar order constituting the final discharge of all obligations to the plaintiff of the settling covered person arising out of the action. The order shall bar all future claims for contribution arising out of the action–

           i.   by any person against the settling covered person; and

          ii.   by the settling covered person against any person, other than a person whose liability has been extinguished by the settlement of the settling covered person.

        B.   Reduction

If a covered person enters into a settlement with the plaintiff prior to final verdict or judgment, the verdict or judgment shall be reduced by the greater of–

           i.   an amount that corresponds to the percentage of responsibility of that covered person; or

          ii.   the amount paid to the plaintiff by that covered person.

8.   Contribution

A covered person who becomes jointly and severally liable for damages in any private action may recover contribution from any other person who, if joined in the original action, would have been liable for the same damages. A claim for contribution shall be determined based on the percentage of responsibility of the claimant and of each person against whom a claim for contribution is made.

9.   Statute of limitations for contribution

In any private action determining liability, an action for contribution shall be brought not later than 6 months after the entry of a final, nonappealable judgment in the action, except that an action for contribution brought by a covered person who was required to make an additional payment pursuant to paragraph (4) may be brought not later than 6 months after the date on which such payment was made.

10.   Definitions

For purposes of this subsection–

        A.   a covered person "knowingly commits a violation of the securities laws"–

      i.   with respect to an action that is based on an untrue statement of material fact or omission of a material fact necessary to make the statement not misleading, if–

         I.   that covered person makes an untrue statement of a material fact, with actual knowledge that the representation is false, or omits to state a fact necessary in order to make the statement made not misleading, with actual knowledge that, as a result of the omission, one of the material representations of the covered person is false; and

        II.   persons are likely to reasonably rely on that misrepresentation or omission; and

      ii.   with respect to an action that is based on any conduct that is not described in clause (i), if that covered person engages in that conduct with actual knowledge of the facts and circumstances that make the conduct of that covered person a violation of the securities laws;

B.   reckless conduct by a covered person shall not be construed to constitute a knowing commission of a violation of the securities laws by that covered person;

C.   the term "covered person" means–

      i.   a defendant in any private action arising under this title; or

      ii.   a defendant in any private action arising under section 11 of the Securities Act of 1933, who is an outside director of the issuer of the securities that are the subject of the action; and

D.   the term "outside director" shall have the meaning given such term by rule or regulation of the Commission.

Section 21E – Application of Safe Harbor for Forward-Looking Statements

a.   **Applicability**

This section shall apply only to a forward-looking statement made by–

1.   an issuer that, at the time that the statement is made, is subject to the reporting requirements of section 13(a) or section 15(d);

2.   a person acting on behalf of such issuer;

3.   an outside reviewer retained by such issuer making a statement on behalf of such issuer; or

4.   an underwriter, with respect to information provided by such issuer or information derived from information provided by such issuer.

b.   **Exclusions**. Except to the extent otherwise specifically provided by rule, regulation, or order of the Commission, this section shall not apply to a forward looking statement—

1.   that is made with respect to the business or operations of the issuer, if the issuer–

   A.   during the 3-year period preceding the date on which the statement was first made–

        i. was convicted of any felony or misdemeanor described in clauses (i) through (iv) of section 15(b)(4)(B); or

        ii. has been made the subject of a judicial or administrative decree or order arising out of a governmental action that–

            I. prohibits future violations of the antifraud provisions of the securities laws;

            II. requires that the issuer cease and desist from violating the antifraud provisions of the securities laws; or

            III. determines that the issuer violated the antifraud provisions of the securities laws;

    B. makes the forward-looking statement in connection with an offering of securities by a blank check company;

    C. issues penny stock;

    D. makes the forward-looking statement in connection with a rollup transaction; or

    E. makes the forward-looking statement in connection with a going private transaction; or

  2. that is–

    A. included in a financial statement prepared in accordance with generally accepted accounting principles;

    B. contained in a registration statement of, or otherwise issued by, an investment company;

    C. made in connection with a tender offer;

    D. made in connection with an initial public offering;

    E. made in connection with an offering by, or relating to the operations of, a partnership, limited liability company, or a direct participation investment program; or

    F. made in a disclosure of beneficial ownership in a report required to be filed with the Commission pursuant to section 13(d).

c. **Safe harbor**

  1. In general

Except as provided in subsection (b) of this section, in any private action arising under this title that is based on an untrue statement of a material fact or omission of a material fact necessary to make the statement not misleading, a person referred to in subsection (a) of this section shall not be liable with respect to any forward-looking statement, whether written or oral, if and to the extent that–

    A. the forward-looking statement is—

        i. identified as a forward-looking statement, and is accompanied by meaningful cautionary statements identifying important factors that could cause actual results to differ materially from those in the forward looking statement; or

        ii. immaterial; or

    B. the plaintiff fails to prove that the forward-looking statement–

        i. if made by a natural person, was made with actual knowledge by that person that the statement was false or misleading; or

        ii. if made by a business entity, was–

> > I.   made by or with the approval of an executive officer of that entity; and
> >
> > II. made or approved by such officer with actual knowledge by that officer that the statement was false or misleading.

> 2.   Oral forward-looking statements
>
> In the case of an oral forward-looking statement made by an issuer that is subject to the reporting requirements of section 13(a) or section 15(d), or by a person acting on behalf of such issuer, the requirement set forth in paragraph (1)(A) shall be deemed to be satisfied–
>
> > A.   if the oral forward-looking statement is accompanied by a cautionary statement–
> >
> > > i.   that the particular oral statement is a forward-looking statement; and
> > >
> > > ii. that the actual results might differ materially from those projected in the forward-looking statement; and
> >
> > B.   if—
> >
> > > i.   the oral forward-looking statement is accompanied by an oral statement that additional information concerning factors that could cause actual results to materially differ from those in the forward-looking statement is contained in a readily available written document, or portion thereof;
> > >
> > > ii.   the accompanying oral statement referred to in clause (i) identifies the document, or portion thereof, that contains the additional information about those factors relating to the forward-looking statement; and
> > >
> > > iii. the information contained in that written document is a cautionary statement that satisfies the standard established in paragraph (1)(A).

> 3.   Availability
>
> Any document filed with the Commission or generally disseminated shall be deemed to be readily available for purposes of paragraph (2).

> 4.   Effect on other safe harbors
>
> The exemption provided for in paragraph (1) shall be in addition to any exemption that the Commission may establish by rule or regulation under subsection (g) of this section.

d.   **Duty to update.**   Nothing in this section shall impose upon any person a duty to update a forward-looking statement.

e.   **Dispositive motion.**   On any motion to dismiss based upon subsection (c)(1) of this section, the court shall consider any statement cited in the complaint and any cautionary statement accompanying the forward-looking statement, which are not subject to material dispute, cited by the defendant.

f.   **Stay pending decision on motion.**   In any private action arising under this title, the court shall stay discovery (other than discovery that is specifically directed to the applicability of the exemption provided for in this section) during the pendency of any motion by a defendant for summary judgment that is based on the grounds that—

1. the statement or omission upon which the complaint is based is a forward-looking statement within the meaning of this section; and

2. the exemption provided for in this section precludes a claim for relief.

g. **Exemption authority.** In addition to the exemptions provided for in this section, the Commission may, by rule or regulation, provide exemptions from or under any provision of this title, including with respect to liability that is based on a statement or that is based on projections or other forward-looking information, if and to the extent that any such exemption is consistent with the public interest and the protection of investors, as determined by the Commission.

h. **Effect on other authority of Commission.** Nothing in this section limits, either expressly or by implication, the authority of the Commission to exercise similar authority or to adopt similar rules and regulations with respect to forward-looking statements under any other statute under which the Commission exercises rulemaking authority.

i. **Definitions.** For purposes of this section, the following definitions shall apply:

1. Forward-looking statement

   The term "forward-looking statement" means—

   A. a statement containing a projection of revenues, income (including income loss), earnings (including earnings loss) per share, capital expenditures, dividends, capital structure, or other financial items;

   B. a statement of the plans and objectives of management for future operations, including plans or objectives relating to the products or services of the issuer;

   C. a statement of future economic performance, including any such statement contained in a discussion and analysis of financial condition by the management or in the results of operations included pursuant to the rules and regulations of the Commission;

   D. any statement of the assumptions underlying or relating to any statement described in subparagraph (A), (B), or (C);

   E. any report issued by an outside reviewer retained by an issuer, to the extent that the report assesses a forward-looking statement made by the issuer; or

   F. a statement containing a projection or estimate of such other items as may be specified by rule or regulation of the Commission.

2. Investment company

   The term "investment company" has the same meaning as in section 3(a) of the Investment Company Act of 1940.

3. Going private transaction

   The term "going private transaction" has the meaning given that term under the rules or regulations of the Commission issued pursuant to section 13(e).

4. Person acting on behalf of an issuer

   The term "person acting on behalf of an issuer" means any officer, director, or employee of such issuer.

5. Other terms
The terms "blank check company", "roll-up transaction", "partnership", "limited liability company", "executive officer of an entity" and "direct participation investment program", have the meanings given those terms by rule or regulation of the Commission.

Section 23 – Rules, Regulations, and Orders; Annual Reports

a. **Power to make rules and regulations; considerations; public disclosure**
1. The Commission, the Board of Governors of the Federal Reserve System, and the other agencies enumerated in section 3(a)(34) shall each have power to make such rules and regulations as may be necessary or appropriate to implement the provisions of this title for which they are responsible or for the execution of the functions vested in them by this title, and may for such purposes classify persons, securities, transactions, statements, applications, reports, and other matters within their respective jurisdictions, and prescribe greater, lesser, or different requirements for different classes thereof. No provision of this title imposing any liability shall apply to any act done or omitted in good faith in conformity with a rule, regulation, or order of the Commission, the Board of Governors of the Federal Reserve System, other agency enumerated in section 3(a)(34), or any self regulatory organization, notwithstanding that such rule, regulation, or order may thereafter be amended or rescinded or determined by judicial or other authority to be invalid for any reason.
2. The Commission and the Secretary of the Treasury, in making rules and regulations pursuant to any provisions of this title, shall consider among other matters the impact any such rule or regulation would have on competition. The Commission and the Secretary of the Treasury shall not adopt any such rule or regulation which would impose a burden on competition not necessary or appropriate in furtherance of the purposes of this title. The Commission and the Secretary of the Treasury shall include in the statement of basis and purpose incorporated in any rule or regulation adopted under this title, the reasons for the Commission's or the Secretary's determination that any burden on competition imposed by such rule or regulation is necessary or appropriate in furtherance of the purposes of this title.
3. The Commission and the Secretary, in making rules and regulations pursuant to any provision of this title, considering any application for registration in accordance with section 19(a), or reviewing any proposed rule change of a self-regulatory organization in accordance with section 19(b), shall keep in a public file and make available for copying all written statements filed with the Commission and the Secretary and all written communications between the Commission or the Secretary and any person relating to the proposed rule, regulation, application, or proposed rule change; *Provided, however,* That the Commission and the Secretary shall not be required to keep in a public file or make available for copying any such statement or communication which it may withhold from the public in accordance with the provisions of section 552 of Title 5.

Section 25 – Court Review of Orders and Rules

a. **Final Commission orders; persons aggrieved; petition; record; findings; affirmance, modification, enforcement, or setting aside of orders; remand to adduce additional evidence**

1. A person aggrieved by a final order of the Commission entered pursuant to this title may obtain review of the order in the United States Court of Appeals for the circuit in which he resides or has his principal place of business, or for the District of Columbia Circuit, by filing in such court, within sixty days after the entry of the order, a written petition requesting that the order be modified or set aside in whole or in part.

2. A copy of the petition shall be transmitted forthwith by the clerk of the court to a member of the Commission or an officer designated by the Commission for that purpose. Thereupon the Commission shall file in the court the record on which the order complained of is entered, as provided in section 2112 of Title 28 and the Federal Rules of Appellate Procedure.

3. On the filing of the petition, the court has jurisdiction, which becomes exclusive on the filing of the record, to affirm or modify and enforce or to set aside the order in whole or in part.

4. The findings of the Commission as to the facts, if supported by substantial evidence, are conclusive.

5. If either party applies to the court for leave to adduce additional evidence and shows to the satisfaction of the court that the additional evidence is material and that there was reasonable ground for failure to adduce it before the Commission, the court may remand the case to the Commission for further proceedings, in whatever manner and on whatever conditions the court considers appropriate. If the case is remanded to the Commission, it shall file in the court a supplemental record containing any new evidence, any further or modified findings, and any new order.

b. **Commission rules; persons adversely affected; petition; record; affirmance, enforcement, or setting aside of rules; findings; transfer of proceedings**

1. A person adversely affected by a rule of the Commission promulgated pursuant to section 6, 9(h)(2), 11, 11A, 15(c)(5) or (6), 15A, 17, 17A, or 19 may obtain review of this rule in the United States Court of Appeals for the circuit in which he resides or has his principal place of business or for the District of Columbia Circuit, by filing in such court, within sixty days after the promulgation of the rule, a written petition requesting that the rule be set aside.

2. A copy of the petition shall be transmitted forthwith by the clerk of the court to a member of the Commission or an officer designated for that purpose. Thereupon, the Commission shall file in the court the rule under review and any documents referred to therein, the Commission's notice of proposed rulemaking and any documents referred to therein, all written submissions and the transcript of any oral presentations in the rulemaking, factual information not included in the foregoing that was considered by the Commission in the promulgation of the rule or proffered by the Commission as pertinent to the rule, the report of any advisory committee received or considered by the

Commission in the rulemaking, and any other materials prescribed by the court.

3. On the filing of the petition, the court has jurisdiction, which becomes exclusive on the filing of the materials set forth in paragraph (2) of this subsection, to affirm and enforce or to set aside the rule.

4. The findings of the Commission as to the facts identified by the Commission as the basis, in whole or in part, of the rule, if supported by substantial evidence, are conclusive. The court shall affirm and enforce the rule unless the Commission's action in promulgating the rule is found to be arbitrary, capricious, an abuse of discretion, or otherwise not in accordance with law; contrary to constitutional right, power, privilege, or immunity; in excess of statutory jurisdiction, authority, or limitations, or short of statutory right; or without observance of procedure required by law.

5. If proceedings have been instituted under this subsection in two or more courts of appeals with respect to the same rule, the Commission shall file the materials set forth in paragraph (2) of this subsection in that court in which a proceeding was first instituted. The other courts shall thereupon transfer all such proceedings to the court in which the materials have been filed. For the convenience of the parties in the interest of justice that court may thereafter transfer all the proceedings to any other court of appeals.

c. **Objections not urged before Commission; stay of orders and rules; transfer of enforcement or review proceedings**

1. No objection to an order or rule of the Commission, for which review is sought under this section, may be considered by the court unless it was urged before the Commission or there was reasonable ground for failure to do so.

2. The filing of a petition under this section does not operate as a stay of the Commission's order or rule. Until the court's jurisdiction becomes exclusive, the Commission may stay its order or rule pending judicial review if it finds that justice so requires. After the filing of a petition under this section, the court, on whatever conditions may be required and to the extent necessary to prevent irreparable injury, may issue all necessary and appropriate process to stay the order or rule or to preserve status or rights pending its review; but (notwithstanding section 705 of Title 5) no such process may be issued by the court before the filing of the record or the materials set forth in subsection (b)(2) of this section unless: (A) the Commission has denied a stay or failed to grant requested relief, (B) a reasonable period has expired since the filing of an application for a stay without a decision by the Commission, or (C) there was reasonable ground for failure to apply to the Commission.

3. When the same order or rule is the subject of one or more petitions for review filed under this section and an action for enforcement filed in a district court of the United States under section 21(d) or (e), that court in which the petition or the action is first filed has jurisdiction with respect to the order or rule to the exclusion of any other court, and thereupon all such proceedings shall be transferred to that court; but, for the convenience of the parties in the interest of justice, that court may thereafter transfer all the proceedings to any other court of appeals or district court of the United States, whether or not a petition for review or an action for enforcement was originally filed in the transferee court.

The scope of review by a district court under section 21(d) or (e) is in all cases the same as by a court of appeals under this section.

d. **Other appropriate regulatory agencies**
    1. For purposes of the preceding subsections of this section, the term "Commission" includes the agencies enumerated in section 3(a)(34) insofar as such agencies are acting pursuant to this title and the Secretary of the Treasury insofar as he is acting pursuant to section 15C.
    2. For purposes of subsection (a)(4) of this section and section 706 of Title 5, an order of the Commission pursuant to section 19(a) denying registration to a clearing agency for which the Commission is not the appropriate regulatory agency or pursuant to section 19(b) disapproving a proposed rule change by such a clearing agency shall be deemed to be an order of the appropriate regulatory agency for such clearing agency insofar as such order was entered by reason of a determination by such appropriate regulatory agency pursuant to section 19(a)(2)(C) or 19(b)(4)(C) that such registration or proposed rule change would be inconsistent with the safeguarding of securities or funds.

Section 27 – Jurisdiction of Offenses and Suits

The district courts of the United States and the United States courts of any Territory or other place subject to the jurisdiction of the United States shall have exclusive jurisdiction of violations of this title or the rules and regulations thereunder, and of all suits in equity and actions at law brought to enforce any liability or duty created by this title or the rules and regulations thereunder. Any criminal proceeding may be brought in the district wherein any act or transaction constituting the violation occurred. Any suit or action to enforce any liability or duty created by this title or rules and regulations thereunder, or to enjoin any violation of such title or rules and regulations, may be brought in any such district or in the district wherein the defendant is found or is an inhabitant or transacts business, and process in such cases may be served in any other district of which the defendant is an inhabitant or wherever the defendant may be found. Judgments and decrees so rendered shall be subject to review as provided in sections 1254, 1291, 1292, and 1294 of Title 28. No costs shall be assessed for or against the Commission in any proceeding under this title brought by or against it in the Supreme Court or such other courts.

Section 28 – Effect on Existing Law

a. **Addition of rights and remedies; recovery of actual damages; State securities commissions**. Except as provided in subsection (f), the rights and remedies provided by this title shall be in addition to any and all other rights and remedies that may exist at law or in equity; but no person permitted to maintain a suit for damages under the provisions of this title shall recover, through satisfaction of judgment in one or more actions, a total amount in excess of his actual damages on account of the act complained of. Except as otherwise specifically provided in this title, nothing in this title shall affect the jurisdiction of the securities commission (or any agency or officer performing like functions) of any State over any security or any person insofar as it does not conflict with the provisions of this title or the rules and regulations thereunder. No State law which prohibits or regulates the making or promoting of wagering or gaming contracts, or the operation of "bucket shops" or other similar or related activities, shall invalidate any put, call, straddle, option, privilege, or other security subject to this title, or apply to any activity which is incidental or related to the offer, purchase, sale, exercise, settlement, or closeout of any such security. No provision of State law regarding the offer, sale, or distribution of securities shall apply to any transaction in a security futures product, except that this sentence shall not be construed as limiting any State antifraud law of general applicability.

b.   **Modification of disciplinary procedures.**   Nothing in this title shall be construed to modify existing law with regard to the binding effect (1) on any member of or participant in any self- regulatory organization of any action taken by the authorities of such organization to settle disputes between its members or participants, (2) on any municipal securities dealer or municipal securities broker of any action taken pursuant to a procedure established by the Municipal Securities Rulemaking Board to settle disputes between municipal securities dealers and municipal securities brokers, or (3) of any action described in paragraph (1) or (2) on any person who has agreed to be bound thereby.

c.   **Continuing validity of disciplinary sanctions.**   The stay, setting aside, or modification pursuant to section 19(e) of any disciplinary sanction imposed by a self-regulatory organization on a member thereof, person associated with a member, or participant therein, shall not affect the validity or force of any action taken as a result of such sanction by the self-regulatory organization prior to such stay, setting aside, or modification: *Provided,* That such action is not inconsistent with the provisions of this title or the rules or regulations thereunder. The rights of any person acting in good faith which arise out of any such action shall not be affected in any way by such stay, setting aside, or modification.

d.   **Physical location of facilities of registered clearing agencies or registered transfer agents not to subject changes in beneficial or record ownership of securities to State or local taxes**.   No State or political subdivision thereof shall impose any tax on any change in beneficial or record ownership of securities effected through the facilities of a registered clearing agency or registered transfer agent or any nominee thereof or custodian therefor or upon the delivery or transfer of securities to or through or receipt from such agency or agent or any nominee thereof or custodian therefor, unless such change is in beneficial or record ownership or such transfer or delivery or receipt would otherwise be taxable by such State or political subdivision if the facilities of such registered clearing agency, registered transfer agent, or any nominee thereof or custodian therefor were not physically located in the taxing State or political subdivision. No State or political subdivision thereof shall impose any tax on securities which are deposited in or retained by a registered clearing agency, registered transfer agent, or any nominee thereof or custodian therefor, unless such securities would otherwise be taxable by such State or political subdivision if the facilities of such registered clearing agency, registered transfer agent, or any nominee thereof or custodian therefor were not physically located in the taxing State or political subdivision.

e.   **Exchange, broker, and dealer commissions; brokerage and research services**

1.   No person using the mails, or any means or instrumentality of interstate commerce, in the exercise of investment discretion with respect to an account shall be deemed to have acted unlawfully or to have breached a fiduciary duty under State or Federal law unless expressly provided to the contrary by a law enacted by the Congress or any State subsequent to June 4, 1975, solely by reason of his having caused the account to pay a member of an exchange, broker, or dealer an amount of commission for effecting a securities transaction in excess of the amount of commission another member of an exchange, broker, or dealer would have charged for effecting that transaction, if such person determined in good faith that such amount of commission was reasonable in relation to the value of the brokerage and research services provided by such member, broker, or dealer, viewed in terms of either that particular transaction or his overall responsibilities with respect to the accounts as to which he exercises investment discretion. This subsection is exclusive and plenary insofar as conduct is covered by the foregoing, unless otherwise expressly provided by contract: *Provided, however,* That nothing in this subsection shall be construed to impair or limit the power of the Commission under any other provision of this title or otherwise.

2.   A person exercising investment discretion with respect to an account shall make such disclosure of his policies and practices with respect to commissions that will be paid for effecting securities transactions, at such times and in such manner, as the appropriate regulatory agency, by rule, may prescribe as necessary or appropriate in the public interest or for the protection of investors.

3.   For purposes of this subsection a person provides brokerage and research services insofar as he–

A.   furnishes advice, either directly or through publications or writings, as to the value of securities, the advisability of investing in, purchasing, or selling securities, and the availability of securities or purchasers or sellers of securities;

B.   furnishes analyses and reports concerning issuers, industries, securities, economic factors and trends, portfolio strategy, and the performance of accounts; or

C.   effects securities transactions and performs functions incidental thereto (such as clearance, settlement, and custody) or required in connection therewith by rules of the Commission or a self-regulatory organization of which such person is a member or person associated with a member or in which such person is a participant.

4.   The provisions of this subsection shall not apply with regard to securities that are security futures products.

f.   **Limitations on remedies**

1.   Class action limitations

No covered class action based upon the statutory or common law of any State or subdivision thereof may be maintained in any State or Federal court by any private party alleging–

A.   a misrepresentation or omission of a material fact in connection with the purchase or sale of a covered security; or

B.   that the defendant used or employed any manipulative or deceptive device or contrivance in connection with the purchase or sale of a covered security.

2.   Removal of covered class actions

Any covered class action brought in any State court involving a covered security, as set forth in paragraph (1), shall be removable to the Federal district court for the district in which the action is pending, and shall be subject to paragraph (1).

3.   Preservation of certain actions

A.   Actions under State law of State of incorporation

    i.   Actions preserved

Notwithstanding paragraph (1) or (2), a covered class action described in clause (ii) of this subparagraph that is based upon the statutory or common law of the State in which the issuer is incorporated (in the case of a corporation) or organized (in the case of any other entity) may be maintained in a State or Federal court by a private party.

    ii.   Permissible actions

A covered class action is described in this clause if it involves–

I.   the purchase or sale of securities by the issuer or an affiliate of the issuer exclusively from or to holders of equity securities of the issuer; or

II.   any recommendation, position, or other communication with respect to the sale of securities of an issuer that–

(aa) is made by or on behalf of the issuer or an affiliate of the issuer to holders of equity securities of the issuer; and (bb) concerns decisions of such equity holders with respect to voting their securities, acting in response to a tender or exchange offer, or exercising dissenters' or appraisal rights.

B.   State actions

    i.   In general

Notwithstanding any other provision of this subsection, nothing in this subsection may be construed to preclude a State or political subdivision thereof or a State pension plan from bringing an action involving a covered security on its own behalf, or as a member of a class comprised solely of other States, political subdivisions, or State pension plans that are named plaintiffs, and that have authorized participation, in such action.

    ii.   State pension plan defined

For purposes of this subparagraph, the term "State pension plan" means a pension plan established and maintained for its employees by the government of a State or political subdivision thereof, or by any agency or instrumentality thereof.

C.   Actions under contractual agreements between issuers and indenture trustees

Notwithstanding paragraph (1) or (2), a covered class action that seeks to enforce a contractual agreement between an issuer and an indenture trustee may be maintained in a State or Federal court by a party to the agreement or a successor to such party.

D. Remand of removed actions

In an action that has been removed from a State court pursuant to paragraph (2), if the Federal court determines that the action may be maintained in State court pursuant to this subsection, the Federal court shall remand such action to such State court.

4. Preservation of State jurisdiction

The securities commission (or any agency or office performing like functions) of any State shall retain jurisdiction under the laws of such State to investigate and bring enforcement actions.

5. Definitions

For purposes of this subsection, the following definitions shall apply:

A. Affiliate of the issuer

The term "affiliate of the issuer" means a person that directly or indirectly, through one or more intermediaries, controls or is controlled by or is under common control with, the issuer.

B. Covered class action

The term "covered class action" means–

i. any single lawsuit in which–

I. damages are sought on behalf of more than 50 persons or prospective class members, and questions of law or fact common to those persons or members of the prospective class, without reference to issues of individualized reliance on an alleged misstatement or omission, predominate over any questions affecting only individual persons or members; or

II. one or more named parties seek to recover damages on a representative basis on behalf of themselves and other unnamed parties similarly situated, and questions of law or fact common to those persons or members of the prospective class predominate over any questions affecting only individual persons or members; or

ii. any group of lawsuits filed in or pending in the same court and involving common questions of law or fact, in which–

I. damages are sought on behalf of more than 50 persons; and

II. the lawsuits are joined, consolidated, or otherwise proceed as a single action for any purpose.

C. Exception for derivative actions

Notwithstanding subparagraph (B), the term "covered class action" does not include an exclusively derivative action brought by one or more shareholders on behalf of a corporation.

D. Counting of certain class members

For purposes of this paragraph, a corporation, investment company, pension plan, partnership, or other entity, shall be treated as one person or prospective class member, but only if the entity is not established for the purpose of participating in the action.

E.   Covered security
        The term "covered security" means a security that satisfies the standards
        for a covered security specified in paragraph (1) or (2) of section 18(b)
        of the Securities Act of 1933, at the time during which it is alleged that
        the misrepresentation, omission, or manipulative or deceptive conduct
        occurred, except that such term shall not include any debt security that is
        exempt from registration under the Securities Act of 1933 pursuant to
        rules issued by the Commission under section 4(2) of the Securities Act
        of 1933.

F.   Rule of construction
        Nothing in this paragraph shall be construed to affect the discretion of a
        State court in determining whether actions filed in such court should be
        joined, consolidated, or otherwise allowed to proceed as a single action

Section 29 – Validity of Contracts

a.   **Waiver provisions.** Any condition, stipulation, or provision binding any person to
     waive compliance with any provision of this title or of any rule or regulation
     thereunder, or of any rule of an exchange required thereby shall be void.

b.   **Contract provisions in violation of title.** Every contract made in violation of any
     provision of this title or of any rule or regulation thereunder, and every contract
     (including any contract for listing a security on an exchange) heretofore or hereafter
     made, the performance of which involves the violation of, or the continuance of any
     relationship or practice in violation of, any provision of this title or any rule or
     regulation thereunder, shall be void (1) as regards the rights of any person who, in
     violation of any such provision, rule, or regulation, shall have made or engaged in the
     performance of any such contract, and (2) as regards the rights of any person who, not
     being a party to such contract, shall have acquired any right thereunder with actual
     knowledge of the facts by reason of which the making or performance of such
     contract was in violation of any such provision, rule, or regulation: Provided, (A) That
     no contract shall be void by reason of this subsection because of any violation of any
     rule or regulation prescribed pursuant to paragraph (3) of subsection (c) of section 15,
     and (B) that no contract shall be deemed to be void by reason of this subsection in any
     action maintained in reliance upon this subsection, by any person to or for whom any
     broker or dealer sells, or from or for whom any broker or dealer purchases, a security
     in violation of any rule or regulation prescribed pursuant to paragraph (1) or (2) of
     subsection (c) of section 15, unless such action is brought within one year after the
     discovery that such sale or purchase involves such violation and within three years
     after such violation. The Commission may, in a rule or regulation prescribed pursuant
     to such paragraph (2) of such section 15(c), designate such rule or regulation, or
     portion thereof, as a rule or regulation, or portion thereof, a contract in violation of
     which shall not be void by reason of this subsection.

c.   **Validity of loans, extensions of credit, and creation of liens; actual knowledge of
     violation.** Nothing in this title shall be construed (1) to affect the validity of any loan
     or extension of credit (or any extension or renewal thereof) made or of any lien
     created prior or subsequent to the enactment of this title, unless at the time of the

making of such loan or extension of credit (or extension or renewal thereof) or the creating of such lien, the person making such loan or extension of credit (or extension or renewal thereof) or acquiring such lien shall have actual knowledge of facts by reason of which the making of such loan or extension of credit (or extension or renewal thereof) or the acquisition of such lien is a violation of the provisions of this title or any rule or regulation thereunder, or (2) to afford a defense to the collection of any debt or obligation or the enforcement of any lien by any person who shall have acquired such debt, obligation, or lien in good faith for value and without actual knowledge of the violation of any provision of this title or any rule or regulation thereunder affecting the legality of such debt, obligation, or lien.

Section 32 – Penalties

a. **Willful violations; false and misleading statements.** Any person who willfully violates any provision of this title (other than section 30A), or any rule or regulation thereunder the violation of which is made unlawful or the observance of which is required under the terms of this title, or any person who willfully and knowingly makes, or causes to be made, any statement in any application, report, or document required to be filed under this title or any rule or regulation thereunder or any undertaking contained in a registration statement as provided in subsection (d) of section 15, or by any self-regulatory organization in connection with an application for membership or participation therein or to become associated with a member thereof, which statement was false or misleading with respect to any material fact, shall upon conviction be fined not more than $5,000,000, or imprisoned not more than 20 years, or both, except that when such person is a person other than a natural person, a fine not exceeding $25,000,000 may be imposed; but no person shall be subject to imprisonment under this section for the violation of any rule or regulation if he proves that he had no knowledge of such rule or regulation.

b. **Failure to file information, documents, or reports.** Any issuer which fails to file information, documents, or reports required to be filed under subsection (d) of section 15 or any rule or regulation thereunder shall forfeit to the United States the sum of $100 for each and every day such failure to file shall continue. Such forfeiture, which shall be in lieu of any criminal penalty for such failure to file which might be deemed to arise under subsection (a) of this section, shall be payable into the Treasury of the United States and shall be recoverable in a civil suit in the name of the United States.

c. **Violations by issuers, officers, directors, stockholders, employees, or agents of issuers**
   1. A. Any issuer that violates subsection (a) or (g) of section 30A shall be fined not more than $2,000,000.
      B. Any issuer that violates subsection (a) or (g) of section 30A shall be subject to a civil penalty of not more than $10,000 imposed in an action brought by the Commission.
   2. A. Any officer, director, employee, or agent of an issuer, or stockholder acting on behalf of such issuer, who willfully violates subsection (a) or (g) of section 30A shall be fined not more than $100,000, or imprisoned not more than 5 years, or both.

    B.   Any officer, director, employee, or agent of an issuer, or stockholder acting on behalf of such issuer, who violates subsection (a) or (g) of section 30A shall be subject to a civil penalty of not more than $10,000 imposed in an action brought by the Commission.

  3.   Whenever a fine is imposed under paragraph (2) upon any officer, director, employee, agent, or stockholder of an issuer, such fine may not be paid, directly or indirectly, by such issuer.

Section 36 – General Exemptive Authority

  a. **Authority**

    1.   In general

    Except as provided in subsection (b) of this section, but notwithstanding any other provision of this title, the Commission, by rule, regulation, or order, may conditionally or unconditionally exempt any person, security, or transaction, or any class or classes of persons, securities, or transactions, from any provision or provisions of this title or of any rule or regulation thereunder, to the extent that such exemption is necessary or appropriate in the public interest, and is consistent with the protection of investors.

    2.   Procedures

    The Commission shall, by rule or regulation, determine the procedures under which an exemptive order under this section shall be granted and may, in its sole discretion, decline to entertain any application for an order of exemption under this section.

  b. **Limitation**. The Commission may not, under this section, exempt any person, security, or transaction, or any class or classes of persons, securities, or transactions from section 15C or the rules or regulations issued thereunder or (for purposes of section 15C and the rules and regulations issued thereunder) from any definition in paragraph (42), (43), (44), or (45) of section 3(a).

Rule 10A-1 – Notice to the Commission Pursuant to Section 10A of the Act

a.

    1.   If any issuer with a reporting obligation under the Act receives a report requiring a notice to the Commission in accordance with section 10A(b)(3) of the Act, the issuer shall submit such notice to the Commission's Office of the Chief Accountant within the time period prescribed in that section. The notice may be provided by facsimile, telegraph, personal delivery, or any other means, provided it is received by the Office of the Chief Accountant within the required time period.

    2.   The notice specified in paragraph (a)(1) of this section shall be in writing and:

        i.   Shall identify the issuer (including the issuer's name, address, phone number, and file number assigned to the issuer's filings by the Commission) and the independent accountant (including the independent accountant's name and phone number, and the address of the independent accountant's principal office);

        ii.   Shall state the date that the issuer received from the independent accountant the report specified in section 10A(b)(2) of the Act;

        iii.   Shall provide, at the election of the issuer, either:

            A.   A summary of the independent accountant's report, including a description of the act that the independent accountant has identified as a likely illegal act and the possible effect of that act on all affected financial statements of the issuer or those related to the most current three-year period, whichever is shorter; or

            B.   A copy of the independent accountant's report; and

        iv.   May provide additional information regarding the issuer's views of and response to the independent accountant's report.

    3.   Reports of the independent accountant submitted by the issuer to the Commission's Office of the Chief Accountant in accordance with paragraph (a)(2)(iii)(B) of this section shall be deemed to have been made pursuant to section 10A(b)(3) or section 10A(b)(4) of the Act, for purposes of the safe harbor provided by section 10A(c) of the Act.

    4.   Submission of the notice in paragraphs (a)(1) and (a)(2) of this section shall not relieve the issuer from its obligations to comply fully with all other reporting requirements, including, without limitation:

        i.   The filing requirements of Form 8-K, and Form N-SAR, regarding a change in the issuer's certifying accountant and

        ii.   The disclosure requirements of Item 304 of Regulation S-K.

b.

    1.   Any independent accountant furnishing to the Commission a copy of a report (or the documentation of any oral report) in accordance with section 10A(b)(3) or section 10A(b)(4) of the Act shall submit that report (or documentation) to the Commission's Office of the Chief Accountant within the time period prescribed by the appropriate section of the Act. The report (or documentation) may be submitted to the Commission's Office of the Chief Accountant by facsimile, telegraph, personal delivery, or any other means, provided it is received by the Office of the Chief Accountant within the time period set forth

in section 10A(b)(3) or 10A(b)(4) of the Act, whichever is applicable in the circumstances.

2. If the report (or documentation) submitted to the Office of the Chief Accountant in accordance with paragraph (b)(1) of this section does not clearly identify both the issuer (including the issuer's name, address, phone number, and file number assigned to the issuer's filings with the Commission) and the independent accountant (including the independent accountant's name and phone number, and the address of the independent accountant's principal office), then the independent accountant shall place that information in a prominent attachment to the report (or documentation) and shall submit that attachment to the Office of the Chief Accountant at the same time and in the same manner as the report (or documentation) is submitted to that Office.

3. Submission of the report (or documentation) by the independent accountant as described in paragraphs (b)(1) and (b)(2) of this section shall not replace, or otherwise satisfy the need for, the newly engaged and former accountants' letters under Items 304(a)(2)(D) and 304(a)(3) of Regulation S-K, respectively, and under items 304(a)(2)(D) and 304(a)(3) of Regulation S-B, respectively, and shall not limit, reduce, or affect in any way the independent accountant's obligations to comply fully with all other legal and professional responsibilities, including, without limitation, those under generally accepted auditing standards and the rules or interpretations of the Commission that modify or supplement those auditing standards.

c. A notice or report submitted to the Office of the Chief Accountant in accordance with paragraphs (a) and (b) of this section shall be deemed to be an investigative record and shall be non-public and exempt from disclosure pursuant to the Freedom of Information Act to the same extent and for the same periods of time that the Commission's investigative records are non-public and exempt from disclosure under, among other applicable provisions, 5 U.S.C. 552(b)(7) and 17 CFR 200.80(b)(7). Nothing in this paragraph, however, shall relieve, limit, delay, or affect in any way, the obligation of any issuer or any independent accountant to make all public disclosures required by law, by any Commission disclosure item, rule, report, or form, or by any applicable accounting, auditing, or professional standard.

Instruction to Paragraph (c). Issuers and independent accountants may apply for additional bases for confidential treatment for a notice, report, or part thereof, in accordance with 17 CFR 200.83. That section indicates, in part, that any person who, pursuant to any requirement of law, submits any information or causes or permits any information to be submitted to the Commission, may request that the Commission afford it confidential treatment by reason of personal privacy or business confidentiality, or for any other reason permitted by Federal law.

Rule 10A-2 – Auditor Independence

It shall be unlawful for an auditor not to be independent under Rule 2-01(c)(2)(iii)(B), (c)(4), (c)(6), (c)(7), and Rule 2-07 of Regulation S-X.

Rule 10A-3 – Listing Standards Relating to Audit Committees

a. Pursuant to section 10A(m) of the Securities Exchange Act of 1934 (the "Act") and section 3 of the Sarbanes-Oxley Act of 2002:

    1. National securities exchanges. The rules of each national securities exchange registered pursuant to section 6 of the Act must, in accordance with the provisions of this section, prohibit the initial or continued listing of any security of an issuer that is not in compliance with the requirements of any portion of paragraph (b) or (c) of this section.

    2. National securities associations. The rules of each national securities association registered pursuant to section 15A of the Act must, in accordance with the provisions of this section, prohibit the initial or continued listing in an automated inter-dealer quotation system of any security of an issuer that is not in compliance with the requirements of any portion of paragraph (b) or (c) of this section.

    3. Opportunity to cure defects. The rules required by paragraphs (a)(1) and (a)(2) of this section must provide for appropriate procedures for a listed issuer to have an opportunity to cure any defects that would be the basis for a prohibition under paragraph (a) of this section, before the imposition of such prohibition. Such rules also may provide that if a member of an audit committee ceases to be independent in accordance with the requirements of this section for reasons outside the member's reasonable control, that person, with notice by the issuer to the applicable national securities exchange or national securities association, may remain an audit committee member of the listed issuer until the earlier of the next annual shareholders meeting of the listed issuer or one year from the occurrence of the event that caused the member to be no longer independent.

    4. Notification of noncompliance. The rules required by paragraphs (a)(1) and (a)(2) of this section must include a requirement that a listed issuer must notify the applicable national securities exchange or national securities association promptly after an executive officer of the listed issuer becomes aware of any material noncompliance by the listed issuer with the requirements of this section.

    5. Implementation.

        i. The rules of each national securities exchange or national securities association meeting the requirements of this section must be operative, and listed issuers must be in compliance with those rules, by the following dates:

            A. July 31, 2005 for foreign private issuers and small business issuers (as defined in Rule 12b-2); and

            B. For all other listed issuers, the earlier of the listed issuer's first annual shareholders meeting after January 15, 2004, or October 31, 2004.

        ii. Each national securities exchange and national securities association must provide to the Commission, no later than July 15, 2003, proposed rules or rule amendments that comply with this section.

    iii.   Each national securities exchange and national securities association must have final rules or rule amendments that comply with this section approved by the Commission no later than December 1, 2003.

b. **Required standards**.
    1.   Independence.
        i.   Each member of the audit committee must be a member of the board of directors of the listed issuer, and must otherwise be independent; provided that, where a listed issuer is one of two dual holding companies, those companies may designate one audit committee for both companies so long as each member of the audit committee is a member of the board of directors of at least one of such dual holding companies.
        ii.   Independence requirements for non-investment company issuers. In order to be considered to be independent for purposes of this paragraph (b)(1), a member of an audit committee of a listed issuer that is not an investment company may not, other than in his or her capacity as a member of the audit committee, the board of directors, or any other board committee:
            A. Accept directly or indirectly any consulting, advisory, or other compensatory fee from the issuer or any subsidiary thereof, provided that, unless the rules of the national securities exchange or national securities association provide otherwise, compensatory fees do not include the receipt of fixed amounts of compensation under a retirement plan (including deferred compensation) for prior service with the listed issuer (provided that such compensation is not contingent in any way on continued service); or
            B. Be an affiliated person of the issuer or any subsidiary thereof.
        iii.   Independence requirements for investment company issuers. In order to be considered to be independent for purposes of this paragraph (b)(1), a member of an audit committee of a listed issuer that is an investment company may not, other than in his or her capacity as a member of the audit committee, the board of directors, or any other board committee:
            A. Accept directly or indirectly any consulting, advisory, or other compensatory fee from the issuer or any subsidiary thereof, provided that, unless the rules of the national securities exchange or national securities association provide otherwise, compensatory fees do not include the receipt of fixed amounts of compensation under a retirement plan (including deferred compensation) for prior service with the listed issuer (provided that such compensation is not contingent in any way on continued service); or
            B. Be an "interested person" of the issuer as defined in section 2(a)(19) of the Investment Company Act of 1940.
        iv.   Exemptions from the independence requirements.
            A. For an issuer listing securities pursuant to a registration statement under section 12 of the Act, or for an issuer that has a registration statement under the Securities Act of 1933 covering an initial public offering of securities to be listed by the issuer, where in each case

the listed issuer was not, immediately prior to the effective date of such registration statement, required to file reports with the Commission pursuant to section 13(a) or 15(d) of the Act:

1.   All but one of the members of the listed issuer's audit committee may be exempt from the independence requirements of paragraph (b)(1)(ii) of this section for 90 days from the date of effectiveness of such registration statement; and

2.   A minority of the members of the listed issuer's audit committee may be exempt from the independence requirements of paragraph (b)(1)(ii) of this section for one year from the date of effectiveness of such registration statement.

B.   An audit committee member that sits on the board of directors of a listed issuer and an affiliate of the listed issuer is exempt from the requirements of paragraph (b)(1)(ii)(B) of this section if the member, except for being a director on each such board of directors, otherwise meets the independence requirements of paragraph (b)(1)(ii) of this section for each such entity, including the receipt of only ordinary-course compensation for serving as a member of the board of directors, audit committee or any other board committee of each such entity.

C.   An employee of a foreign private issuer who is not an executive officer of the foreign private issuer is exempt from the requirements of paragraph (b)(1)(ii) of this section if the employee is elected or named to the board of directors or audit committee of the foreign private issuer pursuant to the issuer's governing law or documents, an employee collective bargaining or similar agreement or other home country legal or listing requirements.

D.   An audit committee member of a foreign private issuer may be exempt from the requirements of paragraph (b)(1)(ii)(B) of this section if that member meets the following requirements:

1.   The member is an affiliate of the foreign private issuer or a representative of such an affiliate;

2.   The member has only observer status on, and is not a voting member or the chair of, the audit committee; and

3.   Neither the member nor the affiliate is an executive officer of the foreign private issuer.

E.   An audit committee member of a foreign private issuer may be exempt from the requirements of paragraph (b)(1)(ii)(B) of this section if that member meets the following requirements:

1.   The member is a representative or designee of a foreign government or foreign governmental entity that is an affiliate of the foreign private issuer; and

2.   The member is not an executive officer of the foreign private issuer.

F.   In addition to paragraphs (b)(1)(iv)(A) through (E) of this section, the Commission may exempt from the requirements of paragraphs (b)(1)(ii) or (b)(1)(iii) of this section a particular relationship with

379

respect to audit committee members, as the Commission determines appropriate in light of the circumstances.

2. *Responsibilities relating to registered public accounting firms.* The audit committee of each listed issuer, in its capacity as a committee of the board of directors, must be directly responsible for the appointment, compensation, retention and oversight of the work of any registered public accounting firm engaged (including resolution of disagreements between management and the auditor regarding financial reporting) for the purpose of preparing or issuing an audit report or performing other audit, review or attest services for the listed issuer, and each such registered public accounting firm must report directly to the audit committee.

3. *Complaints.* Each audit committee must establish procedures for:
   i. The receipt, retention, and treatment of complaints received by the listed issuer regarding accounting, internal accounting controls, or auditing matters; and
   ii. The confidential, anonymous submission by employees of the listed issuer of concerns regarding questionable accounting or auditing matters.

4. *Authority to engage advisers.* Each audit committee must have the authority to engage independent counsel and other advisers, as it determines necessary to carry out its duties.

5. *Funding.* Each listed issuer must provide for appropriate funding, as determined by the audit committee, in its capacity as a committee of the board of directors, for payment of:
   i. Compensation to any registered public accounting firm engaged for the purpose of preparing or issuing an audit report or performing other audit, review or attest services for the listed issuer;
   ii. Compensation to any advisers employed by the audit committee under paragraph (b)(4) of this section; and
   iii. Ordinary administrative expenses of the audit committee that are necessary or appropriate in carrying out its duties.

c. **General exemptions**.
   1. At any time when an issuer has a class of securities that is listed on a national securities exchange or national securities association subject to the requirements of this section, the listing of other classes of securities of the listed issuer on a national securities exchange or national securities association is not subject to the requirements of this section.
   2. At any time when an issuer has a class of common equity securities (or similar securities) that is listed on a national securities exchange or national securities association subject to the requirements of this section, the listing of classes of securities of a direct or indirect consolidated subsidiary or an at least 50% beneficially owned subsidiary of the issuer (except classes of equity securities, other than non-convertible, non-participating preferred securities, of such subsidiary) is not subject to the requirements of this section.
   3. The listing of securities of a foreign private issuer is not subject to the requirements of paragraphs (b)(1) through (b)(5) of this section if the foreign private issuer meets the following requirements:

        i.   The foreign private issuer has a board of auditors (or similar body), or has statutory auditors, established and selected pursuant to home country legal or listing provisions expressly requiring or permitting such a board or similar body;

        ii.   The board or body, or statutory auditors is required under home country legal or listing requirements to be either:
            A. Separate from the board of directors; or
            B. Composed of one or more members of the board of directors and one or more members that are not also members of the board of directors;

        iii.   The board or body, or statutory auditors, are not elected by management of such issuer and no executive officer of the foreign private issuer is a member of such board or body, or statutory auditors;

        iv.   Home country legal or listing provisions set forth or provide for standards for the independence of such board or body, or statutory auditors, from the foreign private issuer or the management of such issuer;

        v.   Such board or body, or statutory auditors, in accordance with any applicable home country legal or listing requirements or the issuer's governing documents, are responsible, to the extent permitted by law, for the appointment, retention and oversight of the work of any registered public accounting firm engaged (including, to the extent permitted by law, the resolution of disagreements between management and the auditor regarding financial reporting) for the purpose of preparing or issuing an audit report or performing other audit, review or attest services for the issuer; and

        vi.   The audit committee requirements of paragraphs (b)(3), (b)(4) and (b)(5) of this section apply to such board or body, or statutory auditors, to the extent permitted by law.

4.   The listing of a security futures product cleared by a clearing agency that is registered pursuant to section 17A of the Act or that is exempt from the registration requirements of section 17A pursuant to paragraph (b)(7)(A) of such section is not subject to the requirements of this section.

5.   The listing of a standardized option, as defined in Rule 9b-1(a)(4), issued by a clearing agency that is registered pursuant to section 17A of the Act is not subject to the requirements of this section.

6.   The listing of securities of the following listed issuers are not subject to the requirements of this section:
        i.   Asset-Backed Issuers (as defined in Rule 13a-14(g) and Rule 15d-14(g));
        ii.   Unit investment trusts (as defined in section 4(2) of the Investment Company Act of 1940); and
        iii.   Foreign governments (as defined in Rule 3b-4(a)).

7.   The listing of securities of a listed issuer is not subject to the requirements of this section if:
        i.   The listed issuer, as reflected in the applicable listing application, is organized as a trust or other unincorporated association that does not have a board of directors or persons acting in a similar capacity; and

ii.   The activities of the listed issuer that is described in paragraph (c)(7)(i) of this section are limited to passively owning or holding (as well as administering and distributing amounts in respect of) securities, rights, collateral or other assets on behalf of or for the benefit of the holders of the listed securities.

d. **Disclosure.** Any listed issuer availing itself of an exemption from the independence standards contained in paragraph (b)(1)(iv) of this section (except paragraph (b)(1)(iv)(B) of this section), the general exemption contained in paragraph (c)(3) of this section or the last sentence of paragraph (a)(3) of this section, must:

1. Disclose its reliance on the exemption and its assessment of whether, and if so, how, such reliance would materially adversely affect the ability of the audit committee to act independently and to satisfy the other requirements of this section in any proxy or information statement for a meeting of shareholders at which directors are elected that is filed with the Commission pursuant to the requirements of section 14 of the Act; and

2. Disclose the information specified in paragraph (d)(1) of this section in, or incorporate such information by reference from such proxy or information statement filed with the Commission into, its annual report filed with the Commission pursuant to the requirements of section 13(a) or 15(d) of the Act.

e. **Definitions.** Unless the context otherwise requires, all terms used in this section have the same meaning as in the Act. In addition, unless the context otherwise requires, the following definitions apply for purposes of this section:

1.

    i.   The term **affiliate** of, or a person **affiliated** with, a specified person, means a person that directly, or indirectly through one or more intermediaries, controls, or is controlled by, or is under common control with, the person specified.

    ii.

        A. A person will be deemed not to be in control of a specified person for purposes of this section if the person:

            1. Is not the beneficial owner, directly or indirectly, of more than 10% of any class of voting equity securities of the specified person; and

            2. Is not an executive officer of the specified person.

        B. Paragraph (e)(1)(ii)(A) of this section only creates a safe harbor position that a person does not control a specified person. The existence of the safe harbor does not create a presumption in any way that a person exceeding the ownership requirement in paragraph (e)(1)(ii)(A)(1) of this section controls or is otherwise an affiliate of a specified person.

    iii.   The following will be deemed to be affiliates:

        A. An executive officer of an affiliate;

        B. A director who also is an employee of an affiliate;

        C. A general partner of an affiliate; and

        D. A managing member of an affiliate.

     iv.   For purposes of paragraph (e)(1)(i) of this section, dual holding companies will not be deemed to be affiliates of or persons affiliated with each other by virtue of their dual holding company arrangements with each other, including where directors of one dual holding company are also directors of the other dual holding company, or where directors of one or both dual holding companies are also directors of the businesses jointly controlled, directly or indirectly, by the dual holding companies (and, in each case, receive only ordinary-course compensation for serving as a member of the board of directors, audit committee or any other board committee of the dual holding companies or any entity that is jointly controlled, directly or indirectly, by the dual holding companies).

2. In the case of foreign private issuers with a two-tier board system, the term **board of directors** means the supervisory or non-management board.

3. In the case of a listed issuer that is a limited partnership or limited liability company where such entity does not have a board of directors or equivalent body, the term **board of directors** means the board of directors of the managing general partner, managing member or equivalent body.

4. The term **control** (including the terms **controlling, controlled by** and under **common control with**) means the possession, direct or indirect, of the power to direct or cause the direction of the management and policies of a person, whether through the ownership of voting securities, by contract, or otherwise.

5. The term **dual holding companies** means two foreign private issuers that:
   i. Are organized in different national jurisdictions;
   ii. Collectively own and supervise the management of one or more businesses which are conducted as a single economic enterprise; and
   iii. Do not conduct any business other than collectively owning and supervising such businesses and activities reasonably incidental thereto.

6. The term **executive officer** has the meaning set forth in Rule 3b-7.

7. The term **foreign private issuer** has the meaning set forth in Rule 3b-4(c).

8. The term **indirect** acceptance by a member of an audit committee of any consulting, advisory or other compensatory fee includes acceptance of such a fee by a spouse, a minor child or stepchild or a child or stepchild sharing a home with the member or by an entity in which such member is a partner, member, an officer such as a managing director occupying a comparable position or executive officer, or occupies a similar position (except limited partners, non-managing members and those occupying similar positions who, in each case, have no active role in providing services to the entity) and which provides accounting, consulting, legal, investment banking or financial advisory services to the issuer or any subsidiary of the issuer.

9. The terms **listed** and **listing** refer to securities listed on a national securities exchange or listed in an automated inter-dealer quotation system of a national securities association or to issuers of such securities.

Instructions to Rule 10A-3:

1. The requirements in paragraphs (b)(2) through (b)(5), (c)(3)(v) and (c)(3)(vi) of this section do not conflict with, and do not affect the application of, any requirement or ability under a listed issuer's governing law or documents or other home country legal or listing provisions that requires or permits shareholders to ultimately vote on, approve or

ratifysuch requirements. The requirements instead relate to the assignment of responsibility as between the audit committee and management. In such an instance, however, if the listed issuer provides a recommendation or nomination regarding such responsibilities to shareholders, the audit committee of the listed issuer, or body performing similar functions, must be responsible for making the recommendation or nomination.

2. The requirements in paragraphs (b)(2) through (b)(5), (c)(3)(v), (c)(3)(vi) and Instruction 1 of this section do not conflict with any legal or listing requirement in a listed issuer'shome jurisdiction that prohibits the full board of directors from delegating such responsibilities to the listed issuer's audit committee or limits the degree of such delegation. In that case, the audit committee, or body performing similar functions, must be granted such responsibilities, which can include advisory powers, with respect to such matters to the extent permitted by law, including submitting nominations or recommendations to the full board.

3. The requirements in paragraphs (b)(2) through (b)(5), (c)(3)(v) and (c)(3)(vi) of this section do not conflict with any legal or listing requirement in a listed issuer's home jurisdiction that vests such responsibilities with a government entity or tribunal. In that case, the audit committee, or body performing similar functions, must be granted such responsibilities, which can include advisory powers, with respect to such matters to the extent permitted by law.

For purposes of this section, the determination of a person's beneficial ownership must be made in accordance with Rule 13d-3.

Rule 10b-5 – Employment of Manipulative and Deceptive Devices

It shall be unlawful for any person, directly or indirectly, by the use of any means or instrumentality of interstate commerce, or of the mails or of any facility of any national securities exchange,

a. To employ any device, scheme, or artifice to defraud,

b. To make any untrue statement of a material fact or to omit to state a material fact necessary in order to make the statements made, in the light of the circumstances under which they were made, not misleading, or

c. To engage in any act, practice, or course of business which operates or would operate as a fraud or deceit upon any person,

in connection with the purchase or sale of any security.

Rule 10b5-1 – Trading "on the Basis of" Material Nonpublic Information in Insider Trading Cases

Preliminary Note:

This provision defines when a purchase or sale constitutes trading "on the basis of" material nonpublic information in insider trading cases brought under Section 10(b) of the Act and Rule 10b-5 thereunder. The law of insider trading is otherwise defined by judicial opinions construing Rule 10b-5, and Rule 10b5-1 does not modify the scope of insider trading law in any other respect.

a. **General**. The "manipulative and deceptive devices" prohibited by Section 10(b) of the Act and Rule 10b-5 thereunder include, among other things, the purchase or sale of a security of any issuer, on the basis of material nonpublic information about that security or issuer, in breach of a duty of trust or confidence that is owed directly, indirectly, or derivatively, to the issuer of that security or the shareholders of that issuer, or to any other person who is the source of the material nonpublic information.

b. **Definition of "on the basis of."** Subject to the affirmative defenses in paragraph (c) of this section, a purchase or sale of a security of an issuer is "on the basis of" material nonpublic information about that security or issuer if the person making the purchase or sale was aware of the material nonpublic information when the person made the purchase or sale.

c. **Affirmative defenses**.
    1.   i.   Subject to paragraph (c)(1)(ii) of this section, a person's purchase or sale is not "on the basis of" material nonpublic information if the person making the purchase or sale demonstrates that:
            A. Before becoming aware of the information, the person had:
                1. Entered into a binding contract to purchase or sell the security,
                2. Instructed another person to purchase or sell the security for the instructing person's account, or
                3. Adopted a written plan for trading securities;
            B. The contract, instruction, or plan described in paragraph (c)(1)(i)(A) of this Section:
                1. Specified the amount of securities to be purchased or sold and the price at which and the date on which the securities were to be purchased or sold;
                2. Included a written formula or algorithm, or computer program, for determining the amount of securities to be purchased or sold and the price at which and the date on which the securities were to be purchased or sold; or
                3. Did not permit the person to exercise any subsequent influence over how, when, or whether to effect purchases or sales; provided, in addition, that any other person who, pursuant to the contract, instruction, or plan, did exercise such influence must not have been aware of the material nonpublic information when doing so; and
            C. The purchase or sale that occurred was pursuant to the contract, instruction, or plan. A purchase or sale is not "pursuant to a contract, instruction, or plan" if, among other things, the person who entered into the contract, instruction, or plan altered or deviated from the contract, instruction, or plan to purchase or sell securities (whether by changing the amount, price, or timing of the purchase or sale), or entered into or altered a corresponding or hedging transaction or position with respect to those securities.
            ii. Paragraph (c)(1)(i) of this section is applicable only when the contract, instruction, or plan to purchase or sell securities was given or entered

385

into in good faith and not as part of a plan or scheme to evade the prohibitions of this section.

    iii. This paragraph (c)(1)(iii) defines certain terms as used in paragraph (c) of this Section.

        A. *Amount.* "Amount" means either a specified number of shares or other securities or a specified dollar value of securities.

        B. *Price.* "Price" means the market price on a particular date or a limit price, or a particular dollar price.

        C. *Date.* "Date" means, in the case of a market order, the specific day of the year on which the order is to be executed (or as soon thereafter as is practicable under ordinary principles of best execution). "Date" means, in the case of a limit order, a day of the year on which the limit order is in force.

2. A person other than a natural person also may demonstrate that a purchase or sale of securities is not "on the basis of" material nonpublic information if the person demonstrates that:

    i. The individual making the investment decision on behalf of the person to purchase or sell the securities was not aware of the information; and

    ii. The person had implemented reasonable policies and procedures, taking into consideration the nature of the person's business, to ensure that individuals making investment decisions would not violate the laws prohibiting trading on the basis of material nonpublic information. These policies and procedures may include those that restrict any purchase, sale, and causing any purchase or sale of any security as to which the person has material nonpublic information, or those that prevent such individuals from becoming aware of such information.

Rule 10b5-2 – Duties of Trust or Confidence in Misappropriation Insider Trading Cases

Preliminary Note:

This section provides a non-exclusive definition of circumstances in which a person has a duty of trust or confidence for purposes of the "misappropriation" theory of insider trading under Section 10(b) of the Act and Rule 10b-5. The law of insider trading is otherwise defined by judicial opinions construing Rule 10b-5, and Rule 10b5-2 does not modify the scope of insider trading law in any other respect.

    a. **Scope of Rule.** This section shall apply to any violation of Section 10(b) of the Act and Rule 10b-5 thereunder that is based on the purchase or sale of securities on the basis of, or the communication of, material nonpublic information misappropriated in breach of a duty of trust or confidence.

    b. **Enumerated "duties of trust or confidence."** For purposes of this section, a *duty of trust or confidence* exists in the following circumstances, among others:

        1. Whenever a person agrees to maintain information in confidence;

        2. Whenever the person communicating the material nonpublic information and the person to whom it is communicated have a history, pattern, or practice of sharing confidences, such that the recipient of the information knows or reasonably should know that the person communicating the material nonpublic information expects that the recipient will maintain its confidentiality; or

3. Whenever a person receives or obtains material nonpublic information from his or her spouse, parent, child, or sibling; *provided, however*, that the person receiving or obtaining the information may demonstrate that no duty of trust or confidence existed with respect to the information, by establishing that he or she neither knew nor reasonably should have known that the person who was the source of the information expected that the person would keep the information confidential, because of the parties' history, pattern, or practice of sharing and maintaining confidences, and because there was no agreement or understanding to maintain the confidentiality of the information.

Rule 10b-9 – Prohibited Representations in Connection with Certain Offerings

a. It shall constitute a *manipulative or deception device or contrivance*, as used in section 10(b) of the Act, for any person, directly or indirectly, in connection with the offer or sale of any security, to make any representation:
   1. To the effect that the security is being offered or sold on an "all-or-none" basis, unless the security is part of an offering or distribution being made on the condition that all or a specified amount of the consideration paid for such security will be promptly refunded to the purchaser unless
      A. all of the securities being offered are sold at a specified price within a specified time, and
      B. the total amount due to the seller is received by him by a specified date; or
   2. To the effect that the security is being offered or sold on any other basis whereby all or part of the consideration paid for any such security will be refunded to the purchaser if all or some of the securities are not sold, unless the security is part of an offering or distribution being made on the condition that all or a specified part of the consideration paid for such security will be promptly refunded to the purchaser unless
      A. a specified number of units of the security are sold at a specified price within a specified time, and
      B. the total amount due to the seller is received by him by a specified date.

b. This rule shall not apply to any offer or sale of securities as to which the seller has a firm commitment from underwriters or others (subject only to customary conditions precedent, including "market outs") for the purchase of all the securities being offered.

Rule 10b-18 – Purchases of Certain Equity Securities by the Issuer and Others

Preliminary Notes:
   1. Rule 10b-18 provides an issuer (and its affiliated purchasers) with a "safe harbor" from liability for manipulation under sections 9(a)(2) of the Act and Rule 10b-5 under the Act solely by reason of the manner, timing, price, and volume of their repurchases when they repurchase the issuer's common stock in the market in accordance with the section's manner, timing, price, and volume conditions. As a safe harbor, compliance with Rule 10b-18 is voluntary. To come within the safe harbor, however, an issuer's repurchases must satisfy (on a daily basis) each of the section's four conditions.

Failure to meet any one of the four conditions will remove all of the issuer's repurchases from the safe harbor for that day. The safe harbor, moreover, is not available for repurchases that, although made in technical compliance with the section, are part of a plan or scheme to evade the federal securities laws.

2. Regardless of whether the repurchases are effected in accordance with Rule 10b-18, reporting issuers must report their repurchasing activity as required by Item 703 of Regulation S-K and Item 15(e) of Form 20-F (regarding foreign private issuers), and closed-end management investment companies that are registered under the Investment Company Act of 1940 must report their repurchasing activity as required by Item 8 of Form N-CSR.

a. **Definitions.** Unless otherwise provided, all terms used in this section shall have the same meaning as in the Act. In addition, the following definitions shall apply:

1. **ADTV** means the average daily trading volume reported for the security during the four calendar weeks preceding the week in which the Rule 10b-18 purchase is to be effected.

2. **Affiliate** means any person that directly or indirectly controls, is controlled by, or is under common control with, the issuer.

3. **Affiliated purchaser** means:
   i.   A person acting, directly or indirectly, in concert with the issuer for the purpose of acquiring the issuer's securities; or
   ii.   An affiliate who, directly or indirectly, controls the issuer's purchases of such securities, whose purchases are controlled by the issuer, or whose purchases are under common control with those of the issuer; *Provided, however*, that "affiliated purchaser" shall not include a broker, dealer, or other person solely by reason of such broker, dealer, or other person effecting Rule 10b-18 purchases on behalf of the issuer or for its account, and shall not include an officer or director of the issuer solely by reason of that officer or director's participation in the decision to authorize Rule 10b-18 purchases by or on behalf of the issuer.

4. **Agent independent of the issuer** has the meaning contained in Rule 100 of this chapter.

5. **Block** means a quantity of stock that either:
   i.   Has a purchase price of $200,000 or more; or
   ii.   Is at least 5,000 shares and has a purchase price of at least $50,000; or
   iii. Is at least 20 round lots of the security and totals 150 percent or more of the trading volume for that security or, in the event that trading volume data are unavailable, is at least 20 round lots of the security and totals at least one-tenth of one percent (.001) of the outstanding shares of the security, exclusive of any shares owned by any affiliate;
   Provided, however, That a block under paragraph (a)(5)(i), (ii), and (iii) shall not include any amount a broker or dealer, acting as principal, has accumulated for the purpose of sale or resale to the issuer or to any affiliated purchaser of the issuer if the issuer or such affiliated purchaser knows or has reason to know that such amount was accumulated for such purpose, nor shall it include any amount that a broker or dealer has sold short to the issuer or to any affiliated purchaser of the issuer if the

issuer or such affiliated purchaser knows or has reason to know that the sale was a short sale.

6. **Consolidated system** means a consolidated transaction or quotation reporting system that collects and publicly disseminates on a current and continuous basis transaction or quotation information in common equity securities pursuant to an effective transaction reporting plan (Rule 11Aa3-1) or a national market system plan (as defined in Rule 11Aa3-2).

7. **Market-wide trading suspension** means a market-wide trading halt of 30 minutes or more that is:
    i. Imposed pursuant to the rules of a national securities exchange or a national securities association in response to a market-wide decline during a single trading session; or
    ii. Declared by the Commission pursuant to its authority under section 12(k) of the Act.

8. **Plan** has the meaning contained in Rule 100 of this chapter.

9. **Principal market for a security** means the single securities market with the largest reported trading volume for the security during the six full calendar months preceding the week in which the Rule 10b-18 purchase is to be effected.

10. **Public float value** has the meaning contained in Rule 100 of this chapter.

11. **Purchase price** means the price paid per share as reported, exclusive of any commission paid to a broker acting as agent, or commission equivalent, mark-up, or differential paid to a dealer.

12. **Riskless principal transaction** means a transaction in which a broker or dealer after having received an order from an issuer to buy its security, buys the security as principal in the market at the same price to satisfy the issuer's buy order. The issuer's buy order must be effected at the same price per-share at which the broker or dealer bought the shares to satisfy the issuer's buy order, exclusive of any explicitly disclosed markup or markdown, commission equivalent, or other fee. In addition, only the first leg of the transaction, when the broker or dealer buys the security in the market as principal, is reported under the rules of a self-regulatory organization or under the Act. For purposes of this section, the broker or dealer must have written policies and procedures in place to assure that, at a minimum, the issuer's buy order was received prior to the offsetting transaction; the offsetting transaction is allocated to a riskless principal account or the issuer's account within 60 seconds of the execution; and the broker or dealer has supervisory systems in place to produce records that enable the broker or dealer to accurately and readily reconstruct, in a time-sequenced manner, all orders effected on a riskless principal basis.

13. **Rule 10b-18 purchase** means a purchase (or any bid or limit order that would effect such purchase) of an issuer's common stock (or an equivalent interest, including a unit of beneficial interest in a trust or limited partnership or a depository share) by or for the issuer or any affiliated purchaser (including riskless principal transactions). However, it does not include any purchase of such security:
    i. Effected during the applicable restricted period of a distribution that is subject to Rule 102 of this chapter;
    ii. Effected by or for an issuer plan by an agent independent of the issuer;

　　　iii. Effected as a fractional share purchase (a fractional interest in a security) evidenced by a script certificate, order form, or similar document;

　　　iv. Effected during the period from the time of public announcement (as defined in Rule 165(f)) of a merger, acquisition, or similar transaction involving a recapitalization, until the earlier of the completion of such transaction or the completion of the vote by target shareholders. This exclusion does not apply to Rule 10b-18 purchases:

　　　　　A. Effected during such transaction in which the consideration is solely cash and there is no valuation period; or

　　　　　B. Where:

　　　　　　　1. The total volume of Rule 10b-18 purchases effected on any single day does not exceed the lesser of 25% of the security's four-week ADTV or the issuer's average daily Rule 10b-18 purchases during the three full calendar months preceding the date of the announcement of such transaction;

　　　　　　　2. The issuer's block purchases effected pursuant to paragraph (b)(4) of this section do not exceed the average size and frequency of the issuer's block purchases effected pursuant to paragraph (b)(4) of this section during the three full calendar months preceding the date of the announcement of such transaction; and

　　　　　　　3. Such purchases are not otherwise restricted or prohibited;

　　　v. Effected pursuant to Rule 13e-1;

　　　vi. Effected pursuant to a tender offer that is subject to Rule 13e-4 or specifically excepted from Rule 13e-4; or

　　　vii. Effected pursuant to a tender offer that is subject to section 14(d) of the Act and the rules and regulations thereunder.

b. **Conditions to be met**. Rule 10b-18 purchases shall not be deemed to have violated the anti-manipulation provisions of sections 9(a)(2) or 10(b) of the Act or Rule 10b-5 under the Act, solely by reason of the time, price, or amount of the Rule 10b-18 purchases, or the number of brokers or dealers used in connection with such purchases, if the issuer or affiliated purchaser of the issuer effects the Rule 10b-18 purchases according to each of the following conditions:

　1. One broker or dealer. Rule 10b-18 purchases must be effected from or through only one broker or dealer on any single day; *Provided, however*, that:

　　　i. The "one broker or dealer" condition shall not apply to Rule 10b-18 purchases that are not solicited by or on behalf of the issuer or its affiliated purchaser(s);

　　　ii. Where Rule 10b-18 purchases are effected by or on behalf of more than one affiliated purchaser of the issuer (or the issuer and one or more of its affiliated purchasers) on a single day, the issuer and all affiliated purchasers must use the same broker or dealer; and

　　　iii. Where Rule 10b-18 purchases are effected on behalf of the issuer by a broker-dealer that is not an electronic communication network (ECN) or other alternative trading system (ATS), that broker-dealer can access

ECN or other ATS liquidity in order to execute repurchases on behalf of the issuer (or any affiliated purchaser of the issuer) on that day.

2.   Time of purchases. Rule 10b-18 purchases must not be:
   i.   The opening (regular way) purchase reported in the consolidated system;
   ii. Effected during the 10 minutes before the scheduled close of the primary trading session in the principal market for the security, and the 10 minutes before the scheduled close of the primary trading session in the market where the purchase is effected, for a security that has an ADTV value of $1 million or more and a public float value of $150 million or more; and
   iii. Effected during the 30 minutes before the scheduled close of the primary trading session in the principal market for the security, and the 30 minutes before the scheduled close of the primary trading session in the market where the purchase is effected, for all other securities;
   iv. However, for purposes of this section, Rule 10b-18 purchases may be effected following the close of the primary trading session until the termination of the period in which last sale prices are reported in the consolidated system so long as such purchases are effected at prices that do not exceed the lower of the closing price of the primary trading session in the principal market for the security and any lower bids or sale prices subsequently reported in the consolidated system, and all of this section's conditions are met. However, for purposes of this section, the issuer may use one broker or dealer to effect Rule 10b-18 purchases during this period that may be different from the broker or dealer that it used during the primary trading session. However, the issuer's Rule 10b-18 purchase may not be the opening transaction of the session following the close of the primary trading session.

3.   Price of purchases. Rule 10b-18 purchases must be effected at a purchase price that:
   i.   Does not exceed the highest independent bid or the last independent transaction price, whichever is higher, quoted or reported in the consolidated system at the time the Rule 10b-18 purchase is effected;
   ii. For securities for which bids and transaction prices are not quoted or reported in the consolidated system, Rule 10b-18 purchases must be effected at a purchase price that does not exceed the highest independent bid or the last independent transaction price, whichever is higher, displayed and disseminated on any national securities exchange or on any inter-dealer quotation system (as defined in Rule.15c2-11) that displays at least two priced quotations for the security, at the time the Rule 10b-18 purchase is effected; and
   iii. For all other securities, Rule 10b-18 purchases must be effected at a price no higher than the highest independent bid obtained from three independent dealers.

4.   Volume of purchases. The total volume of Rule 10b-18 purchases effected by or for the issuer and any affiliated purchasers effected on any single day must not exceed 25 percent of the ADTV for that security; However, once each

week, in lieu of purchasing under the 25% of ADTV limit for that day, the issuer or an affiliated purchaser of the issuer may effect one block purchase if:

    i.   No other Rule 10b-18 purchases are effected that day, and

    ii.   The block purchase is not included when calculating a security's four week ADTV under this section.

c.   **Alternative conditions.** The conditions of paragraph (b) of this section shall apply in connection with Rule 10b-18 purchases effected during a trading session following the imposition of a market-wide trading suspension, except:

    1.   That the time of purchases condition in paragraph (b)(2) of this section shall not apply, either:

        i.   From the reopening of trading until the scheduled close of trading on the day that the market-wide trading suspension is imposed; or

        ii.   At the opening of trading on the next trading day until the scheduled close of trading that day, if a market-wide trading suspension was in effect at the close of trading on the preceding day; and

    2.   The volume of purchases condition in paragraph (b)(4) of this section is modified so that the amount of Rule 10b-18 purchases must not exceed 100 percent of the ADTV for that security.

d.   **Other purchases.** No presumption shall arise that an issuer or an affiliated purchaser has violated the anti-manipulation provisions of sections 9(a)(2) or 10(b) of the Act, or Rule 10b-5 under the Act, if the Rule 10b-18 purchases of such issuer or affiliated purchaser do not meet the conditions specified in paragraph (b) or (c) of this section.

Rule 12b-2 – Definitions

Unless the context otherwise requires, the following terms, when used in the rules contained in this regulation or in Regulation 13A or 15D or in the forms for statements and reports filed pursuant to Sections 12, 13 or 15(d) of the act, shall have the respective meanings indicated in this rule:

Accelerated filer and large accelerated filer.

    1.   The term "accelerated filer" means an issuer after it first meets the following conditions as of the end of its fiscal year:

        i.   The issuer had an aggregate worldwide market value of the voting and non-voting common equity held by its non-affiliates of $75 million or more, but less than $700 million, as of the last business day of the issuer's most recently completed second fiscal quarter;

        ii.   The issuer has been subject to the requirements of section 13(a) or 15(d) of the Act for a period of at least twelve calendar months;

        iii.   The issuer has filed at least one annual report pursuant to section 13(a) or 15(d) of the Act; and

        iv.   The issuer is not eligible to use the requirements for smaller reporting companies in Part 229 of this chapter for its annual and quarterly reports.

    2.   *Large accelerated filer.* The term large accelerated filer means an issuer after it first meets the following conditions as of the end of its fiscal year:

    i.   The issuer had an aggregate worldwide market value of the voting and non-voting common equity held by its non-affiliates of $700 million or more, as of the last business day of the issuer's most recently completed second fiscal quarter;

    ii.   The issuer has been subject to the requirements of section 13(a) or 15(d) of the Act for a period of at least twelve calendar months;

    iii.   The issuer has filed at least one annual report pursuant to section 13(a) or 15(d) of the Act; and

    iv.   The issuer is not eligible to use the requirements for smaller reporting companies in Part 229 of this chapter for its annual and quarterly reports.

3.   *Entering and Exiting Accelerated Filer Status.*

    i.   The determination at the end of the issuer's fiscal year for whether a nonaccelerated filer becomes an accelerated filer, or whether a non-accelerated filer or accelerated filer becomes a large accelerated filer, governs the deadlines for the annual report to be filed for that fiscal year, the quarterly and annual reports to be filed for the subsequent fiscal year and all annual and quarterly reports to be filed thereafter while the issuer remains an accelerated filer or large accelerated filer.

    ii.   Once an issuer becomes an accelerated filer, it will remain an accelerated filer unless the issuer determines at the end of a fiscal year that the aggregate worldwide market value of the voting and non-voting common equity held by non-affiliates of the issuer was less than $50 million, as of the last business day of the issuer's most recently completed second fiscal quarter. An issuer making this determination becomes a nonaccelerated filer. The issuer will not become an accelerated filer again unless it subsequently meets the conditions in paragraph (1) of this definition.

    iii.   Once an issuer becomes a large accelerated filer, it will remain a large accelerated filer unless the issuer determines at the end of a fiscal year that the aggregate worldwide market value of the voting and non-voting common equity held by non-affiliates of the issuer was less than $500 million, as of the last business day of the issuer's most recently completed second fiscal quarter. If the issuer's aggregate worldwide market value was $50 million or more, but less than $500 million, as of the last business day of the issuer's most recently completed second fiscal quarter, the issuer becomes an accelerated filer. If the issuer's aggregate worldwide market value was less than $50 million, as of the last business day of the issuer's most recently completed second fiscal quarter, the issuer becomes a nonaccelerated filer. An issuer will not become a large accelerated filer again unless it subsequently meets the conditions in paragraph (2) of this definition.

    iv.   The determination at the end of the issuer's fiscal year for whether an accelerated filer becomes a nonaccelerated filer, or a large accelerated filer becomes an accelerated filer or a non-accelerated filer, governs the deadlines for the annual report to be filed for that fiscal year, the quarterly and annual reports to be filed for the subsequent fiscal year and all annual and quarterly reports to be filed thereafter while the issuer remains an accelerated filer or non-accelerated filer.

Note to paragraphs (1), (2) and (3): The aggregate worldwide market value of the issuer's outstanding voting and non-voting common equity shall be computed by use of the price at which the common equity was last sold, or the average of the bid and asked prices of such common equity, in the principal market for such common equity.

Affiliate. An "affiliate" of, or a person "affiliated" with, a specified person, is a person that directly, or indirectly through one or more intermediaries, controls, or is controlled by, or is under common control with, the person specified.

Amount. The term "amount," when used in regard to securities, means the principal amount if relating to evidences of indebtedness, the number of shares if relating to shares, and the number of units if relating to any other kind of security.

Associate. The term "associate" used to indicate a relationship with any person, means
1. any corporation or organization (other than the registrant or a majority-owned subsidiary of the registrant) of which such person is an officer or partner or is, directly or indirectly, the beneficial owner of 10 percent or more of any class of equity securities,
2. any trust or other estate in which such person has a substantial beneficial interest or as to which such person serves as trustee or in a similar fiduciary capacity, and
3. any relative or spouse of such person, or any relative of such spouse, who has the same home as such person or who is a director or officer of the registrant or any of its parents or subsidiaries.

Business combination related shell company: The term business combination related shell company means a shell company (as defined in Rule 12b-2) that is:
1. Formed by an entity that is not a shell company solely for the purpose of changing the corporate domicile of that entity solely within the United States; or
2. Formed by an entity that is not a shell company solely for the purpose of completing a business combination transaction (as defined in Rule 230.165(f) of this chapter) among one or more entities other than the shell company, none of which is a shell company.

Certified. The term "certified," when used in regard to financial statements, means examined and reported upon with an opinion expressed by an independent public or certified public accountant.

Charter. The term "charter" includes articles of incorporation, declarations of trust, articles of association or partnership, or any similar instrument, as amended, effecting (either with or without filing with any governmental agency) the organization or creation of an incorporated or unincorporated person.

Common equity. The term "common equity" means any class of common stock or an equivalent interest, including but not limited to a unit of beneficial interest in a trust or a limited partnership interest.

Control. The term "control" (including the terms "controlling," "controlled by" and "under common control with") means the possession, direct or indirect, of the power to direct or cause the direction of the management and policies of a person, whether through the ownership of voting securities, by contract, or otherwise.

Depositary share. The term "depositary share" means a security, evidenced by an American Depositary Receipt, that represents a foreign security or a multiple of or fraction thereof deposited with a depositary.

Employee. The term "employee" does not include a director, trustee, or officer.

Fiscal year. The term "fiscal year" means the annual accounting period or, if no closing date has been adopted, the calendar year ending on December 31.

Majority-owned subsidiary. The term "majority-owned subsidiary" means a subsidiary more than 50 percent of whose outstanding securities representing the right, other than as affected by events of default, to vote for the election of directors, is owned by the subsidiary's parent and/or one or more of the parent's other majority-owned subsidiaries.

Managing underwriter. The term "managing underwriter" includes an underwriter (or underwriters) who, by contract or otherwise, deals with the registrant; organizes the selling effort; receives some benefit directly or indirectly in which all other underwriters similarly situated do not share in proportion to their respective interests in the underwriting; or represents any other underwriters in such matters as maintaining the records of the distribution, arranging the allotments of securities offered or arranging for appropriate stabilization activities, if any.

Material. The term "material," when used to qualify a requirement for the furnishing of information as to any subject, limits the information required to those matters to which there is a substantial likelihood that a reasonable investor would attach importance in determining whether to buy or sell the securities registered.

Material weakness. The term material weakness is a deficiency, or a combination of deficiencies, in internal control over financial reporting such that there is a reasonable possibility that a material misstatement of the registrant's annual or interim financial statements will not be prevented or detected on a timely basis.

Parent. A "parent" of a specified person is an affiliate controlling such person directly, or indirectly through one or more intermediaries.

Predecessor. The term "predecessor" means a person the major portion of the business and assets of which another person acquired in a single succession or in a series of related successions in each of which the acquiring person acquired the major portion of the business and assets of the acquired person.

Previously filed or reported. The terms "previously filed" and "previously reported" mean previously filed with, or reported in, a statement under Section 12, a report under Section 13 or 15(d), a definitive proxy statement or information statement under Section 14 of the act, or a registration statement under the Securities Act of 1933: *Provided,* That information contained in any such document shall be deemed to have been previously filed with, or reported to, an exchange only if such document is filed with such exchange.

Principal underwriter. The term "principal underwriter" means an underwriter in privity of contract with the issuer of the securities as to which he is underwriter.

Promoter.
1. The term "promoter" includes:
   i.   Any person who, acting alone or in conjunction with one or more other persons, directly or indirectly takes initiative in founding and organizing the business or enterprise of an issuer; or
   ii. Any person who, in connection with the founding and organizing of the business or enterprise of an issuer, directly or indirectly receives in consideration of services or property, or both services and property, 10 percent or more of any class of securities of the issuer or 10 percent or more of the proceeds from the sale of any class of such securities. However, a person who receives such securities or proceeds either solely as underwriting commissions or solely in consideration of property shall not be deemed a promoter within the meaning of this paragraph if such person does not otherwise take part in founding and organizing the enterprise.
2. All persons coming within the definition of "promoter" in paragraph 1 of this definition may be referred to as "founders" or "organizers" or by another term provided that such term is reasonably descriptive of those persons' activities with respect to the issuer.

Prospectus. Unless otherwise specified or the context otherwise requires, the term "prospectus" means a prospectus meeting the requirements of Section 10(a) of the Securities Act of 1933 as amended.

Registrant. The term "registrant" means an issuer of securities with respect to which a registration statement or report is to be filed.

Registration statement. The term "registration statement" or "statement", when used with reference to registration pursuant to Section 12 of the act, includes both an application for registration of securities on a national securities exchange pursuant to Section 12(b) of the act and a registration statement filed pursuant to Section 12(g) of the act.

Share. The term "share" means a share of stock in a corporation or unit of interest in an unincorporated person.

Shell Company: The term shell company means a registrant, other than an asset-backed issuer as defined in Item 1101(b) of Regulation AB, that has:
1. No or nominal operations; and
2. Either:
   i.   No or nominal assets;
   ii. Assets consisting solely of cash and cash equivalents; or

iii.   Assets consisting of any amount of cash and cash equivalents and nominal other assets.

Note: For purposes of this definition, the determination of a registrant's assets (including cash and cash equivalents) is based solely on the amount of assets that would be reflected on the registrant's balance sheet prepared in accordance with generally accepted accounting principles on the date of that determination.

Significant deficiency. The term significant deficiency is a deficiency, or a combination of deficiencies, in internal control over financial reporting that is less severe than a material weakness, yet important enough to merit attention by those responsible for oversight of the registrant's financial reporting.

Significant subsidiary. The term "significant subsidiary" means a subsidiary, including its subsidiaries, which meets any of the following conditions:

1.   The registrant's and its other subsidiaries' investments in and advances to the subsidiary exceed 10 percent of the total assets of the registrant and its subsidiaries consolidated as of the end of the most recently completed fiscal year (for a proposed combination between entities under common control, this condition is also met when the number of common shares exchanged or to be exchanged by the registrant exceeds 10 percent of its total common shares outstanding at the date the combination is initiated); or

2.   The registrant's and its other subsidiaries' proportionate share of the total assets (after intercompany eliminations) of the subsidiary exceeds 10 percent of the total assets of the registrant and its subsidiaries consolidated as of the end of the most recently completed fiscal year; or

3.   The registrant's and its other subsidiaries' equity in the income from continuing operations before income taxes, extraordinary items and cumulative effect of a change in accounting principle of the subsidiary exclusive of amounts attributable to any noncontrolling interests exceeds 10 percent of such income of the registrant and its subsidiaries consolidated for the most recently completed fiscal year.

Computational note: For purposes of making the prescribed income test the following guidance should be applied:

1.   When a loss exclusive of amounts attributable to any noncontrolling interests has been incurred by either the parent and its subsidiaries consolidated or the tested subsidiary, but not both, the equity in the income or loss of the tested subsidiary exclusive of amounts attributable to any noncontrolling interests should be excluded from such income of the registrant and its subsidiaries consolidated for purposes of the computation.

2.   If income of the registrant and its subsidiaries consolidated exclusive of amounts attributable to any noncontrolling interests for the most recent fiscal year is at least 10 percent lower than the average of the income for the last five fiscal years, such average income should be substituted for purposes of the computation. Any loss years should be omitted for purposes of computing average income.

Small Business Issuer. The term "small business issuer" means an entity that meets the following criteria:

1.   has revenues of less than $25,000,000;
2.   is a U.S. or Canadian issuer;

3. Is not an investment company and is not an asset-backed issuer (as defined in Rule 1101 of this chapter); and

4. if a majority owned subsidiary, the parent corporation is also a small business issuer.

Provided however, that an entity is not a small business issuer if it has a public float (the aggregate market value of the issuer's outstanding voting and non-voting common equity held by non-affiliates) of $25,000,000 or more.

Note: The public float of a reporting company shall be computed by use of the price at which the stock was last sold, or the average of the bid and asked prices of such stock, on a date within 60 days prior to the end of its most recent fiscal year. The public float of a company filing an initial registration statement under the Exchange Act shall be determined as of a date within 60 days of the date the registration statement is filed. In the case of an initial public offering of securities, public float shall be computed on the basis of the number of shares outstanding prior to the offering and the estimated public offering price of the securities.

Smaller reporting company. As used in this part, the term smaller reporting company means an issuer that is not an investment company, an asset-backed issuer (as defined in Item 1101 of this chapter), or a majority-owned subsidiary of a parent that is not a smaller reporting company and that:

1. Had a public float of less than $ 75 million as of the last business day of its most recently completed second fiscal quarter, computed by multiplying the aggregate worldwide number of shares of its voting and non-voting common equity held by non-affiliates by the price at which the common equity was last sold, or the average of the bid and asked prices of common equity, in the principal market for the common equity; or

2. In the case of an initial registration statement under the Securities Act or Exchange Act for shares of its common equity, had a public float of less than $75 million as of a date within 30 days of the date of the filing of the registration statement, computed by multiplying the aggregate worldwide number of such shares held by non-affiliates before the registration plus, in the case of a Securities Act registration statement, the number of such shares included in the registration statement by the estimated public offering price of the shares; or

3. In the case of an issuer whose public float as calculated under paragraph (1) or (2) of this definition was zero, had annual revenues of less than $50 million during the most recently completed fiscal year for which audited financial statements are available.

4. Determination: Whether or not an issuer is a smaller reporting company is determined on an annual basis.

    i.   For issuers that are required to file reports under section 13(a) or 15(d) of the Exchange Act, the determination is based on whether the issuer came within the definition of smaller reporting company using the amounts specified in paragraph (f)(2)(iii) of Item 10 of Regulation S-K, as of the last business day of the second fiscal quarter of the issuer's previous fiscal year. An issuer in this category must reflect this determination in the information it provides in its quarterly report on Form 10-Q for the first fiscal quarter of the next year, indicating on the cover page of that filing, and in subsequent filings for that fiscal year, whether or not it is a smaller reporting company, except that, if a determination based on public float indicates that the issuer is newly eligible to be a smaller reporting company, the issuer may choose to reflect this determination beginning with its first quarterly report on Form 10-Q following the determination, rather than waiting until the first fiscal quarter of the next year.

ii.   For determinations based on an initial Securities Act or Exchange Act registration statement under paragraph (f)(1)(ii) of Item 10 of Regulation S-K, the issuer must reflect the determination in the information it provides in the registration statement and must appropriately indicate on the cover page of the filing, and subsequent filings for the fiscal year in which the filing is made, whether or not it is a smaller reporting company. The issuer must redetermine its status at the end of its second fiscal quarter and then reflect any change in status as provided in paragraph (4)(i) of this definition. In the case of a determination based on an initial Securities Act registration statement, an issuer that was not determined to be a smaller reporting company has the option to redetermine its status at the conclusion of the offering covered by the registration statement based on the actual offering price and number of shares sold.

iii. Once an issuer fails to qualify for smaller reporting company status, it will remain unqualified unless it determines that its public float, as calculated in accordance with paragraph (f)(1) of this definition, was less than $50 million as of the last business day of its second fiscal quarter or, if that calculation results in zero because the issuer had no public equity outstanding or no market price for its equity existed, if the issuers had annual revenues of less than $ 40 million during its previous fiscal year.

Subsidiary. A "subsidiary" of a specified person is an affiliate controlled by such person directly, or indirectly through one or more intermediaries. (See also "majority-owned subsidiary," "significant subsidiary," and "totally-held subsidiary.")

Succession. The term "succession" means the direct acquisition of the assets comprising a going business, whether by merger, consolidation, purchase, or other direct transfer. The term does not include the acquisition of control of a business unless followed by the direct acquisition of its assets. The terms "succeed" and "successor" have meanings correlative to the foregoing.

Totally held subsidiary. The term "totally held subsidiary" means a subsidiary (1) substantially all of whose outstanding securities are owned by its parent and/or the parent's other totally held subsidiaries, and (2) which is not indebted to any person other than its parent and/or the parent's other totally held subsidiaries in an amount which is material in relation to the particular subsidiary, excepting indebtedness incurred in the ordinary course of business which is not overdue and which matures within one year from the date of its creation, whether evidenced by securities or not.

Voting securities. The term "voting securities" means securities the holders of which are presently entitled to vote for the election of directors.

Wholly-owned subsidiary. The term "wholly-owned subsidiary" means a subsidiary substantially all of whose outstanding voting securities are owned by its parent and/or the parent's other wholly-owned subsidiaries.

Rule 12b-20 – Additional Information

In addition to the information expressly required to be included in a statement or report, there shall be added such further material information, if any, as may be necessary to make the required statements, in the light of the circumstances under which they are made not misleading.

Rule 12g-1 – Exemption from Section 12(g)

An issuer shall be exempt from the requirement to register any class of equity securities pursuant to section 12(g)(1) if on the last day of its most recent fiscal year the issuer had total assets not exceeding $10 million and, with respect to a foreign private issuer, such securities were not quoted in an automated inter-dealer quotation system.

Rule 12g3-2 – Exemptions for American Depositary Receipts and Certain Foreign Securities

a. Securities of any class issued by any foreign private issuer shall be exempt from section 12(g) of the Act if the class has fewer than 300 holders resident in the United States. This exemption shall continue until the next fiscal year end at which the issuer has a class of equity securities held by 300 or more persons resident in the United States. For the purpose of determining whether a security is exempt pursuant to this paragraph:

1. Securities held of record by persons resident in the United States shall be determined as provided in Rule 12g5-1 except that securities held of record by a broker, dealer, bank or nominee for any of them for the accounts of customers resident in the United States shall be counted as held in the United States by the number of separate accounts for which the securities are held. The issuer may rely in good faith on information as to the number of such separate accounts supplied by all owners of the class of its securities which are brokers, dealers, or banks or a nominee for any of them.

2. Persons in the United States who hold the security only through a Canadian Retirement Account (as that term is defined in Rule 237(a)(2) under the Securities Act of 1933, shall not be counted as holders resident in the United States.

b. 1. A foreign private issuer shall be exempt from the requirement to register a class of equity securities under section 12(g) of the Act if:

i. The issuer is not required to file or furnish reports under section 13(a) of the Act or section 15(d) of the Act;

ii. The issuer currently maintains a listing of the subject class of securities on one or more exchanges in a foreign jurisdiction that, either singly or together with the trading of the same class of the issuer's securities in another foreign jurisdiction, constitutes the primary trading market for those securities; and

iii. The issuer has published in English, on its Internet Web site or through an electronic information delivery system generally available to the public in its primary trading market, information that, since the first day of its most recently completed fiscal year, it:

A. Has made public or been required to make public pursuant to the laws of the country of its incorporation, organization or domicile;

B. Has filed or been required to file with the principal stock exchange in its primary trading market on which its securities are traded and which has been made public by that exchange; and

C. Has distributed or been required to distribute to its security holders.

Note 1 to Paragraph (b)(1):

For the purpose of paragraph (b) of this section, primary trading market means that at least 55 percent of the trading in the subject class of securities on a worldwide basis took place in, on or through the facilities of a securities market or markets in a single foreign jurisdiction or in no more than two foreign jurisdictions during the issuer's most recently completed fiscal year. If a foreign private issuer aggregates the trading of its subject class of securities in two foreign jurisdictions for the purpose of this paragraph, the trading for the issuer's securities in at least one of the two foreign jurisdictions must be larger than the trading in the United States for the same class of the issuer's securities. When determining an issuer's primary trading market under this paragraph, calculate average daily trading volume in the United States and on a worldwide basis as under Rule 12h-6 under the Act.

Note 2 to Paragraph (b)(1):

Paragraph (b)(1)(iii) of this section does not apply to an issuer when claiming the exemption under paragraph (b) of this section upon the effectiveness of the termination of its registration of a class of securities under section 12(g) of the Act, or the termination of its obligation to file or furnish reports under section 15(d) of the Act.

Note 3 to Paragraph (b)(1):

Compensatory stock options for which the underlying securities are in a class exempt under paragraph (b) of this section are also exempt under that paragraph.

2.

i. In order to maintain the exemption under paragraph (b) of this section, a foreign private issuer shall publish, on an ongoing basis and for each subsequent fiscal year, in English, on its Internet Web site or through an electronic information delivery system generally available to the public in its primary trading market, the information specified in paragraph (b)(1)(iii) of this section.

ii. An issuer must electronically publish the information required by paragraph (b)(2) of this secti on promptly after the information has been made public.

3.

    i.   The information required to be published electronically under paragraph (b) of this section is information that is material to an investment decision regarding the subject securities, such as information concerning:

        A. Results of operations or financial condition;

        B. Changes in business;

        C. Acquisitions or dispositions of assets;

        D. The issuance, redemption or acquisition of securities;

        E. Changes in management or control;

        F. The granting of options or the payment of other remuneration to directors or officers; and

        G. Transactions with directors, officers or principal security holders.

    ii.   At a minimum, a foreign private issuer shall electronically publish English translations of the following documents required to be published under paragraph (b) of this section if in a foreign language:

        A. Its annual report, including or accompanied by annual financial statements;

        B. Interim reports that include financial statements;

        C. Press releases; and

        D. All other communications and documents distributed directly to security holders of each class of securities to which the exemption relates.

c.   The exemption under paragraph (b) of this section shall remain in effect until:

    1.   The issuer no longer satisfies the electronic publication condition of paragraph (b)(2) of this section;

    2.   The issuer no longer maintains a listing of the subject class of securities on one or more exchanges in a primary trading market, as defined under paragraph (b)(1) of this section; or

    3.   The issuer registers a class of securities under section 12 of the Act or incurs reporting obligations under section 15(d) of the Act.

d.   Depositary shares registered on Form F-6, but not the underlying deposited securities, are exempt from section 12(g) of the Act under this paragraph.

Rule 12g-4 – Certifications of Termination of Registration Under Section 12(g)

a.   Termination of registration of a class of securities shall take effect 90 days, or such shorter period as the Commission may determine, after the issuer certifies to the Commission on Form 15 that:

    1.   Such class of securities is held of record by:

        i.   Less than 300 persons; or

        ii.   By less than 500 persons, where the total assets of the issuer have not exceeded $10 million on the last day of each of the issuer's three most recent fiscal years; or

    2.   Such class of securities of a foreign private issuer, as defined in Rule 3b-4, is held of record by:

        i.   Less than 300 persons resident in the United States or

    ii.   Less than 500 persons resident in the United States where the total assets of the issuer have not exceeded $10 million on the last day of each of the issuer's most recent three fiscal years.

           For purposes of this paragraph, the number of persons resident in the United States shall be determined in accordance with the provisions of Rule 12g3-2(a).

b.   The issuer's duty to file any reports required under section 13(a) shall be suspended immediately upon filing a certification on Form 15. *Provided, however,* That if the certification on Form 15 is subsequently withdrawn or denied, the issuer shall, within 60 days after the date of such withdrawal or denial, file with the Commission all reports which would have been required had the certification on Form 15 not been filed. If the suspension resulted from the issuer's merger into, or consolidation with, another issuer or issuers, the certification shall be filed by the successor issuer

Rule 12g5-1 – Definition of Securities "Held of Record"

a.   For the purpose of determining whether an issuer is subject to the provisions of Sections 12(g) and 15(d) of the Act, securities shall be deemed to be "held of record" by each person who is identified as the owner of such securities on records of security holders maintained by or on behalf of the issuer, subject to the following:

    1.   In any case where the records of security holders have not been maintained in accordance with accepted practice, any additional person who would be identified as such an owner on such records if they had been maintained in accordance with accepted practice shall be included as a holder of record.

    2.   Securities identified as held of record by a corporation, a partnership, a trust whether or not the trustees are named, or other organization shall be included as so held by one person.

    3.   Securities identified as held of record by one or more persons as trustees, executors, guardians, custodians or in other fiduciary capacities with respect to a single trust, estate or account shall be included as held of record by one person.

    4.   Securities held by two or more persons as co-owners shall be included as held by one person.

    5.   Each outstanding unregistered or bearer certificate shall be included as held of record by a separate person, except to the extent that the issuer can establish that, if such securities were registered, they would be held of record, under the provisions of this rule, by a lesser number of persons.

    6.   Securities registered in substantially similar names where the issuer has reason to believe because of the address or other indications that such names represent the same person, may be included as held of record by one person.

b.   Notwithstanding paragraph (a) of this section:

    1.   Securities held, to the knowledge of the issuer, subject to a voting trust, deposit agreement or similar arrangement shall be included as held of record by the record holders of the voting trust certificates, certificates of deposit, receipts or similar evidences of interest in such securities: *Provided, however,* That the

issuer may rely in good faith on such information as is received in response to its request from a non-affiliated issuer of the certificates or evidences of interest.

2. Whole or fractional securities issued by a savings and loan association, building and loan association, cooperative bank, homestead association, or similar institution for the sole purpose of qualifying a borrower for membership in the issuer, and which are to be redeemed or repurchased by the issuer when the borrower's loan is terminated, shall not be included as held of record by any person.

3. If the issuer knows or has reason to know that the form of holding securities of record is used primarily to circumvent the provisions of Section 12(g) or 15(d) of the Act, the beneficial owners of such securities shall be deemed to be the record owners thereof.

Rule 12h-3 – Suspension of Duty to File Reports under Section 15(d)

a. Subject to paragraphs (c) and (d) of this section, the duty under Section 15(d) to file reports required by Section 13(a) of the Act with respect to a class of securities specified in paragraph (b) of this section shall be suspended for such class of securities immediately upon filing with the Commission a certification on Form 15 if the issuer of such class has filed all reports required by Section 13(a), without regard to Rule 12b-25, for the shorter of its most recent three fiscal years and the portion of the current year preceding the date of filing Form 15, or the period since the issuer became subject to such reporting obligation. If the certification on Form 15 is subsequently withdrawn or denied, the issuer shall, within 60 days, file with the Commission all reports which would have been required if such certification had not been filed.

b. The classes of securities eligible for the suspension provided in paragraph (a) of this section are:
   1. Any class of securities held of record by:
      i.   Less than 300 persons; or
      ii. By less then 500 persons, where the total assets of the issuer have not exceeded $10 million on the last day of each of the issuer's three most recent fiscal years; and
   2. Any class or securities deregistered pursuant to Section 12(d) of the Act if such class would not thereupon be deemed registered under Section 12(g) of the Act or the rules thereunder.

c. This section shall not be available for any class of securities for a fiscal year in which a registration statement relating to that class becomes effective under the Securities Act of 1933, or is required to be updated pursuant to Section 10(a)(3) of the Act, and, in the case of paragraph (b)(1)(ii), the two succeeding fiscal years; *Provided, however,* That this paragraph shall not apply to the duty to file reports which arises solely from a registration statement filed by an issuer with no significant assets, for the reorganization of a non-reporting issuer into a one subsidiary holding company in which equity security holders receive the same proportional interest in the holding company as they held in the non-reporting issuer, except for changes resulting from the exercise of dissenting shareholder rights under state law.

d.   The suspension provided by this rule relates only to the reporting obligation under section 15(d) with respect to a class of securities, does not affect any other duties imposed on that class of securities, and shall continue as long as either criteria (i) or (ii) in paragraph (b)(1) is met on the first day of any subsequent fiscal year; *Provided, however,* That such criteria need not be met if the duty to file reports arises solely from a registration statement filed by an issuer with no significant assets in a reorganization of a non-reporting company into a one subsidiary holding company in which equity security holders receive the same proportional interest in the holding company as they held in the non-reporting issuer except for changes resulting from the exercise of dissenting shareholder rights under state law.

e.   If the suspension provided by this rule is discontinued because a class of securities does not meet the eligibility criteria of paragraph (b) on the first day of an issuer's fiscal year, then the issuer shall resume periodic reporting pursuant to Section 15(d) by filing an annual report on Form 10-K for its preceding fiscal year, not later than 120 days after the end of such fiscal year.

Rule 13a-1 – Requirements of Annual Reports

Every issuer having securities registered pursuant to section 12 of the Act shall file an annual report on the appropriate form authorized or prescribed therefor for each fiscal year after the last full fiscal year for which financial statements were filed in its registration statement. Annual reports shall be filed within the period specified in the appropriate form.

Rule 13a-11 – Current Reports on Form 8-K

a.   Except as provided in paragraph (b) of this section, every registrant subject to Rule 13a-1 shall file a current report on Form 8-K within the period specified in that form unless substantially the same information as that required by Form 8-K has been previously reported by the registrant.

b.   This section shall not apply to foreign governments, foreign private issuers required to make reports on Form 6-K pursuant to Rule 13a-16, issuers of American Depositary Receipts for securities of any foreign issuer, or investment companies required to file reports pursuant to Rule 30b1-1 under the Investment Company Act of 1940, except where such investment companies are required to file notice of a blackout period pursuant to Rule 104 of Regulation BTR.

c.   No failure to file a report on Form 8-K that is required solely pursuant to Item 1.01, 1.02, 2.03, 2.04, 2.05, 2.06, 4.02(a), 5.02(e) or 6.03 of Form 8-K shall be deemed to be a violation of Section 10(b) and Rule 10b-5.

Rule 13a-13 – Quarterly Reports on Form 10-Q

a. Except as provided in paragraphs (b) and (c) of this section, every issuer that has securities registered pursuant to section 12 of the Act and is required to file annual reports pursuant to section 13 of the Act, and has filed or intends to file such reports on Form 10-K shall file a quarterly report on Form 10-Q within the period specified in General Instruction A.1. to that form for each of the first three quarters of each fiscal year of the issuer, commencing with the first fiscal quarter following the most recent fiscal year for which full financial statements were included in the registration statement, or, if the registration statement included financial statements for an interim period subsequent to the most recent fiscal year end meeting the requirements of Article 10 of Regulation S-X, for the first fiscal quarter subsequent to the quarter reported upon in the registration statement. The first quarterly report of the issuer shall be filed either within 45 days after the effective date of the registration statement or on or before the date on which such report would have been required to be filed if the issuer has been required to file reports on Form 10-Q as of its last fiscal quarter, whichever is later.

b. The provisions of this rule shall not apply to the following issuers:
    1. Investment companies required to file reports pursuant to Rule 30b1-1; or
    2. Foreign private issuers required to file reports pursuant to Rule 13a-16; and
    3. Asset-backed issuers required to file reports pursuant to Rule 13a-17.

c. Part I of the quarterly reports on Form 10-Q need not be filed by:
    1. Mutual life insurance companies; or
    2. Mining companies not in the production stage but engaged primarily in the exploration for the development of mineral deposits other than oil, gas or coal, if all the following conditions are met:
        i.   The registrant has not been in production during the current fiscal year or the two years immediately prior thereto; except that being in production for an aggregate period of not more than eight months over the three-year period shall not be a violation of this condition.
        ii. Receipts from the sale of mineral products or from the operations of mineral producing properties by the registrant and its subsidiaries combined have not exceeded $500,000 in any of the most recent six years and have not aggregated more than $1,500,000 in the most recent six fiscal years.

d. Notwithstanding the foregoing provisions of this section, the financial information required by Part I of Form 10-Q shall not be deemed to be "filed" for the purpose of section 18 of the Act or otherwise subject to the liabilities of that section of the Act but shall be subject to all other provisions of the Act.

Rule 13a-14 – Certification of Disclosure in Annual and Quarterly Reports

a. Each report, including transition reports, filed on Form 10-Q, Form 10-K, Form 20-F or Form 40-F under section 13(a) of the Act, other than a report filed by an Asset-Backed Issuer (as defined in 1101 of this chapter), must include certifications in the form specified in the applicable exhibit filing requirements of such report and such certifications must be filed as an exhibit to such report. Each principal executive and principal financial officer of the issuer, or persons performing similar functions, at the time of filing of the report must sign a certification.

b. Each periodic report containing financial statements filed by an issuer pursuant to section 13(a) of the Act must be accompanied by the certifications required by Section 1350 of Chapter 63 of Title 18 of the United States Code and such certifications must be furnished as an exhibit to such report as specified in the applicable exhibit requirements for such report. Each principal executive and principal financial officer of the issuer (or equivalent thereof) must sign a certification. This requirement may be satisfied by a single certification signed by an issuer's principal executive and principal financial officers.

c. A person required to provide a certification specified in paragraph (a) or (b) of this section may not have the certification signed on his or her behalf pursuant to a power of attorney or other form of confirming authority.

* * *

f. The certification requirements of this section do not apply to:
  1. An Interactive Data File, as defined in Rule 11 of Regulation S-T; or
  2. XBRL-Related Documents, as defined in Rule 11 of Regulation S-T.

* * *

Rule 13a-15 – Issuer's Disclosure Controls and Procedures Related to Preparation of Required Reports

a. Every issuer that has a class of securities registered pursuant to section 12 of the Act, other than an Asset-Backed Issuer (as defined in Rule 13a-14(g)), a small business investment company registered on Form N-5, or a unit investment trust as defined by section 4(2) of the Investment Company Act of 1940, must maintain disclosure controls and procedures (as defined in paragraph (e) of this section) and internal control over financial reporting (as defined in paragraph (f) of this section).

b. Each such issuer's management must evaluate, with the participation of the issuer's principal executive and principal financial officers, or persons performing similar functions, the effectiveness of the issuer's disclosure controls and procedures, as of the end of each fiscal quarter, except that management must perform this evaluation:
  1. In the case of a foreign private issuer (as defined in Rule 3b-4) as of the end of each fiscal year; and
  2. In the case of an investment company registered under section 8 of the Investment Company Act of 1940, within the 90-day period prior to the filing date of each report requiring certification under Investment Company Act Rule 30a-2.

c.   The management of each such issuer, that either had been required to file an annual report pursuant to section 13(a) or 15(d) of the Act for the prior fiscal year or previously had filed an annual report with the Commission for the prior fiscal year, other than an investment company registered under section 8 of the Investment Company Act of 1940, must evaluate, with the participation of the issuer's principal executive and principal financial officers, or persons performing similar functions, the effectiveness, as of the end of each fiscal year, of the issuer's internal control over financial reporting. The framework on which management's evaluation of the issuer's internal control over financial reporting is based must be a suitable, recognized control framework that is established by a body or group that has followed due-process procedures, including the broad distribution of the framework for public comment. Although there are many different ways to conduct an evaluation of the effectiveness of internal control over financial reporting to meet the requirements of this paragraph, an evaluation that is conducted in accordance with the interpretive guidance issued by the Commission in Release No. 34-55929 will satisfy the evaluation required by this paragraph.

d.   The management of each such issuer, other than an investment company registered under section 8 of the Investment Company Act of 1940, must evaluate, with the participation of the issuer's principal executive and principal financial officers, or persons performing similar functions, any change in the issuer's internal control over financial reporting, that occurred during each of the issuer's fiscal quarters, or fiscal year in the case of a foreign private issuer, that has materially affected, or is reasonably likely to materially affect, the issuer's internal control over financial reporting.

e.   For purposes of this section, the term *disclosure controls and procedures* means controls and other procedures of an issuer that are designed to ensure that information required to be disclosed by the issuer in the reports that it files or submits under the Act is recorded, processed, summarized and reported, within the time periods specified in the Commission's rules and forms. Disclosure controls and procedures include, without limitation, controls and procedures designed to ensure that information required to be disclosed by an issuer in the reports that it files or submits under the Act is accumulated and communicated to the issuer's management, including its principal executive and principal financial officers, or persons performing similar functions, as appropriate to allow timely decisions regarding required disclosure.

f.   The term *internal control over financial reporting* is defined as a process designed by, or under the supervision of, the issuer's principal executive and principal financial officers, or persons performing similar functions, and effected by the issuer's board of directors, management and other personnel, to provide reasonable assurance regarding the reliability of financial reporting and the preparation of financial statements for external purposes in accordance with generally accepted accounting principles and includes those policies and procedures that:
1.   Pertain to the maintenance of records that in reasonable detail accurately and fairly reflect the transactions and dispositions of the assets of the issuer;

2.   Provide reasonable assurance that transactions are recorded as necessary to permit preparation of financial statements in accordance with generally accepted accounting principles, and that receipts and expenditures of the issuer are being made only in accordance with authorizations of management and directors of the issuer; and

3.   Provide reasonable assurance regarding prevention or timely detection of unauthorized acquisition, use or disposition of the issuer's assets that could have a material effect on the financial statements.

Rule 13a-20 – Plain English presentation of specified information.

a.   Any information included or incorporated by reference in a report filed under section 13(a) of the Act that is required to be disclosed pursuant to Item 402, 403, 404 or 407 of Regulation S-B or Item 402, 403, 404 or 407 of Regulation S-K must be presented in a clear, concise and understandable manner. You must prepare the disclosure using the following standards:

1.   Present information in clear, concise sections, paragraphs and sentences;

2.   Use short sentences;

3.   Use definite, concrete, everyday words;

4.   Use the active voice;

5.   Avoid multiple negatives;

6.   Use descriptive headings and subheadings;

7.   Use a tabular presentation or bullet lists for complex material, wherever possible;

8.   Avoid legal jargon and highly technical business and other terminology;

9.   Avoid frequent reliance on glossaries or defined terms as the primary means of explaining information. Define terms in a glossary or other section of the document only if the meaning is unclear from the context. Use a glossary only if it facilitates understanding of the disclosure; and

10. In designing the presentation of the information you may include pictures, logos, charts, graphs and other design elements so long as the design is not misleading and the required information is clear. You are encouraged to use tables, schedules, charts and graphic illustrations that present relevant data in an understandable manner, so long as such presentations are consistent with applicable disclosure requirements and consistent with other information in the document. You must draw graphs and charts to scale. Any information you provide must not be misleading.

b.   Reserved.

Note to Rule 13a-20. In drafting the disclosure to comply with this section, you should avoid the following:

1.   Legalistic or overly complex presentations that make the substance of the disclosure difficult to understand;

2.   Vague "boilerplate" explanations that are imprecise and readily subject to different interpretations;

3.   Complex information copied directly from legal documents without any clear and concise explanation of the provision(s); and

4.   Disclosure repeated in different sections of the document that increases the size of the document but does not enhance the quality of the information.

Rule 13b2-1 – Falsification of Accounting Records

No person shall directly or indirectly, falsify or cause to by falsified, any book, record or account subject to section 13(b)(2)(A) of the Securities Exchange Act.

Rule 13b2-2 – Representations and Conduct in Connection with the Preparation of Required Reports and Documents

a.   No director or officer of an issuer shall, directly or indirectly:
   1.   Make or cause to be made a materially false or misleading statement to an accountant in connection with; or
   2.   Omit to state, or cause another person to omit to state, any material fact necessary in order to make statements made, in light of the circumstances under which such statements were made, not misleading, to an accountant in connection with:
      i.   Any audit, review or examination of the financial statements of the issuer required to be made pursuant to this subpart; or
      ii.   The preparation or filing of any document or report required to be filed with the Commission pursuant to this subpart or otherwise.

b.
   1.   No officer or director of an issuer, or any other person acting under the direction thereof, shall directly or indirectly take any action to coerce, manipulate, mislead, or fraudulently influence any independent public or certified public accountant engaged in the performance of an audit or review of the financial statements of that issuer that are required to be filed with the Commission pursuant to this subpart or otherwise if that person knew or should have known that such action, if successful, could result in rendering the issuer's financial statements materially misleading.
   2.   For purposes of paragraphs (b)(1) and (c)(2) of this section, actions that, "if successful, could result in rendering the issuer's financial statements materially misleading" include, but are not limited to, actions taken at any time with respect to the professional engagement period to coerce, manipulate, mislead, or fraudulently influence an auditor:
      i.   To issue or reissue a report on an issuer's financial statements that is not warranted in the circumstances (due to material violations of generally accepted accounting principles, generally accepted auditing standards, or other professional or regulatory standards);
      ii.   Not to perform audit, review or other procedures required by generally accepted auditing standards or other professional standards;
      iii.   Not to withdraw an issued report; or
      iv.   Not to communicate matters to an issuer's audit committee.

c.   In addition, in the case of an investment company registered under section 8 of the Investment Company Act of 1940, or a business development company as defined in section 2(a)(48) of the Investment Company Act of 1940, no officer or director of the company's investment adviser, sponsor, depositor, trustee, or administrator (or, in the case of paragraph (c)(2) of this section, any other person acting under the direction thereof) shall, directly or indirectly:

1.

    i. Make or cause to be made a materially false or misleading statement to an accountant in connection with; or

    ii. Omit to state, or cause another person to omit to state, any material fact necessary in order to make statements made, in light of the circumstances under which such statements were made, not misleading to an accountant in connection with:

        A. Any audit, review, or examination of the financial statements of the investment company required to be made pursuant to this subpart; or

        B. The preparation or filing of any document or report required to be filed with the Commission pursuant to this subpart or otherwise; or

2. Take any action to coerce, manipulate, mislead, or fraudulently influence any independent public or certified public accountant engaged in the performance of an audit or review of the financial statements of that investment company that are required to be filed with the Commission pursuant to this subpart or otherwise if that person knew or should have known that such action, if successful, could result in rendering the investment company's financial statements materially misleading.

Rule 13d-1 – Filing of Schedules 13D and 13G

a. Any person who, after acquiring directly or indirectly the beneficial ownership of any equity security of a class which is specified in paragraph (i) of this section, is directly or indirectly the beneficial owner of more than five percent of the class shall, within 10 days after the acquisition, file with the Commission, a statement containing the information required by Schedule 13D.

b. 1. A person who would otherwise be obligated under paragraph (a) of this section to file a statement on Schedule 13D may, in lieu thereof, file with the Commission, a short-form statement on Schedule 13G, *Provided,* That:

    i. Such person has acquired such securities in the ordinary course of his business and not with the purpose nor with the effect of changing or influencing the control of the issuer, nor in connection with or as a participant in any transaction having such purpose or effect, including any transaction subject to Rule 13d-3(b); and

    ii. Such person is:

        A. A broker or dealer registered under section 15 of the Act;

        B. A bank as defined in section 3(a)(6) of the Act;

        C. An insurance company as defined in section 3(a)(19) of the Act;

        D. An investment company registered under section 8 of the Investment Company Act of 1940;

        E. Any person registered as an investment adviser under Section 203 of the Investment Advisers Act of 1940 or under the laws of any state;

F. An employee benefit plan as defined in Section 3(3) of the Employee Retirement Income Security Act of 1974 ("ERISA") that is subject to the provisions of ERISA, or any such plan that is not subject to ERISA that is maintained primarily for the benefit of the employees of a state or local government or instrumentality, or an endowment fund;

G. A parent holding company or control person, provided the aggregate amount held directly by the parent or control person, and directly and indirectly by their subsidiaries or affiliates that are not persons specified in Rule 13d- 1(b)(1)(ii)(A) through (I), does not exceed one percent of the securities of the subject class;

H. A savings association as defined in Section 3(b) of the Federal Deposit Insurance Act;

I. A church plan that is excluded from the definition of an investment company under section 3(c)(14) of the Investment Company Act of 1940; and

J. A group, provided that all the members are persons specified in Rule 13d- 1(b)(1)(ii)(A) through (I); and

iii. Such person has promptly notified any other person (or group within the meaning of section 13(d)(3) of the Act) on whose behalf it holds, on a discretionary basis, securities exceeding five percent of the class, of any acquisition or transaction on behalf of such other person which might be reportable by that person under section 13(d) of the Act. This paragraph only requires notice to the account owner of information which the filing person reasonably should be expected to know and which would advise the account owner of an obligation he may have to file a statement pursuant to section 13(d) of the Act or an amendment thereto.

2. The Schedule 13G filed pursuant to paragraph (b)(1) of this section shall be filed within 45 days after the end of the calendar year in which the person became obligated under paragraph (b)(1) of this section to report the person's beneficial ownership as of the last day of the calendar year, *Provided,* That it shall not be necessary to file a Schedule 13G unless the percentage of the class of equity security specified in paragraph (i) of this section beneficially owned as of the end of the calendar year is more than five percent; *However,* if the person's direct or indirect beneficial ownership exceeds 10 percent of the class of equity securities prior to the end of the calendar year, the initial Schedule 13G shall be filed within 10 days after the end of the first month in which the person's direct or indirect beneficial ownership exceeds 10 percent of the class of equity securities, computed as of the last day of the month.

c. A person who would otherwise be obligated under paragraph (a) of this section to file a statement on Schedule 13D may, in lieu thereof, file with the Commission, within 10 days after an acquisition described in paragraph (a) of this section, a short-form statement on Schedule 13G. *Provided,* That the person:

1. Has not acquired the securities with any purpose, or with the effect of, changing or influencing the control of the issuer, or in connection with or as a participant in any transaction having that purpose or effect, including any transaction subject to Rule 13d-3(b);

2. Is not a person reporting pursuant to paragraph (b)(1) of this section; and

3. Is not directly or indirectly the beneficial owner of 20 percent or more of the class.

d. Any person who, as of the end of any calendar year, is or becomes directly or indirectly the beneficial owner of more than five percent of any equity security of a class specified in paragraph (i) of this section and who is not required to file a statement under paragraph (a) of this section by virtue of the exemption provided by Section 13(d)(6)(A) or (B) of the Act, or because the beneficial ownership was acquired prior to December 22, 1970, or because the person otherwise (except for the exemption provided by Section 13(d)(6)(C) of the Act) is not required to file a statement, shall file with the Commission, within 45 days after the end of the calendar year in which the person became obligated to report under this paragraph (d), a statement containing the information required by Schedule 13G.

e. 1. Notwithstanding paragraphs (b) and (c) of this section and Rule 13d-2(b), a person that has reported that it is the beneficial owner of more than five percent of a class of equity securities in a statement on Schedule 13G pursuant to paragraph (b) or (c) of this section, or is required to report the acquisition but has not yet filed the schedule, shall immediately become subject to Rule 13d-1(a) and Rule 13d-2(a) and shall file a statement on Schedule 13D within 10 days if, and shall remain subject to those requirements for so long as, the person:

    i. Has acquired or holds the securities with a purpose or effect of changing or influencing control of the issuer, or in connection with or as a participant in any transaction having that purpose or effect, including any transaction subject to Rule 13d-3(b); and

    ii. Is at that time the beneficial owner of more than five percent of a class of equity securities described in Rule 13d-1(i).

2. From the time the person has acquired or holds the securities with a purpose or effect of changing or influencing control of the issuer, or in connection with or as a participant in any transaction having that purpose or effect until the expiration of the tenth day from the date of the filing of the Schedule 13D pursuant to this section, that person shall not:

    i. Vote or direct the voting of the securities described therein; or

    ii. Acquire an additional beneficial ownership interest in any equity securities of the issuer of the securities, nor of any person controlling the issuer.

f. Notwithstanding paragraph (c) of this section and Rule 13d-2(b), persons reporting on Schedule 13G pursuant to paragraph (c) of this section shall immediately become subject to Rule 13d-1(a) and Rule 13d- 2(a) and shall remain subject to those requirements for so long as, and shall file a statement on Schedule 13D within 10 days of the date on which, the person's beneficial ownership equals or exceeds 20 percent of the class of equity securities.

1. From the time of the acquisition of 20 percent or more of the class of equity securities until the expiration of the tenth day from the date of the filing of the Schedule 13D pursuant to this section, the person shall not:

    i.   Vote or direct the voting of the securities described therein,

    ii.   Acquire an additional beneficial ownership interest in any equity securities of the issuer of the securities, nor of any person controlling the issuer.

g.   Any person who has reported an acquisition of securities in a statement on Schedule 13G pursuant to paragraph (b) of this section, or has become obligated to report on the Schedule 13G but has not yet filed the Schedule, and thereafter ceases to be a person specified in paragraph (b)(1)(ii) of this section or determines that it no longer has acquired or holds the securities in the ordinary course of business shall immediately become subject to Rule 13d-1(a) or Rule 13d-1(c) (if the person satisfies the requirements specified in Rule 13d-1(c)), and Rule 13d-2 (a), (b) or (d), and shall file, within 10 days thereafter, a statement on Schedule 13D or amendment to Schedule 13G, as applicable, if the person is a beneficial owner at that time of more than five percent of the class of equity securities.

h.   Any person who has filed a Schedule 13D pursuant to paragraph (e), (f) or (g) of this section may again report its beneficial ownership on Schedule 13G pursuant to paragraphs (b) or (c) of this section provided the person qualifies thereunder, as applicable, by filing a Schedule 13G once the person determines that the provisions of paragraph (e), (f) or (g) of this section no longer apply.

i.   For the purpose of this regulation, the term "equity security" means any equity security of a class which is registered pursuant to section 12 of that Act, or any equity security of any insurance company which would have been required to be so registered except for the exemption contained in section 12(g) (2) (G) of the Act, or any equity security issued by a closed-end investment company registered under the Investment Company Act of 1940: Provided, such term shall not include securities of a class of non-voting securities.

j.   For the purpose of sections 13(d) and 13(g), any person, in determining the amount of outstanding securities of a class of equity securities, may rely upon information set forth in the issuer's most recent quarterly or annual report, and any current report subsequent thereto, filed with the Commission pursuant to this Act, unless he knows or has reason to believe that the information contained therein is inaccurate.

k. 1.   Whenever two or more persons are required to file a statement containing the information required by Schedule 13D or Schedule 13G with respect to the same securities, only one statement need be filed: *Provided,* That:

    i.   Each person on whose behalf the statement is filed is individually eligible to use the Schedule on which the information is filed;

    ii.   Each person on whose behalf the statement is filed is responsible for the timely filing of such statement and any amendments thereto, and for the completeness and accuracy of the information concerning such person contained therein; such person is not responsible for the completeness or accuracy of the information concerning the other persons making the filing, unless such person knows or has reason to believe that such information is inaccurate; and

iii.   Such statement identifies all such persons, contains the required information with regard to each such person, indicates that such statement is filed on behalf of all such persons, and includes, as an exhibit, their agreement in writing that such a statement is filed on behalf of each of them.

2.   A group's filing obligation may be satisfied either by a single joint filing or by each of the group's members making an individual filing. If the group's members elect to make their own filings, each such filing should identify all members of the group but the information provided concerning the other persons making the filing need only reflect information which the filing person knows or has reason to know.

Rule 13d-2 – Filing of Amendments to Schedules 13D or 13G

a.   If any material change occurs in the facts set forth in the Schedule 13D required by Rule13d-1(a), including, but not limited to, any material increase or decrease in the percentage of the class beneficially owned, the person or persons who were required to file the statement shall promptly file or cause to be filed with the Commission an amendment disclosing that change. An acquisition or disposition of beneficial ownership of securities in an amount equal to one percent or more of the class of securities shall be deemed "material" for purposes of this section; acquisitions or dispositions of less than those amounts may be material, depending upon the facts and circumstances.

b.   Notwithstanding paragraph (a) of this section, and provided that the person filing a Schedule 13G pursuant to Rule 13d-1(b) or Rule 13d-1(c) continues to meet the requirements set forth therein, any person who has filed a Schedule 13G pursuant to Rule 13d-1(b), Rule 13d-1(c) or Rule 13d-1(d) shall amend the statement within forty-five days after the end of each calendar year if, as of the end of the calendar year, there are any changes in the information reported in the previous filing on that Schedule: *Provided, however,* That an amendment need not be filed with respect to a change in the percent of class outstanding previously reported if the change results solely from a change in the aggregate number of securities outstanding. Once an amendment has been filed reflecting beneficial ownership of five percent or less of the class of securities, no additional filings are required unless the person thereafter becomes the beneficial owner of more than five percent of the class and is required to file pursuant to Rule 13d-1.

c.   Any person relying on Rule 13d-1(b) that has filed its initial Schedule 13G pursuant to that paragraph shall, in addition to filing any amendments pursuant to Rule 13d-2(b), file an amendment on Schedule 13G within 10 days after the end of the first month in which the person's direct or indirect beneficial ownership, computed as of the last day of the month, exceeds 10 percent of the class of equity securities. Thereafter, that person shall, in addition to filing any amendments pursuant to Rule 13d-2(b), file an amendment on Schedule 13G within 10 days after the end of the first month in which the person's direct or indirect beneficial ownership, computed as of the last day of the month, increases or decreases by more than five percent of the class of equity securities. Once an amendment has been filed reflecting beneficial ownership of five percent or less of the class of securities, no additional filings are required by this paragraph (c).

d. Any person relying on Rule 13d-1(c) and has filed its initial Schedule 13G pursuant to that paragraph shall, in addition to filing any amendments pursuant to Rule 13d-2(b), file an amendment on Schedule 13G promptly upon acquiring, directly or indirectly, greater than 10 percent of a class of equity securities specified in Rule 13d-1(d), and thereafter promptly upon increasing or decreasing its beneficial ownership by more than five percent of the class of equity securities. Once an amendment has been filed reflecting beneficial ownership of 5 percent or less of the class of securities, no additional filings are required by this paragraph (d).

e. The first electronic amendment to a paper format Schedule 13D or Schedule 13G shall restate the entire text of the Schedule 13D or 13G, but previously filed paper exhibits to such Schedules are not required to be restated electronically. See Rule 102 of Regulation S-T regarding amendments to exhibits previously filed in paper format. Notwithstanding the foregoing, if the sole purpose of filing the first electronic Schedule 13D or 13G amendment is to report a change in beneficial ownership that would terminate the filer's obligation to report, the amendment need not include a restatement of the entire text of the Schedule being amended.

Note to Rule 13d-2: For persons filing a short form statement pursuant to Rule 13d-1 (b) or (c), see also Rules 13d-1(e), (f), and (g).

Rule 13d-3 – Determination of Beneficial Owner

a. For the purposes of sections 13(d) and 13(g) of the Act a beneficial owner of a security includes any person who, directly or indirectly, through any contract, arrangement, understanding, relationship, or otherwise has or shares:
   1. Voting power which includes the power to vote, or to direct the voting of, such security; and/or,
   2. Investment power which includes the power to dispose, or to direct the disposition of, such security.

b. Any person who, directly or indirectly, creates or uses a trust, proxy, power of attorney, pooling arrangement or any other contract, arrangement, or device with the purpose of effect of divesting such person of beneficial ownership of a security or preventing the vesting of such beneficial ownership as part of a plan or scheme to evade the reporting requirements of section 13(d) or (g) of the Act shall be deemed for purposes of such sections to be the beneficial owner of such security.

c. All securities of the same class beneficially owned by a person, regardless of the form which such beneficial ownership takes, shall be aggregated in calculating the number of shares beneficially owned by such person.

d. Notwithstanding the provisions of paragraphs (a) and (c) of this rule:
   1.
      i. A person shall be deemed to be the beneficial owner of a security, subject to the provisions of paragraph (b) of this rule, if that person has

the right to acquire beneficial ownership of such security, as defined in Rule 13d-3(a) within sixty days, including but not limited to any right to acquire:

A. through the exercise of any option, warrant or right;

B. through the conversion of a security;

C. pursuant to the power to revoke a trust, discretionary account, or similar arrangement; or

D. pursuant to the automatic termination of a trust, discretionary account or similar arrangement; *provided, however*, any person who acquires a security or power specified in paragraphs (d)(1)(i)(A), (B) or (C), of this section, with the purpose or effect of changing or influencing the control of the issuer, or in connection with or as a participant in any transaction having such purpose or effect, immediately upon such acquisition shall be deemed to be the beneficial owner of the securities which may be acquired through the exercise or conversion of such security or power. Any securities not outstanding which are subject to such options, warrants, rights or conversion privileges shall be deemed to be outstanding for the purpose of computing the percentage of outstanding securities of the class owned by such person but shall not be deemed to be outstanding for the purpose of computing the percentage of the class by any other person.

ii. Paragraph (d)(1)(i) of this section remains applicable for the purpose of determining the obligation to file with respect to the underlying security even though the option, warrant, right or convertible security is of a class of equity security, as defined in Rule 13d-1(i), and may therefore give rise to a separate obligation to file.

2. A member of a national securities exchange shall not be deemed to be a beneficial owner of securities held directly or indirectly by it on behalf of another person solely because such member is the record holder of such securities and, pursuant to the rules of such exchange, may direct the vote of such securities, without instruction, on other than contested matters or matters that may affect substantially the rights or privileges of the holders of the securities to be voted, but is otherwise precluded by the rules of such exchange from voting without instruction.

3. A person who in the ordinary course of his business is a pledgee of securities under a written pledge agreement shall not be deemed to be the beneficial owner of such pledged securities until the pledgee AE1 has taken all formal steps necessary which are required to declare a default and determines that the power to vote or to direct the vote or to dispose or to direct the disposition of such pledged securities will be exercised, provided, that:

i. The pledgee agreement is bona fide and was not entered into with the purpose nor with the effect of changing or influencing the control of the issuer, nor in connection with any transaction having such purpose or effect, including any transaction subject to Rule 13d-3(b);

ii. The pledgee is a person specified in Rule 13d-1(b)(1)(ii), including persons meeting the conditions set forth in paragraph (G) thereof; and

iii. The pledgee agreement, prior to default, does not grant to the pledgee;

A. The power to vote or to direct the vote of the pledged securities; or

B. The power to dispose or direct the disposition of the pledged securities, other than the grant of such power(s) pursuant to a pledge agreement under which credit is extended subject to regulation T and in which the pledgee is a broker or dealer registered under section 15 of the act.

4. A person engaged in business as an underwriter of securities who acquires securities through his participation in good faith in a firm commitment underwriting registered under the Securities Act of 1933 shall not be deemed to be the beneficial owner of such securities until the expiration of forty days after the date of such acquisition.

Rule 13d-5 – Acquisition of Securities

a. A person who becomes a beneficial owner of securities shall be deemed to have acquired such securities for purposes of section 13(d)(1) of the Act, whether such acquisition was through purchase or otherwise. However, executors or administrators of a decedent's estate generally will be presumed not to have acquired beneficial ownership of the securities in the decedent's estate until such time as such executors or administrators are qualified under local law to perform their duties.

b.

1. When two or more persons agree to act together for the purpose of acquiring, holding, voting or disposing of equity securities of an issuer, the group formed thereby shall be deemed to have acquired beneficial ownership, for purposes of Sections 13(d) and(g) of the Act, as of the date of such agreement, of all equity securities of that issuer beneficially owned by any such persons.

2. Notwithstanding the previous paragraph, a group shall be deemed not to have acquired any equity securities beneficially owned by the other members of the group solely by virtue of their concerted actions relating to the purchase of equity securities directly from an issuer in a transaction not involving a public offering: provided, that:

   i. All the members of the group are persons specified in Rule 13d-1(b)(1)(ii);

   ii. The purchase is in the ordinary course of each member's business and not with the purpose nor with the effect of changing or influencing control of the issuer, nor in connection with or as a participant in any transaction having such purpose or effect, including any transaction subject to Rule 13d-3(b);

   iii. There is no agreement among, or between any members of the group to act together with respect to the issuer or its securities except for the purpose of facilitating the specific purchase involved; and

   iv. The only actions among or between any members of the group with respect to the issuer or its securities subsequent to the closing date of the non-public offering are those which are necessary to conclude ministerial matters directly related to the completion of the offer or sale of the securities.

Rule 13d-7 – Dissemination

One copy of the Schedule filed pursuant to Rule 13d-1 and Rule 13d-2 shall be sent to the issuer of the security at its principal executive office, by registered or certified mail. A copy of Schedules filed pursuant to Rule 13d-1(a) and Rule 13d-2(a) shall also be sent to each national securities exchange where the security is traded.

Rule 13e-1 – Purchase of Securities by the Issuer During a Third-Party Tender Offer

An issuer that has received notice that it is the subject of a tender offer made under Section 14(d)(1) of the Act, that has commenced under Rule 14d-2 must not purchase any of its equity securities during the tender offer unless the issuer first:

  a. Files a statement with the Commission containing the following information:
  1. The title and number of securities to be purchased;
  2. The names of the persons or classes of persons from whom the issuer will purchase the securities;
  3. The name of any exchange, inter-dealer quotation system or any other market on or through which the securities will be purchased;
  4. The purpose of the purchase;
  5. Whether the issuer will retire the securities, hold the securities in its treasury, or dispose of the securities. If the issuer intends to dispose of the securities, describe how it intends to do so; and
  6. The source and amount of funds or other consideration to be used to make the purchase. If the issuer borrows any funds or other consideration to make the purchase or enters any agreement for the purpose of acquiring, holding, or trading the securities, describe the transaction and agreement and identify the parties; and

  b. Pays the fee required by Rule 0-11 when it files the initial statement.

  c. This section does not apply to periodic repurchases in connection with an employee benefit plan or other similar plan of the issuer so long as the purchases are made in the ordinary course and not in response to the tender offer.

Instruction to Rule 13e-1: File eight copies if paper filing is permitted.

Rule 13e-3 – Going Private Transactions by Certain Issuers or Their Affiliates

  a. **Definitions**. Unless indicated otherwise or the context otherwise requires, all terms used in this section and in Schedule 13E-3 shall have the same meaning as in the Act or elsewhere in the General Rules and Regulations thereunder. In addition, the following definitions apply:
  1. An **affiliate** of an issuer is a person that directly or indirectly through one or more intermediaries controls, is controlled by, or is under common control with such issuer. For the purposes of this section only, a person who is not an affiliate of an issuer at the commencement of such person's tender offer for a class of equity securities of such issuer will not be deemed an affiliate of such

issuer prior to the stated termination of such tender offer and any extensions thereof;

2. The term **purchase** means any acquisition for value including, but not limited to,

     i. any acquisition pursuant to the dissolution of an issuer subsequent to the sale or other disposition of substantially all the assets of such issuer to its affiliate,

     ii. any acquisition pursuant to a merger,

     iii. any acquisition of fractional interests in connection with a reverse stock split, and

     iv. any acquisition subject to the control of an issuer or an affiliate of such issuer;

3. A **Rule 13e-3 transaction** is any transaction or series of transactions involving one or more of the transactions described in paragraph (a)3(i) of this section which has either a reasonable likelihood or a purpose of producing, either directly or indirectly, any of the effects described in paragraph (a)(3)(ii) of this section;

     i. The transactions referred to in paragraph (a)3 of this section are:

         A. A purchase of any equity security by the issuer of such security or by an affiliate of such issuer;

         B. A tender offer for or request or invitation for tenders of any equity security made by the issuer of such class of securities or by an affiliate of such issuer; or

         C. A solicitation subject to Regulation 14A [Rule 14a-1 to Rule 14b-1] of any proxy, consent or authorization of, or a distribution subject to Regulation 14C [Rule 14c-1 to Rule 14c-101] of information statements to, any equity security holder by the issuer of the class of securities or by an affiliate of such issuer, in connection with: a merger, consolidation, reclassification, recapitalization, reorganization or similar corporate transaction of an issuer or between an issuer (or its subsidiaries) and its affiliate; a sale of substantially all the assets of an issuer to its affiliate or group of affiliates; or a reverse stock split of any class of equity securities of the issuer involving the purchase of fractional interests.

     ii. The effects referred to in paragraph (a)(3) of this section are:

         A. Causing any class of equity securities of the issuer which is subject to section 12(g) or section 15(d) of the Act to be held of record by less than 300 persons; or

         B. Causing any class of equity securities of the issuer which is either listed on a national securities exchange or authorized to be quoted in an inter-dealer quotation system of a registered national securities association to be neither listed on any national securities exchange nor authorized to be quoted on an inter-dealer quotation system of any registered national securities association.

4. An **unaffiliated security holder** is any security holder of an equity security subject to a Rule 13e-3 transaction who is not an affiliate of the issuer of such security.

b. **Application of section to an issuer (or an affiliate of such issuer) subject to section 12 of the Act.**

    1.   It shall be a fraudulent, deceptive or manipulative act or practice, in connection with a Rule 13e-3 transaction, for an issuer which has a class of equity securities registered pursuant to section 12 of the Act or which is a closed-end investment company registered under the Investment Company Act of 1940, or an affiliate of such issuer, directly or indirectly

        i.   To employ any device, scheme or artifice to defraud any person;

        ii.   To make any untrue statement of a material fact or to omit to state a material fact necessary in order to make the statements made, in light of the circumstances under which they were made, not misleading; or

        iii.   To engage in any act, practice or course of business which operates or would operate as a fraud or deceit upon any person.

    2.   As a means reasonably designed to prevent fraudulent, deceptive or manipulative acts or practices in connection with any Rule 13e-3 transaction, it shall be unlawful for an issuer which has a class of equity securities registered pursuant to section 12 of the Act, or an affiliate of such issuer, to engage, directly or indirectly, in a Rule 13e-3 transaction unless:

        i.   Such issuer or affiliate complies with the requirements of paragraphs (d), (e) and (f) of this section; and

        ii.   The Rule 13e-3 transaction is not in violation of paragraph (b)(1) of this section.

c. **Application of section to an issuer (or an affiliate of such issuer) subject to section 15(d) of the Act.**

    1.   It shall be unlawful as a fraudulent, deceptive or manipulative act or practice for an issuer which is required to file periodic reports pursuant to Section 15(d) of the Act, or an affiliate of such issuer, to engage, directly or indirectly, in a Rule 13e-3 transaction unless such issuer or affiliate complies with the requirements of paragraphs (d), (e) and (f) of this section.

    2.   An issuer or affiliate which is subject to paragraph (c)1 of this section and which is soliciting proxies or distributing information statements in connection with a transaction described in paragraph (a)(3)(i)(A) of this section may elect to use the timing procedures for conducting a solicitation subject to Regulation 14A [Rule 14a-1 to Rule 14b-1] or a distribution subject to Regulation 14C [Rule 14c-1 to Rule 14c-101] in complying with paragraphs (d), (e) and (f) of this section, provided that if an election is made, such solicitation or distribution is conducted in accordance with the requirements of the respective regulations, including the filing of preliminary copies of soliciting materials or an information statement at the time specified in Regulation 14A or 14C, respectively.

d. **Material required to be filed.** The issuer or affiliate engaging in a Rule 13e-3 transaction must file with the Commission:

    1.   A Schedule 13E-3 (Rule 13e-100), including all exhibits;

    2.   An amendment to Schedule 13E-3 reporting promptly any material changes in the information set forth in the schedule previously filed; and

3. A final amendment to Schedule 13E-3 reporting promptly the results of the Rule 13e-3 transaction.

e. **Disclosure of information to security holders.**
    1. In addition to disclosing the information required by any other applicable rule or regulation under the federal securities laws, the issuer or affiliate engaging in a Rule 13e-3 transaction must disclose to security holders of the class that is the subject of the transaction, as specified in paragraph (f) of this section, the following:
        i.   The information required by Item 1 of Schedule 13E-3 (Rule 13e- 100) (Summary Term Sheet);
        ii. The information required by Items 7, 8 and 9 of Schedule 13E-3, which must be prominently disclosed in a "Special Factors" section in the front of the disclosure document;
        iii. A prominent legend on the outside front cover page that indicates that neither the Securities and Exchange Commission nor any state securities commission has: approved or disapproved of the transaction; passed upon the merits or fairness of the transaction; or passed upon the adequacy or accuracy of the disclosure in the document. The legend also must make it clear that any representation to the contrary is a criminal offense;
        iv. The information concerning appraisal rights required by Item 1016(f) of Regulation M-A; and
        v.   The information required by the remaining items of Schedule 13E-3, except for Item 1016 of Regulation M-A (exhibits), or a fair and adequate summary of the information.

        Instructions to paragraph (e)(1):
        1. If the Rule 13e-3 transaction also is subject to Regulation 14A (Rule 14a-1 through Rule 14b-2) or 14C (Rule 14c-1 through Rule 14c-101), the registration provisions and rules of the Securities Act of 1933, Regulation 14D or Rule 13e-4, the information required by paragraph (e)(1) of this section must be combined with the proxy statement, information statement, prospectus or tender offer material sent or given to security holders.
        2. If the Rule 13e-3 transaction involves a registered securities offering, the legend required by Item 501(b)(7) of Regulation S-K must be combined with the legend required by paragraph (e)(1)(iii) of this section.
        3. The required legend must be written in clear, plain language.

    2. If there is any material change in the information previously disclosed to security holders, the issuer or affiliate must disclose the change promptly to security holders as specified in paragraph (f)(1)(iii) of this section.

f. **Dissemination of information to security holders.**
    1. If the Rule 13e-3 transaction involves a purchase as described in paragraph (a)(3)(i)(A) of this section or a vote, consent, authorization, or distribution of information statements as described in paragraph (a)(3)(i)(C) of this section, the issuer or affiliate engaging in the Rule 13e-3 transaction shall:
        i. Provide the information required by paragraph (e) of this section:

A. In accordance with the provisions of any applicable Federal or State law, but in no event later than 20 days prior to: any such purchase; any such vote, consent or authorization; or with respect to the distribution of information statements, the meeting date, or if corporate action is to be taken by means of the written authorization or consent of security holders, the earliest date on which corporate action may be taken: *Provided, however,* That if the purchase subject to this section is pursuant to a tender offer excepted from Rule 13e-4 by paragraph (g)(5) of Rule 13e-4 [Editor's note: It seems this should refer to paragraph (h)(5) of Rule 13e-4.], the information required by paragraph (e) of this section shall be disseminated in accordance with paragraph (e) of Rule 13e-4 no later than 10 business days prior to any purchase pursuant to such tender offer,

B. to each person who is a record holder of a class of equity securities subject to the Rule 13e-3 transaction as of a date not more than 20 days prior to the date of dissemination of such information.

ii. If the issuer or affiliate knows that securities of the class of securities subject to the Rule 13e-3 transaction are held of record by a broker, dealer, bank or voting trustee or their nominees, such issuer or affiliate shall (unless Rule 14a-13(a) or Rule 14c-7 is applicable) furnish the number of copies of the information required by paragraph (e) of this section that are requested by such persons (pursuant to inquiries by or on behalf of the issuer or affiliate), instruct such persons to forward such information to the beneficial owners of such securities in a timely manner and undertake to pay the reasonable expenses incurred by such persons in forwarding such information; and

iii. Promptly disseminate disclosure of material changes to the information required by paragraph (d) of this section in a manner reasonably calculated to inform security holders.

2. If the Rule 13e-3 transaction is a tender offer or a request or invitation for tenders of equity securities which is subject to Regulation 14D or Rule 13e-4, the tender offer containing the information required by paragraph (e) of this section, and any material change with respect thereto, shall be published, sent or given in accordance with Regulation 14D or Rule 13e-4, respectively, to security holders of the class of securities being sought by the issuer or affiliate.

g. **Exceptions**. This section shall not apply to:
1. Any Rule 13e-3 transaction by or on behalf of a person which occurs within one year of the date of termination of a tender offer in which such person was the bidder and became an affiliate of the issuer as a result of such tender offer: *Provided,* That the consideration offered to unaffiliated security holders in such Rule 13e-3 transaction is at least equal to the highest consideration offered during such tender offer and *Provided further,* That:
    i. If such tender offer was made for any or all securities of a class of the issuer;

      A. Such tender offer fully disclosed such person's intention to engage in a Rule 13e-3 transaction, the form and effect of such transaction and, to the extent known, the proposed terms thereof; and

      B. Such Rule 13e-3 transaction is substantially similar to that described in such tender offer; or

    ii. If such tender offer was made for less than all the securities of a class of the issuer:

      A. Such tender offer fully disclosed a plan of merger, a plan of liquidation or a similar binding agreement between such person and the issuer with respect to a Rule 13e-3 transaction; and

      B. Such Rule 13e-3 transaction occurs pursuant to the plan of merger, plan of liquidation or similar binding agreement disclosed in the bidder's tender offer.

  2. Any Rule 13e-3 transaction in which the security holders are offered or receive only an equity security *Provided,* That:

    i. Such equity security has substantially the same rights as the equity security which is the subject of the Rule 13e-3 transaction including, but not limited to, voting, dividends, redemption and liquidation rights except that this requirement shall be deemed to be satisfied if unaffiliated security holders are offered common stock;

    ii. Such equity security is registered pursuant to section 12 of the Act or reports are required to be filed by the issuer thereof pursuant to section 15(d) of the Act; and

    iii. If the security which is the subject of the Rule 13e-3 transaction was either listed on a national securities exchange or authorized to be quoted in an interdealer quotation system of a registered national securities association, such equity security is either listed on a national securities exchange or authorized to be quoted in an inter-dealer quotation system of a registered national securities association.

  3. [Reserved];

  4. Redemptions, calls or similar purchases of an equity security by an issuer pursuant to specific provisions set forth in the instrument(s) creating or governing that class of equity securities; or

  5. Any solicitation by an issuer with respect to a plan of reorganization under Chapter XI of the Bankruptcy Act, as amended, if made after the entry of an order approving such plan pursuant to section 1125(b) of that Act and after, or concurrently with, the transmittal of information concerning such plan as required by section 1125(b) of that Act.

  6. Any tender offer or business combination made in compliance with Securities Act Rule 802, Exchange Act Rules 13e-4(h)(8) or 14d-1(c).

Rule 13e-4 – Tender Offers by Issuers

 a. **Definitions**. Unless the context otherwise requires, all terms used in this section and in Schedule TO shall have the same meaning as in the Act or elsewhere in the General Rules and Regulations thereunder. In addition, the following definitions shall apply:

  1. The term **issuer** means any issuer which has a class of equity security registered pursuant to section 12 of the Act, or which is required to file

periodic reports pursuant to section 15(d) of the Act, or which is a closed-end investment company registered under the Investment Company Act of 1940.

2.   The term **issuer tender offer** refers to a tender offer for, or a request or invitation for tenders of, any class of equity security, made by the issuer of such class of equity security or by an affiliate of such issuer.

3.   As used in this section and in Schedule TO, the term **business day** means any day, other than Saturday, Sunday, or a Federal holiday, and shall consist of the time period from 12:01 a.m. through 12:00 midnight Eastern Time. In computing any time period under this Rule or Schedule TO, the date of the event that begins the running of such time period shall be included *except that* if such event occurs on other than a business day such period shall begin to run on and shall include the first business day thereafter

4.   The term **commencement** means 12:01 a.m. on the date that the issuer or affiliate has first published, sent or given the means to tender to security holders. For purposes of this section, the means to tender includes the transmittal form or a statement regarding how the transmittal form may be obtained.

5.   The term **termination** means the date after which securities may not be tendered pursuant to an issuer tender offer.

6.   The term **security holders** means holders of record and beneficial owners of securities of the class of equity security which is the subject of an issuer tender offer.

7.   The term **security position listing** means, with respect to the securities of any issuer held by a registered clearing agency in the name of the clearing agency or its nominee, a list of those participants in the clearing agency on whose behalf the clearing agency holds the issuer's securities and of the participants' respective positions in such securities as of a specified date.

b.   **Filing, disclosure and dissemination.** As soon as practicable on the date of commencement of the issuer tender offer, the issuer or affiliate making the issuer tender offer must comply with:
1.   The filing requirements of paragraph (c)(2) of this section;
2.   The disclosure requirements of paragraph (d)(1) of this section; and
3.   The dissemination requirements of paragraph (e) of this section.

c.   **Material required to be filed.** The issuer or affiliate making the issuer tender offer must file with the Commission:
1.   All written communications made by the issuer or affiliate relating to the issuer tender offer, from and including the first public announcement, as soon as practicable on the date of the communication;
2.   A Schedule TO, including all exhibits;
3.   An amendment to Schedule TO reporting promptly any material changes in the information set forth in the schedule previously filed; and
4.   A final amendment to Schedule TO reporting promptly the results of the issuer tender offer.

Instructions to Rule 13e-4(c):
1.   Pre-commencement communications must be filed under cover of Schedule TO and the box on the cover page of the schedule must be marked.

2. Any communications made in connection with an exchange offer registered under the Securities Act of 1933 need only be filed under Rule 425 under such Act and will be deemed filed under this section.

3. Each pre-commencement written communication must include a prominent legend in clear, plain language advising security holders to read the tender offer statement when it is available because it contains important information. The legend also must advise investors that they can get the tender offer statement and other filed documents for free at the Commission's web site and explain which documents are free from the issuer.

4. See Rule 135, Rule 165 and Rule 166 under the Securities Act for pre-commencement communications made in connection with registered exchange offers.

5. "Public announcement" is any oral or written communication by the issuer, affiliate or any person authorized to act on their behalf that is reasonably designed to, or has the effect of, informing the public or security holders in general about the issuer tender offer.

d. **Disclosure of tender offer information to security holders.**

1. The issuer or affiliate making the issuer tender offer must disclose, in a manner prescribed by paragraph (e)(1) of this section, the following:

    i.   The information required by Item 1 of Schedule TO (summary term sheet); and

    ii. The information required by the remaining items of Schedule TO for issuer tender offers, except for Item 12 (exhibits), or a fair and adequate summary of the information.

2. If there are any material changes in the information previously disclosed to security holders, the issuer or affiliate must disclose the changes promptly to security holders in a manner specified in paragraph (e)(3) of this section.

3. If the issuer or affiliate disseminates the issuer tender offer by means of summary publication as described in paragraph (e)(1)(iii) of this section, the summary advertisement must not include a transmittal letter that would permit security holders to tender securities sought in the offer and must disclose at least the following information:

    i.   The identity of the issuer or affiliate making the issuer tender offer;

    ii. The information required by Item 1004(a)(1) and Item 1006(a) of Regulation M-A;

    iii. Instructions on how security holders can obtain promptly a copy of the statement required by paragraph (d)(1) of this section, at the issuer or affiliate's expense; and

    iv. A statement that the information contained in the statement required by paragraph (d)(1) of this section is incorporated by reference.

e. **Dissemination of tender offers to security holders.** An issuer tender offer will be deemed to be published, sent or given to security holders if the issuer or affiliate making the issuer tender offer complies fully with one or more of the methods described in this section.

1. For issuer tender offers in which the consideration offered consists solely of cash and/or securities exempt from registration under section 3 of the Securities Act of 1933:

    i. Dissemination of cash issuer tender offers by long-form publication: By making adequate publication of the information required by paragraph (d)(1) of this section in a newspaper or newspapers, on the date of commencement of the issuer tender offer.

    ii. Dissemination of any issuer tender offer by use of stockholder and other lists:

        A. By mailing or otherwise furnishing promptly a statement containing the information required by paragraph (d)(1) of this section to each security holder whose name appears on the most recent stockholder list of the issuer;

        B. By contacting each participant on the most recent security position listing of any clearing agency within the possession or access of the issuer or affiliate making the issuer tender offer, and making inquiry of each participant as to the approximate number of beneficial owners of the securities sought in the offer that are held by the participant;

        C. By furnishing to each participant a sufficient number of copies of the statement required by paragraph (d)(1) of this section for transmittal to the beneficial owners; and

        D. By agreeing to reimburse each participant promptly for its reasonable expenses incurred in forwarding the statement to beneficial owners.

    iii. Dissemination of certain cash issuer tender offers by summary publication:

        A. If the issuer tender offer is not subject to Rule 13e-3, by making adequate publication of a summary advertisement containing the information required by paragraph (d)(3) of this section in a newspaper or newspapers, on the date of commencement of the issuer tender offer; and

        B. By mailing or otherwise furnishing promptly the statement required by paragraph (d)(1) of this section and a transmittal letter to any security holder who requests a copy of the statement or transmittal letter.

    Instruction to paragraph (e)(1):

    For purposes of paragraphs (e)(1)(i) and (e)(1)(iii) of this section, adequate publication of the issuer tender offer may require publication in a newspaper with a national circulation, a newspaper with metropolitan or regional circulation, or a combination of the two, depending upon the facts and circumstances involved.

2. For tender offers in which the consideration consists solely or partially of securities registered under the Securities Act of 1933, a registration statement containing all of the required information, including pricing information, has been filed and a preliminary prospectus or a prospectus that meets the requirements of Section 10(a) of the Securities Act, including a letter of transmittal, is delivered to security holders. However, for going-private

transactions (as defined by Rule 13e-3 under the Securities Exchange Act) and roll-up transactions (as described by Item 901 of Regulation S-K, a registration statement registering the securities to be offered must have become effective and only a prospectus that meets the requirements of Section 10(a) of the Securities Act may be delivered to security holders on the date of commencement.

Instructions to paragraph (e)(2):
    i.   If the prospectus is being delivered by mail, mailing on the date of commencement is sufficient.
    ii. A preliminary prospectus used under this section may not omit information under Rule 430 or Rule 430A under the Securities Act.
    iii. If a preliminary prospectus is used under this section and the issuer must disseminate material changes, the tender offer must remain open for the period specified in paragraph (e)(3) of this section.
    iv. If a preliminary prospectus is used under this section, tenders may be requested in accordance with Rule 162(a) under the Securities Act.

  3.   If a material change occurs in the information published, sent or given to security holders, the issuer or affiliate must disseminate promptly disclosure of the change in a manner reasonably calculated to inform security holders of the change. In a registered securities offer where the issuer or affiliate disseminates the preliminary prospectus as permitted by paragraph (e)(2) of this section, the offer must remain open from the date that material changes to the tender offer materials are disseminated to security holders, as follows:
    i.   Five business days for a prospectus supplement containing a material change other than price or share levels;
    ii. Ten business days for a prospectus supplement containing a change in price, the amount of securities sought, the dealer's soliciting fee, or other similarly significant change;
    iii. Ten business days for a prospectus supplement included as part of a post-effective amendment; and
    Twenty business days for a revised prospectus when the initial prospectus was materially deficient.

f. **Manner of making tender offer**.
  1.   The issuer tender offer, unless withdrawn, shall remain open until the expiration of:
    i.   At least twenty business days from its commencement; and
    ii. At least ten business days from the date that notice of an increase or decrease in the percentage of the class of securities being sought or the consideration offered or the dealer's soliciting fee to be given is first published, sent or given to security holders. *Provided, however,* That, for purposes of this paragraph, the acceptance for payment by the issuer or affiliate of an additional amount of securities not to exceed two percent of the class of securities that is the subject of the tender offer shall not be deemed to be an increase. For purposes of this paragraph, the percentage of a class of securities shall be calculated in accordance with section 14(d)(3) of the Act.

2.   The issuer or affiliate making the issuer tender offer shall permit securities tendered pursuant to the issuer tender offer to be withdrawn:

     i.   At any time during the period such issuer tender offer remains open; and

     ii.   If not yet accepted for payment, after the expiration of forty business days from the commencement of the issuer tender offer.

3.   If the issuer or affiliate makes a tender offer for less than all of the outstanding equity securities of a class, and if a greater number of securities is tendered pursuant thereto than the issuer or affiliate is bound or willing to take up and pay for, the securities taken up and paid for shall be taken up and paid for as nearly as may be pro rata, disregarding fractions, according to the number of securities tendered by each security holder during the period such offer remains open; *Provided, however,* That this provision shall not prohibit the issuer or affiliate making the issuer tender offer from:

     A.   Accepting all securities tendered by persons who own, beneficially or of record, an aggregate of not more than a specified number which is less than one hundred shares of such security and who tender all their securities, before prorating securities tendered by others; or

     B.   Accepting by lot securities tendered by security holders who tender all securities held by them and who, when tendering their securities, elect to have either all or none or at least a minimum amount or none accepted, if the issuer or affiliate first accepts all securities tendered by security holders who do not so elect;

4.   In the event the issuer or affiliate making the issuer tender increases the consideration offered after the issuer tender offer has commenced, such issuer or affiliate shall pay such increased consideration to all security holders whose tendered securities are accepted for payment by such issuer or affiliate.

5.   The issuer or affiliate making the tender offer shall either pay the consideration offered, or return the tendered securities, promptly after the termination or withdrawal of the tender offer.

6.   Until the expiration of at least ten business days after the date of termination of the issuer tender offer, neither the issuer nor any affiliate shall make any purchases, otherwise than pursuant to the tender offer, of:

     i.   Any security which is the subject of the issuer tender offer, or any security of the same class and series, or any right to purchase any such securities; and

     ii.   In the case of an issuer tender offer which is an exchange offer, any security being offered pursuant to such exchange offer, or any security of the same class and series, or any right to purchase any such security.

7.   The time periods for the minimum offering periods pursuant to this section shall be computed on a concurrent as opposed to a consecutive basis.

8.   No issuer or affiliate shall make a tender offer unless:

     i.   The tender offer is open to all security holders of the class of securities subject to the tender offer; and

     ii.   The consideration paid to any security holder for securities tendered in the tender offer is the highest consideration paid to any other security holder for securities tendered in the tender offer.

9.   Paragraph (f)(8)(i) of this section shall not:

     A.   Affect dissemination under paragraph (e) of this section; or

        B.   Prohibit an issuer or affiliate from making a tender offer excluding all security holders in a state where the issuer or affiliate is prohibited from making the tender offer by administrative or judicial action pursuant to a state statute after a good faith effort by the issuer or affiliate to comply with such statute.

10.   Paragraph (f)(8)(ii) of this section shall not prohibit the offer of more than one type of consideration in a tender offer, provided that:

        A.   Security holders are afforded equal right to elect among each of the types of consideration offered; and

        B.   The highest consideration of each type paid to any security holder is paid to any other security holder receiving that type of consideration.

11.   If the offer and sale of securities constituting consideration offered in an issuer tender offer is prohibited by the appropriate authority of a state after a good faith effort by the issuer or affiliate to register or qualify the offer and sale of such securities in such state:

        A.   The issuer or affiliate may offer security holders in such state an alternative form of consideration; and

        B.   Paragraph (f)(10) of this section shall not operate to require the issuer or affiliate to offer or pay the alternative form of consideration to security holders in any other state.

12.   i.   Paragraph (f)(8)(ii) of this section shall not prohibit the negotiation, execution or amendment of an employment compensation, severance or other employee benefit arrangement, or payments made or to be made or benefits granted or to be granted according to such an arrangement, with respect to any security holder of the issuer, where the amount payable under the arrangement:

           A.   Is being paid or granted as compensation for past services performed, future services to be performed, or future services to be refrained from performing, by the security holder (and matters incidental thereto); and

           B.   Is not calculated based on the number of securities tendered or to be tendered in the tender offer by the security holder.

    ii.   The provisions of paragraph (f)(12)(i) of this section shall be satisfied and, therefore, pursuant to this non-exclusive safe harbor, the negotiation, execution or amendment of an arrangement and any payments made or to be made or benefits granted or to be granted according to that arrangement shall not be prohibited by paragraph (f)(8)(ii) of this section, if the arrangement is approved as an employment compensation, severance or other employee benefit arrangement solely by independent directors as follows:

           A.   The compensation committee or a committee of the board of directors that performs functions similar to a compensation committee of the issuer approves the arrangement, regardless of whether the issuer is a party to the arrangement, or, if an affiliate is a party to the arrangement, the compensation committee or a committee of the board of directors that performs functions similar to a compensation committee of the affiliate approves the arrangement; or

B. If the issuer's or affiliate's board of directors, as applicable, does not have a compensation committee or a committee of the board of directors that performs functions similar to a compensation committee or if none of the members of the issuer's or affiliate's compensation committee or committee that performs functions similar to a compensation committee is independent, a special committee of the board of directors formed to consider and approve the arrangement approves the arrangement; or

C. If the issuer or affiliate, as applicable, is a foreign private issuer, any or all members of the board of directors or any committee of the board of directors authorized to approve employment compensation, severance or other employee benefit arrangements under the laws or regulations of the home country approves the arrangement.

Instructions to paragraph (f)(12)(ii): For purposes of determining whether the members of the committee approving an arrangement in accordance with the provisions of paragraph (f)(12)(ii) of this section are independent, the following provisions shall apply:

1. If the issuer or affiliate, as applicable, is a listed issuer (as defined in Rule 10A-3 of this chapter) whose securities are listed either on a national securities exchange registered pursuant to section 6(a) of the Exchange Act or in an inter-dealer quotation system of a national securities association registered pursuant to section 15A(a) of the Exchange Act that has independence requirements for compensation committee members that have been approved by the Commission (as those requirements may be modified or supplemented), apply the issuer's or affiliate's definition of independence that it uses for determining that the members of the compensation committee are independent in compliance with the listing standards applicable to compensation committee members of the listed issuer.

2. If the issuer or affiliate, as applicable, is not a listed issuer (as defined in Rule 10A-3 of this chapter), apply the independence requirements for compensation committee members of a national securities exchange registered pursuant to section 6(a) of the Exchange Act or an inter-dealer quotation system of a national securities association registered pursuant to section 15A(a) of the Exchange Act that have been approved by the Commission (as those requirements may be modified or supplemented). Whatever definition the issuer or affiliate, as applicable, chooses, it must apply that definition consistently to all members of the committee approving the arrangement.

3. Notwithstanding Instructions 1 and 2 to paragraph (f)(12)(ii), if the issuer or affiliate, as applicable, is a closed-end investment company registered under the Investment Company Act of 1940, a director is considered to be independent if the director is not, other than in his or her capacity as a member of the board of directors or any board committee, an "interested person" of the investment company, as defined in section 2(a)(19) of the Investment Company Act of 1940.

4. If the issuer or affiliate, as applicable, is a foreign private issuer, apply either the independence standards set forth in Instructions 1 and 2 to paragraph (f)(12)(ii) or the independence requirements of the laws, regulations, codes or standards of the home country of the issuer or affiliate, as applicable, for members of the board of directors or the committee of the board of directors approving the arrangement.

5. A determination by the issuer's or affiliate's board of directors, as applicable, that the members of the board of directors or the committee of the board of directors, as applicable, approving an arrangement in accordance with the provisions of paragraph (f)(12)(ii) are independent in accordance with the provisions of this instruction to paragraph (f)(12)(ii) shall satisfy the independence requirements of paragraph (f)(12)(ii).

Instruction to paragraph (f)(12): The fact that the provisions of paragraph (f)(12) of this section extend only to employment compensation, severance and other employee benefit arrangements and not to other arrangements, such as commercial arrangements, does not raise any inference that a payment under any such other arrangement constitutes consideration paid for securities in a tender offer.

13. Electronic filings. If the issuer or affiliate is an electronic filer, the minimum offering periods set forth in paragraph (f)(1) of this section shall be tolled for any period during which it fails to file in electronic format, absent a hardship exemption (Rule 201 and Rule 202 of Regulation S-T), the Schedule TO, the tender offer material specified in Item 1016(a)(1) of Regulation M-A, and any amendments thereto. If such documents were filed in paper pursuant to a hardship exemption (see Rule 201 and Rule 202 of Regulation S-T), the minimum offering periods shall be tolled for any period during which a required confirming electronic copy of such Schedule and tender offer material is delinquent.

g. The requirements of section 13(e)(1) of the Act and Rule 13e-4 and Schedule TO thereunder shall be deemed satisfied with respect to any issuer tender offer, including any exchange offer, where the issuer is incorporated or organized under the laws of Canada or any Canadian province or territory, is a foreign private issuer, and is not an investment company registered or required to be registered under the Investment Company Act of 1940, if less than 40 percent of the class of securities that is the subject of the tender offer is held by U. S. holders, and the tender offer is subject to, and the issuer complies with, the laws, regulations and policies of Canada and/or any of its provinces or territories governing the conduct of the offer (unless the issuer has received an exemption(s) from, and the issuer tender offer does not comply with, requirements that otherwise would be prescribed by this section), provided that:

1. Where the consideration for an issuer tender offer subject to this paragraph consists solely of cash, the entire disclosure document or documents required to be furnished to holders of the class of securities to be acquired shall be filed with the Commission on Schedule 13E-4F and disseminated to shareholders residing in the United States in accordance with such Canadian laws, regulations and policies; or

2. Where the consideration for an issuer tender offer subject to this paragraph includes securities to be issued pursuant to the offer, any registration statement

and/or prospectus relating thereto shall be filed with the Commission along with the Schedule 13E-4F referred to in paragraph (g)(1) of this section, and shall be disseminated, together with the home jurisdiction document(s) accompanying such Schedule, to shareholders of the issuer residing in the United States in accordance with such Canadian laws, regulations and policies.

Note: Notwithstanding the grant of an exemption from one or more of the applicable Canadian regulatory provisions imposing requirements that otherwise would be prescribed by this section, the issuer tender offer will be eligible to proceed in accordance with the requirements of this section if the Commission by order determines that the applicable Canadian regulatory provisions are adequate to protect the interest of investors.

    h.   This section shall not apply to:

        1.   Calls or redemptions of any security in accordance with the terms and conditions of its governing instruments;

        2.   Offers to purchase securities evidenced by a scrip certificate, order form or similar document which represents a fractional interest in a share of stock or similar security;

        3.   Offers to purchase securities pursuant to a statutory procedure for the purchase of dissenting security holders' securities;

        4.   Any tender offer which is subject to section 14(d) of the Act;

        5.   Offers to purchase from security holders who own an aggregate of not more than a specified number of shares that is less than one hundred: *Provided, however,* That:

            i.   The offer complies with paragraph (f)(8)(i) of this section with respect to security holders who own a number of shares equal to or less than the specified number of shares, except that an issuer can elect to exclude participants in a plan as that term is defined in Rule 100 of Regulation M, or to exclude security holders who do not own their shares as of a specified date determined by the issuer; and

           ii.   The offer complies with paragraph (f)(8)(ii) of this section or the consideration paid pursuant to the offer is determined on the basis of a uniformly applied formula based on the market price of the subject security;

        6.   An issuer tender offer made solely to effect a rescission offer: *Provided, however,* That the offer is registered under the Securities Act of 1933, and the consideration is equal to the price paid by each security holder, plus legal interest if the issuer elects to or is required to pay legal interest;

        7.   Offers by closed-end management investment companies to repurchase equity securities pursuant to Rule 23c-3 under the Investment Company Act; ...

        9.   Any other transaction or transactions, if the Commission, upon written request or upon its own motion, exempts such transaction or transactions, either unconditionally, or on specified terms and conditions, as not constituting a fraudulent, deceptive or manipulative act or practice comprehended within the purpose of this section.

* * *

    j.   1.   It shall be a fraudulent, deceptive or manipulative act or practice, in connection with an issuer tender offer, for an issuer or an affiliate of such issuer, in connection with an issuer tender offer:

i.   To employ any device, scheme or artifice to defraud any person;

ii. To make any untrue statement of a material fact or to omit to state a material fact necessary in order to make the statements made, in the light of the circumstances under which they were made, not misleading; or

iii. To engage in any act, practice or course of business which operates or would operate as a fraud or deceit upon any person.

2.   As a means reasonably designed to prevent fraudulent, deceptive or manipulative acts or practices in connection with any issuer tender offer, it shall be unlawful for an issuer or an affiliate of such issuer to make an issuer tender offer unless:

i.   Such issuer or affiliate complies with the requirements of paragraphs (b), (c), (d), (e) and (f) of this section; and

ii. The issuer tender offer is not in violation of paragraph (j)(1) of this section.

Rule 14a-1 – Definitions

Unless the context otherwise requires, all terms used in this regulation have the same meanings as in the Act or elsewhere in the general rules and regulations thereunder. In addition, the following definitions apply unless the context otherwise requires:

a.   **Associate**. The term *associate*, used to indicate a relationship with any person, means:

1.   Any corporation or organization (other than the registrant or a majority owned subsidiary of the registrant) of which such person is an officer or partner or is, directly or indirectly, the beneficial owner of 10 percent or more of any class of equity securities;

2.   Any trust or other estate in which such person has a substantial beneficial interest or as to which such person serves as trustee or in a similar fiduciary capacity; and

3.   Any relative or spouse of such person, or any relative of such spouse, who has the same home as such person or who is a director or officer of the registrant or any of its parents or subsidiaries.

b.   **Employee benefit plan**. For purposes of Rules 14a-13, 14b-1 and 14b-2, the term *employee benefit plan* means any purchase, savings, option, bonus, appreciation, profit sharing, thrift, incentive, pension or similar plan primarily for employees, directors, trustees or officers.

c.   **Entity that exercises fiduciary powers.** The term *entity that exercises fiduciary powers* means any entity that holds securities in nominee name or otherwise on behalf of a beneficial owner but does not include a clearing agency registered pursuant to section 17A of the Act or a broker or a dealer.

d.   **Exempt employee benefit plan securities**. For purposes of Rules 14a-13, 14b-1 and 14b-2, the term *exempt employee benefit plan securities* means:

1. Securities of the registrant held by an employee benefit plan, as defined in paragraph (b) of this section, where such plan is established by the registrant; or

2. If notice regarding the current solicitation has been given pursuant to Rule 14a-13(a)(1)(ii)(C) or if notice regarding the current request for a list of names, addresses and securities positions of beneficial owners has been given pursuant to Rule 14a-13(b)(3), securities of the registrant held by an employee benefit plan, as defined in paragraph (b) of this section, where such plan is established by an affiliate of the registrant.

e. **Last fiscal year.** The term *last fiscal year* of the registrant means the last fiscal year of the registrant ending prior to the date of the meeting for which proxies are to be solicited or if the solicitation involves written authorizations or consents in lieu of a meeting, the earliest date they may be used to effect corporate action.

f. **Proxy.** The term *proxy* includes every proxy, consent or authorization within the meaning of section 14(a) of the Act. The consent or authorization may take the form of failure to object or to dissent.

g. **Proxy statement.** The term *proxy statement* means the statement required by Rule 14a-3(a) whether or not contained in a single document.

h. **Record date.** The term *record date* means the date as of which the record holders of securities entitled to vote at a meeting or by written consent or authorization shall be determined.

i. **Record holder.** For purposes of Rules 14a-13, 14b-1 and 14b-2, the term *record holder* means any broker, dealer, voting trustee, bank, association or other entity that exercises fiduciary powers which holds securities of record in nominee name or otherwise or as a participant in a clearing agency registered pursuant to section 17A of the Act.

j. **Registrant.** The term *registrant* means the issuer of the securities in respect of which proxies are to be solicited.

k. **Respondent bank.** For purposes of Rules 14a-13, 14b-1 and 14b-2, the term *respondent bank* means any bank, association or other entity that exercises fiduciary powers which holds securities on behalf of beneficial owners and deposits such securities for safekeeping with another bank, association or other entity that exercises fiduciary powers.

l. **Solicitation.**
    1. The terms *solicit* and *solicitation* include:
        i.   Any request for a proxy whether or not accompanied by or included in a form of proxy:
        ii. Any request to execute or not to execute, or to revoke, a proxy; or

        iii. The furnishing of a form of proxy or other communication to security holders under circumstances reasonably calculated to result in the procurement, withholding or revocation of a proxy.

  2. The terms do not apply, however, to:

        i. The furnishing of a form of proxy to a security holder upon the unsolicited request of such security holder;

        ii. The performance by the registrant of acts required by Rule 14a-7;

        iii. The performance by any person of ministerial acts on behalf of a person soliciting a proxy; or

        iv. A communication by a security holder who does not otherwise engage in a proxy solicitation (other than a solicitation exempt under Rule 14a-2) stating how the security holder intends to vote and the reasons therefor, provided that the communication:

            A. Is made by means of speeches in public forums, press releases, published or broadcast opinions, statements, or advertisements appearing in a broadcast media, or newspaper, magazine or other bona fide publication disseminated on a regular basis,

            B. Is directed to persons to whom the security holder owes a fiduciary duty in connection with the voting of securities of a registrant held by the security holder, or

            C. Is made in response to unsolicited requests for additional information with respect to a prior communication by the security holder made pursuant to this paragraph (l)(2)(iv).

Rule 14a-2 – Solicitations to Which Rule 14a-3 to Rule 14a-15 Apply

Rules 14a-3 to 14a-15, except as specified, apply to every solicitation of a proxy with respect to securities registered pursuant to section 12 of the Act, whether or not trading in such securities has been suspended. To the extent specified below, certain of these sections also apply to roll-up transactions that do not involve an entity with securities registered pursuant to section 12 of the Act.

  a. Rules 14a-3 to 14a-15 do not apply to the following:

    1. Any solicitation by a person in respect to securities carried in his name or in the name of his nominee (otherwise than as voting trustee) or held in his custody, if such person-

        i. Receives no commission or remuneration for such solicitation, directly or indirectly, other than reimbursement of reasonable expenses,

        ii. Furnishes promptly to the person solicited (or such person's household in accordance with Rule 14a-3(e)(1)) a copy of all soliciting material with respect to the same subject matter or meeting received from all persons who shall furnish copies thereof for such purpose and who shall, if requested, defray the reasonable expenses to be incurred in forwarding such material, and

        iii. In addition, does no more than impartially instruct the person solicited to forward a proxy to the person, if any, to whom the person solicited desires to give a proxy, or impartially request from the person solicited instructions as to the authority to be conferred by the proxy and state that a proxy will be given if no instructions are received by a certain date.

2.   Any solicitation by a person in respect of securities of which he is the beneficial owner;

3.   Any solicitation involved in the offer and sale of securities registered under the Securities Act of 1933: *Provided,* That this paragraph shall not apply to securities to be issued in any transaction of the character specified in paragraph (a) of Rule 145 under that Act;

4.   Any solicitation with respect to a plan of reorganization under Chapter 11 of the Bankruptcy Reform Act of 1978, as amended, if made after the entry of an order approving the written disclosure statement concerning a plan of reorganization pursuant to section 1125 of said Act and after, or concurrently with, the transmittal of such disclosure statement as required by section 1125 of said Act;

5.   [Reserved]

6.   Any solicitation through the medium of a newspaper advertisement which informs security holders of a source from which they may obtain copies of a proxy statement, form of proxy and any other soliciting material and does no more than:

      i.   Name the registrant,

      ii. State the reason for the advertisement, and

      iii. Identify the proposal or proposals to be acted upon by security holders.

b.   Rules 14a-3 to 14a-6 (other than Rule 14a-6(g)), Rule 14a-8, and Rule 14a-10 to Rule 14a-15 do not apply to the following:

1.   Any solicitation by or on behalf of any person who does not, at any time during such solicitation, seek directly or indirectly, either on its own or another's behalf, the power to act as proxy for a security holder and does not furnish or otherwise request, or act on behalf of a person who furnishes or requests, a form of revocation, abstention, consent or authorization. *Provided, however,* That the exemption set forth in this paragraph shall not apply to:

      i.   The registrant or an affiliate or associate of the registrant (other than an officer or director or any person serving in a similar capacity);

      ii. An officer or director of the registrant or any person serving in a similar capacity engaging in a solicitation financed directly or indirectly by the registrant;

      iii. An officer, director, affiliate or associate of a person that is ineligible to rely on the exemption set forth in this paragraph (other than persons specified in paragraph (b)(1)(i) of this section), or any person serving in a similar capacity;

      iv. Any nominee for whose election as a director proxies are solicited;

      v. Any person soliciting in opposition to a merger, recapitalization, reorganization, sale of assets or other extraordinary transaction recommended or approved by the board of directors of the registrant who is proposing or intends to propose an alternative transaction to which such person or one of its affiliates is a party;

      vi. Any person who is required to report beneficial ownership of the registrant's equity securities on a Schedule 13D, unless such person has filed a Schedule 13D and has not disclosed pursuant to Item 4 thereto an intent, or reserved the right, to engage in a control transaction, or any contested solicitation for the election of directors;

      vii. Any person who receives compensation from an ineligible person directly related to the solicitation of proxies, other than pursuant to Rule 14a-13;

      viii. Where the registrant is an investment company registered under the Investment Company Act of 1940, an "interested person" of that investment company, as that term is defined in section 2(a)(19) of the Investment Company Act;

      ix. Any person who, because of a substantial interest in the subject matter of the solicitation, is likely to receive a benefit from a successful solicitation that would not be shared pro rata by all other holders of the same class of securities, other than a benefit arising from the person's employment with the registrant; and

      x. Any person acting on behalf of any of the foregoing.

2. Any solicitation made otherwise than on behalf of the registrant where the total number of persons solicited is not more than ten; and

3. The furnishing of proxy voting advice by any person (the "advisor") to any other person with whom the advisor has a business relationship, if:

      i. The advisor renders financial advice in the ordinary course of his business;

      ii. The advisor discloses to the recipient of the advice any significant relationship with the registrant or any of its affiliates, or a security holder proponent of the matter on which advice is given, as well as any material interests of the advisor in such matter;

      iii. The advisor receives no special commission or remuneration for furnishing the proxy voting advice from any person other than a recipient of the advice and other persons who receive similar advice under this subsection; and

      iv. The proxy voting advice is not furnished on behalf of any person soliciting proxies or on behalf of a participant in an election subject to the provisions of Rule 14a-12(c).

4. Any solicitation in connection with a roll-up transaction as defined in Item 901(c) of Regulation S-K in which the holder of a security that is the subject of a proposed roll-up transaction engages in preliminary communications with other holders of securities that are the subject of the same limited partnership roll-up transaction for the purpose of determining whether to solicit proxies, consents, or authorizations in opposition to the proposed limited partnership roll-up transaction; *Provided, however,* that:

      i. This exemption shall not apply to a security holder who is an affiliate of the registrant or general partner or sponsor; and

      ii. This exemption shall not apply to a holder of five percent 5% or more of the outstanding securities of a class that is the subject of the proposed roll-up transaction who engages in the business of buying and selling limited partnership interests in the secondary market unless that holder discloses to the persons to whom the communications are made such ownership interest and any relations of the holder to the parties of the transaction or to the transaction itself, as required by Rule 14a-6(n)(1) and specified in the Notice of Exempt Preliminary Roll-up Communication. If the communication is oral, this disclosure may be provided to the security holder orally. Whether the communication is written or oral, the notice required by Rule 14a-6(n) and Rule 14a-104 shall be furnished to the Commission.

5.   Publication or distribution by a broker or a dealer of a research report in accordance with Rule 138 or Rule 139 during a transaction in which the broker or dealer or its affiliate participates or acts in an advisory role.

6.   Any solicitation by or on behalf of any person who does not seek directly or indirectly, either on its own or another's behalf, the power to act as proxy for a shareholder and does not furnish or otherwise request, or act on behalf of a person who furnishes or requests, a form of revocation, abstention, consent, or authorization in an electronic shareholder forum that is established, maintained or operated pursuant to the provisions of Rule 14a-17, provided that the solicitation is made more than 60 days prior to the date announced by a registrant for its next annual or special meeting of shareholders. If the registrant announces the date of its next annual or special meeting of shareholders less than 60 days before the meeting date, then the solicitation may not be made more than two days following the date of the registrant's announcement of the meeting date. Participation in an electronic shareholder forum does not eliminate a person's eligibility to solicit proxies after the date that this exemption is no longer available, or is no longer being relied upon, provided that any such solicitation is conducted in accordance with this regulation.

Rule 14a-3 – Information to be Furnished to Security Holders

a.   No solicitation subject to this regulation shall be made unless each person solicited is concurrently furnished or has previously been furnished with:

1.   A publicly-filed preliminary or definitive written proxy statement containing the information specified in Schedule 14A;

2.   A preliminary or definitive written proxy statement included in a registration statement filed under the Securities Act of 1933 on Form S-4 or F-4 or Form N–14 and containing the information specified in such Form; or

3.   A publicly-filed preliminary or definitive proxy statement, not in the form and manner described in Rule 14a-16, containing the information specified in Schedule 14A, if:

    i.   The solicitation relates to a business combination transaction as that term is defined in Rule 165 of this chapter, as well as transactions for cash consideration requiring disclosure under Item 14 of Rule 14a-101; or

    ii.   The solicitation may not follow the form and manner described in Rule 14a-16 pursuant to the laws of the state of incorporation of the registrant.

b. If the solicitation is made on behalf of the registrant, other than an investment company registered under the Investment Company Act of 1940, and relates to an annual (or special meeting in lieu of the annual) meeting of security holders, or written consent in lieu of such meeting, at which directors are to be elected, each proxy statement furnished pursuant to paragraph (a) of this section shall be accompanied or preceded by an annual report to security holders as follows:

1. The report shall include, for the registrant and its subsidiaries consolidated, audited balance sheets as of the end of each of the two most recent fiscal years and audited statements of income and cash flows for each of the three most recent fiscal years prepared in accordance with Regulation S-X, except that the provisions of Article 3 (other than Rules 3-03(e), 3-04 and 3-20) and Article 11 shall not apply. Any financial statement schedules or exhibits or separate financial statements which may otherwise be required in filings with the Commission may be omitted. If the financial statements of the registrant and its subsidiaries consolidated in the annual report filed or to be filed with the Commission are not required to be audited, the financial statements required by this paragraph may be unaudited.

    Note 1: If the financial statements for a period prior to the most recently completed fiscal year have been examined by a predecessor accountant, the separate report of the predecessor accountant may be omitted in the report to security holders provided the registrant has obtained from the predecessor accountant a reissued report covering the prior period presented and the successor accountant clearly indicates in the scope paragraph of his report

    a. that the financial statements of the prior period were examined by other accountants,

    b. the date of their report,

    c. the type of opinion expressed by the predecessor accountant and

    d. the substantive reasons therefor, if it was other than unqualified.

    It should be noted, however, that the separate report of any predecessor accountant is required in filings with the Commission. If, for instance, the financial statements in the annual report to security holders are incorporated by reference in a Form 10-K the separate report of a predecessor accountant shall be filed in Part II or in Part IV as a financial statement schedule.

    Note 2: For purposes of complying with Rule 14a-3, if the registrant has changed its fiscal closing date, financial statements covering two years and one period of 9 to 12 months shall be deemed to satisfy the requirements for statements of income and cash flows for the three most recent fiscal years.

2. Financial statements and notes thereto shall be presented in roman type at least as large and as legible as 10-point modern type. If necessary for convenient presentation, the financial statements may be in roman type as large and as legible as 8-point modern type. All type shall be leaded at least 2 points.

3. The report shall contain the supplementary financial information required by Item 302 of Regulation S-K.

4. The report shall contain information concerning changes in and disagreements with accountants on accounting and financial disclosure required by Item 304 of Regulation S-K.

5.

     i.   The report shall contain the selected financial data required by Item 301 of Regulation S-K.

    ii.   The report shall contain management's discussion and analysis of financial condition and results of operations required by Item 303 of Regulation S-K.

  iii.   The report shall contain the quantitative and qualitative disclosures about market risk required by Item 305 of Regulation S-K.

6.   The report shall contain a brief description of the business done by the registrant and its subsidiaries during the most recent fiscal year which will, in the opinion of management, indicate the general nature and scope of the business of the registrant and its subsidiaries.

7.   The report shall contain information relating to the registrant's industry segments, classes of similar products or services, foreign and domestic operations and exports sales required by paragraphs (b), (c)(1)(i) and (d) of Item 101 of Regulation S-K.

8.   The report shall identify each of the registrant's directors and executive officers, and shall indicate the principal occupation or employment of each such person and the name and principal business of any organization by which such person is employed.

9.   The report shall contain the market price of and dividends on the registrant's common equity and related security holder matters required by Items 201(a), (b) and (c) of Regulation S-K. If the report precedes or accompanies a proxy statement or information statement relating to an annual meeting of security holders at which directors are to be elected (or special meeting or written consents in lieu of such meeting), furnish the performance graph required by Item 201(e).

10.   The registrant's proxy statement, or the report, shall contain an undertaking in bold face or otherwise reasonably prominent type to provide without charge to each person solicited upon the written request of any such person, a copy of the registrant's annual report on Form 10-K including the financial statements and the financial statement schedules, required to be filed with the Commission pursuant to Rule 13a-1 under the Act for the registrant's most recent fiscal year, and shall indicate the name and address of the person to whom such a written request is to be directed. In the discretion of management, a registrant need not undertake to furnish without charge copies of all exhibits to its Form 10-K provided the that copy of the annual report on Form 10-K furnished without charge to requesting security holders is accompanied by a list briefly describing all the exhibits not contained therein and indicating that the registrant will furnish any exhibit upon the payment of a specified reasonable fee which fee shall be limited to the registrant's reasonable expenses in furnishing such exhibit. If the registrant's annual report to security holders complies with all of the disclosure requirements of Form 10-K and is filed with the Commission in satisfaction of its Form 10-K filing requirements, such registrant need not furnish a separate Form 10-K to security holders who receive a copy of such annual report.

> **Note:** Pursuant to the undertaking required by paragraph (b)(10) of this section, a registrant shall furnish a copy of its annual report on Form 10-K to a beneficial owner of its securities upon receipt of a written request from such person. Each request must set forth a good faith representation that, as of the record date for the solicitation requiring the furnishing of the annual report to security holders pursuant to paragraph (b) of this section, the person making the request was a beneficial owner of securities entitled to vote.

11. Subject to the foregoing requirements, the report may be in any form deemed suitable by management and the information required by paragraphs (b)(5) to (10) of this section may be presented in an appendix or other separate section of the report, provided that the attention of security holders is called to such presentation.

> **Note:** Registrants are encouraged to utilize tables, schedules, charts and graphic illustrations of present financial information in an understandable manner. Any presentation of financial information must be consistent with the data in the financial statements contained in the report and, if appropriate, should refer to relevant portions of the financial statements and notes thereto.

12. [Reserved]

13. Paragraph (b) of this section shall not apply, however, to solicitations made on behalf of the registrant before the financial statements are available if a solicitation is being made at the same time in opposition to the registrant and if the registrant's proxy statement includes an undertaking in bold face type to furnish such annual report to security holders to all persons being solicited at least 20 calendar days before the date of the meeting or, if the solicitation refers to a written consent or authorization in lieu of a meeting, at least 20 calendar days prior to the earliest date on which it may be used to effect corporate action.

c. Seven copies of the report sent to security holders pursuant to this rule shall be mailed to the Commission, solely for its information, not later than the date on which such report is first sent or given to security holders or the date on which preliminary copies, or definitive copies, if preliminary filing was not required, of solicitation material are filed with the Commission pursuant to Rule 14a-6, whichever date is later. The report is not deemed to be "soliciting material" or to be "filed" with the Commission or subject to this regulation otherwise than as provided in this Rule, or to the liabilities of section 18 of the Act, except to the extent that the registrant specifically requests that it be treated as a part of the proxy soliciting material or incorporates it in the proxy statement or other filed report by reference.

d. An annual report to security holders prepared on an integrated basis pursuant to General Instruction H to Form 10-K may also be submitted in satisfaction of this rule. When filed as the annual report on Form 10-K responses to the Items of that form are subject to section 18 of the Act notwithstanding paragraph (c) of this section.

e.

1. i. A registrant will be considered to have delivered an annual report to security holders, proxy statement or Notice of Internet Availability of

Proxy Materials, as described in Rule 14a-16, to all security holders of record who share an address if:

A. The registrant delivers one annual report to security holders, proxy statement or Notice of Internet Availability of Proxy Materials, as applicable, to the shared address;

B. The registrant addresses the annual report to security holders, proxy statement or Notice of Internet Availability of Proxy Materials, as applicable, to the security holders as a group (for example, "ABC Fund [or Corporation] Security Holders," "Jane Doe and Household," "The Smith Family"), to each of the security holders individually (for example, "John Doe and Richard Jones") or to the security holders in a form to which each of the security holders has consented in writing;

Note to paragraph (e)(1)(i)(B): Unless the registrant addresses the annual report to security holders, proxy statement or Notice of Internet Availability of Proxy Materials to the security holders as a group or to each of the security holders individually, it must obtain, from each security holder to be included in the householded group, a separate affirmative written consent to the specific form of address the registrant will use.

C. The security holders consent, in accordance with paragraph (e)(1)(ii) of this section, to delivery of one annual report to security holders or proxy statement, as applicable;

D. With respect to delivery of the proxy statement or Notice of Internet Availability of Proxy Materials, the registrant delivers, together with or subsequent to delivery of the proxy statement, a separate proxy card for each security holder at the shared address; and

E. The registrant includes an undertaking in the proxy statement to deliver promptly upon written or oral request a separate copy of the annual report to security holders, proxy statement or Notice of Internet Availability of Proxy Materials, as applicable, to a security holder at a shared address to which a single copy of the document was delivered.

ii. Consent.

A. Affirmative written consent. Each security holder must affirmatively consent, in writing, to delivery of one annual report to security holders or proxy statement, as applicable. A security holder's affirmative written consent will be considered valid only if the security holder has been informed of:

1. The duration of the consent;

2. The specific types of documents to which the consent will apply;

3. The procedures the security holder must follow to revoke consent; and

4. The registrant's obligation to begin sending individual copies to a security holder within thirty days after the security holder revokes consent.

B. Implied consent. The registrant need not obtain affirmative written consent from a security holder for purposes of paragraph (e)(1)(ii)(A) of this section if all of the following conditions are met:

1. The security holder has the same last name as the other security holders at the shared address or the registrant reasonably believes that the security holders are members of the same family;

2. The registrant has sent the security holder a notice at least 60 days before the registrant begins to rely on this section concerning delivery of annual reports and proxy statements or Notice of Internet Availability of Proxy Materials to that security holder. The notice must:

   i. Be a separate written document;

   ii. State that only one annual report or proxy statement or Notice of Internet Availability of Proxy Materials, as applicable, will be delivered to the shared address unless the registrant receives contrary instructions;

   iii. Include a toll-free telephone number, or be accompanied by a reply form that is pre-addressed with postage provided, that the security holder can use to notify the registrant that the security holder wishes to receive a separate annual report or proxy statement or Notice of Internet Availability of Proxy Materials,;

   iv. State the duration of the consent;

   v. Explain how a security holder can revoke consent;

   vi. State that the registrant will begin sending individual copies to a security holder within thirty days after the security holder revokes consent; and

   vii. Contain the following prominent statement, or similar clear and understandable statement, in bold-face type: "Important Notice Regarding Delivery of Security Holder Documents." This statement also must appear on the envelope in which the notice is delivered. Alternatively, if the notice is delivered separately from other communications to security holders, this statement may appear either on the notice or on the envelope in which the notice is delivered.

   Note to paragraph (e)(1)(ii)(B)(2): The notice should be written in plain English. See Rule 421(d)(2) for a discussion of plain English principles.

3. The registrant has not received the reply form or other notification indicating that the security holder wishes to continue to receive an individual copy of the annual report or proxy statement or Notice of Internet Availability of Proxy Materials,, as applicable, within 60 days after the registrant sent the notice required by paragraph (e)(1)(ii)(B)(2) of this section; and

4. The registrant delivers the document to a post office box or residential street address.

   Note to paragraph (e)(1)(ii)(B)(4): The registrant can assume that a street address is residential unless the registrant has information that indicates the street address is a business.

iii. Revocation of consent. If a security holder, orally or in writing, revokes consent to delivery of one annual report to security holder, proxy statement or Notice of Internet Availability of Proxy Materials to a shared address, the registrant must begin sending individual copies to that security holder within 30 days after the registrant receives revocation of the security holder's consent.

iv. Definition of address. Unless otherwise indicated, for purposes of this section, address means a street *address,* a post office box number, an electronic mail address, a facsimile telephone number or other similar destination to which paper or electronic documents are delivered, unless otherwise provided in this section. If the registrant has reason to believe that the address is a street address of a multi-unit building, the address must include the unit number.

Note to paragraph (e)(1): A person other than the registrant making a proxy solicitation may deliver a single proxy statement to security holders of record or beneficial owners who have separate accounts and share an address if: (a) the registrant or intermediary has followed the procedures in this section; and (b) the registrant or intermediary makes available the shared address information to the person in accordance with Rule 14a-7(a)(2)(i) and (ii).

2. Notwithstanding paragraphs (a) and (b) of this section, unless state law requires otherwise, a registrant is not required to send an annual report to security holders or proxy statement or Notice of Internet Availability of Proxy Materials to a security holder if:

i. An annual report and a proxy statement, or Notice of Internet Availability of Proxy Materials, for two consecutive annual meetings; or

ii. All, and at least two, payments (if sent by first class mail) of dividends or interest on securities, or dividend reinvestment confirmations, during a twelve month period, have been mailed to such security holder's address and have been returned as undeliverable. If any such security holder delivers or causes to be delivered to the registrant written notice setting forth his then current address for security holder communications purposes, the registrant's obligation to deliver an annual report to security holders or a proxy statement or Notice of Internet Availability of Proxy Materials under this section is reinstated.

f. The provisions of paragraph (a) of this section shall not apply to a communication made by means of speeches in public forums, press releases, published or broadcast opinions, statements, or advertisements appearing in a broadcast media, newspaper, magazine or other bona fide publication disseminated on a regular basis, provided that:
1. No form of proxy, consent or authorization or means to execute the same is provided to a security holder in connection with the communication; and
2. At the time the communication is made, a definitive proxy statement is on file with the Commission pursuant to Rule 14a-6(b).

Rule 14a-4 – Requirements as to a Proxy

a. The form of proxy
1. Shall indicate in bold-face type whether or not the proxy is solicited on behalf of the registrant's board of directors or, if provided other than by a majority of the board of directors, shall indicate in bold-face type on whose behalf the solicitation is made;
2. Shall provide a specifically designated blank space for dating the proxy card; and
3. Shall identify clearly and impartially each separate matter intended to be acted upon, whether or not related to or conditioned on the approval of other matters, and whether proposed by the registrant or by security holders. No reference need be made, however, to proposals as to which discretionary authority is conferred pursuant to paragraph (c) of this section.

Note to paragraph (a)(3) (Electronic filers):
Electronic filers shall satisfy the filing requirements of Rule 14a-6(a) or (b) with respect to the form of proxy by filing the form of proxy as an appendix at the end of the proxy statement. Forms of proxy shall not be filed as exhibits or separate documents within an electronic submission.

b. 1. Means shall be provided in the form of proxy whereby the person solicited is afforded an opportunity to specify by boxes a choice between approval or disapproval of, or abstention with respect to each separate matter referred to therein as intended to be acted upon, other than elections to office. A proxy may confer discretionary authority with respect to matters as to which a choice is not specified by the security holder provided that the form of proxy states in bold-face type how it is intended to vote the shares represented by the proxy in each such case.
2. A form of proxy which provides for the election of directors shall set forth the names of persons nominated for election as directors. Such form of proxy shall clearly provide any of the following means for security holders to withhold authority to vote for each nominee:
    i. A box opposite the name of each nominee which may be marked to indicate that authority to vote for such nominee is withheld; or
    ii. An instruction in bold-face type which indicates that the security holder may withhold authority to vote for any nominee by lining through or otherwise striking out the name of any nominee; or

iii. Designated blank spaces in which the security holder may enter the names of nominees with respect to whom the security holder chooses to withhold authority to vote; or

iv. Any other similar means, provided that clear instructions are furnished indicating how the security holder may withhold authority to vote for any nominee.

Such form of proxy also may provide a means for the security holder to grant authority to vote for the nominees set forth, as a group, provided that there is a similar means for the security holder to withhold authority to vote for such group of nominees. Any such form of proxy which is executed by the security holder in such manner as not to withhold authority to vote for the election of any nominee shall be deemed to grant such authority, provided that the form of proxy so states in bold-face type.

Instructions.

1. Paragraph (2) does not apply in the case of a merger, consolidation or other plan if the election of directors is an integral part of the plan.

2. If applicable state law gives legal effect to votes cast against a nominee, then in lieu of, or in addition to, providing a means for security holders to withhold authority to vote, the registrant should provide a similar means for security holders to vote against each nominee.

c. A proxy may confer discretionary authority to vote on any of the following matters:

1. For an annual meeting of shareholders, if the registrant did not have notice of the matter at least 45 days before the date on which the registrant first sent its proxy materials for the prior year's annual meeting of shareholders (or date specified by an advance notice provision), and a specific statement to that effect is made in the proxy statement or form of proxy. If during the prior year the registrant did not hold an annual meeting, or if the date of the meeting has changed more than 30 days from the prior year, then notice must not have been received a reasonable time before the registrant sends its proxy materials for the current year.

2. In the case in which the registrant has received timely notice in connection with an annual meeting of shareholders (as determined under paragraph (c)(1) of this section), if the registrant includes, in the proxy statement, advice on the nature of the matter and how the registrant intends to exercise its discretion to vote on each matter. However, even if the registrant includes this information in its proxy statement, it may not exercise discretionary voting authority on a particular proposal if the proponent:

i. Provides the registrant with a written statement, within the time-frame determined under paragraph (c)(1) of this section, that the proponent intends to deliver a proxy statement and form of proxy to holders of at least the percentage of the company's voting shares required under applicable law to carry the proposal;

ii. Includes the same statement in its proxy materials filed under Rule 14a-6; and

iii. Immediately after soliciting the percentage of shareholders required to carry the proposal, provides the registrant with a statement from any solicitor or other person with knowledge that the necessary steps have been taken to deliver a proxy statement and form of proxy to holders of at least the percentage of the company's voting shares required under applicable law to carry out the proposal.

3. For solicitations other than for annual meetings or for solicitations by persons other than the registrant, matters which the persons making the solicitation do not know, a reasonable time before the solicitation, are to be presented at the meeting, if a specific statement to that effect is made in the proxy statement or form of proxy.

4. Approval of the minutes of the prior meeting if such approval does not amount to ratification of the action taken at that meeting;

5. The election of any person to any office for which a bona fide nominee is named in the proxy statement and such nominee is unable to serve or for good cause will not serve.

6. Any proposal omitted from the proxy statement and form of proxy pursuant to Rule 14a-8 or 14a-9 of this chapter.

7. Matters incident to the conduct of the meeting.

d. No proxy shall confer authority:

1. To vote for the election of any person to any office for which a bona fide nominee is not named in the proxy statement,

2. To vote at any annual meeting other than the next annual meeting (or any adjournment thereof) to be held after the date on which the proxy statement and form of proxy are first sent or given to security holders,

3. To vote with respect to more than one meeting (and any adjournment thereof) or more than one consent solicitation or

4. To consent to or authorize any action other than the action proposed to be taken in the proxy statement, or matters referred to in paragraph (c) of this rule. A person shall not be deemed to be a bona fide nominee and he shall not be named as such unless he has consented to being named in the proxy statement and to serve if elected. *Provided, however,* That nothing in this Rule 14a-4 shall prevent any person soliciting in support of nominees who, if elected, would constitute a minority of the board of directors, from seeking authority to vote for nominees named in the registrant's proxy statement, so long as the soliciting party:

    i. Seeks authority to vote in the aggregate for the number of director positions then subject to election;

    ii. Represents that it will vote for all the registrant nominees, other than those registrant nominees specified by the soliciting party;

    iii. Provides the security holder an opportunity to withhold authority with respect to any other registrant nominee by writing the name of that nominee on the form of proxy; and

    iv. States on the form of proxy and in the proxy statement that there is no assurance that the registrant's nominees will serve if elected with any of the soliciting party's nominees.

e. The proxy statement or form of proxy shall provide, subject to reasonable specified conditions, that the shares represented by the proxy will be voted and that where the person solicited specifies by means of a ballot provided pursuant to paragraph (b) of this section a choice with respect to any matter to be acted upon, the shares will be voted in accordance with the specifications so made.

f. No person conducting a solicitation subject to this regulation shall deliver a form of proxy, consent or authorization to any security holder unless the security holder concurrently receives, or has previously received, a definitive proxy statement that has been filed with the Commission pursuant to Rule 14a-6(b).

Rule 14a-5 – Presentation of Information in Proxy Statement

a. The information included in the proxy statement shall be clearly presented and the statements made shall be divided into groups according to subject matter and the various groups of statements shall be preceded by appropriate headings. The order of items and sub-items in the schedule need not be followed. Where practicable and appropriate, the information shall be presented in tabular form. All amounts shall be stated in figures. Information required by more than one applicable item need not be repeated. No statement need be made in response to any item or sub-item which is inapplicable.

b. Any information required to be included in the proxy statement as to terms of securities or other subject matter which from a standpoint of practical necessity must be determined in the future may be stated in terms of present knowledge and intention. To the extent practicable, the authority to be conferred concerning each such matter shall be confined within limits reasonably related to the need for discretionary authority. Subject to the foregoing, information which is not known to the persons on whose behalf the solicitation is to be made and which it is not reasonably within the power of such persons to ascertain or procure may be omitted, if a brief statement of the circumstances rendering such information unavailable is made.

c. Any information contained in any other proxy soliciting material which has been furnished to each person solicited in connection with the same meeting or subject matter may be omitted from the proxy statement, if a clear reference is made to the particular document containing such information.

d. 1. All printed proxy statements shall be in roman type at least as large and as legible as 10-point modern type, except that to the extent necessary for convenient presentation financial statements and other tabular data, but not the notes thereto, may be in roman type at least as large and as legible as 8-point modern type. All such type shall be leaded at least 2 points.

    2. Where a proxy statement is delivered through an electronic medium, issuers may satisfy legibility requirements applicable to printed documents, such as type size and font, by presenting all required information in a format readily communicated to investors.

e. All proxy statements shall disclose, under an appropriate caption, the following dates:

1. The deadline for submitting shareholder proposals for inclusion in the registrant's proxy statement and form of proxy for the registrant's next annual meeting, calculated in the manner provided in Rule 14a- 8(d)(Question 4); and

2. The date after which notice of a shareholder proposal submitted outside the processes of Rule 14a-8 is considered untimely, either calculated in the manner provided by Rule 14a-4(c)(1) or as established by the registrant's advance notice provision, if any, authorized by applicable state law.

f. If the date of the next annual meeting is subsequently advanced or delayed by more than 30 calendar days from the date of the annual meeting to which the proxy statement relates, the registrant shall, in a timely manner, inform shareholders of such change, and the new dates referred to in paragraphs (e)(1) and (e)(2) of this section, by including a notice, under Item 5, in its earliest possible quarterly report on Form 10-Q or, in the case of investment companies, in a shareholder report under Rule 30e-1 under the Investment Company Act of 1940, or, if impracticable, any means reasonably calculated to inform shareholders.

Rule 14a-6 – Filing Requirements

a. **Preliminary proxy statement.** Five preliminary copies of the proxy statement and form of proxy shall be filed with the Commission at least 10 calendar days prior to the date definitive copies of such material are first sent or given to security holders, or such shorter period prior to that date as the Commission may authorize upon a showing of good cause thereunder. A registrant, however, shall not file with the Commission a preliminary proxy statement, form of proxy or other soliciting material to be furnished to security holders concurrently therewith if the solicitation relates to an annual (or special meeting in lieu of the annual) meeting, or for an investment company registered under the Investment Company Act of 1940 or a business development company, if the solicitation relates to any meeting of security holders at which the only matters to be acted upon are:

1. The election of directors;
2. The election, approval or ratification of accountant(s);
3. A security holder proposal included pursuant to Rule 14a-8;
4. The approval or ratification of a plan as defined in paragraph (a)(6)(ii) of Item 402 of Regulation S-K or amendments to such a plan;
5. With respect to an investment company registered under the Investment Company Act of 1940 or a business development company, a proposal to continue, without change, any advisory or other contract or agreement that previously has been the subject of a proxy solicitation for which proxy material was filed with the Commission pursuant to this section; and/or
6. With respect to an open-end investment company registered under the Investment Company Act of 1940, a proposal to increase the number of shares authorized to be issued.

This exclusion from filing preliminary proxy material does not apply if the registrant comments upon or refers to a solicitation in opposition in connection with the meeting in its proxy material.

Note 1: The filing of revised material does not recommence the ten day time period unless the revised material contains material revisions or material new proposal(s) that constitute a fundamental change in the proxy material.

Note 2: The official responsible for the preparation of the proxy material should make every effort to verify the accuracy and completeness of the information required by the applicable rules. The preliminary material should be filed with the Commission at the earliest practicable date.

Note 3*: Solicitation in Opposition.*

For purposes of the exclusion from filing preliminary proxy material, a "solicitation in opposition" includes:

a. Any solicitation opposing a proposal supported by the registrant; and

b. any solicitation supporting a proposal that the registrant does not expressly support, other than a security holder proposal included in the registrant's proxy material pursuant to Rule14a-8. The inclusion of a security holder proposal in the registrant's proxy material pursuant to Rule 14a-8 does not constitute a "solicitation in opposition," even if the registrant opposes the proposal and/or includes a statement in opposition to the proposal.

Note 4: A registrant that is filing proxy material in preliminary form only because the registrant has commented on or referred to a solicitation in opposition should indicate that fact in a transmittal letter when filing the preliminary material with the Commission.

b. **Definitive proxy statement and other soliciting material.** Eight definitive copies of the proxy statement, form of proxy and all other soliciting materials, in the same form as the materials sent to security holders, must be filed with the Commission no later than the date they are first sent or given to security holders. Three copies of these materials also must be filed with, or mailed for filing to, each national securities exchange on which the registrant has a class of securities listed and registered.

c. **Personal solicitation materials.** If part or all of the solicitation involves personal solicitation, then eight copies of all written instructions or other materials that discuss, review or comment on the merits of any matter to be acted on, that are furnished to persons making the actual solicitation for their use directly or indirectly in connection with the solicitation, must be filed with the Commission no later than the date the materials are first sent or given to these persons.

d. **Release dates.** All preliminary proxy statements and forms of proxy filed pursuant to paragraph (a) of this section shall be accompanied by a statement of the date on which definitive copies thereof filed pursuant to paragraph (b) of this section are intended to be released to security holders. All definitive material filed pursuant to paragraph (b) of this section shall be accompanied by a statement of the date on which copies of such material were released to security holders, or, if not released, the date on which copies thereof are intended to be released. All material filed pursuant to paragraph (c) of this section shall be accompanied by a statement of the date on which copies thereof were released to the individual who will make the actual solicitation or if not released, the date on which copies thereof are intended to be released.

e.
1. Public availability of information. All copies of preliminary proxy statements and forms of proxy filed pursuant to paragraph (a) of this section shall be clearly marked "Preliminary Copies," and shall be deemed immediately available for public inspection unless confidential treatment is obtained pursuant to paragraph (e)(2) of this section.
2. Confidential treatment. If action will be taken on any matter specified in Item 14 of Schedule 14A, all copies of the preliminary proxy statement and form of proxy filed under paragraph (a) of this section will be for the information of the Commission only and will not be deemed available for public inspection until filed with the Commission in definitive form so long as:
    i. The proxy statement does not relate to a matter or proposal subject to Rule 13e-3 or a roll-up transaction as defined in Item 901(c) of Regulation S-K;
    ii. Neither the parties to the transaction nor any persons authorized to act on their behalf have made any public communications relating to the transaction except for statements where the content is limited to the information specified in Rule 135; and
    iii. The materials are filed in paper and marked "Confidential, For Use of the Commission Only." In all cases, the materials may be disclosed to any department or agency of the United States Government and to the Congress, and the Commission may make any inquiries or investigation into the materials as may be necessary to conduct an adequate review by the Commission.
    Instruction to paragraph (e)(2): If communications are made publicly that go beyond the information specified in Rule 135, the preliminary proxy materials must be re-filed promptly with the Commission as public materials.

f. **Communications not required to be filed**. Copies of replies to inquiries from security holders requesting further information and copies of communications which do no more than request that forms of proxy theretofore solicited be signed and returned need not be filed pursuant to this section.

g. **Solicitations subject to Rule 14a-2(b)(1)**
1. Any person who:
    i. Engages in a solicitation pursuant to Rule 14a-2(b)(1), and
    ii. At the commencement of that solicitation owns beneficially securities of the class which is the subject of the solicitation with a market value of over $5 million,
    shall furnish or mail to the Commission, not later than three days after the date the written solicitation is first sent or given to any security holder, five copies of a statement containing the information specified in the Notice of Exempt Solicitation (Rule 14a-103) which statement shall attach as an exhibit all written soliciting materials. Five copies of an amendment to such statement shall be furnished or mailed to the Commission, in connection with dissemination of any additional communications, not later than three days after

the date the additional material is first sent or given to any security holder. Three copies of the Notice of Exempt Solicitation and amendments thereto shall, at the same time the materials are furnished or mailed to the Commission, be furnished or mailed to each national securities exchange upon which any class of securities of the registrant is listed and registered.

    2.   Notwithstanding paragraph (g)(1) of this section, no such submission need be made with respect to oral solicitations (other than with respect to scripts used in connection with such oral solicitations), speeches delivered in a public forum, press releases, published or broadcast opinions, statements, and advertisements appearing in a broadcast media, or a newspaper, magazine or other bona fide publication disseminated on a regular basis.

h.   **Revised material.** Where any proxy statement, form of proxy or other material filed pursuant to this section is amended or revised, two of the copies of such amended or revised material filed pursuant to this section (or in the case of investment companies registered under the Investment Company Act of 1940, three of such copies) shall be marked to indicate clearly and precisely the changes effected therein. If the amendment or revision alters the text of the material the changes in such text shall be indicated by means of underscoring or in some other appropriate manner.

i.   **Fees.** At the time of filing the proxy solicitation material, the persons upon whose behalf the solicitation is made, other than investment companies registered under the Investment Company Act of 1940, shall pay to the Commission the following applicable fee:

    1.   For preliminary proxy material involving acquisitions, mergers, spinoffs, consolidations or proposed sales or other dispositions of substantially all the assets of the company, a fee established in accordance with Rule 0-11 shall be paid. No refund shall be given.

    2.   For all other proxy submissions and submissions made pursuant to Rule 14a-6(g), no fee shall be required.

j.   **Merger proxy materials.**

    1.   Any proxy statement, form of proxy or other soliciting material required to be filed by this section that also is either

        i.   Included in a registration statement filed under the Securities Act of 1933 on Forms S-4, F-4 or N-14; or

        ii.   Filed under Rule 424, Rule 425 or Rule 497 is required to be filed only under the Securities Act, and is deemed filed under this section.

    2.   Under paragraph (j)(1) of this section, the fee required by paragraph (i) of this section need not be paid.

k.   **Computing time periods.** In computing time periods beginning with the filing date specified in Regulation 14A , the filing date shall be counted as the first day of the time period and midnight of the last day shall constitute the end of the specified time period.

l.   **Roll-up transactions.** If a transaction is a roll-up transaction as defined in Item 901(c) of Regulation S-K and is registered (or authorized to be registered) on Form S-

4 or Form F-4, the proxy statement of the sponsor or the general partner as defined in Item 901(d) and Item 901(a), respectively, of Regulation S-K must be distributed to security holders no later than the lesser of 60 calendar days prior to the date on which the meeting of security holders is held or action is taken, or the maximum number of days permitted for giving notice under applicable state law.

m. **Cover page.** Proxy materials filed with the Commission shall include a cover page in the form set forth in Schedule 14A. The cover page required by this paragraph need not be distributed to security holders.

n. **Solicitations subject to Rule 14a-2(b)(4).** Any person who:
    1. Engages in a solicitation pursuant to Rule 14a-2(b)(4); and
    2. At the commencement of that solicitation both owns five percent 5% or more of the outstanding securities of a class that is the subject of the proposed roll-up transaction, and engages in the business of buying and selling limited partnership interests in the secondary market, shall furnish or mail to the Commission, not later than three days after the date an oral or written solicitation by that person is first made, sent or provided to any security holder, five copies of a statement containing the information specified in the Notice of Exempt Preliminary Roll-up Communication (Rule 14a-104). Five copies of any amendment to such statement shall be furnished or mailed to the Commission not later than three days after a communication containing revised material is first made, sent or provided to any security holder.

o. **Solicitations before furnishing a definitive proxy statement**. Solicitations that are published, sent or given to security holders before they have been furnished a definitive proxy statement must be made in accordance with Rule 14a-12 unless there is an exemption available under Rule 14a-2.

Rule 14a-7 – Obligations of Registrants to Provide a List of, or Mail Soliciting Material to, Security Holders

a. If the registrant has made or intends to make a proxy solicitation in connection with a security holder meeting or action by consent or authorization, upon the written request by any record or beneficial holder of securities of the class entitled to vote at the meeting or to execute a consent or authorization to provide a list of security holders or to mail the requesting security holder's materials, regardless of whether the request references this section, the registrant shall:
    1. Deliver to the requesting security holder within five business days after receipt of the request:
        i.   Notification as to whether the registrant has elected to mail the security holder's soliciting materials or provide a security holder list if the election under paragraph (b) of this section is to be made by the registrant;
        ii. A statement of the approximate number of record holders and beneficial holders, separated by type of holder and class, owning securities in the same class or classes as holders which have been or are to be solicited on management's behalf, or any more limited group of such holders

designated by the security holder if available or retrievable under the registrant's or its transfer agent's security holder data systems; and

 iii. The estimated cost of mailing a proxy statement, form of proxy or other communication to such holders, including to the extent known or reasonably available, the estimated costs of any bank, broker, and similar person through whom the registrant has solicited or intends to solicit beneficial owners in connection with the security holder meeting or action;

2. Perform the acts set forth in either paragraphs (a)(2)(i) or (a)2(ii) of this section, at the registrant's or requesting security holder's option, as specified in paragraph (b) of this section:

 i. Send copies of any proxy statement, form of proxy, or other soliciting material, including a Notice of Internet Availability of Proxy Materials (as described in Rule 14a-16), furnished by the security holder to the record holders, including banks, brokers, and similar entities, designated by the security holder. A sufficient number of copies must be sent to the banks, brokers, and similar entities for distribution to all beneficial owners designated by the security holder. The security holder may designate only record holders and/or beneficial owners who have not requested paper and/or e-mail copies of the proxy statement. If the registrant has received affirmative written or implied consent to deliver a single proxy statement to security holders at a shared address in accordance with the procedures in Rule 14a-3(e)(1), a single copy of the proxy statement or Notice of Internet Availability of Proxy Materials furnished by the security holder shall be sent to that address, provided that if multiple copies of the Notice of Internet Availability of Proxy Materials are furnished by the security holder for that address, the registrant shall deliver those copies in a single envelope to that address. The registrant shall send the security holder material with reasonable promptness after tender of the material to be sent, envelopes or other containers therefore, postage or payment for postage and other reasonable expenses of effecting such distribution. The registrant shall not be responsible for the content of the material; or

 ii. Deliver the following information to the requesting security holder within five business days of receipt of the request:

  A. A reasonably current list of the names, addresses and security positions of the record holders, including banks, brokers and similar entities holding securities in the same class or classes as holders which have been or are to be solicited on management's behalf, or any more limited group of such holders designated by the security holder if available or retrievable under the registrant's or its transfer agent's security holder data systems;

  B. The most recent list of names, addresses and security positions of beneficial owners as specified in Rule 14a-13(b), in the possession, or which subsequently comes into the possession, of the registrant;

  C. The names of security holders at a shared address that have consented to delivery of a single copy of proxy materials to a shared address, if the registrant has received written or implied consent in accordance with Rule 14a-3(e)(1); and

    D. If the registrant has relied on Rule 14a-16, the names of security holders who have requested paper copies of the proxy materials for all meetings and the names of security holders who, as of the date that the registrant receives the request, have requested paper copies of the proxy materials only for the meeting to which the solicitation relates.

iii. All security holder list information shall be in the form requested by the security holder to the extent that such form is available to the registrant without undue burden or expense. The registrant shall furnish the security holder with updated record holder information on a daily basis or, if not available on a daily basis, at the shortest reasonable intervals; provided, however, the registrant need not provide beneficial or record holder information more current than the record date for the meeting or action.

b. 1. The requesting security holder shall have the options set forth in paragraph (a)(2) of this section, and the registrant shall have corresponding obligations, if the registrant or general partner or sponsor is soliciting or intends to solicit with respect to:

    i. A proposal that is subject to Rule 13e-3;

    ii. A roll-up transaction as defined in Item 901(c) of Regulation S-K that involves an entity with securities registered pursuant to Section 12 of the Act; or

    iii. A roll-up transaction as defined in Item 901(c) of Regulation S-K that involves a limited partnership, unless the transaction involves only:

        A. Partnerships whose investors will receive new securities or securities in another entity that are not reported under a transaction reporting plan declared effective before December 17, 1993 by the Commission under Section 11A of the Act; or

        B. Partnerships whose investors' securities are reported under a transaction reporting plan declared effective before December 17, 1993 by the Commission under Section 11A of the Act.

  2. With respect to all other requests pursuant to this section, the registrant shall have the option to either mail the security holder's material or furnish the security holder list as set forth in this section.

c. At the time of a list request, the security holder making the request shall:

  1. If holding the registrant's securities through a nominee, provide the registrant with a statement by the nominee or other independent third party, or a copy of a current filing made with the Commission and furnished to the registrant, confirming such holder's beneficial ownership; and

  2. Provide the registrant with an affidavit, declaration, affirmation or other similar document provided for under applicable state law identifying the proposal or other corporate action that will be the subject of the security holder's solicitation or communication and attesting that:

i. The security holder will not use the list information for any purpose other than to solicit security holders with respect to the same meeting or action by consent or authorization for which the registrant is soliciting or intends to solicit or to communicate with security holders with respect to a solicitation commenced by the registrant; and

ii. The security holder will not disclose such information to any person other than a beneficial owner for whom the request was made and an employee or agent to the extent necessary to effectuate the communication or solicitation.

d. The security holder shall not use the information furnished by the registrant pursuant to paragraph (a)(2)(ii) of this section for any purpose other than to solicit security holders with respect to the same meeting or action by consent or authorization for which the registrant is soliciting or intends to solicit or to communicate with security holders with respect to a solicitation commenced by the registrant; or disclose such information to any person other than an employee, agent, or beneficial owner for whom a request was made to the extent necessary to effectuate the communication or solicitation. The security holder shall return the information provided pursuant to paragraph (a)(2)(ii) of this section and shall not retain any copies thereof or of any information derived from such information after the termination of the solicitation.

e. The security holder shall reimburse the reasonable expenses incurred by the registrant in performing the acts requested pursuant to paragraph (a) of this section.

Notes to Rule 14a-7:

1. Reasonably prompt methods of distribution to security holders may be used instead of mailing. If an alternative distribution method is chosen, the costs of that method should be considered where necessary rather than the costs of mailing.

2. When providing the information required by Rule 14a-7(a)(1)(ii), if the registrant has received affirmative written or implied consent to delivery of a single copy of proxy materials to a shared address in accordance with Rule 14a-3(e)(1), it shall exclude from the number of record holders those to whom it does not have to deliver a separate proxy statement.

Rule 14a-8 – Proposals of Security Holders

This section addresses when a company must include a shareholder's proposal in its proxy statement and identify the proposal in its form of proxy when the company holds an annual or special meeting of shareholders. In summary, in order to have your shareholder proposal included on a company's proxy card, and included along with any supporting statement in its proxy statement, you must be eligible and follow certain procedures. Under a few specific circumstances, the company is permitted to exclude your proposal, but only after submitting its reasons to the Commission. We structured this section in a question-and- answer format so that it is easier to understand. The references to "you" are to a shareholder seeking to submit the proposal.

a. **Question 1:** What is a proposal? A shareholder proposal is your recommendation or requirement that the company and/or its board of directors take action, which you intend to present at a meeting of the company's shareholders. Your proposal should state as clearly as possible the course of action that you believe the company should follow. If your proposal is placed on the company's proxy card, the company must also provide in the form of proxy means for shareholders to specify by boxes a choice between approval or disapproval, or abstention. Unless otherwise indicated, the word "proposal" as used in this section refers both to your proposal, and to your corresponding statement in support of your proposal (if any).

b. **Question 2**: Who is eligible to submit a proposal, and how do I demonstrate to the company that I am eligible?

   1.   In order to be eligible to submit a proposal, you must have continuously held at least $2,000 in market value, or 1%, of the company's securities entitled to be voted on the proposal at the meeting for at least one year by the date you submit the proposal. You must continue to hold those securities through the date of the meeting.

   2.   If you are the registered holder of your securities, which means that your name appears in the company's records as a shareholder, the company can verify your eligibility on its own, although you will still have to provide the company with a written statement that you intend to continue to hold the securities through the date of the meeting of shareholders. However, if like many shareholders you are not a registered holder, the company likely does not know that you are a shareholder, or how many shares you own. In this case, at the time you submit your proposal, you must prove your eligibility to the company in one of two ways:

      i.   The first way is to submit to the company a written statement from the "record" holder of your securities (usually a broker or bank) verifying that, at the time you submitted your proposal, you continuously held the securities for at least one year. You must also include your own written statement that you intend to continue to hold the securities through the date of the meeting of shareholders; or

      ii.   The second way to prove ownership applies only if you have filed a Schedule 13D, Schedule 13G, Form 3, Form 4 and/or Form 5, or amendments to those documents or updated forms, reflecting your ownership of the shares as of or before the date on which the one-year eligibility period begins. If you have filed one of these documents with the SEC, you may demonstrate your eligibility by submitting to the company:

         A.   A copy of the schedule and/or form, and any subsequent amendments reporting a change in your ownership level;

         B.   Your written statement that you continuously held the required number of shares for the one-year period as of the date of the statement; and

         C.   Your written statement that you intend to continue ownership of the shares through the date of the company's annual or special meeting.

c. **Question 3:** How many proposals may I submit: Each shareholder may submit no more than one proposal to a company for a particular shareholders' meeting.

d. **Question 4:** How long can my proposal be?   The proposal, including any accompanying supporting statement, may not exceed 500 words.

e. **Question 5:** What is the deadline for submitting a proposal?
    1. If you are submitting your proposal for the company's annual meeting, you can in most cases find the deadline in last year's proxy statement. However, if the company did not hold an annual meeting last year, or has changed the date of its meeting for this year more than 30 days from last year's meeting, you can usually find the deadline in one of the company's quarterly reports on Form 10-Q or in shareholder reports of investment companies under Rule 30e-1 of the Investment Company Act of 1940. In order to avoid controversy, shareholders should submit their proposals by means, including electronic means, that permit them to prove the date of delivery.
    2. The deadline is calculated in the following manner if the proposal is submitted for a regularly scheduled annual meeting. The proposal must be received at the company's principal executive offices not less than 120 calendar days before the date of the company's proxy statement released to shareholders in connection with the previous year's annual meeting. However, if the company did not hold an annual meeting the previous year, or if the date of this year's annual meeting has been changed by more than 30 days from the date of the previous year's meeting, then the deadline is a reasonable time before the company begins to print and send its proxy materials.
    3. If you are submitting your proposal for a meeting of shareholders other than a regularly scheduled annual meeting, the deadline is a reasonable time before the company begins to print and mail its proxy materials.

f. **Question 6:** What if I fail to follow one of the eligibility or procedural requirements explained in answers to Questions 1 through 4 of this section?
    1. The company may exclude your proposal, but only after it has notified you of the problem, and you have failed adequately to correct it. Within 14 calendar days of receiving your proposal, the company must notify you in writing of any procedural or eligibility deficiencies, as well as of the time frame for your response. Your response must be postmarked, or transmitted electronically, no later than 14 days from the date you received the company's notification. A company need not provide you such notice of a deficiency if the deficiency cannot be remedied, such as if you fail to submit a proposal by the company's properly determined deadline. If the company intends to exclude the proposal, it will later have to make a submission under Rule 14a-8 and provide you with a copy under Question 10 below, Rule 14a-8(j).
    2. If you fail in your promise to hold the required number of securities through the date of the meeting of shareholders, then the company will be permitted to exclude all of your proposals from its proxy materials for any meeting held in the following two calendar years.

g. **Question 7:** Who has the burden of persuading the Commission or its staff that my proposal can be excluded? Except as otherwise noted, the burden is on the company to demonstrate that it is entitled to exclude a proposal.

h. **Question 8:** Must I appear personally at the shareholders' meeting to present the proposal?

   1.   Either you, or your representative who is qualified under state law to present the proposal on your behalf, must attend the meeting to present the proposal. Whether you attend the meeting yourself or send a qualified representative to the meeting in your place, you should make sure that you, or your representative, follow the proper state law procedures for attending the meeting and/or presenting your proposal.

   2.   If the company holds it shareholder meeting in whole or in part via electronic media, and the company permits you or your representative to present your proposal via such media, then you may appear through electronic media rather than traveling to the meeting to appear in person.

   3.   If you or your qualified representative fail to appear and present the proposal, without good cause, the company will be permitted to exclude all of your proposals from its proxy materials for any meetings held in the following two calendar years.

i. **Question 9:** If I have complied with the procedural requirements, on what other bases may a company rely to exclude my proposal?

   1.   Improper under state law: If the proposal is not a proper subject for action by shareholders under the laws of the jurisdiction of the company's organization;

         Note to paragraph (i)(1): Depending on the subject matter, some proposals are not considered proper under state law if they would be binding on the company if approved by shareholders. In our experience, most proposals that are cast as recommendations or requests that the board of directors take specified action are proper under state law. Accordingly, we will assume that a proposal drafted as a recommendation or suggestion is proper unless the company demonstrates otherwise.

   2.   Violation of law: If the proposal would, if implemented, cause the company to violate any state, federal, or foreign law to which it is subject;

         Note to paragraph (i)(2): We will not apply this basis for exclusion to permit exclusion of a proposal on grounds that it would violate foreign law if compliance with the foreign law could result in a violation of any state or federal law.

   3.   Violation of proxy rules: If the proposal or supporting statement is contrary to any of the Commission's proxy rules, including Rule 14a-9, which prohibits materially false or misleading statements in proxy soliciting materials;

   4.   Personal grievance; special interest: If the proposal relates to the redress of a personal claim or grievance against the company or any other person, or if it is designed to result in a benefit to you, or to further a personal interest, which is not shared by the other shareholders at large;

   5.   Relevance: If the proposal relates to operations which account for less than 5 percent of the company's total assets at the end of its most recent fiscal year, and for less than 5 percent of its net earning sand gross sales for its most recent fiscal year, and is not otherwise significantly related to the company's business;

   6.   Absence of power/authority: If the company would lack the power or authority to implement the proposal;

7.   Management functions: If the proposal deals with a matter relating to the company's ordinary business operations;

8.   Relates to election: If the proposal relates to a nomination or an election for membership on the company's board of directors or analogous governing body or a procedure for such nomination or election;

9.   Conflicts with company's proposal: If the proposal directly conflicts with one of the company's own proposals to be submitted to shareholders at the same meeting.

     Note to paragraph (i)(9): Note to paragraph (i)(9): A company's submission to the Commission under this section should specify the points of conflict with the company's proposal.

10. Substantially implemented: If the company has already substantially implemented the proposal;

11. Duplication: If the proposal substantially duplicates another proposal previously submitted to the company by another proponent that will be included in the company's proxy materials for the same meeting;

12. Resubmissions: If the proposal deals with substantially the same subject matter as another proposal or proposals that has or have been previously included in the company's proxy materials within the preceding 5 calendar years, a company may exclude it from its proxy materials for any meeting held within 3 calendar years of the last time it was included if the proposal received:

     i.   Less than 3% of the vote if proposed once within the preceding 5 calendar years;

     ii.   Less than 6% of the vote on its last submission to shareholders if proposed twice previously within the preceding 5 calendar years; or

     iii. Less than 10% of the vote on its last submission to shareholders if proposed three times or more previously within the preceding 5 calendar years; and

13. Specific amount of dividends: If the proposal relates to specific amounts of cash or stock dividends.

j.   **Question 10:** What procedures must the company follow if it intends to exclude my proposal?

     1.   If the company intends to exclude a proposal from its proxy materials, it must file its reasons with the Commission no later than 80 calendar days before it files its definitive proxy statement and form of proxy with the Commission. The company must simultaneously provide you with a copy of its submission. The Commission staff may permit the company to make its submission later than 80 days before the company files its definitive proxy statement and form of proxy, if the company demonstrates good cause for missing the deadline.

     2.   The company must file six paper copies of the following:

          i.   The proposal;

          ii.   An explanation of why the company believes that it may exclude the proposal, which should, if possible, refer to the most recent applicable authority, such as prior Division letters issued under the rule; and

          iii. A supporting opinion of counsel when such reasons are based on matters of state or foreign law.

k. **Question 11:** May I submit my own statement to the Commission responding to the company's arguments?

Yes, you may submit a response, but it is not required. You should try to submit any response to us, with a copy to the company, as soon as possible after the company makes its submission. This way, the Commission staff will have time to consider fully your submission before it issues its response. You should submit six paper copies of your response.

l. **Question 12:** If the company includes my shareholder proposal in its proxy materials, what information about me must it include along with the proposal itself?

1. The company's proxy statement must include your name and address, as well as the number of the company's voting securities that you hold. However, instead of providing that information, the company may instead include a statement that it will provide the information to shareholders promptly upon receiving an oral or written request.

2. The company is not responsible for the contents of your proposal or supporting statement.

m. **Question 13:** What can I do if the company includes in its proxy statement reasons why it believes shareholders should not vote in favor of my proposal, and I disagree with some of its statements?

1. The company may elect to include in its proxy statement reasons why it believes shareholders should vote against your proposal. The company is allowed to make arguments reflecting its own point of view, just as you may express your own point of view in your proposal's supporting statement.

2. However, if you believe that the company's opposition to your proposal contains materially false or misleading statements that may violate our anti-fraud rule, Rule 14a-9, you should promptly send to the Commission staff and the company a letter explaining the reasons for your view, along with a copy of the company's statements opposing your proposal. To the extent possible, your letter should include specific factual information demonstrating the inaccuracy of the company's claims. Time permitting, you may wish to try to work out your differences with the company by yourself before contacting the Commission staff.

3. We require the company to send you a copy of its statements opposing your proposal before it sends its proxy materials, so that you may bring to our attention any materially false or misleading statements, under the following timeframes:

    i. If our no-action response requires that you make revisions to your proposal or supporting statement as a condition to requiring the company to include it in its proxy materials, then the company must provide you with a copy of its opposition statements no later than 5 calendar days after the company receives a copy of your revised proposal; or

    ii. In all other cases, the company must provide you with a copy of its opposition statements no later than 30 calendar days before its files definitive copies of its proxy statement and form of proxy under Rule 14a-6.

Rule 14a-9 – False or Misleading Statements

a. No solicitation subject to this regulation shall be made by means of any proxy statement, form of proxy, notice of meeting or other communication, written or oral, containing any statement which, at the time and in the light of the circumstances under which it is made, is false or misleading with respect to any material fact, or which omits to state any material fact necessary in order to make the statements therein not false or misleading or necessary to correct any statement in any earlier communication with respect to the solicitation of a proxy for the same meeting or subject matter which has become false or misleading.

b. The fact that a proxy statement, form of proxy or other soliciting material has been filed with or examined by the Commission shall not be deemed a finding by the Commission that such material is accurate or complete or not false or misleading, or that the Commission has passed upon the merits of or approved any statement contained therein or any matter to be acted upon by security holders. No representation contrary to the foregoing shall be made.
    Note: The following are some examples of what, depending upon particular facts and circumstances, may be misleading within the meaning of this section.
    a. Predictions as to specific future market values.
    b. Material which directly or indirectly impugns character, integrity or personal reputation, or directly or indirectly makes charges concerning improper, illegal or immoral conduct or associations, without factual foundation.
    c. Failure to so identify a proxy statement, form of proxy and other soliciting material as to clearly distinguish it from the soliciting material of any other person or persons soliciting for the same meeting or subject matter.
    d. Claims made prior to a meeting regarding the results of a solicitation.

Rule 14a-10 – Prohibition of Certain Solicitations

No person making a solicitation which is subject to Rule 14a-1 to Rule 14a-10 shall solicit:

a. Any undated or postdated proxy; or

b. Any proxy which provides that it shall be deemed to be dated as of any date subsequent to the date on which it is signed by the security holder.

Rule 14a-12 – Solicitation Before Furnishing a Proxy Statement

a. Notwithstanding the provisions of Rule 14a-3(a), a solicitation may be made before furnishing security holders with a proxy statement meeting the requirements of Rule 14a-3(a) if:
    1. Each written communication includes:
        i. The identity of the participants in the solicitation (as defined in Instruction 3 to Item 4 of Schedule 14A (Rule 14a-101)) and a description of their direct or indirect interests, by security holdings or

otherwise, or a prominent legend in clear, plain language advising security holders where they can obtain that information; and

ii.   A prominent legend in clear, plain language advising security holders to read the proxy statement when it is available because it contains important information. The legend also must explain to investors that they can get the proxy statement, and any other relevant documents, for free at the Commission's web site and describe which documents are available free from the participants; and

2.   A definitive proxy statement meeting the requirements of Rule 14a-3(a) is sent or given to security holders solicited in reliance on this section before or at the same time as the forms of proxy, consent or authorization are furnished to or requested from security holders.

b.   Any soliciting material published, sent or given to security holders in accordance with paragraph (a) of this section must be filed with the Commission no later than the date the material is first published, sent or given to security holders. Three copies of the material must at the same time be filed with, or mailed for filing to, each national securities exchange upon which any class of securities of the registrant is listed and registered. The soliciting material must include a cover page in the form set forth in Schedule 14A (Rule 14a-101) and the appropriate box on the cover page must be marked. Soliciting material in connection with a registered offering is required to be filed only under Rule 424 or Rule 425, and will be deemed filed under this section.

c.   Solicitations by any person or group of persons for the purpose of opposing a solicitation subject to this regulation by any other person or group of persons with respect to the election or removal of directors at any annual or special meeting of security holders also are subject to the following provisions:

1.   Application of this rule to annual report to security holders. Notwithstanding the provisions of Rule 14a-3(b) and (c), any portion of the annual report to security holders referred to in Rule 14a-3(b) that comments upon or refers to any solicitation subject to this rule, or to any participant in the solicitation, other than the solicitation by the management, must be filed with the Commission as proxy material subject to this regulation. This must be filed in electronic format unless an exemption is available under Rules 201 or 202 of Regulation S-T.

2.   Use of reprints or reproductions. In any solicitation subject to this Rule 14a-12(c), soliciting material that includes, in whole or part, any reprints or reproductions of any previously published material must:

i.   State the name of the author and publication, the date of prior publication, and identify any person who is quoted without being named in the previously published material.

ii.   Except in the case of a public or official document or statement, state whether or not the consent of the author and publication has been obtained to the use of the previously published material as proxy soliciting material.

iii.   If any participant using the previously published material, or anyone on his or her behalf, paid, directly or indirectly, for the preparation or prior publication of the previously published material, or has made or proposes to make any payments or give any other consideration in connection with the publication or republication of the material, state the circumstances.

Instructions to Rule 14a-12

1. If paper filing is permitted, file eight copies of the soliciting material with the Commission, except that only three copies of the material specified by Rule 14a-12(c)(1) need be filed.

2. Any communications made under this section after the definitive proxy statement is on file but before it is disseminated also must specify that the proxy statement is publicly available and the anticipated date of dissemination.

Rule 14a-13 – Obligation of Registrants in Communicating with Beneficial Owners

a. If the registrant knows that securities of any class entitled to vote at a meeting (or by written consents or authorizations if no meeting is held) with respect to which the registrant intends to solicit proxies, consents or authorizations are held of record by a broker, dealer, voting trustee, bank, association, or other entity that exercises fiduciary powers in nominee name or otherwise, the registrant shall:

1. By first class mail or other equally prompt means:

   i.   Inquire of each such record holder:

      A. Whether other persons are the beneficial owners of such securities and if so, the number of copies of the proxy and other soliciting material necessary to supply such material to such beneficial owners;

      B. In the case of an annual (or special meeting in lieu of the annual) meeting, or written consents in lieu of such meeting, at which directors are to be elected, the number of copies of the annual report to security holders necessary to supply such report to beneficial owners to whom such reports are to be distributed by such record holder or its nominee and not by the registrant;

      C. If the record holder has an obligation under Rule 14b-1(b)(3) or Rule 14b-2(b)(4)(ii) and (iii), whether an agent has been designated to act on its behalf in fulfilling such obligation and, if so, the name and address of such agent; and

      D. Whether it holds the registrant's securities on behalf of any respondent bank and, if so, the name and address of each such respondent bank; and

   ii. Indicate to each such record holder:

      A. Whether the registrant, pursuant to paragraph (c) of this section, intends to distribute the annual report to security holders to beneficial owners of its securities whose names, addresses and securities positions are disclosed pursuant to Rule 14b-1(b)(3) or Rule 14b-2(b)(4)(ii) and (iii);

      B. The record date; and

      C. At the option of the registrant, any employee benefit plan established by an affiliate of the registrant that holds securities of the registrant that the registrant elects to treat as exempt employee benefit plan securities;

2. Upon receipt of a record holder's or respondent bank's response indicating, pursuant to Rule 14b-2(b)(1)(i), the names and addresses of its respondent banks, within one business day after the date such response is received, make an inquiry of and give notification to each such respondent bank in the same manner required by paragraph (a)(1) of this section; *Provided, however,* the inquiry required by paragraphs(a)(1) and (a)(2) of this section shall not cover beneficial owners of exempt employee benefit plan securities;

3. Make the inquiry required by paragraph (a)(1) of this section at least 20 business days prior to the record date of the meeting of security holders, or

    i. If such inquiry is impracticable 20 business days prior to the record date of a special meeting, as many days before the record date of such meeting as is practicable or,

    ii. If consents or authorizations are solicited, and such inquiry is impracticable 20 business days before the earliest date on which they may be used to effect corporate action, as many days before that date as is practicable, or

    iii. At such later time as the rules of a national securities exchange on which the class of securities in question is listed may permit for good cause shown;

    Provided, however, That if a record holder or respondent bank has informed the registrant that a designated office(s) or department(s) is to receive such inquiries, the inquiry shall be made to such designated office(s) or department(s); and

4. Supply, in a timely manner, each record holder and respondent bank of whom the inquiries required by paragraphs(a)(1) and (a)(2) of this section are made with copies of the proxy, other proxy soliciting material, and/or the annual report to security holders, in such quantities, assembled in such form and at such place(s), as the record holder or respondent bank may reasonably request in order to send such material to each beneficial owner of securities who is to be furnished with such material by the record holder or respondent bank; and

5. Upon the request of any record holder or respondent bank that is supplied with proxy soliciting material and/or annual reports to security holders pursuant to paragraph (a)(4) of this section, pay its reasonable expenses for completing the sending of such material to beneficial owners.

Note 1: If the registrant's list of security holders indicates that some of its securities are registered in the name of a clearing agency registered pursuant to Section 17A of the Act (e.g., "Cede & Co.", nominee for the Depository Trust Company), the registrant shall make appropriate inquiry of the clearing agency and thereafter of the participants in such clearing agency who may hold on behalf of a beneficial owner or respondent bank, and shall comply with the above paragraph with respect to any such participant (*see* Rule 14a-1(i)).

Note 2: The attention of registrants is called to the fact that each broker, dealer, bank, association, and other entity that exercises fiduciary powers has an obligation pursuant to Rule 14b-1 and Rule 14b-2 (except as provided therein with respect to exempt employee benefit plan securities held in nominee name) and, with respect to brokers and dealers, applicable self-regulatory organization requirements to obtain and forward, within the time periods prescribed therein,

a.   proxies (or in lieu thereof requests for voting instructions) and proxy soliciting materials to beneficial owners on whose behalf it holds securities, and

b.   annual reports to security holders to beneficial owners on whose behalf it holds securities,

unless the registrant has notified the record holder or respondent bank that it has assumed responsibility to send such material to beneficial owners whose names, addresses, and securities positions are disclosed pursuant to Rule 14b-1(b)(3) and Rule 14b-2(b)(4)(ii) and (iii).

Note 3: The attention of registrants is called to the fact that registrants have an obligation, pursuant to paragraph (d) of this section, to cause proxies (or in lieu thereof requests for voting instructions), proxy soliciting material and annual reports to security holders to be furnished, in a timely manner, to beneficial owners of exempt employee benefit plan securities.

b.   Any registrant requesting pursuant to Rule 14b-1(b)(3) or Rule 14b-2(b)(4)(ii) and (iii) a list of names, addresses and securities positions of beneficial owners of its securities who either have consented or have not objected to disclosure of such information shall:

1.   By first class mail or other equally prompt means, inquire of each record holder and each respondent bank identified to the registrant pursuant to Rule 14b-2(b)(4)(i) whether such record holder or respondent bank holds the registrant's securities on behalf of any respondent banks and, if so, the name and address of each such respondent bank;

2.   Request such list to be compiled as of a date no earlier than five business days after the date the registrant's request is received by the record holder or respondent bank; *Provided, however,* That if the record holder or respondent bank has informed the registrant that a designated office(s) or department(s) is to receive such requests, the request shall be made to such designated office(s) or department(s);

3.   Make such request to the following persons that hold the registrant's securities on behalf of beneficial owners: all brokers, dealers, banks, associations and other entities that exercises fiduciary powers; *Provided however,* such request shall not cover beneficial owners of exempt employee benefit plan securities as defined in Rule 14a-1(d)(1); and, at the option of the registrant, such request may give notice of any employee benefit plan established by an affiliate of the registrant that holds securities of the registrant that the registrant elects to treat as exempt employee benefit plan securities;

4.   Use the information furnished in response to such request exclusively for purposes of corporate communications; and

5.   Upon the request of any record holder or respondent bank to whom such request is made, pay the reasonable expenses, both direct and indirect, of providing beneficial owner information.

Note: A registrant will be deemed to have satisfied its obligations under paragraph (b) of this section by requesting consenting and non-objecting beneficial owner lists from a designated agent acting on behalf of the record holder or respondent bank and paying to that designated agent the reasonable expenses of providing the beneficial owner information.

c. A registrant, at its option, may send its annual report to security holders to the beneficial owners whose identifying information is provided by record holders and respondent banks, pursuant to Rule 14b-1(b)(3) or Rule 14b-2(b)(4)(ii) and (iii), provided that such registrant notifies the record holders and respondent banks, at the time it makes the inquiry required by paragraph (a) of this section, that the registrant will send the annual report to security holders to the beneficial owners so identified.

d. If a registrant solicits proxies, consents or authorizations from record holders and respondent banks who hold securities on behalf of beneficial owners, the registrant shall cause proxies (or in lieu thereof requests or voting instructions), proxy soliciting material and annual reports to security holders to be furnished, in a timely manner, to beneficial owners of exempt employee benefit plan securities.

Rule 14a-14 – Modified or Superseded Documents

a. Any statement contained in a document incorporated or deemed to be incorporated by reference shall be deemed to be modified or superseded, for purposes of the proxy statement, to the extent that a statement contained in the proxy statement or in any other subsequently filed document that also is or is deemed to be incorporated by reference modifies or replaces such statement.

b. The modifying or superseding statement may, but need not, state it has modified or superseded a prior statement or include any other information set forth in the document that is not so modified or superseded. The making of a modifying or superseding statement shall not be deemed an admission that the modified or superseded statement, when made, constituted an untrue statement of a material fact, an omission to state a material fact necessary to make a statement not misleading, or the employment of a manipulative, deceptive, or fraudulent device, contrivance, scheme, transaction, act, practice, course of business or artifice to defraud, as those terms are used in the Securities Act of 1933, the Securities Exchange Act of 1934 ("the Act"), the Investment Company Act of 1940, or the rules and regulations thereunder.

c. Any statement so modified shall not be deemed in its unmodified form to constitute part of the proxy statement for purposes of the Act. Any statement so superseded shall not be deemed to constitute a part of the proxy statement for purposes of the Act.

Rule 14a-15 – Differential and Contingent Compensation in Connection with Roll-Up Transactions

a. It shall be unlawful for any person to receive compensation for soliciting proxies, consents, or authorizations directly from security holders in connection with a roll-up transaction as provided in paragraph (b) of this section, if the compensation is:
1. Based on whether the solicited proxy, consent, or authorization either approves or disapproves the proposed roll-up transaction; or
2. Contingent on the approval, disapproval, or completion of the roll-up transaction.

b.   This section is applicable to a roll-up transaction as defined in Item 901(c) of Regulation S-K, except for a transaction involving only:

1.   Finite-life entities that are not limited partnerships;

2.   Partnerships whose investors will receive new securities or securities in another entity that are not reported under a transaction reporting plan declared effective before December 17, 1993 by the Commission under section 11A of the Act; or

3.   Partnerships whose investors' securities are reported under a transaction reporting plan declared effective before December 17, 1993 by the Commission under section 11A of the Act.

Rule 14a-16 – Internet availability of proxy materials.

a.   1.   A registrant shall furnish a proxy statement pursuant to Rule14a–3(a), or an annual report to security holders pursuant to Rule 14a–3(b), to a security holder by sending the security holder a Notice of Internet Availability of Proxy Materials, as described in this section, 40 calendar days or more prior to the security holder meeting date, or if no meeting is to be held, 40 calendar days or more prior to the date the votes, consents or authorizations may be used to effect the corporate action, and complying with all other requirements of this section.

2.   Unless the registrant chooses to follow the full set delivery option set forth in paragraph (n) of this section, it must provide the record holder or respondent bank with all information listed in paragraph (d) of this section in sufficient time for the record holder or respondent bank to prepare, print and send a Notice of Internet Availability of Proxy Materials to beneficial owners at least 40 calendar days before the meeting date.

b.   1.   All materials identified in the Notice of Internet Availability of Proxy Materials must be publicly accessible, free of charge, at the Web site address specified in the notice on or before the time that the notice is sent to the security holder and such materials must remain available on that Web site through the conclusion of the meeting of security holders.

2.   All additional soliciting materials sent to security holders or made public after the Notice of Internet Availability of Proxy Materials has been sent must be made publicly accessible at the specified Web site address no later than the day on which such materials are first sent to security holders or made public.

3.   The Web site address relied upon for compliance under this section may not be the address of the Commission's electronic filing system.

4.   The registrant must provide security holders with a means to execute a proxy as of the time the Notice of Internet Availability of Proxy Materials is first sent to security holders.

c.   The materials must be presented on the Web site in a format, or formats, convenient for both reading online and printing on paper.

d.   The Notice of Internet Availability of Proxy Materials must contain the following:

1.   A prominent legend in bold-face type that states: **"Important Notice Regarding the Availability of Proxy Materials for the Shareholder Meeting to Be Held on [insert meeting date]."**

2.   An indication that the communication is not a form for voting and presents only an overview of the more complete proxy materials, which contain important information and are available on the Internet or by mail, and encouraging a security holder to access and review the proxy materials before voting;

3.   The Internet Web site address where the proxy materials are available;

4.   Instructions regarding how a security holder may request a paper or email copy of the proxy materials at no charge, including the date by which they should make the request to facilitate timely delivery, and an indication that they will not otherwise receive a paper or email copy;

5.   The date, time, and location of the meeting, or if corporate action is to be taken by written consent, the earliest date on which the corporate action may be effected;

6.   A clear and impartial identification of each separate matter intended to be acted on and the soliciting person's recommendations, if any, regarding those matters, but no supporting statements;

7.   A list of the materials being made available at the specified Web site;

8.   A toll-free telephone number, an e-mail address, and an Internet Web site where the security holder can request a copy of the proxy statement, annual report to security holders, and form of proxy, relating to all of the registrant's future security holder meetings and for the particular meeting to which the proxy materials being furnished relate;

9.   Any control/identification numbers that the security holder needs to access his or her form of proxy;

10. Instructions on how to access the form of proxy, provided that such instructions do not enable a security holder to execute a proxy without having access to the proxy statement and, if required by Rule 14a-3(b), the annual report to security holders; and

11. Information on how to obtain directions to be able to attend the meeting and vote in person.

e.   1.   The Notice of Internet Availability of Proxy Materials may not be incorporated into, or combined with, another document, except that it may be incorporated into, or combined with, a notice of security holder meeting required under state law, unless state law prohibits such incorporation or combination.

2.   The Notice of Internet Availability of Proxy Materials may contain only the information required by paragraph (d) of this section and any additional information required to be included in a notice of security holders meeting under state law; provided that:

i.   The registrant must revise the information on the Notice of Internet Availability of Proxy Materials, including any title to the document, to reflect the fact that:

        A. The registrant is conducting a consent solicitation rather than a proxy solicitation; or

        B. The registrant is not soliciting proxy or consent authority, but is furnishing an information statement pursuant to Rule 14c-2; and

   ii. The registrant may include a statement on the Notice to educate security holders that no personal information other than the identification or control number is necessary to execute a proxy.

f. 1. Except as provided in paragraph (h) of this section, the Notice of Internet Availability of Proxy Materials must be sent separately from other types of security holder communications and may not accompany any other document or materials, including the form of proxy.

    2. Notwithstanding paragraph (f)(1) of this section, the registrant may accompany the Notice of Internet Availability of Proxy Materials with:

       i. A pre-addressed, postage-paid reply card for requesting a copy of the proxy materials;

      ii. A copy of any notice of security holder meeting required under state law if that notice is not combined with the Notice of Internet Availability of Proxy Materials; and

     iii. In the case of an investment company registered under the Investment Company Act of 1940, the company's prospectus or a report that is required to be transmitted to stockholders by section 30(e) of the Investment Company Act and the rules thereunder; and

     iv. An explanation of the reasons for a registrant's use of the rules detailed in this section and the process of receiving and reviewing the proxy materials and voting as detailed in this section.

g. Plain English

    1. To enhance the readability of the Notice of Internet Availability of Proxy Materials, the registrant must use plain English principles in the organization, language, and design of the notice.

    2. The registrant must draft the language in the Notice of Internet Availability of Proxy Materials so that, at a minimum, it substantially complies with each of the following plain English writing principles:

       i. Short sentences;

      ii. Definite, concrete, everyday words;

     iii. Active voice;

     iv. Tabular presentation or bullet lists for complex material, whenever possible;

      v. No legal jargon or highly technical business terms; and

     vi. No multiple negatives.

    3. In designing the Notice of Internet Availability of Proxy Materials, the registrant may include pictures, logos, or similar design elements so long as the design is not misleading and the required information is clear.

h. The registrant may send a form of proxy to security holders if:

    1. At least 10 calendar days or more have passed since the date it first sent the Notice of Internet Availability of Proxy Materials to security holders and the

form of proxy is accompanied by a copy of the Notice of Internet Availability of Proxy Materials; or

2. The form of proxy is accompanied or preceded by a copy, via the same medium, of the proxy statement and any annual report to security holders that is required by Rule 14a-3(b).

i. The registrant must file a form of the Notice of Internet Availability of Proxy Materials with the Commission pursuant to Rule 14a-6(b) no later than the date that the registrant first sends the notice to security holders.

j. Obligation to provide copies.

1. The registrant must send, at no cost to the record holder or respondent bank and by U.S. first class mail or other reasonably prompt means, a paper copy of the proxy statement, information statement, annual report to security holders, and form of proxy (to the extent each of those documents is applicable) to any record holder or respondent bank requesting such a copy within three business days after receiving a request for a paper copy.

2. The registrant must send, at no cost to the record holder or respondent bank and via e-mail, an electronic copy of the proxy statement, information statement, annual report to security holders, and form of proxy (to the extent each of those documents is applicable) to any record holder or respondent bank requesting such a copy within three business days after receiving a request for an electronic copy via e-mail.

3. The registrant must provide copies of the proxy materials for one year after the conclusion of the meeting or corporate action to which the proxy materials relate, provided that, if the registrant receives the request after the conclusion of the meeting or corporate action to which the proxy materials relate, the registrant need not send copies via First Class mail and need not respond to such request within three business days.

4. The registrant must maintain records of security holder requests to receive materials in paper or via e-mail for future solicitations and must continue to provide copies of the materials to a security holder who has made such a request until the security holder revokes such request.

k. Security holder information.

1. A registrant or its agent shall maintain the Internet Web site on which it posts its proxy materials in a manner that does not infringe on the anonymity of a person accessing such Web site.

2. The registrant and its agents shall not use any e-mail address obtained from a security holder solely for the purpose of requesting a copy of proxy materials pursuant to paragraph (j) for any purpose other than to send a copy of those materials to that security holder. The registrant shall not disclose such information to any person other than an employee or agent to the extent necessary to send a copy of the proxy materials pursuant to paragraph (j).

l. A person other than the registrant may solicit proxies pursuant to the conditions imposed on registrants by this section, provided that:

    1.   A soliciting person other than the registrant is required to provide copies of its proxy materials only to security holders to whom it has sent a Notice of Internet Availability of Proxy Materials; and

    2.   A soliciting person other than the registrant must send its Notice of Internet Availability of Proxy Materials by the later of:

        i.   40 calendar days prior to the security holder meeting date or, if no meeting is to be held, 40 calendar days prior to the date the votes, consents, or authorizations may be used to effect the corporate action; or

        ii.   The date on which it files its definitive proxy statement with the Commission, provided its preliminary proxy statement is filed no later than 10 calendar days after the date that the registrant files its definitive proxy statement.

    3.   Content of the soliciting person's Notice of Internet Availability of Proxy Materials.

        i.   If, at the time a soliciting person other than the registrant sends its Notice of Internet Availability of Proxy Materials, the soliciting person is not aware of all matters on the registrant's agenda for the meeting of security holders, the soliciting person's Notice on Internet Availability of Proxy Materials must provide a clear and impartial identification of each separate matter on the agenda to the extent known by the soliciting person at that time. The soliciting person's notice also must include a clear statement indicating that there may be additional agenda items of which the soliciting person is not aware and that the security holder cannot direct a vote for those items on the soliciting person's proxy card provided at that time.

        ii.   If a soliciting person other than the registrant sends a form of proxy not containing all matters intended to be acted upon, the Notice of Internet Availability of Proxy Materials must clearly state whether execution of the form of proxy will invalidate a security holder's prior vote on matters not presented on the form of proxy.

m.   This section shall not apply to a proxy solicitation in connection with a business combination transaction, as defined in Rule 165 of this chapter, as well as transactions for cash consideration requiring disclosure under Item 14 of Rule 14a-101.

n.   **Full Set Delivery Option.**

    1.   For purposes of this paragraph (n), the term full set of proxy materials shall include all of the following documents:

        i.   A copy of the proxy statement;

        ii.   A copy of the annual report to security holders if required by14a-3(b); and

        iii.   A form of proxy.

    2.   Notwithstanding paragraphs (e) and (f)(2) of this section, a registrant or other soliciting person may:

        i.   Accompany the Notice of Internet Availability of Proxy Materials with a full set of proxy materials; or

        ii.   Send a full set of proxy materials without a Notice of Internet Availability of Proxy Materials if all of the information required in a

Notice of Internet Availability of Proxy Materials pursuant to paragraphs (d) and (n)(4) is incorporated in the proxy statement and the form of proxy.

3. A registrant or other soliciting person that sends a full set of proxy materials to a security holder pursuant to this paragraph (n) need not comply with
    i.   The timing provisions of paragraphs (a) and (l)(2); and
    ii. The obligation to provide copies pursuant to paragraph (j).

4. A registrant or other soliciting person that sends a full set of proxy materials to a security holder pursuant to this paragraph (n) need not include in its Notice of Internet Availability of Proxy Materials, proxy statement, or form of proxy the following disclosures:
    i.   Instructions regarding the nature of the communication pursuant to paragraph (d)(2) of this section;
    ii. Instructions on how to request a copy of the proxy materials; and
    iii. Instructions on how to access the form of proxy pursuant to paragraph (d)(7).

Rule 14a-17 – Electronic shareholder forums

a. A shareholder, registrant, or third party acting on behalf of a shareholder or registrant may establish, maintain, or operate an electronic shareholder forum to facilitate interaction among the registrant's shareholders and between the registrant and its shareholders as the shareholder or registrant deems appropriate. Subject to paragraphs (b) and (c) of this section, the forum must comply with the federal securities laws, including Section 14(a) of the Act and its associated regulations, other applicable federal laws, applicable state laws, and the registrant's governing documents.

b. No shareholder, registrant, or third party acting on behalf of a shareholder or registrant, by reason of establishing, maintaining, or operating an electronic shareholder forum, will be liable under the federal securities laws for any statement or information provided by another person to the electronic shareholder forum. Nothing in this section prevents or alters the application of the federal securities laws, including the provisions for liability for fraud, deception, or manipulation, or other applicable federal and state laws to the person or persons that provide a statement or information to an electronic shareholder forum.

c. Reliance on the exemption in Rule 14a-2(b)(6) to participate in an electronic shareholder forum does not eliminate a person's eligibility to solicit proxies after the date that the exemption in Rule 14a-2(b)(6) is no longer available, or is no longer being relied upon, provided that any such solicitation is conducted in accordance with this regulation.

Rule 14d-1 – Scope of and Definitions Applicable to Regulations 14D and 14E

a. **Scope**. Regulation 14D shall apply to any tender offer which is subject to section 14(d)(1) of the Act, including, but not limited to, any tender offer for securities of a class described in that section which is made by an affiliate of the issuer of such class.

Regulation 14E shall apply to any tender offer for securities (other than exempted securities) unless otherwise noted therein.

b. The requirements imposed by sections 14(d)(1) through 14(d)(7) of the Act, Regulation 14D and Schedules TO and 14D-9 thereunder, and Rule 14e-1 of Regulation 14E under the Act, shall be deemed satisfied with respect to any tender offer, including any exchange offer, for the securities of an issuer incorporated or organized under the laws of Canada or any Canadian province or territory, if such issuer is a foreign private issuer and is not an investment company registered or required to be registered under the Investment Company Act of 1940, if less than 40 percent of the class of securities outstanding that is the subject of the tender offer is held by U.S. holders, and the tender offer is subject to, and the bidder complies with, the laws, regulations and policies of Canada and/or any of its provinces or territories governing the conduct of the offer (unless the bidder has received an exemption(s) from, and the tender offer does not comply with, requirements that otherwise would be prescribed by Regulation 14D or 14E, provided that:

1. In the case of tender offers subject to section 14(d)(1) of the Act, where the consideration for a tender offer subject to this section consists solely of cash, the entire disclosure document or documents required to be furnished to holders of the class of securities to be acquired shall be filed with the Commission on Schedule 14D-1F and disseminated to shareholders of the subject company residing in the United States in accordance with such Canadian laws, regulations and policies; or

2. Where the consideration for a tender offer subject to this section includes securities of the bidder to be issued pursuant to the offer, any registration statement and/or prospectus relating thereto shall be filed with the Commission along with the Schedule 14D-1F referred to in paragraph (b)(1) of this section, and shall be disseminated, together with the home jurisdiction document(s) accompanying such Schedule, to shareholders of the subject company residing in the United States in accordance with such Canadian laws, regulations and policies.

Notes:

1. For purposes of any tender offer, including any exchange offer, otherwise eligible to proceed in accordance with Rule 14d-1(b) under the Act, the issuer of the subject securities will be presumed to be a foreign private issuer and U.S. holders will be presumed to hold less than 40 percent of such outstanding securities, unless

    a. the aggregate trading volume of that class on national securities exchanges in the United States and on NASDAQ exceeded its aggregate trading volume on securities exchanges in Canada and on the Canadian Dealing Network, Inc. ("CDN") over the 12 calendar month period prior to commencement of this offer, or if commenced in response to a prior offer, over the 12 calendar month period prior to the commencement of the initial offer (based on volume figures published by such exchanges and NASDAQ and CDN);

    b. the most recent annual report or annual information form filed or submitted by the issuer with securities regulators of Ontario,

Quebec, British Columbia or Alberta (or, if the issuer of the subject securities is not a reporting issuer in any of such provinces, with any other Canadian securities regulator) or with the Commission indicates that U.S. holders hold 40 percent or more of the outstanding subject class of securities; or

c.   the offeror has actual knowledge that the level of U.S. ownership equals or exceeds 40 percent of such securities.

2.   Notwithstanding the grant of an exemption from one or more of the applicable Canadian regulatory provisions imposing requirements that otherwise would be prescribed by Regulation 14D or 14E, the tender offer will be eligible to proceed in accordance with the requirements of this section if the Commission by order determines that the applicable Canadian regulatory provisions are adequate to protect the interest of investors.

e.   Notwithstanding paragraph (a) of this section, the requirements imposed by sections 14(d)(1) through 14(d)(7) of the Act, Regulation 14D promulgated thereunder (Rule 14d-1 through Rule 14d- 10), and Rule 14e-1 and Rule 14e-2 shall not apply by virtue of the fact that a bidder for the securities of a foreign private issuer, as defined in Rule 3b-4, the subject company of such a tender offer, their representatives, or any other person specified in Rule 14d-9(d), provides any journalist with access to its press conferences held outside of the United States, to meetings with its representatives conducted outside of the United States, or to written press- related materials released outside the United States, at or in which a present or proposed tender offer is discussed, if:

1.   Access is provided to both U.S. and foreign journalists; and

2.   With respect to any written press-related materials released by the bidder or its representatives that discuss a present or proposed tender offer for equity securities registered under Section 12 of the Act, the written press-related materials must state that these written press-related materials are not an extension of a tender offer in the United States for a class of equity securities of the subject company. If the bidder intends to extend the tender offer in the United States at some future time, a statement regarding this intention, and that the procedural and filing requirements of the Williams Act will be satisfied at that time, also must be included in these written press-related materials. No means to tender securities, or coupons that could be returned to indicate interest in the tender offer, may be provided as part of, or attached to, these written press-related materials.

f.   For the purpose of paragraph (c), a bidder may presume that a target company qualifies as a foreign private issuer if the target company is a foreign issuer and files registration statements or reports on the disclosure forms specifically designated for foreign private issuers, claims the exemption from registration under the Act pursuant to Rule 12g3-2(b), or is not reporting in the United States.

g.   **Definitions**. Unless the context otherwise requires, all terms used in Regulation 14D and Regulation 14E have the same meaning as in the Act and in Rule 12b-2 promulgated thereunder. In addition, for purposes of sections 14(d) and 14(e) of the Act and Regulation 14D or 14E, the following definitions apply:

1. The term **beneficial owner** shall have the same meaning as that set forth in Rule 13d-3: *Provided, however,* That, except with respect to Rule 14d-3 and Rule 14d-9(d), the term shall not include a person who does not have or share investment power or who is deemed to be a beneficial owner by virtue of Rule 13d-3(d)(1);

2. The term **bidder** means any person who makes a tender offer or on whose behalf a tender offer is made: *Provided, however,* That the term does not include an issuer which makes a tender offer for securities of any class of which it is the issuer;

3. The term **business day** means any day, other than Saturday, Sunday or a federal holiday, and shall consist of the time period from 12:01 a.m. through 12:00 midnight Eastern time. In computing any time period under section 14(d)(5) or section 14(d)(6) of the Act or under Regulation 14D or Regulation 14E, the date of the event which begins the running of such time period shall be included *except that* if such event occurs on other than a business day such period shall begin to run on and shall include the first business day thereafter; and

4. The term **initial offering period** means the period from the time the offer commences until all minimum time periods, including extensions, required by Regulations 14D and 14E have been satisfied and all conditions to the offer have been satisfied or waived within these time periods.

5. The term **security holders** means holders of record and beneficial owners of securities which are the subject of a tender offer;

6. The term **security position listing** means, with respect to securities of any issuer held by a registered clearing agency in the name of the clearing agency or its nominee, a list of those participants in the clearing agency on whose behalf the clearing agency holds the issuer's securities and of the participants' respective positions in such securities as of a specified date.

7. The term **subject company** means any issuer of securities which are sought by a bidder pursuant to a tender offer;

8. The term **subsequent offering period** means the period immediately following the initial offering period meeting the conditions specified in Rule 14d-11.

9. The term **tender offer material** means:
    i.   The bidder's formal offer, including all the material terms and conditions of the tender offer and all amendments thereto;
    ii. The related transmittal letter (whereby securities of the subject company which are sought in the tender offer may be transmitted to the bidder or its depositary) and all amendments thereto; and
    iii. Press releases, advertisements, letters and other documents published by the bidder or sent or given by the bidder to security holders which, directly or indirectly, solicit, invite or request tenders of the securities being sought in the tender offer;

h. **Signatures.** Where the Act or the rules, forms, reports or schedules thereunder require a document filed with or furnished to the Commission to be signed, such document shall be manually signed, or signed using either typed signatures or duplicated or facsimile versions of manual signatures. Where typed, duplicated or facsimile signatures are used, each signatory to the filing shall manually sign a signature page or other document authenticating, acknowledging or otherwise adopting his or her signature that appears in the filing. Such document shall be executed before or at the time the filing is made and shall be retained by the filer for a period of five years. Upon request, the filer shall furnish to the Commission or its staff a copy of any or all documents retained pursuant to this section.

Rule 14d-2 – Commencement of a Tender Offer

a. **Date of commencement**. A bidder will have commenced its tender offer for purposes of section 14(d) of the Act and the rules under that section at 12:01 a.m. on the date when the bidder has first published, sent or given the means to tender to security holders. For purposes of this section, the means to tender includes the transmittal form or a statement regarding how the transmittal form may be obtained.

b. **Pre-commencement communications**. A communication by the bidder will not be deemed to constitute commencement of a tender offer if:
   1. It does not include the means for security holders to tender their shares into the offer; and
   2. All written communications relating to the tender offer, from and including the first public announcement, are filed under cover of Schedule TO with the Commission no later than the date of the communication. The bidder also must deliver to the subject company and any other bidder for the same class of securities the first communication relating to the transaction that is filed, or required to be filed, with the Commission.

   Instructions to paragraph (b)(2)
   1. The box on the front of Schedule TO indicating that the filing contains pre-commencement communications must be checked.
   2. Any communications made in connection with an exchange offer registered under the Securities Act of 1933 need only be filed under Rule 425 and will be deemed filed under this section.
   3. Each pre-commencement written communication must include a prominent legend in clear, plain language advising security holders to read the tender offer statement when it is available because it contains important information. The legend also must advise investors that they can get the tender offer statement and other filed documents for free at the Commission's web site and explain which documents are free from the offeror.
   4. See Rule 135, Rule 165 and Rule 166 for pre-commencement communications made in connection with registered exchange offers.
   5. "Public announcement" is any oral or written communication by the bidder, or any person authorized to act on the bidder's behalf, that is reasonably designed to, or has the effect of, informing the public or security holders in general about the tender offer.

c. **Filing and other obligations triggered by commencement**. As soon as practicable on the date of commencement, a bidder must comply with the filing requirements of Rule 14d-3(a), the dissemination requirements of Rule 14d-4(a) or (b), and the disclosure requirements of Rule 14d-6(a).

Rule 14d-3 – Filing and Transmission of Tender Offer Statement

a. **Filing and transmittal.** No bidder shall make a tender offer if, after consummation thereof, such bidder would be the beneficial owner of more than 5 percent of the class of the subject company's securities for which the tender offer is made, unless as soon as practicable on the date of the commencement of the tender offer such bidder:

    1.   Files with the Commission a Tender Offer Statement on Schedule TO, including all exhibits thereto;

    2.   Delivers a copy of such Schedule TO, including all exhibits thereto:

        i.   To the subject company at its principal executive office; and

        ii.   To any other bidder, which has filed a Schedule TO with the Commission relating to a tender offer which has not yet terminated for the same class of securities of the subject company, at such bidder's principal executive office or at the address of the person authorized to receive notices and communications (which is disclosed on the cover sheet of such other bidder's Schedule TO);

    3.   Gives telephonic notice of the information required by Rule 14d-6(d)(2)(i) and (ii) and mails by means of first class mail a copy of such Schedule TO, including all exhibits thereto:

        i.   To each national securities exchange where such class of the subject company's securities is registered and listed for trading (which may be based upon information contained in the subject company's most recent Annual Report on Form 10-K filed with the Commission unless the bidder has reason to believe that such information is not current) which telephonic notice shall be made when practicable prior to the opening of each such exchange; and

        ii.   To the National Association of Securities Dealers, Inc. ("NASD") if such class of the subject company's securities is authorized for quotation in the NASDAQ interdealer quotation system.

b. **Post-commencement amendments and additional materials**. The bidder making the tender offer must file with the Commission:

    1.   An amendment to Schedule TO reporting promptly any material changes in the information set forth in the schedule previously filed and including copies of any additional tender offer materials as exhibits; and

    2.   A final amendment to Schedule TO reporting promptly the results of the tender offer.

Instruction to paragraph (b): A copy of any additional tender offer materials or amendment filed under this section must be sent promptly to the subject company and to any exchange and/or NASD, as required by paragraph (a) of this section, but in no event later than the date the materials are first published, sent or given to security holders.

c. **Certain announcements.** Notwithstanding the provisions of paragraph (b) of this section, if the additional tender offer material or an amendment to Schedule TO discloses only the number of shares deposited to date, and/or announces an extension of the time during which shares may be tendered, then the bidder may file such tender offer material or amendment and send a copy of such tender offer material or amendment to the subject company, any exchange and/or the NASD, as required by paragraph (a) of this section, promptly after the date such tender offer material is first published or sent or given to security holders.

Rule 14d-4 – Dissemination of Tender Offers to Security Holders

As soon as practicable on the date of commencement of a tender offer, the bidder must publish, send or give the disclosure required by Rule 14d-6 to security holders of the class of securities that is the subject of the offer, by complying with all of the requirements of any of the following:

a. **Cash tender offers and exempt securities offers**. For tender offers in which the consideration consists solely of cash and/or securities exempt from registration under section 3 of the Securities Act of 1933:
   1. *Long-form publication.* The bidder makes adequate publication in a newspaper or newspapers of long-form publication of the tender offer.
   2. *Summary publication.*
      i. If the tender offer is not subject to Rule 13e-3, the bidder makes adequate publication in a newspaper or newspapers of a summary advertisement of the tender offer; and
      ii. Mails by first class mail or otherwise furnishes with reasonable promptness the bidder's tender offer materials to any security holder who requests such tender offer materials pursuant to the summary advertisement or otherwise.
   3. *Use of stockholder lists and security position listings.* Any bidder using stockholder lists and security position listings under Rule 14d-5 must comply with paragraph (a)(1) or (2) of this section on or before the date of the bidder's request under Rule 14d-5(a).

   Instruction to paragraph (a): Tender offers may be published or sent or given to security holders by other methods, but with respect to summary publication and the use of stockholder lists and security position listings under Rule 14d-5, paragraphs (a)(2) and (a)(3) of this section are exclusive.

b. **Registered securities offers**. For tender offers in which the consideration consists solely or partially of securities registered under the Securities Act of 1933, a registration statement containing all of the required information, including pricing information, has been filed and a preliminary prospectus or a prospectus that meets the requirements of section 10(a) of the Securities Act, including a letter of transmittal, is delivered to security holders. However, for going-private transactions (as defined by Rule 13e-3) and roll-up transactions (as described by Item 901 of Regulation S-K), a registration statement registering the securities to be offered must have become effective and only a prospectus that meets the requirements of section 10(a) of the Securities Act may be delivered to security holders on the date of commencement.

   Instructions to paragraph (b):
   1. If the prospectus is being delivered by mail, mailing on the date of commencement is sufficient.

2. A preliminary prospectus used under this section may not omit information under Rule 430 or Rule 430A of this chapter.
3. If a preliminary prospectus is used under this section and the bidder must disseminate material changes, the tender offer must remain open for the period specified in paragraph (d)(2) of this section.
4. If a preliminary prospectus is used under this section, tenders may be requested in accordance with Rule 162(a) of this chapter.

c. **Adequate publication**. Depending on the facts and circumstances involved, adequate publication of a tender offer pursuant to this section may require publication in a newspaper with a national circulation or may only require publication in a newspaper with metropolitan or regional circulation or may require publication in a combination thereof: *Provided, however,* that publication in all editions of a daily newspaper with a national circulation shall be deemed to constitute adequate publication.

d. **Publication of changes and extension of the offer.**
1. If a tender offer has been published or sent or given to security holders by one or more of the methods enumerated in paragraph (a) of this section, a material change in the information published or sent or given to security holders shall be promptly disseminated to security holders in a manner reasonably designed to inform security holders of such change; *Provided, however,* That if the bidder has elected pursuant to Rule 14d-5 (f)(1) of this section to require the subject company to disseminate amendments disclosing material changes to the tender offer materials pursuant to Rule 14d-5, the bidder shall disseminate material changes in the information published or sent or given to security holders at least pursuant to Rule 14d-5.
2. In a registered securities offer where the bidder disseminates the preliminary prospectus as permitted by paragraph (b) of this section, the offer must remain open from the date that material changes to the tender offer materials are disseminated to security holders, as follows:
   i. Five business days for a prospectus supplement containing a material change other than price or share levels;
   ii. Ten business days for a prospectus supplement containing a change in price, the amount of securities sought, the dealer's soliciting fee, or other similarly significant change;
   iii. Ten business days for a prospectus supplement included as part of a post-effective amendment; and
   iv. Twenty business days for a revised prospectus when the initial prospectus was materially deficient.

Rule 14d-5 – Dissemination of Certain Tender Offers by the Use of Stockholder Lists and Security Position Listings

a. **Obligations of the subject company**. Upon receipt by a subject company at its principal executive offices of a bidder's written request, meeting the requirements of paragraph (e) of this section, the subject company shall comply with the following sub-paragraphs.

1. The subject company shall notify promptly transfer agents and any other person who will assist the subject company in complying with the requirements of this section of the receipt by the subject company of a request by a bidder pursuant to this section.

2. The subject company shall promptly ascertain whether the most recently prepared stockholder list, written or otherwise, within the access of the subject company was prepared as of a date earlier than ten business days before the date of the bidder's request and, if so, the subject company shall promptly prepare or cause to be prepared a stockholder list as of the most recent practicable date which shall not be more than ten business days before the date of the bidder's request.

3. The subject company shall make an election to comply and shall comply with all of the provisions of either paragraph (b) or paragraph (c) of this section. The subject company's election once made shall not be modified or revoked during the bidder's tender offer and extensions thereof.

4. No later than the second business day after the date of the bidder's request, the subject company shall orally notify the bidder, which notification shall be confirmed in writing, of the subject company's election made pursuant to paragraph(a)(3) of this section. Such notification shall indicate
    i.   the approximate number of security holders of the class of securities being sought by the bidder and,
    ii. if the subject company elects to comply with paragraph (b) of this section, appropriate information concerning the location for delivery of the bidder's tender offer materials and the approximate direct costs incidental to the mailing to security holders of the bidder's tender offer materials computed in accordance with paragraph (g)(2) of this section.

b. **Mailing of tender offer materials by the subject company.** A subject company which elects pursuant to paragraph (a)(3) of this section to comply with the provisions of this paragraph shall perform the acts prescribed by the following paragraphs.

    1. The subject company shall promptly contact each participant named on the most recent security position listing of any clearing agency within the access of the subject company and make inquiry of each such participant as to the approximate number of beneficial owners of the subject company securities being sought in the tender offer held by each such participant.

    2. No later than the third business day after delivery of the bidder's tender offer materials pursuant to paragraph (g)(1) of this section, the subject company shall begin to mail or cause to be mailed by means of first class mail a copy of the bidder's tender offer materials to each person whose name appears as a record holder of the class of securities for which the offer is made on the most recent stockholder list referred to in paragraph (a)(2) of this section. The subject company shall use its best efforts to complete the mailing in a timely manner but in no event shall such mailing be completed in a substantially greater period of time than the subject company would complete a mailing to security holders of its own materials relating to the tender offer.

    3. No later than the third business day after the delivery of the bidder's tender offer materials pursuant to paragraph (g)(1) of this section, the subject company shall begin to transmit or cause to be transmitted a sufficient number

of sets of the bidder's tender offer materials to the participants named on the security position listings described in paragraph (b)(1) of this section. The subject company shall use its best efforts to complete the transmittal in a timely manner but in no event shall such transmittal be completed in a substantially greater period of time than the subject company would complete a transmittal to such participants pursuant to security position listings of clearing agencies of its own material relating to the tender offer.

4. The subject company shall promptly give oral notification to the bidder, which notification shall be confirmed in writing, of the commencement of the mailing pursuant to paragraph (b)(2) of this section and of the transmittal pursuant to paragraph (b)(3) of this section.

5. During the tender offer and any extension thereof the subject company shall use reasonable efforts to update the stockholder list and shall mail or cause to be mailed promptly following each update a copy of the bidder's tender offer materials (to the extent sufficient sets of such materials have been furnished by the bidder) to each person who has become a record holder since the later of

 i. the date of preparation of the most recent stockholder list referred to in paragraph (a)(2) of this section or

 ii. the last preceding update.

6. If the bidder has elected pursuant to paragraph (f)(1) of this section to require the subject company to disseminate amendments disclosing material changes to the tender offer materials pursuant to this section, the subject company, promptly following delivery of each such amendment, shall mail or cause to be mailed a copy of each such amendment to each record holder whose name appears on the shareholder list described in paragraphs (a)(2) and (b)(5) of this section and shall transmit or cause to be transmitted sufficient copies of such amendment to each participant named on security position listings who received sets of the bidder's tender offer materials pursuant to paragraph (b)(3) of this section.

7. The subject company shall not include any communication other than the bidder's tender offer materials or amendments thereto in the envelopes or other containers furnished by the bidder.

8. Promptly following the termination of the tender offer, the subject company shall reimburse the bidder the excess, if any, of the amounts advanced pursuant to paragraph (f)(3)(iii) over the direct costs incidental to compliance by the subject company and its agents in performing the acts required by this section computed in accordance with paragraph (g)(2) of this section.

c. **Delivery of stockholder lists and security position listings.** A subject company which elects pursuant to paragraph (a)(3) of this section to comply with the provisions of this paragraph shall perform the acts prescribed by the following paragraphs.

1. No later than the third business day after the date of the bidder's request, the subject company must furnish to the bidder at the subject company's principal executive office a copy of the names and addresses of the record holders on the most recent stockholder list referred to in paragraph (a)(2) of this section; the names and addresses of participants identified on the most recent security position listing of any clearing agency that is within the access of the subject company; and the most recent list of names, addresses and security positions of

beneficial owners as specified in Rule 14a-13(b), in the possession of the subject company, or that subsequently comes into its possession. All security holder list information must be in the format requested by the bidder to the extent the format is available to the subject company without undue burden or expense.

2.   If the bidder has elected pursuant to paragraph (f)(1) of this section to require the subject company to disseminate amendments disclosing material changes to the tender offer materials, the subject company shall update the stockholder list by furnishing the bidder with the name and address of each record holder named on the stockholder list, and not previously furnished to the bidder, promptly after such information becomes available to the subject company during the tender offer and any extensions thereof.

d.   **Liability of subject company and others.** Neither the subject company nor any affiliate or agent of the subject company nor any clearing agency shall be:

1.   Deemed to have made a solicitation or recommendation respecting the tender offer within the meaning of section 14(d)(4) based solely upon the compliance or noncompliance by the subject company or any affiliate or agent of the subject company with one or more requirements of this section;

2.   Liable under any provision of the Federal securities laws to the bidder or to any security holder based solely upon the inaccuracy of the current names or addresses on the stockholder list or security position listing, unless such inaccuracy results from a lack of reasonable care on the part of the subject company or any affiliate or agent of the subject company;

3.   Deemed to be an "underwriter" within the meaning of section 211 of the Securities Act of 1933 for any purpose of that Act or any rule or regulation promulgated thereunder based solely upon the compliance or noncompliance by the subject company or any affiliate or agent of the subject company with one or more of the requirements of this section;

4.   Liable under any provision of the Federal securities laws for the disclosure in the bidder's tender offer materials, including any amendment thereto, based solely upon the compliance or noncompliance by the subject company or any affiliate or agent of the subject company with one or more of the requirements of this section.

e.   **Content of the bidder's request.** The bidder's written request referred to in paragraph (a) of this section shall include the following:

1.   The identity of the bidder;

2.   The title of the class of securities which is the subject of the bidder's tender offer;

3.   A statement that the bidder is making a request to the subject company pursuant to paragraph (a) of this section for the use of the stockholder list and security position listings for the purpose of disseminating a tender offer to security holders;

4.   A statement that the bidder is aware of and will comply with the provisions of paragraph (f) of this section;

5. A statement as to whether or not it has elected pursuant to paragraph (f)(1) of this section to disseminate amendments disclosing material changes to the tender offer materials pursuant to this section; and

6. The name, address and telephone number of the person whom the subject company shall contact pursuant to paragraph (a)(4) of this section.

f. **Obligations of the bidder.** Any bidder who requests that a subject company comply with the provisions of paragraph (a) of this section shall comply with the following paragraphs.

1. The bidder shall make an election whether or not to require the subject company to disseminate amendments disclosing material changes to the tender offer materials pursuant to this section, which election shall be included in the request referred to in paragraph (a) of this section and shall not be revocable by the bidder during the tender offer and extensions thereof.

2. With respect to a tender offer subject to section 14(d)(1) of the Act in which the consideration consists solely of cash and/or securities exempt from registration under section 3 of the Securities Act of 1933, the bidder shall comply with the requirements of Rule 14d-4(a)3.

3. If the subject company elects to comply with paragraph (b) of this section,

    i.   The bidder shall promptly deliver the tender offer materials after receipt of the notification from the subject company as provided in paragraph (a)(4) of this section;

    ii. The bidder shall promptly notify the subject company of any amendment to the bidder's tender offer materials requiring compliance by the subject company with paragraph (b)(6) of this section and shall promptly deliver such amendment to the subject company pursuant to paragraph (g)(1) of this section;

    iii. The bidder shall advance to the subject company an amount equal to the approximate cost of conducting mailings to security holders computed in accordance with paragraph (g)(2) of this section;

    iv. The bidder shall promptly reimburse the subject company for the direct costs incidental to compliance by the subject company and its agents in performing the acts required by this section computed in accordance with paragraph (g)(2) of this section which are in excess of the amount advanced pursuant to paragraph (f)(2)(iii) of this section; and

    v.   The bidder shall mail be means of first class mail or otherwise furnish with reasonable promptness the tender offer materials to any security holder who requests such materials.

4. If the subject company elects to comply with paragraph (c) of this section,

    i.   The bidder shall use the stockholder list and security position listings furnished to the bidder pursuant to paragraph (c) of this section exclusively in the dissemination of tender offer materials to security holders in connection with the bidder's tender offer and extensions thereof;

    ii. The bidder shall return the stockholder lists and security position listings furnished to the bidder pursuant to paragraph (c) of this section promptly after the termination of the bidder's tender offer;

iii.   The bidder shall accept, handle and return the stockholder lists and security position listings furnished to the bidder pursuant to paragraph (c) of this section to the subject company on a confidential basis;

iv.   The bidder shall not retain any stockholder list or security position listing furnished by the subject company pursuant to paragraph (c) of this section, or any copy thereof, nor retain any information derived from any such list or listing or copy thereof after the termination of the bidder's tender offer;

v.   The bidder shall mail by means of first class mail, at its own expense, a copy of its tender offer materials to each person whose identity appears on the stockholder list as furnished and updated by the subject company pursuant to paragraphs (c)(1) and (2) of this section;

vi.   The bidder shall contact the participants named on the security position listing of any clearing agency, make inquiry of each participant as to the approximate number of sets of tender offer materials required by each such participant, and furnish, at its own expense, sufficient sets of tender offer materials and any amendment thereto to each such participant for subsequent transmission to the beneficial owners of the securities being sought by the bidder;

vii.   The bidder shall mail by means of first class mail or otherwise furnish with reasonable promptness the tender offer materials to any security holder who requests such materials; and

viii.   The bidder shall promptly reimburse the subject company for direct costs incidental to compliance by the subject company and its agents in performing the acts required by this section computed in accordance with paragraph (g)(2) of this section.

g.   **Delivery of materials, computation of direct costs.**

1.   Whenever the bidder is required to deliver tender offer materials or amendments to tender offer materials, the bidder shall deliver to the subject company at the location specified by the subject company in its notice given pursuant to paragraph (a)(4) of this section a number of sets of the materials or of the amendment, as the case may be, at least equal to the approximate number of security holders specified by the subject company in such notice, together with appropriate envelopes or other containers therefor: *Provided, however,* That such delivery shall be deemed not to have been made unless the bidder has complied with paragraph (f)(3)(iii) of this section at the time the materials or amendments, as the case may be, are delivered.

2.   The approximate direct cost of mailing the bidder's tender offer materials shall be computed by adding

i.   the direct cost incidental to the mailing of the subject company's last annual report to shareholders (excluding employee time), less the costs of preparation and printing of the report, and postage, plus

ii.   the amount of first class postage required to mail the bidder's tender offer materials. The approximate direct costs incidental to the mailing of the amendments to the bidder's tender offer materials shall be computed by adding

iii.   the estimated direct costs of preparing mailing labels, of updating shareholder lists and of third party handling charges plus

iv.   the amount of first class postage required to mail the bidder's amendment. Direct costs incidental to the mailing of the bidder's tender offer materials and amendments thereto when finally computed may include all reasonable charges paid by the subject company to third parties for supplies or services, including costs attendant to preparing shareholder lists, mailing labels, handling the bidder's materials, contacting participants named on security position listings and for postage, but shall exclude indirect costs, such as employee time which is devoted to either contesting or supporting the tender offer on behalf of the subject company. The final billing for direct costs shall be accompanied by an appropriate accounting in reasonable detail.

Note to Rule 14d-5. Reasonably prompt methods of distribution to security holders may be used instead of mailing. If alternative methods are chosen, the approximate direct costs of distribution shall be computed by adding the estimated direct costs of preparing the document for distribution through the chosen medium (including updating of shareholder list) plus the estimated reasonable cost of distribution through that medium. Direct costs incidental to the distribution of tender offer materials and amendments thereto may include all reasonable charges paid by the subject company to third parties for supplies or services, including costs attendant to preparing shareholder lists, handling the bidder's materials, and contacting participants named on security position listings, but shall not including indirect cost, such as employee time which is devoted to either contesting or supporting the tender offer on behalf of the subject company.

Rule 14d-6 – Disclosure Requirements with Respect to Tender Offers

a.   **Information required on date of commencement–**

    1.   Long-form publication. If a tender offer is published, sent or given to security holders on the date of commencement by means of long-form publication under Rule 14d-4(a)(1), the long-form publication must include the information required by paragraph (d)(1) of this section.

    2.   Summary publication. If a tender offer is published, sent or given to security holders on the date of commencement by means of summary publication under Rule 14d-4(a)(2):

        i.   The summary advertisement must contain at least the information required by paragraph (d)(2) of this section; and

        ii.   The tender offer materials furnished by the bidder upon request of any security holder must include the information required by paragraph (d)(1) of this section.

    3.   Use of stockholder lists and security position listings. If a tender offer is published, sent or given to security holders on the date of commencement by the use of stockholder lists and security position listings under Rule 14d-4(a)(3):

        i.   The summary advertisement must contain at least the information required by paragraph (d)(2) of this section; and

        ii.   The tender offer materials transmitted to security holders pursuant to such lists and security position listings and furnished by the bidder upon the request of any security holder must include the information required by paragraph (d)(1) of this section.

4. *Other tender offers.* If a tender offer is published or sent or given to security holders other than pursuant to Rule 14d-4(a), the tender offer materials that are published or sent or given to security holders on the date of commencement of such offer must include the information required by paragraph (d)(1) of this section.

b. **Information required in other tender offer materials published after commencement**. Except for tender offer materials described in paragraphs (a)(2)(ii) and (a)(3)(ii) of this section, additional tender offer materials published, sent or given to security holders after commencement must include:

1. The identities of the bidder and subject company;
2. The amount and class of securities being sought;
3. The type and amount of consideration being offered; and
4. The scheduled expiration date of the tender offer, whether the tender offer may be extended and, if so, the procedures for extension of the tender offer.

Instruction to paragraph (b): If the additional tender offer materials are summary advertisements, they also must include the information required by paragraphs (d)(2)(v) of this section.

c. **Material changes**. A material change in the information published or sent or given to security holders must be promptly disclosed to security holders in additional tender offer materials.

d. **Information to be included–**

1. *Tender offer materials other than summary publication.* The following information is required by paragraphs (a)(1), (a)(2)(ii), (a)(3)(ii) and (a)(4) of this section:

   i. The information required by Item 1 of Schedule TO (Rule 14d-100) (Summary Term Sheet); and

   ii. The information required by the remaining items of Schedule TO (Rule 14d-100) for third-party tender offers, except for Item 12 (exhibits) of Schedule TO (Rule 14d-100), or a fair and adequate summary of the information.

2. *Summary Publication.* The following information is required in a summary advertisement under paragraphs (a)(2)(i) and (a)(3)(i) of this section:

   i. The identity of the bidder and the subject company;

   ii. The information required by Item 1004(a)(1) of Regulation M-A;

   iii. If the tender offer is for less than all of the outstanding securities of a class of equity securities, a statement as to whether the purpose or one of the purposes of the tender offer is to acquire or influence control of the business of the subject company;

   iv. A statement that the information required by paragraph (d)(1) of this section is incorporated by reference into the summary advertisement;

   v. Appropriate instructions as to how security holders may obtain promptly, at the bidder's expense, the bidder's tender offer materials; and

vi. In a tender offer published or sent or given to security holders by use of stockholder lists and security position listings under Rule 14d-4(a)(3), a statement that a request is being made for such lists and listings. The summary publication also must state that tender offer materials will be mailed to record holders and will be furnished to brokers, banks and similar persons whose name appears or whose nominee appears on the list of security holders or, if applicable, who are listed as participants in a clearing agency's security position listing for subsequent transmittal to beneficial owners of such securities. If the list furnished to the bidder also included beneficial owners pursuant to Rule 14d-5(c)(1) and tender offer materials will be mailed directly to beneficial holders, include a statement to that effect.

3. No transmittal letter. Neither the initial summary advertisement nor any subsequent summary advertisement may include a transmittal letter (the letter furnished to security holders for transmission of securities sought in the tender offer) or any amendment to the transmittal letter.

Rule 14d-7 – Additional Withdrawal Rights

a.

1. *Rights.* In addition to the provisions of section 14(d)(5) of the Act, any person who has deposited securities pursuant to a tender offer has the right to withdraw any such securities during the period such offer request or invitation remains open.

2. *Exemption during subsequent offering period.* Notwithstanding the provisions of section 14(d)(5) of the Act and paragraph (a) of this section, the bidder need not offer withdrawal rights during a subsequent offering period.

b. **Notice of withdrawal.** Notice of withdrawal pursuant to this section shall be deemed to be timely upon the receipt by the bidder's depositary of a written notice of withdrawal specifying the name(s) of the tendering stockholder(s), the number or amount of the securities to be withdrawn and the name(s) in which the certificate(s) is (are) registered, if different from that of the tendering security holder(s). A bidder may impose other reasonable requirements, including certificate numbers and a signed request for withdrawal accompanied by a signature guarantee, as conditions precedent to the physical release of withdrawn securities.

Rule 14d-8 – Exemption from Statutory Pro Rata Requirements

Notwithstanding the pro rata provisions of section 14(d)6 of the Act, if any person makes a tender offer or request or invitation for tenders, for less than all of the outstanding equity securities of a class, and if a greater number of securities are deposited pursuant thereto than such person is bound or willing to take up and pay for, the securities taken up and paid for shall be taken up and paid for as nearly as may be pro rata, disregarding fractions, according to the number of securities deposited by each depositor during the period such offer, request or invitation remains open.

Rule 14d-9 – Recommendation or Solicitation by the Subject Company and Others

a.   **Pre-commencement communications**. A communication by a person described in paragraph (e) of this section with respect to a tender offer will not be deemed to constitute a recommendation or solicitation under this section if:

1.   The tender offer has not commenced under Rule 14d-2; and
2.   The communication is filed under cover of Schedule 14D-9 with the Commission no later than the date of the communication.
     Instructions to paragraph (a)(2):
     1.   The box on the front of Schedule 14D-9 indicating that the filing contains pre-commencement communications must be checked.
     2.   Any communications made in connection with an exchange offer registered under the Securities Act of 1933 need only be filed under Rule 425 and will be deemed filed under this section.
     3.   Each pre-commencement written communication must include a prominent legend in clear, plain language advising security holders to read the company's solicitation/recommendation statement when it is available because it contains important information. The legend also must advise investors that they can get the recommendation and other filed documents for free at the Commission's web site and explain which documents are free from the filer.
     4.   See Rule 135, Rule 165 and Rule 166 of this chapter for pre-commencement communications made in connection with registered exchange offers.

b.   **Post-commencement communications**. After commencement by a bidder under Rule 14d-2, no solicitation or recommendation to security holders may be made by any person described in paragraph (e) of this section with respect to a tender offer for such securities unless as soon as practicable on the date such solicitation or recommendation is first published or sent or given to security holders such person complies with the following:

1.   Such person shall file with the Commission a Tender Offer Solicitation/Recommendation Statement on Schedule 14D-9, including all exhibits thereto; and
2.   If such person is either the subject company or an affiliate of the subject company,
     i.   Such person shall hand deliver a copy of the Schedule 14D-9 to the bidder at its principal office or at the address of the person authorized to receive notices and communications (which is set forth on the cover sheet of the bidder's Schedule TO filed with the Commission; and
     ii. Such person shall give telephonic notice (which notice to the extent possible shall be given prior to the opening of the market) of the information required by Items 1003(d) and 1012(a) of Regulation M-A and shall mail a copy of the Schedule to each national securities exchange where the class of securities is registered and listed for trading and, if the class is authorized for quotation in the NASDAQ interdealer

quotation system, to the National Association of Securities Dealers, Inc. ("NASD").

3.   If such person is neither the subject company nor an affiliate of the subject company,

    i.   Such person shall mail a copy of the schedule to the bidder at its principal office or at the address of the person authorized to receive notices and communications (which is set forth on the cover sheet of the bidder's Schedule TO; and

    ii.   Such person shall mail a copy of the Schedule to the subject company at its principal office.

c.   **Amendments**. If any material change occurs in the information set forth in the Schedule 14D-9 required by this section, the person who filed such Schedule 14D-9 shall:

1.   File with the Commission an amendment on Schedule 14D-9 disclosing such change promptly, but not later than the date such material is first published, sent or given to security holders; and

2.   Promptly deliver copies and give notice of the amendment in the same manner as that specified in paragraph (b)(2) or (3) of this section, whichever is applicable; and

3.   Promptly disclose and disseminate such change in a manner reasonably designed to inform security holders of such change.

d.   **Information required in solicitation or recommendation**. Any solicitation or recommendation to holders of a class of securities referred to in section 14(d)(1) of the Act with respect to a tender offer for such securities shall include the name of the person making such solicitation or recommendation and the information required by Items 1 through 8 of Schedule 14D-9 or a fair and adequate summary thereof: *Provided, however,* That such solicitation or recommendation may omit any of such information previously furnished to security holders of such class of securities by such person with respect to such tender offer.

e.   **Applicability**.

1.   Except as is provided in paragraphs (e)(2) and (f) of this section, this section shall only apply to the following persons:

    i.   The subject company, any director, officer, employee, affiliate or subsidiary of the subject company;

    ii.   Any record holder or beneficial owner of any security issued by the subject company, by the bidder, or by any affiliate of either the subject company or the bidder; and

    iii.   Any person who makes a solicitation or recommendation to security holders on behalf of any of the foregoing or on behalf of the bidder other than by means of a solicitation or recommendation to security holders which has been filed with the Commission pursuant to this section or Rule 14d-3.

2.   Notwithstanding paragraph (e)(1) of this section, this section shall not apply to the following persons:

    i.   A bidder who has filed a Schedule TO pursuant to Rule 14d-3 ;

      ii.   Attorneys, banks, brokers, fiduciaries or investment advisers who are not participating in a tender offer in more than a ministerial capacity and who furnish information and/or advice regarding such tender offer to their customers or clients on the unsolicited request of such customers or clients or solely pursuant to a contract or a relationship providing for advice to the customer or client to whom the information and/or advice is given.

      iii.   Any person specified in paragraph (e)(1) of this section if:

         A.   The subject company is the subject of a tender offer conducted under Rule 14d-1(c);

         B.   Any person specified in paragraph (e)(1) of this section furnishes to the Commission on Form CB the entire informational document it publishes or otherwise disseminates to holders of the class of securities in connection with the tender offer no later than the next business day after publication or dissemination;

         C.   Any person specified in paragraph (e)(1) of this section disseminates any informational document to U.S. holders, including any amendments thereto, in English, on a comparable basis to that provided to security holders in the issuer's home jurisdiction; and

         D.   Any person specified in paragraph (e)(1) of this section disseminates by publication in its home jurisdiction, such person must publish the information in the United States in a manner reasonably calculated to inform U.S. security holders of the offer.

f.   **Stop-look-and-listen communication**. This section shall not apply to the subject company with respect to a communication by the subject company to its security holders which only:

   1.   Identifies the tender offer by the bidder;

   2.   States that such tender offer is under consideration by the subject company's board of directors and/or management;

   3.   States that on or before a specified date (which shall be no later than 10 business days from the date of commencement of such tender offer) the subject company will advise such security holders of

      i.   whether the subject company recommends acceptance or rejection of such tender offer; expresses no opinion and remains neutral toward such tender offer; or is unable to take a position with respect to such tender offer and

      ii.   the reason(s) for the position taken by the subject company with respect to the tender offer (including the inability to take a position); and

   4.   Requests such security holders to defer making a determination whether to accept or reject such tender offer until they have been advised of the subject company's position with respect thereto pursuant to paragraph (f)(3) of this section.

g.   **Statement of management's position**. A statement by the subject company's of its position with respect to a tender offer which is required to be published or sent or given to security holders pursuant to Rule 14e-2 shall be deemed to constitute a solicitation or recommendation within the meaning of this section and section 14(d)(1) of the Act.

Rule 14d-10 – Equal Treatment of Security Holders

a. No bidder shall make a tender offer unless:
1. The tender offer is open to all security holders of the class of securities subject to the tender offer; and
2. The consideration paid to any security holder for securities tendered in the tender offer is the highest consideration paid to any other security holder for securities tendered in the tender offer.

b. Paragraph (a)(1) of this section shall not:
1. Affect dissemination under Rule 14d-4; or
2. Prohibit a bidder from making a tender offer excluding all security holders in a state where the bidder is prohibited from making the tender offer by administrative or judicial action pursuant to a state statute after a good faith effort by the bidder to comply with such statute.

c. Paragraph (a)(2) of this section shall not prohibit the offer of more than one type of consideration in a tender offer, *Provided,* That:
1. Security holders are afforded equal right to elect among each of the types of consideration offered; and
2. The highest consideration of each type paid to any security holder is paid to any other security holder receiving that type of consideration.

d. 1. Paragraph (a)(2) of this section shall not prohibit the negotiation, execution or amendment of an employment compensation, severance or other employee benefit arrangement, or payments made or to be made or benefits granted or to be granted according to such an arrangement, with respect to any security holder of the subject company, where the amount payable under the arrangement:
    i. Is being paid or granted as compensation for past services performed, future services to be performed, or future services to be refrained from performing, by the security holder (and matters incidental thereto); and
    ii. Is not calculated based on the number of securities tendered or to be tendered in the tender offer by the security holder.
  2. The provisions of paragraph (d)(1) of this section shall be satisfied and, therefore, pursuant to this non-exclusive safe harbor, the negotiation, execution or amendment of an arrangement and any payments made or to be made or benefits granted or to be granted according to that arrangement shall not be prohibited by paragraph (a)(2) of this section, if the arrangement is approved as an employment compensation, severance or other employee benefit arrangement solely by independent directors as follows:
    i. The compensation committee or a committee of the board of directors that performs functions similar to a compensation committee of the subject company approves the arrangement, regardless of whether the subject company is a party to the arrangement, or, if the bidder is a party to the arrangement, the compensation committee or a committee of the

board of directors that performs functions similar to a compensation committee of the bidder approves the arrangement; or

ii.   If the subject company's or bidder's board of directors, as applicable, does not have a compensation committee or a committee of the board of directors that performs functions similar to a compensation committee or if none of the members of the subject company's or bidder's compensation committee or committee that performs functions similar to a compensation committee is independent, a special committee of the board of directors formed to consider and approve the arrangement approves the arrangement; or

iii. If the subject company or bidder, as applicable, is a foreign private issuer, any or all members of the board of directors or any committee of the board of directors authorized to approve employment compensation, severance or other employee benefit arrangements under the laws or regulations of the home country approves the arrangement.

Instructions to paragraph (d)(2): For purposes of determining whether the members of the committee approving an arrangement in accordance with the provisions of paragraph (d)(2) of this section are independent, the following provisions shall apply:

1.   If the bidder or subject company, as applicable, is a listed issuer (as defined in Rule 10A-3 of this chapter) whose securities are listed either on a national securities exchange registered pursuant to section 6(a) of the Exchange Act or in an inter-dealer quotation system of a national securities association registered pursuant to section 15A(a) of the Exchange Act that has independence requirements for compensation committee members that have been approved by the Commission (as those requirements may be modified or supplemented), apply the bidder's or subject company's definition of independence that it uses for determining that the members of the compensation committee are independent in compliance with the listing standards applicable to compensation committee members of the listed issuer.

2.   If the bidder or subject company, as applicable, is not a listed issuer (as defined in Rule 10A-3 of this chapter), apply the independence requirements for compensation committee members of a national securities exchange registered pursuant to section 6(a) of the Exchange Act or an inter-dealer quotation system of a national securities association registered pursuant to section 15A(a) of the Exchange Act that have been approved by the Commission (as those requirements may be modified or supplemented). Whatever definition the bidder or subject company, as applicable, chooses, it must apply that definition consistently to all members of the committee approving the arrangement.

3.   Notwithstanding Instructions 1 and 2 to paragraph (d)(2), if the bidder or subject company, as applicable, is a closed-end investment company registered under the Investment Company Act of 1940, a director is considered to be independent if the director is not, other than in his or her capacity as a member of the board of directors or any board committee, an

"interested person" of the investment company, as defined in section 2(a)(19) of the Investment Company Act of 1940.

4. If the bidder or the subject company, as applicable, is a foreign private issuer, apply either the independence standards set forth in Instructions 1 and 2 to paragraph (d)(2) or the independence requirements of the laws, regulations, codes or standards of the home country of the bidder or subject company, as applicable, for members of the board of directors or the committee of the board of directors approving the arrangement.

5. A determination by the bidder's or the subject company's board of directors, as applicable, that the members of the board of directors or the committee of the board of directors, as applicable, approving an arrangement in accordance with the provisions of paragraph (d)(2) are independent in accordance with the provisions of this instruction to paragraph (d)(2) shall satisfy the independence requirements of paragraph (d)(2).

Instruction to paragraph (d): The fact that the provisions of paragraph (d) of this section extend only to employment compensation, severance and other employee benefit arrangements and not to other arrangements, such as commercial arrangements, does not raise any inference that a payment under any such other arrangement constitutes consideration paid for securities in a tender offer.

e. If the offer and sale of securities constituting consideration offered in a tender offer is prohibited by the appropriate authority of a state after a good faith effort by the bidder to register or qualify the offer and sale of such securities in such state:

1. The bidder may offer security holders in such state an alternative form of consideration; and

2. Paragraph (c) of this section shall not operate to require the bidder to offer or pay the alternative form of consideration to security holders in any other state.

f. This section shall not apply to any tender offer with respect to which the Commission, upon written request or upon its own motion, either unconditionally or on specified terms and conditions, determines that compliance with this section is not necessary or appropriate in the public interest or for the protection of investors.

Rule 14d-11 – Subsequent Offering Period

A bidder may elect to provide a subsequent offering period of 3 business days to 20 business days during which tenders will be accepted if:

a. The initial offering period of at least 20 business days has expired;

b. The offer is for all outstanding securities of the class that is the subject of the tender offer, and if the bidder is offering security holders a choice of different forms of consideration, there is no ceiling on any form of consideration offered;

c. The bidder immediately accepts and promptly pays for all securities tendered during the initial offering period;

    d.   The bidder announces the results of the tender offer, including the approximate number and percentage of securities deposited to date, no later than 9:00 a.m. Eastern time on the next business day after the expiration date of the initial offering period and immediately begins the subsequent offering period;

    e.   The bidder immediately accepts and promptly pays for all securities as they are tendered during the subsequent offering period; and

    f.   The bidder offers the same form and amount of consideration to security holders in both the initial and the subsequent offering period.

Note for Rule 14d-11: No withdrawal rights apply during the subsequent offering period in accordance with Rule 14d-7(a)(2).

Regulation 14E

Note: For the scope of and definitions applicable to Regulation 14E, refer to Rule 14d-1.

Rule 14e-1 – Unlawful Tender Offer Practices

As a means reasonably designed to prevent fraudulent, deceptive or manipulative acts or practices within the meaning of section 14(e) of the Act, no person who makes a tender offer shall:

    a.   Hold such tender offer open for less than twenty business days from the date such tender offer is first published or sent to security holders; *provided, however*, that if the tender offer involves a roll-up transaction as defined in Item 901(c) of Regulation S-K and the securities being offered are registered (or authorized to be registered) on Form S-4 or Form F-4, the offer shall not be open for less than sixty calendar days from the date the tender offer is first published or sent to security holders;

    b.   Increase or decrease the percentage of the class of securities being sought or the consideration offered or the dealer's soliciting fee to be given in a tender offer unless such tender offer remains open for at least ten business days from the date that notice of such increase or decrease is first published or sent or given to security holders. *Provided, however,* That, for purposes of this paragraph, the acceptance for payment of an additional amount of securities not to exceed two percent of the class of securities that is the subject of the tender offer shall not be deemed to be an increase. For purposes of this paragraph, the percentage of a class of securities shall be calculated in accordance with section 14(d)(3) of the Act.

    c.   Fail to pay the consideration offered or return the securities deposited by or on behalf of security holders promptly after the termination or withdrawal of a tender offer. This paragraph does not prohibit a bidder electing to offer a subsequent offering period under Rule 14d-11 from paying for securities during the subsequent offering period in accordance with that section.

    d.   Extend the length of a tender offer without issuing a notice of such extension by press release or other public announcement, which notice shall include disclosure of the approximate number of securities deposited to date and shall be issued no later than the earlier of:

    i.   9:00 a.m. Eastern time, on the next business day after the scheduled expiration date of the offer or,

    ii.   if the class of securities which is the subject of the tender offer is registered on one or more national securities exchanges, the first opening of any one of such exchanges on the next business day after the scheduled expiration date of the offer.

e.   The periods of time required by paragraphs (a) and (b) of this section shall be tolled for any period during which the bidder has failed to file in electronic format, absent a hardship exemption (Rules 201 and 202 of this chapter), the Schedule TO Tender Offer Statement, any tender offer material required to be filed by Item 12 of that Schedule pursuant to paragraph (a) of Item 1016 of Regulation M-A, and any amendments thereto. If such documents were filed in paper pursuant to a hardship exemption (see Rules 201 and Rule 202(d)), the minimum offering periods shall be tolled for any period during which a required confirming electronic copy of such Schedule and tender offer material is delinquent.

Rule 14e-2 – Position of Subject Company with Respect to a Tender Offer

a.   **Position of subject company**. As a means reasonably designed to prevent fraudulent, deceptive or manipulative acts or practices within the meaning of section 14(e) of the Act, the subject company, no later than 10 business days from the date the tender offer is first published or sent or given, shall publish, send or give to security holders a statement disclosing that the subject company:

    1.   Recommends acceptance or rejection of the bidder's tender offer;

    2.   Expresses no opinion and is remaining neutral toward the bidder's tender offer; or

    3.   Is unable to take a position with respect to the bidder's tender offer. Such statement shall also include the reason(s) for the position (including the inability to take a position) disclosed therein.

b.   **Material change.** If any material change occurs in the disclosure required by paragraph (a) of this section, the subject company shall promptly publish or send or give a statement disclosing such material change to security holders.

c.   Any issuer, a class of the securities of which is the subject of a tender offer filed with the Commission on Schedule 14D-1F and conducted in reliance upon and in conformity with Rule 14d-1(b) under the Act, and any director or officer of such issuer where so required by the laws, regulations and policies of Canada and/or any of its provinces or territories, in lieu of the statements called for by paragraph (a) of this section and Rule 14d-9 under the Act, shall file with the Commission on Schedule 14D-9F the entire disclosure document(s) required to be furnished to holders of securities of the subject issuer by the laws, regulations and policies of Canada and/or any of its provinces or territories governing the conduct of the tender offer, and shall disseminate such document(s) in the United States in accordance with such laws, regulations and policies.

   d.   **Exemption for cross-border tender offers**. The subject company shall be exempt from this section with respect to a tender offer conducted under Rule 14d-1(c).

Rule 14e-3 – Transactions in Securities on the Basis of Material, Nonpublic Information in the Context of Tender Offers

   a.   If any person has taken a substantial step or steps to commence, or has commenced, a tender offer (the "offering person"), it shall constitute a fraudulent, deceptive or manipulative act or practice within the meaning of section 14(e) of the Act for any other person who is in possession of material information relating to such tender offer which information he knows or has reason to know is nonpublic and which he knows or has reason to know has been acquired directly or indirectly from:

      1.   The offering person,

      2.   The issuer of the securities sought or to be sought by such tender offer, or

      3.   Any officer, director, partner or employee or any other person acting on behalf of the offering person or such issuer, to purchase or sell or cause to be purchased or sold any of such securities or any securities convertible into or exchangeable for any such securities or any option or right to obtain or to dispose of any of the foregoing securities, unless within a reasonable time prior to any purchase or sale such information and its source are publicly disclosed by press release or otherwise.

   b.   A person other than a natural person shall not violate paragraph (a) of this section if such person shows that:

      1.   The individual(s) making the investment decision on behalf of such person to purchase or sell any security described in paragraph (a) of this section or to cause any such security to be purchased or sold by or on behalf of others did not know the material, nonpublic information; and

      2.   Such person had implemented one or a combination of policies and procedures, reasonable under the circumstances, taking into consideration the nature of the person's business, to ensure that individual(s) making investment decision(s) would not violate paragraph (a) of this section, which policies and procedures may include, but are not limited to,

         i.   those which restrict any purchase, sale and causing any purchase and sale of any such security or

        ii.   those which prevent such individual(s) from knowing such information.

   c.   Notwithstanding anything in paragraph (a) of this section to contrary, the following transactions shall not be violations of paragraph (a) of this section:

      1.   Purchase(s) of any security described in paragraph (a) of this section by a broker or by another agent on behalf of an offering person; or

      2.   Sale(s) by any person of any security described in paragraph (a) of this section to the offering person.

   d.

      1.   As a means reasonably designed to prevent fraudulent, deceptive or manipulative acts or practices within the meaning of section 14(e) of the Act, it

shall be unlawful for any person described in paragraph (d)(2) of this section to communicate material, nonpublic information relating to a tender offer to any other person under circumstances in which it is reasonably foreseeable that such communication is likely to result in a violation of this section *except* that this paragraph shall not apply to a communication made in good faith,

  i.   To the officers, directors, partners or employees of the offering person, to its advisors or to other persons, involved in the planning, financing, preparation or execution of such tender offer;

  ii. To the issuer whose securities are sought or to be sought by such tender offer, to its officers, directors, partners, employees or advisors or to other persons, involved in the planning, financing, preparation or execution of the activities of the issuer with respect to such tender offer; or

  iii. To any person pursuant to a requirement of any statute or rule or regulation promulgated thereunder.

2.   The persons referred to in paragraph (d)(1) of this section are:

  i.   The offering person or its officers, directors, partners, employees or advisors;

  ii. The issuer of the securities sought or to be sought by such tender offer or its officers, directors, partners, employees or advisors;

  iii. Anyone acting on behalf of the persons in paragraph (d)(2)(i) of this section or the issuer or persons in paragraph (d)(2)(ii) of this section; and

  iv. Any person in possession of material information relating to a tender offer which information he knows or has reason to know is nonpublic and which he knows or has reason to know has been acquired directly or indirectly from any of the above.

Rule 14e-4 – Prohibited Transactions in Connection with Partial Tender Offers

a.   **Definitions**. For purposes of this section:

1.   The amount of a person's **net long position** in a subject security shall equal the excess, if any, of such person's "long position" over such person's "short position." For the purposes of determining the net long position as of the end of the proration period and for tendering concurrently to two or more partial tender offers, securities that have been tendered in accordance with the rule and not withdrawn are deemed to be part of the person's long position.

  i.   Such person's *long position* is the amount of subject securities that such person:

    A. Or his agent has title to or would have title to but for having lent such securities; or

    B. Has purchased, or has entered into an unconditional contract, binding on both parties thereto, to purchase but has not yet received; or

    C. Has exercised a standardized call option for; or

    D. Has converted, exchanged, or exercised an equivalent security for; or

    E. Is entitled to receive upon conversion, exchange, or exercise of an equivalent security.

      ii. Such person's *short position,* is the amount of subject securities or subject securities underlying equivalent securities that such person:

        A. Has sold, or has entered into an unconditional contract, binding on both parties thereto, to sell; or

        B. Has borrowed; or

        C. Has written a non-standardized call option, or granted any other right pursuant to which his shares may be tendered by another person; or

        D. Is obligated to deliver upon exercise of a standardized call option sold on or after the date that a tender offer is first publicly announced or otherwise made known by the bidder to holders of the security to be acquired, if the exercise price of such option is lower than the highest tender offer price or stated amount of the consideration offered for the subject security. For the purpose of this paragraph, if one or more tender offers for the same security are ongoing on such date, the announcement date shall be that of the first announced offer.

2.   The term **equivalent security** means:

      i. Any security (including any option, warrant, or other right to purchase the subject security), issued by the person whose securities are the subject of the offer, that is immediately convertible into, or exchangeable or exercisable for, a subject security, or

      ii. Any other right or option (other than a standardized call option) that entitles the holder thereof to acquire a subject security, but only if the holder thereof reasonably believes that the maker or writer of the right or option has title to and possession of the subject security and upon exercise will promptly deliver the subject security.

3.   The term **subject security** means a security that is the subject of any tender offer or request or invitation for tenders.

4.   For purposes of this rule, a person shall be deemed to **tender** a security if he:

      i. Delivers a subject security pursuant to an offer,

      ii. Causes such delivery to be made,

      iii. Guarantees delivery of a subject security pursuant to a tender offer,

      iv. Causes a guarantee of such delivery to be given by another person, or

      v. Uses any other method by which acceptance of a tender offer may be made.

5.   The term **partial tender offer** means a tender offer or request or invitation for tenders for less than all of the outstanding securities subject to the offer in which tenders are accepted either by lot or on a *pro rata* basis for a specified period, or a tender offer for all of the outstanding shares that offers a choice of consideration in which tenders for different forms of consideration may be accepted either by lot or on a *pro rata* basis for a specified period.

6.   The term **standardized call option** means any call option that is traded on an exchange, or for which quotation information is disseminated in an electronic interdealer quotation system of a registered national securities association.

b. It shall be unlawful for any person acting alone or in concert with others, directly or indirectly, to tender any subject security in a partial tender offer:

1.   For his own account unless at the time of tender, and at the end of the proration period or period during which securities are accepted by lot (including any extensions thereof), he has a net long position equal to or greater than the amount tendered in:

     i.   The subject security and will deliver or cause to be delivered such security for the purpose of tender to the person making the offer within the period specified in the offer; or

     ii.   An equivalent security and, upon the acceptance of his tender will acquire the subject security by conversion, exchange, or exercise of such equivalent security to the extent required by the terms of the offer, and will deliver or cause to be delivered the subject security so acquired for the purpose of tender to the person making the offer within the period specified in the offer; or

2.   For the account of another person unless the person making the tender:

     i.   Possesses the subject security or an equivalent security, or

     ii.   Has a reasonable belief that, upon information furnished by the person on whose behalf the tender is made, such person owns the subject security or an equivalent security and will promptly deliver the subject security or such equivalent security for the purpose of tender to the person making the tender.

c.   This rule shall not prohibit any transaction or transactions which the Commission, upon written request or upon its own motion, exempts, either unconditionally or on specified terms and conditions.

Rule 14e-5 – Prohibiting Purchases Outside of a Tender Offer

a.   **Unlawful activity**. As a means reasonably designed to prevent fraudulent, deceptive or manipulative acts or practices in connection with a tender offer for equity securities, no covered person may directly or indirectly purchase or arrange to purchase any subject securities or any related securities except as part of the tender offer. This prohibition applies from the time of public announcement of the tender offer until the tender offer expires. This prohibition does not apply to any purchases or arrangements to purchase made during the time of any subsequent offering period as provided for in Rule 14d-11 if the consideration paid or to be paid for the purchases or arrangements to purchase is the same in form and amount as the consideration offered in the tender offer.

b.   **Excepted activity**. The following transactions in subject securities or related securities are not prohibited by paragraph (a) of this section:

1.   Exercises of securities. Transactions by covered persons to convert, exchange, or exercise related securities into subject securities, if the covered person owned the related securities before public announcement;

2.   Purchases for plans. Purchases or arrangements to purchase by or for a plan that are made by an agent independent of the issuer;

3.   Purchases during odd-lot offers. Purchases or arrangements to purchase if the tender offer is excepted under Rule 13e-4(h)(5);

4. Purchases as intermediary. Purchases by or through a dealer-manager or its affiliates that are made in the ordinary course of business and made either:
    i.   On an agency basis not for a covered person; or
    ii. As principal for its own account if the dealer-manager or its affiliate is not a market maker, and the purchase is made to offset a contemporaneous sale after having received an unsolicited order to buy from a customer who is not a covered person;

5. Basket transactions. Purchases or arrangements to purchase a basket of securities containing a subject security or a related security if the following conditions are satisfied:
    i.   The purchase or arrangement to purchase is made in the ordinary course of business and not to facilitate the tender offer;
    ii. The basket contains 20 or more securities; and
    iii. Covered securities and related securities do not comprise more than 5% of the value of the basket;

6. Covering transactions. Purchases or arrangements to purchase that are made to satisfy an obligation to deliver a subject security or a related security arising from a short sale or from the exercise of an option by a non- covered person if:
    i.   The short sale or option transaction was made in the ordinary course of business and not to facilitate the offer;
    ii. In the case of a short sale, the short sale was entered into before public announcement of the tender offer; and
    iii. In the case of an exercise of an option, the covered person wrote the option before public announcement of the tender offer;

7. Purchases pursuant to contractual obligations. Purchases or arrangements to purchase pursuant to a contract if the following conditions are satisfied:
    i.   The contract was entered into before public announcement of the tender offer;
    ii. The contract is unconditional and binding on both parties; and
    iii. The existence of the contract and all material terms including quantity, price and parties are disclosed in the offering materials;

8. Purchases or arrangements to purchase by an affiliate of the dealer- manager. Purchases or arrangements to purchase by an affiliate of a dealer-manager if the following conditions are satisfied:
    i.   The dealer-manager maintains and enforces written policies and procedures reasonably designed to prevent the flow of information to or from the affiliate that might result in a violation of the federal securities laws and regulations;
    ii. The dealer-manager is registered as a broker or dealer under Section 15(a) of the Act;
    iii. The affiliate has no officers (or persons performing similar functions) or employees (other than clerical, ministerial, or support personnel) in common with the dealer-manager that direct, effect, or recommend transactions in securities; and
    iv. The purchases or arrangements to purchase are not made to facilitate the tender offer;

9. Purchases by connected exempt market makers or connected exempt principal traders. Purchases or arrangements to purchase if the following conditions are satisfied:
   i. The issuer of the subject security is a foreign private issuer, as defined in Rule 3b-4(c);
   ii. The tender offer is subject to the United Kingdom's City Code on Takeovers and Mergers;
   iii. The purchase or arrangement to purchase is effected by a connected exempt market maker or a connected exempt principal trader, as those terms are used in the United Kingdom's City Code on Takeovers and Mergers;
   iv. The connected exempt market maker or the connected exempt principal trader complies with the applicable provisions of the United Kingdom's City Code on Takeovers and Mergers; and
   v. The tender offer documents disclose the identity of the connected exempt market maker or the connected exempt principal trader and disclose, or describe how U.S. security holders can obtain, information regarding market making or principal purchases by such market maker or principal trader to the extent that this information is required to be made public in the United Kingdom; and

10. Purchases during cross-border tender offers. Purchases or arrangements to purchase if the following conditions are satisfied:
    i. The tender offer is excepted under Rule 13e-4(h)(8) or Rule 14d-1(c);
    ii. The offering documents furnished to U.S. holders prominently disclose the possibility of any purchases, or arrangements to purchase, or the intent to make such purchases;
    iii. The offering documents disclose the manner in which any information about any such purchases or arrangements to purchase will be disclosed;
    iv. The offeror discloses information in the United States about any such purchases or arrangements to purchase in a manner comparable to the disclosure made in the home jurisdiction, as defined in Rule 13e-4(i)(3) [Editor's note: There is no subparagraph (3) to paragraph (i) of Rule 13e-4.]; and
    v. The purchases comply with the applicable tender offer laws and regulations of the home jurisdiction.

c. **Definitions**. For purposes of this section, the term:
   1. **Affiliate** has the same meaning as in Rule 12b-2;
   2. **Agent independent of the issuer** has the same meaning as in Rule 100(b);
   3. **Covered person** means:
      i. The offeror and its affiliates;
      ii. The offeror's dealer-manager and its affiliates;
      iii. Any advisor to any of the persons specified in paragraph (c)(3)(i) and (ii) of this section, whose compensation is dependent on the completion of the offer; and
      iv. Any person acting, directly or indirectly, in concert with any of the persons specified in this paragraph (c)(3) in connection with any

purchase or arrangement to purchase any subject securities or any related securities;

4. **Plan** has the same meaning as in Rule 100(b);

5. **Public announcement** is any oral or written communication by the offeror or any person authorized to act on the offeror's behalf that is reasonably designed to, or has the effect of, informing the public or security holders in general about the tender offer;

6. **Related securities** means securities that are immediately convertible into, exchangeable for, or exercisable for subject securities; and

7. **Subject securities** has the same meaning as in Item 1000.

d. *Exemptive authority*. Upon written application or upon its own motion, the Commission may grant an exemption from the provisions of this section, either unconditionally or on specified terms or conditions, to any transaction or class of transactions or any security or class of security, or any person or class of persons.

Rule 14e-8 – Prohibited Conduct in Connection with Pre-commencement Communications

It is a fraudulent, deceptive or manipulative act or practice within the meaning of section 14(e) of the Act for any person to publicly announce that the person (or a party on whose behalf the person is acting) plans to make a tender offer that has not yet been commenced, if the person:

a. Is making the announcement of a potential tender offer without the intention to commence the offer within a reasonable time and complete the offer;

b. Intends, directly or indirectly, for the announcement to manipulate the market price of the stock of the bidder or subject company; or

c. Does not have the reasonable belief that the person will have the means to purchase securities to complete the offer.

Rule 15c2-8 – Delivery of Prospectus

a. It shall constitute a deceptive act or practice, as those terms are used in Section 15(c)(2) of the Act, for a broker or dealer to participate in a distribution of securities with respect to which a registration statement has been filed under the Securities Act of 1933 unless he complies with the requirements set forth in paragraphs (b) through (g) of this section. For the purposes of this section, a broker or dealer participating in the distribution shall mean any underwriter and any member or proposed member of the selling group.

b. In connection with an issue of securities, the issuer of which has not previously been required to file reports pursuant to Sections 13(a) or 15(d) of the Securities Exchange Act of 1934, unless such issuer has been exempted from the requirement to file reports thereunder pursuant to Section 12(h) of the Act, such broker or dealer shall deliver a copy of the preliminary prospectus to any person who is expected to receive a confirmation of sale at least 48 hours prior to the sending of such confirmation.

c. Such broker or dealer shall take reasonable steps to furnish to any person who makes written request for a preliminary prospectus between the filing date and a reasonable time prior to the effective date of the registration statement to which such prospectus relates, a copy of the latest preliminary prospectus on file with the Commission. Reasonable steps shall include receiving an undertaking by the managing underwriter or underwriters to send such copy to the address given in the requests.

d. Such broker or dealer shall take reasonable steps to comply promptly with the written request of any person for a copy of the final prospectus relating to such securities during the period between the effective date of the registration statement and the later of either the termination of such distribution, or the expiration of the applicable 40- or 90-day period under Section 4(3) of the Securities Act of 1933. Reasonable steps shall include receiving an undertaking by the managing underwriter or underwriters to send such copy to the address given in the requests. (The 40-day and 90-day periods referred to above shall be deemed to apply for purposes of this rule irrespective of the provisions of paragraphs (b) and (d) of Rule 174 under the Securities Act of 1933).

e. Such broker or dealer shall take reasonable steps
    i. to make available a copy of the preliminary prospectus relating to such securities to each of his associated persons who is expected, prior to the effective date, to solicit customers' order for such securities before the making of any such solicitation by such associated persons and 2 to make available to each such associated person a copy of any amended preliminary prospectus promptly after the filing thereof.

f. Such broker or dealer shall take reasonable steps to make available a copy of the final prospectus relating to such securities to each of his associated persons who is expected, after the effective date, to solicit customers orders for such securities prior to the making of any such solicitation by such associated persons, unless a preliminary prospectus which is substantially the same as the final prospectus except for matters relating to the price of the stocks, has been so made available.

g. If the broker or dealer is a managing underwriter of such distribution, he shall take reasonable steps to see to it that all other brokers or dealers participating in such distribution are promptly furnished with sufficient copies, as requested by them, of each preliminary prospectus, each amended preliminary prospectus and the final prospectus to enable them to comply with paragraphs (b), (c), (d), and (e) of this section.

h. If the broker or dealer is a managing underwriter of such distribution, he shall take reasonable steps to see that any broker or dealer participating in the distribution or trading in the registered security is furnished reasonable quantities of the final prospectus relating to such securities, as requested by him, in order to enable him to comply with the prospectus delivery requirements of Section 5(b)(1) and (2) of the Securities Act of 1933.

i. This rule shall not require the furnishing of prospectuses in any state where such furnishing would be unlawful under the laws of such state: *Provided, however,* That this provision is not to be construed to relieve a broker or dealer from complying with the requirements of Section 5(b)(1) and (2) of the Securities Act of 1933. Prospectuses shall not be furnished pursuant to this rule while the registration statement is subject to an examination, proceeding, or stop order pursuant to Section 8 of the securities act of 1933.

j. For purposes of this section, the term **preliminary prospectus** shall include the term *prospectus subject to completion* as used in Rule 434(a), and the term *final prospectus* shall include the term *Section 10(a) prospectus* as used in Rule 434(a).

Rule 15c2-11 – Initiation or Resumption of Quotations without Specific Information

Preliminary Note: Brokers and dealers may wish to refer to Securities Exchange Act Release No. 29094 (April 17, 1991), for a discussion of procedures for gathering and reviewing the information required by this rule and the requirement that a broker or dealer have a reasonable basis for believing that the information is accurate and obtained from reliable sources.

a. As a means reasonably designed to prevent fraudulent, deceptive, or manipulative acts or practices, it shall be unlawful for a broker or dealer to publish any quotation for a security or, directly or indirectly, to submit any such quotation for publication, in any quotation medium (as defined in this section) unless such broker or dealer has in its records the documents and information required by this paragraph (for purposes of this section, "paragraph (a) information"), and, based upon a review of the paragraph (a) information together with any other documents and information required by paragraph (b) of this section, has a reasonable basis under the circumstances for believing that the paragraph (a) information is accurate in all material respects, and that the sources of the paragraph (a) information are reliable. The information required pursuant to this paragraph is:

1. A copy of the prospectus specified by Section 10(a) of the Securities Act of 1933 for an issuer that has filed a registration statement under the Securities Act of 1933, other than a registration statement on Form F-6, which became effective less than 90 calendar days prior to the day on which such broker or dealer publishes or submits the quotation to the quotation medium, *Provided* That such registration statement has not thereafter been the subject of a stop order which is still in effect when the quotation is published or submitted; or

2. A copy of the offering circular provided for under Regulation A under the Securities Act of 1933 for an issuer that has filed a notification under Regulation A and was authorized to commence the offering less than 40 calendar days prior to the day on which such broker or dealer publishes or submits the quotation to the quotation medium, *Provided* That the offering circular provided for under Regulation A has not thereafter become the subject of a suspension order which is still in effect when the quotation is published or submitted; or

3. A copy of the issuer's most recent annual report filed pursuant to Section 13 or 15(d) of the Act or a copy of the annual statement referred to in Section 12(g)(2)(G)(i) of the Act, in the case of an issuer required to file reports

pursuant to Section 13 or 15(d) of the Act or an issuer of a security covered by Section 12(g)(2)(B) or (G) of the Act, together with any quarterly and current reports that have been filed under the provisions of the Act by the issuer after such annual report or annual statement; *Provided, however,* That until such issuer has filed its first annual report pursuant to Section 13 or 15(d) of the Act or annual statement referred to in Section 12(g)(2)(G)(i) of the Act, the broker or dealer has in its records a copy of the prospectus specified by Section 10(a) of the Securities Act of 1933 included in a registration statement filed by the issuer under the Securities Act of 1933, other than a registration statement on Form F-6, that became effective within the prior 16 months, or a copy of any registration statement filed by the issuer under Section 12 of the Act that became effective within the prior 16 months, together with any quarterly and current reports filed thereafter under Section 13 or 15(d) of the Act; and *Provided further,* That the broker or dealer has a reasonable basis under the circumstances for believing that the issuer is current in filing annual, quarterly, and current reports filed pursuant to Section 13 or 15(d) of the Act, or, in the case of an insurance company exempted from Section 12(g) of the Act by reason of Section 12(g)(2)(G) thereof, the annual statement referred to in Section 12(g)(2)(G)(i) of the Act; or

4. The information that, since the beginning of its last fiscal year, the issuer has published pursuant to Rule 12g3-2(b), and which the broker or dealer shall make reasonably available upon the request of a person expressing an interest in a proposed transaction in the issuer's security with the broker or dealer, such as by providing the requesting person with appropriate instructions regarding how to obtain the information electronically; or

5. The following information, which shall be reasonably current in relation to the day the quotation is submitted and which the broker or dealer shall make reasonably available upon request to any person expressing an interest in a proposed transaction in the security with such broker or dealer:
    i. the exact name of the issuer and its predecessor (if any);
    ii. the address of its principal executive offices;
    iii. the state of incorporation, if it is a corporation;
    iv. the exact title and class of the security;
    v. the par or stated value of the security;
    vi. the number of shares or total amount of the securities outstanding as of the end of the issuer's most recent fiscal year;
    vii. the name and address of the transfer agent;
    viii. the nature of the issuer's business;
    ix. the nature of products or services offered;
    x. the nature and extent of the issuer's facilities;
    xi. the name of the chief executive officer and members of the board of directors;
    xii. the issuer's most recent balance sheet and profit and loss and retained earnings statements;
    xiii. similar financial information for such part of the 2 preceding fiscal years as the issuer or its predecessor has been in existence;
    xiv. whether the broker or dealer or any associated person is affiliated, directly or indirectly with the issuer;

xv.   whether the quotation is being published or submitted on behalf of any other broker or dealer, and, if so, the name of such broker or dealer; and

xvi.   whether the quotation is being submitted or published directly or indirectly on behalf of the issuer, or any director, officer or any person, directly or indirectly the beneficial owner of more than 10 percent of the outstanding units or shares of any equity security of the issuer, and, if so, the name of such person, and the basis for any exemption under the federal securities laws for any sales of such securities on behalf of such person.

If such information is made available to others upon request pursuant to this paragraph, such delivery, unless otherwise represented, shall not constitute a representation by such broker or dealer that such information is accurate, but shall constitute a representation by such broker or dealer that the information is reasonably current in relation to the day the quotation is submitted, that the broker or dealer has a reasonable basis under the circumstances for believing the information is accurate in all material respects, and that the information was obtained from sources which the broker or dealer has a reasonable basis for believing are reliable. This paragraph (a)(5) shall not apply to any security of an issuer included in paragraph (a)(3) of this Section unless a report or statement of such issuer described in paragraph (a)(3) of this Section is not reasonably available to the broker or dealer. A report or statement of an issuer described in paragraph (a)(3) of this Section shall be "reasonably available" when such report or statement is filed with the Commission.

b.   With respect to any security the quotation of which is within the provisions of this Section, the broker or dealer submitting or publishing such quotation shall have in its records the following documents and information:

1.   A record of the circumstances involved in the submission of publication of such quotation, including the identity of the person or persons for whom the quotation is being submitted or published and any information regarding the transactions provided to the broker or dealer by such person or persons;

2.   A copy of any trading suspension order issued by the Commission pursuant to Section 12(k) of the Act respecting any securities of the issuer or its predecessor (if any) during the 12 months preceding the date of the publication or submission of the quotation, or a copy of the public release issued by the Commission announcing such trading suspension order; and

3.   A copy or a written record of any other material information (including adverse information) regarding the issuer which comes to the broker's or dealer's knowledge or possession before the publication or submission of the quotation.

c.   The broker or dealer shall preserve the documents and information required under paragraphs (a) and (b) of this Section for a period of not less than three years, the first two years in an easily accessible place.

d.   1.   For any security of an issuer included in paragraph (a)(5) of this Section, the broker or dealer submitting the quotation shall furnish to the interdealer quotation system (as defined in paragraph (e)(2) of this Section), in such form as such system shall prescribe, at least 3 business days before the quotation is published or submitted, the information regarding the security and the issuer which such broker or dealer is required to maintain pursuant to said paragraph (a)(5) of this Section.

2. For any security of an issuer included in paragraph (a)(3) of this Section,

    i. a broker-dealer shall be in compliance with the requirement to obtain current reports filed by the issuer if the broker-dealer obtains all current reports filed with the Commission by the issuer as of a date up to five business days in advance of the earlier of the date of submission of the quotation to the quotation medium and the date of submission of the paragraph (a) information pursuant to Schedule H of the By-Laws of the National Association of Securities Dealers, Inc.; and

    ii. a broker-dealer shall be in compliance with the requirement to obtain the annual, quarterly, and current reports filed by the issuer, if the broker-dealer has made arrangements to receive all such reports when filed by the issuer and it has regularly received reports from the issuer on a timely basis, unless the broker-dealer has a reasonable basis under the circumstances for believing that the issuer has failed to file a required report or has filed a report but has not sent it to the broker-dealer.

e. For purposes of this Section:

    1. **Quotation medium** shall mean any "interdealer quotation system" or any publication or electronic communications network or other device which is used by brokers or dealers to make known to others their interest in transactions in any security, including offers to buy or sell at a stated price or otherwise, or invitations of offers to buy or sell.

    2. **inter-dealer quotation system** shall mean any system of general circulation to brokers or dealers which regularly disseminates quotations of identified brokers or dealers.

    3. Except as otherwise specified in this rule, **quotation** shall mean any bid or offer at a specified price with respect to a security, or any indication of interest by a broker or dealer in receiving bids or offers from others for a security, or any indication by a broker or dealer that he wishes to advertise his general interest in buying or selling a particular security.

    4. **Issuer**, in the case of quotations for American Depositary Receipts, shall mean the issuer of the deposited shares represented by such American Depositary Receipts.

f. The provisions of this Section shall not apply to:

    1. The publication or submission of a quotation respecting a security admitted to trading on a national securities exchange and which is traded on such an exchange on the same day as, or on the business day next preceding, the day the quotation is published or submitted.

    2. The publication or submission by a broker or dealer, solely on behalf of a customer (other than a person acting as or for a dealer), of a quotation that represents the customer's indication of interest and does not involve the solicitation of the customer's interest; *Provided, however,* That this paragraph

(f)(2) shall not apply to a quotation consisting of both a bid and an offer, each of which is at a specified price, unless the quotation medium specifically identifies the quotation as representing such an unsolicited customer interest.

3.

    i. The publication or submission, in an interdealer quotation system that specifically identifies as such unsolicited customer indications of interest of the kind described in paragraph (f)(2) of this Section, of a quotation respecting a security which has been the subject of quotations (exclusive of any identified customer interests) in such a system on each of at least 12 days within the previous 30 calendar days, with no more than 4 business days in succession without a quotation; or

    ii. The publication or submission, in an interdealer quotation system that does not so identify any such unsolicited customer indications of interest, of a quotation respecting a security which has been the subject of both bid and ask quotations in an interdealer quotation system at specified prices on each of at least 12 days within the previous 30 calendar days, with no more than 4 business days in succession without such a two-way quotation;

    iii. A dealer acting in the capacity of market maker, as defined in Section 3(a)(38) of the Act, that has published or submitted a quotation respecting a security in an interdealer quotation system and such quotation has qualified for an exception provided in this paragraph (f)(3), may continue to publish or submit quotations for such security in the interdealer quotation system without compliance with this Section unless and until such dealer ceases to submit or publish a quotation or ceases to act in the capacity of market maker respecting such security.

4. The publication or submission of a quotation respecting a municipal security.

5. The publication or submission of a quotation respecting a security that is authorized for quotation in the NASDAQ system (as defined in Rule 11Ac1-2(a)(3) of this chapter), and such authorization is not suspended, terminated, or prohibited.

g. The requirement in subparagraph (a)(5) that the information with respect to the issuer be "reasonably current" will be presumed to be satisfied, unless the broker or dealer has information to the contrary, if:

1. The balance sheet is as of a date less than 16 months before the publication or submission of the quotation, the statements of profit and loss and retained earnings are for the 12 months preceding the date of such balance sheet, and if such balance sheet is not as of a date less than 6 months before the publication or submission of the quotation, it shall be accompanied by additional statements of profit and loss and retained earnings for the period from the date of such balance sheet to a date less than 6 months before the publication or submission of the quotation.

2. Other information regarding the issuer specified in subparagraph (a)(5) is as of a date within 12 months prior to the publication or submission of the quotation.

h. This Section shall not prohibit any publication or submission of any quotation if the Commission, upon written request or upon its own motion, exempts such quotation either unconditionally or on specified terms and conditions, as not constituting a fraudulent, manipulative or deceptive practice comprehended within the purpose of this Rule.

Rule 15d-3 – Reports for Depositary Shares Registered on Form F-6

Annual and other reports are not required with respect to Depositary Shares registered on Form F-6. The exemption in this section does not apply to any deposited securities registered on any other form under the Securities Act of 1933.

Rule 15d-14 – Certification of Disclosure in Annual and Quarterly Reports

a.   Each report, including transition reports, filed on Form 10-Q, Form 10-K, Form 20-F or Form 40-F under section 15(d) of the Act, other than a report filed by an Asset-Backed Issuer (as defined in paragraph (g) of this section), must include certifications in the form specified in the applicable exhibit filing requirements of such report and such certifications must be filed as an exhibit to such report. Each principal executive and principal financial officer of the issuer, or persons performing similar functions, at the time of filing of the report must sign a certification.

b.   Each periodic report containing financial statements filed by an issuer pursuant to section 15(d) of the Act must be accompanied by the certifications required by Section 1350 of Chapter 63 of Title 18 of the United States Code and such certifications must be furnished as an exhibit to such report as specified in the applicable exhibit requirements for such report. Each principal executive and principal financial officer of the issuer (or equivalent thereof) must sign a certification. This requirement may be satisfied by a single certification signed by an issuer's principal executive and principal financial officers.

c.   A person required to provide a certification specified in paragraph (a) or (b) of this section may not have the certification signed on his or her behalf pursuant to a power of attorney or other form of confirming authority.

* * *

f.   The certification requirements of this section do not apply to:
1.   An Interactive Data File, as defined in Rule 11 of Regulation S-T; or
2.   XBRL-Related Documents, as defined in Rule 11 of Regulation S-T.

* * *

Rule 15d-15 – Controls and Procedures

a. Every issuer that files reports under section 15(d) of the Act, other than an Asset-Backed Issuer (as defined in Rule 15d-14(g)), a small business investment company registered on Form N-5, or a unit investment trust as defined in section 4(2) of the Investment Company Act of 1940, must maintain disclosure controls and procedures (as defined in paragraph (e) of this section) and internal control over financial reporting (as defined in paragraph (f) of this section).

b. Each such issuer's management must evaluate, with the participation of the issuer's principal executive and principal financial officers, or persons performing similar functions, the effectiveness of the issuer's disclosure controls and procedures, as of the end of each fiscal quarter, except that management must perform this evaluation:
    1. In the case of a foreign private issuer (as defined in Rule 3b-4) as of the end of each fiscal year; and
    2. In the case of an investment company registered under section 8 of the Investment Company Act of 1940, within the 90-day period prior to the filing date of each report requiring certification under Investment Company Act Rule 30a-2.

c. The management of each such issuer, that either had been required to file an annual report pursuant to section 13(a) or 15(d) of the Act for the prior fiscal year or previously had filed an annual report with the Commission for the prior fiscal year, other than an investment company registered under section 8 of the Investment Company Act of 1940, must evaluate, with the participation of the issuer's principal executive and principal financial officers, or persons performing similar functions, the effectiveness, as of the end of each fiscal year, of the issuer's internal control over financial reporting. The framework on which management's evaluation of the issuer's internal control over financial reporting is based must be a suitable, recognized control framework that is established by a body or group that has followed due-process procedures, including the broad distribution of the framework for public comment. Although there are many different ways to conduct an evaluation of the effectiveness of internal control over financial reporting to meet the requirements of this paragraph, an evaluation that is conducted in accordance with the interpretive guidance issued by the Commission in Release No. 34-55929 will satisfy the evaluation required by this paragraph.

d. The management of each such issuer, other than an investment company registered under section 8 of the Investment Company Act of 1940, must evaluate, with the participation of the issuer's principal executive and principal financial officers, or persons performing similar functions, any change in the issuer's internal control over financial reporting, that occurred during each of the issuer's fiscal quarters, or fiscal year in the case of a foreign private issuer, that has materially affected, or is reasonably likely to materially affect, the issuer's internal control over financial reporting.

e. For purposes of this section, the term *disclosure controls and procedures* means controls and other procedures of an issuer that are designed to ensure that information required to be disclosed by the issuer in the reports that it files or submits under the Act is recorded, processed, summarized and reported, within the time periods specified in the Commission's rules and forms. Disclosure controls and procedures include, without limitation, controls and procedures designed to ensure that information required to be disclosed by an issuer in the reports that it files or submits under the Act is accumulated and communicated to the issuer's management, including its principal executive and principal financial officers, or persons performing similar functions, as appropriate to allow timely decisions regarding required disclosure.

f.   The term *internal control over financial reporting* is defined as a process designed by, or under the supervision of, the issuer's principal executive and principal financial officers, or persons performing similar functions, and effected by the issuer's board of directors, management and other personnel, to provide reasonable assurance regarding the reliability of financial reporting and the preparation of financial statements for external purposes in accordance with generally accepted accounting principles and includes those policies and procedures that:

1.   Pertain to the maintenance of records that in reasonable detail accurately and fairly reflect the transactions and dispositions of the assets of the issuer;

2.   Provide reasonable assurance that transactions are recorded as necessary to permit preparation of financial statements in accordance with generally accepted accounting principles, and that receipts and expenditures of the issuer are being made only in accordance with authorizations of management and directors of the issuer; and

3.   Provide reasonable assurance regarding prevention or timely detection of unauthorized acquisition, use or disposition of the issuer's assets that could have a material effect on the financial statements.

Rule 16a-1 – Definitions of Terms

Terms defined in this rule shall apply solely to section 16 of the Act and the rules thereunder. These terms shall not be limited to section 16(a) of the Act but also shall apply to all other subsections under section 16 of the Act.

a.   The term **beneficial owner** shall have the following applications:

1.   Solely for purposes of determining whether a person is a beneficial owner of more than ten percent of any class of equity securities registered pursuant to section 12 of the Act, the term "beneficial owner" shall mean any person who is deemed a beneficial owner pursuant to section 13(d) of the Act and the rules thereunder; *provided, however,* that the following institutions or persons shall not be deemed the beneficial owner of securities of such class held for the benefit of third parties or in customer or fiduciary accounts in the ordinary course of business (or in the case of an employee benefit plan specified in paragraph (a)(1)(vi) of this section, of securities of such class allocated to plan participants where participants have voting power) as long as such shares are acquired by such institutions or persons without the purpose or effect of changing or influencing control of the issuer or engaging in any arrangement subject to Rule 13d-3(b):

i.   A broker or dealer registered under section 15 of the Act;

ii.   A bank as defined in section 3(a)(6) of the Act;

iii.   An insurance company as defined in section 3(a)(19) of the Act;

iv.   An investment company registered under section 8 of the Investment Company Act of 1940;

v.   Any person registered as an investment adviser under Section 203 of the Investment Advisers Act of 1940 or under the laws of any state;

vi.   An employee benefit plan as defined in Section 3(3) of the Employee Retirement Income Security Act of 1974 ("ERISA") that is subject to the provisions of ERISA, or any such plan that is not subject to ERISA that is maintained primarily for the benefit of the employees of a state or local government or instrumentality, or an endowment fund;

vii.   A parent holding company or control person, provided the aggregate amount held directly by the parent or control person, and directly and indirectly by their subsidiaries or affiliates that are not persons specified in paragraphs (a)(1)(i) through (ix), does not exceed one percent of the securities of the subject class;

viii.   A savings association as defined in Section 3(b) of the Federal Deposit Insurance Act;

ix.   A church plan that is excluded from the definition of an investment company under section 3(c)(14) of the Investment Company Act of 1940; and

x.   A group, provided that all the members are persons specified in Rule 16a-1(a)(1)(i) through (ix).

xi.   A group, provided that all the members are persons specified in Rule 16a-1(a)(1) (i) through (vii).

Note to paragraph (a). Pursuant to this section, a person deemed a beneficial owner of more than ten percent of any class of equity securities registered under section 12 of the Act would file a Form 3, but the securities holdings disclosed on Form 3, and changes in beneficial ownership reported on subsequent Forms 4 or 5, would be determined by the definition of "beneficial owner" in paragraph (a)(2) of this section.

2.   Other than for purposes of determining whether a person is a beneficial owner of more than ten percent of any class of equity securities registered under Section 12 of the Act, the term *beneficial owner* shall mean any person who, directly or indirectly, through any contract, arrangement, understanding, relationship or otherwise, has or shares a direct or indirect pecuniary interest in the equity securities, subject to the following:

i.   The term *pecuniary interest* in any class of equity securities shall mean the opportunity, directly or indirectly, to profit or share in any profit derived from a transaction in the subject securities.

ii.   The term *indirect pecuniary interest* in any class of equity securities shall include, but not be limited to:

A.   Securities held by members of a person's immediate family sharing the same household; *provided, however*, that the presumption of such beneficial ownership may be rebutted; *see* also Rule 16a-1(a)(4);

    B. A general partner's proportionate interest in the portfolio securities held by a general or limited partnership. The general partner's proportionate interest, as evidenced by the partnership agreement in effect at the time of the transaction and the partnership's most recent financial statements, shall be the greater of:

       1. The general partner's share of the partnership's profits, including profits attributed to any limited partnership interests held by the general partner and any other interests in profits that arise from the purchase and sale of the partnership's portfolio securities; or

       2. The general partner's share of the partnership capital account, including the share attributable to any limited partnership interest held by the general partner.

    C. A performance-related fee, other than an asset-based fee, received by any broker, dealer, bank, insurance company, investment company, investment adviser, investment manager, trustee or person or entity performing a similar function; *provided, however,* that no pecuniary interest shall be present where:

       1. The performance-related fee, regardless of when payable, is calculated based upon net capital gains and/or net capital appreciation generated from the portfolio or from the fiduciary's overall performance over a period of one year or more; and

       2. Equity securities of the issuer do not account for more than ten percent of the market value of the portfolio. A right to a nonperformance-related fee alone shall not represent a pecuniary interest in the securities;

    D. A person's right to dividends that is separated or separable from the underlying securities. Otherwise, a right to dividends alone shall not represent a pecuniary interest in the securities;

    E. A person's interest in securities held by a trust, as specified in Rule 16a-8(b); and

    F. A person's right to acquire equity securities through the exercise or conversion of any derivative security, whether or not presently exercisable.

  iii.   A shareholder shall not be deemed to have a pecuniary interest in the portfolio securities held by a corporation or similar entity in which the person owns securities if the shareholder is not a controlling shareholder of the entity and does not have or share investment control over the entity's portfolio.

3.   Where more than one person subject to section 16 of the Act is deemed to be a beneficial owner of the same equity securities, all such persons must report as beneficial owners of the securities, either separately or jointly, as provided in Rule 16a-3(j). In such cases, the amount of short-swing profit recoverable shall not be increased above the amount recoverable if there were only one beneficial owner.

4. Any person filing a statement pursuant to section 16(a) of the Act may state that the filing shall not be deemed an admission that such person is, for purposes of section 16 of the Act or otherwise, the beneficial owner of any equity securities covered by the statement.

5. The following interests are deemed not to confer beneficial ownership for purposes of section 16 of the Act:

    i. Interests in portfolio securities held by any holding company registered under the Public Utility Holding Company Act of 1935;

    ii. Interests in portfolio securities held by any investment company registered under the Investment Company Act of 1940; and

    iii. Interests in securities comprising part of a broad-based, publicly traded market basket or index of stocks, approved for trading by the appropriate federal governmental authority.

b. The term **call equivalent position** shall mean a derivative security position that increases in value as the value of the underlying equity increases, including, but not limited to, a long convertible security, a long call option, and a short put option position.

c. The term **derivative securities** shall mean any option, warrant, convertible security, stock appreciation right, or similar right with an exercise or conversion privilege at a price related to an equity security, or similar securities with a value derived from the value of an equity security, but shall not include:

1. Rights of a pledgee of securities to sell the pledged securities;

2. Rights of all holders of a class of securities of an issuer to receive securities pro rata, or obligations to dispose of securities, as a result of a merger, exchange offer, or consolidation involving the issuer of the securities;

3. Rights or obligations to surrender a security, or have a security withheld, upon the receipt or exercise of a derivative security or the receipt or vesting of equity securities, in order to satisfy the exercise price or the tax withholding consequences of receipt, exercise or vesting;

4. Interests in broad-based index options, broad-based index futures, and broad-based publicly traded market baskets of stocks approved for trading by the appropriate federal governmental authority;

5. Interests or rights to participate in employee benefit plans of the issuer;

6. Rights with an exercise or conversion privilege at a price that is not fixed; or

7. Options granted to an underwriter in a registered public offering for the purpose of satisfying over-allotments in such offering.

d. The term **equity security of such issuer** shall mean any equity security or derivative security relating to an issuer, whether or not issued by that issuer.

e. The term **immediate family** shall mean any child, stepchild, grandchild, parent, stepparent, grandparent, spouse, sibling, mother-in-law, father-in-law, son-in-law, daughter-in-law, brother-in-law, or sister-in-law, and shall include adoptive relationships.

f.   The term **officer** shall mean an issuer's president, principal financial officer, principal accounting officer (or, if there is no such accounting officer, the controller), any vice-president of the issuer in charge of a principal business unit, division or function (such as sales, administration or finance), any other officer who performs a policy-making function, or any other person who performs similar policy-making functions for the issuer. Officers of the issuer's parent(s) or subsidiaries shall be deemed officers of the issuer if they perform such policy-making functions for the issuer. In addition, when the issuer is a limited partnership, officers or employees of the general partner(s) who perform policy-making functions for the limited partnership are deemed officers of the limited partnership. When the issuer is a trust, officers or employees of the trustee(s) who perform policy-making functions for the trust are deemed officers of the trust.

    Note: "Policy-making function" is not intended to include policy-making functions that are not significant. If pursuant to Item 401(b) of Regulation S-K the issuer identifies a person as an "executive officer," it is presumed that the Board of Directors has made that judgment and that the persons so identified are the officers for purposes of Section 16 of the Act, as are such other persons enumerated in this paragraph (f) but not in Item 401(b).

g.   The term **portfolio securities** shall mean all securities owned by an entity, other than securities issued by the entity.

h.   The term **put equivalent position** shall mean a derivative security position that increases in value as the value of the underlying equity decreases, including, but not limited to, a long put option and a short call option position.

Rule 16a-2 – Persons and Transactions Subject to Section 16

Any person who is the beneficial owner, directly or indirectly, of more than ten percent of any class of equity securities ("ten percent beneficial owner") registered pursuant to section 12 of the Act, any director or officer of the issuer of such securities, and any person specified in section 30(h) of the Investment Company Act of 1940, including any person specified in Rule 16a-8, shall be subject to the provisions of section 16 of the Act. The rules under section 16 of the Act apply to any class of equity securities of an issuer whether or not registered under section 12 of the Act. The rules under section 16 of the Act also apply to non-equity securities as provided by the Investment Company Act of 1940. With respect to transactions by persons subject to section 16 of the Act:

a.   A transaction(s) carried out by a director or officer in the six months prior to the director or officer becoming subject to section 16 of the Act shall be subject to section 16 of the Act and reported on the first required Form 4 only if the transaction(s) occurred within six months of the transaction giving rise to the Form 4 filing obligation and the director or officer became subject to section 16 of the Act solely as a result of the issuer registering a class of equity securities pursuant to section 12 of the Act.

b.   A transaction(s) following the cessation of director or officer status shall be subject to section 16 of the Act only if :

1. Executed within a period of less than six months of an opposite transaction subject to section 16(b) of the Act that occurred while that person was a director or officer.

2. Not otherwise exempted form section 16(b) of the Act pursuant to the provisions of this chapter.

Note to Paragraph (b): For the purposes of this paragraph, an acquisition and a disposition each shall be an opposite transaction with respect to the other.

c. The transaction that results in a person becoming a ten percent beneficial owner is not subject to section 16 of the Act unless the person otherwise is subject to section 16 of the Act. A ten percent beneficial owner not otherwise subject to section 16 of the Act must report only those transactions conducted while the beneficial owner of more than ten percent of a class of equity securities of the issuer registered pursuant to section 12 of the Act.

d.

1. Transactions by a person or entity shall be exempt from the provisions of section 16 of the Act for the 12 months following appointment and qualification, to the extent such person or entity is acting as:

 i. Executor or administrator of the estate of a decedent;

 ii. Guardian or member of a committee for an incompetent;

 iii. Receiver, trustee in bankruptcy, assignee for the benefit of creditors, conservator, liquidating agent, or other similar person duly authorized by law to administer the estate or assets of another person; or

 iv. Fiduciary in a similar capacity.

2. Transactions by such person or entity acting in a capacity specified in paragraph (d)(1) of this section after the period specified in that paragraph shall be subject to section 16 of the Act only where the estate, trust or other entity is a beneficial owner of more than ten percent of any class of equity security registered pursuant to section 12 of the Act.

Rule 16a-3 – Reporting Transactions and Holdings

a. Initial statements of beneficial ownership of equity securities required by section 16(a) of the Act shall be filed on Form 3. Statements of changes in beneficial ownership required by that section shall be filed on Form 4. Annual statements shall be filed on Form 5. At the election of the reporting person, any transaction required to be reported on Form 5 may be reported on an earlier filed Form 4. All such statements shall be prepared and filed in accordance with the requirements of the applicable form.

b. A person filing statements pursuant to section 16(a) of the Act with respect to any class of equity securities registered pursuant to section 12 of the Act need not file an additional statement on Form 3:

1. When an additional class of equity securities of the same issuer becomes registered pursuant to section 12 of the Act; or

2. When such person assumes a different or an additional relationship to the same issuer (for example, when an officer becomes a director).

c.   Any issuer that has equity securities listed on more than one national securities exchange may designate one exchange as the only exchange with which reports pursuant to section 16(a) of the Act need be filed. Such designation shall be made in writing and shall be filed with the Commission and with each national securities exchange on which any equity security of the issuer is listed at the time of such election. The reporting person's obligation to file reports with each national securities exchange on which any equity security of the issuer is listed shall be satisfied by filing with the exchange so designated.

d.   Any person required to file a statement with respect to securities of a single issuer under both section 16(a) of the Act and section 30(h) of the Investment Company Act of 1940 may file a single statement containing the required information, which will be deemed to be filed under both Acts.

e.   Any person required to file a statement under section 16(a) of the Act shall, not later than the time the statement is transmitted for filing with the Commission, send or deliver a duplicate to the person designated by the issuer to receive such statements, or, in the absence of such a designation, to the issuer's corporate secretary or person performing equivalent functions.

f.

   1.   A Form 5 shall be filed by every person who at any time during the issuer's fiscal year was subject to section 16 of the Act with respect to such issuer, except as provided in paragraph (f)(2) of this section. The Form shall be filed within 45 days after the issuer's fiscal year end, and shall disclose the following holdings and transactions not reported previously on Forms 3, 4 or 5:

      i.   All transactions during the most recent fiscal year that were exempt from Section 16(b) of the Act, except:

         A.   Exercises and conversions of derivative securities exempt under either Rule 16b-3 or Rule 16b-6(b), and any transaction exempt under Rule 16b-3(d), Rule 16b-3(e), or Rule 16b-3(f) (these are required to be reported on Form 4);

         B.   Transactions exempt from Section 16(b) of the Act pursuant to Rule 16b-3(c) which shall be exempt from Section 16(a) of the Act; and

         C.   Transactions exempt from Section 16(a) of the Act pursuant to another rule;

      ii.   Transactions that constituted small acquisitions pursuant to Rule 16a-6(a);

      iii.   All holdings and transactions that should have been reported during the most recent fiscal year, but were not; and

      iv.   With respect to the first Form 5 requirement for a reporting person, all holdings and transactions that should have been reported in each of the issuer's last two fiscal years but were not, based on the reporting person's reasonable belief in good faith in the completeness and accuracy of the information.

2.   Notwithstanding the above, no Form 5 shall be required where all transactions otherwise required to be reported on the Form 5 have been reported before the due date of the Form 5.

Note: Persons no longer subject to section 16 of the Act, but who were subject to the Section at any time during the issuer's fiscal year, must file a Form 5 unless paragraph (f)(2) is satisfied. *See also* Rule 16a-2(b) regarding the reporting obligations of persons ceasing to be officers or directors.

g.

1.   A Form 4 must be filed to report: All transactions not exempt from section 16(b) of the Act; All transactions exempt from section 16(b) of the Act pursuant to Rule 16b-3(d), Rule 16b-3(e), or Rule 16b-3(f); and all exercises and conversions of derivative securities, regardless of whether exempt from section 16(b) of the Act. Form 4 must be filed before the end of the second business day following the day on which the subject transaction has been executed.

2.   Solely for purposes of section 16(a)(2)(C) of the Act and paragraph (g)(1) of this section, the date on which the executing broker, dealer or plan administrator notifies the reporting person of the execution of the transaction is deemed the date of execution for a transaction where the following conditions are satisfied:

    i.   the transaction is pursuant to a contract, instruction or written plan for the purchase or sale of equity securities of the issuer (as defined in Rule 16a-1(d)) that satisfies the affirmative defense conditions of Rule 10b5-1(c); and

    ii.   the reporting person does not select the date of execution.

3.   Solely for purposes of section 16(a)(2)(C) of the Act and paragraph (g)(1) of this section, the date on which the plan administrator notifies the reporting person that the transaction has been executed is deemed the date of execution for a discretionary transaction (as defined in Rule 16b-3(b)(1)) for which the reporting person does not select the date of execution.

4.   In the case of the transactions described in paragraphs (g)(2) and (g)(3) of this section, if the notification date is later than the third business day following the trade date of the transaction, the date of execution is deemed to be the third business day following the trade date of the transaction.

5.   At the option of the reporting person, transactions that are reportable on Form 5 may be reported on Form 4, so long as the Form 4 is filed no later than the due date of the Form 5 on which the transaction is otherwise required to be reported.

h.   The date of filing with the Commission shall be the date of receipt by the Commission.

i.   Duplicated or facsimile versions of manual signatures of persons required to sign any document pursuant to Section 16 of the Act that is filed or submitted to the Commission under the Act shall be considered manual signatures for purposes of the Act and rules and regulations thereunder; provided that, the original signed document is retained by the filer for a period of five years and, upon request, the filer furnishes to the Commission or the staff the original manually signed document.

j.   Where more than one person subject to section 16 of the Act is deemed to be a beneficial owner of the same equity securities, all such persons must report as beneficial owners of the securities, either separately or jointly. Where persons in a group are deemed to be beneficial owners of equity securities pursuant to Rule 16a-1(a)(1) due to the aggregation of holdings, a single Form 3, 4 or 5 may be filed on behalf of all persons in the group. Joint and group filings must include all required information for each beneficial owner, and such filings must be signed by each beneficial owner, or on behalf of such owner by an authorized person.

k.   Any issuer that maintains a corporate Web site shall post on that Web site by the end of the business day after filing any Form 3, 4, or 5 filed under section 16(a) of the Act as to the equity securities of that issuer. Each such form shall remain accessible on such issuer's Web site for at least a 12-month period. In the case of an issuer that is an investment company and that does not maintain its own Web site, if any of the issuer's investment adviser, sponsor, depositor, trustee, administrator, principal underwriter, or any affiliated person of the investment company maintains a Web site that includes the name of the issuer, the issuer shall comply with the posting requirements by posting the forms on one such Web site.

Rule 16a-4 – Derivative Securities

a.   For purposes of section 16 of the Act, both derivative securities and the underlying securities to which they relate shall be deemed to be the same class of equity securities, except that the acquisition or disposition of any derivative security shall be separately reported.

b.   The exercise or conversion of a call equivalent position shall be reported on Form 4 and be treated for reporting purposes as:
1.   A purchase of the underlying security; and
2.   A closing of the derivative security position.

c.   The exercise or conversion of a put equivalent position shall be reported on Form 4 and shall be treated for reporting purposes as:
1.   A sale of the underlying security; and
2.   A closing of the derivative security position.

d.   The disposition or closing of a long derivative security position, as a result of cancellation or expiration, shall be exempt from section 16(a) of the Act if exempt from section 16(b) of the Act pursuant to Rule .

Note: Under Rule 16b-6(b), a purchase or sale resulting from an exercise or conversion of a derivative security generally is exempt from section 16(b) of the Act.

Rule 16b-3 – Transactions Between an Issuer and its Officers or Directors

Transactions between an issuer and its officers or directors.

a.   **General**. A transaction between the issuer (including an employee benefit plan sponsored by the issuer) and an officer or director of the issuer that involves issuer equity securities shall be exempt from Section 16(b) of the Act if the transaction satisfies the applicable conditions set forth in this section.

b.   **Definitions**.
1.   A **Discretionary Transaction** shall mean a transaction pursuant to an employee benefit plan that:
     i.   Is at the volition of a plan participant;
     ii. Is not made in connection with the participant's death, disability, retirement or termination of employment;
     iii. Is not required to be made available to a plan participant pursuant to a provision of the Internal Revenue Code; and
     iv. Results in either an intra-plan transfer involving an issuer equity securities fund, or a cash distribution funded by a volitional disposition of an issuer equity security.
2.   An **Excess Benefit Plan** shall mean an employee benefit plan that is operated in conjunction with a Qualified Plan, and provides only the benefits or contributions that would be provided under a Qualified Plan but for any benefit or contribution limitations set forth in the Internal Revenue Code of 1986, or any successor provisions thereof.
     i.   A **Non-Employee Director** shall mean a director who:
          A.   Is not currently an officer (as defined in Rule 16a-1(f)) of the issuer or a parent or subsidiary of the issuer, or otherwise currently employed by the issuer or a parent or subsidiary of the issuer;
          B.   Does not receive compensation, either directly or indirectly, from the issuer or a parent or subsidiary of the issuer, for services rendered as a consultant or in any capacity other than as a director, except for an amount that does not exceed the dollar amount for which disclosure would be required pursuant to Item 404(a) of Regulation S-K.
          C.   Does not possess an interest in any other transaction for which disclosure would be required pursuant to Item 404(a) of Regulation S-K; and
          D.   Is not engaged in a business relationship for which disclosure would be required pursuant to Item 404(b) of Regulation S-K.
     ii. Notwithstanding paragraph (b)(3)(i) of this section, a Non-Employee Director of a closed-end investment company shall mean a director who is not an interested person of the issuer, as that term is defined in Section 2(a)(19) of the Investment Company Act of 1940.
3.   A **Qualified Plan** shall mean an employee benefit plan that satisfies the coverage and participation requirements of Sections 410 and 401(a)(26) of the Internal Revenue Code of 1986, or any successor provisions thereof.

4.   A **Stock Purchase Plan** shall mean an employee benefit plan that satisfies the coverage and participation requirements of Sections 423(b)(3) and 423(b)(5), or Section 410, of the Internal Revenue Code of 1986, or any successor provisions thereof.

c.   **Tax-conditioned plans**. Any transaction (other than a Discretionary Transaction) pursuant to a Qualified Plan, an Excess Benefit Plan, or a Stock Purchase Plan shall be exempt without condition.

d.   **Acquisitions from the issuer**. Any transaction, other than a Discretionary Transaction, involving an acquisition from the issuer (including without limitation a grant or award), whether or not intended for a compensatory or other particular purpose, shall be exempt if:

1.   The transaction is approved by the board of directors of the issuer, or a committee of the board of directors that is composed solely of two or more Non-Employee Directors;

2.   The transaction is approved or ratified, in compliance with Section 14 of the Act, by either: the affirmative votes of the holders of a majority of the securities of the issuer present, or represented, and entitled to vote at a meeting duly held in accordance with the applicable laws of the state or other jurisdiction in which the issuer is incorporated; or the written consent of the holders of a majority of the securities of the issuer entitled to vote; provided that such ratification occurs no later than the date of the next annual meeting of shareholders; or

3.   The issuer equity securities so acquired are held by the officer or director for a period of six months following the date of such acquisition, provided that this condition shall be satisfied with respect to a derivative security if at least six months elapse from the date of acquisition of the derivative security to the date of disposition of the derivative security (other than upon exercises or conversion) or its underlying equity security.

e.   **Dispositions to the issuer**. Any transaction, other than a Discretionary Transaction, involving the disposition to the issuer of issuer equity securities, whether or not intended for a compensatory or other particular purpose, shall be exempt, provided that the terms of such disposition are approved in advance in the manner prescribed by either paragraph (d)(1) or paragraph (d)(2) of this section.

f.   **Discretionary Transactions**. A Discretionary Transaction shall be exempt only if effected pursuant to an election made at least six months following the date of the most recent election, with respect to any plan of the issuer, that effected a Discretionary Transaction that was:

1.   An acquisition, if the transaction to be exempted would be a disposition; or

2.   A disposition, if the transaction to be exempted would be an acquisition.

Notes to Rule 16b-3:

1.   The exercise or conversion of a derivative security that does not satisfy the conditions of this section is eligible for exemption from Section 16(b) of the Act to the extent that the conditions of Rule 16b-6(b) are satisfied.

2. Section 16(a) reporting requirements applicable to transactions exempt pursuant to this section are set forth in Rule 16a-3(f) and (g) and Rule 16a-4.

3. The approval conditions of paragraphs (d)(1), (d)(2) and (e) of this section require the approval of each specific transaction, and are not satisfied by approval of a plan in its entirety except for the approval of a plan pursuant to which the terms and conditions of each transaction are fixed in advance, such as a formula plan. Where the terms of a subsequent transaction (such as the exercise price of an option, or the provision of an exercise or tax with-holding right) are provided for in a transaction as initially approved pursuant to paragraphs (d)(1), (d)(2) or (e), such subsequent transaction shall not require further specific approval.

4. For purposes of determining a director's status under those portions of paragraph (b)(3)(i) that reference Item 404(a) of this chapter, an issuer may rely on the disclosure provided under Item 404(a) of this chapter for the issuer's most recent fiscal year contained in the most recent filing in which disclosure required under Item 404(a) is presented. Where a transaction disclosed in that filing was terminated before the director's proposed service as a Non-Employee Director, that transaction will not bar such service. The issuer must believe in good faith that any current or contemplated transaction in which the director participates will not be required to be disclosed under Item 404(a) of this chapter, based on information readily available to the issuer and the director at the time such director proposes to act as a Non-Employee Director. At such time as the issuer believes in good faith, based on readily available information, that a current or contemplated transaction with a director will be required to be disclosed under Item 404(a) in a future filing, the director no longer is eligible to serve as a Non-Employee Director; provided, however, that this determination does not result in retroactive loss of a Rule 16b-3 exemption for a transaction previously approved by the director while serving as a Non-Employee Director consistent with this note. In making the determinations specified in this Note, the issuer may rely on information it obtains from the director, for example, pursuant to a response to an inquiry.

Rule 16b-6 – Derivative Securities

a. The establishment of or increase in a call equivalent position or liquidation of or decrease in a put equivalent position shall be deemed a purchase of the underlying security for purposes of Section 16(b) of the Act, and the establishment of or increase in a put equivalent position or liquidation of or decrease in a call equivalent position shall be deemed a sale of the underlying securities for purposes of Section 16(b) of the Act; *Provided, however,* That if the increase or decrease occurs as a result of the fixing of the exercise price of a right initially issued without a fixed price, where the date the price is fixed is not known in advance and is outside the control of the recipient, the increase or decrease shall be exempt from Section 16(b) of the Act with respect to any offsetting transaction within the six months prior to the date the price is fixed.

b. The closing of a derivative security position as a result of its exercise or conversion shall be exempt from the operation of Section 16(b) of the Act, and the acquisition of underlying securities at a fixed exercise price due to the exercise or conversion of a call equivalent position or the disposition of underlying securities at a fixed exercise price due to the exercise of a put equivalent position shall be exempt from the operation of Section 16(b) of the Act: *Provided, however,* That the acquisition of underlying securities from the exercise of an out-of-the-money option, warrant, or right shall not be exempt unless the exercise is necessary to comport with the sequential exercise provisions of the Internal Revenue Code.

c. In determining the short-swing profit recoverable pursuant to Section 16(b) of the Act from transactions involving the purchase and sale or sale and purchase of derivative and other securities, the following rules apply:

 1. Short-swing profits in transactions involving the purchase and sale or sale and purchase of derivative securities that have identical characteristics (*e.g.,* purchases and sales of call options of the same strike price and expiration date, or purchases and sales of the same series of convertible debentures) shall be measured by the actual prices paid or received in the short-swing transactions.

 2. Short-swing profits in transactions involving the purchase and sale or sale and purchase of derivative securities having different characteristics but related to the same underlying security (*e.g.,* the purchase of a call option and the sale of a convertible debenture) or derivative securities and underlying securities shall not exceed the difference in price of the underlying security on the date of purchase or sale and the date of sale or purchase. Such profits may be measured by calculating the short-swing profits that would have been realized had the subject transactions involved purchases and sales solely of the derivative security that was purchased or solely of the derivative security that was sold, valued as of the time of the matching purchase or sale, and calculated for the lesser of the number of underlying securities actually purchased or sold.

d. Upon cancellation or expiration of an option within six months of the writing of the option, any profit derived from writing the option shall be recoverable under Section 16(b) of the Act. The profit shall not exceed the premium received for writing the option. The disposition or closing of a long derivative security position, as a result of cancellation or expiration, shall be exempt from Section 16(b) of the Act where no value is received from the cancellation or expiration.

Regulation FD

Rule 100 – General Rule Regarding Selective Disclosure

a. Whenever an issuer, or any person acting on its behalf, discloses any material nonpublic information regarding that issuer or its securities to any person described in paragraph (b)(1) of this section, the issuer shall make public disclosure of that information as provided in Rule 101(e):

    1. Simultaneously, in the case of an intentional disclosure; and
    2. Promptly, in the case of a non-intentional disclosure.

b.

    1. Except as provided in paragraph (b)(2) of this section, paragraph (a) of this section shall apply to a disclosure made to any person outside the issuer:

        i.   Who is a broker or dealer, or a person associated with a broker or dealer, as those terms are defined in Section 3(a) of the Securities Exchange Act of 1934;

        ii. Who is an investment adviser, as that term is defined in Section 202(a)(11) of the Investment Advisers Act of 1940; an institutional investment manager, as that term is defined in Section 13(f)(5) of the Securities Exchange Act of 1934, that filed a report on Form 13F with the Commission for the most recent quarter ended prior to the date of the disclosure; or a person associated with either of the foregoing. For purposes of this paragraph, a "person associated with an investment adviser or institutional investment manager" has the meaning set forth in Section 202(a)(17) of the Investment Advisers Act of 1940, assuming for these purposes that an institutional investment manager is an investment adviser;

        iii. Who is an investment company, as defined in Section 3 of the Investment Company Act of 1940, or who would be an investment company but for Section 3(c)(1) or Section 3(c)(7) thereof, or an affiliated person of either of the foregoing. For purposes of this paragraph, "affiliated person" means only those persons described in Section 2(a)(3)(C), (D), (E), and (F) of the Investment Company Act of 1940, assuming for these purposes that a person who would be an investment company but for Section 3(c)(1) or Section 3(c)(7) of the Investment Company Act of 1940 is an investment company; or

        iv. Who is a holder of the issuer's securities, under circumstances in which it is reasonably foreseeable that the person will purchase or sell the issuer's securities on the basis of the information.

    2. Paragraph (a) of this section shall not apply to a disclosure made:

        i.   To a person who owes a duty of trust or confidence to the issuer (such as an attorney, investment banker, or accountant);

        ii. To a person who expressly agrees to maintain the disclosed information in confidence;

        iii. To an entity whose primary business is the issuance of credit ratings, provided the information is disclosed solely for the purpose of developing a credit rating and the entity's ratings are publicly available; or

iv. In connection with a securities offering registered under the Securities Act, other than an offering of the type described in any of Rule 415(a)(1)(i) through (vi) under the Securities Act (except an offering of the type described in Rule 415(a)(1)(i) under the Securities Act also involving a registered offering, whether or not underwritten, for capital formation purposes for the account of the issuer (unless the issuer's offering is being registered for the purpose of evading the requirements of this section)), if the disclosure is by any of the following means:

(A) A registration statement filed under the Securities Act, including a prospectus contained therein;

(B) A free writing prospectus used after filing of the registration statement for the offering or a communication falling within the exception to the definition of prospectus contained in clause (a) of section 2(a)(10) of the Securities Act;

(C) Any other Section 10(b) prospectus;

(D) A notice permitted by Rule 135 under the Securities Act;

(E) A communication permitted by Rule 134 under the Securities Act; or

(F) An oral communication made in connection with the registered securities offering after filing of the registration statement for the offering under the Securities Act.

Rule 101 – Definitions

This section defines certain terms as used in Regulation FD (Rule 100 through Rule 103).

a. **Intentional.** A selective disclosure of material nonpublic information is *intentional* when the person making the disclosure either knows, or is reckless in not knowing, that the information he or she is communicating is both material and nonpublic.

b. **Issuer.** An *issuer* subject to this regulation is one that has a class of securities registered under Section 12 of the Securities Exchange Act of 1934, or is required to file reports under Section 15(d) of the Securities Exchange Act of 1934, including any closed-end investment company (as defined in Section 5(a)(2) of the Investment Company Act of 1940), but not including any other investment company or any foreign government or foreign private issuer, as those terms are defined in Rule 405 under the Securities Act.

c. **Person acting on behalf of an issuer.** *Person acting on behalf of an issuer* means any senior official of the issuer (or, in the case of a closed-end investment company, a senior official of the issuer's investment adviser), or any other officer, employee, or agent of an issuer who regularly communicates with any person described in Rule 100(b)(1)(i), (ii), or (iii), or with holders of the issuer's securities. An officer, director, employee, or agent of an issuer who discloses material nonpublic information in breach of a duty of trust or confidence to the issuer shall not be considered to be acting on behalf of the issuer.

d.   **Promptly.** *Promptly* means as soon as reasonably practicable (but in no event after the later of 24 hours or the commencement of the next day's trading on the New York Stock Exchange) after a senior official of the issuer (or, in the case of a closed-end investment company, a senior official of the issuer's investment adviser) learns that there has been a non-intentional disclosure by the issuer or person acting on behalf of the issuer of information that the senior official knows, or is reckless in not knowing, is both material and nonpublic.

e.   **Public disclosure.**
   1.   Except as provided in paragraph (e)(2) of this section, an issuer shall make the *public disclosure* of information required by Rule 100(a) by furnishing to or filing with the Commission a Form 8-K disclosing that information.
   2.   An issuer shall be exempt from the requirement to furnish or file a Form 8-K if it instead disseminates the information through another method (or combination of methods) of disclosure that is reasonably designed to provide broad, non-exclusionary distribution of the information to the public.

f.   **Senior official.** *Senior official* means any director, executive officer (as defined in Rule 3b-7 under the Securities Exchange Act of 1934), investor relations or public relations officer, or other person with similar functions.

g.   **Securities offering.** For purposes of Rule 100(b)(2)(iv):
   1.   Underwritten offerings. A *securities offering* that is underwritten commences when the issuer reaches an understanding with the broker-dealer that is to act as managing underwriter and continues until the later of the end of the period during which a dealer must deliver a prospectus or the sale of the securities (unless the offering is sooner terminated);
   2.   Non-underwritten offerings. A securities offering that is not underwritten:
      i.   If covered by Rule 415(a)(1)(x), commences when the issuer makes its first bona fide offer in a takedown of securities and continues until the later of the end of the period during which each dealer must deliver a prospectus or the sale of the securities in that takedown (unless the takedown is sooner terminated);
      ii.   If a business combination as defined in Rule 165(f)(1), commences when the first public announcement of the transaction is made and continues until the completion of the vote or the expiration of the tender offer, as applicable (unless the transaction is sooner terminated);
      iii. If an offering other than those specified in paragraphs (a) and (b) of this section, commences when the issuer files a registration statement and continues until the later of the end of the period during which each dealer must deliver a prospectus or the sale of the securities (unless the offering is sooner terminated).

Rule 102 – No Effect on Antifraud Liability

No failure to make a public disclosure required solely by Rule 100 shall be deemed to be a violation of Rule 10b-5 under the Securities Exchange Act.

Rule 103 – No Effect on Exchange Act Reporting Status

A failure to make a public disclosure required solely by Rule 100 shall not affect whether:
  a. For purposes of Forms S-2, S-3 and S-8 under the Securities Act, an issuer is deemed to have filed all the material required to be filed pursuant to Section 13 or 15(d) of the Securities Exchange Act of 1934 or, where applicable, has made those filings in a timely manner; or
  b. There is adequate current public information about the issuer for purposes of Rule 144(c).

Regulation G

Rule 100 – General Rules Regarding Disclosure of Non-GAAP Financial Measures

a. Whenever a registrant, or person acting on its behalf, publicly discloses material information that includes a non-GAAP financial measure, the registrant must accompany that non-GAAP financial measure with:
    1. A presentation of the most directly comparable financial measure calculated and presented in accordance with Generally Accepted Accounting Principles (GAAP); and
    2. A reconciliation (by schedule or other clearly understandable method), which shall be quantitative for historical non-GAAP measures presented, and quantitative, to the extent available without unreasonable efforts, for forward-looking information, of the differences between the non-GAAP financial measure disclosed or released with the most comparable financial measure or measures calculated and presented in accordance with GAAP identified in paragraph (a)(1) of this section.

b. A registrant, or a person acting on its behalf, shall not make public a non-GAAP financial measure that, taken together with the information accompanying that measure and any other accompanying discussion of that measure, contains an untrue statement of a material fact or omits to state a material fact necessary in order to make the presentation of the non-GAAP financial measure, in light of the circumstances under which it is presented, not misleading.

c. This section shall not apply to a disclosure of a non-GAAP financial measure that is made by or on behalf of a registrant that is a foreign private issuer if the following conditions are satisfied:
    1. The securities of the registrant are listed or quoted on a securities exchange or inter-dealer quotation system outside the United States;
    2. The non-GAAP financial measure is not derived from or based on a measure calculated and presented in accordance with generally accepted accounting principles in the United States; and
    3. The disclosure is made by or on behalf of the registrant outside the United States, or is included in a written communication that is released by or on behalf of the registrant outside the United States.

d. This section shall not apply to a non-GAAP financial measure included in disclosure relating to a proposed business combination, the entity resulting therefrom or an entity that is a party thereto, if the disclosure is contained in a communication that is subject to Rule 425 under the Securities Act, Rules 14a-12 or 14d-2(b)(2) under the Exchange Act or Item 1015 of Regulation M-A.

Notes to Rule 100:

1. If a non-GAAP financial measure is made public orally, telephonically, by Web cast, by broadcast, or by similar means, the requirements of paragraphs (a)(1)(i) and (a)(1)(ii) of this section will be satisfied if:

i.   The required information in those paragraphs is provided on the registrant's Web site at the time the non-GAAP financial measure is made public; and

ii.   The location of the web site is made public in the same presentation in which the non-GAAP financial measure is made public.

2.   The provisions of paragraph (c) of this section shall apply notwithstanding the existence of one or more of the following circumstances:

    i.   A written communication is released in the United States as well as outside the United States, so long as the communication is released in the United States contemporaneously with or after the release outside the United States and is not otherwise targeted at persons located in the United States;

    ii.   Foreign journalists, U.S. journalists or other third parties have access to the information;

    iii.   The information appears on one or more web sites maintained by the registrant, so long as the web sites, taken together, are not available exclusively to, or targeted at, persons located in the United States; or

    iv.   Following the disclosure or release of the information outside the United States, the information is included in a submission by the registrant to the Commission made under cover of a Form 6-K.

Rule 101 – Definitions

This section defines certain terms as used in Regulation G (Rule 100 through Rule 102).

a.

    1.   **Non-GAAP financial measure**. A *non-GAAP financial measure* is a numerical measure of a registrant's historical or future financial performance, financial position or cash flows that:

        i.   Excludes amounts, or is subject to adjustments that have the effect of excluding amounts, that are included in the most directly comparable measure calculated and presented in accordance with GAAP in the statement of income, balance sheet or statement of cash flows (or equivalent statements) of the issuer; or

        ii.   Includes amounts, or is subject to adjustments that have the effect of including amounts, that are excluded from the most directly comparable measure so calculated and presented.

    2.   A non-GAAP financial measure does not include operating and other financial measures and ratios or statistical measures calculated using exclusively one or both of:

        i.   Financial measures calculated in accordance with GAAP; and

        ii.   Operating measures or other measures that are not non-GAAP financial measures.

    3.   A non-GAAP financial measure does not include financial measures required to be disclosed by GAAP, Commission rules, or a system of regulation of a government or governmental authority or self-regulatory organization that is applicable to the registrant.

b.   **GAAP.** *GAAP* refers to generally accepted accounting principles in the United States, except that:
1.   In the case of foreign private issuers whose primary financial statements are prepared in accordance with non-U.S. generally accepted accounting principles, GAAP refers to the principles under which those primary financial statements are prepared; and
2.   In the case of foreign private issuers that include a non-GAAP financial measure derived from a measure calculated in accordance with U.S. generally accepted accounting principles, GAAP refers to U.S. generally accepted accounting principles for purposes of the application of the requirements of Regulation G to the disclosure of that measure.

c.   **Registrant.** A *registrant* subject to this regulation is one that has a class of securities registered under Section 12 of the Securities Exchange Act of 1934, or is required to file reports under Section 15(d) of the Securities Exchange Act of 1934, excluding any investment company registered under Section 8 of the Investment Company Act of 1940.

d.   **United States.** *United States* means the United States of America, its territories and possessions, any State of the United States, and the District of Columbia.

Rule 102 – No Effect on Antifraud Liability

Neither the requirements of this Regulation G nor a person's compliance or non-compliance with the requirements of this Regulation shall in itself affect any person's liability under Section 10(b) of the Securities Exchange Act of 1934 or Rule 10b-5 under such Act.

Regulation M

Rule 100 – Preliminary Note; Definitions

a. *Preliminary note:* Any transaction or series of transactions, whether or not effected pursuant to the provisions of Regulation M, remain subject to the antifraud and antimanipulation provisions of the securities laws, including, without limitation, Section 17(a) of the Securities Act of 1933 and Sections 9, 10(b), and 15(c) of the Securities Exchange Act of 1934.

b. For purposes of Regulation M the following definitions shall apply:

    ADTV means the worldwide average daily trading volume during the two full calendar months immediately preceding, or any 60 consecutive calendar days ending within the 10 calendar days preceding, the filing of the registration statement; or, if there is no registration statement or if the distribution involves the sale of securities on a delayed basis pursuant to Rule 415 under the Securities Act, two full calendar months immediately preceding, or any consecutive 60 calendar days ending within the 10 calendar days preceding, the determination of the offering price.

    Affiliated purchaser means:
    1. A person acting, directly or indirectly, in concert with a distribution participant, issuer, or selling security holder in connection with the acquisition or distribution of any covered security; or
    2. An affiliate, which may be a separately identifiable department or division of a distribution participant, issuer, or selling security holder, that, directly or indirectly, controls the purchases of any covered security by a distribution participant, issuer, or selling security holder, whose purchases are controlled by any such person, or whose purchases are under common control with any such person; or
    3. An affiliate, which may be a separately identifiable department or division of a distribution participant, issuer, or selling security holder, that regularly purchases securities for its own account or for the account of others, or that recommends or exercises investment discretion with respect to the purchase or sale of securities; *Provided, however,* That this paragraph (3) shall not apply to such affiliate if the following conditions are satisfied:
        i.   The distribution participant, issuer, or selling security holder:
             A. Maintains and enforces written policies and procedures reasonably designed to prevent the flow of information to or from the affiliate that might result in a violation of Rules 101, 102, and 104 of Regulation M; and
             B. Obtains an annual, independent assessment of the operation of such policies and procedures; and
        ii. The affiliate has no officers (or persons performing similar functions) or employees (other than clerical, ministerial, or support personnel) in common with the distribution participant, issuer, or selling security holder that direct, effect, or recommend transactions in securities; and

iii.   The affiliate does not, during the applicable restricted period, act as a market maker (other than as a specialist in compliance with the rules of a national securities exchange), or engage, as a broker or a dealer, in solicited transactions or proprietary trading, in covered securities.

Agent independent of the issuer means a trustee or other person who is independent of the issuer. The agent shall be deemed to be independent of the issuer only if:

1.   The agent is not an affiliate of the issuer; and
2.   Neither the issuer nor any affiliate of the issuer exercises any direct or indirect control or influence over the prices or amounts of the securities to be purchased, the timing of, or the manner in which, the securities are to be purchased, or the selection of a broker or dealer (other than the independent agent itself) through which purchases may be executed; *Provided, however,* That the issuer or its affiliate will not be deemed to have such control or influence solely because it revises not more than once in any three-month period the source of the shares to fund the plan, the basis or determining the amount of its contributions to a plan, or the basis for determining the frequency of its allocations to a plan, or any formula specified in a plan that determines the amount or timing of securities to be purchased by the agent.

Asset-backed security has the meaning contained in General Instruction I.B.5. to Form S-3.

At-the-market offering means an offering of securities at other than a fixed price.

Business day refers to a 24 hour period determined with reference to the principal market for the securities to be distributed, and that includes a complete trading session for that market.

Completion of participation in a distribution. Securities acquired in the distribution for investment by any person participating in a distribution, or any affiliated purchaser of such person, shall be deemed to be distributed. A person shall be deemed to have completed its participation in a distribution as follows:

1.   An issuer or selling security holder, when the distribution is completed;
2.   An underwriter, when such person's participation has been distributed, including all other securities of the same class that are acquired in connection with the distribution, and any stabilization arrangements and trading restrictions in connection with the distribution have been terminated; *Provided, however,* That an underwriter's participation will not be deemed to have been completed if a syndicate overallotment option is exercised in an amount that exceeds the net syndicate short position at the time of such exercise; and
3.   Any other person participating in the distribution, when such person's participation has been distributed.

Covered security means any security that is the subject of a distribution, or any reference security.

Current exchange rate means the current rate of exchange between two currencies, which is obtained from at least one independent entity that provides or disseminates foreign exchange quotations in the ordinary course of its business.

Distribution means an offering of securities, whether or not subject to registration under the Securities Act, that is distinguished from ordinary trading transactions by the magnitude of the offering and the presence of special selling efforts and selling methods.

Distribution participant means an underwriter, prospective underwriter, broker, dealer, or other person who has agreed to participate or is participating in a distribution.

Electronic communications network has the meaning contained in Rule 11Ac1-1(a)(8) under the Exchange Act.

Employee has the meaning contained in Form S-8.

Exchange Act means the Securities Exchange Act of 1934.

Independent bid means a bid by a person who is not a distribution participant, issuer, selling security holder, or affiliated purchaser.

NASD means the National Association of Securities Dealers, Inc. or any of its subsidiaries.

Nasdaq means the Nasdaq system electronic dealer quotation system owned and operated by The Nasdaq Stock Market, Inc.

Nasdaq security means a security that is authorized for quotation on Nasdaq, and such authorization is not suspended, terminated, or prohibited.

Net purchases means the amount by which a passive market maker's purchases exceed its sales.

Offering price means the price at which the security is to be or is being distributed.

Passive market maker means a market maker that effects bids or purchases in accordance with the provisions of Rule 103.

Penalty bid means an arrangement that permits the managing underwriter to reclaim a selling concession from a syndicate member in connection with an offering when the securities originally sold by the syndicate member are purchased in syndicate covering transactions.

Plan means any bonus, profit-sharing, pension, retirement, thrift, savings, incentive, stock purchase, stock option, stock ownership, stock appreciation, dividend reinvestment, or similar plan; or any dividend or interest reinvestment plan or employee benefit plan as defined in Rule 405 under the Securities Act.

Principal market means the single securities market with the largest aggregate reported trading volume for the class of securities during the 12 full calendar months immediately preceding the filing of the registration statement; or, if there is no registration statement or if the distribution involves the sale of securities on a delayed basis pursuant to Rule 415, during the 12 full calendar months immediately preceding the determination of the offering price. For the purpose of determining the aggregate trading volume in a security, the trading volume of depositary shares representing such security shall be included, and shall be multiplied by the multiple or fraction of the security represented by the depositary share. For purposes of this paragraph, depositary share means a security, evidenced by a depositary receipt, that represents another security, or a multiple or fraction thereof, deposited with a depositary.

Prospective underwriter means a person:
1. Who has submitted a bid to the issuer or selling security holder, and who knows or is reasonably certain that such bid will be accepted, whether or not the terms and conditions of the underwriting have been agreed upon; or
2. Who has reached, or is reasonably certain to reach, an understanding with the issuer or selling security holder, or managing underwriter that such person will become an underwriter, whether or not the terms and conditions of the underwriting have been agreed upon.

Public float value shall be determined in the manner set forth on the front page of Form 10-K, even if the issuer of such securities is not required to file Form 10-K, relating to the aggregate market value of common equity securities held by non-affiliates of the issuer.

Reference period means the two full calendar months immediately preceding the filing of the registration statement or, if there is no registration statement or if the distribution involves the sale of securities on a delayed basis pursuant to Rule 415, the two full calendar months immediately preceding the determination of the offering price.

Reference security means a security into which a security that is the subject of a distribution ("subject security") may be converted, exchanged, or exercised or which, under the terms of the subject security, may in whole or in significant part determine the value of the subject security.

Restricted period means:
1. For any security with an ADTV value of $100,000 or more of an issuer whose common equity securities have a public float value of $25 million or more, the period beginning on the later of one business day prior to the determination of the offering price or such time that a person becomes a distribution participant, and ending upon such person's completion of participation in the distribution; and

2.　For all other securities, the period beginning on the later of five business days prior to the determination of the offering price or such time that a person becomes a distribution participant, and ending upon such person's completion of participation in the distribution.

3.　In the case of a distribution involving a merger, acquisition, or exchange offer, the period beginning on the day proxy solicitation or offering materials are first disseminated to security holders, and ending upon the completion of the distribution.

Securities Act means the Securities Act of 1933.

Selling security holder means any person on whose behalf a distribution is made, other than an issuer.

Stabilize or **stabilizing** means the placing of any bid, or the effecting of any purchase, for the purpose of pegging, fixing, or maintaining the price of a security.

Syndicate covering transaction means the placing of any bid or the effecting of any purchase on behalf of the sole distributor or the underwriting syndicate or group to reduce a short position created in connection with the offering.

30% ADTV limitation means 30 percent of the market maker's ADTV in a covered security during the reference period, as obtained from the NASD.

Underwriter means a person who has agreed with an issuer or selling security holder:

1.　To purchase securities for distribution; or

2.　To distribute securities for or on behalf of such issuer or selling security holder; or

3.　To manage or supervise a distribution of securities for or on behalf of such issuer or selling security holder.

Rule 101 – Activities by Distribution Participants

a.　**Unlawful Activity.** In connection with a distribution of securities, it shall be unlawful for a distribution participant or an affiliated purchaser of such person, directly or indirectly, to bid for, purchase, or attempt to induce any person to bid for or purchase, a covered security during the applicable restricted period; *Provided, however,* That if a distribution participant or affiliated purchaser is the issuer or selling security holder of the securities subject to the distribution, such person shall be subject to the provisions of Rule 102, rather than this section.

b.　**Excepted Activity.** The following activities shall not be prohibited by paragraph (a) of this section:

1.　Research. The publication or dissemination of any information, opinion, or recommendation, if the conditions of Rule 138 or Rule 139 under the Securities Act of 1933 are met; or

2.   Transactions complying with certain other sections. Transactions complying with Rule 103 or Rule 104; or

3.   Odd-lot transactions. Transactions in odd-lots; or transactions to offset odd-lots in connection with an odd-lot tender offer conducted pursuant to Rule 13e-4(h)(5) under the Securities Exchange Act of 1934; or

4.   Exercises of securities. The exercise of any option, warrant, right, or any conversion privilege set forth in the instrument governing a security; or

5.   Unsolicited transactions. Unsolicited brokerage transactions; or unsolicited purchases that are not effected from or through a broker or dealer, on a securities exchange, or through an inter-dealer quotation system or electronic communications network; or

6.   Basket transactions.

   i.   Bids or purchases, in the ordinary course of business, in connection with a basket of 20 or more securities in which a covered security does not comprise more than 5% of the value of the basket purchased; or

   ii.   Adjustments to such a basket in the ordinary course of business as a result of a change in the composition of a standardized index; or

7.   De minimis transactions. Purchases during the restricted period, other than by a passive market maker, that total less than 2% of the ADTV of the security being purchased, or unaccepted bids; *Provided, however,* That the person making such bid or purchase has maintained and enforces written policies and procedures reasonably designed to achieve compliance with the other provisions of this section; or

8.   Transactions in connection with a distribution. Transactions among distribution participants in connection with a distribution, and purchases of securities from an issuer or selling security holder in connection with a distribution, that are not effected on a securities exchange, or through an inter-dealer quotation system or electronic communications network; or

9.   Offers to sell or the solicitation of offers to buy. Offers to sell or the solicitation of offers to buy the securities being distributed (including securities acquired in stabilizing), or securities offered as principal by the person making such offer or solicitation; or

10.   Transactions in Rule 144A securities. Transactions in securities eligible for resale under Rule 144A(d)(3) under the Securities Act of 1933, or any reference security, if the Rule 144A securities are offered or sold in the United States solely to:

   i.   Qualified institutional buyers, as defined in Rule 144A(a)(1) under the Securities Act of 1933, or to offerees or purchasers that the seller and any person acting on behalf of the seller reasonably believes are qualified institutional buyers, in transactions exempt from registration under section 4(2) of the Securities Act or Rule 144A or Rule 501 through Rule 508 under such Act; or

   ii.   Persons not deemed to be "U.S. persons" for purposes of Rule 902(o)(2) or Rule 902(o)(7) under the Securities Act of 1933 [Editor's note: It appears this should be Rule 902(k)(2) and Rule 902 (k)(7).], during a distribution qualifying under paragraph (b)(10)(i) of this section.

c. **Excepted Securities.** The provisions of this section shall not apply to any of the following securities:

1. Actively-traded securities. Securities that have an ADTV value of at least $1 million and are issued by an issuer whose common equity securities have a public float value of at least $150 million; *Provided, however,* That such securities are not issued by the distribution participant or an affiliate of the distribution participant; or

2. Investment grade nonconvertible and asset-backed securities. Nonconvertible debt securities, nonconvertible preferred securities, and asset- backed securities, that are rated by at least one nationally recognized statistical rating organization, as that term is used in Rule 15c3-1 under the Securities Exchange Act of 1934, in one of its generic rating categories that signifies investment grade; or

3. Exempted securities. "Exempted securities" as defined in section 3(a)(12) of the Exchange Act; or

4. Face-amount certificates or securities issued by an open-end management investment company or unit investment trust. Face-amount certificates issued by a face-amount certificate company, or redeemable securities issued by an open-end management investment company or a unit investment trust. Any terms used in this paragraph (c)(4) that are defined in the Investment Company Act of 1940 shall have the meanings specified in such Act.

d. **Exemptive Authority.** Upon written application or upon its own motion, the Commission may grant an exemption from the provisions of this section, either unconditionally or on specified terms and conditions, to any transaction or class of transactions, or to any security or class of securities.

Rule 102 – Activities by Issuers and Selling Security Holders During a Distribution

a. **Unlawful Activity.** In connection with a distribution of securities effected by or on behalf of an issuer or selling security holder, it shall be unlawful for such person, or any affiliated purchaser of such person, directly or indirectly, to bid for, purchase, or attempt to induce any person to bid for or purchase, a covered security during the applicable restricted period; Except That if an affiliated purchaser is a distribution participant, such affiliated purchaser may comply with Rule 101, rather than this section.

b. **Excepted Activity.** The following activities shall not be prohibited by paragraph (a) of this section:

1. Odd-lot transactions. Transactions in odd-lots, or transactions to offset odd-lots in connection with an odd-lot tender offer conducted pursuant to Rule 13e-4(h)(5) under the Securities Exchange Act of 1934; or

2. Transactions by closed-end investment companies.

    i. Transactions complying with Rule 23c-3 under the Investment Company Act of 1940; or

    ii. Periodic tender offers of securities, at net asset value, conducted pursuant to Rule 13e-4 under the Securities Exchange Act of 1934 by a closed-end investment company that engages in a continuous offering of its securities pursuant to Rule 415 under the Securities Act of 1933; *Provided, however,* That such securities are not traded on a securities exchange or through an inter-dealer quotation system or electronic communications network; or

3. Redemptions by commodity pools or limited partnerships. Redemptions by commodity pools or limited partnerships, at a price based on net asset value, which are effected in accordance with the terms and conditions of the instruments governing the securities; *Provided, however,* That such securities are not traded on a securities exchange, or through an inter-dealer quotation system or electronic communications network; or

4. Exercises of securities. The exercise of any option, warrant, right, or any conversion privilege set forth in the instrument governing a security; or

5. Offers to sell or the solicitation of offers to buy. Offers to sell or the solicitation of offers to buy the securities being distributed; or

6. Unsolicited purchases. Unsolicited purchases that are not effected from or through a broker or dealer, on a securities exchange, or through an inter- dealer quotation system or electronic communications network; or

7. Transactions in Rule 144A securities. Transactions in securities eligible for resale under Rule 144A(d)(3) under the Securities Act of 1933, or any reference security, if the Rule 144A securities are offered or sold in the United States solely to:

    i. Qualified institutional buyers, as defined in Rule 144A(a)(1) under the Securities Act of 1933, or to offerees or purchasers that the seller and any person acting on behalf of the seller reasonably believes are qualified institutional buyers, in transactions exempt from registration under section 4(2) of the Securities Act or Rule 144A or Rule 501 through Rule 508 under such Act; or

    ii. Persons not deemed to be "U.S. persons" for purposes of Rule 902(k)(2) during a distribution qualifying under paragraph (b)(7)(i) of this section.

c. **Plans.**

    1. Paragraph (a) of this section shall not apply to distributions of securities pursuant to a plan, which are made:

        i. Solely to employees or security holders of an issuer or its subsidiaries, or to a trustee or other person acquiring such securities for the accounts of such persons; or

        ii. To persons other than employees or security holders, if bids for or purchases of securities pursuant to the plan are effected solely by an agent independent of the issuer and the securities are from a source other than the issuer or an affiliated purchaser of the issuer.

    2. Bids for or purchases of any security made or effected by or for a plan shall be deemed to be a purchase by the issuer unless the bid is made, or the purchase is effected, by an agent independent of the issuer.

d. **Excepted Securities.** The provisions of this section shall not apply to any of the following securities:

1. Actively-traded reference securities. Reference securities with an ADTV value of at least $1 million that are issued by an issuer whose common equity securities have a public float value of at least $150 million; *Provided, however,* That such securities are not issued by the issuer, or any affiliate of the issuer, of the security in distribution.

2. Investment grade nonconvertible and asset-backed securities. Nonconvertible debt securities, nonconvertible preferred securities, and asset- backed securities, that are rated by at least one nationally recognized statistical rating organization, as that term is used in Rule 15c3-1 under the Securities Exchange Act of 1934, in one of its generic rating categories that signifies investment grade; or

3. Exempted securities. "Exempted securities" as defined in section 3(a)(12) of the Exchange Act; or

4. Face-amount certificates or securities issued by an open-end management investment company or unit investment trust. Face-amount certificates issued by a face-amount certificate company, or redeemable securities issued by an open-end management investment company or a unit investment trust. Any terms used in this paragraph (d)(4) that are defined in the Investment Company Act of 1940 shall have the meanings specified in such Act.

e. **Exemptive Authority.** Upon written application or upon its own motion, the Commission may grant an exemption from the provisions of this section, either unconditionally or on specified terms and conditions, to any transaction or class of transactions, or to any security or class of securities.

Rule 103 – Nasdaq Passive Market Making

a. **Scope of Section.** This section permits broker-dealers to engage in market making transactions in covered securities that are Nasdaq securities without violating the provisions of Rule 101; Except That this section shall not apply to any security for which a stabilizing bid subject to Rule 104 is in effect, or during any at-the-market offering or best efforts offering.

b. **Conditions to be Met.**

1. General limitations. A passive market maker must effect all transactions in the capacity of a registered market maker on Nasdaq. A passive market maker shall not bid for or purchase a covered security at a price that exceeds the highest independent bid for the covered security at the time of the transaction, except as permitted by paragraph (b)(3) of this section or required by a rule promulgated by the Commission or the NASD governing the handling of customer orders.

2. Purchase limitation. On each day of the restricted period, a passive market maker's net purchases shall not exceed the greater of its 30% ADTV limitation or 200 shares (together, "purchase limitation"); *Provided, however,* That a passive market maker may purchase all of the securities that are part of a single order that, when executed, results in its purchase limitation being equaled or exceeded. If a passive market maker's net purchases equal or exceed its purchase limitation, it shall withdraw promptly its quotations from Nasdaq. If a

passive market maker withdraws its quotations pursuant to this paragraph, it may not effect any bid or purchase in the covered security for the remainder of that day, irrespective of any later sales during that day, unless otherwise permitted by Rule 101.

3. Requirement to lower the bid. If all independent bids for a covered security are reduced to a price below the passive market maker's bid, the passive market maker must lower its bid promptly to a level not higher than the then highest independent bid; *Provided, however,* That a passive market maker may continue to bid and effect purchases at its bid at a price exceeding the then highest independent bid until the passive market maker purchases an aggregate amount of the covered security that equals or, through the purchase of all securities that are part of a single order, exceeds the lesser of two times the minimum quotation size for the security, as determined by NASD rules, or the passive market maker's remaining purchasing capacity under paragraph (b)(2) of this section.

4. Limitation on displayed size. At all times, the passive market maker's displayed bid size may not exceed the lesser of the minimum quotation size for the covered security, or the passive market maker's remaining purchasing capacity under paragraph (b)(2) of this section; *Provided, however*, That a passive market maker whose purchasing capacity at any time is between one and 99 shares may display a bid size of 100 shares.

5. Identification of a passive market making bid. The bid displayed by a passive market maker shall be designated as such.

6. Notification and reporting to the NASD. A passive market maker shall notify the NASD in advance of its intention to engage in passive market making, and shall submit to the NASD information regarding passive market making purchases, in such form as the NASD shall prescribe.

7. Prospectus disclosure. The prospectus for any registered offering in which any passive market maker intends to effect transactions in any covered security shall contain the information required in Items 502 and 508 of Regulation S-B, and Items 502, and 508 of Regulation S-K.

c. **Transactions at Prices Resulting from Unlawful Activity.** No transaction shall be made at a price that the passive market maker knows or has reason to know is the result of activity that is fraudulent, manipulative, or deceptive under the securities laws, or any rule or regulation thereunder.

Rule 104 – Stabilizing and Other Activities in Connection with an Offering

a. **Unlawful Activity.** It shall be unlawful for any person, directly or indirectly, to stabilize, to effect any syndicate covering transaction, or to impose a penalty bid, in connection with an offering of any security, in contravention of the provisions of this section. No stabilizing shall be effected at a price that the person stabilizing knows or has reason to know is in contravention of this section, or is the result of activity that is fraudulent, manipulative, or deceptive under the securities laws, or any rule or regulation thereunder.

b. **Purpose**. Stabilizing is prohibited except for the purpose of preventing or retarding a decline in the market price of a security.

c. **Priority**. To the extent permitted or required by the market where stabilizing occurs, any person stabilizing shall grant priority to any independent bid at the same price irrespective of the size of such independent bid at the time that it is entered.

d. **Control of Stabilizing**. No sole distributor or syndicate or group stabilizing the price of a security or any member or members of such syndicate or group shall maintain more than one stabilizing bid in any one market at the same price at the same time.

e. **At-the-Market Offerings**. Stabilizing is prohibited in an at-the-market offering.

f. **Stabilizing Levels.**
    1. Maximum stabilizing bid. Notwithstanding the other provisions of this paragraph (f), no stabilizing shall be made at a price higher than the lower of the offering price or the stabilizing bid for the security in the principal market (or, if the principal market is closed, the stabilizing bid in the principal market at its previous close).
    2. Initiating stabilizing.
        i.   Initiating stabilizing when the principal market is open. After the opening of quotations for the security in the principal market, stabilizing may be initiated in any market at a price no higher than the last independent transaction price for the security in the principal market if the security has traded in the principal market on the day stabilizing is initiated or on the most recent prior day of trading in the principal market and the current asked price in the principal market is equal to or greater than the last independent transaction price. If both conditions of the preceding sentence are not satisfied, stabilizing may be initiated in any market after the opening of quotations in the principal market at a price no higher than the highest current independent bid for the security in the principal market.
        ii. Initiating stabilizing when the principal market is closed.
             A. When the principal market for the security is closed, but immediately before the opening of quotations for the security in the market where stabilizing will be initiated, stabilizing may be initiated at a price no higher than the lower of:
                 1. The price at which stabilizing could have been initiated in the principal market for the security at its previous close; or
                 2. The most recent price at which an independent transaction in the security has been effected in any market since the close of the principal market, if the person stabilizing knows or has reason to know of such transaction.
             B. When the principal market for the security is closed, but after the opening of quotations in the market where stabilizing will be initiated, stabilizing may be initiated at a price no higher than the lower of:

543

1. The price at which stabilization could have been initiated in the principal market for the security at its previous close; or

2. The last independent transaction price for the security in that market if the security has traded in that market on the day stabilizing is initiated or on the last preceding business day and the current asked price in that market is equal to or greater than the last independent transaction price. If both conditions of the preceding sentence are not satisfied, under this paragraph (f)(2)(ii)(B)(2), stabilizing may be initiated at a price no higher than the highest current independent bid for the security in that market.

   iii. Initiating stabilizing when there is no market for the security or before the offering price is determined. If no bona fide market for the security being distributed exists at the time stabilizing is initiated, no stabilizing shall be initiated at a price in excess of the offering price. If stabilizing is initiated before the offering price is determined, then stabilizing may be continued after determination of the offering price at the price at which stabilizing then could be initiated.

3. Maintaining or carrying over a stabilizing bid. A stabilizing bid initiated pursuant to paragraph (f)(2) of this section, which has not been discontinued, may be maintained, or carried over into another market, irrespective of changes in the independent bids or transaction prices for the security.

4. Increasing or reducing a stabilizing bid. A stabilizing bid may be increased to a price no higher than the highest current independent bid for the security in the principal market if the principal market is open, or, if the principal market is closed, to a price no higher than the highest independent bid in the principal market at the previous close thereof. A stabilizing bid may be reduced, or carried over into another market at a reduced price, irrespective of changes in the independent bids or transaction prices for the security. If stabilizing is discontinued, it shall not be resumed at a price higher than the price at which stabilizing then could be initiated.

5. Initiating, maintaining, or adjusting a stabilizing bid to reflect the current exchange rate. If a stabilizing bid is expressed in a currency other than the currency of the principal market for the security, such bid may be initiated, maintained, or adjusted to reflect the current exchange rate, consistent with the provisions of this section. If, in initiating, maintaining, or adjusting a stabilizing bid pursuant to this paragraph (f)(5), the bid would be at or below the midpoint between two trading differentials, such stabilizing bid shall be adjusted downward to the lower differential.

6. Adjustments to stabilizing bid. If a security goes ex-dividend, ex-rights, or ex-distribution, the stabilizing bid shall be reduced by an amount equal to the value of the dividend, right, or distribution. If, in reducing a stabilizing bid pursuant to this paragraph (f)(6), the bid would be at or below the midpoint between two trading differentials, such stabilizing bid shall be adjusted downward to the lower differential.

7. Stabilizing of components. When two or more securities are being offered as a unit, the component securities shall not be stabilized at prices the sum of which exceeds the then permissible stabilizing price for the unit.

8.   Special prices. Any stabilizing price that otherwise meets the requirements of this section need not be adjusted to reflect special prices available to any group or class of persons (including employees or holders of warrants or rights).

g.   **Offerings with no U.S. Stabilizing Activities**

1.   Stabilizing to facilitate an offering of a security in the United States shall not be deemed to be in violation of this section if all of the following conditions are satisfied:

   i.   No stabilizing is made in the United States;

   ii.   Stabilizing outside the United States is made in a jurisdiction with statutory or regulatory provisions governing stabilizing that are comparable to the provisions of this section; and

   iii.   No stabilizing is made at a price above the offering price in the United States, except as permitted by paragraph (f)(5) of this section.

2.   For purposes of this paragraph (g), the Commission by rule, regulation, or order may determine whether a foreign statute or regulation is comparable to this section considering, among other things, whether such foreign statute or regulation: specifies appropriate purposes for which stabilizing is permitted; provides for disclosure and control of stabilizing activities; places limitations on stabilizing levels; requires appropriate recordkeeping; provides other protections comparable to the provisions of this section; and whether procedures exist to enable the Commission to obtain information concerning any foreign stabilizing transactions.

h.   **Disclosure and Notification**

1.   Any person displaying or transmitting a bid that such person knows is for the purpose of stabilizing shall provide prior notice to the market on which such stabilizing will be effected, and shall disclose its purpose to the person with whom the bid is entered.

2.   Any person effecting a syndicate covering transaction or imposing a penalty bid shall provide prior notice to the self-regulatory organization with direct authority over the principal market in the United States for the security for which the syndicate covering transaction is effected or the penalty bid is imposed.

3.   Any person subject to this section who sells to, or purchases for the account of, any person any security where the price of such security may be or has been stabilized, shall send to the purchaser at or before the completion of the transaction, a prospectus, offering circular, confirmation, or other document containing a statement similar to that comprising the statement provided for in Item 502(b) of Regulation S-K.

i.   **Recordkeeping Requirements**. A person subject to this section shall keep the information and make the notification required by Rule 17a-2 under the Securities Exchange Act of 1934.

j. **Excepted Securities**. The provisions of this section shall not apply to:
1. Exempted Securities. "Exempted securities," as defined in section 3(a)(12) of the Exchange Act; or
2. Transactions of Rule 144A securities. Transactions in securities eligible for resale under Rule 144A(d)(3) under the Securities Act of 1933, if such securities are offered or sold in the United States solely to:
   i. Qualified institutional buyers, as defined in Rule 144A(a)(1) under the Securities Act of 1933, or to offerees or purchasers that the seller and any person acting on behalf of the seller reasonably believes are qualified institutional buyers, in a transaction exempt from registration under section 4(2) of the Securities Act or Rule 144A or Rule 501 through Rule 508 under such Act; or
   ii. Persons not deemed to be "U.S. persons" for purposes of Rule 902(k)(2), during a distribution qualifying under paragraph (j)(2)(i) of this section.

k. **Exemptive Authority**. Upon written application or upon its own motion, the Commission may grant an exemption from the provisions of this section, either unconditionally or on specified terms and conditions, to any transaction or class of transactions, or to any security or class of securities.

Rule 105 – Short Selling in Connection with a Public Offering

a. **Unlawful Activity**. In connection with an offering of equity securities for cash pursuant to a registration statement or a notification on Form 1-A or Form 1-E filed under the Securities Act of 1933 ("offered securities"), it shall be unlawful for any person to sell short (as defined in Rule 200(a)) the security that is the subject of the offering and purchase the offered securities from an underwriter or broker or dealer participating in the offering if such short sale was effected during the period ("Rule 105 restricted period") that is the shorter of the period:
1. Beginning five business days before the pricing of the offered securities and ending with such pricing; or
2. Beginning with the initial filing of such registration statement or notification on Form 1-A or Form 1-E and ending with the pricing.

b. **Excepted Activity.**
1. Bona Fide Purchase. It shall not be prohibited for such person to purchase the offered securities as provided in paragraph (a) of this section if:
   i. Such person makes a bona fide purchase(s) of the security that is the subject of the offering that is:
      A. At least equivalent in quantity to the entire amount of the Rule 105 restricted period short sale(s);
      B. Effected during regular trading hours;
      C. Reported to an "effective transaction reporting plan" (as defined in Rule 600(b)(22)); and
      D. Effected after the last Rule 105 restricted period short sale, and no later than the business day prior to the day of pricing; and

ii.   Such person did not effect a short sale, that is reported to an effective transaction reporting plan, within the 30 minutes prior to the close of regular trading hours (as defined in Rule 600(b)(64)) on the business day prior to the day of pricing.

2.   Separate Accounts. Paragraph (a) of this section shall not prohibit the purchase of the offered security in an account of a person where such person sold short during the Rule 105 restricted period in a separate account, if decisions regarding securities transactions for each account are made separately and without coordination of trading or cooperation among or between the accounts.

3.   Investment Companies. Paragraph (a) of this section shall not prohibit an investment company (as defined by Section 3 of the Investment Company Act) that is registered under Section 8 of the Investment Company Act, or a series of such company (investment company) from purchasing an offered security where any of the following sold the offered security short during the Rule 105 restricted period:

i.   An affiliated investment company, or any series of such a company; or

ii.   A separate series of the investment company.

c.   **Excepted Offerings.** This section shall not apply to offerings filed under Rule 415 of this chapter or to offerings that are not conducted on a firm commitment basis.

d.   **Exemptive Authority.** Upon written application or upon its own motion, the Commission may grant an exemption from the provisions of this section, either unconditionally or on specified terms and conditions, to any transaction or class of transactions, or to any security or class of securities.

SCHEDULES
Schedules 13D, 13G, 14A, 14D-9, TO

13D – Information to be Included in Statements Filed Pursuant to Rule 13d-1(a) and Amendments Thereto Filed Pursuant to Rule 13d-2(a)

SECURITIES AND EXCHANGE COMMISSION
Washington, D.C. 20549
SCHEDULE 13D

Under the Securities Exchange Act of 1934 (Amendment No. –)*

(Name of Issuer)

....

(Title of Class of Securities)

....

(CUSIP Number)

....

(Name, Address and Telephone Number of Person Authorized to Receive Notices and Communications)

....

(Date of Event Which Requires Filing of This Statement)

If the filing person has previously filed a statement on Schedule 13G to report the acquisition that is the subject of this Schedule 13D, and is filing this schedule because of Rule 13d-1(e), Rule 13d-1(f) or Rule 13d-1(g), check the following box.[ ]

Note: Schedules filed in paper format shall include a signed original and five copies of the schedule, including all exhibits. See Rule 13d-7(b) for other parties to whom copies are to be sent.

*The remainder of this cover page shall be filled out for a reporting person's initial filing on this form with respect to the subject class of securities, and for any subsequent amendment containing information which would alter disclosures provided in a prior cover page.

The information required on the remainder of this cover page shall not be deemed to be "filed" for the purpose of Section 18 of the Securities Exchange Act of 1934 ("Act") or otherwise subject to the liabilities of that section of the Act but shall be subject to all other provisions of the Act (however, see the Notes).

CUSIP No. ....

(1) Names of reporting persons..

I.R.S. Identification Nos. of above persons (entities only)...................................

(2) Check the appropriate box if a member of a group (see instructions)...

(a)...

(b)...

(3) SEC use only ....

(4) Source of funds (see instructions) ....

(5) Check if disclosure of legal proceedings is required pursuant to Items 2(d) or 2(e).........

(6) Citizenship or place of organization..

Number of shares beneficially owned by each reporting person with.....................................

(7) Sole Voting Power...

(8) Shared Voting Power...

(9) Sole Dispositive Power...

(10) Shared Dispositive Power...

(11) Aggregate Amount Beneficially Owned by Each Reporting Person ....

(12) Check if the Aggregate Amount in Row (11) Excludes Certain Shares (See Instructions)

(13) Percent of Class Represented by Amount in Row (11).......................

(14) Type of Reporting Person (See Instructions)..................................

Instructions for Cover Page

(1) *Names and I.R.S. Identification Numbers of Reporting Persons* Furnish the full legal name of each person for whom the report is filed-i.e., each person required to sign the schedule itself-including each member of a group. Do not include the name of a person required to be identified in the report but who is not a reporting person. Reporting persons are also requested to furnish their I.R.S. identification numbers, although disclosure of such numbers is voluntary, not mandatory (see "SPECIAL INSTRUCTIONS FOR COMPLYING WITH SCHEDULE 13-D" below).

(2) If any of the shares beneficially owned by a reporting person are held as a member of a group and the membership is expressly affirmed, please check row 2(a). If the reporting person disclaims membership in a group or describes a relationship with other person but does not affirm the existence of a group, please check row 2(b) [unless it is a joint filing pursuant to Rule 13d-1(k)(1) in which case it may not be necessary to check row 2(b)].

(3) The 3rd row is for SEC internal use; please leave blank.

(4) Classify the source of funds or other consideration used or to be used in making the purchases as required to be disclosed pursuant to Item 3 of Schedule 13D and insert the appropriate symbol (or symbols if more than one is necessary in row (4):

Category of Source	Symbol
Subject Company (Company whose securities are being acquired)	SC
Bank	BK
Affiliate (of reporting person)	AF
Working Capital (of reporting person)	WC
Personal Funds (of reporting person)	PF
Other	OO

(5) If disclosure of legal proceedings or actions is required pursuant to either Items 2(d) or 2(e) of Schedule 13D, row 5 should be checked.

(6) *Citizenship or Place of Organization*—Furnish citizenship if the named reporting person is a natural person. Otherwise, furnish place of organization. (See Item 2 of Schedule 13D).

(7)-(11) [Reserved]

(13) *Aggregate Amount Beneficially Owned by Each Reporting Person, Etc.*-Rows 7 through 11, inclusive, and (13) are to be completed in accordance with the provisions of Item 5 of Schedule 13D. All percentages are to be rounded off to nearest tenth (one place after decimal point).

(12) Check if the aggregate amount reported as beneficially owned in row 11 does not include shares which the reporting person discloses in the report but as to which beneficial ownership is disclaimed pursuant to Rule 13d-4 under the Securities Exchange Act of 1934.

(14) *Type of Reporting Person*-Please classify each "reporting person" according to the following breakdown and place the appropriate symbol (or symbols, i.e., if more than one is applicable, insert all applicable symbols) on the form:

Category	Symbol
Broker Dealer	BD
Bank	BK
Insurance Company	IC
Investment Company	IV
Investment Adviser	IA
Employee Benefit Plan or Endowment Fund	EP
Parent Holding Company/ Control Person	HC
Savings Association	SA
Church Plan	CP
Corporation	CO
Partnership	PN
Individual	IN
Other	OO

Notes:
Attach as many copies of the second part of the cover page as are needed, one reporting person per page.

Filing persons may, in order to avoid unnecessary duplication, answer items on the schedules (Schedule 13D, 13G, or TO) by appropriate cross references to an item or items on the cover page(s). This approach may only be used where the cover page item or items provide all the disclosure required by the schedule item. Moreover, such a use of a cover page item will result in the item becoming a part of the schedule and accordingly being considered as "filed" for purposes of Section 18 of the Securities Exchange Act or otherwise subject to the liabilities of that section of the Act.

Reporting persons may comply with their cover page filing requirements by filing either completed copies of the blank forms available from the Commission, printed or typed facsimiles, or computer printed facsimiles, provided the documents filed have identical formats to the forms prescribed in the Commission's regulations and meet existing Securities Exchange Act rules as to such matters as clarity and size (Securities Exchange Act Rule 12b-12).

SPECIAL INSTRUCTIONS FOR COMPLYING
WITH SCHEDULE 13D

Under Sections 13(d) and 23 of the Securities Exchange Act of 1934 and the rules and regulations thereunder, the Commission is authorized to solicit the information required to be supplied by this schedule by certain security holders of certain issuers.

Disclosure of the information specified in this schedule is mandatory, except for Social Security or I.R.S. identification numbers, disclosure of which is voluntary. The information will be used for the primary purpose of determining and disclosing the holdings of certain beneficial owners of certain equity securities. This statement will be made a matter of public record. Therefore, any information given will be available for inspection by any member of the public.

Because of the public nature of the information, the Commission can utilize it for a variety of purposes, including referral to other governmental authorities or securities self-regulatory organizations for investigatory purposes or in connection with litigation involving the Federal securities laws or other civil, criminal or regulatory statements or provisions. Social Security or I.R.S. identification numbers, if furnished, will assist the Commission in identifying security holders and, therefore, in promptly processing statements of beneficial ownership of securities.

Failure to disclose the information requested by this schedule, except for Social Security or I.R.S. identification numbers, may result in civil or criminal action against the persons involved for violation of the Federal securities laws and rules promulgated thereunder.

General Instructions
    A.   The item numbers and captions of the items shall be included but the text of the items is to be omitted. The answers to the items shall be so prepared as to indicate clearly

the coverage of the items without referring to the text of the items. Answer every item. If an item is inapplicable or the answer is in the negative, so state.

B. Information contained in exhibits to the statement may be incorporated by reference in answer or partial answer to any item or sub-item of the statement unless it would render such answer misleading, incomplete, unclear or confusing. Matter incorporated by reference shall be clearly identified in the reference by page, paragraph, caption or otherwise. An express statement that the specified matter is incorporated by reference shall be made at the particular place in the statement where the information is required. A copy of any information or a copy of the pertinent pages of a document containing such information which is incorporated by reference shall be submitted with this statement as an exhibit and shall be deemed to be filed with the Commission for all purposes of the Act.

C. If the statement is filed by a general or limited partnership, syndicate, or other group, the information called for by Items 2-6, inclusive, shall be given with respect to

     i.   each partner of such general partnership;

     ii.   each partner who is denominated as a general partner or who functions as a general partner of such limited partnership;

     iii.   each member of such syndicate or group; and

     iv.   each person controlling such partner or member. If the statement is filed by a corporation or if a person referred to in (i),(ii), (iii) or (iv) of this Instruction is a corporation, the information called for by the above mentioned items shall be given with respect to

         a.   each executive officer and director of such corporation;

         b.   each person controlling such corporation; and

         c.   each executive officer and director of any corporation or other person ultimately in control of such corporation.

Item 1. Security and Issuer

State the title of the class of equity securities to which this statement relates and the name and address of the principal executive offices of the issuer of such securities.

Item 2. Identity and Background

If the person filing this statement or any person enumerated in Instruction C of this statement is a corporation, general partnership, limited partnership, syndicate or other group of persons, state its name, the state or other place of its organization, its principal business, the address of its principal office and the information required by (d) and (e) of this Item. If the person filing this statement or any person enumerated in Instruction C is a natural person, provide the information specified in (a) through (f) of this Item with respect to such person(s).

     a.   Name;

     b.   Residence or business address;

     c.   Present principal occupation or employment and the name, principal business and address of any corporation or other organization in which such employment is conducted;

    d.   Whether or not, during the last five years, such person has been convicted in a criminal proceeding (excluding traffic violations or similar misdemeanors) and, if so, give the dates, nature of conviction, name and location of court, any penalty imposed, or other disposition of the case;

    e.   Whether or not, during the last five years, such person was a party to a civil proceeding of a judicial or administrative body of competent jurisdiction and as a result of such proceeding was or is subject to a judgment, decree or final order enjoining future violations of, or prohibiting or mandating activities subject to, federal or state securities laws or finding any violation with respect to such laws; and, if so, identify and describe such proceedings and summarize the terms of such judgment, decree or final order; and

    f.   Citizenship.

Item 3. Source and Amount of Funds or Other Consideration

State the source and the amount of funds or other consideration used or to be used in making the purchases, and if any part of the purchase price is or will be represented by funds or other consideration borrowed or otherwise obtained for the purpose of acquiring, holding, trading or voting the securities, a description of the transaction and the names of the parties thereto. Where material, such information should also be provided with respect to prior acquisitions not previously reported pursuant to this regulation. If the source of all or any part of the funds is a loan made in the ordinary course of business by a bank, as defined in Section 3(a)(6) of the Act, the name of the bank shall not be made available to the public if the person at the time of filing the statement so requests in writing and files such request, naming such bank, with the Secretary of the Commission. If the securities were acquired other than by purchase, describe the method of acquisition.

Item 4. Purpose of Transaction

State the purpose or purposes of the acquisition of securities of the issuer. Describe any plans or proposals which the reporting persons may have which relate to or would result in:

    a.   The acquisition by any person of additional securities of the issuer, or the disposition of securities of the issuer;

    b.   An extraordinary corporate transaction, such as a merger, reorganization or liquidation, involving the issuer or any of its subsidiaries;

    c.   A sale or transfer of a material amount of assets of the issuer or any of its subsidiaries;

    d.   Any change in the present board of directors or management of the issuer, including any plans or proposals to change the number or term of directors or to fill any existing vacancies on the board;

    e.   Any material change in the present capitalization or dividend policy of the issuer;

    f.   Any other material change in the issuer's business or corporate structure, including but not limited to, if the issuer is a registered closed-end investment company, any plans or proposals to make any changes in its investment policy for which a vote is required by Section 13 of the Investment Company Act of 1940;

    g.   Changes in the issuer's charter, bylaws or instruments corresponding thereto or other actions which may impede the acquisition of control of the issuer by any person;

h.   Causing a class of securities of the issuer to be delisted from a national securities exchange or to cease to be authorized to be quoted in an inter-dealer quotation system of a registered national securities association;

i.   A class of equity securities of the issuer becoming eligible for termination of registration pursuant to Section 12(g)(4) of the Act; or

j.   Any action similar to any of those enumerated above.

Item 5. Interest in Securities of the Issuer.

a.   State the aggregate number and percentage of the class of securities identified pursuant to Item 1 (which may be based on the number of securities outstanding as contained in the most recently available filing with the Commission by the issuer unless the filing person has reason to believe such information is not current) beneficially owned (identifying those shares which there is a right to acquire) by each person named in Item 2. The above mentioned information should also be furnished with respect to persons who, together with any of the persons named in Item 2, comprise a group within the meaning of Section 13(d)(3) of the Act;

b.   For each person named in response to paragraph (a), indicate the number of shares as to which there is sole power to vote or to direct the vote, sole power to dispose or to direct the disposition, or shared power to dispose or to direct the disposition. Provide the applicable information required by Item 2 with respect to each person with whom the power to vote or to direct the vote or to dispose or direct the disposition is shared;

c.   Describe any transactions in the class of securities reported on that were effected during the past sixty days or since the most recent filing of Schedule 13D, whichever is less, by the persons named in response to paragraph (a).

Instruction. The description of a transaction required by Item 5(c) shall include, but not necessarily be limited to:

1.   The identity of the person covered by Item 5(c) who effected the transaction;
2.   the date of transaction;
3.   the amount of securities involved;
4.   the price per share or unit; and
5.   where and how the transaction was effected.

d.   If any other person is known to have the right to receive or the power to direct the receipt of dividends from, or the proceeds from the sale of, such securities, a statement to that effect should be included in response to this item and, if such interest relates to more than five percent of the class, such person should be identified. A listing of the shareholders of an investment company registered under the Investment Company Act of 1940 or the beneficiaries of an employee benefit plan, pension fund or endowment fund is not required.

e.   If applicable, state the date on which the reporting person ceased to be the beneficial owner of more than five percent of the class of securities.

Instruction. For computations regarding securities which represent a right to acquire an underlying security, see Rule 13d-3(d)(1) and the note thereto.

Item 6. Contracts, Arrangements, Understandings or Relationships With Respect to Securities of the Issuer.

Describe any contracts, arrangements, understandings or relationships (legal or otherwise) among the persons named in Item 2 and between such persons and any person with respect to any securities of the issuer, including but not limited to transfer or voting of any of the securities, finder's fees, joint ventures, loan or option arrangements, puts or calls, guarantees of profits, division of profits or loss, or the giving or withholding of proxies, naming the persons with whom such contracts, arrangements, understandings or relationships have been entered into. Include such information for any of the securities that are pledged or otherwise subject to a contingency the occurrence of which would give another person voting power or investment power over such securities except that disclosure of standard default and similar provisions contained in loan agreements need not be included.

Item 7. Material to be Filed as Exhibits.

The following shall be filed as exhibits: Copies of written agreements relating to the filing of joint acquisition statements as required by Rule 13d-1(k) and copies of all written agreements, contracts, arrangements, understanding, plans or proposals relating to:
1. The borrowing of funds to finance the acquisition as disclosed in Item 3;
2. the acquisition of issuer control, liquidation, sale of assets, merger, or change in business or corporate structure, or any other matter as disclosed in Item 4; and
3. the transfer or voting of the securities, finder's fees, joint ventures, options, puts, calls, guarantees of loans, guarantees against loss or of profit, or the giving or withholding of any proxy as disclosed in Item 6.

Signature. After reasonable inquiry and to the best of my knowledge and belief, I certify that the information set forth in this statement is true, complete and correct.

....
Date

....
Signature

....
Name/Title

The original statement shall be signed by each person on whose behalf the statement is filed or his authorized representative. If the statement is signed on behalf of a person by his authorized representative (other than an executive officer or general partner of this filing person) , evidence of the representative's authority to sign on behalf of such person shall be filed with the statement, *provided, however,* that a power of attorney for this purpose which is already on file with the Commission may be incorporated by reference. The name and any title of each person who signs the statement shall be typed or printed beneath his signature.

Attention: Intentional misstatements or omissions of fact constitute Federal criminal violations (See 18 U.S.C. 1001).

Schedule 13G – Information to Be Included in Statements Filed Pursuant to Rule 13d-1(b) and (c) and Amendments Thereto Filed Pursuant to Rule 13d-2(b)

SECURITIES AND EXCHANGE COMMISSION
Washington, D.C. 20549
SCHEDULE 13G
Under the Securities Exchange Act of 1934

(Amendment No....) ....

(Name of Issuer) ....

(Title of Class of Securities) ....

(CUSIP Number) ....

(Date of Event Which Requires Filing of this Statement) ....

Check the appropriate box to designate the rule pursuant to which this Schedule is filed:

[ ] Rule 13d-1(b)

[ ] Rule 13d-1(c)

[ ] Rule 13d-1(d)

*The remainder of this cover page shall be filled out for a reporting person's initial filing on this form with respect to the subject class of securities, and for any subsequent amendment containing information which would alter the disclosures provided in a prior cover page.

The information required in the remainder of this cover page shall not be deemed to be "filed" for the purpose of Section 18 of the Securities Exchange Act of 1934 ("Act") or otherwise subject to the liabilities of that section of the Act but shall be subject to all other provisions of the Act (however, see the Notes).

CUSIP No.		
(1) Names of reporting persons. I.R.S. Identification Nos. of above persons (entities only)		
(2) Check the appropriate box if a member of a group (see instructions) (a) (b)		
(3) SEC use only		
(4) Citizenship or place of organization		
Number of shares beneficially owned by each reporting person with:	(5) Sole voting power	
	(6) Shared voting power	
	(7) Sole dispositive power	
	(8) Shared dispositive power	
(9) Aggregate amount beneficially owned by each reporting person		

(10) Check if the aggregate amount in Row (9) excludes certain shares (see instructions)
(11) Percent of class represented by amount in Row 9
(12) Type of reporting person (see instructions)

Instructions for Cover Page

(1) *Names and I.R.S. Identification Numbers of Reporting Persons*—Furnish the full legal name of each person for whom the report is filed—i.e., each person required to sign the schedule itself—including each member of a group. Do not include the name of a person required to be identified in the report but who is not a reporting person. Reporting persons are also requested to furnish their I.R.S. identification numbers, although disclosure of such numbers is voluntary, not mandatory (see "SPECIAL INSTRUCTIONS FOR COMPLYING WITH SCHEDULE 13G", below).

(2) If any of the shares beneficially owned by a reporting person are held as a member of a group and that membership is expressly affirmed, please check row 2(a). If the reporting person disclaims membership in a group or describes a relationship with other person but does not affirm the existence of a group, please check row 2(b) [unless it is a joint filing pursuant to Rule 13d-1(k)(1) in which case it may not be necessary to check row 2(b)].

(3) The third row is for SEC internal use; please leave blank.

(4) *Citizenship or Place of Organization*—Furnish citizenship if the named reporting person is a natural person. Otherwise, furnish place of organization.

(5)-(9), (11) *Aggregated Amount Beneficially Owned By Each Reporting Person, etc.*—Rows (5) through (9) inclusive, and (11) are to be completed in accordance with the provisions of Item 4 of Schedule 13G. All percentages are to be rounded off to the nearest tenth (one place after decimal point).

(10) Check if the aggregate amount reported as beneficially owned in row 9 does not include shares as to which beneficial ownership is disclaimed pursuant to Rule 13d-4 under the Securities Exchange Act of 1934.

(12) *Type of Reporting Person*—Please classify each "reporting person" according to the following breakdown (see Item 3 of Schedule 13G) and place the appropriate symbol on the form:

Category	Symbol
Broker Dealer	BD
Bank	BK
Insurance Company	IC
Investment Company	IV
Investment Adviser	IA
Employee Benefit Plan or Endowment Fund	EP

Parent Holding Company/Control Person	HC
Savings Association	SA
Church Plan	CP
Corporation	CO
Partnership	PN
Individual	IN
Other	OO

Notes: Attach as many copies of the second part of the cover page as are needed, one reporting person per page.

Filing persons may, in order to avoid unnecessary duplication, answer items on the schedules (Schedule 13D, 13G, or TO) by appropriate cross references to an item or items on the cover page(s). This approach may only be used where the cover page item or items provide all the disclosure required by the schedule item. Moreover, such a use of a cover page item will result in the item becoming a part of the schedule and accordingly being considered as "filed" for purposes of Section 18 of the Securities Exchange Act or otherwise subject to the liabilities of that section of the Act.

Reporting persons may comply with their cover page filing requirements by filing either completed copies of the blank forms available from the Commission, printed or typed facsimiles, or computer printed facsimiles, provided the documents filed have identical formats to the forms prescribed in the Commission's regulations and meet existing Securities Exchange Act rules as to such matters as clarity and size (Securities Exchange Act Rule 12b-12).

SPECIAL INSTRUCTIONS FOR COMPLYING
WITH SCHEDULE 13G

Under Sections 13(d), 13(g), and 23 of the Securities Exchange Act of 1934 and the rules and regulations thereunder, the Commission is authorized to solicit the information required to be supplied by this schedule by certain security holders of certain issuers.

Disclosure of the information specified in this schedule is mandatory, except for I.R.S. identification numbers disclosure of which is voluntary. The information will be used for the primary purpose of determining and disclosing the holdings of certain beneficial owners of certain equity securities. This statement will be made a matter of public record. Therefore, any information given will be available for inspection by any member of the public.

Because of the public nature of the information, the Commission can utilize it for a variety of purposes, including referral to other governmental authorities or securities self-regulatory organizations for investigatory purposes or in connection with litigation involving the Federal securities laws or other civil, criminal or regulatory statues or provisions. I.R.S. identification numbers, if furnished, will assist the commission in identifying security holders and, therefore, in promptly processing statements of beneficial ownership of securities.

Failure to disclose the information requested by this schedule, except for I.R.S. identification numbers, may result in civil or criminal action against the persons involved for violation of the Federal securities laws and rules promulgated thereunder.

General Instructions

A. Statements filed pursuant to Rule 13d-1(b) containing the information required by this schedule shall be filed not later than February 14 following the calendar year covered by the statement or within the time specified in Rules 13d-1(b)(2) and 13d-2(c). Statements filed pursuant to Rule 13d-1(c) shall be filed within the time specified in Rules 13d-1(c), 13d- 2(b) and 13d-2(d). Statements filed pursuant to Rule 13d-1(d) shall be filed not later than February 14 following the calendar year covered by the statement pursuant to Rules 13d-1(d) and 13d-2(b).

B. Information contained in a form which is required to be filed by rules under Section 13(f) for the same calendar year as that covered by a statement on this schedule may be incorporated by reference in response to any of the items of this schedule. If such information is incorporated by reference in this schedule, copies of the relevant pages of such form shall be filed as an exhibit to this schedule.

C. The item numbers and captions of the items shall be included but the text of the items is to be omitted. The answers to the items shall be so prepared as to indicate clearly the coverage of the items without referring to the text of the items. Answer every item. If an item is inapplicable or the answer is in the negative, so state.

Item 1.

Item 1(a) Name of issuer:

Item 1(b) Address of issuer's principal executive offices:

Item 2.

2(a) Name of person filing:

2(b) Address or principal business office or, if none, residence:

2(c) Citizenship:

2(d) Title of class of securities:

2(e) CUSIP No.:

Item 3. If this statement is filed pursuant to Rules 13d-1(b), or 13d-2(b) or (c), check whether the person filing is a:

a.   [ ] Broker or dealer registered under Section 15 of the Act.
b.   [ ] Bank as defined in Section 3(a)(6) of the Act.
c.   [ ] Insurance company as defined in Section 3(a)(19) of the Act.
d.   [ ] Investment company registered under Section 8 of the Investment Company Act of 1940.
e.   [ ] An investment adviser in accordance with Rule 13d-1(b)(1)(ii)(E);

    f.   [ ] An employee benefit plan or endowment fund in accordance with Rule 13d-1(b)(1)(ii)(F);

    g.   [ ] A parent holding company or control person in accordance with Rule 13d-1(b)(1)(ii)(G);

    h.   [ ] A savings associations as defined in Section 3(b) of the Federal Deposit Insurance Act (;

    i.   [ ] A church plan that is excluded from the definition of an investment company under section 3(c)(14) of the Investment Company Act of 1940;

    j.   [ ] Group, in accordance with Rule 13d-1(b)(1)(ii)(J).

Item 4. Ownership

Provide the following information regarding the aggregate number and percentage of the class of securities of the issuer identified in Item 1.

    a.   Amount beneficially owned:

    b.   Percent of class

    c.   Number of shares as to which such person has:

        i.   Sole power to vote or to direct the vote

       ii.   Shared power to vote or to direct the vote

     iii.   Sole power to dispose or to direct the disposition of

     iv.   Shared power to dispose or to direct the disposition of

Instruction. For computations regarding securities which represent a right to acquire an underlying security see Rule 13d-3(d)(1).

Item 5. Ownership of 5 Percent or Less of a Class.

If this statement is being filed to report the fact that as of the date hereof the reporting person has ceased to be the beneficial owner of more than 5 percent of the class of securities, check the following [ ].

Instruction. Dissolution of a group requires a response to this item.

Item 6. Ownership of More than 5 Percent on Behalf of Another Person

If any other person is known to have the right to receive or the power to direct the receipt of dividends from, or the proceeds from the sale of, such securities, a statement to that effect should be included in response to this item and, if such interest relates to more than 5 percent of the class, such person should be identified. A listing of the shareholders of an investment company registered under the Investment Company Act of 1940 or the beneficiaries of employee benefit plan, pension fund or endowment fund is not required.

Item 7. Identification and Classification of the Subsidiary Which Acquired the Security Being Reported on by the Parent Holding Company or Control Person.

If a parent holding company or control person has filed this schedule pursuant to Rule 13d-1(b)(1)(ii)(G), so indicate under Item 3(g) and attach an exhibit stating the identity and the Item 3 classification of the relevant subsidiary. If a parent holding company or control person has filed this schedule pursuant to Rule 13d-1(c) or Rule 13d-1(d), attach an exhibit stating the identification of the relevant subsidiary.

Item 8. Identification and Classification of Members of the Group.

If a group has filed this schedule pursuant to Rule 13d-1(b)(ii)(J), so indicate under Item 3(j) and attach an exhibit stating the identity and Item 3 classification of each member of the group. If a group has filed this schedule pursuant to Rule 13d-1(c) or Rule 13d-1(d), attach an exhibit stating the identity of each member of the group.

Item 9. Notice of Dissolution of Group

Notice of dissolution of a group may be furnished as an exhibit stating the date of the dissolution and that all further filings with respect to transactions in the security reported on will be filed, if required, by members of the group, in their individual capacity. See Item 5.

Item 10. Certifications

a. The following certification shall be included if the statement is filed pursuant to Rule 13d-1(b):
    By signing below I certify that, to the best of my knowledge and belief, the securities referred to above were acquired and are held in the ordinary course of business and were not acquired and are not held for the purpose of or with the effect of changing or influencing the control of the issuer of the securities and were not acquired and are not held in connection with or as a participant in any transaction having that purpose or effect.

b. The following certification shall be included if the statement is filed pursuant to Rule 13d-1(c):
    By signing below I certify that, to the best of my knowledge and belief, the securities referred to above were not acquired and are not held for the purpose of or with the effect of changing or influencing the control of the issuer of the securities and were not acquired and are not held in connection with or as a participant in any transaction having that purpose or effect.

Signature. After reasonable inquiry and to the best of my knowledge and belief, I certify that the information set forth in this statement is true, complete and correct.

....
Date

....
Signature

....
Name/Title

The original statement shall be signed by each person on whose behalf the statement is filed or his authorized representative. If the statement is signed on behalf of a person by his authorized representative other than an executive officer or general partner of the filing person, evidence of the representative's authority to sign on behalf of such person shall be filed with the statement, *provided, however,* that a power of attorney for this purpose which is already on file with the Commission may be incorporated by reference. The name and any title of each person who signs the statement shall be typed or printed beneath his signature.

Note: Schedules filed in paper format shall include a signed original and five copies of the schedule, including all exhibits. See Rule 13d-7 for other parties for whom copies are to be sent.

Attention: Intentional misstatements or omissions of fact constitute Federal criminal violations (see 18 U.S.C. 1001).

Schedule 14A – Information Required in Proxy Statement

Proxy Statement Pursuant to Section 14(a)
of the Securities Exchange Act of 1934
(Amendment No.)

Filed by the Registrant [ ]

Filed by a Party other than the Registrant [ ]

Check the appropriate box:
[ ] Preliminary Proxy Statement
[ ] Confidential, for Use of the Commission Only (as permitted by Rule 14a-6(e)(2))
[ ] Definitive Proxy Statement
[ ] Definitive Additional Materials
[ ] Soliciting Material under Rule 14a-12

....

Name of the Registrant as Specified In Its Charter

....

(Name of Person(s) Filing Proxy Statement, if other than the Registrant)

Payment of Filing Fee (Check the appropriate box):
[ ] No fee required.
[ ] Fee computed on table below per Exchange Act Rules 14a-6(i)(4) and 0-11.

1. Title of each class of securities to which transaction applies:
   ....

2. Aggregate number of securities to which transaction applies:
   ....

3. Per unit price or other underlying value of transaction computed pursuant to Exchange Act Rule 0-11 (Set forth the amount on which the filing fee is calculated and state how it was determined):
   ....

4. Proposed maximum aggregate value of transaction:
   ....

5. Total fee paid:
   ....

[ ] Fee paid previously with preliminary materials.

[ ] Check box if any part of the fee is offset as provided by Exchange Act Rule 0-11(a)(2) and identify the filing for which the offsetting fee was paid previously. Identify the previous filing by registration statement number, or the Form or Schedule and the date of its filing.

1. Amount Previously Paid:
   ....

2. Form, Schedule or Registration Statement No.:
   ....

3. Filing Party:
   ....

4. Date Filed:
   ....

Notes:

A. Where any item calls for information with respect to any matter to be acted upon and such matter involves other matters with respect to which information is called for by other items of this schedule, the information called for by such other items also shall be given. For example, where a solicitation of security holders is for the purpose of approving the authorization of additional securities which are to be used to acquire another specified company, and the registrants' security holders will not have a separate opportunity to vote upon the transaction, the solicitation to authorize the securities is also a solicitation with respect to the acquisition. Under those facts, information required by Items 11, 13 and 14 shall be furnished.

B. Where any item calls for information with respect to any matter to be acted upon at the meeting, such item need be answered in the registrant's soliciting material only with respect to proposals to be made by or on behalf of the registrant.

C. Except as otherwise specifically provided, where any item calls for information for a specified period with regard to directors, executive officers, officers or other persons holding specified positions or relationships, the information shall be given with regard to any person who held any of the specified positions or relationship at any time during the period. Information, other than information required by Item 404 of Regulation S-K, need not be included for any portion of the period during which such person did not hold any such position or relationship, provided a statement to that effect is made.

D. Information may be incorporated by reference only in the manner and to the extent specifically permitted in the items of this schedule. Where incorporation by reference is used, the following shall apply:

   1. Any incorporation by reference of information pursuant to the provisions of this schedule shall be subject to the provisions of Item 10(d) of this chapter restricting incorporation by reference of documents which incorporate by reference other information. A registrant incorporating any documents, or portions of documents, shall include a statement on the last page(s) of the proxy statement as to which documents, or portions of documents, are incorporated by reference. Information shall not be incorporated by reference in any case where such incorporation would render the statement incomplete, unclear or confusing.

   2. If a document is incorporated by reference but not delivered to security holders, include an undertaking to provide, without charge, to each person to whom a proxy statement is delivered, upon written or oral request of such person and by first class mail or other equally prompt means within one business day of receipt of such request, a copy of any and all of the information that has been incorporated by reference in the proxy statement (not including exhibits to the information that is incorporated by reference unless such exhibits are specifically incorporated by reference into the information that the proxy statement incorporates), and the address and telephone numbers to which such a request is to be directed. This includes information contained in documents filed subsequent to the date on which definitive copies of the proxy statement are sent or given to security holders, up to the date of responding to the request.

3. If a document or portion of a document other than an annual report sent to security holders pursuant to the requirements of Rule 14a-3 with respect to the same meeting or solicitation of consents or authorizations as that to which the proxy statement relates is incorporated by reference in the manner permitted by Item 13(b) or 14(e)(1) of this schedule, the proxy statement must be sent to security holders no later than 20 business days prior to the date on which the meeting of such security holders is held or, if no meeting is held, at least 20 business days prior to the date the votes, consents or authorizations may be used to effect the corporate action.

4. *Electronic filings.* If any of the information required by Items 13 or 14 of this Schedule is incorporated by reference from an annual or quarterly report to security holders, such report, or any portion thereof incorporated by reference, shall be filed in electronic format with the proxy statement. This provision shall not apply to registered investment companies.

E. In Item 13 of this Schedule, the reference to "meets the requirement of Form S-3" shall refer to a registrant which meets the following requirements:

1. the registrant meets the requirements of General Instruction I.A. of Form S-3; and

2. one of the following is met:

    i. The registrant meets the aggregate market value requirement of General Instruction I.B.1 of Form S-3; or

    ii. Action is to be taken as described in Items 11, 12 and 14 of this schedule which concerns non-convertible debt or preferred securities which are "investment grade securities" as defined in General Instruction I.B.2 of Form S-3, except that the time by which the rating must be assigned shall be the date on which definitive copies of the proxy statement are first sent or given to security holders; or

    iii. The registrant is a majority-owned subsidiary and one of the conditions of General Instruction I.C. of Form S-3 is met.

Item 1. Date, time and place information.

a. State the date, time and place of the meeting of security holders, and the complete mailing address, including ZIP Code, of the principal executive offices of the registrant, unless such information is otherwise disclosed in material furnished to security holders with or preceding the proxy statement. If action is to be taken by written consent, state the date by which consents are to be submitted if state law requires that such a date be specified or if the person soliciting intends to set a date.

b. On the first page of the proxy statement, as delivered to security holders, state the approximate date on which the proxy statement and form of proxy are first sent or given to security holders.

c. Furnish the information required to be in the proxy statement by Rule 14a-5(e).

Item 2. Revocability of proxy.

State whether or not the person giving the proxy has the power to revoke it. If the right of revocation before the proxy is exercised is limited or is subject to compliance with any formal procedure, briefly describe such limitation or procedure.

Item 3. Dissenters' right of appraisal.

Outline briefly the rights of appraisal or similar rights of dissenters with respect to any matter to be acted upon and indicate any statutory procedure required to be followed by dissenting security holders in order to perfect such rights. Where such rights may be exercised only within a limited time after the date of adoption of a proposal, the filing of a charter amendment or other similar act, state whether the persons solicited will be notified of such date.

Instructions.

1.   Indicate whether a security holder's failure to vote against a proposal will constitute a waiver of his appraisal or similar rights and whether a vote against a proposal will be deemed to satisfy any notice requirements under State law with respect to appraisal rights. If the State law is unclear, state what position will be taken in regard to these matters.

2.   Open-end investment companies registered under the Investment Company Act of 1940 are not required to respond to this item.

Item 4. Persons Making the Solicitation

a.   *Solicitations not subject to Rule 14a-12(c)*

1.   If the solicitation is made by the registrant, so state. Give the name of any director of the registrant who has informed the registrant in writing that he intends to oppose any action intended to be taken by the registrant and indicate the action which he intends to oppose.

2.   If the solicitation is made otherwise than by the registrant, so state and give the names of the participants in the solicitation, as defined in paragraphs (a)(iii), (iv), (v) and (vi) of Instruction 3 to this Item.

3.   If the solicitation is to be made otherwise than by the use of the mails or pursuant to Rule14a-16, describe the methods to be employed.. If the solicitation is to be made by specially, engaged employees or paid solicitors, state

i.   the material features of any contract or arrangement for such solicitation and identify the parties, and

ii.   the cost or anticipated cost thereof.

4.   State the names of the persons by whom the cost of solicitation has been or will be borne, directly or indirectly.

b.   *Solicitations subject to Rule 14a-12(c)*

1.   State by whom the solicitation is made and describe the methods employed and to be employed to solicit security holders.

2.   If regular employees of the registrant or any other participant in a solicitation have been or are to be employed to solicit security holders, describe the class or classes of employees to be so employed, and the manner and nature of their employment for such purpose.

3.   If specially engaged employees, representatives or other persons have been or are to be employed to solicit security holders, state

i.   the material features of any contract or arrangement for such solicitation and the identity of the parties,

ii.   the cost or anticipated cost thereof and

iii.   the approximate number of such employees of employees or any other person (naming such other person) who will solicit security holders).

4.   State the total amount estimated to be spent and the total expenditures to date for, in furtherance of, or in connection with the solicitation of security holders.

5.   State by whom the cost of the solicitation will be borne. If such cost is to be borne initially by any person other than the registrant, state whether reimbursement will be sought from the registrant, and, if so, whether the question of such reimbursement will be submitted to a vote of security holders.

6.   If any such solicitation is terminated pursuant to a settlement between the registrant and any other participant in such solicitation, describe the terms of such settlement, including the cost or anticipated cost thereof to the registrant.

Instructions.

1.   With respect to solicitations subject to Rule 14a-12(c), costs and expenditures within the meaning of this Item 4 shall include fees for attorneys, accountants, public relations or financial advisers, solicitors, advertising, printing, transportation, litigation and other costs incidental to the solicitation, except that the registrant may exclude the amount of such costs represented by the amount normally expended for a solicitation for an election of directors in the absence of a contest, and costs represented by salaries and wages of regular employees and officers, provided a statement to that effect is included in the proxy statement.

2.   The information required pursuant to paragraph (b)(6) of this Item should be included in any amended or revised proxy statement or other soliciting materials relating to the same meeting or subject matter furnished to security holders by the registrant subsequent to the date of settlement.

3.   For purposes of this Item 4 and Item 5 of this Schedule 14A:

    a.   The terms "participant" and "participant in a solicitation" include the following:

        i.   The registrant;

        ii.   Any director of the registrant, and any nominee for whose election as a director proxies are solicited;

        iii.   Any committee or group which solicits proxies, any member of such committee or group, and any person whether or not named as a member who, acting alone or with one or more other persons, directly or indirectly takes the initiative, or engages, in organizing, directing, or arranging for the financing of any such committee or group;

        iv.   Any person who finances or joins with another to finance the solicitation of proxies, except persons who contribute not more than $500 and who are not otherwise participants;

        v.   Any person who lends money or furnishes credit or enters into any other arrangements, pursuant to any contract or understanding with a participant, for the purpose of financing or otherwise inducing the purchase, sale, holding or voting of securities of the registrant by any participant or other persons, in support of or in opposition to a participant; except that such terms do not include a bank, broker or dealer who, in the ordinary course of business, lends money or executes orders for the purchase or sale of securities and who is not otherwise a participant; and

vi. Any person who solicits proxies.

b. The terms "participant" and "participant in a solicitation" do not include:

i. Any person or organization retained or employed by a participant to solicit security holders and whose activities are limited to the duties required to be performed in the course of such employment;

ii. Any person who merely transmits proxy soliciting material or performs other ministerial or clerical duties;

iii. Any person employed by a participant in the capacity of attorney, accountant, or advertising, public relations or financial adviser, and whose activities are limited to the duties required to be performed in the course of such employment;

iv. Any person regularly employed as an officer or employee of the registrant or any of its subsidiaries who is not otherwise a participant; or

v. Any officer or director of, or any person regularly employed by, any other participant, if such officer, director or employee is not otherwise a participant.

Item 5. Interest of Certain Persons in Matters to Be Acted Upon

a. *Solicitations not subject to Rule 14a-12(c).*

Describe briefly any substantial interest, direct or indirect, by security holdings or otherwise, of each of the following persons in any matter to be acted upon, other than elections to office:

1. If the solicitation is made on behalf of the registrant, each person who has been a director or executive officer of the registrant at any time since the beginning of the last fiscal year.

2. If the solicitation is made otherwise than on behalf of the registrant, each participant in the solicitation, as defined in paragraphs (a)(iii), (iv), and (v) and (vi) of Instruction 3 to Item 4 of this Schedule 14A.

3. Each nominee for election as a director of the registrant.

4. Each associate of any of the foregoing persons.

Instruction.

Except in the case of a solicitation subject to this regulation made in opposition to another solicitation subject to this regulation, this sub-item (a) shall not apply to any interest arising from the ownership of securities of the registrant where the security holder receives no extra or special benefit not shared on a pro rata basis by all other holders of the same class.

b. *Solicitation subject to Rule 14a-12(c).*

With respect to any solicitation subject to Rule 14a-12(c) :

1. Describe briefly any substantial interest, direct or indirect, by security holdings or otherwise, of each participant as defined in paragraphs (a)(ii), (iii), (iv), (v) and (vi) of Instruction 3 to Item 4 of this Schedule 14A, in any matter to be acted upon at the meeting, and include with respect to each participant the following information, or a fair and accurate summary thereof:

i. Name and business address of the participant.

ii. The participant's present principal occupation or employment and the name, principal business and address of any corporation or other organization in which such employment is carried on.

iii. State whether or not, during the past ten years, the participant has been convicted in a criminal proceeding (excluding traffic violations or similar misdemeanors) and, if so, give dates, nature of conviction, name and location of court, and penalty imposed or other disposition of the case. A negative answer need not be included in the proxy statement or other soliciting material.

iv. State the amount of each class of securities of the registrant which the participant owns beneficially, directly or indirectly.

v. State the amount of each class of securities of the registrant which the participant owns of record but not beneficially.

vi. State with respect to all securities of the registrant purchased or sold within the past two years, the dates on which they were purchased or sold and the amount purchased or sold on each such date.

vii. If any part of the purchase price or market value of any of the shares specified in paragraph (b)(1)(vi) of this Item is represented by funds borrowed or otherwise obtained for the purpose of acquiring or holding such securities, so state and indicate the amount of the indebtedness as of the latest practicable date. If such funds were borrowed or obtained otherwise than pursuant to a margin account or bank loan in the regular course of business of a bank, broker or dealer, briefly describe the transaction, and state the names of the parties.

viii. State whether or not the participant is, or was within the past year, a party to any contract, arrangements or understandings with any person with respect to any securities of the registrant, including, but not limited to joint ventures, loan or option arrangements, puts or calls, guarantees against loss or guarantees of profit, division of losses or profits, or the giving or withholding of proxies. If so, name the parties to such contracts, arrangements or understandings and give the details thereof.

ix. State the amount of securities of the registrant owned beneficially, directly or indirectly, by each of the participant's associates and the name and address of each such associate.

x. State the amount of each class of securities of any parent or subsidiary of the registrant which the participant owns beneficially, directly or indirectly.

xi. Furnish for the participant and associates of the participant the information required by Item 404(a) of Regulation S-K.

xii. State whether or not the participant or any associates of the participant have any arrangement or understanding with any person-

    A. with respect to any future employment by the registrant or its affiliates; or

    B. with respect to any future transactions to which the registrant or any of its affiliates will or may be a party.

If so, describe such arrangement or understanding and state the names of the parties thereto.

2. With respect to any person, other than a director or executive officer of the registrant acting solely in that capacity, who is a party to an arrangement or understanding pursuant to which a nominee for election as director is proposed to be elected, describe any substantial interest, direct or indirect, by security holdings or otherwise, that such person has in any matter to be acted upon at the meeting, and furnish the information called for by paragraphs (b)(1)(xi) and (xii) of this Item.

Instruction:

For purposes of this Item 5, beneficial ownership shall be determined in accordance with Rule 13d-3 under the Act.

Item 6. Voting Securities and Principal Holders Thereof

a. As to each class of voting securities of the registrant entitled to be voted at the meeting (or by written consents or authorizations if no meeting is held), state the number of shares outstanding and the number of votes to which each class is entitled.

b. State the record date, if any, with respect to this solicitation. If the right to vote or give consent is not to be determined, in whole or in part, by reference to a record date, indicate the criteria for the determination of security holders entitled to vote or give consent.

c. If action is to be taken with respect to the election of directors and if the persons solicited have cumulative voting rights:
   1. Make a statement that they have such rights,
   2. briefly describe such rights,
   3. state briefly the conditions precedent to the exercise thereof, and
   4. if discretionary authority to cumulate votes is solicited, so indicate.

d. Furnish the information required by Item 403 of Regulation S-K to the extent known by the persons on whose behalf the solicitation is made.

e. If, to the knowledge of the persons on whose behalf the solicitation is made, a change in control of the registrant has occurred since the beginning of its last fiscal year, state the name of the person(s) who acquired such control, the amount and the source of the consideration used by such person or persons; the basis of the control, the date and a description of the transaction(s) which resulted in the change of control and the percentage of voting securities of the registrant now beneficially owned directly or indirectly by the person(s) who acquired control; and the identity of the person(s) from whom control was assumed. If the source of all or any part of the consideration used is a loan made in the ordinary course of business by a bank as defined by section 3(a)(6) of the Act, the identity of such bank shall be omitted provided a request for confidentiality has been made pursuant to section 13(d)(1)(B) of the Act by the person(s) who acquired control. In lieu thereof, the material shall indicate that the identity of the bank has been so omitted and filed separately with the Commission.

Instruction.
   1. State the terms of any loans or pledges obtained by the new control group for the purpose of acquiring control, and the names of the lenders or pledgees.
   2. Any arrangements or understandings among members of both the former and new control groups and their associates with respect to election of directors or other matters should be described.

Item 7. Directors and Executive Officers

If action is to be taken with respect to the election of directors, furnish the following information in tabular form to the extent practicable. If, however, the solicitation is made on behalf of persons other than the registrant, the information required need be furnished only as to nominees of the persons making the solicitation.

a. The information required by instruction 4 to Item 103 of Regulation S-K with respect to directors and executive officers.

b. The information required by Items 401, 404(a) and (b), 405 and 407(d)(4), (d)(5) and (h) of Regulation S–K.

c. The information required by Item 407(a) of Regulation S-K.

d. The information required by Item 407(b), (c)(1), (c)(2), (d)(1), (d)(2), (d)(3), (e)(1), (e)(2), (e)(3) and (f) of Regulation S-K.

e. In lieu of the information required by this Item 7, investment companies registered under the Investment Company Act of 1940 must furnish the information required by Item 22(b) of this Schedule 14A.

Item 8. Compensation of Directors and Executive Officers.

Furnish the information required by Item 402 of Regulation S-K and paragraphs (e)(4) and (e)(5) of Item 407 of Regulation S-K if action is to be taken with regard to:

a. The election of directors;

b. Any bonus, profit sharing or other compensation plan, contract or arrangement in which any director, nominee for election as a director, or executive officer of the registrant will participate;

c. Any pension or retirement plan in which any such person will participate; or

d. The granting or extension to any such person of any options, warrants or rights to purchase any securities, other than warrants or rights issued to security holders as such, on a pro rata basis.

However, if the solicitation is made on behalf of persons other than the registrant, the information required need be furnished only as to nominees of the persons making the solicitation and associates of such nominees. In the case of investment companies registered under the Investment Company Act of 1940, furnish the information required by Item 22(b)(13) of this Schedule 14A.

Instruction.

If an otherwise reportable compensation plan became subject to such requirements because of an acquisition or merger and, within one year of the acquisition or merger, such plan was terminated for purposes of prospective eligibility, the registrant may furnish a description of its obligation to the designated individuals pursuant to the compensation plan. Such description may be furnished in lieu of a description of the compensation plan in the proxy statement.

Item 9. Independent Public Accountants.

If the solicitation is made on behalf of the registrant and relates to: (1) The annual (or special meeting in lieu of annual) meeting of security holders at which directors are to be elected, or a solicitation of consents or authorizations in lieu of such meeting or (2) the election, approval or ratification of the registrant's accountant, furnish the following information describing the registrant's relationship with its independent public accountant:

a. The name of the principal accountant selected or being recommended to security holders for election, approval or ratification for the current year. If no accountant has been selected or recommended, so state and briefly describe the reasons therefor.

b. The name of the principal accountant for the fiscal year most recently completed if different from the accountant selected or recommended for the current year or if no accountant has yet been selected or recommended for the current year.

c. The proxy statement shall indicate:

    1. Whether or not representatives of the principal accountant for the current year and for the most recently completed fiscal year are expected to be present at the security holders' meeting,

    2. whether or not they will have the opportunity to make a statement if they desire to do so, and

    3. whether or not such representatives are expected to be available to respond to appropriate questions.

d. If during the registrant's two most recent fiscal years or any subsequent interim period,

    1. an independent accountant who was previously engaged as the principal accountant to audit the registrant's financial statements, or an independent accountant on whom the principal accountant expressed reliance in its report regarding a significant subsidiary, has resigned (or indicated it has declined to stand for re-election after the completion of the current audit) or was dismissed, or

    2. a new independent accountant has been engaged as either the principal accountant to audit the registrant's financial statements or as an independent accountant on whom the principal accountant has expressed or is expected to express reliance in its report regarding a significant subsidiary, then, notwithstanding any previous disclosure, provide the information required by Item 304(a) of Regulation S-K.

e.

    1. Disclose, under the caption Audit Fees, the aggregate fees billed for each of the last two fiscal years for professional services rendered by the principal accountant for the audit of the registrant's annual financial statements and review of financial statements included in the registrant's Form 10-Q or services that are normally provided by the accountant in connection with statutory and regulatory filings or engagements for those fiscal years.

    2. Disclose, under the caption Audit-Related Fees, the aggregate fees billed in each of the last two fiscal years for assurance and related services by the principal accountant that are reasonably related to the performance of the audit or review of the registrant's financial statements and are not reported under paragraph (e)(1) of this section. Registrants shall describe the nature of the services comprising the fees disclosed under this category.

    3. Disclose, under the caption Tax Fees, the aggregate fees billed in each of the last two fiscal years for professional services rendered by the principal accountant for tax compliance, tax advice, and tax planning. Registrants shall describe the nature of the services comprising the fees disclosed under this category.

4.   Disclose, under the caption All Other Fees, the aggregate fees billed in each of the last two fiscal years for products and services provided by the principal accountant, other than the services reported in paragraphs (e)(1) through (e)(3) of this section. Registrants shall describe the nature of the services comprising the fees disclosed under this category.

5.

    i.   Disclose the audit committee's pre-approval policies and procedures described in Rule 2-01(c)(7)(i) of Regulation S-X.

    ii.   Disclose the percentage of services described in each of paragraphs (e)(2) - (e)(4) of this section that were approved by the audit committee pursuant to Rule 2-01(c)(7)(i)(C) of Regulation S-X.

6.   If greater than 50 percent, disclose the percentage of hours expended on the principal accountant's engagement to audit the registrant's financial statements for the most recent fiscal year that were attributed to work performed by persons other than the principal accountant's full-time, permanent employees.

7.   If the registrant is an investment company, disclose the aggregate non-audit fees billed by the registrant's accountant for services rendered to the registrant, and to the registrant's investment adviser (not including any subadviser whose role is primarily portfolio management and is subcontracted with or overseen by another investment adviser), and any entity controlling, controlled by, or under common control with the adviser that provides ongoing services to the registrant for each of the last two fiscal years of the registrant.

8.   If the registrant is an investment company, disclose whether the audit committee of the board of directors has considered whether the provision of non-audit services that were rendered to the registrant's investment adviser (not including any subadviser whose role is primarily portfolio management and is subcontracted with or overseen by another investment adviser), and any entity controlling, controlled by, or under common control with the investment adviser that provides ongoing services to the registrant that were not pre-approved pursuant to Rule 2-01(c)(7)(ii) of Regulation S-X is compatible with maintaining the principal accountant's independence.

Instruction to Item 9(e).

For purposes of Item 9(e)(2), (3), and (4), registrants that are investment companies must disclose fees billed for services rendered to the registrant and separately, disclose fees required to be approved by the investment company registrant's audit committee pursuant to Rule 2-01(c)(7)(ii) of Regulation S-X. Registered investment companies must also disclose the fee percentages as required by item 9(e)(5)(ii) for the registrant and separately, disclose the fee percentages as required by item 9(e)(5)(ii) for the fees required to be approved by the investment company registrant's audit committee pursuant to Rule 2-01(c)(7)(ii) of Regulation S-X.

Item 10. Compensation Plans.

If action is to be taken with respect to any plan pursuant to which cash or noncash compensation may be paid or distributed, furnish the following information:

    a. *Plans subject to security holder action.*

        1. Describe briefly the material features of the plan being acted upon, identify each class of persons who will be eligible to participate therein, indicate the approximate number of persons in each such class, and state the basis of such participation.

        2.

            i. In the tabular format specified below, disclose the benefits or amounts that will be received by or allocated to each of the following under the plan being acted upon, if such benefits or amounts are determinable:

NEW PLAN BENEFITS Plan Name		
Name and Position	**Dollar Value ($)**	**Number of Units**
CEO		
#A		
#B		
#C		
#D		
Executive Group		
Non-Executive Director Group		
Non-Executive Officer Employee Group		

           ii. The table required by paragraph (a)(2)(i) of this Item shall provide information as to the following persons:

              A. Each person (stating name and position) specified in paragraph (a)(3) of Item 402 of Regulation S-K;

                Instruction:

                In the case of investment companies registered under the Investment Company Act of 1940, furnish the information for Compensated Persons as defined in Item 22(b)(13) of this Schedule in lieu of the persons specified in paragraph (a)(3) of Item 402 of Regulation S-K.

              B. All current executive officers as a group;

              C. All current directors who are not executive officers as a group; and

              D. All employees, including all current officers who are not executive officers, as a group.

Instruction to New Plan Benefits Table.
Additional columns should be added for each plan with respect to which security holder action is to be taken.

      iii.   If the benefits or amounts specified in paragraph (a)(2)(i) of this item are not determinable, state the benefits or amounts which would have been received by or allocated to each of the following for the last completed fiscal year if the plan had been in effect, if such benefits or amounts may be determined, in the table specified in paragraph (a)(2)(i) of this Item:

         A.   Each person (stating name and position) specified in paragraph (a)(3) of Item 402 of Regulation S-K;

         B.   All current executive officers as a group;

         C.   All current directors who are not executive officers as a group; and

         D.   All employees, including all current officers who are not executive officers, as a group.

    3.   If the plan to be acted upon can be amended, otherwise than by a vote of security holders, to increase the cost thereof to the registrant or to alter the allocation of the benefits as between the persons and groups specified in paragraph (a)(2) of this item, state the nature of the amendments which can be so made.

  b.   *Additional information regarding specified plans subject to security holder action.*

    1.   With respect to any pension or retirement plan submitted for security holder action, state:

      i.   The approximate total amount necessary to fund the plan with respect to past services, the period over which such amount is to be paid and the estimated annual payments necessary to pay the total amount over such period; and

      ii.   The estimated annual payment to be made with respect to current services. In the case of a pension or retirement plan, information called for by paragraph (a)(2) of this Item may be furnished in the format specified by paragraph (h)(2) of Item 402 of Regulation S-K.

         Instruction.
In the case of investment companies registered under the Investment Company Act of 1940, refer to instruction 4 in Item 22(b)(13)(i) of this Schedule in lieu of paragraph (h)(2) of Item 402 of Regulation S-K.

    2.

      i.   With respect to any specific grant of or any plan containing options, warrants or rights submitted for security holder action, state:

         A.   The title and amount of securities underlying such options, warrants or rights;

         B.   The prices, expiration dates and other material conditions upon which the options, warrants or rights may be exercised;

         C.   The consideration received or to be received by the registrant or subsidiary for the granting or extension of the options, warrants or rights;

               D.   The market value of the securities underlying the options, warrants, or rights as of the latest practicable date; and

               E.   In the case of options, the federal income tax consequences of the issuance and exercise of such options to the recipient and the registrant; and

      ii.   State separately the amount of such options received or to be received by the following persons if such benefits or amounts are determinable:

               A.   Each person (stating name and position) specified in paragraph (a)3 of Item 402 of Regulation S-K;

               B.   All current executive officers as a group;

               C.   All current directors who are not executive officers as a group;

               D.   Each nominee for election as a director;

               E.   Each associate of any of such directors, executive officers or nominees;

               F.   Each other person who received or is to receive 5 percent of such options, warrants or rights; and

               G.   All employees, including all current officers who are not executive officers, as a group.

c.   *Information regarding plans and other arrangements not subject to security holder action.* Furnish the information required by Item 201(d) of Regulation S-K.

Instructions to paragraph (c):

    1.   If action is to be taken as described in paragraph (a) of this Item with respect to the approval of a new compensation plan under which equity securities of the registrant are authorized for issuance, information about the plan shall be disclosed as required under paragraphs (a) and (b) of this Item and shall not be included in the disclosure required by Item 201(d) of Regulation S-K. If action is to be taken as described in paragraph (a) of this Item with respect to the amendment or modification of an existing plan under which equity securities of the registrant are authorized for issuance, the registrant shall include information about securities previously authorized for issuance under the plan (including any outstanding options, warrants and rights previously granted pursuant to the plan and any securities remaining available for future issuance under the plan) in the disclosure required by Item 201(d) of Regulation S-K. Any additional securities that are the subject of the amendments or modification of the existing plan shall be disclosed as required under paragraphs (a) and (b) of this Item and shall not be included in the Item 201(d) disclosure.

Instructions

    1.   The term "plan" as used in this Item means any plan as defined in paragraph (a)(7)(ii) of Item 402 of Regulation S-K.

    2.   If action is to be taken with respect to a material amendment or modification of an existing plan, the item shall be answered with respect to the plan as proposed to be amended or modified and shall indicate any material differences from the existing plan.

    3.   If the plan to be acted upon is set forth in a written document, three copies thereof shall be filed with the Commission at the time copies of the proxy statement and form

of proxy are first filed pursuant to paragraph (a) or (b) of Rule 14a-6. Electronic filers shall file with the Commission a copy of such written plan document in electronic format as an appendix to the proxy statement. It need not be provided to security holders unless it is a part of the proxy statement.

4. Paragraph (b)(2)(ii) does not apply to warrants or rights to be issued to security holders as such on a pro rata basis.

5. The Commission shall be informed, as supplemental information, when the proxy statement is first filed, as to when the options, warrants or rights and the shares called for thereby will be registered under the Securities Act or, if such registration is not contemplated, the section of the Securities Act or rule of the Commission under which exemption from such registration is claimed and the facts relied upon to make the exemption available.

Item 11. Authorization or Issuance of Securities Otherwise than for Exchange.

If action is to be taken with respect to the authorization or issuance of any securities otherwise than for exchange for outstanding securities of the registrant, furnish the following information:

a. State the title and amount of securities to be authorized or issued.

b. Furnish the information required by Item 202 of Regulation S-K. If the terms of the securities cannot be stated or estimated with respect to any or all of the securities to be authorized, because no offering thereof is contemplated in the proximate future, and if no further authorization by security holders for the issuance thereof is to be obtained, it should be stated that the terms of the securities to be authorized, including dividend or interest rates, conversion prices, voting rights, redemption prices, maturity dates, and similar matters will be determined by the board of directors. If the securities are additional shares of common stock of a class outstanding, the description may be omitted except for a statement of the preemptive rights, if any. Where the statutory provisions with respect to preemptive rights are so indefinite or complex that they cannot be stated in summarized form, it will suffice to make a statement in the form of an opinion of counsel as to the existence and extent of such rights.

c. Describe briefly the transaction in which the securities are to be issued including a statement as to

     1. the nature and approximate amount of consideration received or to be received by the registrant and

     2. the approximate amount devoted to each purpose so far as determinable for which the net proceeds have been or are to be used.

If it is impracticable to describe the transaction in which the securities are to be issued, state the reason, indicate the purpose of the authorization of the securities, and state whether further authorization for the issuance of the securities by a vote of security holders will be solicited prior to such issuance.

d. If the securities are to be issued otherwise than in a public offering for cash, state the reasons for the proposed authorization or issuance and the general effect thereof upon the rights of existing security holders.

e. Furnish the information required by Item 13(a) of this schedule.

Item 12. Modification or Exchange of Securities.

If action is to be taken with respect to the modification of any class of securities of the registrant, or the issuance or authorization for issuance of securities of the registrant in exchange for outstanding securities of the registrant furnish the following information:

a. If outstanding securities are to be modified, state the title and amount thereof. If securities are to be issued in exchange for outstanding securities, state the title and amount of securities to be so issued, the title and amount of outstanding securities to be exchanged therefor and the basis of the exchange.

b. Describe any material differences between the outstanding securities and the modified or new securities in respect of any of the matters concerning which information would be required in the description of the securities in Item 202 of Regulation S-K.

c. State the reasons for the proposed modification or exchange and the general effect thereof upon the rights of existing security holders.

d. Furnish a brief statement as to arrears in dividends or as to defaults in principal or interest in respect to the outstanding securities which are to be modified or exchanged and such other information as may be appropriate in the particular case to disclose adequately the nature and effect of the proposed action.

e. Outline briefly any other material features of the proposed modification or exchange. If the plan of proposed action is set forth in a written document, file copies thereof with the Commission in accordance with Rule 14a-6.

f. Furnish the information required by Item 13(a) of this Schedule.

Instruction.
If the existing security is presently listed and registered on a national securities exchange, state whether the registrant intends to apply for listing and registration of the new or reclassified security on such exchange or any other exchange. If the registrant does not intend to make such application, state the effect of the termination of such listing and registration.

Item 13. Financial and Other Information. (*See* Notes D and E at the beginning of this Schedule.)

a. *Information required.* If action is to be taken with respect to any matter specified in Item 11 or 12, furnish the following information:

1. Financial statements meeting the requirements of Regulation S-X, including financial information required by Rule 3-05 and Article 11 of Regulation S-X with respect to transactions other than that pursuant to which action is to be taken as described in this proxy statement;

2. Item 302 of Regulation S-K, supplementary financial information;

3. Item 303 of Regulation S-K, management's discussion and analysis of financial condition and results of operations;

4. Item 304 of Regulation S-K, changes in and disagreements with accountants on accounting and financial disclosure;

5. Item 305 of Regulation S-K, quantitative and qualitative disclosures about market risk; and

6. A statement as to whether or not representatives of the principal accountants for the current year and for the most recently completed fiscal year:

    i.   Are expected to be present at the security holders' meeting;

> ii.   Will have the opportunity to make a statement if they desire to do so; and
>
> iii.   Are expected to be available to respond to appropriate questions.

b. *Incorporation by reference.* The information required pursuant to paragraph (a) of this Item may be incorporated by reference into the proxy statement as follows:

1. *S-3 registrants.* If the registrant meets the requirements of Form S-3 (*see* Note E to this Schedule), it may incorporate by reference to previously-filed documents any of the information required by paragraph (a) of this Item, provided that the requirements of paragraph (c) are met. Where the registrant meets the requirements of Form S-3 and has elected to furnish the required information by incorporation by reference, the registrant may elect to update the information so incorporated by reference to information in subsequently-filed documents.

2. *All registrants.* The registrant may incorporate by reference any of the information required by paragraph (a) of this Item, provided that the information is contained in an annual report to security holders or a previously-filed statement or report, such report or statement is delivered to security holders with the proxy statement and the requirements of paragraph (c) are met.

c. *Certain conditions applicable to incorporation by reference.* Registrants eligible to incorporate by reference into the proxy statement the information required by paragraph (a) of this Item in the manner specified by paragraphs (b)(1) and (b)(2) may do so only if:

1. The information is not required to be included in the proxy statement pursuant to the requirement of another Item;

2. The proxy statement identifies on the last page(s) the information incorporated by reference; and

3. The material incorporated by reference substantially meets the requirements of this Item or the appropriate portions of this Item.

Instructions to Item 13.

1. Notwithstanding the provisions of this Item, any or all of the information required by paragraph (a) of this Item not material for the exercise of prudent judgment in regard to the matter to be acted upon may be omitted. In the usual case the information is deemed material to the exercise of prudent judgment where the matter to be acted upon is the authorization or issuance of a material amount of senior securities, but the information is not deemed material where the matter to be acted upon is the authorization or issuance of common stock, otherwise than in an exchange, merger, consolidation, acquisition or similar transaction, the authorization of preferred stock without present intent to issue or the authorization of preferred stock for issuance for cash in an amount constituting fair value.

2. In order to facilitate compliance with Rule 2-02(a) of Regulation S-X, one copy of the definitive proxy statement filed with the Commission shall include a manually signed copy of the accountant's report. If the financial statements are incorporated by reference, a manually signed copy of the accountant's report shall be filed with the definitive proxy statement.

3. Notwithstanding the provisions of Regulation S-X, no schedules other than those prepared in accordance with Rules 12-15, 12-28 and 12-29 (or, for management

investment companies, Rules 12-12 through 12-14) of that regulation need be furnished in the proxy statement.

4. Unless registered on a national securities exchange or otherwise required to furnish such information, registered investment companies need not furnish the information required by paragraph (a)(2) or (3) of this Item.

5. If the registrant submits preliminary proxy material incorporating by reference financial statements required by this Item, the registrant should furnish a draft of the financial statements if the document from which they are incorporated has not been filed with or furnished to the Commission.

6. A registered investment company need not comply with items (a)(2), (a)(3), and (a)(5) of this Item 13.

Item 14. Mergers, Consolidations, Acquisitions and Similar Matters. (*See* Notes A and D at the beginning of this Schedule.)

Instructions to Item 14.

1. In transactions in which the consideration offered to security holders consists wholly or in part of securities registered under the Securities Act of 1933, furnish the information required by Form S-4, Form F-4, or Form N-14, as applicable, instead of this Item. Only a Form S-4, Form F-4, or Form N-14 must be filed in accordance with Rule 14a-6(j).

2.
    a. In transactions in which the consideration offered to security holders consists wholly of cash, the information required by paragraph (c)(1) of this Item for the acquiring company need not be provided unless the information is material to an informed voting decision (e.g., the security holders of the target company are voting and financing is not assured).

    b. Additionally, if only the security holders of the target company are voting:
        i. The financial information in paragraphs (b)(8)–(11) of this Item for the acquiring company and the target need not be provided; and
        ii. The information in paragraph (c)(2) of this Item for the target company need not be provided.
        If, however, the transaction is a going-private transaction (as defined by Rule 13e-3), then the information required by paragraph (c)(2) of this Item must be provided and to the extent that the going-private rules require the information specified in paragraph (b)(8)–(b)(11) of this Item, that information must be provided as well.

3. In transactions in which the consideration offered to security holders consists wholly of securities exempt from registration under the Securities Act of 1933 or a combination of exempt securities and cash, information about the acquiring company required by paragraph (c)(1) of this Item need not be provided if only the security holders of the acquiring company are voting, unless the information is material to an informed voting decision. If only the security holders of the target company are voting, information about the target company in paragraph (c)(2) of this Item need not be provided. However, the information required by paragraph (c)(2) of this Item must be provided if the transaction is a going-private (as defined by Rule 13e-3) or roll-up (as described by Item 901 of Regulation S-K) transaction.

4. The information required by paragraphs (b)(8)–(11) and (c) need not be provided if the plan being voted on involves only the acquiring company and one or more of its totally held subsidiaries and does not involve a liquidation or a spin-off.

5. To facilitate compliance with Rule 2-02(a) of Regulation S-X (technical requirements relating to accountants' reports), one copy of the definitive proxy statement filed with the Commission must include a signed copy of the accountant's report. If the financial statements are incorporated by reference, a signed copy of the accountant's report must be filed with the definitive proxy statement. Signatures may be typed if the document is filed electronically on EDGAR. See Rule 302 of Regulation S-T.

6. Notwithstanding the provisions of Regulation S-X, no schedules other than those prepared in accordance with Rule 12-15, Rule 12-28 and Rule 12-29(or, for management investment companies, Rule 12-12 through Rule 12-14) of that regulation need be furnished in the proxy statement.

7. If the preliminary proxy material incorporates by reference financial statements required by this Item, a draft of the financial statements must be furnished to the Commission staff upon request if the document from which they are incorporated has not been filed with or furnished to the Commission.

   a. Applicability. If action is to be taken with respect to any of the following transactions, provide the information required by this Item:

      1. A merger or consolidation;
      2. An acquisition of securities of another person;
      3. An acquisition of any other going business or the assets of a going business;
      4. A sale or other transfer of all or any substantial part of assets; or
      5. A liquidation or dissolution.

   b. Transaction information. Provide the following information for each of the parties to the transaction unless otherwise specified:

      1. Summary term sheet. The information required by Item 1001 of Regulation M-A.
      2. Contact information. The name, complete mailing address and telephone number of the principal executive offices.
      3. Business conducted. A brief description of the general nature of the business conducted.
      4. Terms of the transaction. The information required by Item 1004(a)(2) of Regulation M-A.
      5. Regulatory approvals. A statement as to whether any federal or state regulatory requirements must be complied with or approval must be obtained in connection with the transaction and, if so, the status of the compliance or approval.
      6. Reports, opinions, appraisals. If a report, opinion or appraisal materially relating to the transaction has been received from an outside party, and is referred to in the proxy statement, furnish the information required by Item 1015(b) of Regulation M-A.
      7. Past contacts, transactions or negotiations. The information required by Items 1005(b) and 1011(a)(1) of Regulation M-A, for the parties to the transaction and their affiliates during the periods for which financial statements are presented or incorporated by reference under this Item.

8. Selected financial data. The selected financial data required by Item 301 of Regulation S-K.

9. Pro forma selected financial data. If material, the information required by Item 301 of Regulation S-K for the acquiring company, showing the pro forma effect of the transaction.

10. Pro forma information. In a table designed to facilitate comparison, historical and pro forma per share data of the acquiring company and historical and equivalent pro forma per share data of the target company for the following Items:

   i. Book value per share as of the date financial data is presented pursuant to Item 301 of Regulation S-K;

   ii. Cash dividends declared per share for the periods for which financial data is presented pursuant to Item 301 of Regulation S-K; and

   iii. Income (loss) per share from continuing operations for the periods for which financial data is presented pursuant to Item 301 of Regulation S-K.

Instructions to paragraphs (b)(8), (b)(9) and (b)(10):

   1. For a business combination, present the financial information required by paragraphs (b)(9) and (b)(10) only for the most recent fiscal year and interim period. For a combination between entities under common control, present the financial information required by paragraphs (b)(9) and (b)(10) (except for information with regard to book value) for the most recent three fiscal years and interim period. For purposes of these paragraphs, book value information need only be provided for the most recent balance sheet date.

   2. Calculate the equivalent pro forma per share amounts for one share of the company being acquired by multiplying the exchange ratio times each of:

      i. The pro forma income (loss) per share before non-recurring charges or credits directly attributable to the transaction;

      ii. The pro forma book value per share; and

      iii. The pro forma dividends per share of the acquiring company.

   3. Unless registered on a national securities exchange or otherwise required to furnish such information, registered investment companies need not furnish the information required by paragraphs (b)(8) and (b)(9) of this Item.

11. Financial information. If material, financial information required by Article 11 of Regulation S-X with respect to this transaction.

Instructions to paragraph (b)(11):

   1. Present any Article 11 information required with respect to transactions other than those being voted upon (where not incorporated by reference) together with the pro forma information relating to the transaction being voted upon. In presenting this

> information, you must clearly distinguish between the transaction being voted upon and any other transaction.
>
> 2. If current pro forma financial information with respect to all other transactions is incorporated by reference, you need only present the pro forma effect of this transaction.

c. Information about the parties to the transaction.

> 1. Acquiring company. Furnish the information required by Part B (Registrant Information) of Form S-4 or Form F-4, as applicable, for the acquiring company. However, financial statements need only be presented for the latest two fiscal years and interim periods.
>
> 2. Acquired company. Furnish the information required by Part C (Information with Respect to the Company Being Acquired) of Form S-4 or Form F-4, as applicable.

d. Information about parties to the transaction: registered investment companies and business development companies. If the acquiring company or the acquired company is an investment company registered under the Investment Company Act of 1940 or a business development company as defined by Section 2(a)(48) of the Investment Company Act of 1940, provide the following information for that company instead of the information specified by paragraph (c) of this Item:

> 1. Information required by Item 101 of Regulation S-K, description of business;
>
> 2. Information required by Item 102 of Regulation S-K, description of property;
>
> 3. Information required by Item 103 of Regulation S-K, legal proceedings;
>
> 4. Information required by Item 201(a), (b) and (c) of Regulation S-K, market price of and dividends on the registrant's common equity and related stockholder matters;
>
> 5. Financial statements meeting the requirements of Regulation S-X, including financial information required by Rule 3-05 and Article 11 of Regulation S-X with respect to transactions other than that as to which action is to be taken as described in this proxy statement;
>
> 6. Information required by Item 301 of Regulation S-K, selected financial data;
>
> 7. Information required by Item 302 of Regulation S-K, supplementary financial information;
>
> 8. Information required by Item 303 of Regulation S-K, management's discussion and analysis of financial condition and results of operations; and
>
> 9. Information required by Item 304 of Regulation S-K, changes in and disagreements with accountants on accounting and financial disclosure.

Instruction to paragraph 14(d): Unless registered on a national securities exchange or otherwise required to furnish such information, registered investment companies need not furnish the information required by paragraphs (d)(6), (d)(7) and (d)(8) of this Item.

e. Incorporation by reference.

> 1. The information required by paragraph (c) of this section may be incorporated by reference into the proxy statement to the same extent as would be permitted by Form S-4 or Form F-4, as applicable.
>
> 2. Alternatively, the registrant may incorporate by reference into the proxy statement the information required by paragraph (c) of this Item if it is

contained in an annual report sent to security holders in accordance with Rule 14a-3 with respect to the same meeting or solicitation of consents or authorizations that the proxy statement relates to and the information substantially meets the disclosure requirements of Item 14 or Item 17 of Form S-4 or Form F-4, as applicable.

Item 15. Acquisition or Disposition of Property.

If action is to be taken with respect to the acquisition or disposition of any property, furnish the following information:

a. Describe briefly the general character and location of the property.

b. State the nature and amount of consideration to be paid or received by the registrant or any subsidiary. To the extent practicable, outline briefly the facts bearing upon the question of the fairness of the consideration.

c. State the name and address of the transferer or transferee, as the case may be and the nature of any material relationship of such person to the registrant or any affiliate of the registrant.

d. Outline briefly any other material features of the contract or transaction.

Item 16. Restatement of Accounts.

If action is to be taken with respect to the restatement of any asset, capital, or surplus account of the registrant furnish the following information:

a. State the nature of the restatement and the date as of which it is to be effective.

b. Outline briefly the reasons for the restatement and for the selection of the particular effective date.

c. State the name and amount of each account (including any reserve accounts) affected by the restatement and the effect of the restatement thereon. Tabular presentation of the amounts shall be made when appropriate, particularly in the case of recapitalizations.

d. To the extent practicable, state whether and the extent, if any, to which, the restatement will, as of the date thereof, alter the amount available for distribution to the holders of equity securities.

Item 17. Action with Respect to Reports.

If action is to be taken with respect to any report of the registrant or of its directors, officers or committees or any minutes of a meeting of its security holders, furnish the following information:

a. State whether or not such action is to constitute approval or disapproval of any of the matters referred to in such reports or minutes.

b. Identify each of such matters which it is intended will be approved or disapproved, and furnish the information required by the appropriate item or items of this schedule with respect to each such matter.

Item 18. Matters not Required to be Submitted.

If action is to be taken with respect to any matter which is not required to be submitted to a vote of security holders, state the nature of such matter, the reasons for submitting it to a vote of security holders and what action is intended to be taken by the registrant in the event of a negative vote on the matter by the security holders.

Item 19. Amendment of Charter, Bylaws or Other Documents.

If action is to be taken with respect to any amendment of the registrant's charter, bylaws or other documents as to which information is not required above, state briefly the reasons for and the general effect of such amendment.
Instructions.
1. Where the matter to be acted upon is the classification of directors, state whether vacancies which occur during the year may be filled by the board of directors to serve only until the next annual meeting or may be so filled for the remainder of the full term.
2. Attention is directed to the discussion of disclosure regarding anti-takeover and similar proposals in Release No. 34-15230 (October 13, 1978).

Item 20. Other Proposed Action.

If action is to be taken on any matter not specifically referred to in this Schedule 14A, describe briefly the substance of each such matter in substantially the same degree of detail as is required by Items 5 to 19, inclusive, of this Schedule, and, with respect to investment companies registered under the Investment Company Act of 1940, Item 22 of this Schedule.

Item 21. Voting Procedures.

As to each matter which is to be submitted to a vote of security holders, furnish the following information:
a. State the vote required for approval or election, other than for the approval of auditors.
b. Disclose the method by which votes will be counted, including the treatment and effect of abstentions and broker non-votes under applicable state law as well as registrant charter and by-law provisions.

Item 22. [Intentionally Omitted]

Item 23. Delivery of Documents to Security Holders Sharing an Address.

If one annual report to security holders, proxy statement, or Notice of Internet Availability of Proxy Materials is being delivered to two or more security holders who share an address in accordance with Rule14a-3(e)(1), furnish the following information:
a. State that only one annual report to security holders, proxy statement, or Notice of Internet Availability of Proxy Materials, as applicable, is being delivered to multiple security holders sharing an address unless the registrant has received contrary instructions from one or more of the security holders;

b. Undertake to deliver promptly upon written or oral request a separate copy of the annual report to security holders, proxy statement, or Notice of Internet Availability of Proxy Materials, as applicable, to a security holder at a shared address to which a single copy of the documents was delivered and provide instructions as to how a security holder can notify the registrant that the security holder wishes to receive a separate copy of an annual report to security holders, proxy statement, or Notice of Internet Availability of Proxy Materials, as applicable;

c. Provide the phone number and mailing address to which a security holder can direct a notification to the registrant that the security holder wishes to receive a separate annual report to security holders, proxy statement, or Notice of Internet Availability of Proxy Materials, as applicable, in the future; and

d. Provide instructions how security holders sharing an address can request delivery of a single copy of annual reports to security holders, proxy statements, or Notices of Internet Availability of Proxy Materials if they are receiving multiple copies of annual reports to security holders, proxy statements, or Notices of Internet Availability of Proxy Materials.

Schedule 14D-9 Solicitation/Recommendation Statement Under Section 14(d)(4) of the Securities Exchange Act of 1934

<table>
<tr><td colspan="1" align="center">SECURITIES AND EXCHANGE COMMISSION</td></tr>
<tr><td align="center">Washington, DC 20549</td></tr>
<tr><td align="center">SCHEDULE 14D-9</td></tr>
<tr><td align="center">Solicitation/Recommendation Statement Under Section 14(d)(4) of the
Securities Exchange Act of 1934</td></tr>
<tr><td>(Amendment No. _____)</td></tr>
<tr><td> </td></tr>
<tr><td>(Name of Subject Company)</td></tr>
<tr><td> </td></tr>
<tr><td>(Name of Persons Filing Statement)</td></tr>
<tr><td> </td></tr>
<tr><td>(Title of Class of Securities)</td></tr>
<tr><td> </td></tr>
<tr><td>(CUSIP Number of Class of Securities)</td></tr>
<tr><td> </td></tr>
<tr><td>(Name, address and telephone numbers of person authorized to receive notices and communications on behalf of the persons filing statement)</td></tr>
<tr><td>[ ] Check the box if the filing relates solely to preliminary communications made before the commencement of a tender offer.</td></tr>
</table>

General Instructions:

    A.   File eight copies of the statement, including all exhibits, with the Commission if paper filing is permitted.

    B.   If the filing contains only preliminary communications made before the commencement of a tender offer, no signature is required. The filer need not respond to the items in the schedule. Any pre-commencement communications that are filed under cover of this schedule need not be incorporated by reference into the schedule.

    C.   If an item is inapplicable or the answer is in the negative, so state. The statement published, sent or given to security holders may omit negative and not applicable responses. If the schedule includes any information that is not published, sent or given to security holders, provide that information or specifically incorporate it by reference under the appropriate item number and heading in the schedule. Do not recite the text of disclosure requirements in the schedule or any document published, sent or given to security holders. Indicate clearly the coverage of the requirements without referring to the text of the items.

    D.   Information contained in exhibits to the statement may be incorporated by reference in answer or partial answer to any item unless it would render the answer misleading, incomplete, unclear or confusing. A copy of any information that is incorporated by reference or a copy of the pertinent pages of a document containing the information must be submitted with this statement as an exhibit, unless it was previously filed with the Commission electronically on EDGAR. If an exhibit contains information responding to more than one item in the schedule, all information in that exhibit may be incorporated by reference once in response to the several items in the schedule for which it provides an answer. Information incorporated by reference is deemed filed with the Commission for all purposes of the Act.

E. Amendments disclosing a material change in the information set forth in this statement may omit any information previously disclosed in this statement.

Item 1. Subject Company Information

Furnish the information required by Item 1002(a) and (b) of Regulation M-A.

Item 2. Identity and Background of Filing Person

Furnish the information required by Item 1003(a) and (d) of Regulation M-A.

Item 3. Past Contacts, Transactions, Negotiations and Agreements

Furnish the information required by Item 1005(d) of Regulation M-A.

Item 4. The Solicitation or Recommendation

Furnish the information required by Item 1012(a) through (c) of Regulation M-A.

Item 5. Person/Assets, Retained, Employed, Compensated or Used

Furnish the information required by Item 1009(a) of Regulation M-A.

Item 6. Interest in Securities of the Subject Company

Furnish the information required by Item 1008(b) of Regulation M-A.

Item 7. Purposes of the Transaction and Plans or Proposals

Furnish the information required by Item 1006(d) of Regulation M-A.

Item 8. Additional Information

Furnish the information required by Item 1011(b) of Regulation M-A.

Item 9. Exhibits

File as an exhibit to the Schedule all documents specified by Item 1016(a), (e) and (g) of Regulation M-A.

Signature: After due inquiry and to the best of my knowledge and belief, I certify that the information set forth in this statement is true, complete and correct.

....

Date

....

Signature

....

Name/Title

Instruction to Signature:
The statement must be signed by the filing person or that person's authorized representative. If the statement is signed on behalf of a person by an authorized representative (other than an executive officer of a corporation or general partner of a partnership), evidence of the representative's authority to sign on behalf of the person must be filed with the statement. The name and any title of each person who signs the statement must be typed or printed beneath the signature. See Rule 14d-1(h) with respect to signature requirements.

Schedule TO – Tender Offer Statement Under Section 14(d)(1) or 13(e)(1) of the Securities Exchange Act of 1934

SECURITIES AND EXCHANGE COMMISSION

Washington, DC 20549

SCHEDULE TO

Tender Offer Statement Under Section 14(d)(1) or 13(e)(1) of the
Securities Exchange Act of 1934

(Amendment No. –)*

....
(Name of Subject Company [Issuer])

....
(Names of Filing Persons (identifying status as offeror, issuer or other person))

....
(Title of Class of Securities)

....
(CUSIP Number of Class of Securities)

....
(Name, Address, and Telephone Numbers of Person Authorized to Receive Notices and Communications on Behalf of filing persons)

Calculation of Filing Fee	
Transaction valuation*	Amount of Filing Fee

*Set forth the amount on which the filing fee is calculated and state how it was determined.

[ ] Check box if any part of the fee is offset as provided by Rule 0-11(a)(2) and identify the filing with which the offsetting fee was previously paid. Identify the previous filing by registration statement number, or the Form or Schedule and the date of its filing.

Amount Previously Paid:...

Form or Registration No.:...

Filing Party:...

DATE FILED:...

[ ] Check the box if the filing relates solely to preliminary communications made before the commencement of a tender offer.

Check the appropriate boxes below to designate any transactions to which the statement relates:

[ ] third-party tender offer subject to Rule 14d-1.

[ ] issuer tender offer subject to Rule 13e-4.

[ ] going-private transaction subject to Rule 13e-3.

[ ] amendment to Schedule 13D under Rule 13d-2.

Check the following box if the filing is a final amendment reporting the results of the tender offer: [ ]

General Instructions

A. File eight copies of the statement, including all exhibits, with the Commission if paper filing is permitted.

B. This filing must be accompanied by a fee payable to the Commission as required by Rule 0-11.

C. If the statement is filed by a general or limited partnership, syndicate or other group, the information called for by Items 3 and 5-8 for a third-party tender offer and Items 5-8 for an issuer tender offer must be given with respect to: (i) Each partner of the general partnership; (ii) each partner who is, or functions as, a general partner of the limited partnership; (iii) each member of the syndicate or group; and (iv) each person controlling the partner or member. If the statement is filed by a corporation or if a person referred to in (i), (ii), (iii) or (iv) of this Instruction is a corporation, the information called for by the items specified above must be given with respect to: (a) Each executive officer and director of the corporation; (b) each person controlling the corporation; and (c) each executive officer and director of any corporation or other person ultimately in control of the corporation.

D. If the filing contains only preliminary communications made before the commencement of a tender offer, no signature or filing fee is required. The filer need not respond to the items in the schedule. Any pre-commencement communications that are filed under cover of this schedule need not be incorporated by reference into the schedule.

E. If an item is inapplicable or the answer is in the negative, so state. The statement published, sent or given to security holders may omit negative and not applicable responses. If the schedule includes any information that is not published, sent or given to security holders, provide that information or specifically incorporate it by reference under the appropriate item number and heading in the schedule. Do not recite the text of disclosure requirements in the schedule or any document published, sent or given to security holders. Indicate clearly the coverage of the requirements without referring to the text of the items.

F. Information contained in exhibits to the statement may be incorporated by reference in answer or partial answer to any item unless it would render the answer misleading, incomplete, unclear or confusing. A copy of any information that is incorporated by reference or a copy of the pertinent pages of a document containing the information must be submitted with this statement as an exhibit, unless it was previously filed with the Commission electronically on EDGAR. If an exhibit contains information responding to more than one item in the schedule, all information in that exhibit may be incorporated by reference once in response to the several items in the schedule for which it provides an answer. Information incorporated by reference is deemed filed with the Commission for all purposes of the Act.

G. A filing person may amend its previously filed Schedule 13D on Schedule TO if the appropriate box on the cover page is checked to indicate a combined filing and the information called for by the fourteen disclosure items on the cover page of Schedule

13D is provided on the cover page of the combined filing with respect to each filing person.

H. The final amendment required by Rule 14d-3(b)(2) and Rule 13e-4(c)(4) will satisfy the reporting requirements of section 13(d) of the Act with respect to all securities acquired by the offeror in the tender offer.

I. Amendments disclosing a material change in the information set forth in this statement may omit any information previously disclosed in this statement.

J. If the tender offer disclosed on this statement involves a going-private transaction, a combined Schedule TO and Schedule 13E-3 may be filed with the Commission under cover of Schedule TO. The Rule 13e-3 box on the cover page of the Schedule TO must be checked to indicate a combined filing. All information called for by both schedules must be provided except that Items 1–3, 5, 8 and 9 of Schedule TO may be omitted to the extent those items call for information that duplicates the item requirements in Schedule 13E-3.

K. For purposes of this statement, the following definitions apply:

1. The term offeror means any person who makes a tender offer or on whose behalf a tender offer is made;

2. The term issuer tender offer has the same meaning as in Rule 13e-4(a)(2); and

3. The term third-party tender offer means a tender offer that is not an issuer tender offer.

SPECIAL INSTRUCTIONS FOR COMPLYING WITH SCHEDULE TO

Under Sections 13(e), 14(d) and 23 of the Act and the rules and regulations of the Act, the Commission is authorized to solicit the information required to be supplied by this schedule.

Disclosure of the information specified in this schedule is mandatory, except for I.R.S. identification numbers, disclosure of which is voluntary. The information will be used for the primary purpose of disclosing tender offer and going-private transactions. This statement will be made a matter of public record. Therefore, any information given will be available for inspection by any member of the public.

Because of the public nature of the information, the Commission can use it for a variety of purposes, including referral to other governmental authorities or securities self-regulatory organizations for investigatory purposes or in connection with litigation involving the Federal securities laws or other civil, criminal or regulatory statutes or provisions. I.R.S. identification numbers, if furnished, will assist the Commission in identifying security holders and, therefore, in promptly processing tender offer and going-private statements.

Failure to disclose the information required by this schedule, except for I.R.S. identification numbers, may result in civil or criminal action against the persons involved for violation of the Federal securities laws and rules.

Item 1. Summary Term Sheet

Furnish the information required by Item 1001 of Regulation M-A unless information is disclosed to security holders in a prospectus that meets the requirements of Rule 421(d) under the Securities Act.

Item 2. Subject Company Information

Furnish the information required by Item 1002(a) through (c) of Regulation M-A.

Item 3. Identity and Background of Filing Person

Furnish the information required by Item 1003(a) through (c) of Regulation M-A for a third-party tender offer and the information required by Item 1003(a) of Regulation M-A for an issuer tender offer.

Item 4. Terms of the Transaction

Furnish the information required by Item 1004(a) of Regulation M-A for a third-party tender offer and the information required by Item 1004(a) through (b) of Regulation M-A for an issuer tender offer.

Item 5. Past Contacts, Transactions, Negotiations and Agreements

Furnish the information required by Item 1005(a) and (b) of Regulation M-A for a third-party tender offer and the information required by Item 1005(e) of Regulation M-A for an issuer tender offer.

Item 6. Purposes of the Transaction and Plans or Proposals

Furnish the information required by Item 1006(a) and (c)(1) through (7) of Regulation M-A for a third-party tender offer and the information required by Item 1006(a) through (c) of Regulation M-A for an issuer tender offer.

Item 7. Source and Amount of Funds or Other Consideration

Furnish the information required by Item 1007(a), (b) and (d) of Regulation M-A.

Item 8. Interest in Securities of the Subject Company

Furnish the information required by Item 1008 of Regulation M-A.

Item 9. Persons/Assets, Retained, Employed, Compensated or Used

Furnish the information required by Item 1009(a) of Regulation M-A.

Item 10. Financial Statements

If material, furnish the information required by Item 1010(a) and (b) of Regulation M-A for the issuer in an issuer tender offer and for the offeror in a third-party tender offer.

Instructions to Item 10:

1. Financial statements must be provided when the offeror's financial condition is material to security holder's decision whether to sell, tender or hold the securities sought. The facts and circumstances of a tender offer, particularly the terms of the tender offer, may influence a determination as to whether financial statements are material, and thus required to be disclosed.

2. Financial statements are not considered material when: (a) The consideration offered consists solely of cash; (b) the offer is not subject to any financing condition; and either: (c) the offeror is a public reporting company under Section 13(a) or 15(d) of the Act that files reports electronically on EDGAR, or (d) the offer is for all outstanding securities of the subject class. Financial information may be required, however, in a two-tier transaction. See Instruction 5 below.

3. The filing person may incorporate by reference financial statements contained in any document filed with the Commission, solely for the purposes of this schedule, if: (a) The financial statements substantially meet the requirements of this item; (b) an express statement is made that the financial statements are incorporated by reference; (c) the information incorporated by reference is clearly identified by page, paragraph, caption or otherwise; and (d) if the information incorporated by reference is not filed with this schedule, an indication is made where the information may be inspected and copies obtained. Financial statements that are required to be presented in comparative form for two or more fiscal years or periods may not be incorporated by reference unless the material incorporated by reference includes the entire period for which the comparative data is required to be given. See General Instruction F to this schedule.

4. If the offeror in a third-party tender offer is a natural person, and such person's financial information is material, disclose the net worth of the offeror. If the offeror's net worth is derived from material amounts of assets that are not readily marketable or there are material guarantees and contingencies, disclose the nature and approximate amount of the individual's net worth that consists of illiquid assets and the magnitude of any guarantees or contingencies that may negatively affect the natural person's net worth.

5. Pro forma financial information is required in a negotiated third-party cash tender offer when securities are intended to be offered in a subsequent merger or other transaction in which remaining target securities are acquired and the acquisition of the subject company is significant to the offeror under Rule 11-01(b)(1) of Regulation S-X. The offeror must disclose the financial information specified in Item 3(f) and Item 5 of Form S-4 in the schedule filed with the Commission, but may furnish only the summary financial information specified in Item 3(d), (e) and (f) of Form S-4 in the disclosure document sent to security holders. If pro forma financial information is required by this instruction, the historical financial statements specified in Item 1010 of Regulation M-A are required for the bidder.

6. The disclosure materials disseminated to security holders may contain the summarized financial information specified by Item 1010(c) of Regulation M-A instead of the financial information required by Item 1010(a) and (b). In that case, the

financial information required by Item 1010(a) and (b) of Regulation M-A must be disclosed in the statement. If summarized financial information is disseminated to security holders, include appropriate instructions on how more complete financial information can be obtained. If the summarized financial information is prepared on the basis of a comprehensive body of accounting principles other than U.S. GAAP, the summarized financial information must be accompanied by a reconciliation as described in Instruction 8 of this Item.

7. If the offeror is not subject to the periodic reporting requirements of the Act, the financial statements required by this Item need not be audited if audited financial statements are not available or obtainable without unreasonable cost or expense. Make a statement to that effect and the reasons for their unavailability.

8. If the financial statements required by this Item are prepared on the basis of a comprehensive body of accounting principles other than U.S. GAAP, provide a reconciliation to U.S. GAAP in accordance with Item 17 of Form 20-F, unless a reconciliation is unavailable or not obtainable without unreasonable cost or expense. At a minimum, however, when financial statements are prepared on a basis other than U.S. GAAP, a narrative description of all material variations in accounting principles, practices and methods used in preparing the non-U.S. GAAP financial statements from those accepted in the U.S. must be presented.

Item 11. Additional Information

Furnish the information required by Item 1011 of Regulation M-A.

Item 12. Exhibits

File as an exhibit to the Schedule all documents specified by Item 1016 (a), (b), (d), (g) and (h) of Regulation M-A.

Item 13. Information Required by Schedule 13E-3

If the Schedule TO is combined with Schedule 13E-3, set forth the information required by Schedule 13E-3 that is not included or covered by the items in Schedule TO.

Signature: After due inquiry and to the best of my knowledge and belief, I certify that the information set forth in this statement is true, complete and correct.

....
Date

....
Signature

....
Name/Title

Instruction to Signature:

The statement must be signed by the filing person or that person's authorized representative. If the statement is signed on behalf of a person by an authorized representative (other than an executive officer of a corporation or general partner of a partnership), evidence of the representative's authority to sign on behalf of the person must be filed with the statement. The name and any title of each person who signs the statement must be typed or printed beneath the signature. See Rule 12b-11 and Rule 14d-1(h) with respect to signature requirements.

Exchange Act – Forms 8-K, 10, 10-K, 10-Q

EFFECTIVE AUGUST 23RD, 2004

**UNITED STATES
SECURITIES AND EXCHANGE COMMISSION
Washington, D.C. 20549**

FORM 8-K

CURRENT REPORT

Pursuant to Section 13 or 15(d) of The Securities Exchange Act of 1934

Date of Report (Date of earliest event reported) _____

(Exact name of registrant as specified in its charter)

| (State or other jurisdiction of incorporation or organization) | (Commission File No.) | (IRS Employer Identification No) |

| (Address of principal executive offices) | (Zip Code) |

Registrant's telephone number, including area code

(Former name, former address and former fiscal year, if changed since last report)

Check the appropriate box below if the Form 8-K filing is intended to simultaneously satisfy the filing obligation of the registrant under any of the following provisions (see General Instruction A.2. below):

[ ]   Written communications pursuant to Rule 425 under the Securities Act
[ ]   Soliciting material pursuant to Rule 14a-12 under the Exchange Act
[ ]   Pre-commencement communications pursuant to Rule 14d-2(b) under the Exchange Act
[ ]   Pre-commencement communications pursuant to Rule 13e-4(c) under the Exchange Act

GENERAL INSTRUCTIONS

A.   **Rule as to Use of Form 8-K.**

1.   Form 8-K shall be used for current reports under Section 13 or 15(d) of the Securities Exchange Act of 1934, filed pursuant to Rule 13 a-11 or Rule 15d-11 and for reports of nonpublic information required to be disclosed by Regulation FD.

2.   Form 8-K may be used by a registrant to satisfy its filing obligations pursuant to Rule 425 under the Securities Act, regarding written communications related to business combination transactions, or Rules 14a-12 or Rule 14d-2(b) under the Exchange Act, relating to soliciting materials and pre-commencement communications pursuant to tender offers, respectively, provided that the Form 8-K filing satisfies all the substantive requirements of those rules (other than the Rule 425(c) requirement to include certain specified information in any prospectus filed pursuant to such rule). Such filing is also deemed to be filed pursuant to any rule for which the box is checked. A registrant is not required to check the box in connection with Rule 14a-12 or Rule 14d-2(b) if the communication is filed pursuant to Rule 425. Communications filed pursuant to Rule 425 are deemed filed under the other applicable sections. See Note 2 to Rule 425, Rule 14a-12 and Instruction 2 to Rule 14d-2(b)(2).

B.   **Events to be Reported and Time for Filing of Reports.**

1.   A report on this form is required to be filed or furnished, as applicable, upon the occurrence of any one or more of the events specified in the items in Sections 1-6 and 9 of this form. Unless otherwise specified, a report is to be filed or furnished within four business days after occurrence of the event. If the event occurs on a Saturday, Sunday or holiday on which the Commission is not open for business, then the four business day period shall begin to run on, and include, the first business day thereafter. A registrant either furnishing a report on this form under Item 7.01 (Regulation FD Disclosure) or electing to file a report on this form under Item 8.01 (Other Events) solely to satisfy its obligations under Regulation FD must furnish such report or make such filing, as applicable, in accordance with the requirements of Rule 100(a) of Regulation FD, including the deadline for furnishing or filing such report.

2.   The information in a report furnished pursuant to Item 2.02 (Results of Operations and Financial Condition) or Item 7.01 (Regulation FD Disclosure) shall not be deemed to be "filed" for purposes of Section 18 of the Exchange Act or otherwise subject to the liabilities of that section, unless the registrant specifically states that the information is to be considered "filed" under the Exchange Act or incorporates it by reference into a filing under the Securities Act or the Exchange Act. If a report on Form 8-K contains disclosures under Item 2.02 or Item 7.01, whether or not the report contains disclosures regarding other items, all exhibits to such report relating to Item 2.02 or Item 7.01 will be deemed furnished, and not filed, unless the registrant specifies, under Item 9.01 (Financial Statements and Exhibits), which exhibits, or portions of exhibits, are intended to be deemed filed rather than furnished pursuant to this instruction.

3.   If the registrant previously has reported substantially the same information as required by this form, the registrant need not make an additional report of the information on this form. To the extent that an item calls for disclosure of developments concerning a previously reported event or transaction, any information required in the new report or amendment about the previously reported event or transaction may be provided by incorporation by reference to

the previously filed report. The term previously reported is defined in Rule 12b-2.

4. Copies of agreements, amendments or other documents or instruments required to be filed pursuant to Form 8-K are not required to be filed or furnished as exhibits to the Form 8-K unless specifically required to be filed or furnished by the applicable Item. This instruction does not affect the requirement to otherwise file such agreements, amendments or other documents or instruments, including as exhibits to registration statements and periodic reports pursuant to the requirements of Item 601 of Regulation S-K or Item 601 of Regulation S-B, as applicable.

5. When considering current reporting on this form, particularly of other events of material importance pursuant to Item 7.01 (Regulation FD Disclosure) and Item 8.01(Other Events), registrants should have due regard for the accuracy, completeness and currency of the information in registration statements filed under the Securities Act which incorporate by reference information in reports filed pursuant to the Exchange Act, including reports on this form.

6. A registrant's report under Item 7.01 (Regulation FD Disclosure) or Item 8.01 (Other Events) will not be deemed an admission as to the materiality of any information in the report that is required to be disclosed solely by Regulation FD.

C.   Application of General Rules and Regulations.

1. The General Rules and Regulations under the Act contain certain general requirements which are applicable to reports on any form. These general requirements should be carefully read and observed in the preparation and filing of reports on this form.

2. Particular attention is directed to Regulation 12B which contains general requirements regarding matters such as the kind and size of paper to be used, the legibility of the report, the information to be given whenever the title of securities is required to be stated, and the filing of the report. The definitions contained in Rule 12b-2 should be especially noted. See also Regulations 13A and 15D.

D.   Preparation of Report.

This form is not to be used as a blank form to be filled in, but only as a guide in the preparation of the report on paper meeting the requirements of Rule 12b-12. The report shall contain the number and caption of the applicable item, but the text of such item may be omitted, provided the answers thereto are prepared in the manner specified in Rule 12b-13. To the extent that Item 1.01 and one or more other items of the form are applicable, registrants need not provide the number and caption of Item 1.01 so long as the substantive disclosure required by Item 1.01 is disclosed in the report and the number and caption of the other applicable item(s) are provided. All items that are not required to be answered in a particular report may be omitted and no reference thereto need be made in the report. All instructions should also be omitted.

E.   Signature and Filing of Report.

Three complete copies of the report, including any financial statements, exhibits or other papers or documents filed as a part thereof, and five additional copies which need not include exhibits, shall be filed with the Commission. At least one complete copy of the report, including any financial statements, exhibits or other papers or documents filed as a part thereof, shall be filed, with each exchange on which any class of securities of the registrant is registered. At least one complete copy of the report filed with the Commission and one such copy filed with each exchange shall be manually signed. Copies not manually signed shall bear typed or printed signatures.

F.   Incorporation by Reference.

If the registrant makes available to its stockholders or otherwise publishes, within the period prescribed for filing the report, a press release or other document or statement containing information meeting some or all of the requirements of this form, the information called for may be incorporated by reference to such published document or statement, in answer or partial answer to any item or items of this form, provided copies thereof are filed as an exhibit to the report on this form.

* * *

INFORMATION TO BE INCLUDED IN THE REPORT

Section 1 - Registrant's Business and Operations

Item 1.01 Entry into a Material Definitive Agreement.

(a) If the registrant has entered into a material definitive agreement not made in the ordinary course of business of the registrant, or into any amendment of such agreement that is material to the registrant, disclose the following information:

    (1) the date on which the agreement was entered into or amended, the identity of the parties to the agreement or amendment and a brief description of any material relationship between the registrant or its affiliates and any of the parties, other than in respect of the material definitive agreement or amendment; and

    (2) a brief description of the terms and conditions of the agreement or amendment that are material to the registrant.

(b) For purposes of this Item 1.01, a material definitive agreement means an agreement that provides for obligations that are material to and enforceable against the registrant, or rights that are material to the registrant and enforceable by the registrant against one or more other parties to the agreement, in each case whether or not subject to conditions.

Instructions.

1. Any material definitive agreement of the registrant not made in the ordinary course of the registrant's business must be disclosed under this Item 1.01. An agreement is deemed to be not made in the ordinary course of a registrant's business even if the agreement is such as

600

ordinarily accompanies the kind of business conducted by the registrant if it involves the subject matter identified in Item 601(b)(10)(ii)(A) - (D) of Regulation S-K. An agreement involving the subject matter identified in Item 601(b)(10)(iii)(A) or (B) need not be disclosed under this Item.

2. A registrant must provide disclosure under this Item 1.01 if the registrant succeeds as a party to the agreement or amendment to the agreement by assumption or assignment (other than in connection with a merger or acquisition or similar transaction).

Item 1.02 Termination of a Material Definitive Agreement.

(a) If a material definitive agreement which was not made in the ordinary course of business of the registrant and to which the registrant is a party is terminated otherwise than by expiration of the agreement on its stated termination date, or as a result of all parties completing their obligations under such agreement, and such termination of the agreement is material to the registrant, disclose the following information:

    (1) the date of the termination of the material definitive agreement, the identity of the parties to the agreement and a brief description of any material relationship between the registrant or its affiliates and any of the parties other than in respect of the material definitive agreement;

    (2) a brief description of the terms and conditions of the agreement that are material to the registrant;

    (3) a brief description of the material circumstances surrounding the termination; and

    (4) any material early termination penalties incurred by the registrant.

(b) For purposes of this Item 1.02, the term material definitive agreement shall have the same meaning as set forth in Item 1.01(b).

Instructions.
1. No disclosure is required solely by reason of this Item 1.02 during negotiations or discussions regarding termination of a material definitive agreement unless and until the agreement has been terminated.

2. No disclosure is required solely by reason of this Item 1.02 if the registrant believes in good faith that the material definitive agreement has not been terminated, unless the registrant has received a notice of termination pursuant to the terms of agreement.

Item 1.03 Bankruptcy or Receivership.

(a) If a receiver, fiscal agent or similar officer has been appointed for a registrant or its parent, in a proceeding under the U.S. Bankruptcy Code or in any other proceeding under state or federal law in which a court or governmental authority has assumed jurisdiction over substantially all of the assets or business of the registrant or its parent, or if such jurisdiction has been assumed by leaving the existing directors and officers in possession but subject to the supervision and orders of a court or governmental authority, disclose the following information:

    (1) the name or other identification of the proceeding;

(2) the identity of the court or governmental authority;

(3) the date that jurisdiction was assumed; and

(4) the identity of the receiver, fiscal agent or similar officer and the date of his or her appointment.

(b) If an order confirming a plan of reorganization, arrangement or liquidation has been entered by a court or governmental authority having supervision or jurisdiction over substantially all of the assets or business of the registrant or its parent, disclose the following;

(1) the identity of the court or governmental authority;

(2) the date that the order confirming the plan was entered by the court or governmental authority;

(3) a summary of the material features of the plan and, pursuant to Item 9.01 (Financial Statements and Exhibits), a copy of the plan as confirmed;

(4) the number of shares or other units of the registrant or its parent issued and outstanding, the number reserved for future issuance in respect of claims and interests filed and allowed under the plan, and the aggregate total of such numbers; and

(5) information as to the assets and liabilities of the registrant or its parent as of the date that the order confirming the plan was entered, or a date as close thereto as practicable.

Instruction.

The information called for in paragraph (b)(5) of this Item 1.03 may be presented in the form in which it was furnished to the court or governmental authority.

Section 2 - Financial Information

Item 2.01 Completion of Acquisition or Disposition of Assets.

If the registrant or any of its majority-owned subsidiaries has completed the acquisition or disposition of a significant amount of assets, otherwise than in the ordinary course of business, disclose the following information:

(a) the date of completion of the transaction;

(b) a brief description of the assets involved;

(c) the identity of the person(s) from whom the assets were acquired or to whom they were sold and the nature of any material relationship, other than in respect of the transaction, between such person(s) and the registrant or any of its affiliates, or any director or officer of the registrant, or any associate of any such director or officer;

(d) the nature and amount of consideration given or received for the assets and, if any material relationship is disclosed pursuant to paragraph (c) of this Item 2.01, the formula or principle followed in determining the amount of such consideration; and

(e) if the transaction being reported is an acquisition and if a material relationship exists between the registrant or any of its affiliates and the source(s) of the funds used in the acquisition, the identity of the source(s) of the funds unless all or any part of the consideration used is a loan made in the ordinary course of business by a bank as defined by Section 3(a)(6) of the Act, in which case the identity of such bank may be omitted provided the registrant:

(1) has made a request for confidentiality pursuant to Section 13(d)(1)(B) of the Act;

(2) states in the report that the identity of the bank has been so omitted and filed separately with the Commission.

Instructions.

1. No information need be given as to:

(i) any transaction between any person and any wholly-owned subsidiary of such person;

(ii) any transaction between two or more wholly-owned subsidiaries of any person; or

(iii) the redemption or other acquisition of securities from the public, or the sale or other disposition of securities to the public, by the issuer of such securities or by a wholly-owned subsidiary of that issuer.

2. The term acquisition includes every purchase, acquisition by lease, exchange, merger, consolidation, succession or other acquisition, except that the term does not include the construction or development of property by or for the registrant or its subsidiaries or the acquisition of materials for such purpose. The term disposition includes every sale, disposition by lease, exchange, merger, consolidation, mortgage, assignment or hypothecation of assets, whether for the benefit of creditors or otherwise, abandonment, destruction, or other disposition.

3. The information called for by this Item 2.01 is to be given as to each transaction or series of related transactions of the size indicated. The acquisition or disposition of securities is deemed the indirect acquisition or disposition of the assets represented by such securities if it results in the acquisition or disposition of control of such assets.

4. An acquisition or disposition shall be deemed to involve a significant amount of assets:

(i) if the registrant's and its other subsidiaries' equity in the net book value of such assets or the amount paid or received for the assets upon such acquisition or disposition exceeded 10% of the total assets of the registrant and its consolidated subsidiaries; or

(ii) if it involved a business (see 17 CFR 210.11-01(d)) that is significant (see 17 CFR 210.11-01(b)).

Acquisitions of individually insignificant businesses are not required to be reported pursuant to this Item 2.01 unless they are related businesses (see 17 CFR 210.3-05(a)(3)) and are significant in the aggregate.

5. Attention is directed to the requirements in Item 9.01 (Financial Statements and Exhibits) with respect to the filing of:

(i) financial statements of businesses acquired;

(ii) pro forma financial information; and

(iii) copies of the plans of acquisition or disposition as exhibits to the report.

Item 2.02 Results of Operations and Financial Condition.

(a) If a registrant, or any person acting on its behalf, makes any public announcement or release (including any update of an earlier announcement or release) disclosing material non-public information regarding the registrant's results of operations or financial condition for a completed quarterly or annual fiscal period, the registrant shall disclose the date of the announcement or release, briefly identify the announcement or release and include the text of that announcement or release as an exhibit.

(b) A Form 8-K is not required to be furnished to the Commission under this Item 2.02 in the case of disclosure of material non-public information that is disclosed orally, telephonically, by webcast, by broadcast, or by similar means if:

  (1) the information is provided as part of a presentation that is complementary to, and initially occurs within 48 hours after, a related, written announcement or release that has been furnished on Form 8-K pursuant to this Item 2.02 prior to the presentation;

  (2) the presentation is broadly accessible to the public by dial-in conference call, by webcast, by broadcast or by similar means;

  (3) the financial and other statistical information contained in the presentation is provided on the registrant's website, together with any information that would be required under 17 CFR 244.100; and

  (4) the presentation was announced by a widely disseminated press release, that included instructions as to when and how to access the presentation and the location on the registrant's website where the information would be available.

Instructions.

1. The requirements of this Item 2.02 are triggered by the disclosure of material non-public information regarding a completed fiscal year or quarter. Release of additional or updated material non-public information regarding a completed fiscal year or quarter would trigger an additional Item 2.02 requirement.

2. The requirements of paragraph(e)(1)(i) of Item 10 of Regulation S-K shall apply to disclosures under this Item 2.02.

3. Issuers that make earnings announcements or other disclosures of material non-public information regarding a completed fiscal year or quarter in an interim or annual report to shareholders are permitted to specify which portion of the report contains the information required to be furnished under this Item 2.02.

4. This Item 2.02 does not apply in the case of a disclosure that is made in a quarterly report filed with the Commission on Form 10-Q or an annual report filed with the Commission on Form 10-K.

Item 2.03 Creation of a Direct Financial Obligation or an Obligation under an Off-Balance Sheet Arrangement of a Registrant.

    (a) If the registrant becomes obligated on a direct financial obligation that is material to the registrant, disclose the following information:

        (1) the date on which the registrant becomes obligated on the direct financial obligation and a brief description of the transaction or agreement creating the obligation;

        (2) the amount of the obligation, including the terms of its payment and, if applicable, a brief description of the material terms under which it may be accelerated or increased and the nature of any recourse provisions that would enable the registrant to recover from third parties; and

        (3) a brief description of the other terms and conditions of the transaction or agreement that are material to the registrant.

    (b) If the registrant becomes directly or contingently liable for an obligation that is material to the registrant arising out of an off-balance sheet arrangement, disclose the following information:

        (1) the date on which the registrant becomes directly or contingently liable on the obligation and a brief description of the transaction or agreement creating the arrangement and obligation;

        (2) a brief description of the nature and amount of the obligation of the registrant under the arrangement, including the material terms whereby it may become a direct obligation, if applicable, or may be accelerated or increased and the nature of any recourse provisions that would enable the registrant to recover from third parties;

        (3) the maximum potential amount of future payments (undiscounted) that the registrant may be required to make, if different; and

        (4) a brief description of the other terms and conditions of the obligation or arrangement that are material to the registrant.

    (c) For purposes of this Item 2.03, direct financial obligation means any of the following:

        (1) a long-term debt obligation, as defined in Item 303 (a)(5)(ii)(A) of Regulation S-K;

        (2) a capital lease obligation, as defined in Item 303(a)(5)(ii)(B) of Regulation S-K;

        (3) an operating lease obligation, as defined in Item 303(a)(5)(ii)(C) of Regulation S-K; or

        (4) a short-term debt obligation that arises other than in the ordinary course of business.

    (d) For purposes of this Item 2.03, off-balance sheet arrangement has the meaning set forth in Item 303 (a)(4)(ii) of Regulation S-K.

    (e) For purposes of this Item 2.03, short-term debt obligation means a payment obligation under a borrowing arrangement that is scheduled to mature within one year, or, for those registrants that use the operating cycle concept of working capital, within a registrant's operating cycle that is longer than one year, as discussed in Accounting Research Bulletin No. 43, Chapter 3A, Working Capital.

Instructions.

1. A registrant has no obligation to disclose information under this Item 2.03 until the registrant enters into an agreement enforceable against the registrant, whether or not subject to conditions, under which the direct financial obligation will arise or be created or issued. If there is no such agreement, the registrant must provide the disclosure within four business days after the occurrence of the closing or settlement of the transaction or arrangement under which the direct financial obligation arises or is created.

2. A registrant must provide the disclosure required by paragraph (b) of this Item 2.03 whether or not the registrant is also a party to the transaction or agreement creating the contingent obligation arising under the off-balance sheet arrangement. In the event that neither the registrant nor any affiliate of the registrant is also a party to the transaction or agreement creating the contingent obligation arising under the off-balance sheet arrangement in question, the four business day period for reporting the event under this Item 2.03 shall begin on the earlier of (i) the fourth business day after the contingent obligation is created or arises, and (ii) the day on which an executive officer, as defined in Rule 3b-7, of the registrant becomes aware of the contingent obligation.

3. In the event that an agreement, transaction or arrangement requiring disclosure under this Item 2.03 comprises a facility, program or similar arrangement that creates or may give rise to direct financial obligations of the registrant in connection with multiple transactions, the registrant shall:
(i) disclose the entering into of the facility, program or similar arrangement if the entering into of the facility is material to the registrant; and
(ii) as direct financial obligations arise or are created under the facility or program, disclose the required information under this Item 2.03 to the extent that the obligations are material to the registrant (including when a series of previously undisclosed individually immaterial obligations become material in the aggregate).

4. For purposes of Item 2.03(b)(3), the maximum amount of future payments shall not be reduced by the effect of any amounts that may possibly be recovered by the registrant under recourse or collateralization provisions in any guarantee agreement, transaction or arrangement.

5. If the obligation required to be disclosed under this Item 2.03 is a security, or a term of a security, that has been or will be sold pursuant to an effective registration statement of the registrant, the registrant is not required to file a Form 8-K pursuant to this Item 2.03, provided that the prospectus relating to that sale contains the information required by this Item 2.03 and is filed within the required time period under Securities Act Rule 424.

Item 2.04 Triggering Events That Accelerate or Increase a Direct Financial Obligation or an Obligation under an Off-Balance Sheet Arrangement.

(a) If a triggering event causing the increase or acceleration of a direct financial obligation of the registrant occurs and the consequences of the event, taking into account those described in paragraph (a)(4) of this Item 2.04, are material to the registrant, disclose the following information:

    (1) the date of the triggering event and a brief description of the agreement or transaction under which the direct financial obligation was created and is increased or accelerated;

    (2) a brief description of the triggering event;

    (3) the amount of the direct financial obligation, as increased if applicable, and the terms of payment or acceleration that apply; and

    (4) any other material obligations of the registrant that may arise, increase, be accelerated or become direct financial obligations as a result of the triggering event or the increase or acceleration of the direct financial obligation.

(b) If a triggering event occurs causing an obligation of the registrant under an off-balance sheet arrangement to increase or be accelerated, or causing a contingent obligation of the registrant under an off-balance sheet arrangement to become a direct financial obligation of the registrant, and the consequences of the event, taking into account those described in paragraph (b)(4) of this Item 2.04, are material to the registrant, disclose the following information:

    (1) the date of the triggering event and a brief description of the off-balance sheet arrangement;

    (2) a brief description of the triggering event;

    (3) the nature and amount of the obligation, as increased if applicable, and the terms of payment or acceleration that apply; and

    (4) any other material obligations of the registrant that may arise, increase, be accelerated or become direct financial obligations as a result of the triggering event or the increase or acceleration of the obligation under the off-balance sheet arrangement or its becoming a direct financial obligation of the registrant.

(c) For purposes of this Item 2.04, the term direct financial obligation has the meaning provided in Item 2.03 of this form, but shall also include an obligation arising out of an off-balance sheet arrangement that is accrued under FASB Statement of Financial Accounting Standards No. 5 Accounting for Contingencies (SFAS No. 5) as a probable loss contingency.

(d) For purposes of this Item 2.04, the term off-balance sheet arrangement has the meaning provided in Item 2.03 of this form.

(e) For purposes of this Item 2.04, a triggering event is an event, including an event of default, event of acceleration or similar event, as a result of which a direct financial obligation of the registrant or an obligation of the registrant arising under an off-balance sheet arrangement is increased or becomes accelerated or as a result of which a contingent obligation of the registrant arising out of an off-balance sheet arrangement becomes a direct financial obligation of the registrant.

Instructions.

1. Disclosure is required if a triggering event occurs in respect of an obligation of the registrant under an off-balance sheet arrangement and the consequences are material to the registrant,

whether or not the registrant is also a party to the transaction or agreement under which the triggering event occurs.

2. No disclosure is required under this Item 2.04 unless and until a triggering event has occurred in accordance with the terms of the relevant agreement, transaction or arrangement, including, if required, the sending to the registrant of notice of the occurrence of a triggering event pursuant to the terms of the agreement, transaction or arrangement and the satisfaction of all conditions to such occurrence, except the passage of time.

3. No disclosure is required solely by reason of this Item 2.04 if the registrant believes in good faith that no triggering event has occurred, unless the registrant has received a notice described in Instruction 2 to this Item 2.04.

4. Where a registrant is subject to an obligation arising out of an off-balance sheet arrangement, whether or not disclosed pursuant to Item 2.03 of this form, if a triggering event occurs as a result of which under that obligation an accrual for a probable loss is required under SFAS No. 5, the obligation arising out of the off-balance sheet arrangement becomes a direct financial obligation as defined in this Item 2.04. In that situation, if the consequences as determined under Item 2.04(b) are material to the registrant, disclosure is required under this Item 2.04.

Item 2.05 Costs Associated with Exit or Disposal Activities.
If the registrant's board of directors, a committee of the board of directors or the officer or officers of the registrant authorized to take such action if board action is not required, commits the registrant to an exit or disposal plan, or otherwise disposes of a long-lived asset or terminates employees under a plan of termination described in paragraph 8 of FASB Statement of Financial Accounting Standards No. 146 Accounting for Costs Associated with Exit or Disposal Activities (SFAS No. 146), under which material charges will be incurred under generally accepted accounting principles applicable to the registrant, disclose the following information:

(a) the date of the commitment to the course of action and a description of the course of action, including the facts and circumstances leading to the expected action and the expected completion date;

(b) for each major type of cost associated with the course of action (for example, one-time termination benefits, contract termination costs and other associated costs), an estimate of the total amount or range of amounts expected to be incurred in connection with the action;

(c) an estimate of the total amount or range of amounts expected to be incurred in connection with the action; and

(d) the registrant's estimate of the amount or range of amounts of the charge that will result in future cash expenditures,

provided, however, that if the registrant determines that at the time of filing it is unable in good faith to make a determination of an estimate required by paragraphs (b), (c) or (d) of this Item 2.05, no disclosure of such estimate shall be required; *provided further*, however, that in any such event, the registrant shall file an amended report on Form 8-K under this Item 2.05 within four business days after it makes a determination of such an estimate or range of estimates.

Item 2.06 Material Impairments.

If the registrant's board of directors, a committee of the board of directors or the officer or officers of the registrant authorized to take such action if board action is not required, concludes that a material charge for impairment to one or more of its assets, including, without limitation, impairments of securities or goodwill, is required under generally accepted accounting principles applicable to the registrant, disclose the following information:

(a) the date of the conclusion that a material charge is required and a description of the impaired asset or assets and the facts and circumstances leading to the conclusion that the charge for impairment is required;

(b) the registrant's estimate of the amount or range of amounts of the impairment charge; and

(c) the registrant's estimate of the amount or range of amounts of the impairment charge that will result in future cash expenditures,

provided, however, that if the registrant determines that at the time of filing it is unable in good faith to make a determination of an estimate required by paragraphs (b) or (c) of this Item 2.06, no disclosure of such estimate shall be required; *provided further,* however, that in any such event, the registrant shall file an amended report on Form 8-K under this Item 2.06 within four business days after it makes a determination of such an estimate or range of estimates.

Instruction.

No filing is required under this Item 2.06 if the conclusion is made in connection with the preparation, review or audit of financial statements required to be included in the next periodic report due to be filed under the Exchange Act, the periodic report is filed on a timely basis and such conclusion is disclosed in the report.

Section 3 - Securities and Trading Markets

Item 3.01 Notice of Delisting or Failure to Satisfy a Continued Listing Rule or Standard; Transfer of Listing.

(a) If the registrant has received notice from the national securities exchange or national securities association (or a facility thereof) that maintains the principal listing for any class of the registrant's common equity (as defined in Exchange Act Rule 12b-2 that:

- the registrant or such class of the registrant's securities does not satisfy a rule or standard for continued listing on the exchange or association;
- the exchange has submitted an application under Exchange Act Rule 12d2-2 to the Commission to delist such class of the registrant's securities; or
- the association has taken all necessary steps under its rules to delist the security from its automated inter-dealer quotation system,

the registrant must disclose:

    (i) the date that the registrant received the notice;

    (ii) the a rule or standard for continued listing on the national securities exchange or national securities association that the registrant fails, or has failed to, satisfy; and

    (iii) any action or response that, at the time of filing, the registrant has determined to take in response to the notice.

(b) If the registrant has notified the national securities exchange or national securities association (or a facility thereof) that maintains the principal listing for any class of the registrant's common equity (as defined in Exchange Act Rule 12b-2 that the registrant is aware of any material noncompliance with a rule or standard for continued listing on the exchange or association, the registrant must disclose:

    (i) the date that the registrant provided such notice to the exchange or association;

    (ii) the rule or standard for continued listing on the exchange or association that the registrant fails, or has failed, to satisfy; and

    (iii) any action or response that, at the time of filing, the registrant has determined to take regarding its noncompliance.

(c) If the national securities exchange or national securities association (or a facility thereof) that maintains the principal listing for any class of the registrant's common equity (as defined in Exchange Act Rule 12b-2, in lieu of suspending trading in or delisting such class of the registrant's securities, issues a public reprimand letter or similar communication indicating that the registrant has violated a rule or standard for continued listing on the exchange or association, the registrant must state the date, and summarize the contents of the letter or communication.

(d) If the registrant's board of directors, a committee of the board of directors or the officer or officers of the registrant authorized to take such action if board action is not required, has taken definitive action to cause the listing of a class of its common equity to be withdrawn from the national securities exchange, or terminated from the automated inter-dealer quotation system of a registered national securities association, where such exchange or association maintains the principal listing, for such class of securities, including by reason of a transfer of the listing or quotation to another securities exchange or quotation system, describe the action taken and state the date of the action.

Instructions.

1. The registrant is not required to disclose any information required by paragraph (a) of this Item 3.01 where the delisting is a result of one of the following:

- the entire class of the security has been called for redemption, maturity or retirement; appropriate notice thereof has been given; if required by the terms of the securities, funds sufficient for the payment of all such securities have been deposited with an agency authorized to make such payments; and such funds have been made available to security holders;

- the entire class of the security has been redeemed or paid at maturity or retirement;

- the instruments representing the entire class of securities have come to evidence, by operation of law or otherwise, other securities in substitution therefore and represent no other right, except, if true, the right to receive an immediate cash payment (the right of dissenters to receive the appraised or fair value of their holdings shall not prevent the application of this provision); or

- all rights pertaining to the entire class of the security have been extinguished; *provided, however,* that where such an event occurs as the result of an order of a court or other governmental authority, the order shall be final, all applicable appeal periods shall have expired and no appeals shall be pending.

2. A registrant must provide the disclosure required by paragraph (a) or (b) of this Item 3.01, as applicable, regarding any failure to satisfy a rule or standard for continued listing on the national securities exchange or national securities association (or a facility thereof) that maintains the principal listing for any class of the registrant's common equity (as defined in Exchange Act Rule 12b-2 even if the registrant has the benefit of a grace period or similar extension period during which it may cure the deficiency that triggers the disclosure requirement.

3. Notices or other communications subsequent to an initial notice sent to, or by, a registrant under Item 3.01(a), (b) or (c) that continue to indicate that the registrant does not comply with the same rule or standard for continued listing that was the subject of the initial notice are not required to be filed, but may be filed voluntarily.

4. Registrants whose securities are quoted exclusively (i.e., the securities are not otherwise listed on an exchange or association) on automated inter-dealer quotation systems are not subject to this Item 3.01 and such registrants are thus not required to file a Form 8-K pursuant to this Item 3.01 if the securities are no longer quoted on such quotation system. If a security is listed on an exchange or association and is also quoted on an automated inter-dealer quotation system, the registrant is subject to the disclosure obligations of Item 3.01 if any of the events specified in Item 3.01 occur.

Item 3.02 Unregistered Sales of Equity Securities.

(a) If the registrant sells equity securities in a transaction that is not registered under the Securities Act, furnish the information set forth in paragraphs (a) and (c) through (e) of Item 701 of Regulation S-K. For purposes of determining the required filing date for the Form 8-K under this Item 3.02(a), the registrant has no obligation to disclose information under this Item 3.02 until the registrant enters into an agreement enforceable against the registrant, whether or not subject to conditions, under which the equity securities are to be sold. If there is no such agreement, the registrant must provide the disclosure within four business days after the occurrence of the closing or settlement of the transaction or arrangement under which the equity securities are to be sold.

(b) No report need be filed under this Item 3.02 if the equity securities sold, in the aggregate since its last report filed under this Item 3.02 or its last periodic report, whichever is more recent, constitute less than 1% of the number of shares outstanding of the class of equity securities sold. In the case of a smaller reporting company, no report need be filed if the equity securities sold, in the aggregate since its last report filed under this Item 3.02 or its last periodic report, whichever is more recent, constitute less than 5% of the number of shares outstanding of the class of equity securities sold.

Instructions.

1. For purposes of this Item 3.02, "the number of shares outstanding" refers to the actual number of shares of equity securities of the class outstanding and does not include outstanding securities convertible into or exchangeable for such equity securities.

2. Smaller reporting company is defined in Item 10(f)(1) of Regulation S-K.

Item 3.03 Material Modification to Rights of Security Holders.

(a) If the constituent instruments defining the rights of the holders of any class of registered securities of the registrant have been materially modified, disclose the date of the modification, the title of the class of securities involved and briefly describe the general effect of such modification upon the rights of holders of such securities.

(b) If the rights evidenced by any class of registered securities have been materially limited or qualified by the issuance or modification of any other class of securities by the registrant, briefly disclose the date of the issuance or modification, the general effect of the issuance or modification of such other class of securities upon the rights of the holders of the registered securities.

Instruction.

Working capital restrictions and other limitations upon the payment of dividends must be reported pursuant to this Item 3.03.

Section 4 - Matters Related to Accountants and Financial Statements

Item 4.01 Changes in Registrant's Certifying Accountant.

(a) If an independent accountant who was previously engaged as the principal accountant to audit the registrant's financial statements, or an independent accountant upon whom the principal accountant expressed reliance in its report regarding a significant subsidiary, resigns (or indicates that it declines to stand for re-appointment after completion of the current audit) or is dismissed, disclose the information required by Item 304(a)(1) of Regulation S-K, including compliance with Item 304(a)(3) of Regulation S-K.

(b) If a new independent accountant has been engaged as either the principal accountant to audit the registrant's financial statements or as an independent accountant on whom the principal accountant is expected to express reliance in its report regarding a significant subsidiary, the registrant must disclose the information required by Item 304(a)(2) of Regulation S-K.

Instruction.

The resignation or dismissal of an independent accountant, or its refusal to stand for re-appointment, is a reportable event separate from the engagement of a new independent accountant. On some occasions, two reports on Form 8-K are required for a single change in accountants, the first on the resignation (or refusal to stand for re-appointment) or dismissal of the former accountant and the second when the new accountant is engaged. Information required in the second Form 8-K in such situations need not be provided to the extent that it has been reported previously in the first Form 8-K.

Item 4.02 Non-Reliance on Previously Issued Financial Statements or a Related Audit Report or Completed Interim Review.

(a) If the registrant's board of directors, a committee of the board of directors or the officer or officers of the registrant authorized to take such action if board action is not required, concludes that any previously issued financial statements, covering one or more years or interim periods for which the registrant is required to provide financial statements under Regulation S-X should no longer be relied upon because of an error in such financial statements as addressed in Accounting Principles Board Opinion No. 20, as may be modified, supplemented or succeeded, disclose the following information:

    (1) the date of the conclusion regarding the non-reliance and an identification of the financial statements and years or periods covered that should no longer be relied upon;

    (2) a brief description of the facts underlying the conclusion to the extent known to the registrant at the time of filing; and

    (3) a statement of whether the audit committee, or the board of directors in the absence of an audit committee, or authorized officer or officers, discussed with the registrant's independent accountant the matters disclosed in the filing pursuant to this Item 4.02(a).

(b) If the registrant is advised by, or receives notice from, its independent accountant that disclosure should be made or action should be taken to prevent future reliance on a previously issued audit report or completed interim review related to previously issued financial statements, disclose the following information:

    (1) the date on which the registrant was so advised or notified;

    (2) identification of the financial statements that should no longer be relied upon;

    (3) a brief description of the information provided by the accountant; and

    (4) a statement of whether the audit committee, or the board of directors in the absence of an audit committee, or authorized officer or officers, discussed with the independent accountant the matters disclosed in the filing pursuant to this Item 4.02(b).

(c) If the registrant receives advisement or notice from its independent accountant requiring disclosure under paragraph (b) of this Item 4.02, the registrant must:

    (1) provide the independent accountant with a copy of the disclosures it is making in response to this item 4.02 that the independent accountant shall receive no later than the day that the disclosures are filed with the Commission;

    (2) request the independent accountant to furnish to the registrant as promptly as possible a letter addressed to the Commission stating whether the independent accountant agrees with the statements made by the registrant in

response to this Item 4.02 and, if not, stating the respects in which it does not agree; and

(3) amend the registrant's previously filed Form 8-K by filing the independent accountant's letter as an exhibit to the filed Form 8-K no later than two business days after the registrant's receipt of the letter.

Section 5 - Corporate Governance and Management

Item 5.01 Changes in Control of Registrant.

(a) If, to the knowledge of the registrant's board of directors, a committee of the board of directors or authorized officer or officers of the registrant, a change in control of the registrant has occurred, furnish the following information:

(1) the identity of the person(s) who acquired such control;

(2) the date and a description of the transaction(s) which resulted in the change in control;

(3) the basis of the control, including the percentage of voting securities of the registrant now beneficially owned directly or indirectly by the person(s) who acquired control;

(4) the amount of the consideration used by such person(s);

(5) the source(s) of funds used by the person(s), unless all or any part of the consideration used is a loan made in the ordinary course of business by a bank as defined by Section 3(a)(6) of the Act, in which case the identity of such bank may be omitted provided the person who acquired control:

(i) has made a request for confidentiality pursuant to Section 13(d)(1)(B) of the Act; and

(ii) states in the report that the identity of the bank has been so omitted and filed separately with the Commission.

(6) the identity of the person(s) from whom control was assumed; and

(7) any arrangements or understandings among members of both the former and new control groups and their associates with respect to election of directors or other matters.

(b) Furnish the information required by Item 403(c) of Regulation S-K.

Item 5.02 Departure of Directors or Principal Officers; Election of Directors; Appointment of Principal Officers.

(a)(1) If a director has resigned or refuses to stand for re-election to the board of directors since the date of the last annual meeting of shareholders because of a disagreement with the registrant, known to an executive officer of the registrant, as defined in Rule 3b-7, on any matter relating to the registrant's operations, policies or practices, or if a director has been removed for cause from the board of directors, disclose the following information:

(i) the date of such resignation, refusal to stand for re-election or removal;

(ii) any positions held by the director on any committee of the board of directors at the time of the director's resignation, refusal to stand for re-election or removal; and

(2) a brief description of the circumstances representing the disagreement that the registrant believes caused, in whole or in part, the director's resignation, refusal to stand for re-election or removal.If the director has furnished the registrant with any written correspondence concerning the circumstances surrounding his or her resignation, refusal or removal, the registrant shall file a copy of the document as an exhibit to the report on Form 8-K.

(3) The registrant also must:

    (i) provide the director with a copy of the disclosures it is making in response to this Item 5.02 no later than the day the registrant files the disclosures with the Commission;

    (ii) provide the director with the opportunity to furnish the registrant as promptly as possible with a letter addressed to the registrant stating whether he or she agrees with the statements made by the registrant in response to this Item 5.02 and, if not, stating the respects in which he or she does not agree; and

    (iii) file any letter received by the registrant from the director with the Commission as an exhibit by an amendment to the previously filed Form 8-K within two business days after receipt by the registrant.

(b) If the registrant's principal executive officer, president, principal financial officer, principal accounting officer, principal operating officer, or any person performing similar functions, or any named executive officer, retires, resigns or is terminated from that position, or if a director retires, resigns, is removed, or refuses to stand for re-election (except in circumstances described in paragraph (a) of this Item 5.02), disclose the fact that the event has occurred and the date of the event.

(c) If the registrant appoints a new principal executive officer, president, principal financial officer, principal accounting officer, principal operating officer, or person performing similar functions, disclose the following information with respect to the newly appointed officer:

(1) the name and position of the newly appointed officer and the date of the appointment;

(2) the information required by Items 401(b), (d), (e) and Item 404(a) of Regulation S-K; and

(3) a brief description of any material plan, contract or arrangement (whether or not written) to which a covered officer is a party or in which he or she participates that is entered into or material amendment in connection with the triggering event or any grant or award to any such covered person or modification thereto, under any such plan, contract or arrangement in connection with any such event.

Instruction to paragraph (c).

If the registrant intends to make a public announcement of the appointment other than by means of a report on Form 8-K, the registrant may delay filing the Form 8-K containing the disclosures required by this Item 5.02(c) until the day on which the registrant otherwise makes public announcement of the appointment of such officer.

(d) If the registrant elects a new director, except by a vote of security holders at an annual meeting or special meeting convened for such purpose, disclose the following information:

(1) the name of the newly elected director and the date of election;

(2) a brief description of any arrangement or understanding between the new director and any other persons, naming such persons, pursuant to which such director was selected as a director;

(3) the committees of the board of directors to which the new director has been, or at the time of this disclosure is expected to be, named; and

(4) the information required by Item 404(a) of Regulation S-K.

(5) a brief description of any material plan, contract or arrangement (whether or not written) to which the director is a party or in which he or she participates that is entered into or material amendment in connection with the triggering event or any grant or award to any such covered person or modification thereto, under any such plan, contract or arrangement in connection with any such event.

(e) If the registrant enters into, adopts, or otherwise commences a material compensatory plan, contract or arrangement (whether or not written), as to which the registrant's principal executive officer, principal financial officer, or a named executive officer participates or is a party, or such compensatory plan, contract or arrangement is materially amended or modified, or a material grant or award under any such plan, contract or arrangement to any such person is made or materially modified, then the registrant shall provide a brief description of the terms and conditions of the plan, contract or arrangement and the amounts payable to the officer thereunder.

Instructions to paragraph (e).

(1) Disclosure under this Item 5.02(e) shall be required whether or not the specified event is in connection with events otherwise triggering disclosure pursuant to this Item 5.02.

(2) Grants or awards (or modifications thereto) made pursuant to a plan, contract or arrangement (whether involving cash or equity), that are materially consistent with the previously disclosed terms of such plan, contract or arrangement, need not be disclosed under this Item 5.02(e), provided the registrant has previously disclosed such terms and the grant, award or modification is disclosed when Item 402 of Regulation S-K requires such disclosure.

(f) If the salary or bonus of a named executive officer cannot be calculated as of the most recent practicable date and is omitted from the Summary Compensation Table as specified in Instruction 1 to Item 402(c)(2)(iii) and (iv) of Regulation S-K, disclose the appropriate information under this Item 5.02(f) when there is a payment, grant, award, decision or other occurrence as a result of which such amounts become calculable in whole or part. Disclosure under this Item 5.02(f) shall include a new total compensation figure for the named executive officer, using the new salary or bonus information to recalculate the information that was previously provided with respect to the named executive officer in the registrant's Summary Compensation Table for which the salary and bonus information was omitted in reliance on Instruction 1 to Item 402(c)(2)(iii) and (iv) of Regulation S-K.

Instructions to Item 5.02.

1. The disclosure requirements of this Item 5.02 do not apply to a registrant that is a wholly-owned subsidiary of an issuer with a class of securities registered under Section 12 of the Exchange Act, or that is required to file reports under Section 15(d) of the Exchange Act.

2. To the extent that any information called for in Item 5.02(c)(3) or Item 5.02(d)(3) or Item 5.02(d)(4) is not determined or is unavailable at the time of the required filing, the registrant shall include a statement to this effect in the filing and then must file an amendment to its Form 8-K filing under this Item 5.02 containing such information within four business days after the information is determined or becomes available.

3. The registrant need not provide information with respect to plans, contracts, and arrangements to the extent they do not discriminate in scope, terms or operation, in favor of executive officers or directors of the registrant and that are available generally to all salaried employees.

4. For purposes of this Item, the term "named executive officer" shall refer to those executive officers for whom disclosure was required in the registrant's most recent filing with the Commission under the Securities Act or Exchange Act that required disclosure pursuant to Item 402(c) of Regulation S-K.

Item 5.03 Amendments to Articles of Incorporation or Bylaws; Change in Fiscal Year.

    (a) If a registrant with a class of equity securities registered under Section 12 of the Exchange Act amends its articles of incorporation or bylaws and a proposal for the amendment was not disclosed in a proxy statement or information statement filed by the registrant, disclose the following information:

        (1) the effective date of the amendment; and

        (2) a description of the provision adopted or changed by amendment and, if applicable, the previous provision.

    (b) If the registrant determines to change the fiscal year from that used in its most recent filing with the Commission other than by means of:

        (1) a submission to a vote of security holders through the solicitation of proxies or otherwise; or

        (2) an amendment to its articles of incorporation or bylaws,

disclose the date of such determination, the date of the new fiscal year end and the form (for example, Form 10-K or Form 10-Q) on which the report covering the transition period will be filed.

Instruction to Item 5.03.

Refer to Item 601(b)(3) of Regulation S-K regarding the filing of exhibits to this Item 5.03.

Item 5.04 Temporary Suspension of Trading Under Registrant's Employee Benefit Plans.

(a) No later than the fourth business day after which the registrant receives the notice required by section 101(i)(2)(E) of the Employment Retirement Income Security Act of 1974, or, if such notice is not received by the registrant, on the same date by which the registrant transmits a timely notice to an affected officer or director within the time period prescribed by Rule 104(b)(2)(i)(B) or 104(b)(2)(ii) of Regulation BTR, provide the information specified in Rule 104(b) and the date the registrant received the notice required by section 101(i)(2)(E) of the Employment Retirement Income Security Act of 1974, if applicable.

(b) On the same date by which the registrant transmits a timely updated notice to an affected officer or director, as required by the time period under Rule 104(b)(2)(iii) of Regulation BTR, provide the information specified in Rule 104(b)(3)(iii).

Item 5.05 Amendments to the Registrant's Code of Ethics, or Waiver of a Provision of the Code of Ethics.

(a) Briefly describe the date and nature of any amendment to a provision of the registrant's code of ethics that applies to the registrant's principal executive officer, principal financial officer, principal accounting officer or controller or persons performing similar functions and that relates to any element of the code of ethics definition enumerated in Item 406(b) of Regulation S-K.

(b) If the registrant has granted a waiver, including an implicit waiver, from a provision of the code of ethics to an officer or person described in paragraph (a) of this Item 5.05, and the waiver relates to one or more of the elements of the code of ethics definition referred to in paragraph (a) of this Item 5.05, briefly describe the nature of the waiver, the name of the person to whom the waiver was granted, and the date of the waiver.

(c) The registrant does not need to provide any information pursuant to this Item 5.05 if it discloses the required information on its Internet website within four business days following the date of the amendment or waiver and the registrant has disclosed in its most recently filed annual report its Internet address and intention to provide disclosure in this manner. If the registrant elects to disclose the information required by this Item 5.05 through its website, such information must remain available on the website for at least a 12-month period. Following the 12-month period, the registrant must retain the information for a period of not less than five years. Upon request, the registrant must furnish to the Commission or its staff a copy of any or all information retained pursuant to this requirement.

Instructions.

1. The registrant does not need to disclose technical, administrative or other non-substantive amendments to its code of ethics.

2. For purposes of this Item 5.05:
(i)   The term waiver means the approval by the registrant of a material departure from a provision of the code of ethics; and
(ii)   The term implicit waiver means the registrant's failure to take action within a reasonable period of time regarding a material departure from a provision of the code of ethics that has been made known to an executive officer, as defined in Rule 3b-7 of the registrant.

* * *

Item 5.07 Submission of Matters to a Vote of Security Holders. If any matter was submitted to a vote of security holders, through the solicitation of proxies or otherwise, provide the following information:

(a) The date of the meeting and whether it was an annual or special meeting. This information must be provided only if a meeting of security holders was held

(b) If the meeting involved the election of directors, the name of each director elected at the meeting, as well as a brief description of each other matter voted upon at the meeting; and state the number of votes cast for, against or withheld, as well as the number of abstentions and broker non-votes as to each such matter, including a separate tabulation with respect to each nominee for office.

(c) A description of the terms of any settlement between the registrant and any other participant (as defined in Instruction 3 to Item 4 of Schedule 14A) terminating any solicitation subject to Rule 14a-12(c), including the cost or anticipated cost to the registrant.

Instruction 1 to Item 5.07. The four business day period for reporting the event under this Item 5.07 shall begin to run on the day on which the meeting ended. The registrant shall disclose on Form 8-K under this Item 5.07 the preliminary voting results. The registrant shall file an amended report on Form 8-K under this Item 5.07 to disclose the final voting results within four business days after the final voting results are known. *However*, no preliminary voting results need be disclosed under this Item 5.07 if the registrant has disclosed final voting results on Form 8-K under this Item.
Instruction 2 to Item 5.07. If any matter has been submitted to a vote of security holders otherwise than at a meeting of such security holders, corresponding information with respect to such submission shall be provided. The solicitation of any authorization or consent (other than a proxy to vote at a stockholders' meeting) with respect to any matter shall be deemed a submission of such matter to a vote of security holders within the meaning of this item.
Instruction 3 to Item 5.07. If the registrant did not solicit proxies and the board of directors as previously reported to the Commission was re-elected in its entirety, a statement to that effect in answer to paragraph (b) will suffice as an answer thereto regarding the election of directors.
Instruction 4 to Item 5.07. If the registrant has furnished to its security holders proxy soliciting material containing the information called for by paragraph (c), the paragraph may be answered by reference to the information contained in such material.
Instruction 5 to Item 5.07. A registrant may omit the information called for by this Item 5.07 if, on the date of the filing of its report on Form 8-K, the registrant meets the following conditions:

1. All of the registrant's equity securities are owned, either directly or indirectly, by a single person which is a reporting company under the Exchange Act and which has filed all the material required to be filed pursuant to Section 13, 14 or 15(d) thereof, as applicable; and

2. During the preceding thirty-six calendar months and any subsequent period of days, there has not been any material default in the payment of principal, interest, a sinking or purchase fund installment, or any other material default not cured within thirty days, with respect to any indebtedness of the registrant or its subsidiaries, and there has not been any material default in the payment of rentals under material long-term leases."

Section 6 - [Reserved]

Section 7 - Regulation FD

Item 7.01 Regulation FD Disclosure.
Unless filed under Item 8.01, disclose under this item only information that the registrant elects to disclose through Form 8-K pursuant to Regulation FD.

Section 8 - Other Events

Item 8.01 Other Events.
The registrant may, at its option, disclose under this Item 8.01 any events, with respect to which information is not otherwise called for by this form, that the registrant deems of importance to security holders. The registrant may, at its option, file a report under this Item 8.01 disclosing the nonpublic information required to be disclosed by Regulation FD.

Section 9 - Financial Statements and Exhibits

Item 9.01 Financial Statements and Exhibits.
List below the financial statements, pro forma financial information and exhibits, if any, filed as a part of this report.

(a) Financial statements of businesses acquired.

(1) For any business acquisition required to be described in answer to Item 2.01 of this form, financial statements of the business acquired shall be filed for the periods specified in Rule 3-05(b) of Regulation S-X.

(2) The financial statements shall be prepared pursuant to Regulation S-X except that supporting schedules need not be filed. A manually signed accountant's report should be provided pursuant to Rule 2-02 of Regulation S-X.

(3) With regard to the acquisition of one or more real estate properties, the financial statements and any additional information specified by Rule 3-14 of Regulation S-X shall be filed.

(4) Financial statements required by this item may be filed with the initial report, or by amendment not later than 71 calendar days after the date that the initial report on Form 8-K must be filed. If the financial statements are not included in the initial report, the registrant should so indicate in the Form 8-K report and state when the required financial statements will be filed. The

registrant may, at its option, include unaudited financial statements in the initial report on Form 8-K.

(b) Pro forma financial information.

    (1) For any transaction required to be described in answer to Item 2.01 of this form, furnish any pro forma financial information that would be required pursuant to Article 11 of Regulation S-X.

    (2) The provisions of paragraph (a)(4) of this Item 9.01 shall also apply to pro forma financial information relative to the acquired business.

* * *

(d) Exhibits. The exhibits shall be deemed to be filed or furnished, depending on the relevant item requiring such exhibit, in accordance with the provisions of Item 601 of Regulation S-K and Instruction B.2 to this form.

Instruction.

During the period after a registrant has reported a business combination pursuant to Item 2.01 of this form, until the date on which the financial statements specified by this Item 9.01 must be filed, the registrant will be deemed current for purposes of its reporting obligations under Section 13(a) or 15(d) of the Exchange Act. With respect to filings under the Securities Act, however, registration statements will not be declared effective and post-effective amendments to registrations statements will not be declared effective unless financial statements meeting the requirements of Rule 3-05 of Regulation S-X are provided. In addition, offerings should not be made pursuant to effective registration statements, or pursuant to Rules 505 and 506 of Regulation D where any purchasers are not accredited investors under Rule 501(a) of that Regulation, until the audited financial statements required by Rule 3-05 of Regulation S-X are filed; *provided, however*, that the following offerings or sales of securities may proceed notwithstanding that financial statements of the acquired business have not been filed:

    (a) offerings or sales of securities upon the conversion of outstanding convertible securities or upon the exercise of outstanding warrants or rights;

    (b) dividend or interest reinvestment plans;

    (c) employee benefit plans;

    (d) transactions involving secondary offerings; or

    (e) sales of securities pursuant to Rule 144.

SIGNATURES

Pursuant to the requirements of the Securities Exchange Act of 1934, the registrant has duly caused this report to be signed on its behalf by the undersigned hereunto duly authorized.

_____
(Registrant)

Date _____   _____

(Signature)*

*Print name and title of the signing officer under his signature.

**UNITED STATES
SECURITIES AND EXCHANGE COMMISSION
Washington, D.C. 20549**

FORM 10

GENERAL FORM FOR REGISTRATION OF SECURITIES
Pursuant to Section 12(b) or (g) of The Securities Exchange Act of 1934

_____

(Exact name of registrant as specified in its charter)

(State or other jurisdiction of incorporation or organization)	(I.R.S. Employer Identification No.)

(Address of principal executive offices)   (Zip Code)

Registrant's telephone number, including area code _____

Securities to be registered pursuant to Section 12(b) of the Act:

Title of each class to be so registered	Name of each exchange on which each class is to be registered

Securities to be registered pursuant to Section 12(g) of the Act:

_____

(Title of class)

_____

(Title of class)

INFORMATION REQUIRED IN REGISTRATION STATEMENT

Item 1.   Business.

Furnish the information required by Item 101 of Regulation S-K.

Item 1A.   Risk Factors.

Set forth, under the caption "Risk Factors," where appropriate, the risk factors described in Item 503(c) of Regulation S-K applicable to the registrant. Provide any discussion of risk factors in plain English in accordance with Rule 421(d) of the Securities Act of 1933.

Item 2.   Financial Information.

Furnish the information required by Items 301, 303, and 305 of Regulation S-K.

Item 3.   Properties.

Furnish the information required by Item 102 of Regulation S-K.

Item 4.   Security Ownership of Certain Beneficial Owners and Management.

Furnish the information required by Item 403 of Regulation S-K.

Item 5.   Directors and Executive Officers.

Furnish the information required by Item 401 of Regulation S-K.

Item 6.   Executive Compensation.

Furnish the information required by Item 402 of Regulation S-K and paragraph (e)(4) of Item 407 of Regulation S-K.

Item 7.   Certain Relationships and Related Transactions.

Furnish the information required by Item 404 of Regulation S-K and Item 407(a) of Regulation S-K.

Item 8.   Legal Proceedings.

Furnish the information required by Item 103 of Regulation S-K.

Item 9.   Market Price of and Dividends on the Registrant's Common Equity and Related Stockholder Matters.

Furnish the information required by Item 201 of Regulation S-K.

Item 10.   Recent Sales of Unregistered Securities.

Furnish the information required by item 701 of Regulation S-K.

Item 11.   Description of Registrant's Securities to be Registered.

Furnish the information required by Item 202 of Regulation S-K. If the class of securities to be registered will trade in the form of American Depositary Receipts, furnish Item 202(f) disclosure for such American Depositary Receipts as well.

Item 12.   Indemnification of Directors and Officers.

Furnish the information required by Item 702 of Regulation S-K.

Item 13.   Financial Statements and Supplementary Data.

Furnish all financial statements required by Regulation S-X and the supplementary financial information required by Item 302 of Regulation S-K.

Item 14.   Changes in and Disagreements with Accountants on Accounting and Financial Disclosure.

Furnish the information required by Item 304 of Regulation S-K.

Item 15   Financial Statements and Exhibits.

(a)   List separately all financial statements filed as part of the registration statement.
(b)   Furnish the exhibits required by Item 601 of Regulation S-K.

SIGNATURES

Pursuant to the requirements of Section 12 of the Securities Exchange Act of 1934, the registrant has duly caused this registration statement to be signed on its behalf by the undersigned, thereunto duly authorized.

_____
(Registrant)

Date:_____   By:_____
(Signature)*

*Print name and title of the signing officer under his signature.

GENERAL INSTRUCTIONS

A.   Rule as to Use of Form 10.

Form 10 shall be used for registration pursuant to Section 12(b) or (g) of the Securities Exchange Act of 1934 of classes of securities of issuers for which no other form is prescribed.

B. **Application of General Rules and Regulations.**

(a) The General Rules and Regulations under the Act contain certain general requirements which are applicable to registration on any form. These general requirements should be carefully read and observed in the preparation and filing of registration statements on this form.

(b) Particular attention is directed to Regulation 12B which contains general requirements regarding matters such as the kind and size of paper to be used, the legibility of the registration statement, the information to be given whenever the title of securities is required to be stated, and the filing of the registration statement. The definitions contained in Rule 12b-2 should be especially noted.

C. **Preparation of Registration Statement.**

(a) This form is not to be used as a blank form to be filled in, but only as a guide in the preparation of the registration statement on paper meeting the requirements of Rule 12b-12. The registration statement shall contain the item numbers and captions, but the text of the items may be omitted. The answers to the items shall be prepared in the manner specified in Rule 12b-13.

(b) Unless otherwise stated, the information required shall be given as of a date reasonably close to the date of filing the registration statement.

(c) Attention is directed to Rule 12b-20 which states: "In addition to the information expressly required to be included in a statement or report, there shall be added such further material information, if any, as may be necessary to make the required statements, in light of the circumstances under which they are made, not misleading.

D. **Signature and Filing of Registration Statement.**

Three complete copies of the registration statement, including financial statements, exhibits and all other papers and documents filed as a part thereof, and five additional copies which need not include exhibits, shall be filed with the Commission. At least one complete copy of the registration statement, including financial statements, exhibits and all other papers and documents filed as a part thereof, shall be filed with each exchange on which any class of securities is to be registered. At least one complete copy of the registration statement filed with the Commission and one such copy filed with each exchange shall be manually signed. Copies not manually signed shall bear typed or printed signatures.

E. **Omission of Information Regarding Foreign Subsidiaries.**

Information required by any item or other requirement of this form with respect to any foreign subsidiary may be omitted to the extent that the required disclosure would be detrimental to the registrant. However, financial statements, otherwise required, shall not be omitted pursuant to this instruction. Where information is omitted pursuant to this instruction, a statement shall be made that such information has been omitted and the names of the subsidiaries involved shall be separately furnished to the Commission. The Commission may, in its discretion, call for justification that the required disclosure would be detrimental.

F.   **Incorporation by Reference.**

Attention is directed to Rule 12b-23 which provides for the incorporation by reference of information contained in certain documents in answer or partial answer to any item of a registration statement.

**UNITED STATES
SECURITIES AND EXCHANGE COMMISSION
Washington, D.C. 20549**

FORM 10-K

ANNUAL REPORT PURSUANT TO SECTION 13 OR 15(d)
OF THE SECURITIES EXCHANGE ACT OF 1934

GENERAL INSTRUCTIONS

A.   **Rule as to Use of Form 10-K.**

(1)   This Form shall be used for annual reports pursuant to Section 13 or 15(d) of the Securities Exchange Act of 1934 (the "Act") for which no other form is prescribed. This Form also shall be used for transition reports filed pursuant to Section 13 or 15(d) of the Act

(2)   Annual reports on this Form shall be filed within the following period:

(a)   60 days after the end of the fiscal year covered by the report (75 days for fiscal years ending before December 15, 2006) for large accelerated filers (as defined in Rule 12b-2):

(b)   75 days after the end of the fiscal year covered by the report for accelerated filers (as defined in Rule 12b-2); and

(c)   90 days after the end of the fiscal year covered by the report for all other registrants.

(3)   Transition reports on this Form shall be filed in accordance with the requirements set forth in Rule 13a-10 or Rule 15d-10 applicable when the registrant changes its fiscal year end.

(4)   Notwithstanding paragraphs (2) and (3) of this General Instruction A., all schedules required by Article 12 of Regulation S-X may, at the option of the registrant, be filed as an amendment to the report not later than 30 days after the applicable due date of the report.

B.   **Application of General Rules and Regulations.**

(1)   The General Rules and Regulations under the Act contain certain general requirements which are applicable to reports on any form. These general requirements should be carefully read and observed in the preparation and filing of reports on this Form.

(2)   Particular attention is directed to Regulation 12B which contains general requirements regarding matters such as the kind and size of paper to be used, the legibility of the report, the information to be given whenever the title of securities is required to be stated, and the filing of the report. The definitions contained in Rule 12b-2 should be especially noted. *See also* Regulations 13A and 15D.

C.   Preparation of Report.

(1) This form is not to be used as a blank form to be filled in, but only as a guide in the preparation of the report on paper meeting the requirements of Rule 12b-12. Except as provided in General Instruction G, the answers to the items shall be prepared in the manner specified in Rule 12b-13.

(2) Except where information is required to be given for the fiscal year or as of a specified date, it shall be given as of the latest practicable date.

(3) Attention is directed to Rule 12b-20, which states: "In addition to the information expressly required to be included in a statement or report, there shall be added such further material information, if any, as may be necessary to make the required statements, in the light of the circumstances under which they are made, not misleading."

D.   Signature and Filing of Report.

(1) Three complete copies of the report, including financial statements, financial statement schedules, exhibits, and all other papers and documents filed as a part thereof, and five additional copies which need not include exhibits, shall be filed with the Commission. At least one complete copy of the report, including financial statements, financial statement schedules, exhibits, and all other papers and documents filed as a part thereof, shall be filed with each exchange on which any class of securities of the registrant is registered. At least one complete copy of the report filed with the Commission and one such copy filed with each exchange shall be manually signed. Copies not manually signed shall bear typed or printed signatures.

(2) (a) The report must be signed by the registrant, and on behalf of the registrant by its principal executive officer or officers, its principal financial officer or officers, its controller or principal accounting officer, and by at least the majority of the board of directors or persons performing similar functions. Where the registrant is a limited partnership, the report must be signed by the majority of the board of directors of any corporate general partner who signs the report.

(b) The name of each person who signs the report shall be typed or printed beneath his signature. Any person who occupies more than one of the specified positions shall indicate each capacity in which he signs the report. Attention is directed to Rule 12b-11 concerning manual signatures and signatures pursuant to powers of attorney.

(3) Registrants are requested to indicate in a transmittal letter with the Form 10-K whether the financial statements in the report reflect a change from the preceding year in any accounting principles or practices, or in the method of applying any such principles or practices.

E.   Disclosure With Respect to Foreign Subsidiaries.

Information required by any item or other requirement of this form with respect to any foreign subsidiary may be omitted to the extent that the required disclosure would be detrimental to the registrant. However, financial statements and financial statement schedules, otherwise required, shall not be omitted pursuant to this Instruction. Where information is omitted pursuant to this Instruction, a statement shall be made that such information has been omitted and the names of the subsidiaries involved shall be separately furnished to the Commission. The Commission may, in its discretion, call for justification that the required disclosure would be detrimental.

F.   Information as to Employee Stock Purchase, Savings and Similar Plans.

Attention is directed to Rule 15d-21 which provides that separate annual and other reports need not be filed pursuant to Section 15(d) of the Act with respect to any employee stock purchase, savings or similar plan if the issuer of the stock or other securities offered to employees pursuant to the plan furnishes to the Commission the information and documents specified in the Rule.

G.   Information to be Incorporated by Reference.

(1)   Attention is directed to Rule 12b-23 which provides for the incorporation by reference of information contained in certain documents in answer or partial answer to any item of a report.

(2)   The information called for by Parts I and II of this form (Items 1 through 9A or any portion thereof) may, at the registrant's option, be incorporated by reference from the registrant's annual report to security holders furnished to the Commission pursuant to Rule 14a-3(b) or Rule 14c-3(a) or from the registrant's annual report to security holders, even if not furnished to the Commission pursuant to Rule 14a-3(b) or 14c-3(a), provided such annual report contains the information required by Rule 14a-3.
Note 1. In order to fulfill the requirements of Part I of Form 10-K, the incorporated portion of the annual report to security holders must contain the information required by Items 1-3 of Form 10-K; to the extent applicable.
Note 2. If any information required by Part I or Part II is incorporated by reference into an electronic format document from the annual report to security holders as provided in General Instruction G, any portion of the annual report to security holders incorporated by reference shall be filed as an exhibit in electronic format, as required by Item 601(b)(13) of Regulation S-K.

(3)   The information required by Part III (Items 10, 11, 12, 13 and 14) may be incorporated by reference from the registrant's definitive proxy statement (filed or required to be filed pursuant to Regulation 14A) or definitive information statement (filed or to be filed pursuant to Regulation 14C) which involves the election of directors, if such definitive proxy statement or information statement is filed with the Commission not later than 120 days after the end of the fiscal year covered by the Form 10-K. However, if such definitive proxy statement or

information statement is not filed with the Commission in the 120-day period or is not required to be filed with the Commission by virtue of Rule 3a12-3(b) under the Exchange Act, the Items comprising the Part III information must be filed as part of the Form 10-K, or as an amendment to the Form 10-K, not later than the end of the 120-day period. It should be noted that the information regarding executive officers required by Item 401 of Regulation S-K (may be included in Part I of Form 10-K under an appropriate caption. See Instruction 3 to Item 401(b) of Regulation S-K.

(4) No item numbers of captions of items need be contained in the material incorporated by reference into the report. However, the registrant's attention is directed to Rule 12b-23(e) regarding the specific disclosure required in the report concerning information incorporated by reference. When the registrant combines all of the information in Parts I and II of this Form (Items 1 through 9A) by incorporation by reference from the registrant's annual report to security holders and all of the information in Part III of this Form (Items 10 through 14) by incorporating by reference from a definitive proxy statement or information statement involving the election of directors, then, notwithstanding General Instruction C(1), this Form shall consist of the facing or cover page, those sections incorporated from the annual report to security holders, the proxy or information statement, and the information, if any, required by Part IV of this Form, signatures, and a cross-reference sheet setting forth the item numbers and captions in Parts I, II and III of this Form and the page and/or pages in the referenced materials where the corresponding information appears.

H.   Integrated Reports to Security Holders.

Annual reports to security holders may be combined with the required information of Form 10-K and will be suitable for filing with the Commission if the following conditions are satisfied:

(1) The combined report contains full and complete answers to all items required by Form 10-K. When responses to a certain item of required disclosure are separated within the combined report, an appropriate cross-reference should be made. If the information required by Part III of Form 10-K is omitted by virtue of General Instruction G, a definitive proxy or information statement shall be filed.

(2) The cover page and the required signatures are included. As appropriate, a cross-reference sheet should be filed indicating the location of information required by the items of the Form.

(3) If an electronic filer files any portion of an annual report to security holders in combination with the required information of Form 10-K, as provided in this instruction, only such portions filed in satisfaction of the Form 10-K requirements shall be filed in electronic format.

I. **Omission of Information by Certain Wholly-Owned Subsidiaries.**

If, on the date of the filing of its report on Form 10-K, the registrant meets the conditions specified in paragraph (1) below, then such registrant may furnish the abbreviated narrative disclosure specified in paragraph (2) below.

(1) Conditions for availability of the relief specified in paragraph (2) below.

(a) All of the registrant's equity securities are owned, either directly or indirectly, by a single person which is a reporting company under the Act and which has filed all the material required to be filed pursuant to section 13, 14, or 15(d) thereof, as applicable, and which is named in conjunction with the registrant's description of its business;

(b) During the preceding thirty-six calendar months and any subsequent period of days, there has not been any material default in the payment of principal, interest, a sinking or purchase fund installment, or any other material default not cured within thirty days, with respect to any indebtedness of the registrant or its subsidiaries, and there has not been any material default in the payment of rentals under material long-term leases; and

(c) There is prominently set forth, on the cover page of the Form 10-K, a statement that the registrant meets the conditions set forth in General Instruction (I)(1)(a) and (b) of Form 10-K and is therefore filing this Form with the reduced disclosure format.

(2) Registrants meeting the conditions specified in paragraph (1) above are entitled to the following relief:

(a) Such registrants may omit the information called for by Item 6, Selected Financial Data, and Item 7, Management's Discussion and Analysis of Financial Condition and Results of Operations provided that the registrant includes in the Form 10-K a management's narrative analysis of the results of operations explaining the reasons for material changes in the amount of revenue and expense items between the most recent fiscal year presented and the fiscal year immediately preceding it. Explanations of material changes should include, but not be limited to, changes in the various elements which determine revenue and expense levels such as unit sales volume, prices charged and paid, production levels, production cost variances, labor costs and discretionary spending programs. In addition, the analysis should include an explanation of the effect of any changes in accounting principles and practices or method of application that have a material effect on net income as reported.

(b) Such registrants may omit the list of subsidiaries exhibit required by Item 601 of Regulation S-K.

(c) Such registrants may omit the information called for by the following otherwise required Items: Item 4, Submission of Matters to a Vote of Security Holders; Item 10, Directors and Executive Officers of the Registrant; Item 11, Executive Compensation; Item 12, Security Ownership of Certain Beneficial Owners and Management; and Item 13, Certain Relationships and Related Transactions.

(d) In response to Item 1, Business, such registrant only need furnish a brief description of the business done by the registrant and its subsidiaries during the most recent fiscal year which will, in the opinion of management, indicate the general nature and scope of the business of the registrant and its subsidiaries, and in response to Item 2, Properties, such registrant only need furnish a brief description of the material properties of the registrant and its subsidiaries to the extent, in the opinion of the management, necessary to an understanding of the business done by the registrant and its subsidiaries.

* * *

**UNITED STATES
SECURITIES AND EXCHANGE COMMISSION
Washington, D.C. 20549**

FORM 10-K

(Mark One)

[ ] ANNUAL REPORT PURSUANT TO SECTION 13 OR 15(D) OF THE SECURITIES EXCHANGE ACT OF 1934

For the fiscal year ended _____

Or

[ ] TRANSITION REPORT PURSUANT TO SECTION 13 OR 15(d) OF THE SECURITIES EXCHANGE ACT OF 1934

For the transition period from _____ to _____

Commission file number _____

_____

(Exact name of registrant as specified in its charter)

_____

(State or other jurisdiction of incorporation or organization)	(I.R.S. Employer Identification No.)

_____

(Address of principal executive offices)	(Zip Code)

Registrant's telephone number, including area code _____

Securities to be registered pursuant to Section 12(b) of the Act:

Title of each class	Name of each exchange on which registered

Securities to be registered pursuant to Section 12(g) of the Act:

_____

(Title of class)

_____

(Title of class)

Indicate by check mark if the registrant is a well-known seasoned issuer, as defined in Rule 405 of the Securities Act. ❑ Yes   ❑ No

Indicate by check mark if the registrant is not required to file reports pursuant to Section 13 or Section 15(d) of the Act. ❑ Yes   ❑ No

Note: Checking the box above will not relieve any registrant required to file reports pursuant to Section 13 or 15(d) of the Exchange Act from their obligations under those Sections.

Indicate by check mark whether the registrant (1) has filed all reports required to be filed by Section 13 or 15(d) of the Securities Exchange Act of 1934 during the preceding 12 months (or for such shorter period that the registrant was required to file such reports), and (2) has been subject to such filing requirements for the past 90 days. ❑ Yes   ❑ No

Indicate by check mark whether the registrant has submitted electronically and posted on its corporate Web site, if any, every Interactive Data File required to be submitted and posted pursuant to Rule 405 of Regulation S-T during the preceding 12 months (or for such shorter period that the registrant was required to submit and post such files). ❑ Yes   ❑ No

Indicate by check mark if disclosure of delinquent filers pursuant to Item 405 of Regulation S-K is not contained herein, and will not be contained, to the best of registrant's knowledge, in definitive proxy or information statements incorporated by reference in Part III of this Form 10-K or any amendment to this Form 10-K. ❑

Indicate by check mark whether the registrant is a large accelerated filer, an accelerated filer, a non-accelerated filer, or a smaller reporting company. See the definitions of "large accelerated filer," "accelerated filer" and "smaller reporting company" in Rule 12b-2 of the Exchange Act.
Large accelerated filer ❑   Accelerated filer ❑
Non-accelerated filer ❑   Smaller reporting company ❑
(Do not check if a smaller reporting company)

Indicate by check mark whether the registrant is a shell company (as defined in Rule 12b-2 of the Act). ❑ Yes   ❑ No

State the aggregate market value of the voting and non-voting common equity held by non-affiliates computed by reference to the price at which the common equity was last sold, or the average bid and asked price of such common equity, as of the last business day of the registrant's most recently completed second fiscal quarter.
Note: If a determination as to whether a particular person or entity is an affiliate cannot be made without involving unreasonable effort and expense, the aggregate market value of the common stock held by non-affiliates may be calculated on the basis of assumptions reasonable under the circumstances, provided that the assumptions are set forth in this Form.

APPLICABLE ONLY TO REGISTRANTS INVOLVED IN BANKRUPTCY
PROCEEDINGS DURING THE PRECEDING FIVE YEARS:

Indicate by check mark whether the registrant has filed all documents and reports required to be filed by Section 12, 13 or 15(d) of the Securities Exchange Act of 1934 subsequent to the distribution of securities under a plan confirmed by a court. ❑ Yes   ❑ No

(APPLICABLE ONLY TO CORPORATE REGISTRANTS)

Indicate the number of shares outstanding of each of the registrant's classes of common stock, as of the latest practicable date.

DOCUMENTS INCORPORATED BY REFERENCE

List hereunder the following documents if incorporated by reference and the Part of the Form 10-K (e.g., Part I, Part II, etc.) into which the document is incorporated: (1) Any annual report to security holders; (2) Any proxy or information statement; and (3) Any prospectus filed pursuant to Rule 424(b) or (c) under the Securities Act of 1933. The listed documents should be clearly described for identification purposes (e.g., annual report to security holders for fiscal year ended December 24, 1980).

PART I
[See General Instruction G(2)]

Item 1.   Business.

Furnish the information required by Item 101 of Regulation S-K except that the discussion of the development of the registrant's business need only include developments since the beginning of the fiscal year for which this report is filed.

Item 1A.   Risk Factors.

Set forth, under the caption "Risk Factors," where appropriate, the risk factors described in Item 503(c) of Regulation S-K applicable to the registrant. Provide any discussion of risk factors in plain English in accordance with Rule 421(d) of the Securities Act of 1933.

Item 1B.   Unresolved Staff Comments.

If the registrant is an accelerated filer as defined in Rule 12b-2 of the Exchange Act or is a well-known seasoned issuer as defined in Rule 405 of the Securities Act and has received written comments from the Commission staff regarding its periodic or current reports under the Act not less than 180 days before the end of its fiscal year to which the annual report relates, and such comments remain unresolved, disclose the substance of any such unresolved comments that the registrant believes are material. Such disclosure may provide other information including the position of the registrant with respect to any such comment.

Item 2.   Properties.

Furnish the information required by Item 102 of Regulation S-K.

Item 3.   Legal Proceedings.

(a) Furnish the information required by Item 103 of Regulation S-K.

(b) As to any proceeding that was terminated during the fourth quarter of the fiscal year covered by this report, furnish information similar to that required by Item 103 of Regulation S-K, including the date of termination and a description of the disposition thereof with respect to the registrant and its subsidiaries.

Item 4.   [Reserved[

PART II
[(See General Instruction G(2)]

Item 5.   Market for Registrant's Common Equity, Related Stockholder Matters and Issuer Purchases of Equity Securities.

   (a) Furnish the information required by Item 201 of Regulation S-K and Item 701 of Regulation S-K as to all equity securities of the registrant sold by the registrant during the period covered by the report that were not registered under the Securities Act. *Provided* that if the Item 701 information previously has been included in a Quarterly Report on Form 10-Q or in a current report on Form 8-K, it need not be furnished.

   (b) If required pursuant to Rule 463 of the Securities Act of 1933, furnish the information required by Item 701(f) of Regulation S-K.

   (c) Furnish the information required by Item 703 of Regulation S-Kfor any repurchase made in a month within the fourth quarter of the fiscal year covered by the report. Provide disclosures covering repurchases made on a monthly basis. For example, if the fourth quarter began on January 16 and ended on April 15, the chart would show repurchases for the months from January 16 through February 15, February 16 through March 15, and March 16 through April 15.

Item 6.   Selected Financial Data.

   Furnish the information required by Item 301 of Regulation S-K.

Item 7.   Management's Discussion and Analysis of Financial Condition and Results of Operation.

   Furnish the information required by Item 303 of Regulation S-K.

Item 7A.   Quantitative and Qualitative Disclosures About Market Risk.

   Furnish the information required by Item 305 of Regulation S-K.

Item 8.   Financial Statements and Supplementary Data.

   Furnish financial statements meeting the requirements of Regulation S-X, except §210.3-05 and Article 11 thereof, and the supplementary financial information required by Item 302 of Regulation S-K. Financial statements of the registrant and its subsidiaries consolidated (as required by Rule 14a-3(b)) shall be filed under this item. Other financial statements and schedules required under Regulation S-X may be filed as "Financial Statement Schedules" pursuant to Item 13, Exhibits, Financial Statement Schedules, and Reports on Form 8-K, of this form.

Notwithstanding the above, if the issuer is subject to the reporting provisions of Section 15(d) and such obligation results solely from the issuer having filed a registration statement on Form S-18 which became effective under the Securities Act of 1933 during the last fiscal year, or such obligation applies as to the first or second fiscal year after the registration statement on Form S-18 became effective solely because the issuer had on the first day of the pertinent fiscal year 300 or more record holders of any of its securities to which the Form S-18 related, audited financial statements for the issuer, or for the issuer and its predecessors, may be presented as provided below. The report of the independent accountant shall in all events comply with the requirements of Article 2 of Regulation S-X.

(a) A Form 10-K filed for the fiscal year during which the registrant had a registration statement on Form S-18 become effective may include the following financial statements prepared in accordance with generally accepted accounting principles:

    (1) A balance sheet as of the end of each of the two most recent fiscal years; and

    (2) Consolidated statements of income, statements of cash flows, and statements of other stockholders' equity for each of the two fiscal years preceding the date of the most recent audited balance sheet being filed.

(b) A Form 10-K filed for the first fiscal year after the registrant had a registration statement on Form S-18 become effective may include financial statements prepared as follows:

    (1) Financial statements for the most recent fiscal year prepared in accordance with Regulation S-X, Form and Content of and Requirements for Financial Statements; and

    (2) Financial statements previously disclosed in accordance with paragraph (a) for the prior year. These statements do not need to include the compliance items and schedules of Regulation S-X, but should be recast to show the same line items as are set forth for the most recent fiscal year.

(c) A Form 10-K filed for the second fiscal year after the registrant had a registration statement on Form S-18 become effective may include financial statements for the two most recent fiscal years prepared in accordance with Regulation S-X.

Item 9. Changes in and Disagreements With Accountants on Accounting and Financial Disclosure.

Furnish the information required by Item 304 of Regulation S-K.

Item 9A.   Controls and Procedures.

Furnish the information required by Item 307 and 308 of Regulation S-K.

PART III
[See General Instruction G(3)]

Item 10.   Directors and Executive Officers of the Registrant.

Furnish the information required by Items 401,405 and 406 of Regulation S-K.

Instruction

Checking the box provided on the cover page of this Form to indicate that Item 405 disclosure of delinquent Form 3, 4, or 5 filers is not contained herein is intended to facilitate Form processing and review. Failure to provide such indication will not create liability for violation of the federal securities laws. The space should be checked only if there is no disclosure in this Form of reporting person delinquencies in response to Item 405 and the registrant, at the time of filing the Form 10-K, has reviewed the information necessary to ascertain, and has determined that, Item 405 disclosure is not expected to be contained in Part III of the Form 10-K or incorporated by reference.

Item 11.   Executive Compensation.

Furnish the information required by Item 402 of Regulation S-K.

Item 12.   Security Ownership of Certain Beneficial Owners and Management.

Furnish the information required by Item 201(d) of Regulation S-K and Item 403 of Regulation S-K.

Item 13.   Certain Relationships and Related Transactions.

Furnish the information required by Item 404 of Regulation S-K.

Item 14.   Principal Accounting Fees and Services.

Furnish the information required by Item 9(e) of Schedule 14A.

(1) Disclose, under the caption Audit Fees, the aggregate fees billed for each of the last two fiscal years for professional services rendered by the principal accountant for the audit of the registrant's annual financial statements and review of financial statements included in the registrant's Form 10-Q or services that are normally provided by the accountant in connection with statutory and regulatory filings or engagements for those fiscal years.

(2) Disclose, under the caption Audit-Related Fees, the aggregate fees billed in each of the last two fiscal years for assurance and related services by the

principal accountant that are reasonably related to the performance of the audit or review of the registrant's financial statements and are not reported under Item 9(e)(1) of Schedule 14A. Registrants shall describe the nature of the services comprising the fees disclosed under this category.

(3) Disclose, under the caption Tax Fees, the aggregate fees billed in each of the last two fiscal years for professional services rendered by the principal accountant for tax compliance, tax advice, and tax planning. Registrants shall describe the nature of the services comprising the fees disclosed under this category.

(4) Disclose, under the caption All Other Fees, the aggregate fees billed in each of the last two fiscal years for products and services provided by the principal accountant, other than the services reported in Items 9(e)(1) through 9(e)(3) of Schedule 14A. Registrants shall describe the nature of the services comprising the fees disclosed under this category.

(5) (i) Disclose the audit committee's pre-approval policies and procedures described in paragraph (c)(7)(i) of Rule 2-01 of Regulation S-X.

(ii) Disclose the percentage of services described in each of Items 9(e)(2) through 9(e)(4) of Schedule 14A that were approved by the audit committee pursuant to paragraph (c)(7)(i)(C) of Rule 2-01 of Regulation S-X.

(6) If greater than 50 percent, disclose the percentage of hours expended on the principal accountant's engagement to audit the registrant's financial statements for the most recent fiscal year that were attributed to work performed by persons other than the principal accountant's full-time, permanent employees.

Instructions to Item 14. A registrant that is an Asset-Backed Issuer (as defined in Rule 13a-14(g) and Rule 15d-14(g) of this chapter) is not required to disclose the information required by this Item.

PART IV

Item 15   **Exhibits, Financial Statement Schedules, and Reports on Form 8-K.**

(a) List the following documents filed as a part of the report:

(1) All financial statements;

(2) Those financial statement schedules required to be filed by Item 8 of this form, and by paragraph (d) below.

(3) Those exhibits required by Item 601 of Regulation S-K and by paragraph (c) below. Identify in the list each management contract or compensatory plan or arrangement required to be filed as an exhibit to this form pursuant to Item 14(c) of this report.

(b) Reports on Form 8-K. State whether any reports on Form 8-K have been filed during the last quarter of the period covered by this report, listing the items reported, any financial statements filed and the dates of any such reports.

(c) Registrants shall file, as exhibits to this form, the exhibits required by Item 601 of Regulation S-K.

(d) Registrants shall file, as financial statement schedules to this form, the financial statements required by Regulation S-X which are excluded from the annual report to shareholders by Rule 14a-3(b) including (1) separate financial statements of subsidiaries not consolidated and fifty percent or less owned persons; (2) separate financial statements of affiliates whose securities are pledged as collateral; and (3) schedules.

SIGNATURES

[See General Instruction D]

Pursuant to the requirements of Section 13 or 15(d) of the Securities Exchange Act of 1934, the registrant has duly caused this report to be signed on its behalf by the undersigned, thereunto duly authorized.

(Registrant) _____

By (Signature and Title)* _____

Date _____

Pursuant to the requirements of the Securities Exchange Act of 1934, this report has been signed below by the following persons on behalf of the registrant and in the capacities and on the dates indicated.

By (Signature and Title)*_____

Date _____

By (Signature and Title)*_____

Date _____

**Supplemental Information to be Furnished with Reports Filed
Pursuant to Section 15(d) of the Act by Registrants Which Have Not Registered
Securities Pursuant to Section 12 of the Act**

(a) Except to the extent that the materials enumerated in (1) and/or (2) below are specifically incorporated into this Form by reference (in which case *see* Rule 12b-23(d)), every registrant which files an annual report on this Form pursuant to Section 15(d) of the Act shall furnish to the Commission for its information, at the time of filing its report on this Form, four copies of the following:

   (1) Any annual report to security holders covering the registrant's last fiscal year; and

   (2) Every proxy statement, form of proxy or other proxy soliciting material sent to more than ten of the registrant's security holders with respect to any annual or other meeting of security holders.

(b) The foregoing material shall not be deemed to be "filed" with the Commission or otherwise subject to the liabilities of Section 18 of the Act, except to the extent that the registrant specifically incorporates it in its annual report on this Form by reference.

(c) If no such annual report material has been sent to security holders, a statement to that effect shall be included under this caption. If such report or proxy material is to be furnished to security holders subsequent to the filing of the annual report of this Form, the registrant shall so state under this caption and shall furnish copies of such material to the Commission when it is sent to security holders.

UNITED STATES
SECURITIES AND EXCHANGE COMMISSION
Washington, D.C. 20549

FORM 10-Q

GENERAL INSTRUCTIONS

A.   **Rule as to Use of Form 10-Q.**

    1.   Form 10-Q shall be used for quarterly reports under Section 13 or 15(d) of the Securities Exchange Act of 1934, required to be filed pursuant to Rule 13a-13 or Rule15d-13 of this chapter. A quarterly report on this form pursuant to Rule 13a-13 or Rule 15d-13 of this chapter shall be filed within the following period after the end of the first three fiscal quarters of each fiscal year, but no quarterly report need be filed for the fourth quarter of any fiscal year:

        a.   40 days after the end of the fiscal quarter for large accelerated filers and accelerated filers (as defined in 12b-2); and

        b.   45 days after the end of the fiscal quarter for all other registrants.

B.   **Application of General Rules and Regulations.**

    1.   The General Rules and Regulations under the Act contain certain general requirements which are applicable to reports on any form. These general requirements should be carefully read and observed in the preparation and filing of reports on this form.

    2.   Particular attention is directed to Regulation 12B which contains general requirements regarding matters such as the kind and size of paper to be used, the legibility of the report, the information to be given whenever the title of securities is required to be stated, and the filing of the report. The definitions contained in Rule 12b-2 should be especially noted. See also Regulations 13A and 15D.

C.   **Preparation of Report.**

    1.   This is not a blank form to be filled in. It is a guide copy to be used in preparing the report in accordance with Rules 12b-11 and 12b-12. The Commission does not furnish blank copies of this form to be filled in for filing.

    2.   These general instructions are not to be filed with the report. The instructions to the various captions of the form are also to be omitted from the report as filed.

D.   **Incorporation by Reference.**

    1.   If the registrant makes available to its stockholders or otherwise publishes, within the period prescribed for filing the report, a document or statement containing

information meeting some or all of the requirements of Part I of this form, the information called for may be incorporated by reference from such published document or statement, in answer or partial answer to any item or items of Part I of this form, provided copies thereof are filed as an exhibit to Part I of the report on this form.

2. Other information may be incorporated by reference in answer or partial answer to any item or items of Part II of this form in accordance with the provisions of Rule 12b-23.

3. If any information required by Part I or Part II is incorporated by reference into an electronic format document from the quarterly report to security holders as provided in General Instruction D, any portion of the quarterly report to security holders incorporated by reference shall be filed as an exhibit in electronic format, as required by Item 601(b)(13) of Regulation S-K.

E.   Integrated Reports to Security Holders.

Quarterly reports to security holders may be combined with the required information of Form 10-Q and will be suitable for filing with the Commission if the following conditions are satisfied:

1. The combined report contains full and complete answers to all items required by Part I of this form. When responses to a certain item of required disclosure are separated within the combined report, an appropriate cross-reference should be made.

2. If not included in the combined report, the cover page, appropriate responses to Part II, and the required signatures shall be included in the Form 10-Q. Additionally, as appropriate, a cross-reference sheet should be filed indicating the location of information required by the items of the form.

3. If an electronic filer files any portion of a quarterly report to security holders in combination with the required information of Form 10-Q, as provided in this instruction, only such portions filed in satisfaction of the Form 10-Q requirements shall be filed in electronic format.

F.   Filed Status of Information Presented.

1. Pursuant to Rule 13a-13(d) and Rule 15d-13(d), the information presented in satisfaction of the requirements of Items 1, 2 and 3 of Part I of this form, whether included directly in a report on this form, incorporated therein by reference from a report, document or statement filed as an exhibit to Part I of this form pursuant to Instruction D(1) above, included in an integrated report pursuant to Instruction E above, or contained in a statement regarding computation of per share earnings or a letter regarding a change in accounting principles filed as an exhibit to Part I pursuant to Item 601 of Regulation S-K, except as provided by Instruction F(2) below, shall not be deemed filed for the purpose of Section 18 of the Act or

otherwise subject to the liabilities of that section of the Act but shall be subject to the other provisions of the Act.

2.   Information presented in satisfaction of the requirements of this form other than those of Items 1, 2 and 3 of Part I shall be deemed filed for the purpose of Section 18 of the Act; except that, where information presented in response to Item 1 or 2 of Part I (or as an exhibit thereto) is also used to satisfy Part II requirements through incorporation by reference, only that portion of Part I (or exhibit thereto) consisting of the information required by Part II shall be deemed so filed.

G.   Signature and Filing of Report.

If the report is filed in paper pursuant to a hardship exemption from electronic filing (see Item 201 et seq. of Regulation S-T), three complete copies of the report, including any financial statements, exhibits or other papers or documents filed as a part thereof, and five additional copies which need not include exhibits must be filed with the Commission. At least one complete copy of the report, including any financial statements, exhibits or other papers or documents filed as a part thereof, must be filed with each exchange on which any class of securities of the registrant is registered. At least one complete copy of the report filed with the Commission and one such copy filed with each exchange must be manually signed on the registrant's behalf by a duly authorized officer of the registrant and by the principal financial or chief accounting officer of the registrant. (See Rule 12b-11(d).) Copies not manually signed must bear typed or printed signatures. In the case where the principal executive officer, principal financial officer or chief accounting officer is also duly authorized to sign on behalf of the registrant, one signature is acceptable provided that the registrant clearly indicates the dual responsibilities of the signatory.

H.   Omission of Information by Certain Wholly-Owned Subsidiaries.

If on the date of the filing of its report on Form 10-Q, the registrant meets the conditions specified in paragraph (1) below, then such registrant may omit the information called for in the items specified in paragraph (2) below.

1.   Conditions for availability of the relief specified in paragraph (2) below:

a.   All of the registrant's equity securities are owned, either directly or indirectly, by a single person which is a reporting company under the Act and which has filed all the material required to be filed pursuant to Section 13, 14 or 15(d) thereof, as applicable;

b.   During the preceding thirty-six calendar months and any subsequent period of days, there has not been any material default in the payment of principal, interest, a sinking or purchase fund installment, or any other material default not cured within thirty days, with respect to any indebtedness of the registrant or its subsidiaries, and there has not been any material default in the payment of rentals under material long-term leases; and

    c.   There is prominently set forth, on the cover page of the Form 10-Q, a statement that the registrant meets the conditions set forth in General Instruction H(1)(a) and (b) of Form 10-Q and is therefore filing this form with the reduced disclosure format.

2.   Registrants meeting the conditions specified in paragraph (1) above are entitled to the following relief.

    a.   Such registrants may omit the information called for by Item 2 of Part I, Management's Discussion and Analysis of Financial Condition and Results of Operations, provided that the registrant includes in the Form 10-Q a management's narrative analysis of the results of operations explaining the reasons for material changes in the amount of revenue and expense items between the most recent fiscal year-to-date period presented and the corresponding year-to-date period in the preceding fiscal year. Explanations of material changes should include, but not be limited to, changes in the various elements which determine revenue and expense levels such as unit sales volume, prices charged and paid, production levels, production cost variances, labor costs and discretionary spending programs. In addition, the analysis should include an explanation of the effect of any changes in accounting principles and practices or method of application that have a material effect on net income as reported.

    b.   Such registrants may omit the information called for in the following Part II Items: Item 2, Changes in Securities; Item 3, Defaults Upon Senior Securities; and Item 4, Submission of Matters to a Vote of Security Holders.

    c.   Such registrants may omit the information called for by Item 3 of Part I, Quantitative and Qualitative Disclosures About Market Risk.

UNITED STATES
SECURITIES AND EXCHANGE COMMISSION
Washington, D.C. 20549

FORM 10-Q

(Mark One)

[ ] ANNUAL REPORT PURSUANT TO SECTION 13 OR 15(d) OF THE SECURITIES
EXCHANGE ACT OF 1934

For the quarterly period ended _____

or

[ ] TRANSITION REPORT PURSUANT TO SECTION 13 OR 15(d) OF THE SECURITIES
EXCHANGE ACT OF 1934

For the transition period from _____ to _____

Commission file number _____

_____
(Exact name of registrant as specified in its charter)

(State or other jurisdiction of incorporation or organization)	(I.R.S. Employer Identification No)

_____
(Address of principal executive offices)   (Zip Code)

Registrant's telephone number, including area code
_____
(Former name, former address and former fiscal year, if changed since last report)

Indicate by check mark whether the registrant (1) has filed all reports required to be filed by Section 13 or 15(d) of the Securities Exchange Act of 1934 during the preceding 12 months (or for such shorter period that the registrant was required to file such reports), and (2) has been subject to such filing requirements for the past 90 days. ❑ Yes   ❑ No

Indicate by check mark whether the registrant has submitted electronically and posted on its corporate Web site, if any, every Interactive Data File required to be submitted and posted pursuant to Rule 405 of Regulation S-T during the preceding 12 months (or for such shorter period that the registrant was required to submit and post such files). ❑ Yes   ❑ No

Indicate by check mark whether the registrant is an accelerated filer (as defined in Rule 12b-2 of the Exchange Act). ❑ Yes   ❑ No

APPLICABLE ONLY TO ISSUERS INVOLVED IN BANKRUPTCY PROCEEDINGS
DURING THE PRECEDING FIVE YEARS:

Indicate by check mark whether the registrant has filed all documents and reports required to be filed by Sections 12, 13 or 15(d) of the Securities Exchange Act of 1934 subsequent to the distribution of securities under a plan confirmed by a court. ❏ Yes   ❏ No

APPLICABLE ONLY TO CORPORATE ISSUERS:

Indicate the number of shares outstanding of each of the issuer's classes of common stock, as of the latest practicable date.

PART I—FINANCIAL INFORMATION

Item 1.   Financial Statements.

Provide the information required by Rule 10-01 of Regulation S-X.

Item 2.   Management's Discussion and Analysis of Financial Condition and Results of Operations.

Furnish the information required by Item 303 of Regulation S-K.

Item 3.   Quantitative and Qualitative Disclosures About Market Risk.

Furnish the information required by Item 305 of Regulation S-K.

Item 4:   Controls and Procedures.

Furnish the information required by Item 307 of Regulation S-K and Item 308(c) of Regulation S-K.

PART II—OTHER INFORMATION

Instruction. The report shall contain the item numbers and captions of all applicable items of Part II, but the text of such items may be omitted provided the responses clearly indicate the coverage of the item. Any item which is inapplicable or to which the answer is negative may be omitted and no reference thereto need be made in the report. If substantially the same information has been previously reported by the registrant, an additional report of the information on this form need not be made. The term "previously reported" is defined in Rule 12b-2. A separate response need not be presented in Part II where information called for is already disclosed in the financial information provided in Part I and is incorporated by reference into Part II of the report by means of a statement to that effect in Part II which specifically identifies the incorporated information.

Item 1.   Legal Proceedings.

Furnish the information required by Item 103 of Regulation S-K. As to such proceedings which have been terminated during the period covered by the report, provide similar information, including the date of termination and a description of the disposition thereof with respect to the registrant and its subsidiaries.

Instruction. A legal proceeding need only be reported in the 10-Q filed for the quarter in which it first became a reportable event and in subsequent quarters in which there have been material developments. Subsequent Form 10-Q filings in the same fiscal year in which a legal proceeding or a material development is reported should reference any previous reports in that year.

Item 1A. Risk Factors.

Set forth any material changes from risk factors as previously disclosed in the registrant's Form 10-K in response to Item 1A. to Part I of Form 10-K.

Item 2.   Changes in Securities and Use of Proceeds.

(a) If the constituent instruments defining the rights of the holders of any class of registered securities have been materially modified, give the title of the class of securities involved and state briefly the general effect of such modification upon the rights of holders of such securities.

(b) If the rights evidenced by any class of registered securities have been materially limited or qualified by the issuance or modification of any other class of securities, state briefly the general effect of the issuance or modification of such other class of securities upon the rights of the holders of the registered securities.

(c) Furnish the information required by Item 701 of Regulation S-K as to all equity securities of the registrant sold by the registrant during the period covered by the report that were not registered under the Securities Act.

(d) If required pursuant to Rule 463 of the Securities Act of 1933, furnish the information required by Item 701(f) of Regulation S-K.

(e) Furnish the information required by Item 703 of Regulation S-K for any repurchase made in the quarter covered by the report. Provide disclosures covering repurchases made on a monthly basis. For example, if the quarter began on January 16 and ended on April 15, the chart would show repurchases for the months from January 16 through February 15, February 16 through March 15, and March 16 through April 15.

Instruction. Working capital restrictions and other limitations upon the payment of dividends are to be reported hereunder.

Item 3.   **Defaults Upon Senior Securities.**

(a) If there has been any material default in the payment of principal, interest, a sinking or purchase fund installment, or any other material default not cured within 30 days, with respect to any indebtedness of the registrant or any of its significant subsidiaries exceeding 5 percent of the total assets of the registrant and its consolidated subsidiaries, identify the indebtedness and state the nature of the default. In the case of such a default in the payment of principal, interest, or a sinking or purchase fund installment, state the amount of the default and the total arrearage on the date of filing this report.

Instruction. This paragraph refers only to events which have become defaults under the governing instruments, i.e., after the expiration of any period of grace and compliance with any notice requirements.

(b) If any material arrearage in the payment of dividends has occurred or if there has been any other material delinquency not cured within 30 days, with respect to any class of preferred stock of the registrant which is registered or which ranks prior to any class of registered securities, or with respect to any class of preferred stock of any significant subsidiary of the registrant, give the title of the class and state the nature of the arrearage or delinquency. In the case of an arrearage in the payment of dividends, state the amount and the total arrearage on the date of filing this report.

Instruction. Item 3 need not be answered as to any default or arrearage with respect to any class of securities all of which is held by, or for the account of, the registrant or its totally held subsidiaries.

Item 4.   **[Reserved]**

Item 5   **Other Information.**

(a) The registrant may, at its option, report under this item any information, not previously reported in a report on Form 8-K, with respect to which information is not otherwise called for by this form. If disclosure of such information is made under this item, it need not be repeated in a report on Form 8-K which would otherwise be required to be filed with respect to such information or in a subsequent report on Form 10-Q; and

(b) Furnish the information required by Item 407(c)(3) of Regulation S-K.

Item 6.   **Exhibits and Reports on Form 8-K.**

(a) Furnish the exhibits required by Item 601 of Regulation S-K.

(b) Reports on Form 8-K. State whether any reports on Form 8-K have been filed during the quarter for which this report is filed.

SIGNATURES**

Pursuant to the requirements of the Securities Exchange Act of 1934, the registrant has duly caused this report to be signed on its behalf by the undersigned thereunto duly authorized.

_____
(Registrant)

_____   _____
Date   (Signature) **

_____   _____
Date   (Signature) **

SEC RULES OF PRACTICE

Rule 102 – Appearance and Practice Before the Commission.

A person shall not be represented before the Commission or a hearing officer except as stated in paragraphs (a) and (b) of this rule or as otherwise permitted by the Commission or a hearing officer.

e. **Suspension and Disbarment**.
1. Generally. The Commission may censure a person or deny, temporarily or permanently, the privilege of appearing or practicing before it in any way to any person who is found by the Commission after notice and opportunity for hearing in the matter:
   i. not to possess the requisite qualifications to represent others; or
   ii. to be lacking in character or integrity or to have engaged in unethical or improper professional conduct; or
   iii. to have willfully violated, or willfully aided and abetted the violation of any provision of the Federal securities laws or the rules and regulations thereunder.
   iv. with respect to persons licensed to practice as accountants, "improper professional conduct" under Rule 102(e)(1)(ii) means:
      A. intentional or knowing conduct, including reckless conduct, that results in a violation of applicable professional standards; or
      B. either of the following two types of negligent conduct:
         1. a single instance of highly unreasonable conduct that results in a violation of applicable professional standards in circumstances in which an accountant knows, or should know, that heightened scrutiny is warranted.
         2. repeated instances of unreasonable conduct, each resulting in a violation of applicable professional standards, that indicate a lack of competence to practice before the Commission.
2. Certain Professionals and Convicted Persons. Any attorney who has been suspended or disbarred by a court of the United States or of any State; or any person whose license to practice as an accountant, engineer, or other professional or expert has been revoked or suspended in any State; or any person who has been convicted of a felony or a misdemeanor involving moral turpitude shall be forthwith suspended from appearing or practicing before the Commission. A disbarment, suspension, revocation or conviction within the meaning of this rule shall be deemed to have occurred when the disbarring, suspending, revoking or convicting agency or tribunal enters its judgment or order, including a judgment or order on a plea of nolo contendere, regardless of whether an appeal of such judgment or order is pending or could be taken.
3. Temporary Suspensions. An order of temporary suspension shall become effective upon service on the respondent. No order of temporary suspension shall be entered by the Commission pursuant to paragraph (e)(3)(i) of this rule more than 90 days after the date on which the final judgment or order entered in a judicial or administrative proceeding described in paragraph (e)(3)(i)(A) or (e)(3)(i)(B) has become effective, whether upon completion of review or

appeal procedures or because further review or appeal procedures are no longer available.

i. The Commission, with due regard to the public interest and without preliminary hearing, may, by order, temporarily suspend from appearing or practicing before it any attorney, accountant, engineer, or other professional or expert who has been by name:

    A. permanently enjoined by any court of competent jurisdiction, by reason of his or her misconduct in an action brought by the Commission, from violating or aiding and abetting the violation of any provision of the Federal securities laws or of the rules and regulations thereunder; or

    B. found by any court of competent jurisdiction in an action brought by the Commission to which he or she is a party or found by the Commission in any administrative proceeding to which he or she is a party to have violated (unless the violation was found not to have been willful) or aided and abetted the violation of any provision of the Federal securities laws or of the rules and regulations thereunder.

ii. Any person temporarily suspended from appearing and practicing before the Commission in accordance with paragraph (e)(3)(i) of this rule may, within 30 days after service upon him or her of the order of temporary suspension, petition the Commission to lift the temporary suspension. If no petition has been received by the Commission within 30 days after service of the order, the suspension shall become permanent.

iii. Within 30 days after the filing of a petition in accordance with paragraph (e)(3)(ii) of this rule, the Commission shall either lift the temporary suspension, or set the matter down for hearing at a time and place designated by the Commission, or both, and, after opportunity for hearing, may censure the petitioner or disqualify the petitioner from appearing or practicing before the Commission for a period of time or permanently. In every case in which the temporary suspension has not been lifted, every hearing held and other action taken pursuant to this paragraph (e)(3) shall be expedited in accordance with Rule 500. If the hearing is held before a hearing officer, the time limits set forth in Rule 531 will govern review of the hearing officer's initial decision.

iv. In any hearing held on a petition filed in accordance with paragraph (e)(3)(ii) of this rule, the staff of the Commission shall show either that the petitioner has been enjoined as described in paragraph (e)(3)(i)(A) of this rule or that the petitioner has been found to have committed or aided and abetted violations as described in paragraph (e)(3)(i)(B) of this rule and that showing, without more, may be the basis for censure or disqualification. Once that showing has been made, the burden shall be upon the petitioner to show cause why he or she should not be censured or temporarily or permanently disqualified from appearing and practicing before the Commission. In any such hearing, the petitioner may not contest any finding made against him or her or fact admitted by him or her in the judicial or administrative proceeding upon which the proceeding under this paragraph (e)(3) is predicated. A person who has consented to the entry of a permanent injunction as described in paragraph (e)(3)(i)(A) of this rule without admitting the facts set forth in the complaint shall be presumed for all purposes under this paragraph (e)(3) to have been enjoined by reason of the misconduct alleged in the complaint.

4.   Filing of Prior Orders. Any person appearing or practicing before the Commission who has been the subject of an order, judgment, decree, or finding as set forth in paragraph (e)(3) of this rule shall promptly file with the Secretary a copy thereof (together with any related opinion or statement of the agency or tribunal involved). Failure to file any such paper, order, judgment, decree or finding shall not impair the operation of any other provision of this rule.

5.   Reinstatement.

i.   An application for reinstatement of a person permanently suspended or disqualified under paragraph (e)(1) or (e)(3) of this rule may be made at any time, and the applicant may, in the Commission's discretion, be afforded a hearing; however, the suspension or disqualification shall continue unless and until the applicant has been reinstated by the Commission for good cause shown.

ii.   Any person suspended under paragraph (e)(2) of this rule shall be reinstated by the Commission, upon appropriate application, if all the grounds for application of the provisions of that paragraph are subsequently removed by a reversal of the conviction or termination of the suspension, disbarment, or revocation. An application for reinstatement on any other grounds by any person suspended under paragraph (e)(2) of this rule may be filed at any time and the applicant shall be accorded an opportunity for a hearing in the matter; however, such suspension shall continue unless and until the applicant has been reinstated by order of the Commission for good cause shown.

6.   Other Proceedings Not Precluded. A proceeding brought under paragraph (e)(1), (e)(2) or (e)(3) of this rule shall not preclude another proceeding brought under these same paragraphs.

7.   Public Hearings. All hearings held under this paragraph (e) shall be public unless otherwise ordered by the Commission on its own motion or after considering the motion of a party.

Rule 205 – Standards of Professional Conduct for Attorneys

Rule 1 – Purpose and Scope

This part sets forth minimum standards of professional conduct for attorneys appearing and practicing before the Commission in the representation of an issuer. These standards supplement applicable standards of any jurisdiction where an attorney is admitted or practices and are not intended to limit the ability of any jurisdiction to impose additional obligations on an attorney not inconsistent with the application of this part. Where the standards of a state or other United States jurisdiction where an attorney is admitted or practices conflict with this part, this part shall govern.

Rule 2 – Definitions

For purposes of this part, the following definitions apply:

a. **Appearing and practicing before the Commission**:
    1.   Means:
        i.   Transacting any business with the Commission, including communications in any form;
        ii.   Representing an issuer in a Commission administrative proceeding or in connection with any Commission investigation, inquiry, information request, or subpoena;
        iii.   Providing advice in respect of the United States securities laws or the Commission's rules or regulations thereunder regarding any document that the attorney has notice will be filed with or submitted to, or incorporated into any document that will be filed with or submitted to, the Commission, including the provision of such advice in the context of preparing, or participating in the preparation of, any such document; or
        iv.   Advising an issuer as to whether information or a statement, opinion, or other writing is required under the United States securities laws or the Commission's rules or regulations thereunder to be filed with or submitted to, or incorporated into any document that will be filed with or submitted to, the Commission; but
    2.   Does not include an attorney who:
        i.   Conducts the activities in paragraphs (a)(1)(i) through (a)(1)(iv) of this section other than in the context of providing legal services to an issuer with whom the attorney has an attorney-client relationship; or
        ii.   Is a non-appearing foreign attorney.

b. **Appropriate response** means a response to an attorney regarding reported evidence of a material violation as a result of which the attorney reasonably believes:
    1.   That no material violation, as defined in paragraph (i) of this section, has occurred, is ongoing, or is about to occur;
    2.   That the issuer has, as necessary, adopted appropriate remedial measures, including appropriate steps or sanctions to stop any material violations that are ongoing, to prevent any material violation that has yet to occur, and to remedy or otherwise appropriately address any material violation that has already occurred and to minimize the likelihood of its recurrence; or
    3.   That the issuer, with the consent of the issuer's board of directors, a committee thereof to whom a report could be made pursuant to Rule 3(b)(3), or a qualified legal compliance committee, has retained or directed an attorney to review the reported evidence of a material violation and either:
        i.   Has substantially implemented any remedial recommendations made by such attorney after a reasonable investigation and evaluation of the reported evidence; or
        ii.   Has been advised that such attorney may, consistent with his or her professional obligations, assert a colorable defense on behalf of the issuer (or the issuer's officer, director, employee, or agent, as the case

may be) in any investigation or judicial or administrative proceeding relating to the reported evidence of a material violation.

c. **Attorney** means any person who is admitted, licensed, or otherwise qualified to practice law in any jurisdiction, domestic or foreign, or who holds himself or herself out as admitted, licensed, or otherwise qualified to practice law.

d. **Breach of fiduciary duty** refers to any breach of fiduciary or similar duty to the issuer recognized under an applicable Federal or State statute or at common law, including but not limited to misfeasance, nonfeasance, abdication of duty, abuse of trust, and approval of unlawful transactions.

e. **Evidence of a material violation** means credible evidence, based upon which it would be unreasonable, under the circumstances, for a prudent and competent attorney not to conclude that it is reasonably likely that a material violation has occurred, is ongoing, or is about to occur.

f. **Foreign government issuer** means a foreign issuer as defined in Rule 405 under the Securities Act of 1933 eligible to register securities on Schedule B of the Securities Act of 1933.

g. **In the representation of an issuer** means providing legal services as an attorney for an issuer, regardless of whether the attorney is employed or retained by the issuer.

h. **Issuer** means an issuer (as defined in section 3 of the Securities Exchange Act of 1934, the securities of which are registered under section 12 of that Act, or that is required to file reports under section 15(d) of that Act, or that files or has filed a registration statement that has not yet become effective under the Securities Act of 1933, and that it has not withdrawn, but does not include a foreign government issuer. For purposes of paragraphs (a) and (g) of this section, the term "issuer" includes any person controlled by an issuer, where an attorney provides legal services to such person on behalf of, or at the behest, or for the benefit of the issuer, regardless of whether the attorney is employed or retained by the issuer.

i. **Material violation** means a material violation of an applicable United States federal or state securities law, a material breach of fiduciary duty arising under United States federal or state law, or a similar material violation of any United States federal or state law.

j. **Non-appearing foreign attorney** means an attorney:
    1. Who is admitted to practice law in a jurisdiction outside the United States;
    2. Who does not hold himself or herself out as practicing, and does not give legal advice regarding, United States federal or state securities or other laws (except as provided in paragraph (j)(3)(ii) of this section); and
    3. Who:
        i. Conducts activities that would constitute appearing and practicing before the Commission only incidentally to, and in the ordinary course of, the practice of law in a jurisdiction outside the United States; or

    ii. Is appearing and practicing before the Commission only in consultation with counsel, other than a non-appearing foreign attorney, admitted or licensed to practice in a state or other United States jurisdiction.

k. **Qualified legal compliance committee** means a committee of an issuer (which also may be an audit or other committee of the issuer) that:
1. Consists of at least one member of the issuer's audit committee (or, if the issuer has no audit committee, one member from an equivalent committee of independent directors) and two or more members of the issuer's board of directors who are not employed, directly or indirectly, by the issuer and who are not, in the case of a registered investment company, "interested persons" as defined in section 2(a)(19) of the Investment Company Act of 1940;
2. Has adopted written procedures for the confidential receipt, retention, and consideration of any report of evidence of a material violation under Rule 3;
3. Has been duly established by the issuer's board of directors, with the authority and responsibility:
    i. To inform the issuer's chief legal officer and chief executive officer (or the equivalents thereof) of any report of evidence of a material violation (except in the circumstances described in Rule 3(b)(4));
    ii. To determine whether an investigation is necessary regarding any report of evidence of a material violation by the issuer, its officers, directors, employees or agents and, if it determines an investigation is necessary or appropriate, to:
        A. Notify the audit committee or the full board of directors;
        B. Initiate an investigation, which may be conducted either by the chief legal officer (or the equivalent thereof) or by outside attorneys; and
        C. Retain such additional expert personnel as the committee deems necessary; and
    iii. At the conclusion of any such investigation, to:
        A. Recommend, by majority vote, that the issuer implement an appropriate response to evidence of a material violation; and
        B. Inform the chief legal officer and the chief executive officer (or the equivalents thereof) and the board of directors of the results of any such investigation under this section and the appropriate remedial measures to be adopted; and
4. Has the authority and responsibility, acting by majority vote, to take all other appropriate action, including the authority to notify the Commission in the event that the issuer fails in any material respect to implement an appropriate response that the qualified legal compliance committee has recommended the issuer to take.

l. **Reasonable or reasonably** denotes, with respect to the actions of an attorney, conduct that would not be unreasonable for a prudent and competent attorney.

m. **Reasonably believes** means that an attorney believes the matter in question and that the circumstances are such that the belief is not unreasonable.

n.   **Report** means to make known to directly, either in person, by telephone, by e-mail, electronically, or in writing.

Rule 3 – Issuer as Client

a.   **Representing an issuer.**   An attorney appearing and practicing before the Commission in the representation of an issuer owes his or her professional and ethical duties to the issuer as an organization. That the attorney may work with and advise the issuer's officers, directors, or employees in the course of representing the issuer does not make such individuals the attorney's clients.

b.   **Duty to report evidence of a material violation.**
   1.   If an attorney, appearing and practicing before the Commission in the representation of an issuer, becomes aware of evidence of a material violation by the issuer or by any officer, director, employee, or agent of the issuer, the attorney shall report such evidence to the issuer's chief legal officer (or the equivalent thereof) or to both the issuer's chief legal officer and its chief executive officer (or the equivalents thereof) forthwith. By communicating such information to the issuer's officers or directors, an attorney does not reveal client confidences or secrets or privileged or otherwise protected information related to the attorney's representation of an issuer.
   2.   The chief legal officer (or the equivalent thereof) shall cause such inquiry into the evidence of a material violation as he or she reasonably believes is appropriate to determine whether the material violation described in the report has occurred, is ongoing, or is about to occur. If the chief legal officer (or the equivalent thereof) determines no material violation has occurred, is ongoing, or is about to occur, he or she shall notify the reporting attorney and advise the reporting attorney of the basis for such determination. Unless the chief legal officer (or the equivalent thereof) reasonably believes that no material violation has occurred, is ongoing, or is about to occur, he or she shall take all reasonable steps to cause the issuer to adopt an appropriate response, and shall advise the reporting attorney thereof. In lieu of causing an inquiry under this paragraph (b), a chief legal officer (or the equivalent thereof) may refer a report of evidence of a material violation to a qualified legal compliance committee under paragraph (c)(2) of this section if the issuer has duly established a qualified legal compliance committee prior to the report of evidence of a material violation.
   3.   Unless an attorney who has made a report under paragraph (b)(1) of this section reasonably believes that the chief legal officer or the chief executive officer of the issuer (or the equivalent thereof) has provided an appropriate response within a reasonable time, the attorney shall report the evidence of a material violation to:
      i.   The audit committee of the issuer's board of directors;
      ii.   Another committee of the issuer's board of directors consisting solely of directors who are not employed, directly or indirectly, by the issuer and are not, in the case of a registered investment company, "interested persons" as defined in section 2(a)(19) of the Investment Company Act of 1940 (if the issuer's board of directors has no audit committee); or

      iii. The issuer's board of directors (if the issuer's board of directors has no committee consisting solely of directors who are not employed, directly or indirectly, by the issuer and are not, in the case of a registered investment company, "interested persons" as defined in section 2(a)(19) of the Investment Company Act of 1940).

4.   If an attorney reasonably believes that it would be futile to report evidence of a material violation to the issuer's chief legal officer and chief executive officer (or the equivalents thereof) under paragraph (b)(1) of this section, the attorney may report such evidence as provided under paragraph (b)(3) of this section.

5.   An attorney retained or directed by an issuer to investigate evidence of a material violation reported under paragraph (b)(1), (b)(3), or (b)(4) of this section shall be deemed to be appearing and practicing before the Commission. Directing or retaining an attorney to investigate reported evidence of a material violation does not relieve an officer or director of the issuer to whom such evidence has been reported under paragraph (b)(1), (b)(3), or (b)(4) of this section from a duty to respond to the reporting attorney.

6.   An attorney shall not have any obligation to report evidence of a material violation under this paragraph (b) if:

      i.   The attorney was retained or directed by the issuer's chief legal officer (or the equivalent thereof) to investigate such evidence of a material violation and:

         A. The attorney reports the results of such investigation to the chief legal officer (or the equivalent thereof); and

         B. Except where the attorney and the chief legal officer (or the equivalent thereof) each reasonably believes that no material violation has occurred, is ongoing, or is about to occur, the chief legal officer (or the equivalent thereof) reports the results of the investigation to the issuer's board of directors, a committee thereof to whom a report could be made pursuant to paragraph (b)(3) of this section, or a qualified legal compliance committee; or

      ii. The attorney was retained or directed by the chief legal officer (or the equivalent thereof) to assert, consistent with his or her professional obligations, a colorable defense on behalf of the issuer (or the issuer's officer, director, employee, or agent, as the case may be) in any investigation or judicial or administrative proceeding relating to such evidence of a material violation, and the chief legal officer (or the equivalent thereof) provides reasonable and timely reports on the progress and outcome of such proceeding to the issuer's board of directors, a committee thereof to whom a report could be made pursuant to paragraph (b)(3) of this section, or a qualified legal compliance committee.

7.   An attorney shall not have any obligation to report evidence of a material violation under this paragraph (b) if such attorney was retained or directed by a qualified legal compliance committee:

      i.   To investigate such evidence of a material violation; or

      ii. To assert, consistent with his or her professional obligations, a colorable defense on behalf of the issuer (or the issuer's officer, director, employee, or agent, as the case may be) in any investigation or judicial or administrative proceeding relating to such evidence of a material violation.

8. An attorney who receives what he or she reasonably believes is an appropriate and timely response to a report he or she has made pursuant to paragraph (b)(1), (b)(3), or (b)(4) of this section need do nothing more under this section with respect to his or her report.

9. An attorney who does not reasonably believe that the issuer has made an appropriate response within a reasonable time to the report or reports made pursuant to paragraph (b)(1), (b)(3), or (b)(4) of this section shall explain his or her reasons therefor to the chief legal officer (or the equivalent thereof), the chief executive officer (or the equivalent thereof), and directors to whom the attorney reported the evidence of a material violation pursuant to paragraph (b)(1), (b)(3), or (b)(4) of this section.

10. An attorney formerly employed or retained by an issuer who has reported evidence of a material violation under this part and reasonably believes that he or she has been discharged for so doing may notify the issuer's board of directors or any committee thereof that he or she believes that he or she has been discharged for reporting evidence of a material violation under this section.

c. **Alternative reporting procedures for attorneys retained or employed by an issuer that has established a qualified legal compliance committee.**

1. If an attorney, appearing and practicing before the Commission in the representation of an issuer, becomes aware of evidence of a material violation by the issuer or by any officer, director, employee, or agent of the issuer, the attorney may, as an alternative to the reporting requirements of paragraph (b) of this section, report such evidence to a qualified legal compliance committee, if the issuer has previously formed such a committee. An attorney who reports evidence of a material violation to such a qualified legal compliance committee has satisfied his or her obligation to report such evidence and is not required to assess the issuer's response to the reported evidence of a material violation.

2. A chief legal officer (or the equivalent thereof) may refer a report of evidence of a material violation to a previously established qualified legal compliance committee in lieu of causing an inquiry to be conducted under paragraph (b)(2) of this section. The chief legal officer (or the equivalent thereof) shall inform the reporting attorney that the report has been referred to a qualified legal compliance committee. Thereafter, pursuant to the requirements under Rule 2(k), the qualified legal compliance committee shall be responsible for responding to the evidence of a material violation reported to it under this paragraph (c).

d. **Issuer confidences.**

1. Any report under this section (or the contemporaneous record thereof) or any response thereto (or the contemporaneous record thereof) may be used by an attorney in connection with any investigation, proceeding, or litigation in which the attorney's compliance with this part is in issue.

2. An attorney appearing and practicing before the Commission in the representation of an issuer may reveal to the Commission, without the issuer's

consent, confidential information related to the representation to the extent the attorney reasonably believes necessary:

    i.   To prevent the issuer from committing a material violation that is likely to cause substantial injury to the financial interest or property of the issuer or investors;

    ii.   To prevent the issuer, in a Commission investigation or administrative proceeding from committing perjury, proscribed in 18 U.S.C. 1621; suborning perjury, proscribed in 18 U.S.C. 1622; or committing any act proscribed in 18 U.S.C. 1001 that is likely to perpetrate a fraud upon the Commission; or

    iii.   To rectify the consequences of a material violation by the issuer that caused, or may cause, substantial injury to the financial interest or property of the issuer or investors in the furtherance of which the attorney's services were used.

Rule 4 – Responsibilities of Supervisory Attorneys

a.   An attorney supervising or directing another attorney who is appearing and practicing before the Commission in the representation of an issuer is a supervisory attorney. An issuer's chief legal officer (or the equivalent thereof) is a supervisory attorney under this section.

b.   A supervisory attorney shall make reasonable efforts to ensure that a subordinate attorney, as defined in Rule 5(a), that he or she supervises or directs conforms to this part. To the extent a subordinate attorney appears and practices before the Commission in the representation of an issuer, that subordinate attorney's supervisory attorneys also appear and practice before the Commission.

c.   A supervisory attorney is responsible for complying with the reporting requirements in Rule 3 when a subordinate attorney has reported to the supervisory attorney evidence of a material violation.

d.   A supervisory attorney who has received a report of evidence of a material violation from a subordinate attorney under Rule 3 may report such evidence to the issuer's qualified legal compliance committee if the issuer has duly formed such a committee.

Rule 5 – Responsibilities of a Subordinate Attorney

a.   An attorney who appears and practices before the Commission in the representation of an issuer on a matter under the supervision or direction of another attorney (other than under the direct supervision or direction of the issuer's chief legal officer (or the equivalent thereof)) is a subordinate attorney.

b.   A subordinate attorney shall comply with this part notwithstanding that the subordinate attorney acted at the direction of or under the supervision of another person.

c. A subordinate attorney complies with Rule 3 if the subordinate attorney reports to his or her supervising attorney under Rule 3(b) evidence of a material violation of which the subordinate attorney has become aware in appearing and practicing before the Commission.

d. A subordinate attorney may take the steps permitted or required by Rule 3(b) or (c) if the subordinate attorney reasonably believes that a supervisory attorney to whom he or she has reported evidence of a material violation under Rule 3(b) has failed to comply with Rule 3.

Rule 6 – Sanctions and Discipline

a. A violation of this part by any attorney appearing and practicing before the Commission in the representation of an issuer shall subject such attorney to the civil penalties and remedies for a violation of the federal securities laws available to the Commission in an action brought by the Commission thereunder.

b. An attorney appearing and practicing before the Commission who violates any provision of this part is subject to the disciplinary authority of the Commission, regardless of whether the attorney may also be subject to discipline for the same conduct in a jurisdiction where the attorney is admitted or practices. An administrative disciplinary proceeding initiated by the Commission for violation of this part may result in an attorney being censured, or being temporarily or permanently denied the privilege of appearing or practicing before the Commission.

c. An attorney who complies in good faith with the provisions of this part shall not be subject to discipline or otherwise liable under inconsistent standards imposed by any state or other United States jurisdiction where the attorney is admitted or practices.

d. An attorney practicing outside the United States shall not be required to comply with the requirements of this part to the extent that such compliance is prohibited by applicable foreign law.

Rule 7 – No Private Right of Action
a. Nothing in this part is intended to, or does, create a private right of action against any attorney, law firm, or issuer based upon compliance or noncompliance with its provisions.

b. Authority to enforce compliance with this part is vested exclusively in the Commission.

CRIMINAL STATUTES

18 USC 1348 – Securities Fraud

Whoever knowingly executes, or attempts to execute, a scheme or artifice–

(1)   to defraud any person in connection with any security of an issuer with a class of securities registered under section 12 of the Securities Exchange Act of 1934 or that is required to file reports under section 15(d) of the Securities Exchange Act of 1934; or

(2)   to obtain, by means of false or fraudulent pretenses, representations, or promises, any money or property in connection with the purchase or sale of any security of an issuer with a class of securities registered under section 12 of the Securities Exchange Act of 1934 or that is required to file reports under section 15(d) of the Securities Exchange Act of 1934;

shall be fined under this title, or imprisoned not more than 25 years, or both.

18 USC 1349 – Attempt and Conspiracy

Any person who attempts or conspires to commit any offense under this chapter shall be subject to the same penalties as those prescribed for the offense, the commission of which was the object of the attempt or conspiracy.

18 USC 1350 – Failure of Corporate Officers to Certify Financial Reports

a.   **Certification of periodic financial reports.**–Each periodic report containing financial statements filed by an issuer with the Securities Exchange Commission pursuant to section 13(a) or 15(d) of the Securities Exchange Act of 1934 shall be accompanied by a written statement by the chief executive officer and chief financial officer (or equivalent thereof) of the issuer.

b.   **Content.**–The statement required under subsection (a) shall certify that the periodic report containing the financial statements fully complies with the requirements of section 13(a) or 15(d) of the Securities Exchange Act of 1934 and that information contained in the periodic report fairly presents, in all material respects, the financial condition and results of operations of the issuer.

c.   **Criminal penalties.**–Whoever–

1.   certifies any statement as set forth in subsections (a) and (b) of this section knowing that the periodic report accompanying the statement does not comport with all the requirements set forth in this section shall be fined not more than $1,000,000 or imprisoned not more than 10 years, or both; or

2.   willfully certifies any statement as set forth in subsections (a) and (b) of this section knowing that the periodic report accompanying the statement does not comport with all the requirements set forth in this section shall be fined not more than $5,000,000, or imprisoned not more than 20 years, or both.

18 USC 1514A – Civil Action to Protect against Retaliation in Fraud Cases

a. **Whistleblower protection for employees of publicly traded companies.**–No company with a class of securities registered under section 12 of the Securities Exchange Act of 1934, or that is required to file reports under section 15(d) of the Securities Exchange Act of 1934, or any officer, employee, contractor, subcontractor, or agent of such company, may discharge, demote, suspend, threaten, harass, or in any other manner discriminate against an employee in the terms and conditions of employment because of any lawful act done by the employee–

1. to provide information, cause information to be provided, or otherwise assist in an investigation regarding any conduct which the employee reasonably believes constitutes a violation of section 1341, 1343, 1344, or 1348, any rule or regulation of the Securities and Exchange Commission, or any provision of Federal law relating to fraud against shareholders, when the information or assistance is provided to or the investigation is conducted by–

    A. a Federal regulatory or law enforcement agency;
    B. any Member of Congress or any committee of Congress; or
    C. a person with supervisory authority over the employee (or such other person working for the employer who has the authority to investigate, discover, or terminate misconduct); or

2. to file, cause to be filed, testify, participate in, or otherwise assist in a proceeding filed or about to be filed (with any knowledge of the employer) relating to an alleged violation of section 1341, 1343, 1344, or 1348, any rule or regulation of the Securities and Exchange Commission, or any provision of Federal law relating to fraud against shareholders.

b. **Enforcement action.**–

1. In general.–A person who alleges discharge or other discrimination by any person in violation of subsection (a) may seek relief under subsection (c), by–

    A. filing a complaint with the Secretary of Labor; or
    B. if the Secretary has not issued a final decision within 180 days of the filing of the complaint and there is no showing that such delay is due to the bad faith of the claimant, bringing an action at law or equity for de novo review in the appropriate district court of the United States, which shall have jurisdiction over such an action without regard to the amount in controversy.

2. Procedure.–

    A. In general.–An action under paragraph (1)(A) shall be governed under the rules and procedures set forth in section 42121(b) of title 49, United States Code.
    B. Exception.–Notification made under section 42121(b)(1) of title 49, United States Code, shall be made to the person named in the complaint and to the employer.
    C. Burdens of proof.–An action brought under paragraph (1)(B) shall be governed by the legal burdens of proof set forth in section 42121(b) of title 49, United States Code.

D.   Statute of limitations.–An action under paragraph (1) shall be commenced not later than 90 days after the date on which the violation occurs.

c. **Remedies**.–
    1.   In general.–An employee prevailing in any action under subsection (b)(1) shall be entitled to all relief necessary to make the employee whole.
    2.   Compensatory damages.–Relief for any action under paragraph (1) shall include–
          A.   reinstatement with the same seniority status that the employee would have had, but for the discrimination;
          B.   the amount of back pay, with interest; and
          C.   compensation for any special damages sustained as a result of the discrimination, including litigation costs, expert witness fees, and reasonable attorney fees.

d. **Rights retained by employee**.–Nothing in this section shall be deemed to diminish the rights, privileges, or remedies of any employee under any Federal or State law, or under any collective bargaining agreement.

SARBANES-OXLEY ACT OF 2002

Section 304 – Forfeiture of Certain Bonuses and Profits

a. **Additional Compensation Prior to Noncompliance With Commission Financial Reporting Requirements.** If an issuer is required to prepare an accounting restatement due to the material noncompliance of the issuer, as a result of misconduct, with any financial reporting requirement under the securities laws, the chief executive officer and chief financial officer of the issuer shall reimburse the issuer for–
   1. any bonus or other incentive-based or equity-based compensation received by that person from the issuer during the 12-month period following the first public issuance or filing with the Commission (whichever first occurs) of the financial document embodying such financial reporting requirement; and
   2. any profits realized from the sale of securities of the issuer during that 12-month period.

b. **Commission Exemption Authority.** The Commission may exempt any person from the application of subsection (a), as it deems necessary and appropriate.

Section 404 – Management Assessment of Internal Controls

a. **Rules Required.** The Commission shall prescribe rules requiring each annual report required by section 13(a) or 15(d) of the Securities Exchange Act of 1934 to contain an internal control report, which shall–
   1. state the responsibility of management for establishing and maintaining an adequate internal control structure and procedures for financial reporting; and
   2. contain an assessment, as of the end of the most recent fiscal year of the issuer, of the effectiveness of the internal control structure and procedures of the issuer for financial reporting.

b. **Internal Control Evaluation and Reporting.** With respect to the internal control assessment required by subsection (a), each registered public accounting firm that prepares or issues the audit report for the issuer shall attest to, and report on, the assessment made by the management of the issuer. An attestation made under this subsection shall be made in accordance with standards for attestation engagements issued or adopted by the Board. Any such attestation shall not be the subject of a separate engagement.

Section 408 – Enhanced Review of Periodic Disclosures by Issuers

a. **Regular and Systematic Review.** The Commission shall review disclosures made by issuers reporting under section 13(a) of the Securities Exchange Act of 1934 (including reports filed on Form 10-K), and which have a class of securities listed on a national securities exchange or traded on an automated quotation facility of a national securities association, on a regular and systematic basis for the protection of investors. Such review shall include a review of an issuer's financial statement.

b. **Review Criteria.** For purposes of scheduling the reviews required by subsection (a), the Commission shall consider, among other factors–
  1. issuers that have issued material restatements of financial results;
  2. issuers that experience significant volatility in their stock price as compared to other issuers;
  3. issuers with the largest market capitalization;
  4. emerging companies with disparities in price to earning ratios;
  5. issuers whose operations significantly affect any material sector of the economy; and
  6. any other factors that the Commission may consider relevant.

c. **Minimum Review Period.** In no event shall an issuer required to file reports under section 13(a) or 15(d) of the Securities Exchange Act of 1934 be reviewed under this section less frequently than once every 3 years.